Brant Parker, Don Wilder and Bill Rechin

The Best of CROCK

Titan Comics

The Best of CROCK

ISBN: 9781785862120

Published by Titan Comics, a division of Titan Publishing Group Ltd. 144 Southwark St, London, SE1 0UP

A CIP catalogue record for this title is available from the British Library.

Foreword & History of Crock © Kevin Rechin 2017

This edition first published: Novembert 2017

Special thanks to Kevin Rechin, Tolly Maggs, Russell Seal, David Leach, and Brendan Burford at KFS.

1 3 5 7 9 10 8 6 4 2

Printed in China

CONTENTS

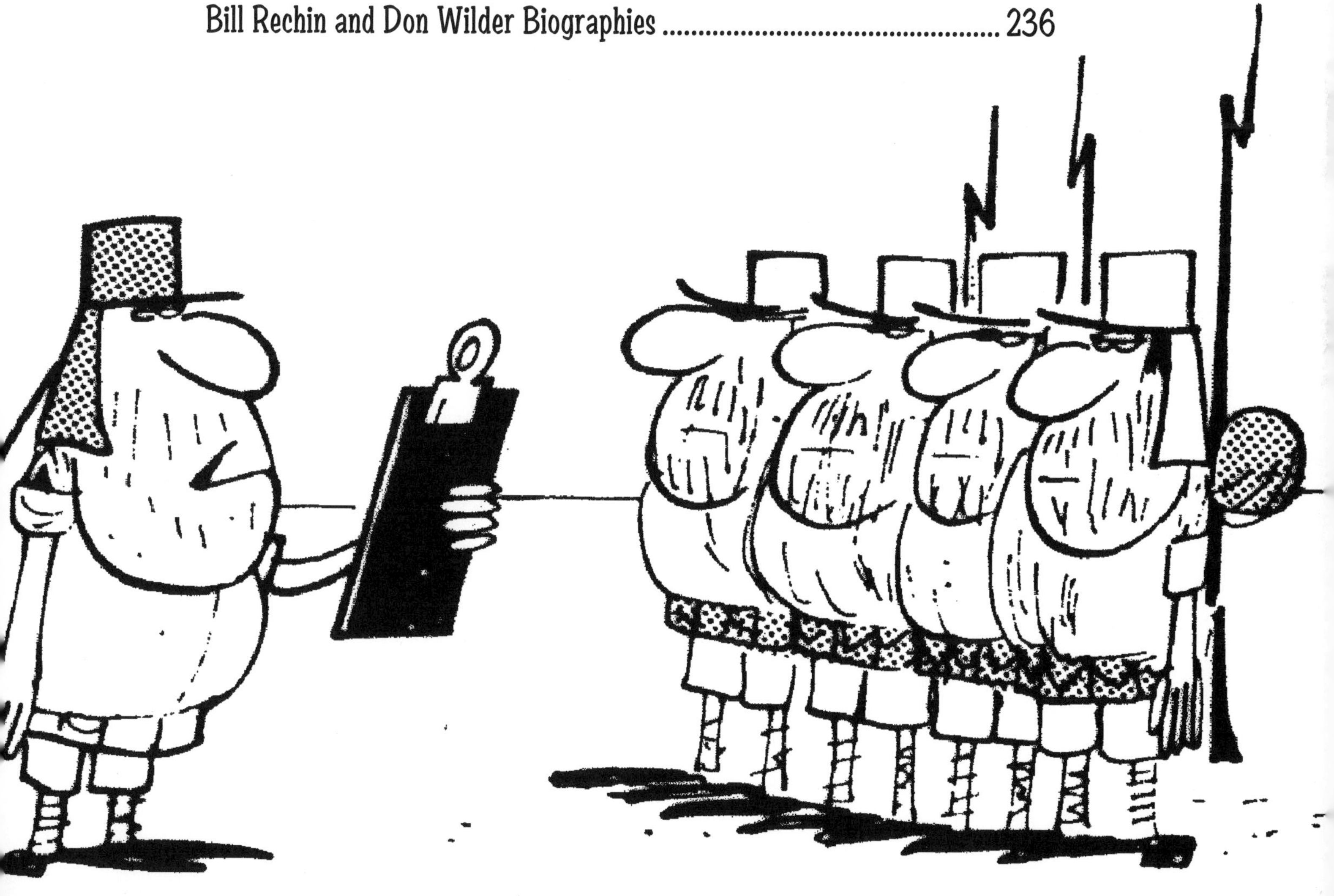

FOREWORD BY KEVIN RECHIN

Bill Rechin (right) was born into a world of pipes, wrenches and faucets. His father, Joe, was a plumber. He probably expected his sons to become plumbers too. But the wrench never quite fit into Bill's grip. However, the crow quill artist's pen did fit. Bill's brothers did go on to become plumbers while Bill became a renowned artist in the world of comic strips, illustration, design and all things funny.

Bill Rechin was my dad and like his dad before him, he had hopes for me, and for all of my six siblings. I'm not sure if he ever really said it out loud to me or my two brothers or four sisters, but in his own way he told each of us to follow our talent. We all did, and today a similar artist's pen fits comfortably in my hand too.

I cannot remember a time when Dad was not drawing, designing or creating. Other dads went to work. My dad went off to draw more than 18,000 daily comic strips. I was not yet 10 when Crock was "born." Dad was driven to make it succeed; and to make it his own. He had an uncanny ability to see each character and the world in which they lived. They lived, in a real sense, in three dimensions, like you and I. This was part of his genius. If Poulet was sitting in Le Cess Pool, then he was perched on a real bar stool, by the real bar. And the inanely stupid comment he made was real. Dad liked to say he "drew big noses" for a living. Actually he created life.

Working as an artist is a blessing. And a curse.

He knew. I know. Deadlines were his nemesis. Mine too. Creativity doesn't always flow.

My Father is responsible for the artist in me. I grew up immersed in cartoons and cartoonists. His home studio had all the cartoonist aromas: rubber cement, magic marker, india ink. I was surrounded by these trappings. Dad was not. But he had a vision from childhood in Buffalo, NY, of being an artist. I think there was a purity about his desire to be a cartoonist and it showed in everything he drew.

My father was a serious artist and designer. Some of what he created as an art director in the late 1950s

4

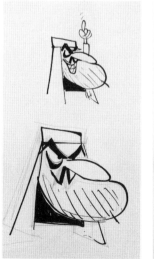

and early 1960s is timeless. But his greatest talent was bringing characters to life. One morning, when I wasn't yet five years old, I asked him to draw me a cowboy. The memory is indelibly etched in my mind. He immediately began to sketch it. Dad's face would transform in unison with the expression he was drawing. He started with the eyes, then a nose and mustache then the giant hat. And the cowboy, in full regalia, came to life. It was simple and straight forward but also complex and subtle. My cowboy was astride a brilliantly funny horse and as the pen rode across the paper my cowboy rode across the prairie. Even now, four decades later, I remember the moment so vividly. In these years I came to understand his economy of line, his simple yet elegant pen strokes that tell so much. I didn't know it then but from that moment forward I was destined to be an artist, like my dad.

This book offers you the opportunity to see what my siblings and I saw over all these years. "I draw big noses." That was dad's lexicon for his work. And he did draw big noses, but as he created the look and character of Crock, it was the huge chin and jaw that ultimately brought this seminal character to life. You can see it in these early development sketches (left) showing how Vermin P. Crock came into being.

Welcome to Crock's very real world.

Kevin Rechin, June 2017

5

CROCK - A POTTED HISTORY BY BOB MORGAN AND KEVIN RECHIN

In 1970, Brandt Parker had an idea. In 1974, Bill Rechin had an inspiration. And in 1975 their collaboration gave birth to *Crock*, one of the most enduring comic strips created in the second Golden Age of Comics that was the 1970s and 1980s.

Parker, already the successful cartoonist of *The Wizard of Id*, was somewhat inspired by the film *Beau Geste*, a classic about the French Foreign Legion. The desert, he felt, was fertile ground for a comic strip. However, it was Rechin, also a successful cartoonist with his comic strip *Pluribus*, who made this citadel in the desert bloom.

"For years I had these visions of funny Frenchmen zapping around in the desert," Parker said once when explaining the idea. He shared the concept with Rechin in some early meetings about the project. For the cartoonists, the meetings were productive if the result was laughter. Early on they simply just tried to make one another laugh, hopefully out loud. Rechin's evolving character sketches are what brought the strip to life. The "aha" moment or, perhaps more descriptively apt, the Frankenstein "It is ALIVE!!!" moment, came when Rechin added the prominent jaw and short stature to Commandant Vermin P. Crock. He was immediately both sinister and silly. From there the strip, the humor, the supporting characters and the gags simply went forth and multiplied.

The comic debuted in early spring of 1975, distributed by Field Newspaper Syndicate. It quickly found a following and appeared in more than 150 newspapers within 14 months. International syndication started in early 1976. Don Wilder, who also assisted with the early collaborations, took over the writing duties that same year. By 1977, Parker returned his focus to *Wizard of Id* and was soon bought out by my Rechin and Don Wilder.

"Sometimes I saw *Crock* as my childhood in sand instead of snow," said Rechin, who grew up in Buffalo, NY. He drew inspiration for many of the strip's characters,

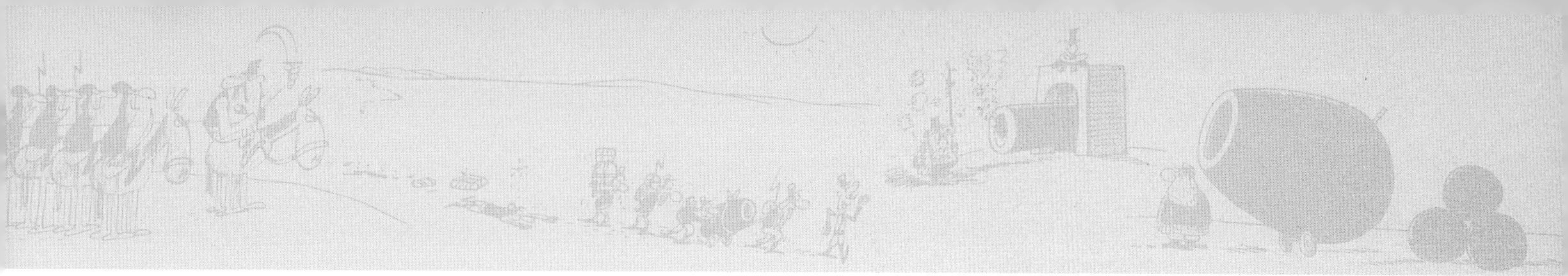

from shapes and sizes to personality and persona, from those surrounding him as he grew up in the 1930s and 40s in and around Buffalo's ethnic neighborhoods. His 1950s stint in the Army helped hone the military depictions and absurdities defining Crock's command.

Wilder, who always said he was better with words than drawing, despite having cartoons accepted and published by *The New Yorker*, said his approach for the gags was attempting to "turn pathos into laughter and misery into comedy."

Rechin, Wilder and Parker all had an affinity for the movies they saw as children and teenagers. Each continued to enjoy these classics as they grew older, one suspects because the black and white images made them feel young again. This likely contributed to the mélange of classic, topical and juvenile humor blended into the characters and gags. The genius of the strip, once described as "a full bubble off level" by fellow cartoonist Mel Lazarus, is that it manages to turn the expected into the unexpected and the sensible into the silly.

Set at a desolate fort in the middle of a barren desert, the tyrannical Crock commands the besieged and beleaguered legionnaires while fighting off bands of would-be plundering hordes. There is the cowardly Captain Poulet, the narcissistic Captain Preppie, the less-than sophisticated Maggot, the hopelessly inept Figowitz, the unquenchable camel Quench and camp follower Grossie. Through the strip's many years, Rechin and Wilder surrounded these core characters and luckless legionnaires with a curious and ever-evolving assortment of supporting players. Among them were Mario the Bartender, the ever-wandering Lost Patrol, outpost sentry duo Buford and Vern, always-to-be-executed-but-never-ever-shot criminal mastermind Jules Schmeese, a Hot Box prisoner twosome, and of course Le Cess Poole, the decrepit, ramshackle local saloon.

The comic strip had its greatest distribution and circulation in the late 1990s when it was published in more than 250 newspapers in 14 countries. By that time, distribution was handled by King Features Syndicate. In 1999, Crock's Fort became a featured part of "Toon Lagoon" at Universal Studios' Florida Island of Adventure theme park.

The strip was produced uninterrupted until 2012. After Wilder's death in 2008, the scripting was often done as a collaboration involving Rechin and his youngest son Kevin Rechin, like his father a Rueben Award-winning artist, and son-in-law Bob Morgan.

Bill Rechin died in 2011. For the next 13 months the strip was drawn by Kevin Rechin and scripted by Morgan. Publication of new original *Crock* strips ended on May 20, 2012. The final "live" Sunday strip paid tribute to Bill Rechin's timeless cast of characters. Because of *Crock*'s popularity, best-of original strips by Bill Rechin continue to be syndicated daily through King Features and the strip retains an international following.

Bob Morgan and Kevin Rechin. 2017.

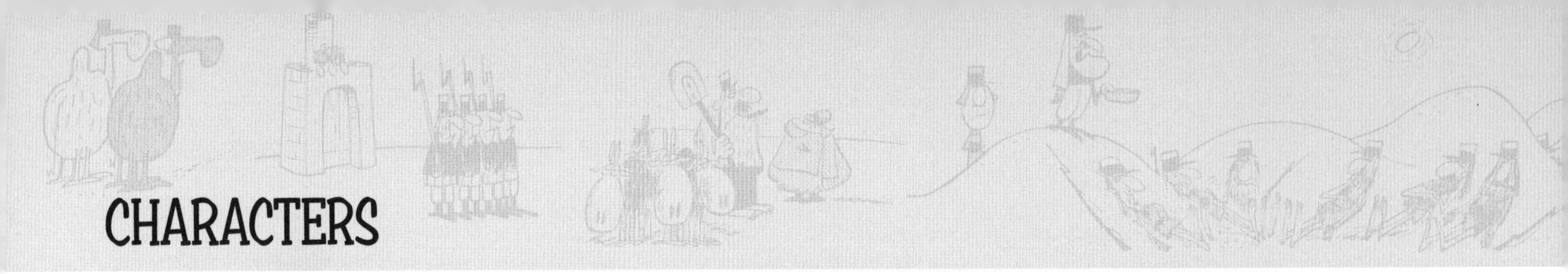

CHARACTERS

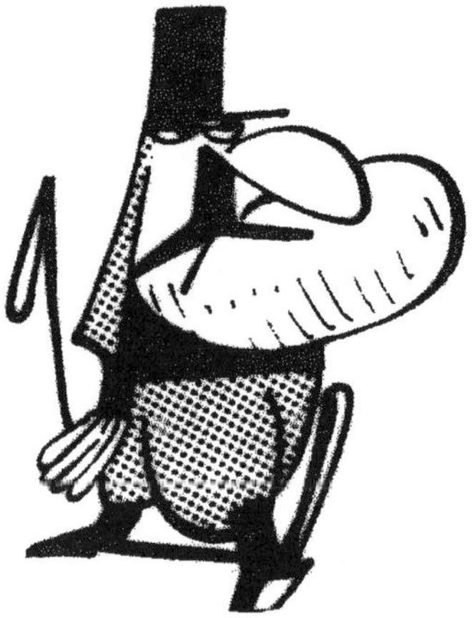

COMMANDANT CROCK

A gleefully cruel and tyrannical leader. Vermin P. Crock's harsh and brutal treatment of his men surpasses even that of the barren and unforgiving desert in which they toil.

PRETTY BOY

The leader of the Arab bandits who is anything but pretty. Matching Crock in his stubbornness to win, Pretty Boy leads his men bravely on the front lines.

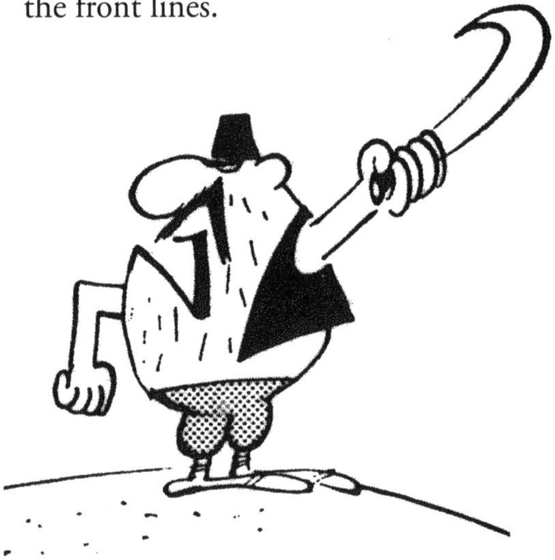

CAPTAIN POULET

Crock's cowardly second in command. Shown little to no respect by the troops, Poulet's loyalty to Crock is an ill-advised act of desperation! To Crock's wicked delight!

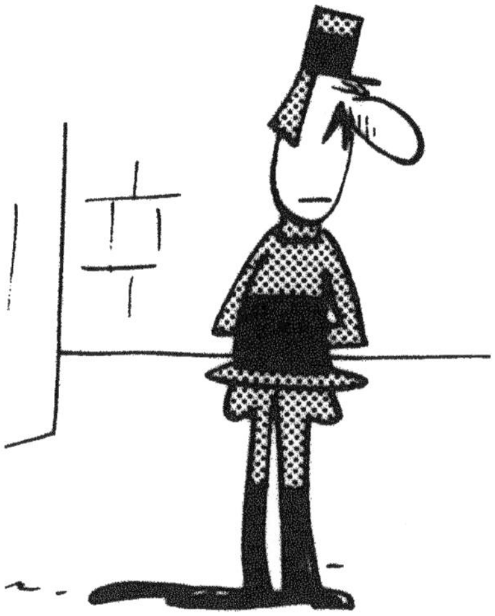

MAGGOT

A grimy, simple-minded grunt, only good for digging garbage holes. Although, if you told his mother that, she'd say you were giving him far too much credit.

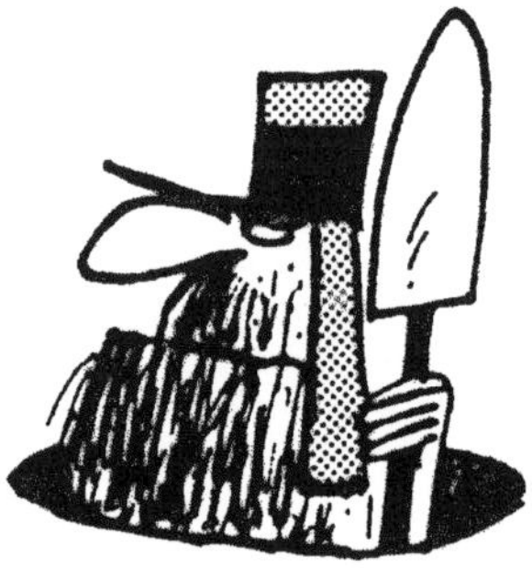

GROSSIE

A camp follower, and sister to Pretty Boy. A courtesan temptress of nobody's desires, Grossie hangs around the fort in the hopes of nabbing a man, or at the very least, some attention. Attracts the worst of both!

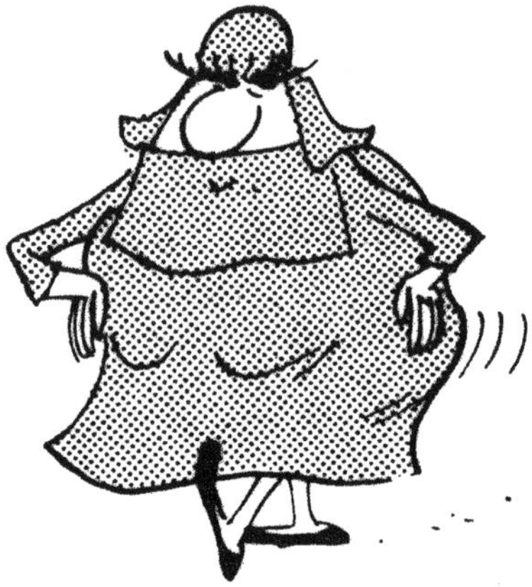

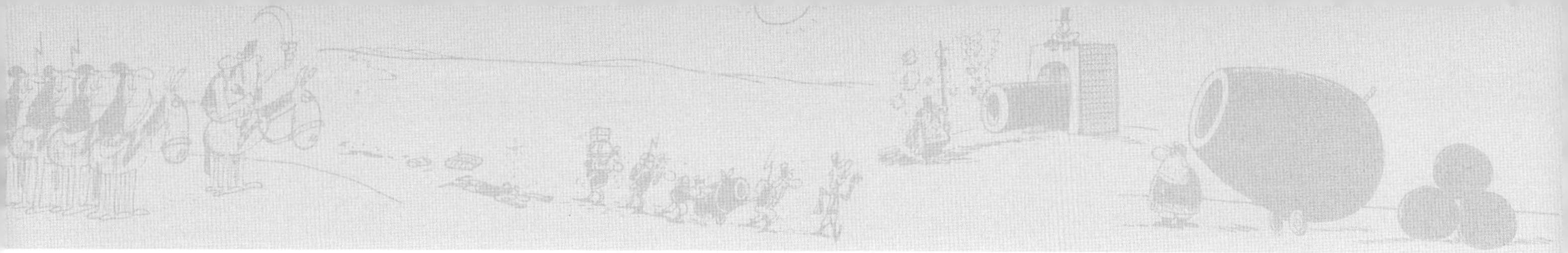

QUENCH

Life would be impossible in the desert without a useful steed to share the load. Unfortunately, Crock's army is stuck with Quench instead, the world's laziest camel.

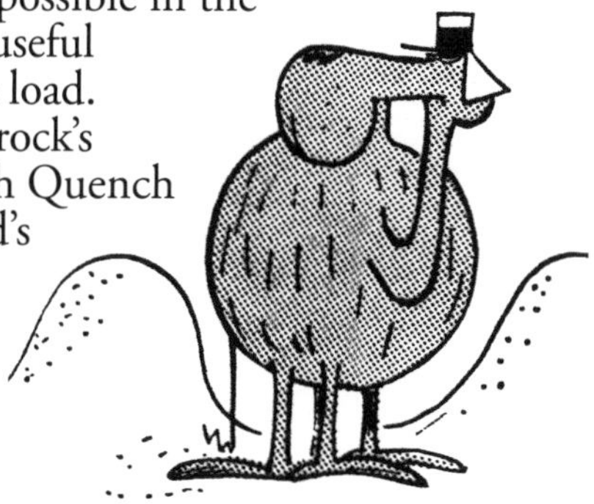

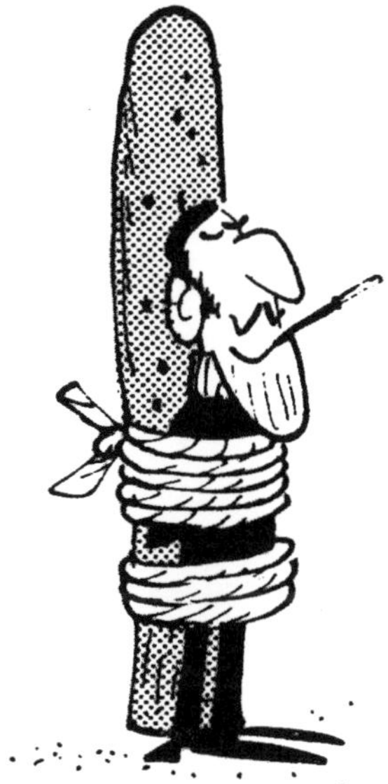

JULES SCHMEESE

Permanently for the firing squad, Crock dreams to one day successfully execute the sneaky thief, but Jules is far too crafty for these daft legionnaires.

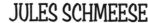

MANCHEZ

Bandito and demolitions expert. Manchez is good for one thing and one thing only. And for everyone's sake, they wish he wasn't.

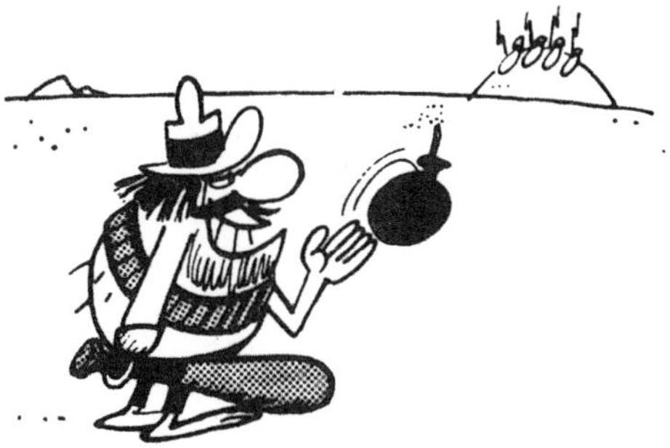

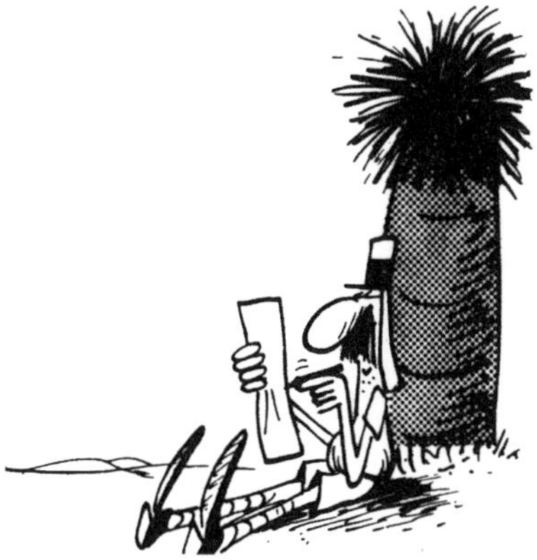

FIGOWITZ

Crock's personal whipping boy, constantly (and literally) getting tread on! Tries to assuage himself reading love notes from his sweetheart back home… detailing all the fun she's having without him.

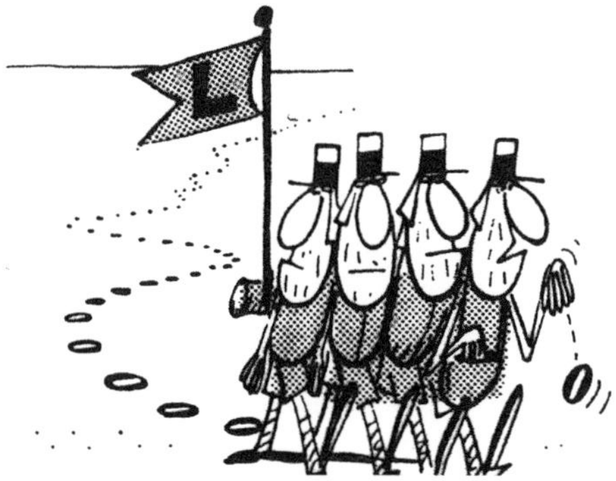
L

THE LOST PATROL

If there's one thing you can count on with this small squad, it's their fantastic ability to never be where Crock needs them to be.

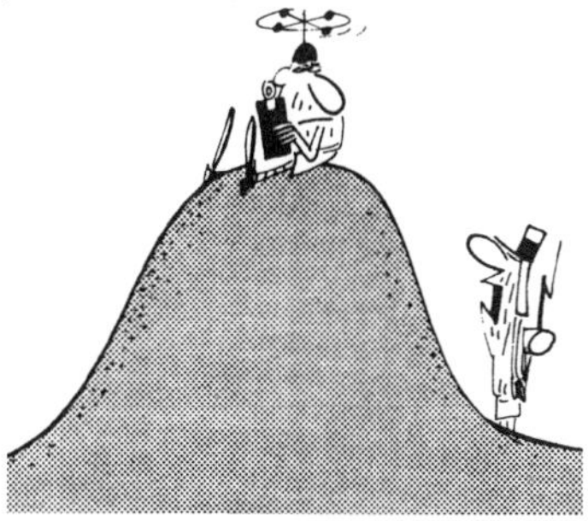

ALVIN

In charge of weather forecast for the desert, Alvin is as hopeless as the chances of rain.

CHARACTERS

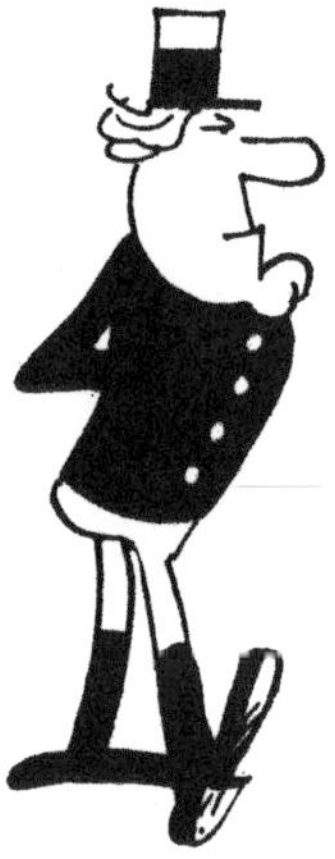

CAPTAIN PREPPIE

A vain and useless officer, handsome Captain Preppie drives the women wild. A shame for them, he's only interested in himself!

THE HOT BOXES

The punishment for insubordination. Forever locked away with no chance to escape, madness is all that is left to keep these poor souls company.

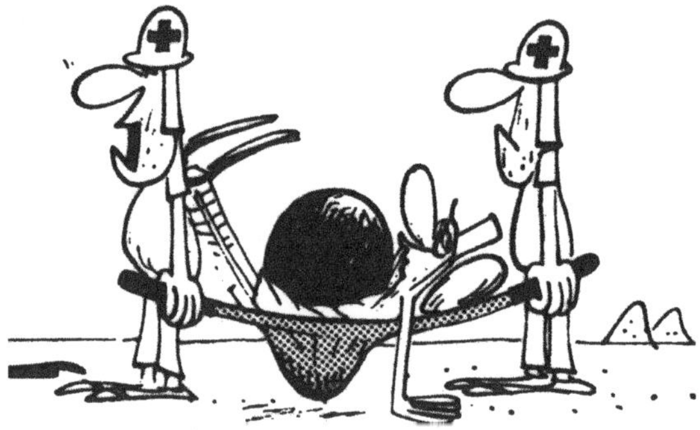

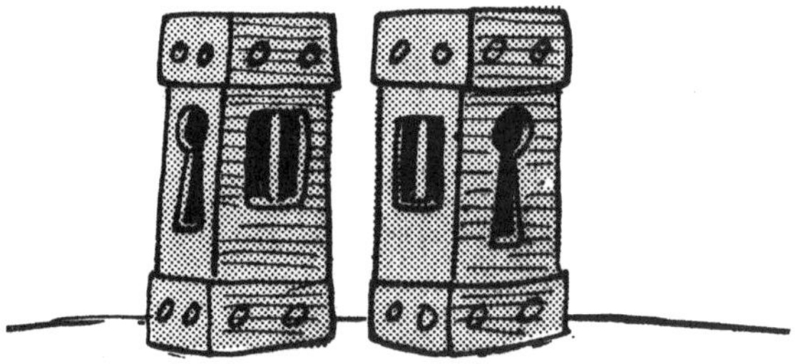

OUTPOST 5

Buford and Vern. Awaiting fresh orders for decades. The only thing worse than living under Crock's tyrannical rule is the excruciating boredom of the outpost.

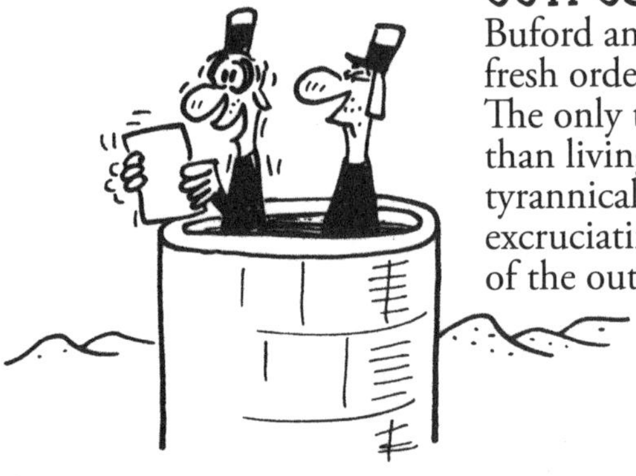

CLEEVIS

Permanently suffering from a cannonball to the gut, Cleevis' chances of survival are poor, even before you meet his slipshod surgeon.

LE CESS POOLE

A favorite hangout of the legionnaires. Or rather, the only hangout. A sordid and dilapidated den of iniquity.

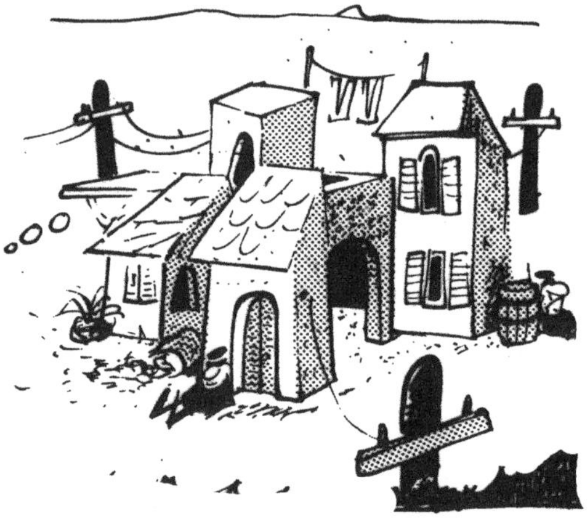

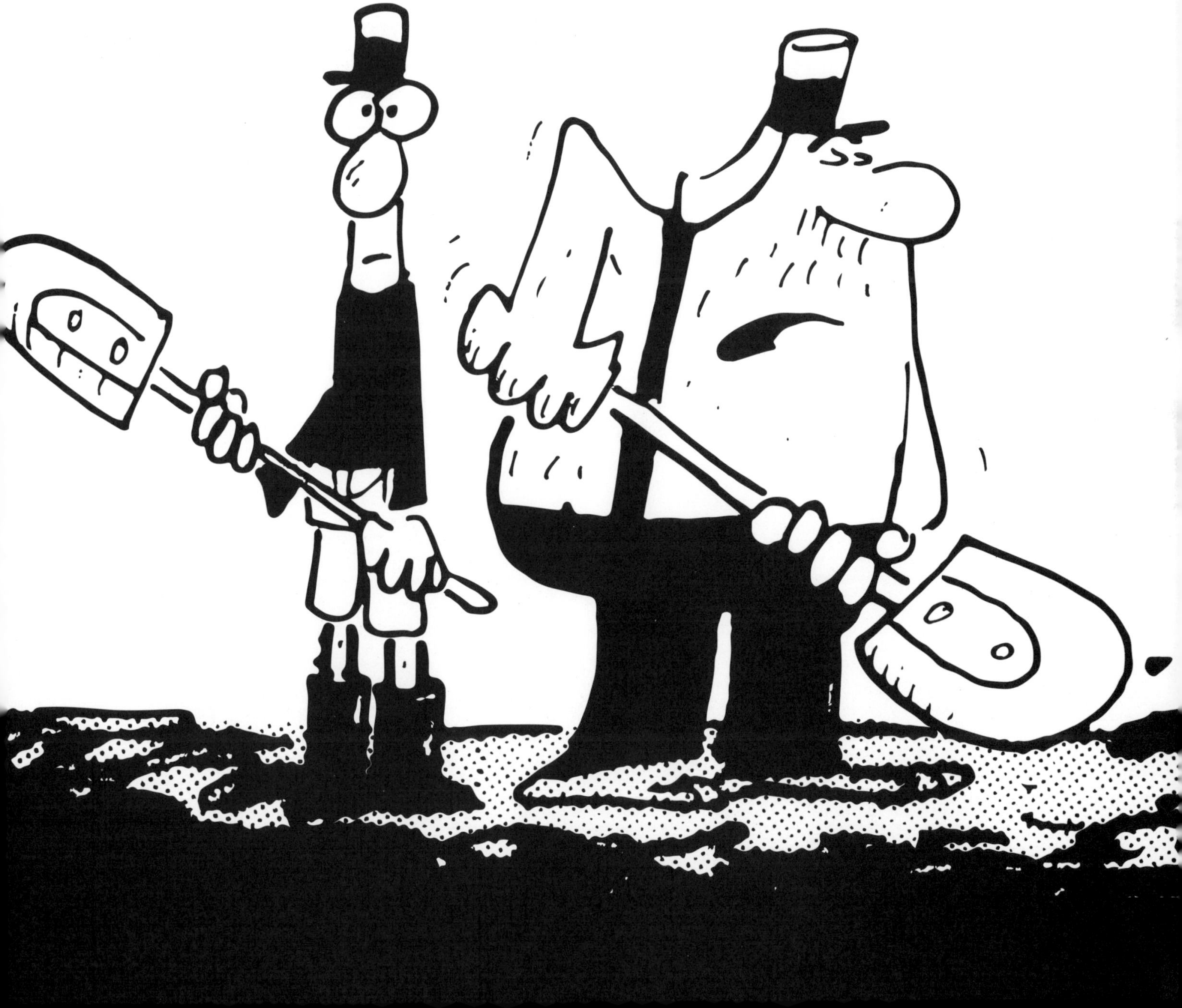

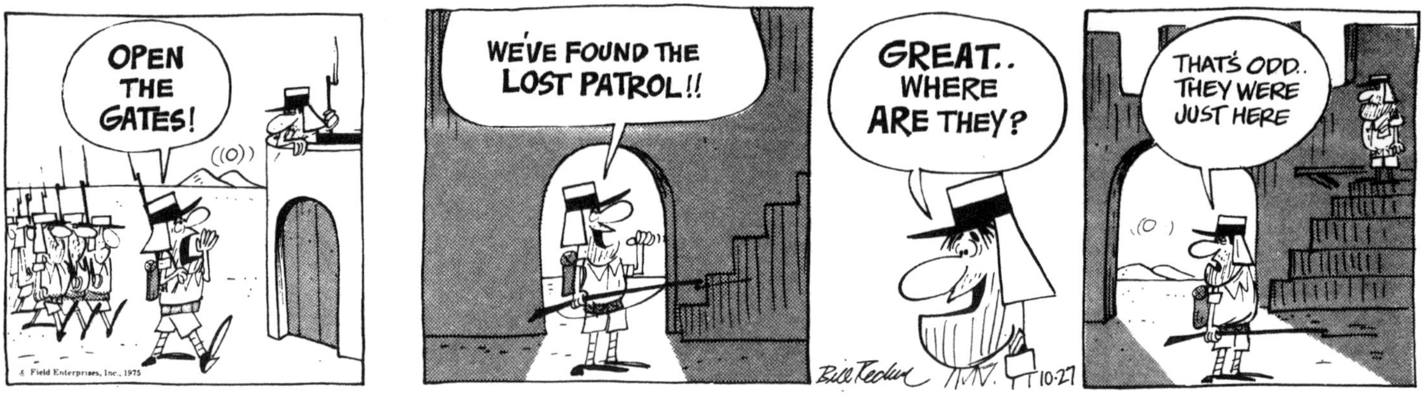
OPEN THE GATES!
WE'VE FOUND THE LOST PATROL!!
GREAT.. WHERE ARE THEY?
THAT'S ODD.. THEY WERE JUST HERE
© Field Enterprises, Inc., 1975
10-27

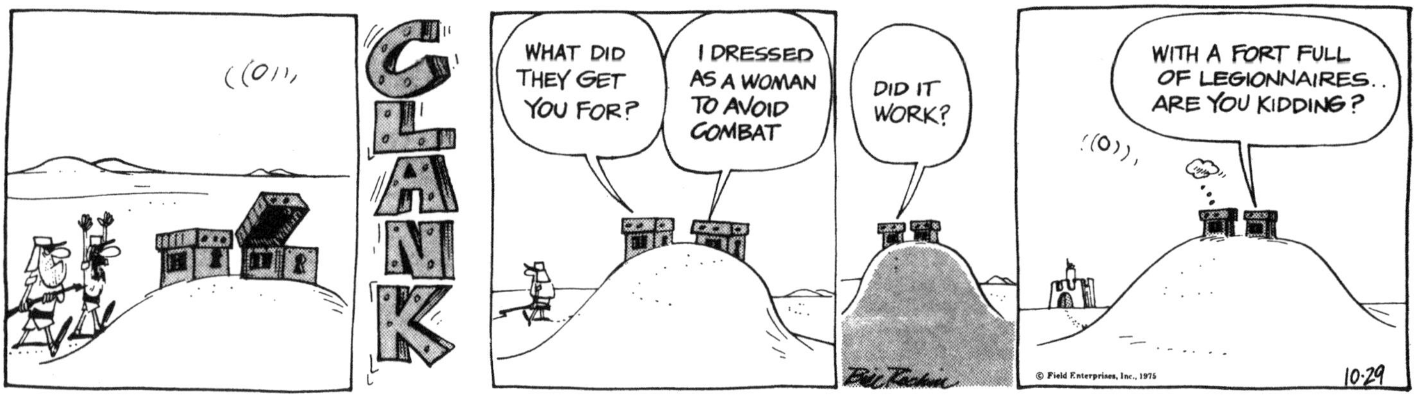
CLANK
WHAT DID THEY GET YOU FOR?
I DRESSED AS A WOMAN TO AVOID COMBAT
DID IT WORK?
WITH A FORT FULL OF LEGIONNAIRES.. ARE YOU KIDDING?
© Field Enterprises, Inc., 1975
10-29

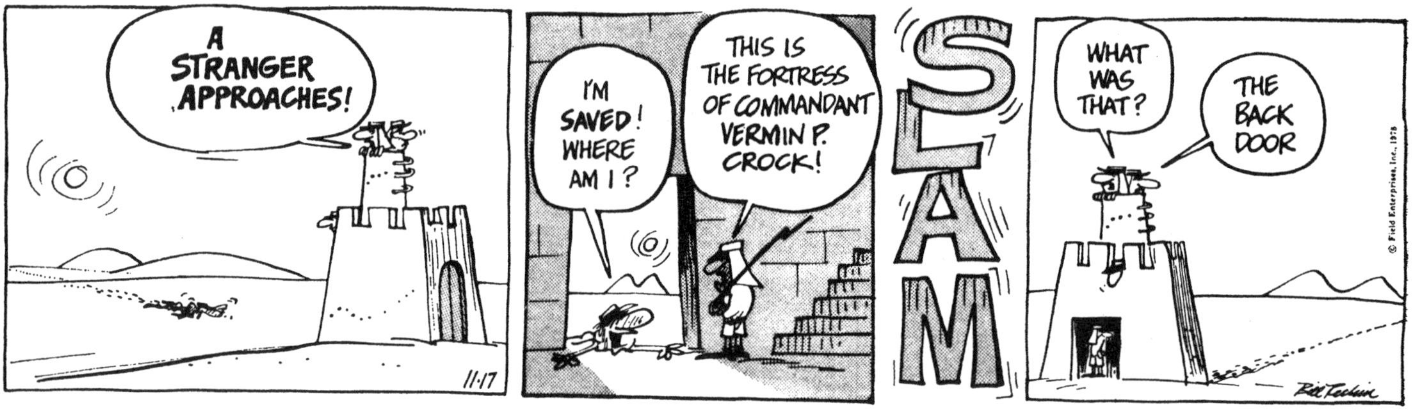
A STRANGER APPROACHES!
11-17
I'M SAVED! WHERE AM I?
THIS IS THE FORTRESS OF COMMANDANT VERMIN P. CROCK!
SLAM
WHAT WAS THAT?
THE BACK DOOR
© Field Enterprises, Inc., 1975

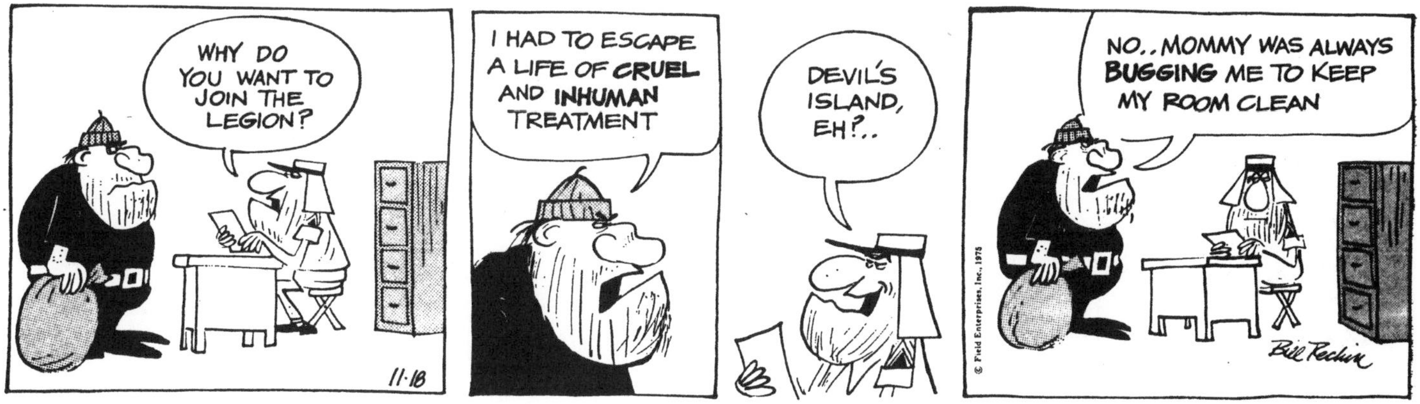
WHY DO YOU WANT TO JOIN THE LEGION?
11·18
I HAD TO ESCAPE A LIFE OF CRUEL AND INHUMAN TREATMENT
DEVIL'S ISLAND, EH?..
NO.. MOMMY WAS ALWAYS BUGGING ME TO KEEP MY ROOM CLEAN
© Field Enterprises, Inc., 1975
Bill Rechin

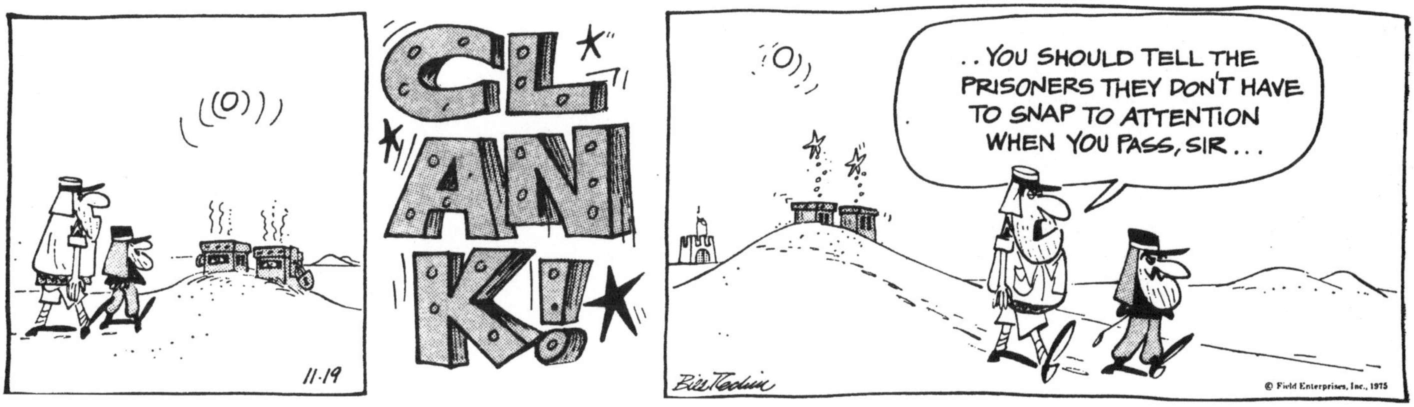
11·19
CLANK!
..YOU SHOULD TELL THE PRISONERS THEY DON'T HAVE TO SNAP TO ATTENTION WHEN YOU PASS, SIR...
Bill Rechin
© Field Enterprises, Inc., 1975

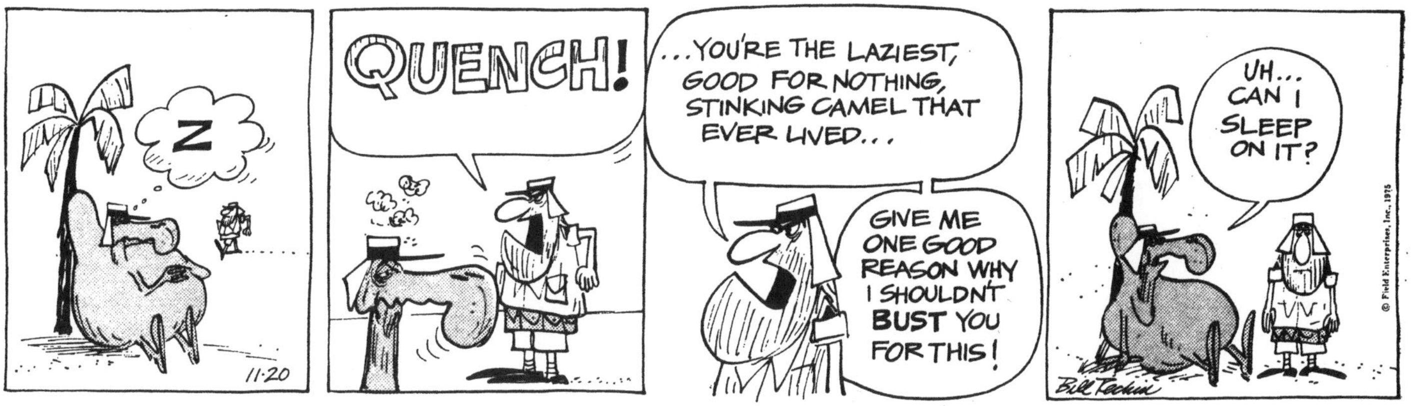
Z
11·20
QUENCH!
...YOU'RE THE LAZIEST, GOOD FOR NOTHING, STINKING CAMEL THAT EVER LIVED...
GIVE ME ONE GOOD REASON WHY I SHOULDN'T BUST YOU FOR THIS!
UH... CAN I SLEEP ON IT?
© Field Enterprises, Inc., 1975
Bill Rechin

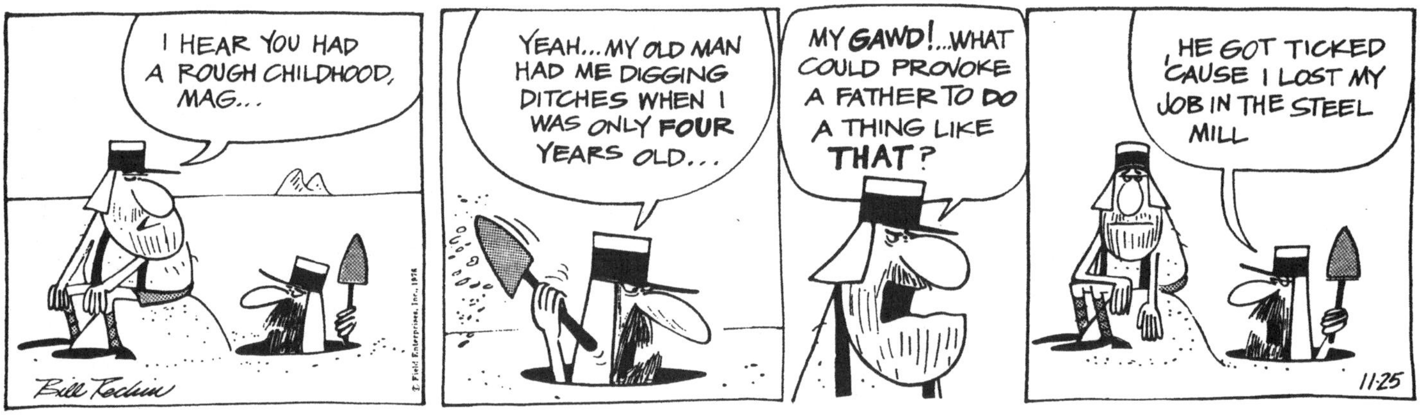
I HEAR YOU HAD A ROUGH CHILDHOOD, MAG...
YEAH... MY OLD MAN HAD ME DIGGING DITCHES WHEN I WAS ONLY FOUR YEARS OLD...
MY GAWD!...WHAT COULD PROVOKE A FATHER TO DO A THING LIKE THAT?
HE GOT TICKED 'CAUSE I LOST MY JOB IN THE STEEL MILL
Bill Rechin
© Field Enterprises, Inc., 1975
11·25

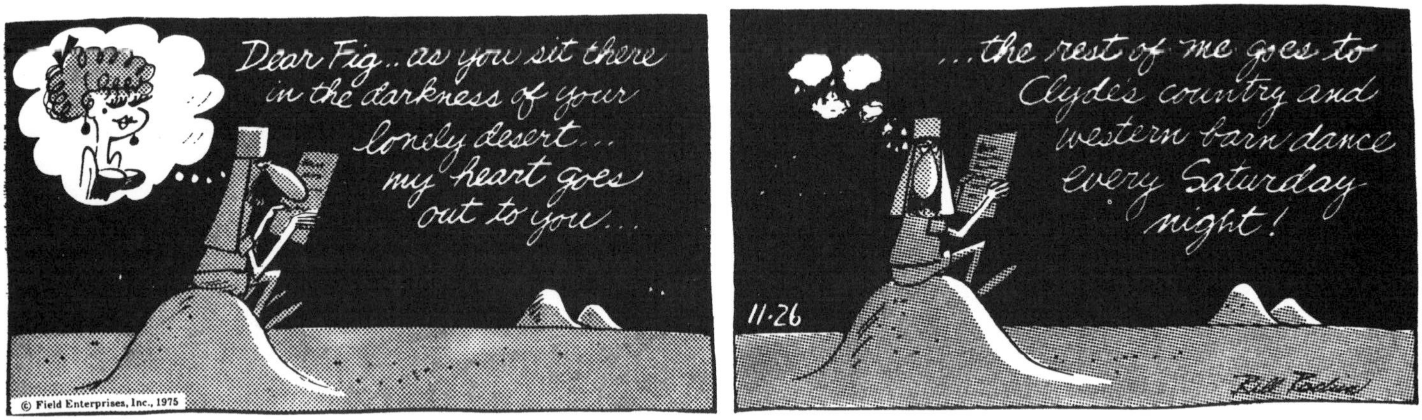
Dear Fig.. as you sit there in the darkness of your lonely desert... my heart goes out to you...
...the rest of me goes to Clyde's country and western barn dance every Saturday night!
11·26
© Field Enterprises, Inc., 1975
Bill Rechin

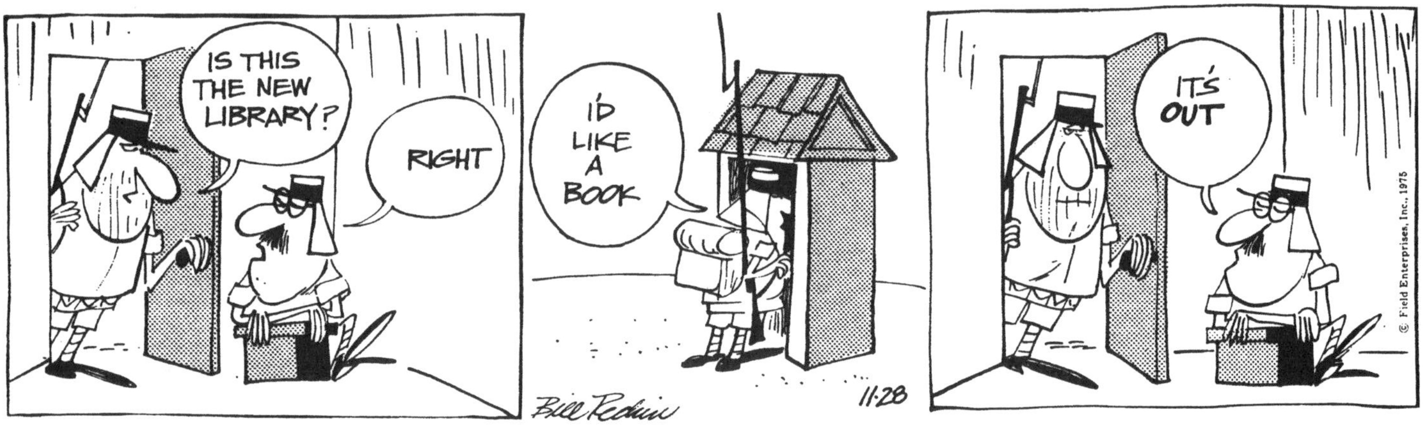
IS THIS THE NEW LIBRARY?
RIGHT
I'D LIKE A BOOK
IT'S OUT
Bill Rechin
11·28
© Field Enterprises, Inc., 1975

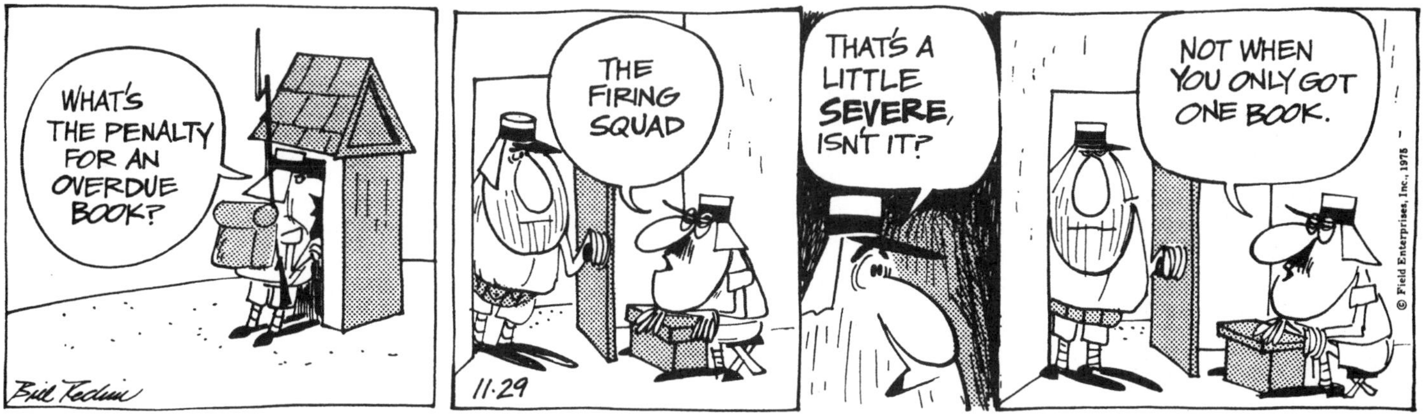
WHAT'S THE PENALTY FOR AN OVERDUE BOOK?
Bill Rechin
THE FIRING SQUAD
11-29
THAT'S A LITTLE SEVERE, ISN'T IT?
NOT WHEN YOU ONLY GOT ONE BOOK.
© Field Enterprises, Inc., 1975

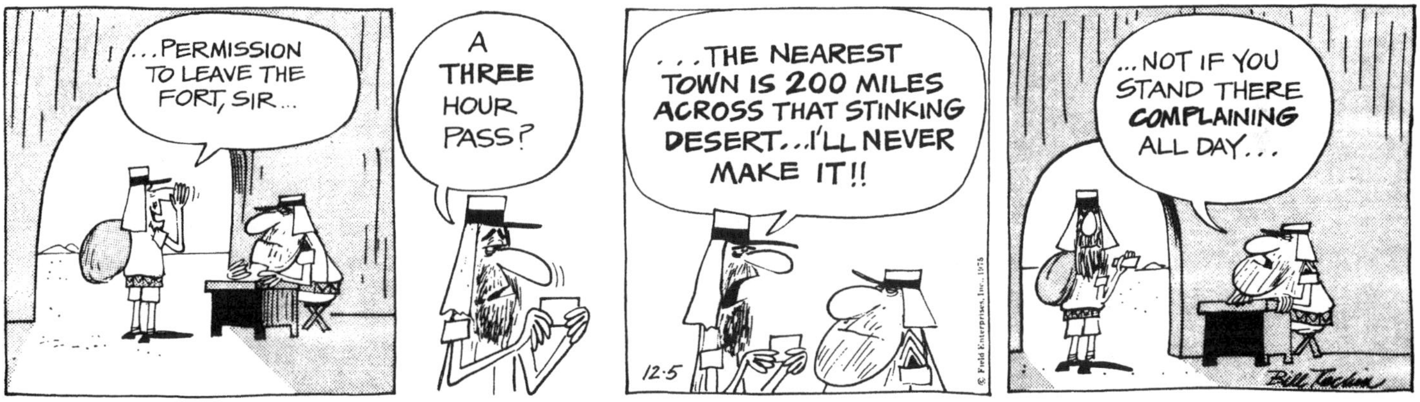
...PERMISSION TO LEAVE THE FORT, SIR...
A THREE HOUR PASS?
...THE NEAREST TOWN IS 200 MILES ACROSS THAT STINKING DESERT...I'LL NEVER MAKE IT!!
12-5
© Field Enterprises, Inc., 1975
...NOT IF YOU STAND THERE COMPLAINING ALL DAY...
Bill Rechin

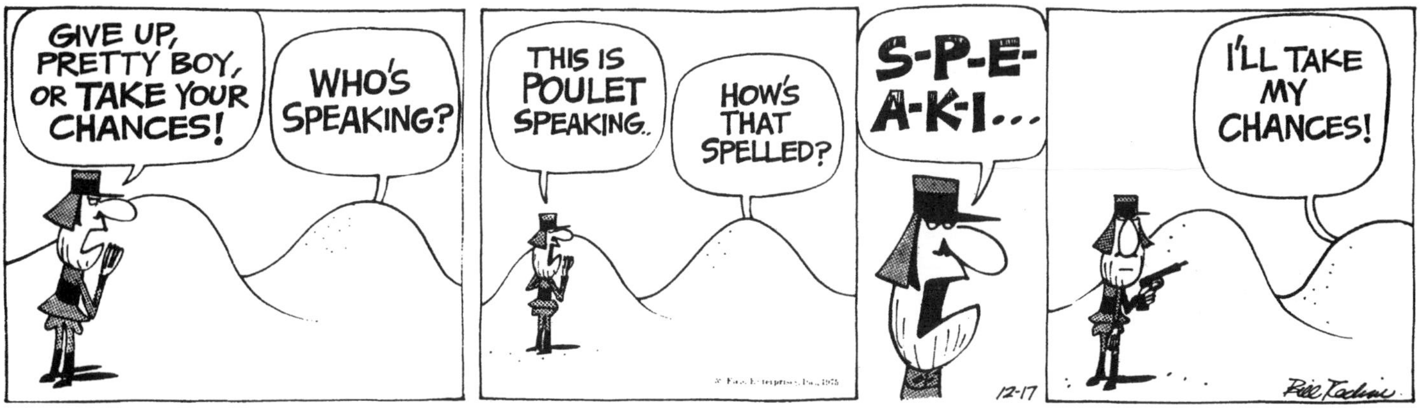
GIVE UP, PRETTY BOY, OR TAKE YOUR CHANCES!
WHO'S SPEAKING?
THIS IS POULET SPEAKING..
HOW'S THAT SPELLED?
S-P-E-A-K-I...
12-17
I'LL TAKE MY CHANCES!
Bill Rechin

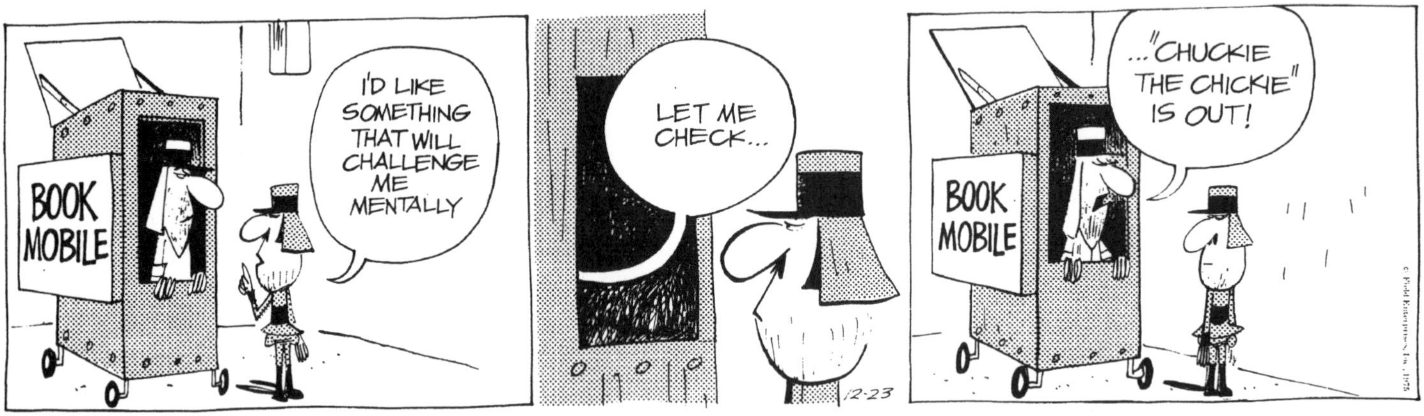
BOOK MOBILE
I'D LIKE SOMETHING THAT WILL CHALLENGE ME MENTALLY
LET ME CHECK...
12-23
BOOK MOBILE
..."CHUCKIE THE CHICKIE" IS OUT!

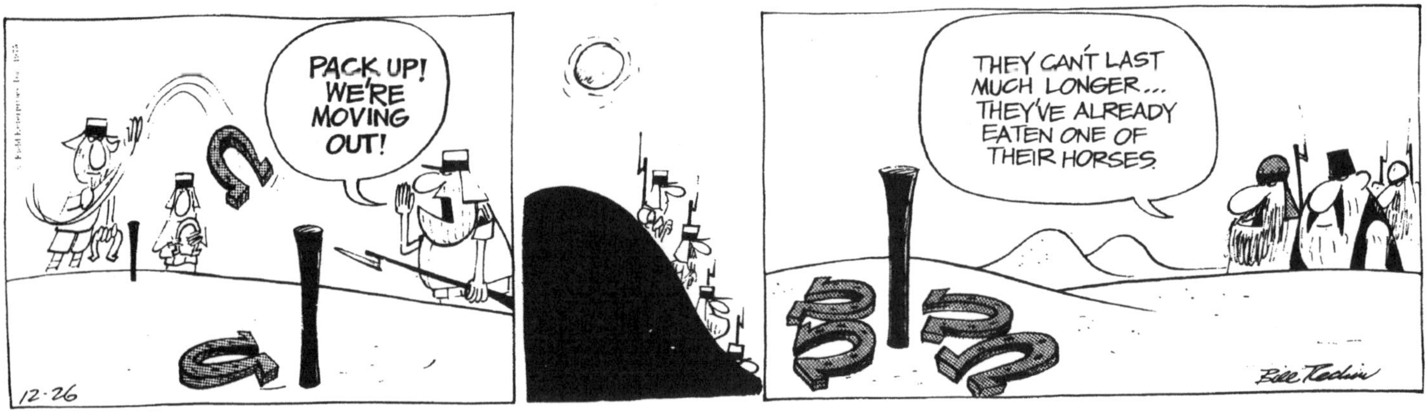
PACK UP! WE'RE MOVING OUT!
12-26
THEY CAN'T LAST MUCH LONGER... THEY'VE ALREADY EATEN ONE OF THEIR HORSES.

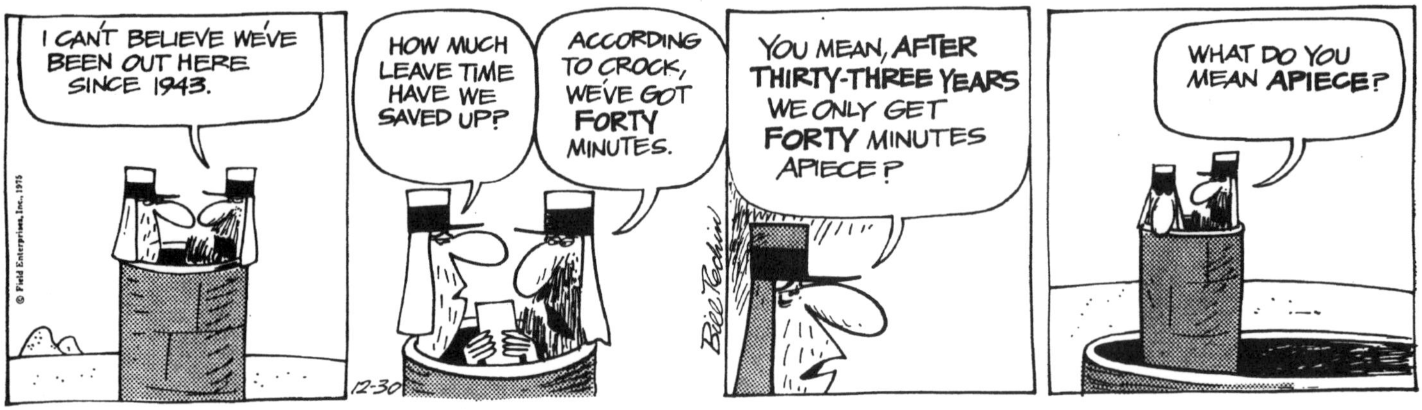
I CAN'T BELIEVE WE'VE BEEN OUT HERE SINCE 1943.
© Field Enterprises, Inc., 1975
HOW MUCH LEAVE TIME HAVE WE SAVED UP?
ACCORDING TO CROCK, WE'VE GOT FORTY MINUTES.
12-30
YOU MEAN, AFTER THIRTY-THREE YEARS WE ONLY GET FORTY MINUTES APIECE?
WHAT DO YOU MEAN APIECE?

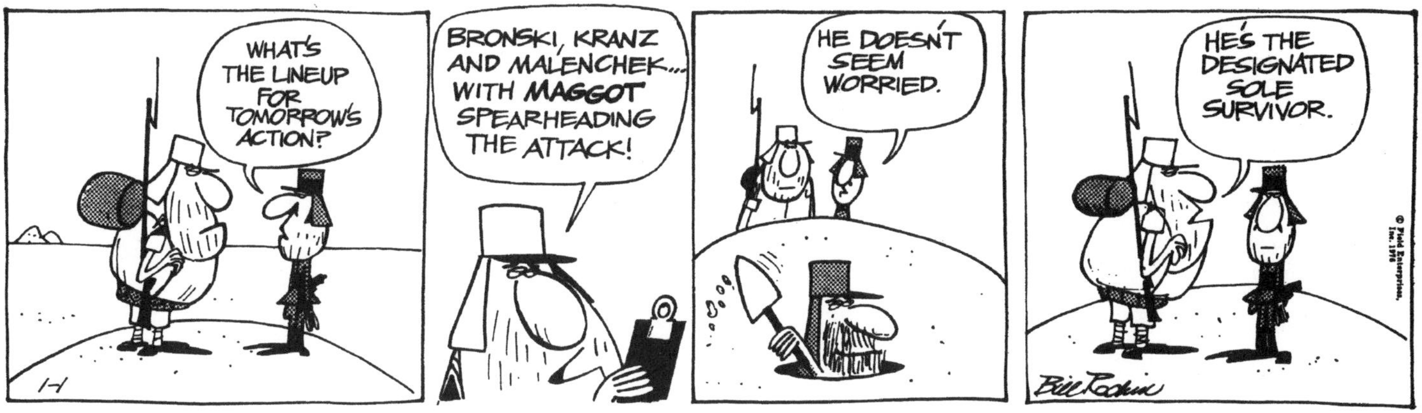
WHAT'S THE LINEUP FOR TOMORROW'S ACTION?
1-1
BRONSKI, KRANZ AND MALENCHEK... WITH MAGGOT SPEARHEADING THE ATTACK!
HE DOESN'T SEEM WORRIED.
HE'S THE DESIGNATED SOLE SURVIVOR.
© Field Enterprises, Inc. 1976
Bill Rechin

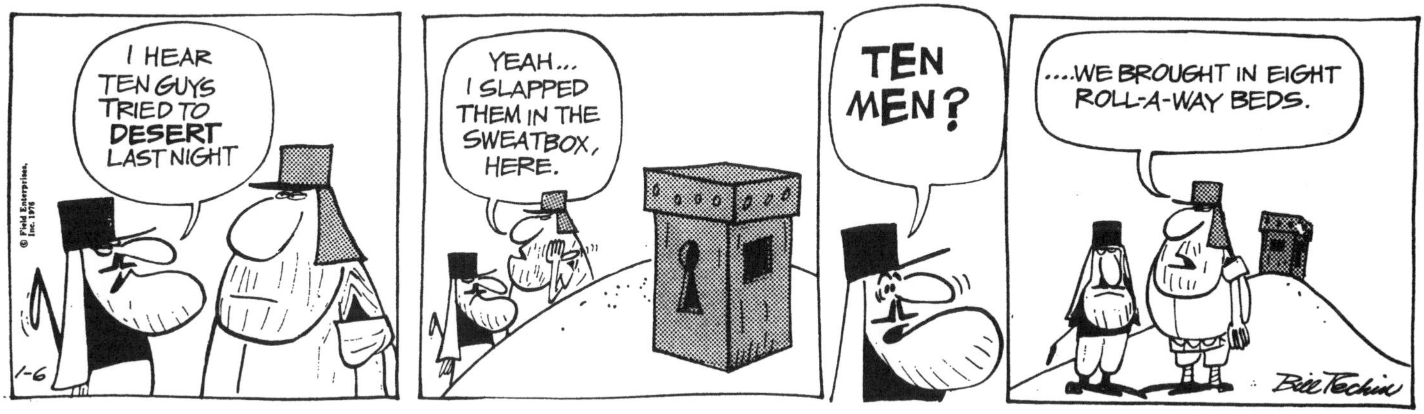
I HEAR TEN GUYS TRIED TO DESERT LAST NIGHT
© Field Enterprises, Inc. 1976
1-6
YEAH... I SLAPPED THEM IN THE SWEATBOX, HERE.
TEN MEN?
....WE BROUGHT IN EIGHT ROLL-A-WAY BEDS.
Bill Rechin

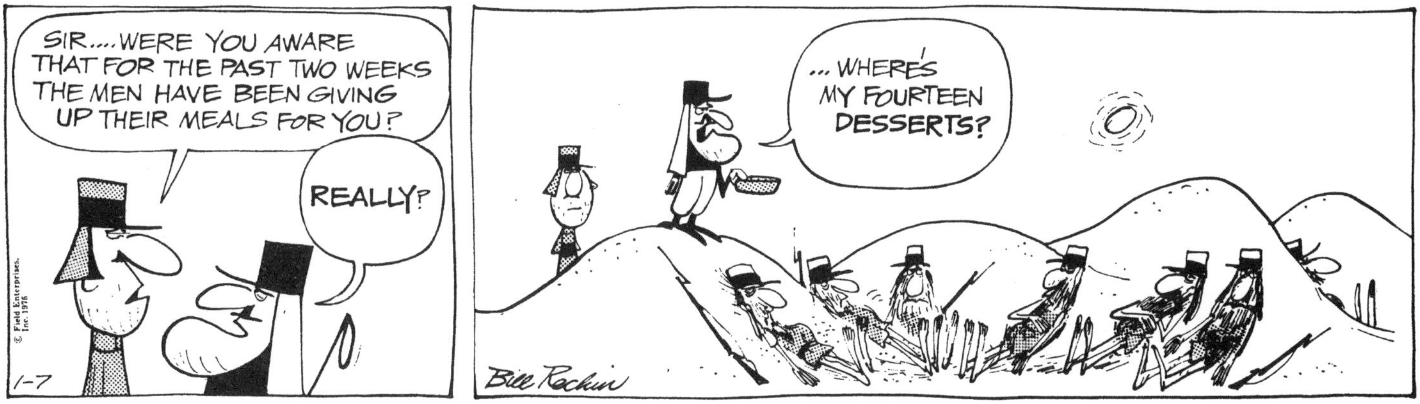
SIR....WERE YOU AWARE THAT FOR THE PAST TWO WEEKS THE MEN HAVE BEEN GIVING UP THEIR MEALS FOR YOU?
REALLY?
© Field Enterprises, Inc. 1976
1-7
...WHERE'S MY FOURTEEN DESSERTS?
Bill Rechin

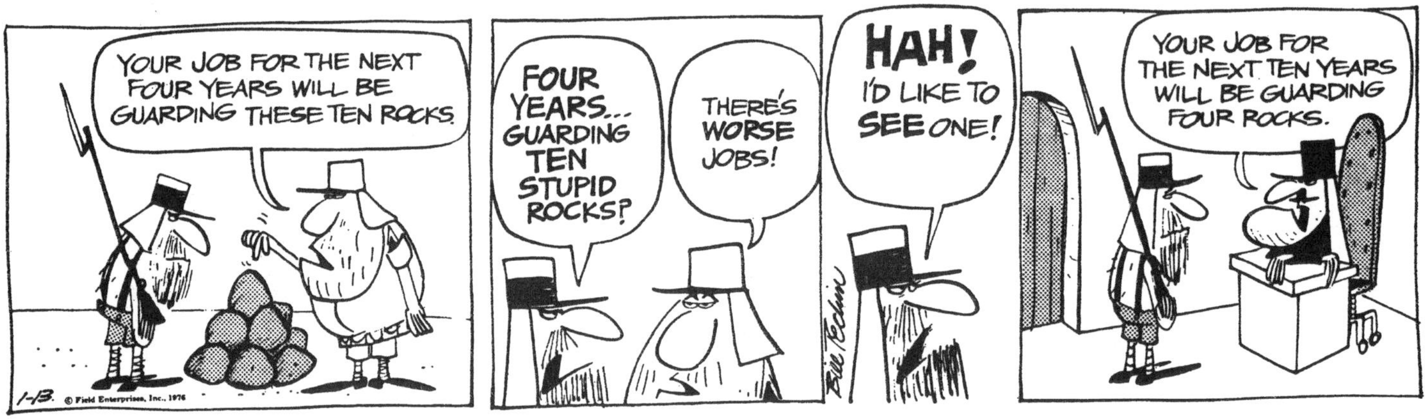
YOUR JOB FOR THE NEXT FOUR YEARS WILL BE GUARDING THESE TEN ROCKS.
1-13. © Field Enterprises, Inc., 1976
FOUR YEARS... GUARDING TEN STUPID ROCKS?
THERE'S WORSE JOBS!
HAH! I'D LIKE TO SEE ONE!
Bill Rechin
YOUR JOB FOR THE NEXT TEN YEARS WILL BE GUARDING FOUR ROCKS.

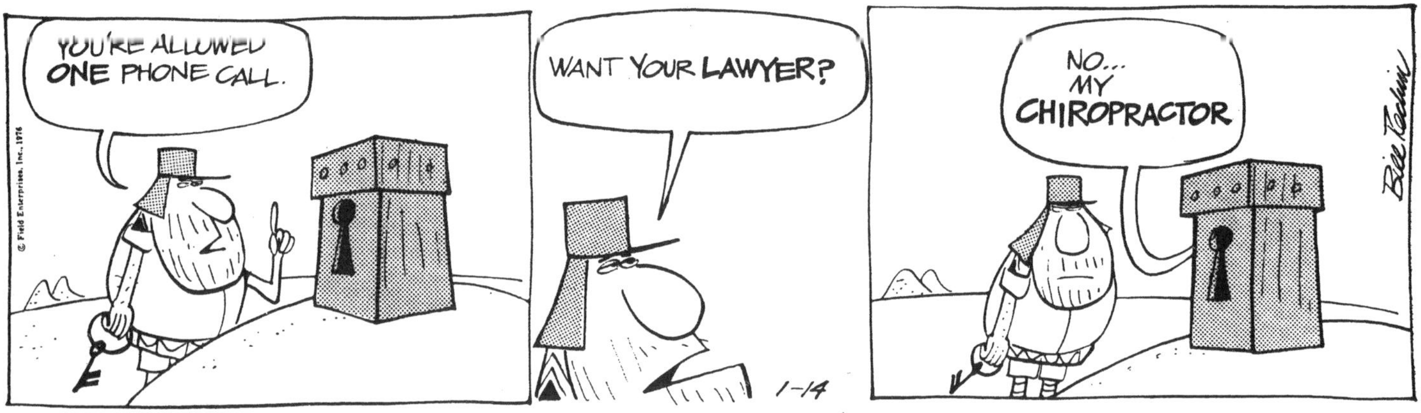
YOU'RE ALLOWED ONE PHONE CALL.
© Field Enterprises, Inc., 1976
WANT YOUR LAWYER?
1-14
NO... MY CHIROPRACTOR
Bill Rechin

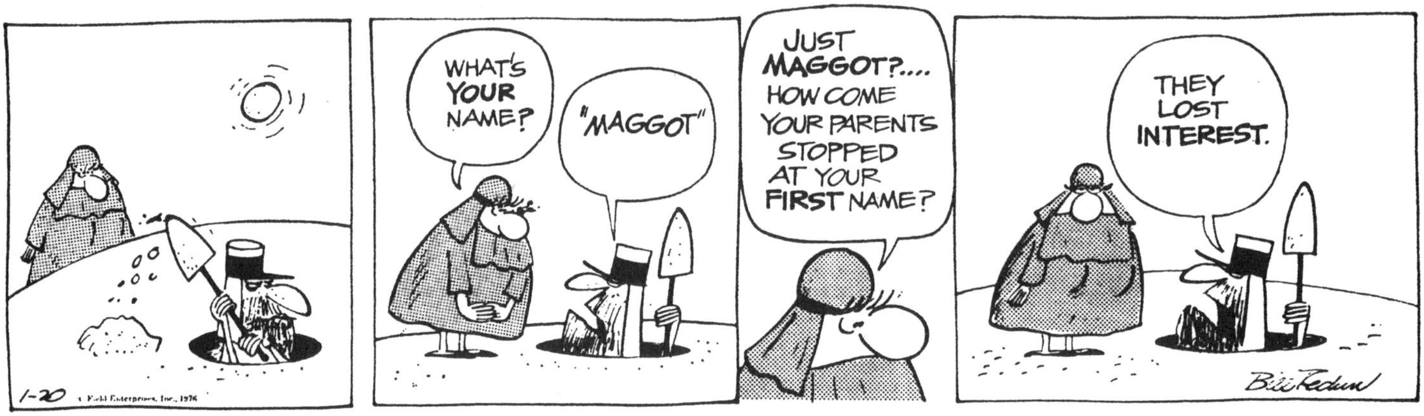
1-20
WHAT'S YOUR NAME?
"MAGGOT"
JUST MAGGOT?.... HOW COME YOUR PARENTS STOPPED AT YOUR FIRST NAME?
THEY LOST INTEREST.
Bill Rechin

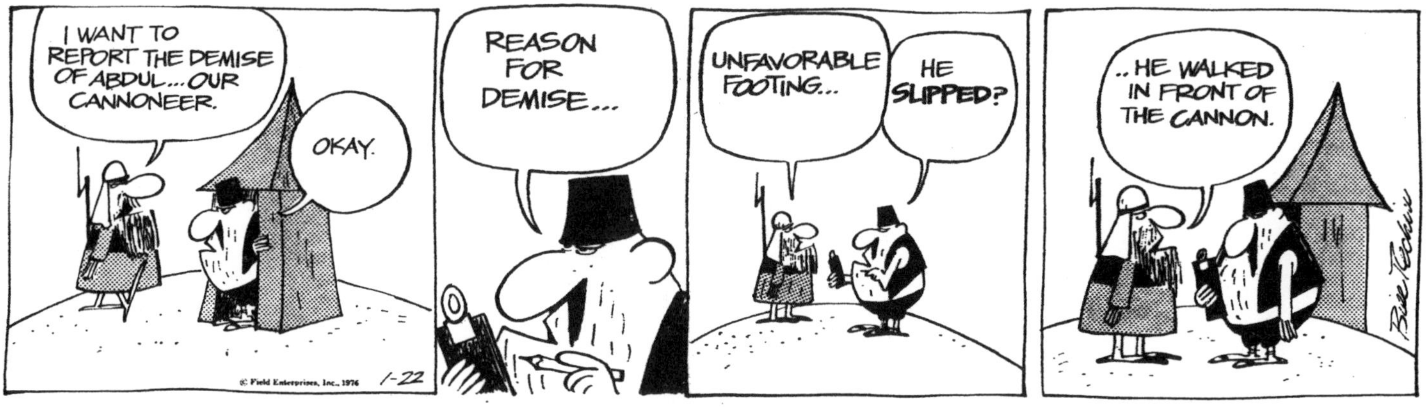
I WANT TO REPORT THE DEMISE OF ABDUL...OUR CANNONEER.
OKAY.
REASON FOR DEMISE...
UNFAVORABLE FOOTING...
HE SLIPPED?
..HE WALKED IN FRONT OF THE CANNON.
© Field Enterprises, Inc., 1976
1-22

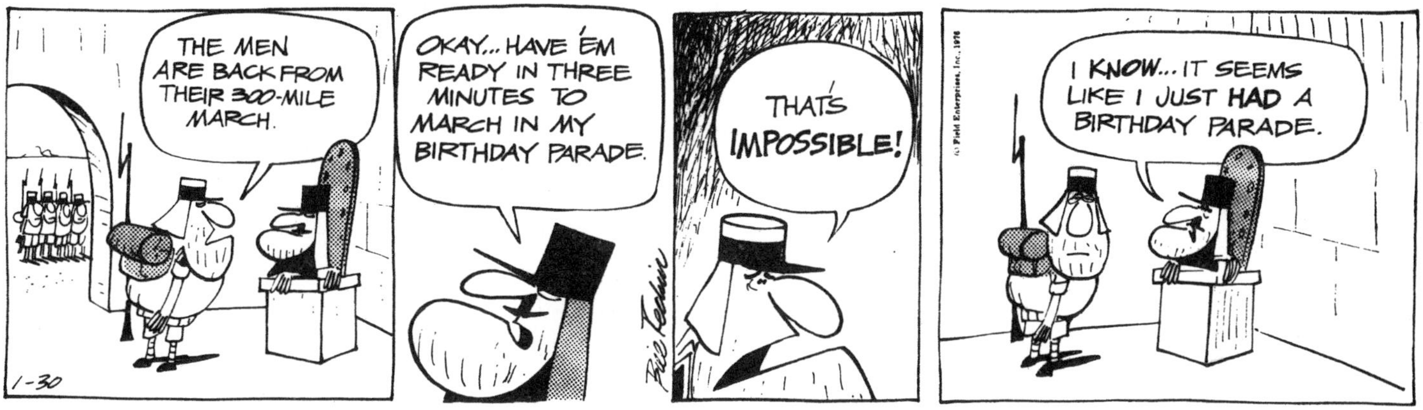
THE MEN ARE BACK FROM THEIR 300-MILE MARCH.
OKAY... HAVE 'EM READY IN THREE MINUTES TO MARCH IN MY BIRTHDAY PARADE.
THAT'S IMPOSSIBLE!
I KNOW... IT SEEMS LIKE I JUST HAD A BIRTHDAY PARADE.
© Field Enterprises, Inc., 1976
1-30

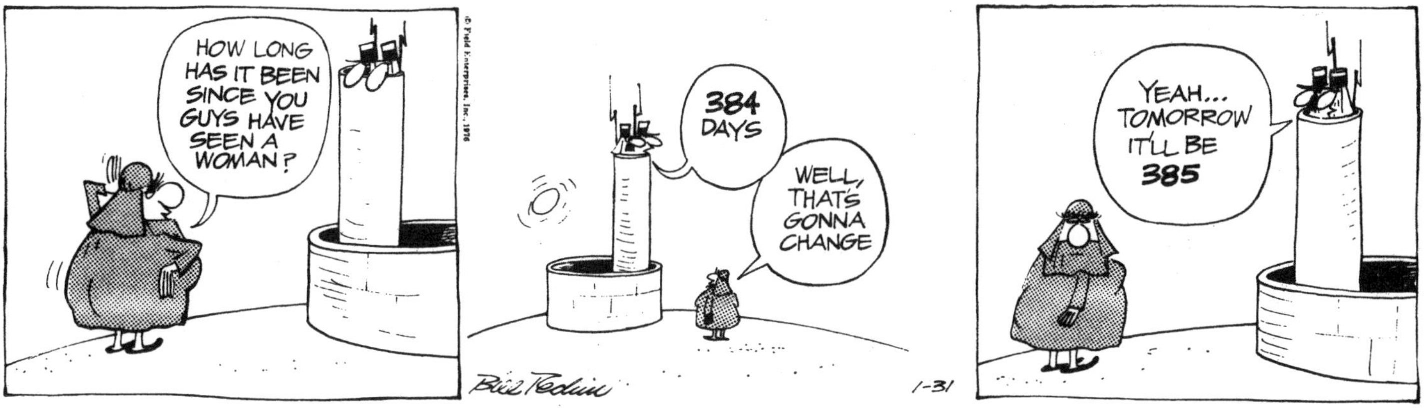
HOW LONG HAS IT BEEN SINCE YOU GUYS HAVE SEEN A WOMAN?
384 DAYS
WELL, THAT'S GONNA CHANGE
YEAH... TOMORROW IT'LL BE 385
© Field Enterprises, Inc., 1976
1-31

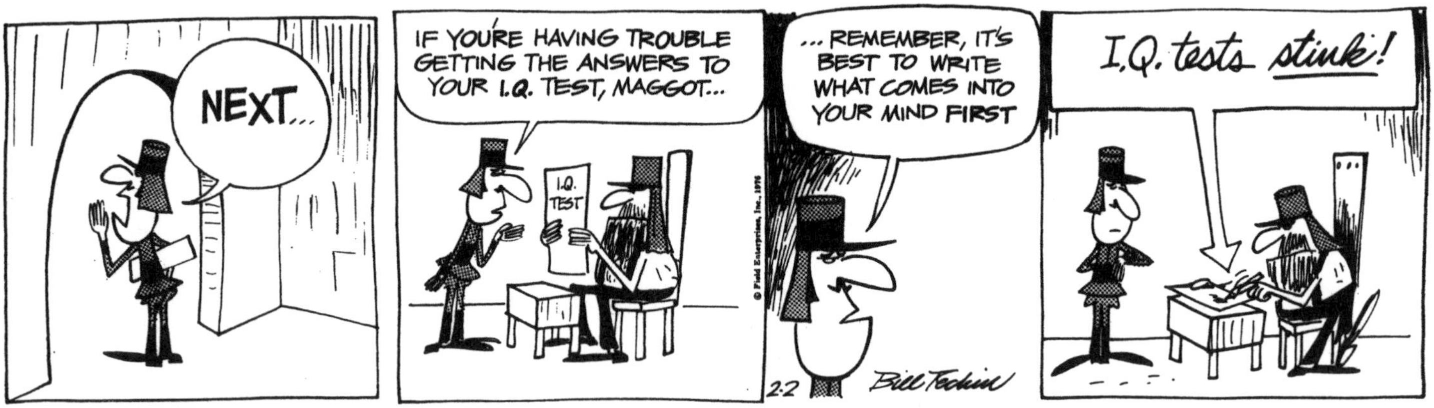
NEXT...
IF YOU'RE HAVING TROUBLE GETTING THE ANSWERS TO YOUR I.Q. TEST, MAGGOT...
I.Q. TEST
... REMEMBER, IT'S BEST TO WRITE WHAT COMES INTO YOUR MIND FIRST
2-2
I.Q. tests stink!

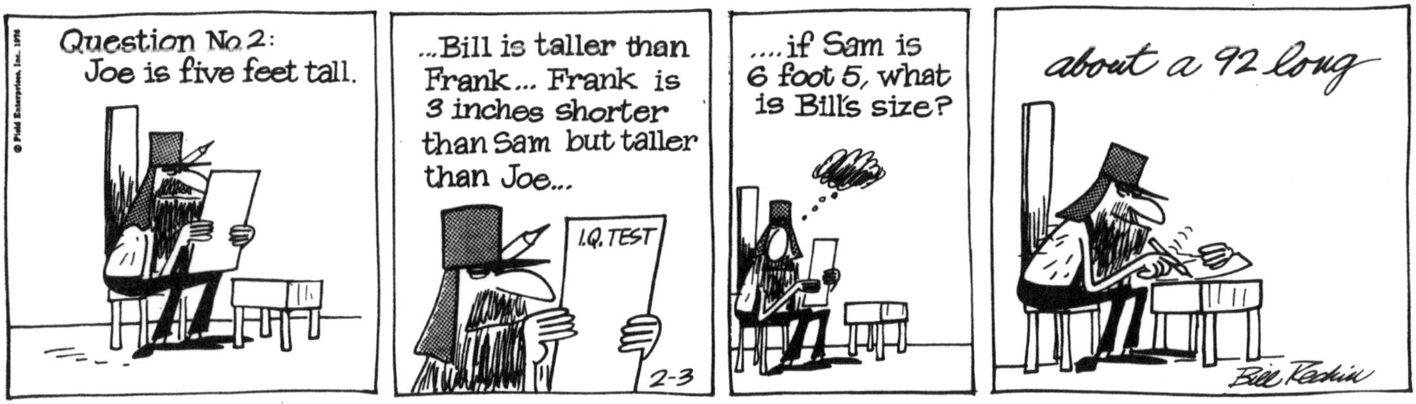
Question No. 2: Joe is five feet tall.
...Bill is taller than Frank... Frank is 3 inches shorter than Sam but taller than Joe...
I.Q. TEST
2-3
....if Sam is 6 foot 5, what is Bill's size?
about a 92 long

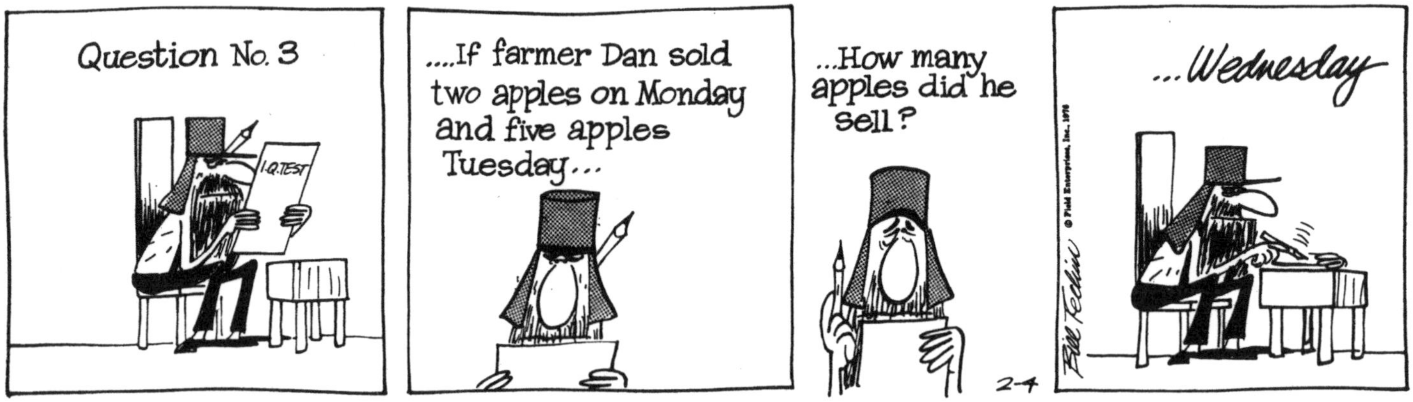
Question No. 3
I.Q. TEST
....If farmer Dan sold two apples on Monday and five apples Tuesday...
...How many apples did he sell?
2-4
...Wednesday

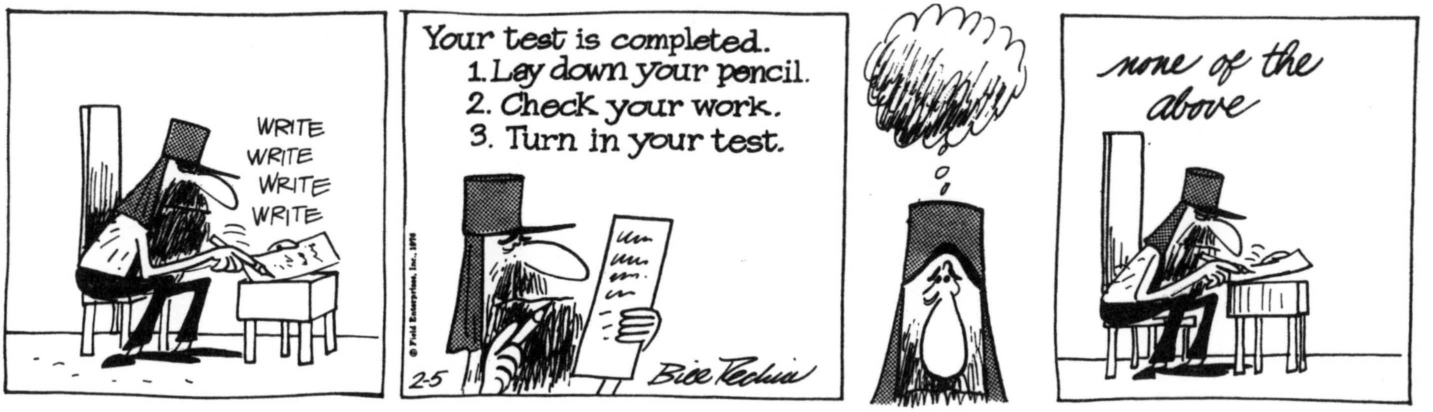
WRITE
WRITE
WRITE
WRITE
Your test is completed.
1. Lay down your pencil.
2. Check your work.
3. Turn in your test.
© Field Enterprises, Inc., 1976
2-5
Bill Rechin
none of the above

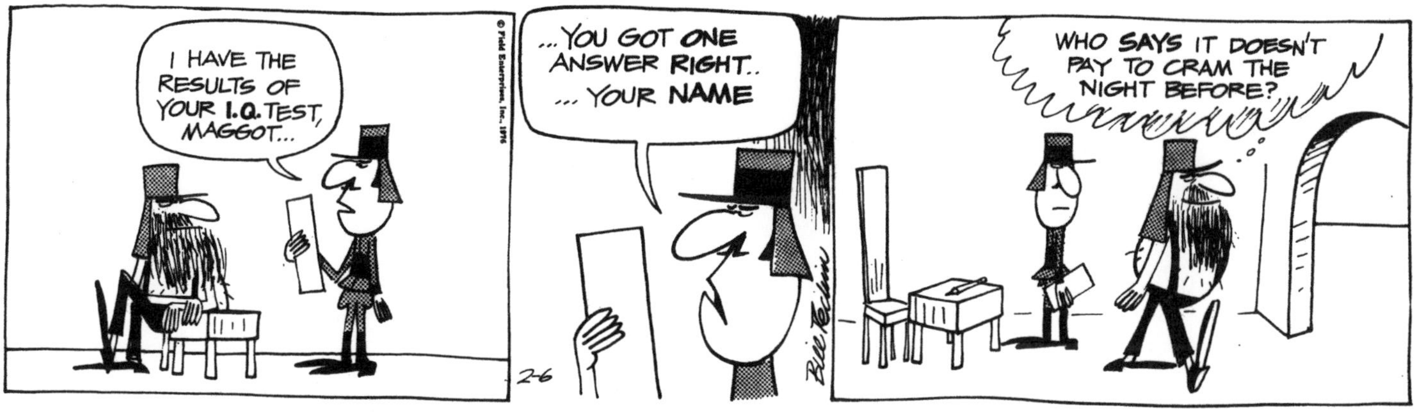
I HAVE THE RESULTS OF YOUR I.Q. TEST, MAGGOT...
© Field Enterprises, Inc., 1976
...YOU GOT ONE ANSWER RIGHT.. ...YOUR NAME
2-6
Bill Rechin
WHO SAYS IT DOESN'T PAY TO CRAM THE NIGHT BEFORE?

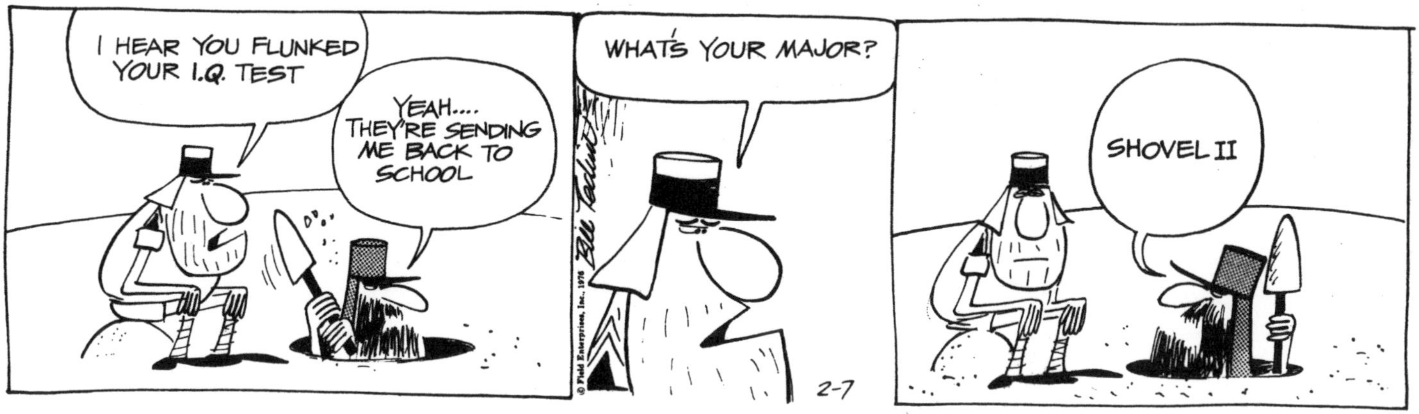
I HEAR YOU FLUNKED YOUR I.Q. TEST
YEAH.... THEY'RE SENDING ME BACK TO SCHOOL
Bill Rechin
© Field Enterprises, Inc., 1976
WHAT'S YOUR MAJOR?
2-7
SHOVEL II

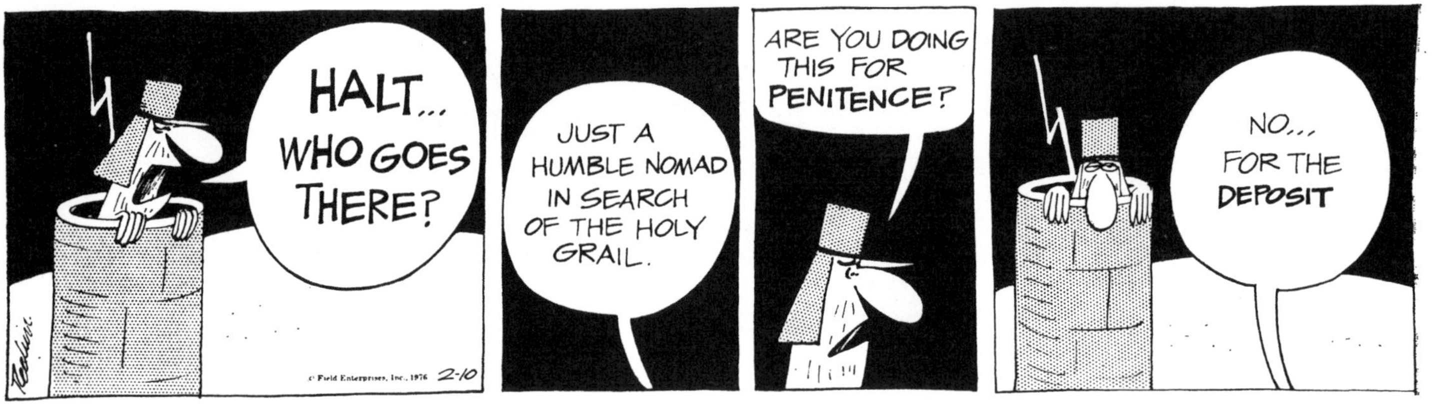
HALT... WHO GOES THERE?
JUST A HUMBLE NOMAD IN SEARCH OF THE HOLY GRAIL.
ARE YOU DOING THIS FOR PENITENCE?
NO... FOR THE DEPOSIT
© Field Enterprises, Inc., 1976 2-10

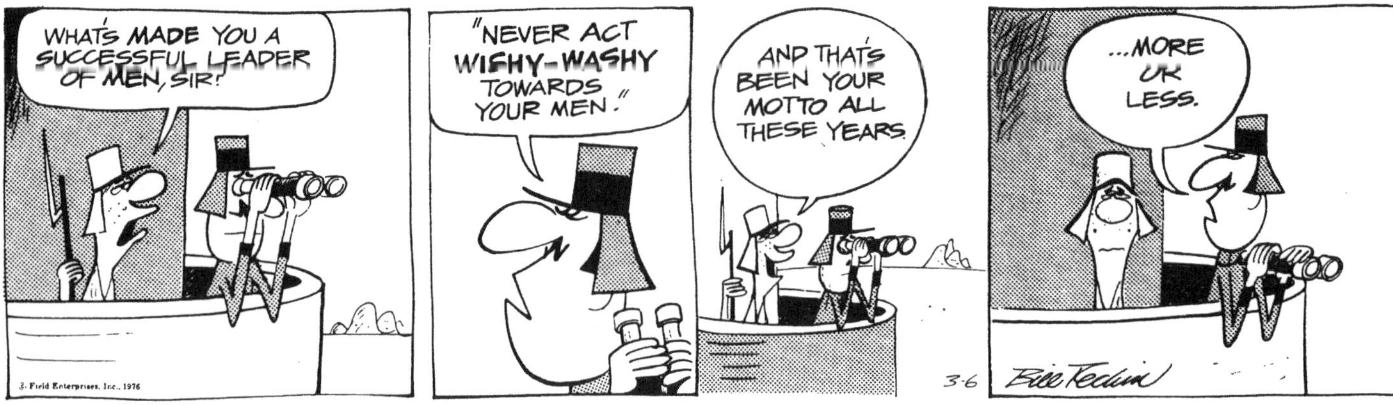
WHAT'S MADE YOU A SUCCESSFUL LEADER OF MEN, SIR?
"NEVER ACT WISHY-WASHY TOWARDS YOUR MEN."
AND THAT'S BEEN YOUR MOTTO ALL THESE YEARS.
...MORE OR LESS.
© Field Enterprises, Inc., 1976
3-6
Bill Rechin

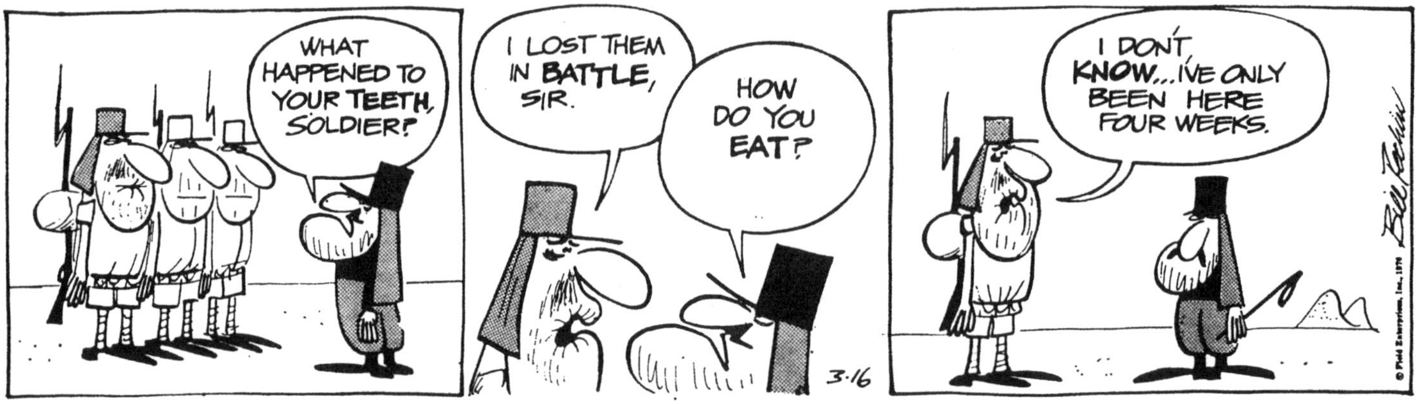
WHAT HAPPENED TO YOUR TEETH, SOLDIER?
I LOST THEM IN BATTLE, SIR.
HOW DO YOU EAT?
3-16
I DON'T KNOW... I'VE ONLY BEEN HERE FOUR WEEKS.
Bill Rechin
© Field Enterprises, Inc., 1976

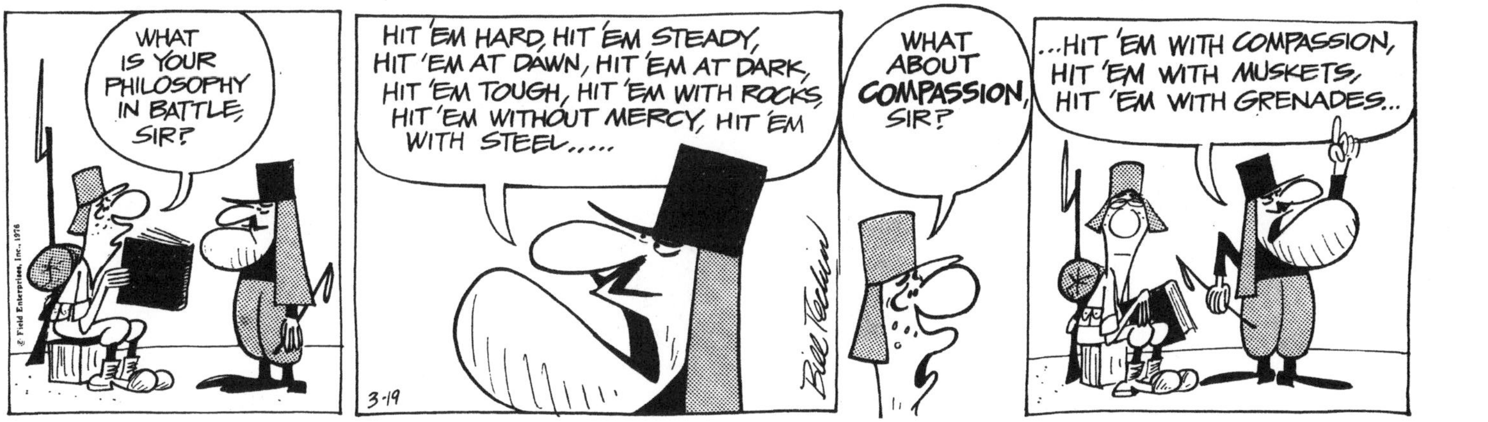

WHAT IS YOUR PHILOSOPHY IN BATTLE, SIR?
HIT 'EM HARD, HIT 'EM STEADY, HIT 'EM AT DAWN, HIT 'EM AT DARK, HIT 'EM TOUGH, HIT 'EM WITH ROCKS, HIT 'EM WITHOUT MERCY, HIT 'EM WITH STEEL.....
WHAT ABOUT COMPASSION, SIR?
...HIT 'EM WITH COMPASSION, HIT 'EM WITH MUSKETS, HIT 'EM WITH GRENADES...
3-19
© Field Enterprises, Inc., 1976

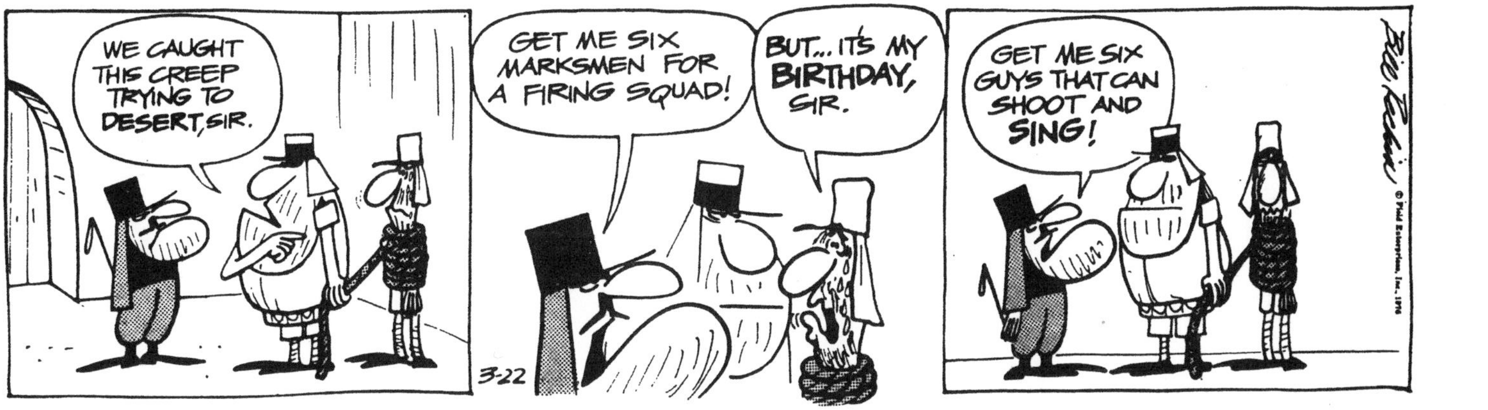

WE CAUGHT THIS CREEP TRYING TO DESERT, SIR.
GET ME SIX MARKSMEN FOR A FIRING SQUAD!
BUT... IT'S MY BIRTHDAY, SIR.
GET ME SIX GUYS THAT CAN SHOOT AND SING!
3-22
© Field Enterprises, Inc., 1976

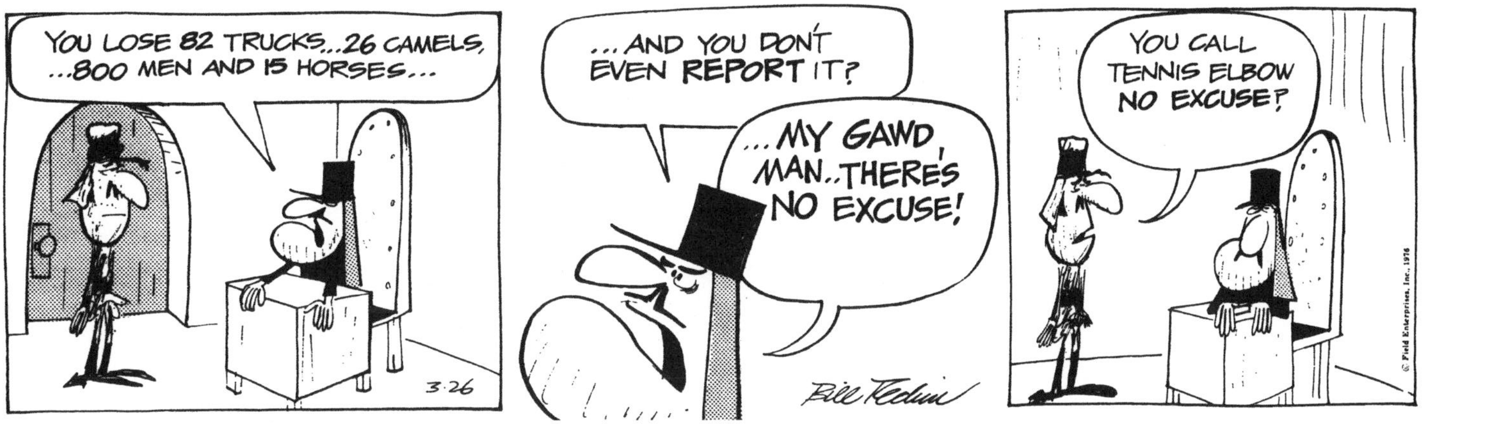

YOU LOSE 82 TRUCKS...26 CAMELS, ...800 MEN AND 15 HORSES...
...AND YOU DON'T EVEN REPORT IT?
...MY GAWD, MAN...THERE'S NO EXCUSE!
YOU CALL TENNIS ELBOW NO EXCUSE?
3-26
© Field Enterprises, Inc., 1976

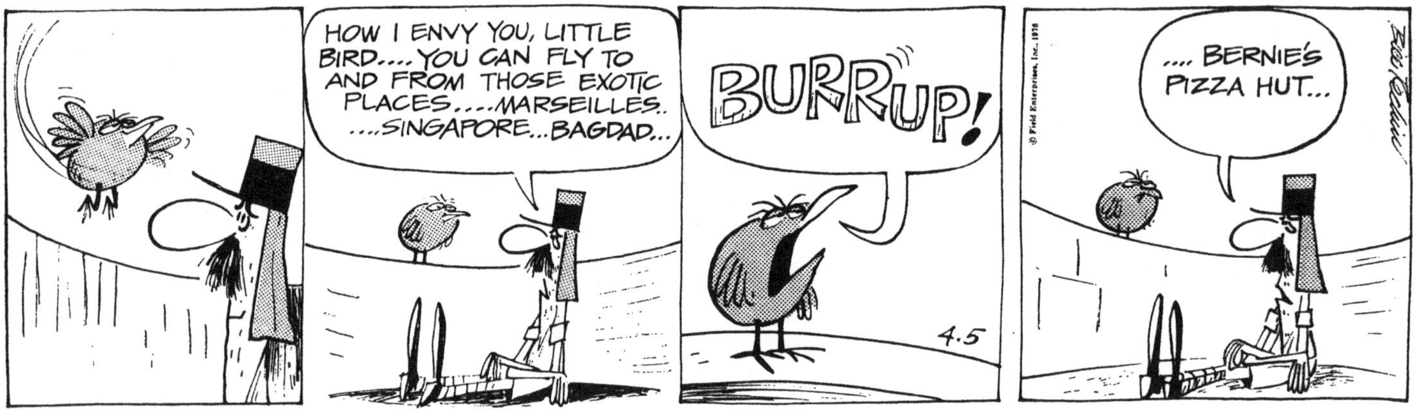
HOW I ENVY YOU, LITTLE BIRD.... YOU CAN FLY TO AND FROM THOSE EXOTIC PLACES.... MARSEILLES.. ....SINGAPORE...BAGDAD...
BURRUP!
4.5
.... BERNIE'S PIZZA HUT...
© Field Enterprises, Inc., 1976
Bill Rechin

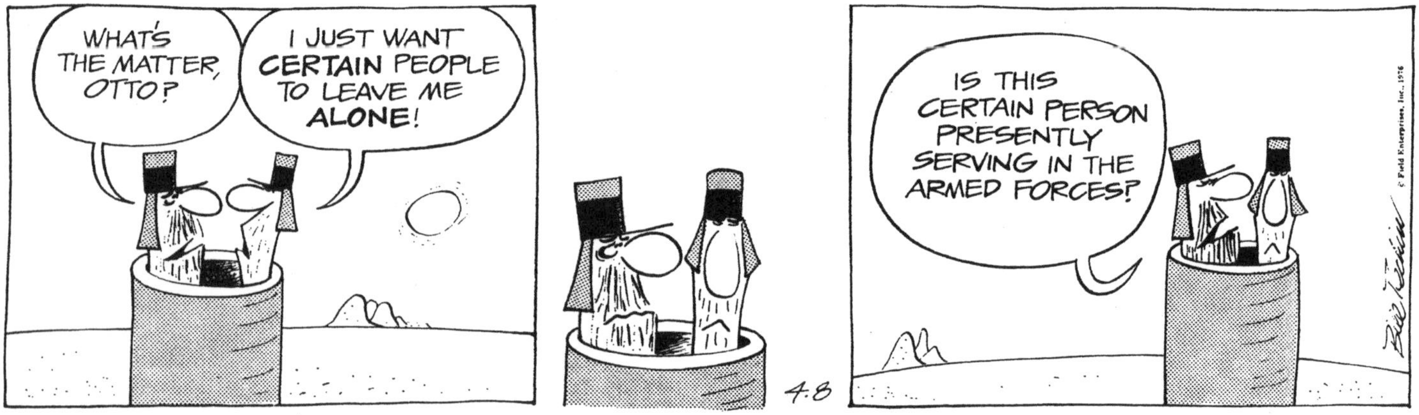
WHAT'S THE MATTER, OTTO?
I JUST WANT **CERTAIN** PEOPLE TO LEAVE ME **ALONE**!
4.8
IS THIS CERTAIN PERSON PRESENTLY SERVING IN THE ARMED FORCES?
© Field Enterprises, Inc., 1976
Bill Rechin

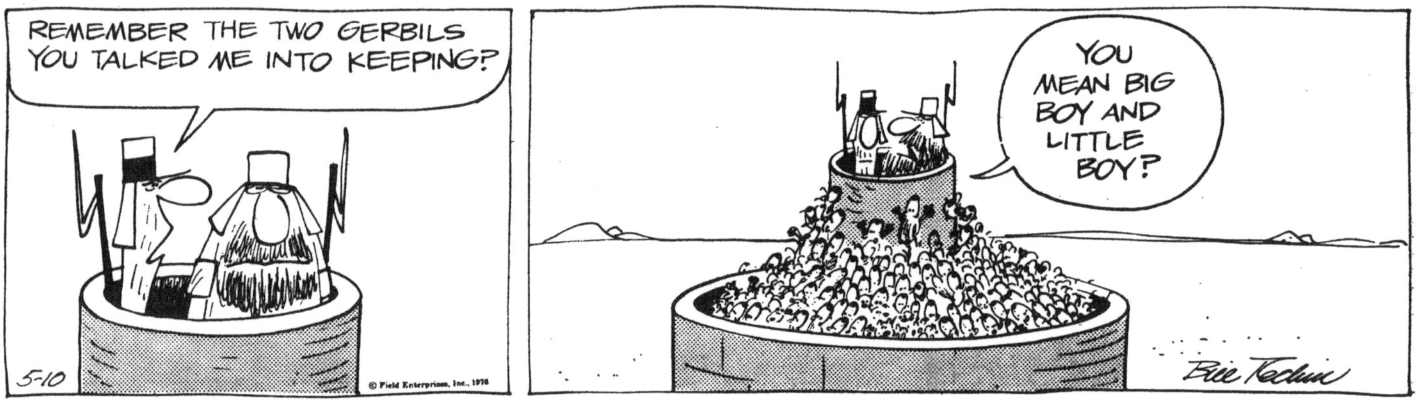
REMEMBER THE TWO GERBILS YOU TALKED ME INTO KEEPING?
5-10
© Field Enterprises, Inc., 1976
YOU MEAN BIG BOY AND LITTLE BOY?
Bill Rechin

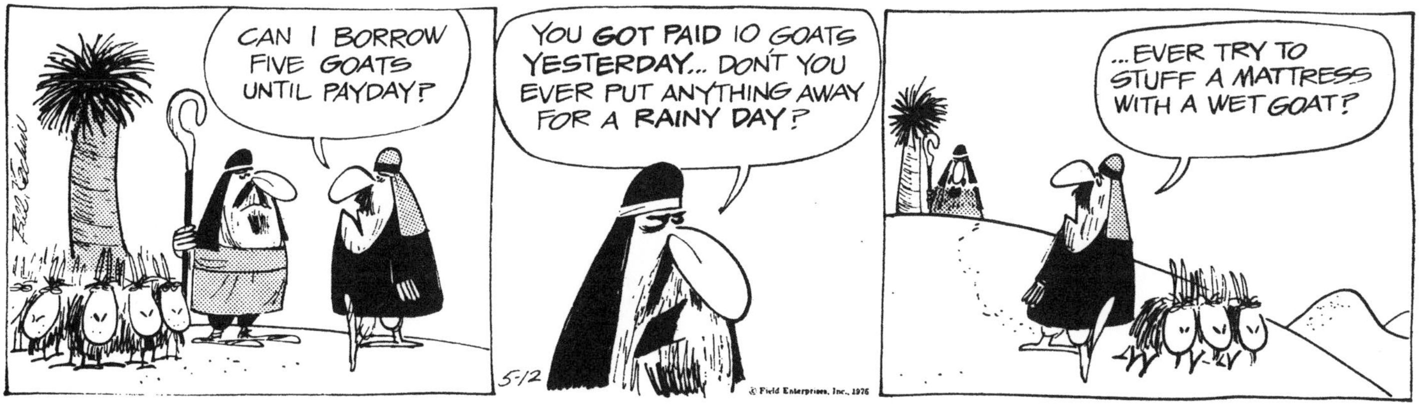
CAN I BORROW FIVE GOATS UNTIL PAYDAY?
YOU GOT PAID 10 GOATS YESTERDAY... DON'T YOU EVER PUT ANYTHING AWAY FOR A RAINY DAY?
...EVER TRY TO STUFF A MATTRESS WITH A WET GOAT?
5-12
© Field Enterprises, Inc., 1976

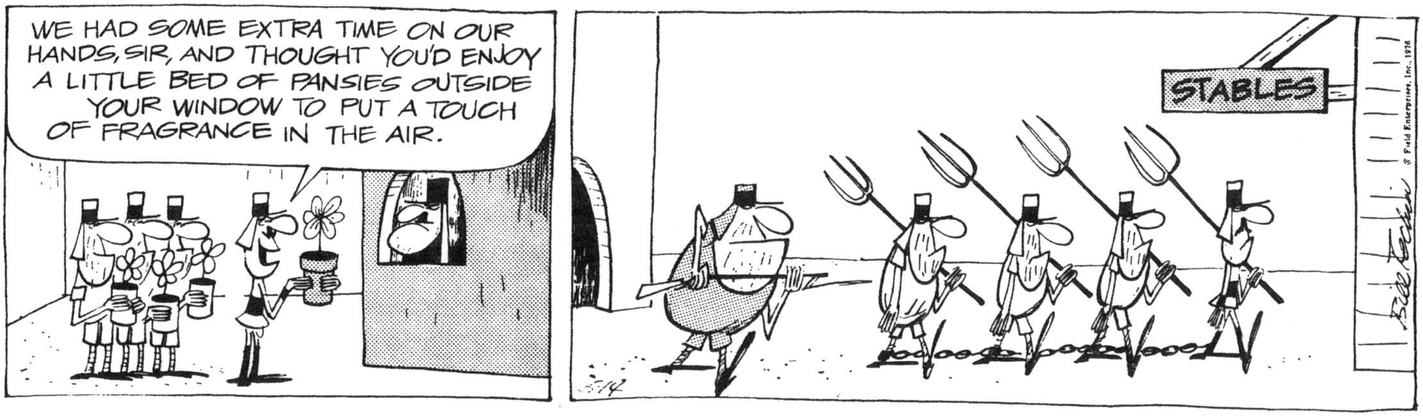
WE HAD SOME EXTRA TIME ON OUR HANDS, SIR, AND THOUGHT YOU'D ENJOY A LITTLE BED OF PANSIES OUTSIDE YOUR WINDOW TO PUT A TOUCH OF FRAGRANCE IN THE AIR.
STABLES
5-14

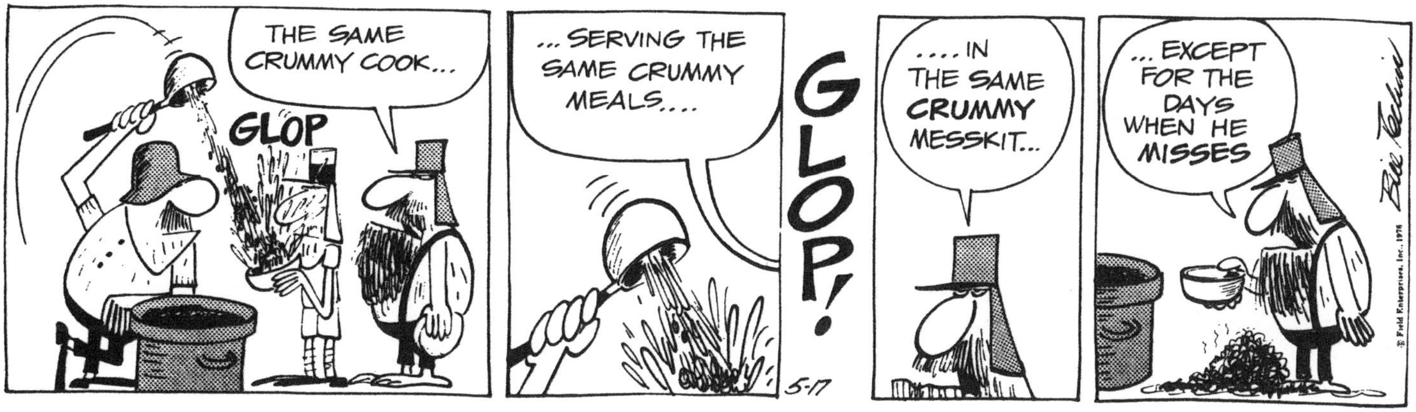
THE SAME CRUMMY COOK...
GLOP
...SERVING THE SAME CRUMMY MEALS....
GLOP!
....IN THE SAME CRUMMY MESSKIT...
...EXCEPT FOR THE DAYS WHEN HE MISSES
5-17

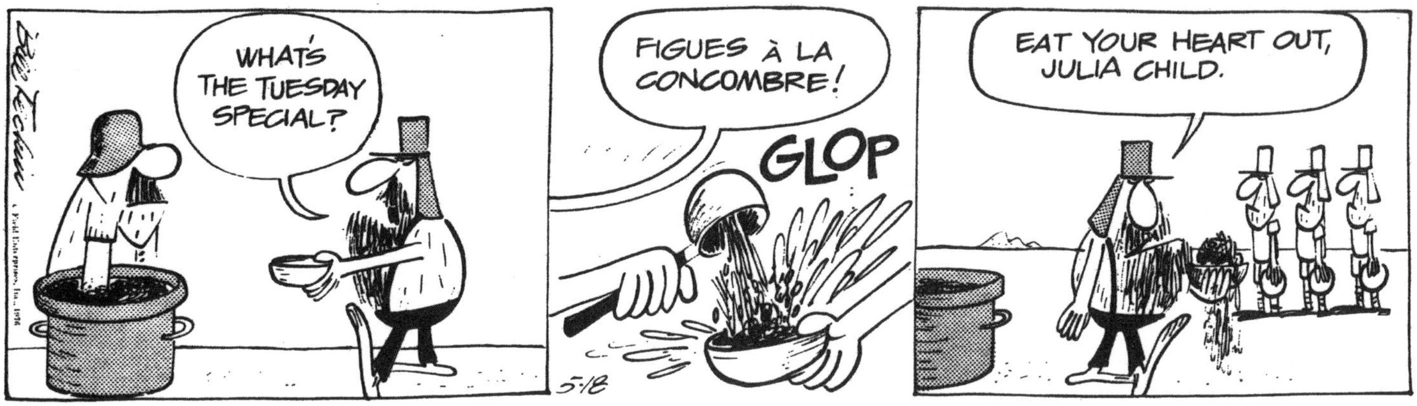
WHAT'S THE TUESDAY SPECIAL?
FIGUES À LA CONCOMBRE!
GLOP
5-18
EAT YOUR HEART OUT, JULIA CHILD.

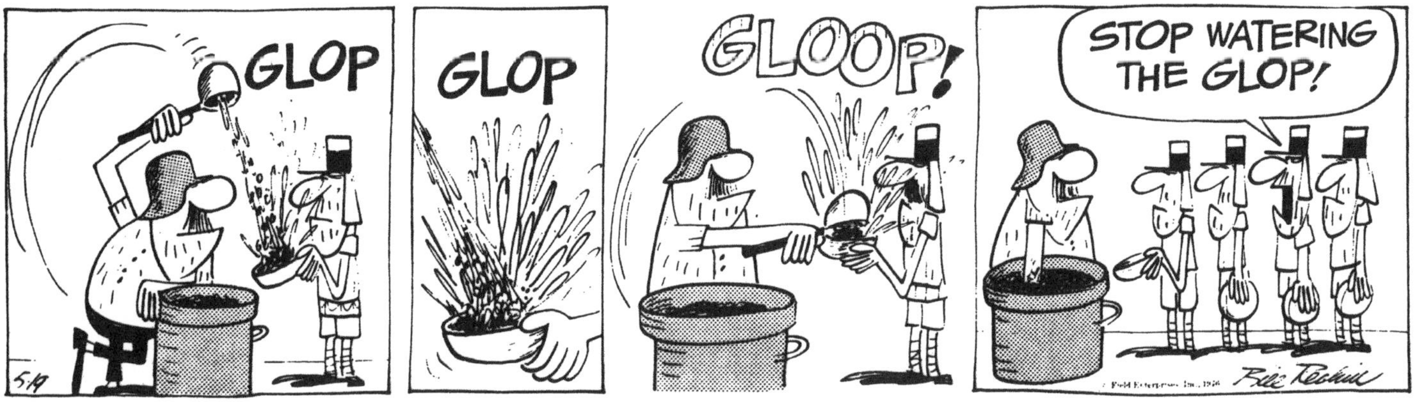
GLOP
5-19
GLOP
GLOOP!
STOP WATERING THE GLOP!

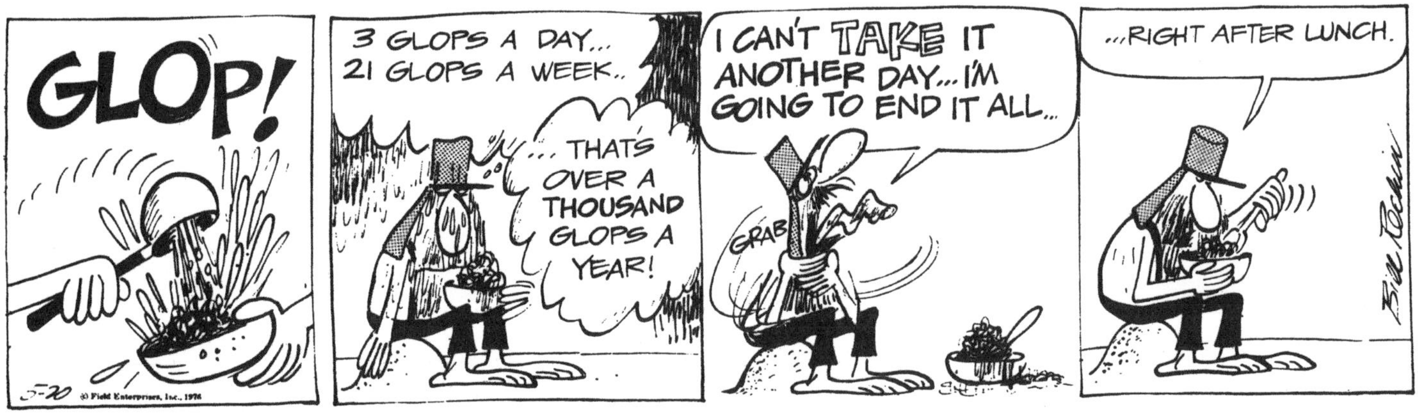
GLOP!
5-20
© Field Enterprises, Inc., 1976
3 GLOPS A DAY... 21 GLOPS A WEEK..
...THAT'S OVER A THOUSAND GLOPS A YEAR!
I CAN'T TAKE IT ANOTHER DAY... I'M GOING TO END IT ALL...
GRAB
...RIGHT AFTER LUNCH.

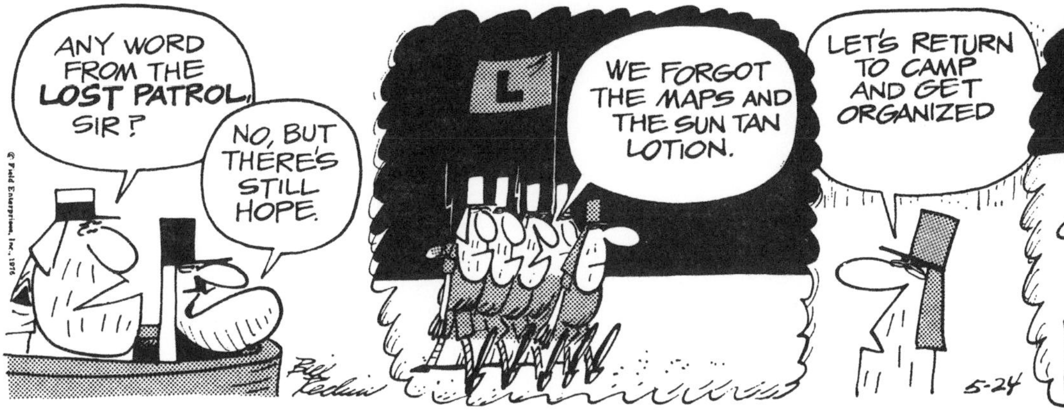
ANY WORD FROM THE **LOST PATROL**, SIR?
NO, BUT THERE'S STILL HOPE.
WE FORGOT THE MAPS AND THE SUN TAN LOTION.
LET'S RETURN TO CAMP AND GET ORGANIZED
5-24

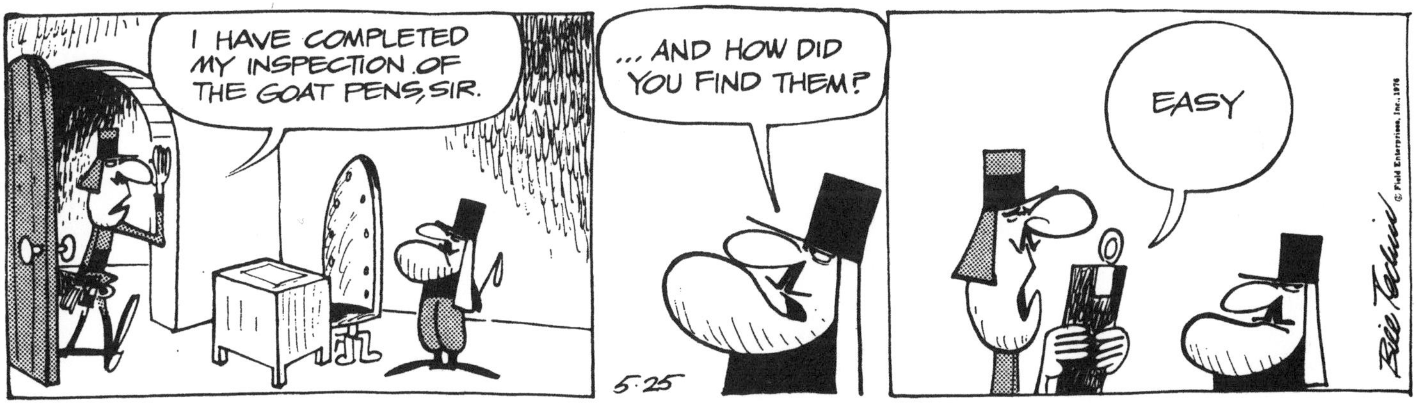
I HAVE COMPLETED MY INSPECTION OF THE GOAT PENS, SIR.
... AND HOW DID YOU FIND THEM?
EASY
5-25

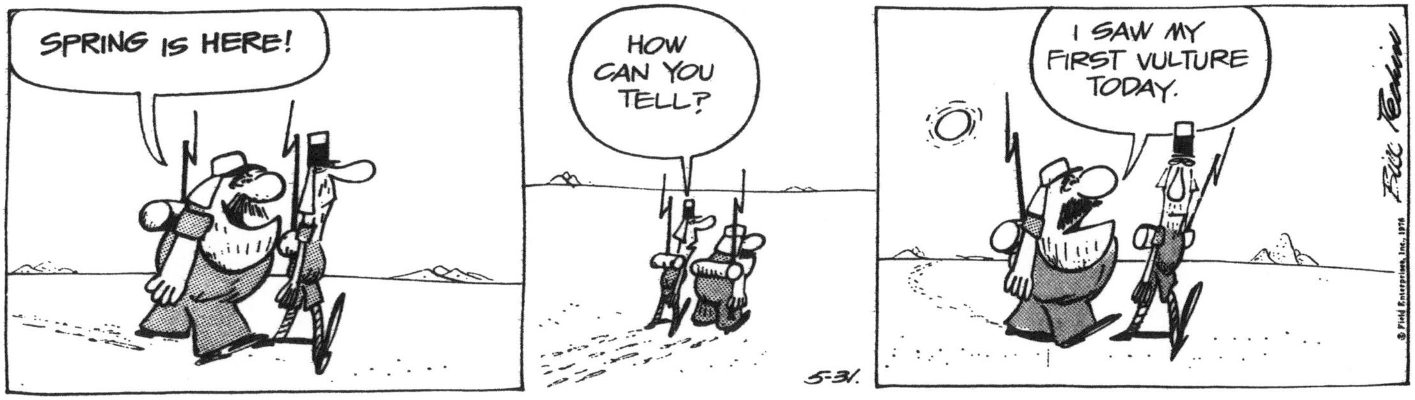
SPRING IS HERE!
HOW CAN YOU TELL?
I SAW MY FIRST VULTURE TODAY.
5-31

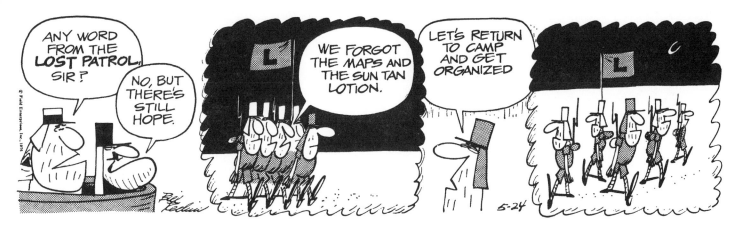

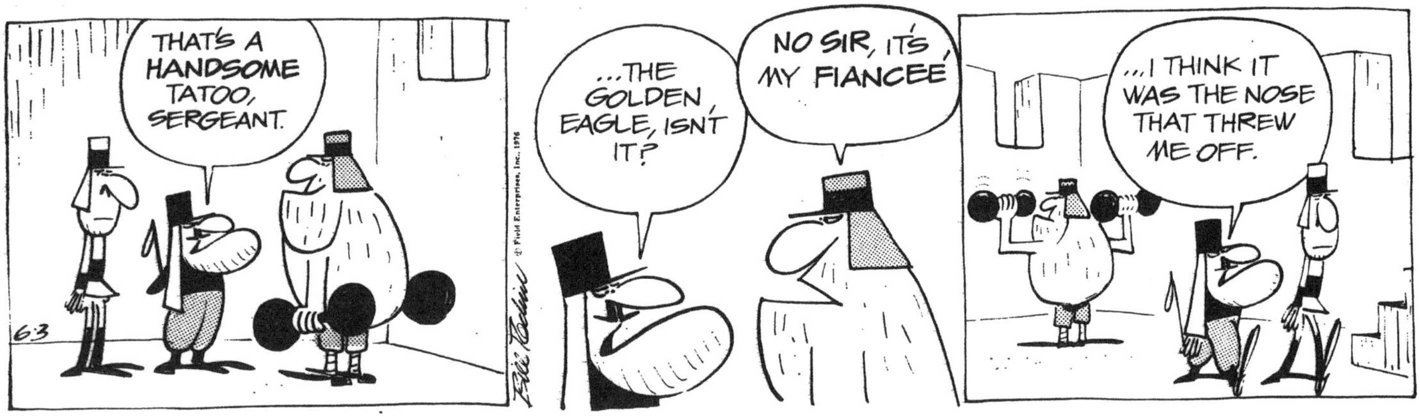

THAT'S A HANDSOME TATOO, SERGEANT.
6·3
...THE GOLDEN EAGLE, ISN'T IT?
NO SIR, IT'S MY FIANCEE
...I THINK IT WAS THE NOSE THAT THREW ME OFF.

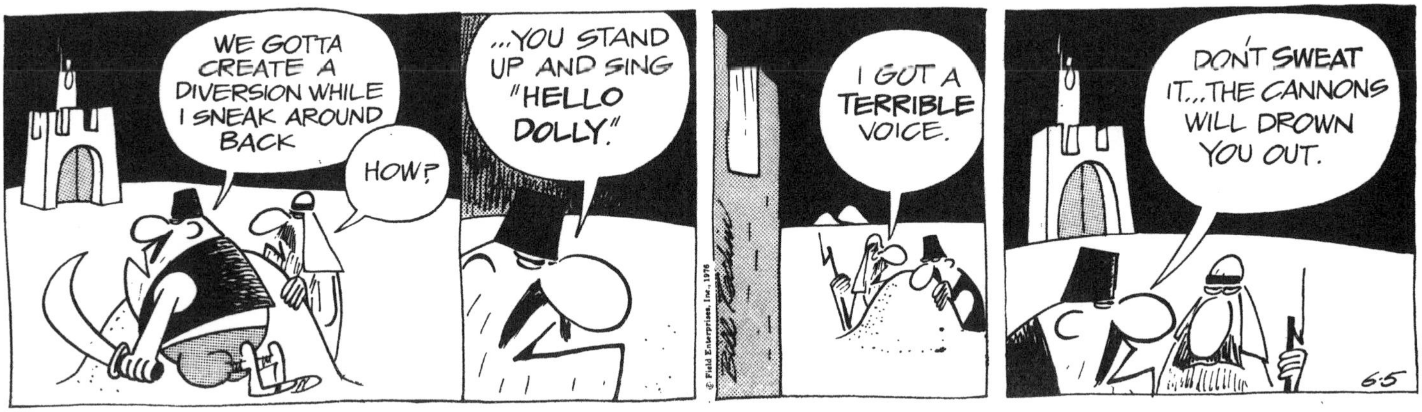

WE GOTTA CREATE A DIVERSION WHILE I SNEAK AROUND BACK
HOW?
...YOU STAND UP AND SING "HELLO DOLLY."
I GOT A TERRIBLE VOICE.
DON'T SWEAT IT...THE CANNONS WILL DROWN YOU OUT.
6·5

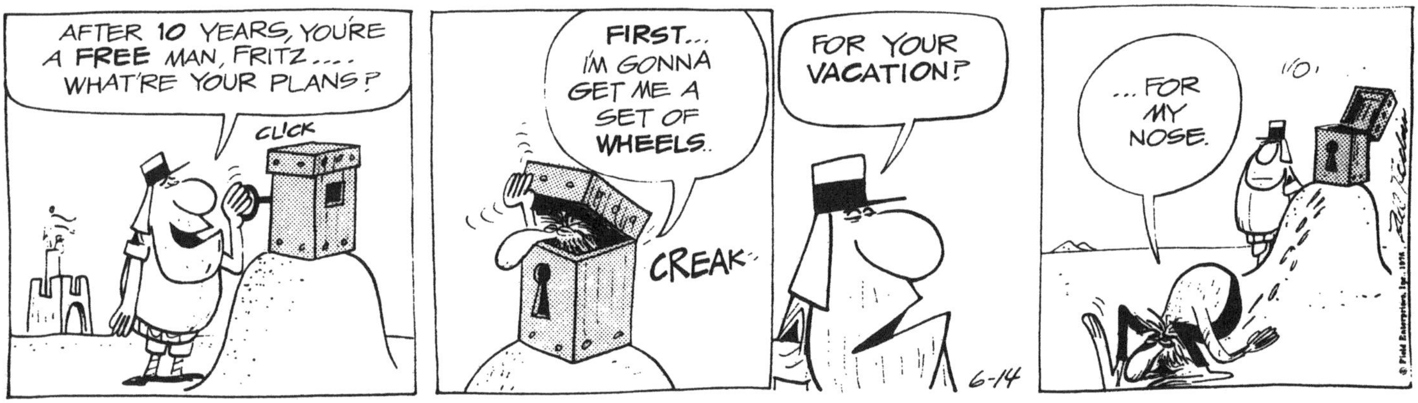

AFTER 10 YEARS, YOU'RE A FREE MAN, FRITZ.... WHAT'RE YOUR PLANS?
CLICK
FIRST... I'M GONNA GET ME A SET OF WHEELS.
CREAK
FOR YOUR VACATION?
6-14
...FOR MY NOSE.

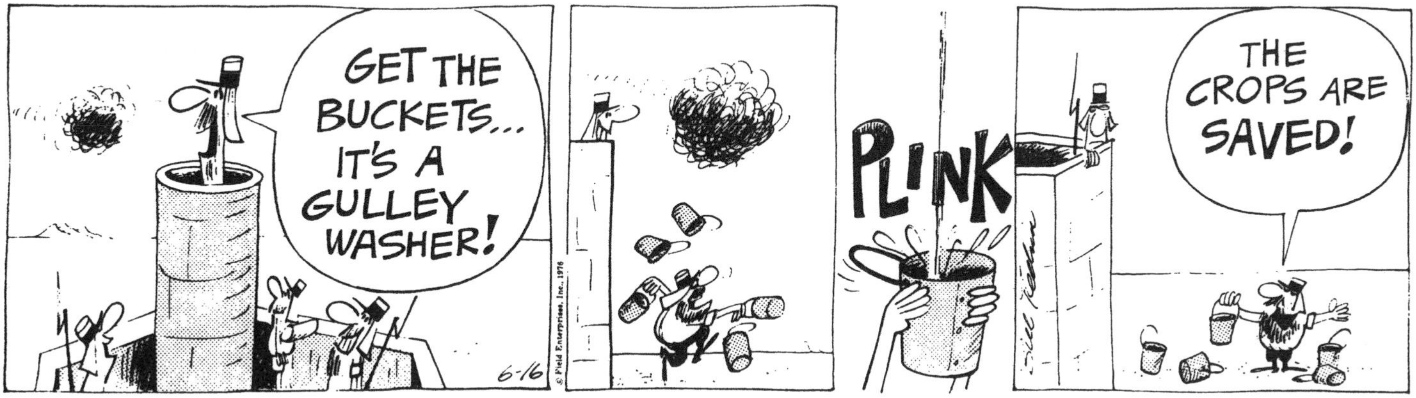
GET THE BUCKETS... IT'S A GULLEY WASHER!
6-16
© Field Enterprises, Inc., 1976
PLINK
THE CROPS ARE SAVED!

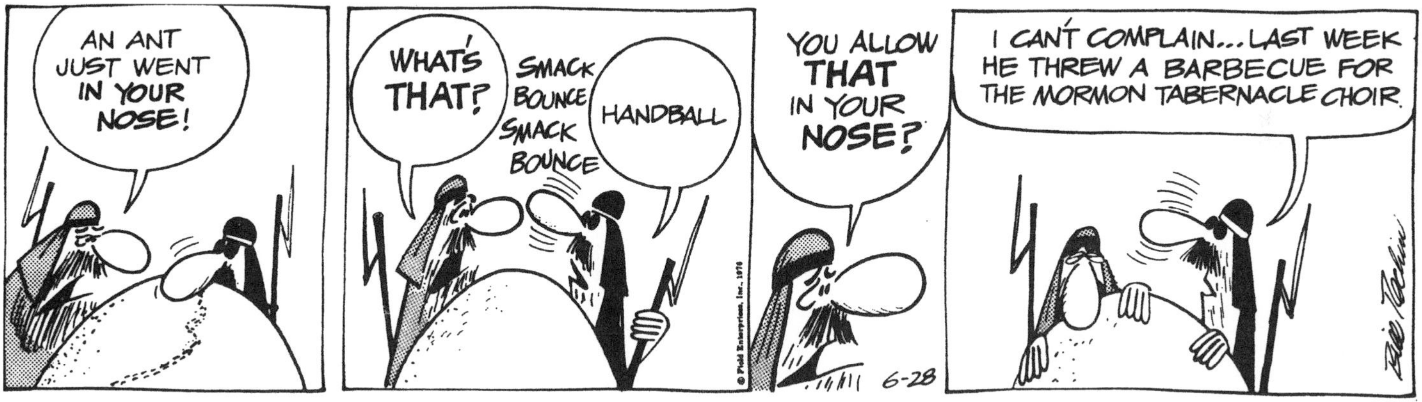
AN ANT JUST WENT IN YOUR NOSE!
WHAT'S THAT?
SMACK BOUNCE SMACK BOUNCE
HANDBALL
© Field Enterprises, Inc., 1976
YOU ALLOW THAT IN YOUR NOSE?
6-28
I CAN'T COMPLAIN... LAST WEEK HE THREW A BARBECUE FOR THE MORMON TABERNACLE CHOIR.

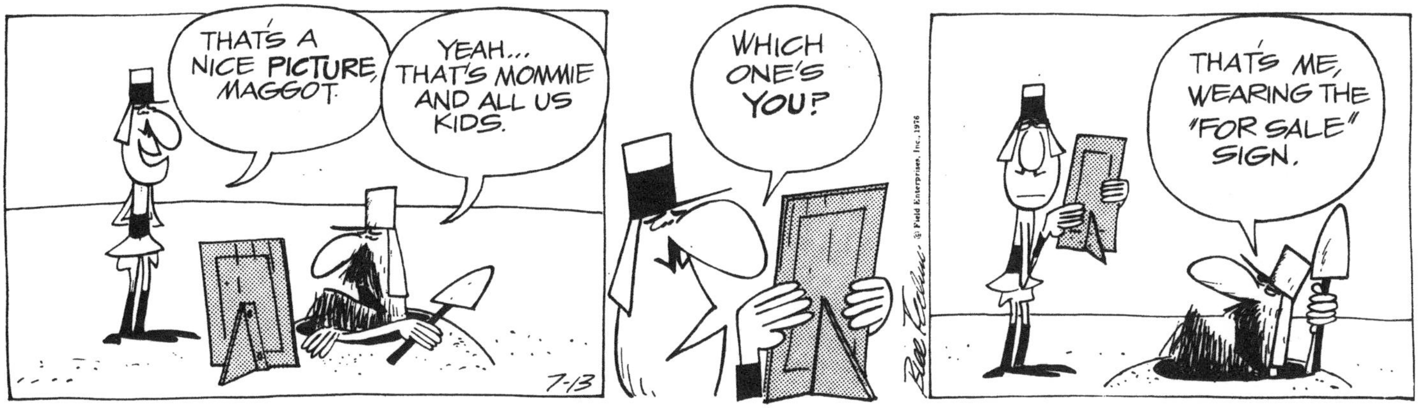
THAT'S A NICE PICTURE, MAGGOT.
YEAH... THAT'S MOMMIE AND ALL US KIDS.
7-13
WHICH ONE'S YOU?
© Field Enterprises, Inc., 1976
THAT'S ME, WEARING THE "FOR SALE" SIGN.

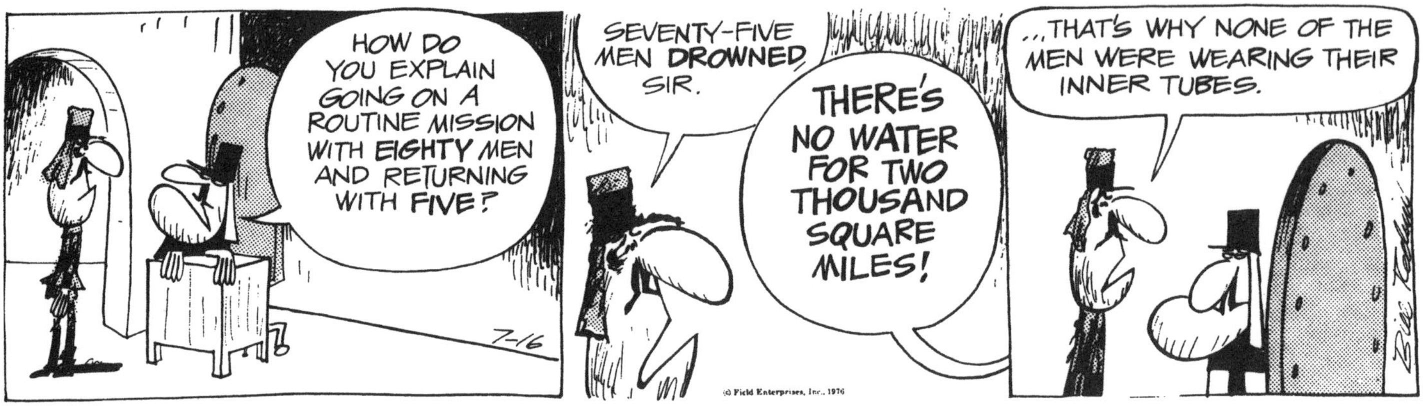
HOW DO YOU EXPLAIN GOING ON A ROUTINE MISSION WITH EIGHTY MEN AND RETURNING WITH FIVE?
7-16
SEVENTY-FIVE MEN DROWNED, SIR.
THERE'S NO WATER FOR TWO THOUSAND SQUARE MILES!
(c) Field Enterprises, Inc., 1976
...THAT'S WHY NONE OF THE MEN WERE WEARING THEIR INNER TUBES.

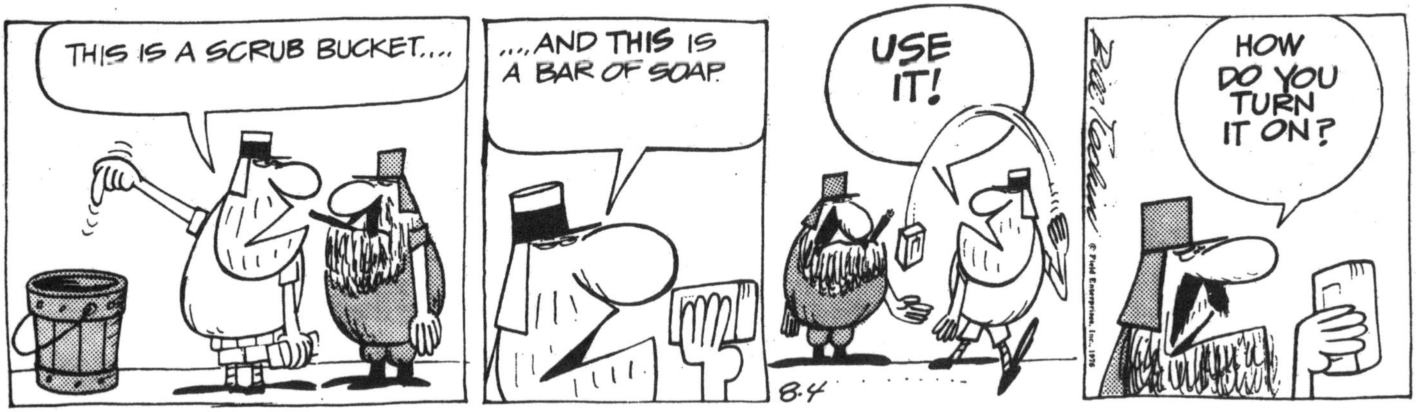
THIS IS A SCRUB BUCKET....
....AND THIS IS A BAR OF SOAP.
USE IT!
8-4
HOW DO YOU TURN IT ON?
© Field Enterprises, Inc., 1976

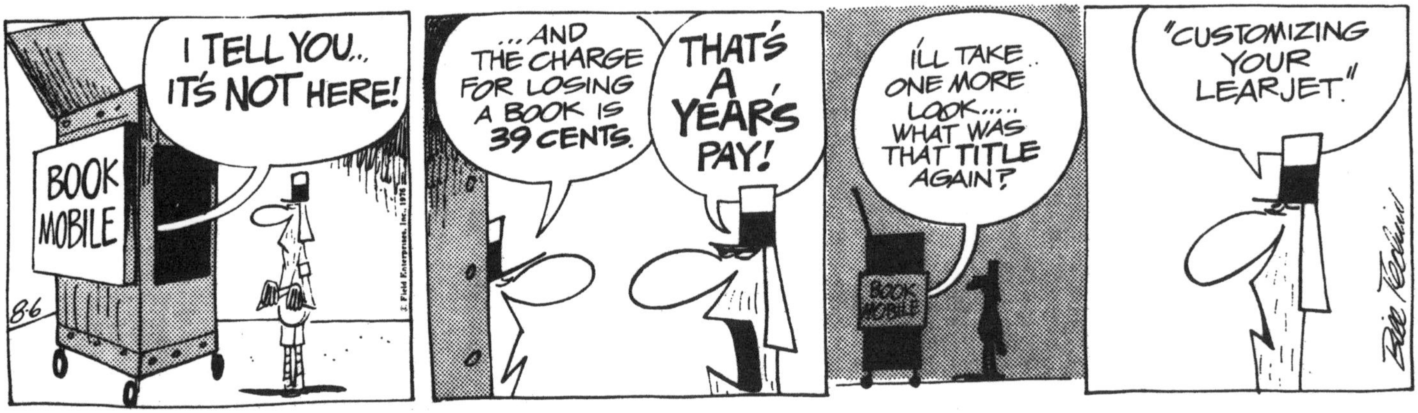
I TELL YOU.. IT'S NOT HERE!
BOOK MOBILE
8-6
© Field Enterprises, Inc., 1976
...AND THE CHARGE FOR LOSING A BOOK IS 39 CENTS.
THAT'S A YEAR'S PAY!
I'LL TAKE ONE MORE LOOK..... WHAT WAS THAT TITLE AGAIN?
BOOK MOBILE
"CUSTOMIZING YOUR LEARJET."

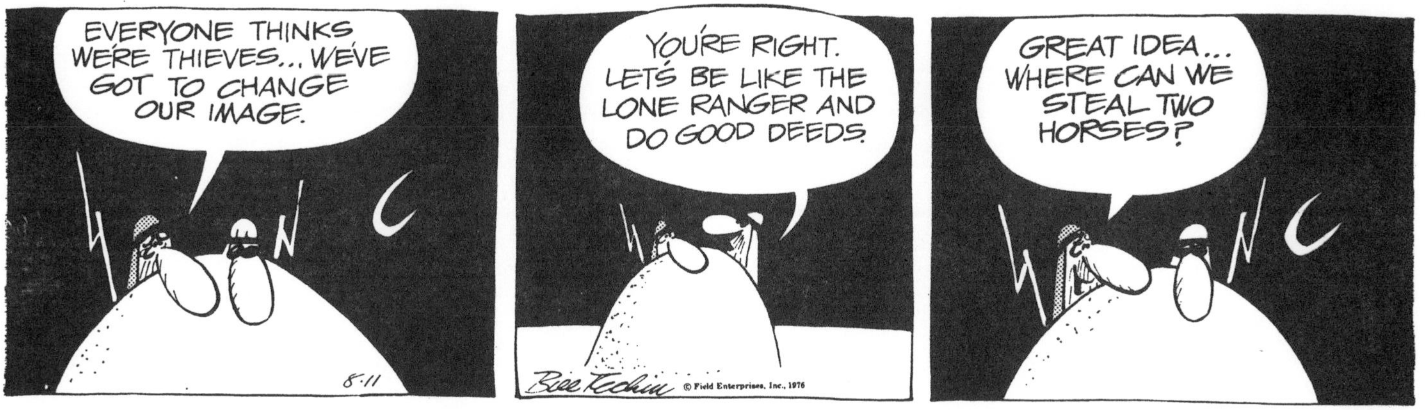
EVERYONE THINKS WE'RE THIEVES... WE'VE GOT TO CHANGE OUR IMAGE.
8·11
YOU'RE RIGHT. LET'S BE LIKE THE LONE RANGER AND DO GOOD DEEDS.
© Field Enterprises, Inc., 1976
GREAT IDEA... WHERE CAN WE STEAL TWO HORSES?

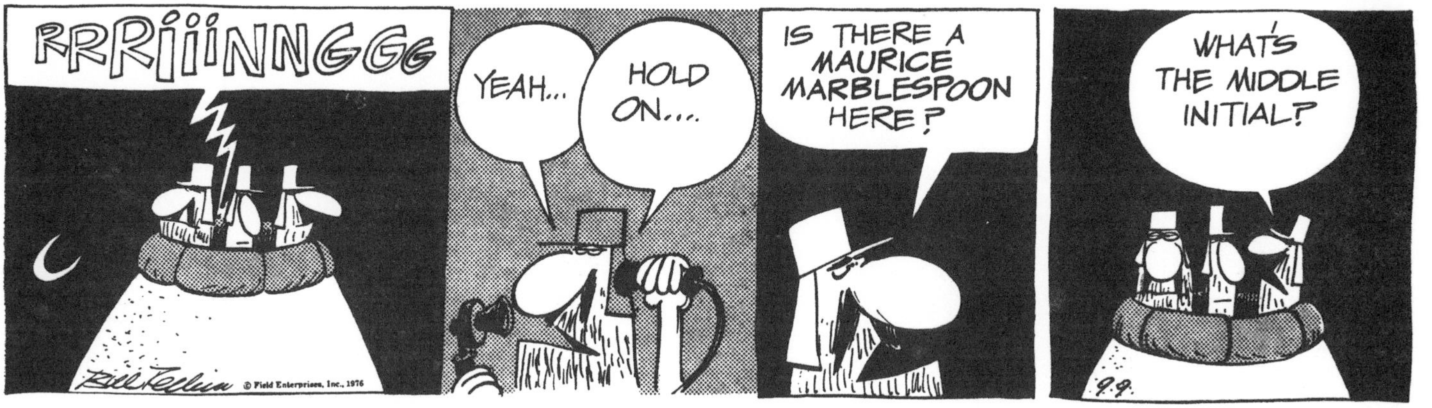
RRRiiiNNGGG
© Field Enterprises, Inc., 1976
YEAH...
HOLD ON....
IS THERE A MAURICE MARBLESPOON HERE?
WHAT'S THE MIDDLE INITIAL?
9·9

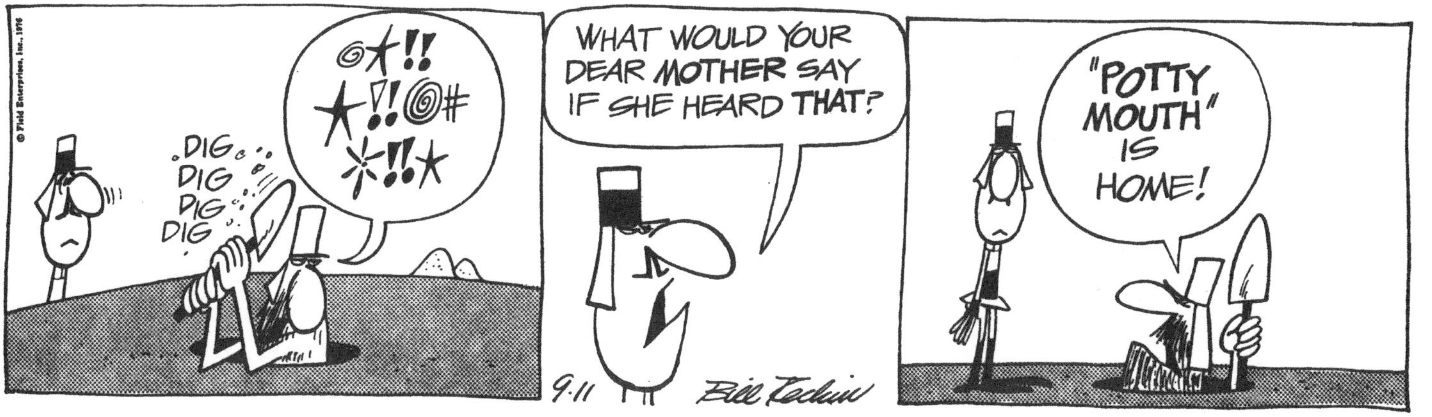
© Field Enterprises, Inc., 1976
DIG
DIG
DIG
DIG
WHAT WOULD YOUR DEAR MOTHER SAY IF SHE HEARD THAT?
9·11
"POTTY MOUTH" IS HOME!

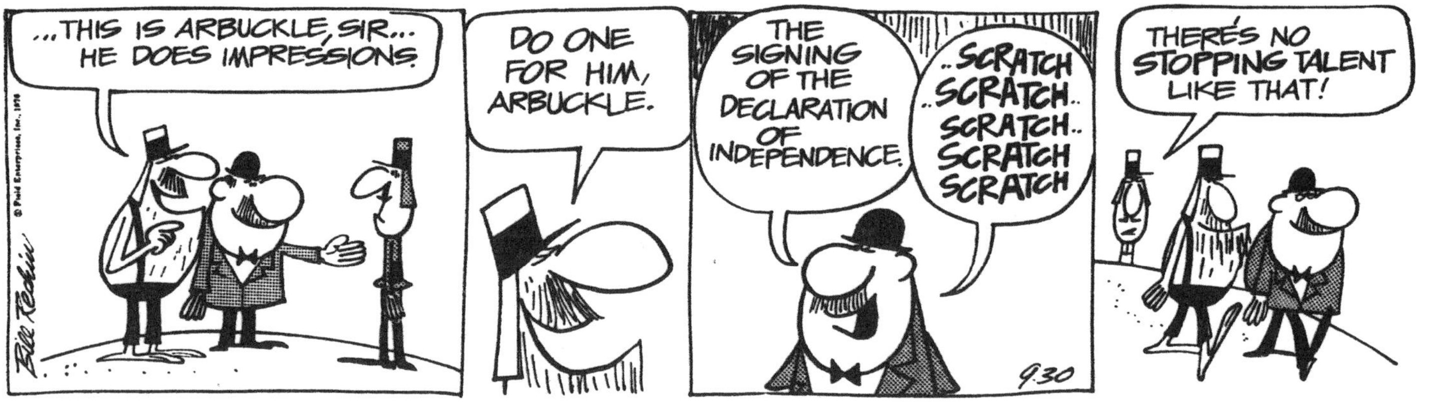
...THIS IS ARBUCKLE, SIR... HE DOES IMPRESSIONS.
DO ONE FOR HIM, ARBUCKLE.
THE SIGNING OF THE DECLARATION OF INDEPENDENCE.
..SCRATCH SCRATCH.. ..SCRATCH.. SCRATCH SCRATCH
THERE'S NO STOPPING TALENT LIKE THAT!
9·30

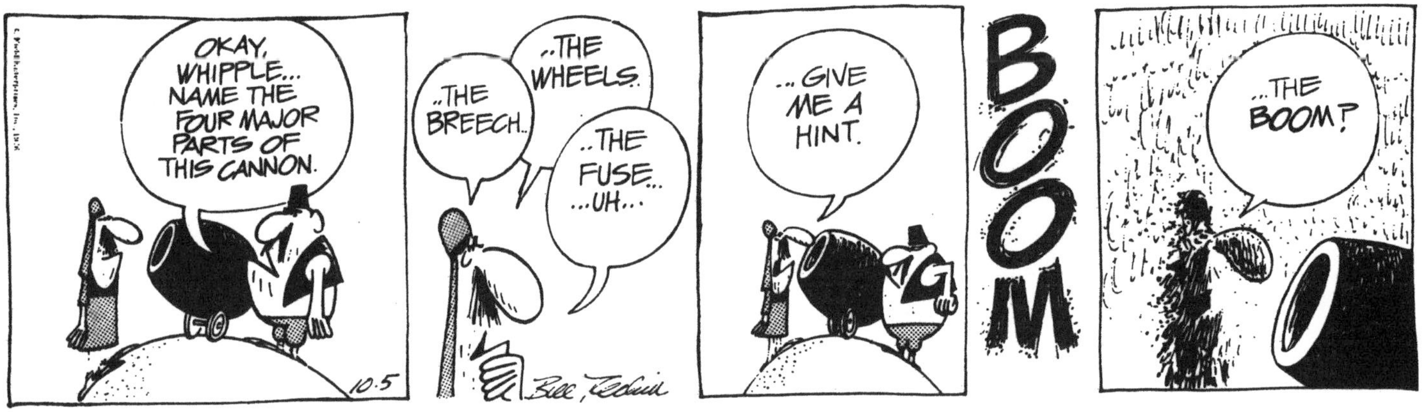
OKAY, WHIPPLE... NAME THE FOUR MAJOR PARTS OF THIS CANNON.
10·5
..THE BREECH..
..THE WHEELS.
..THE FUSE... ...UH...
...GIVE ME A HINT.
BOOOM
...THE BOOM?

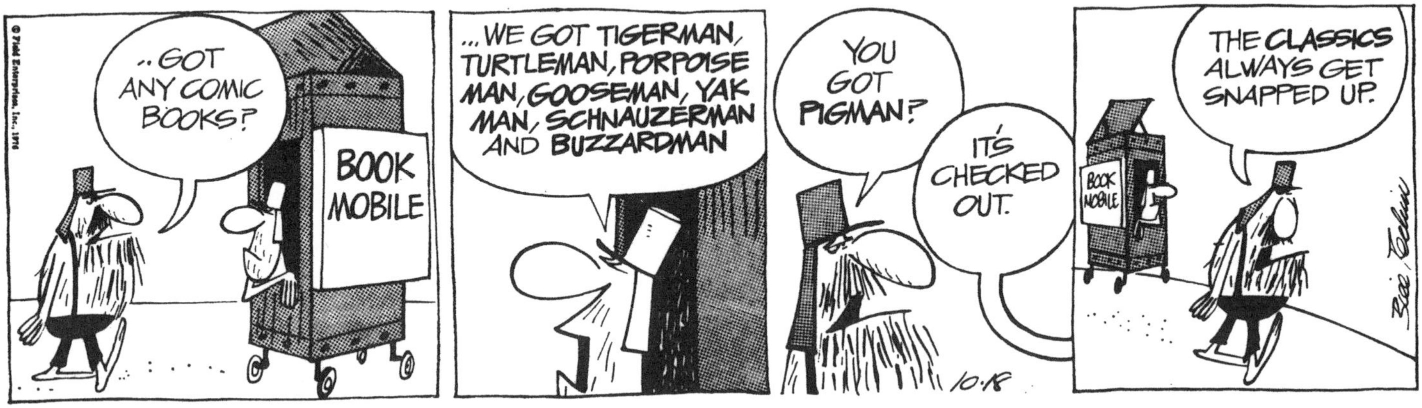
..GOT ANY COMIC BOOKS?
BOOK MOBILE
...WE GOT TIGERMAN, TURTLEMAN, PORPOISE MAN, GOOSEMAN, YAK MAN, SCHNAUZERMAN AND BUZZARDMAN
YOU GOT PIGMAN?
IT'S CHECKED OUT.
10·18
BOOK MOBILE
THE CLASSICS ALWAYS GET SNAPPED UP.

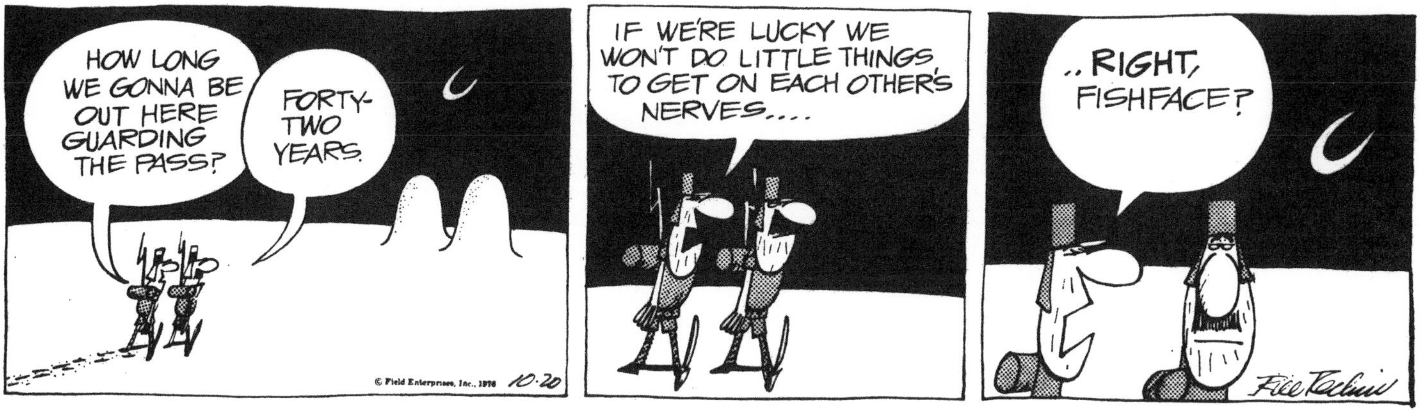
HOW LONG WE GONNA BE OUT HERE GUARDING THE PASS?
FORTY-TWO YEARS.
© Field Enterprises, Inc., 1976
10-20
IF WE'RE LUCKY WE WON'T DO LITTLE THINGS TO GET ON EACH OTHER'S NERVES....
..RIGHT, FISHFACE?

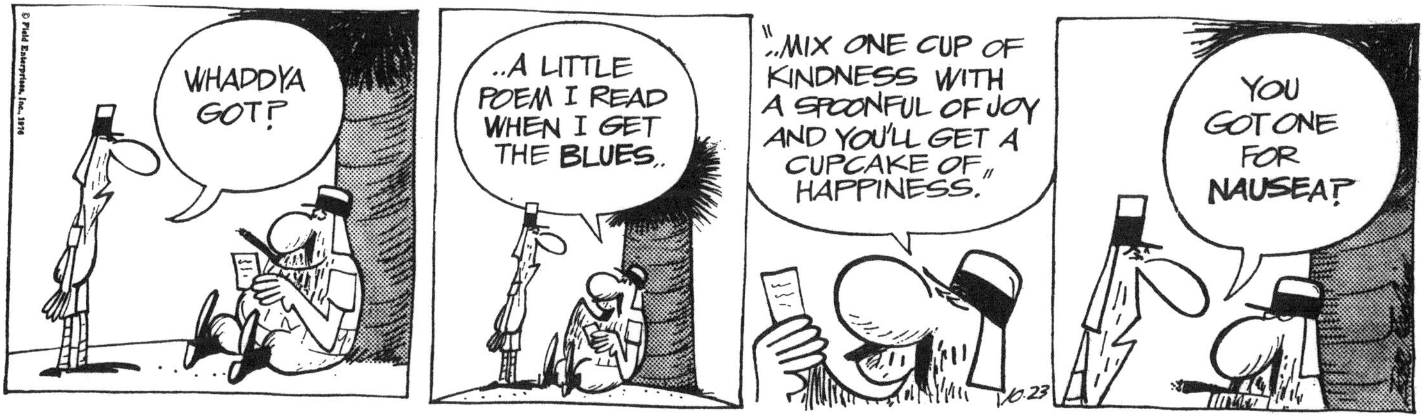
© Field Enterprises, Inc., 1976
WHADDYA GOT?
..A LITTLE POEM I READ WHEN I GET THE BLUES..
"..MIX ONE CUP OF KINDNESS WITH A SPOONFUL OF JOY AND YOU'LL GET A CUPCAKE OF HAPPINESS."
10-23
YOU GOT ONE FOR NAUSEA?

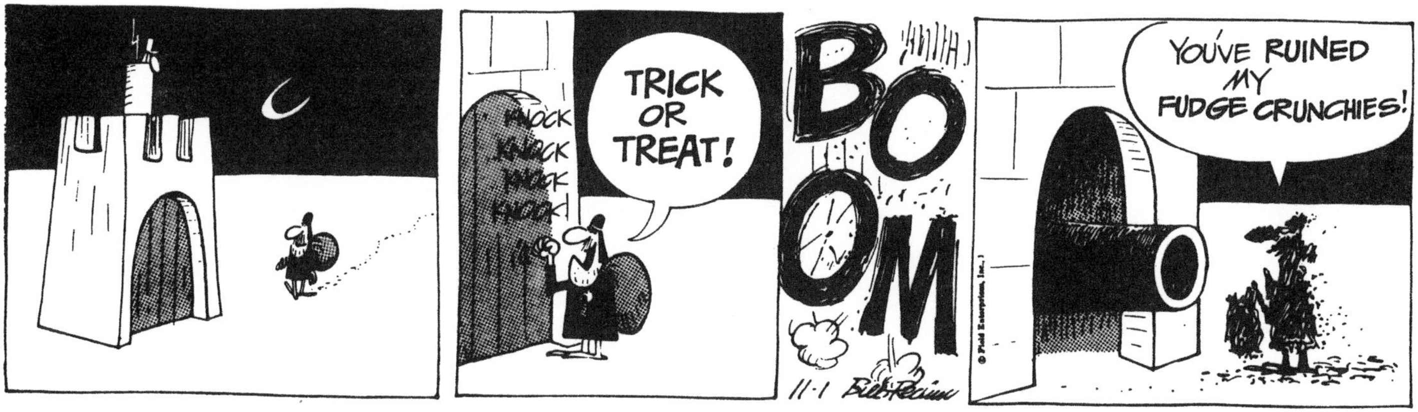
KNOCK KNOCK KNOCK KNOCK
TRICK OR TREAT!
BOOM
11-1
YOU'VE RUINED MY FUDGE CRUNCHIES!

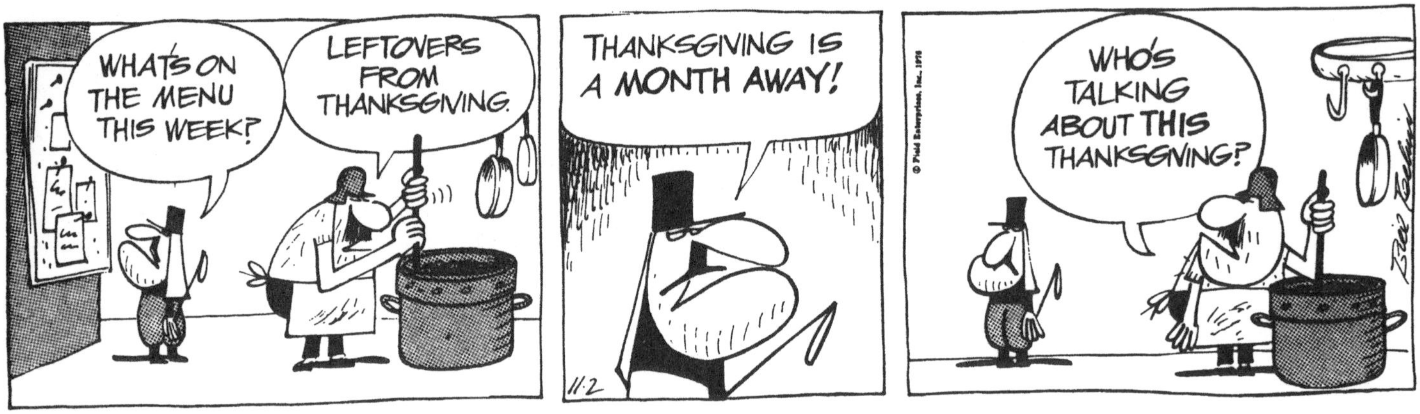
WHAT'S ON THE MENU THIS WEEK?
LEFTOVERS FROM THANKSGIVING.
THANKSGIVING IS A MONTH AWAY!
WHO'S TALKING ABOUT THIS THANKSGIVING?
11-2

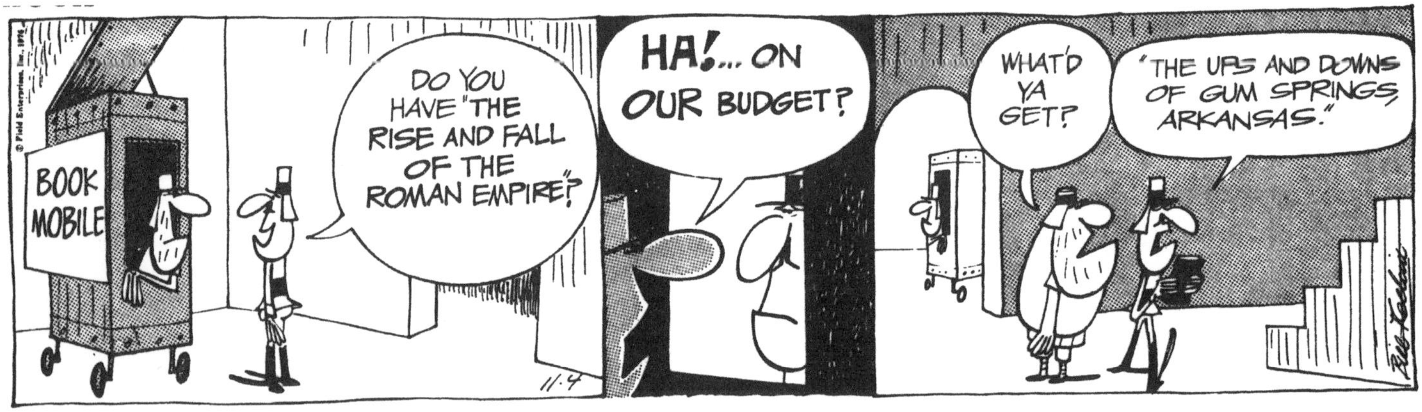
BOOK MOBILE
DO YOU HAVE "THE RISE AND FALL OF THE ROMAN EMPIRE"?
HA!... ON OUR BUDGET?
WHAT'D YA GET?
"THE UPS AND DOWNS OF GUM SPRINGS, ARKANSAS."
11-4

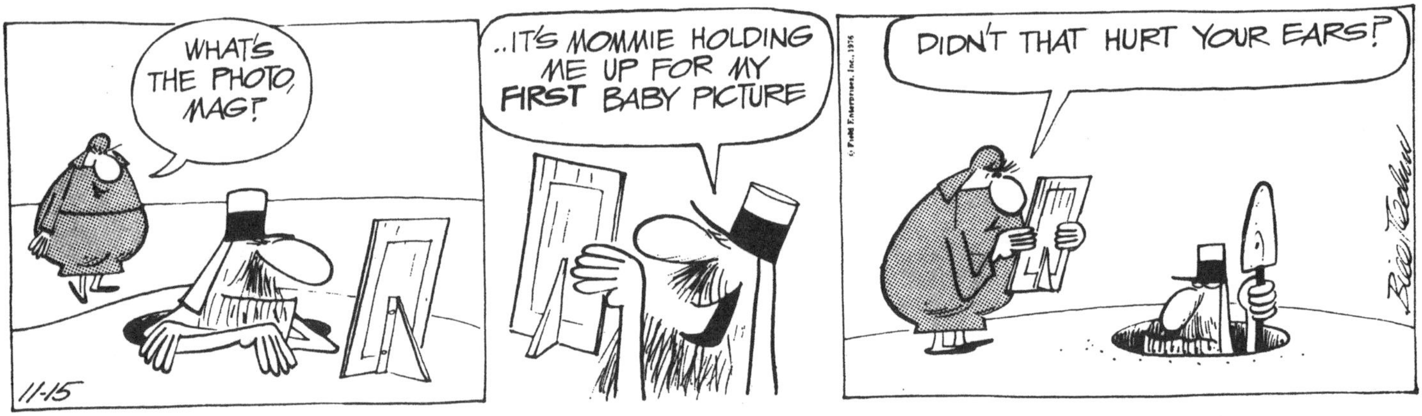
WHAT'S THE PHOTO, MAG?
..IT'S MOMMIE HOLDING ME UP FOR MY FIRST BABY PICTURE
DIDN'T THAT HURT YOUR EARS?
11-15

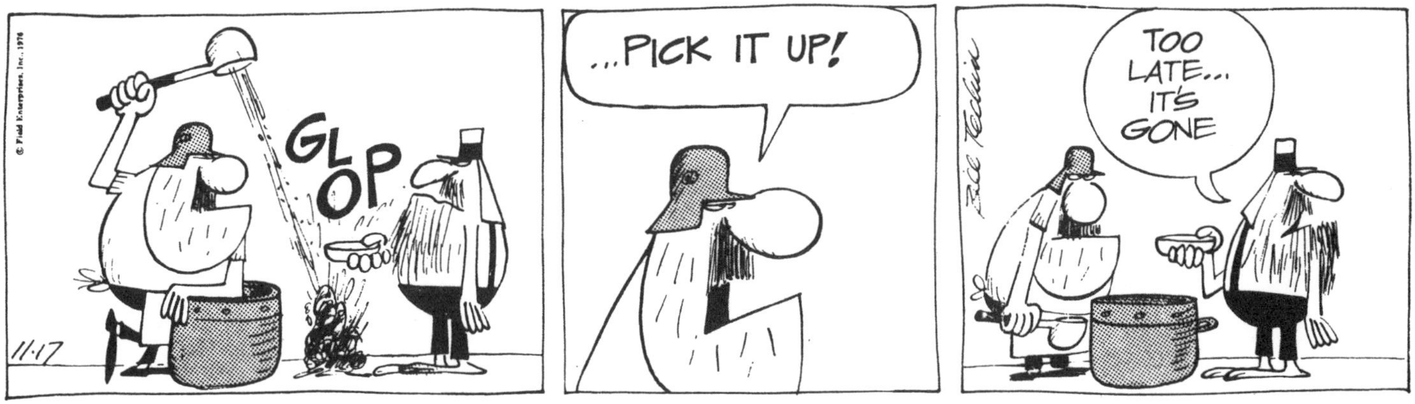
© Field Enterprises, Inc., 1976
GLOP
11·17
...PICK IT UP!
TOO LATE... IT'S GONE

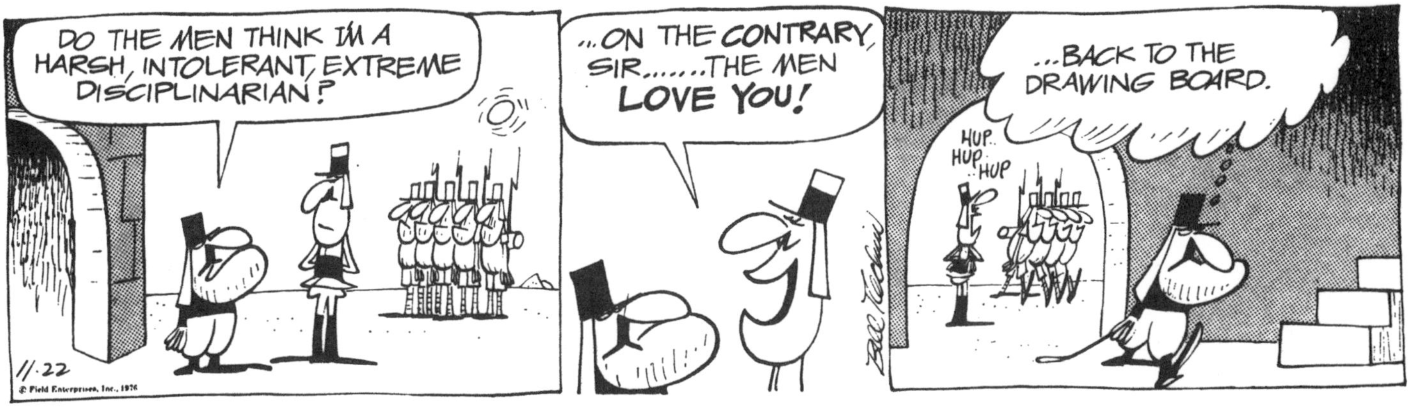
DO THE MEN THINK I'M A HARSH, INTOLERANT, EXTREME DISCIPLINARIAN?
11·22
© Field Enterprises, Inc., 1976
...ON THE CONTRARY, SIR.......THE MEN LOVE YOU!
...BACK TO THE DRAWING BOARD.
HUP.. HUP.. HUP

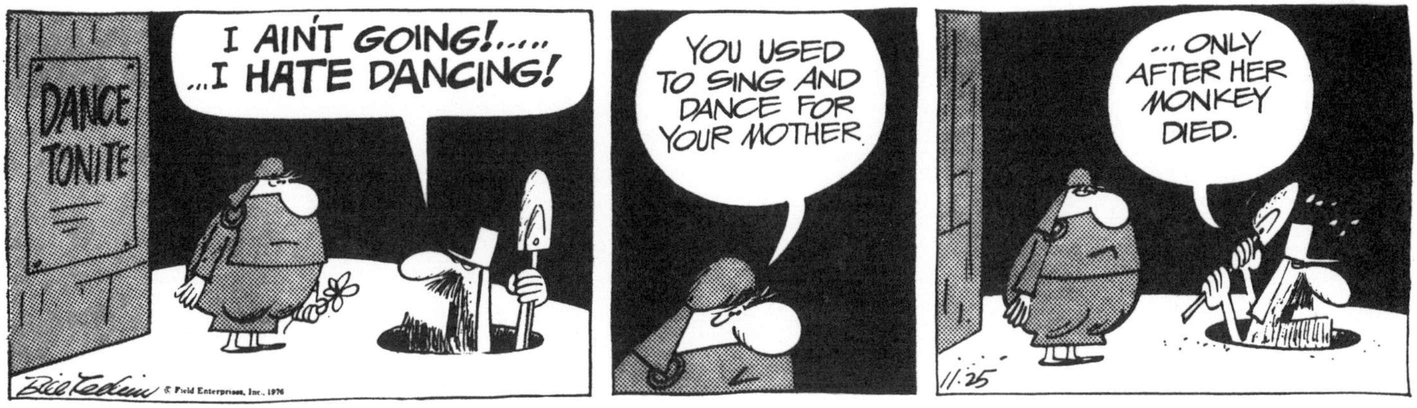
DANCE TONITE
I AIN'T GOING!.....
...I HATE DANCING!
© Field Enterprises, Inc., 1976
YOU USED TO SING AND DANCE FOR YOUR MOTHER.
...ONLY AFTER HER MONKEY DIED.
11·25

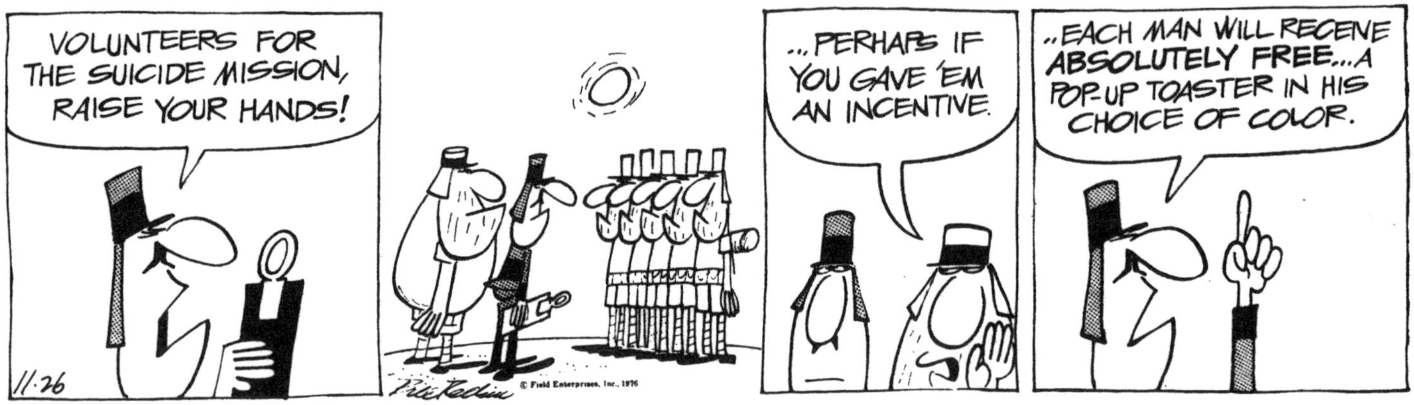
VOLUNTEERS FOR THE SUICIDE MISSION, RAISE YOUR HANDS!
11·26
© Field Enterprises, Inc., 1976
...PERHAPS IF YOU GAVE 'EM AN INCENTIVE.
..EACH MAN WILL RECEIVE ABSOLUTELY FREE...A POP-UP TOASTER IN HIS CHOICE OF COLOR.

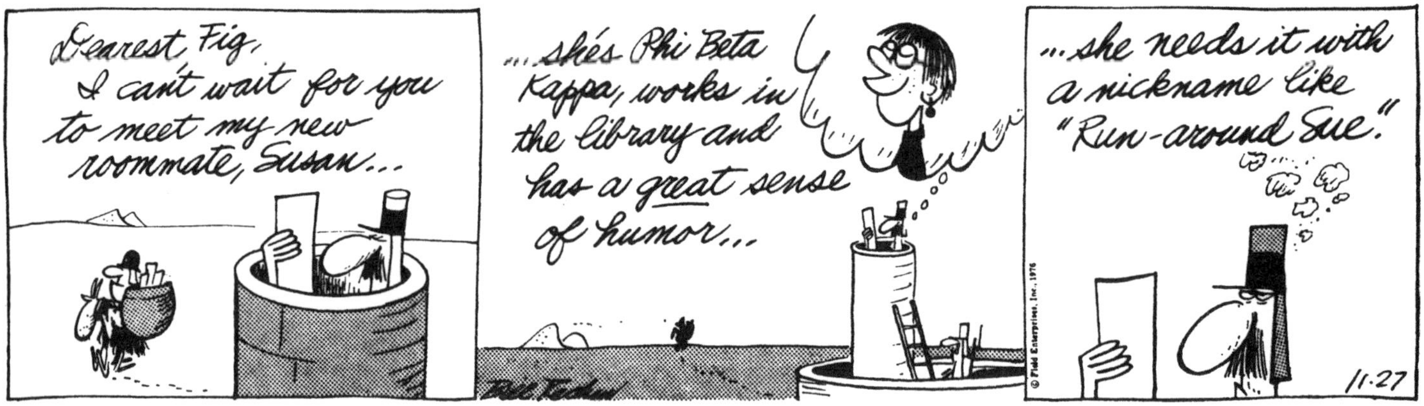
Dearest Fig,
I can't wait for you to meet my new roommate, Susan...
...she's Phi Beta Kappa, works in the library and has a great sense of humor...
...she needs it with a nickname like "Run-around Sue".
11·27

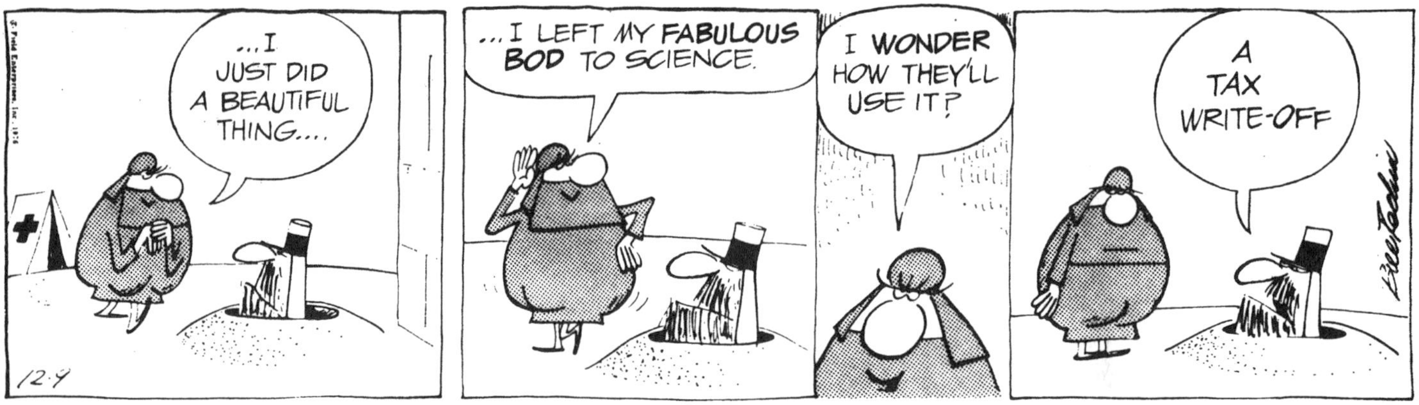
...I JUST DID A BEAUTIFUL THING....
12·4
...I LEFT MY FABULOUS BOD TO SCIENCE.
I WONDER HOW THEY'LL USE IT?
A TAX WRITE-OFF

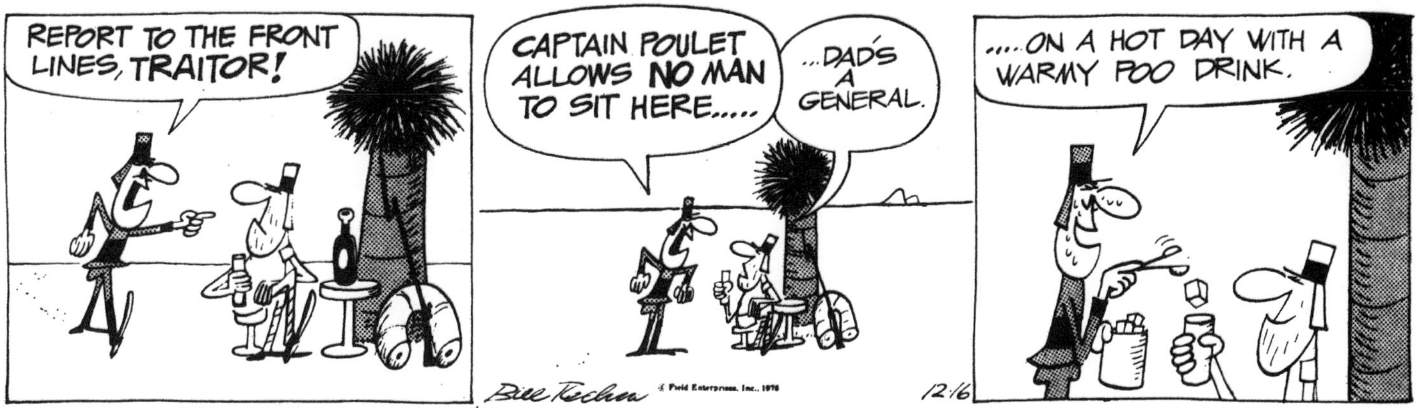
REPORT TO THE FRONT LINES, TRAITOR!
CAPTAIN POULET ALLOWS NO MAN TO SIT HERE.....
...DAD'S A GENERAL.
.....ON A HOT DAY WITH A WARMY POO DRINK.
Bill Rechin
© Field Enterprises, Inc., 1976
12·16

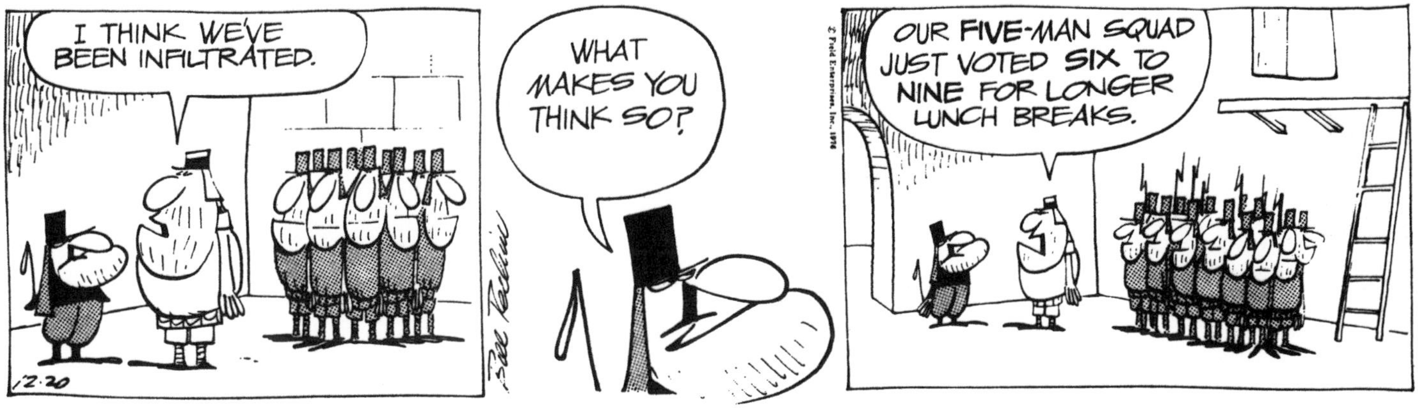
I THINK WE'VE BEEN INFILTRATED.
12·20
Bill Rechin
WHAT MAKES YOU THINK SO?
© Field Enterprises, Inc., 1976
OUR FIVE-MAN SQUAD JUST VOTED SIX TO NINE FOR LONGER LUNCH BREAKS.

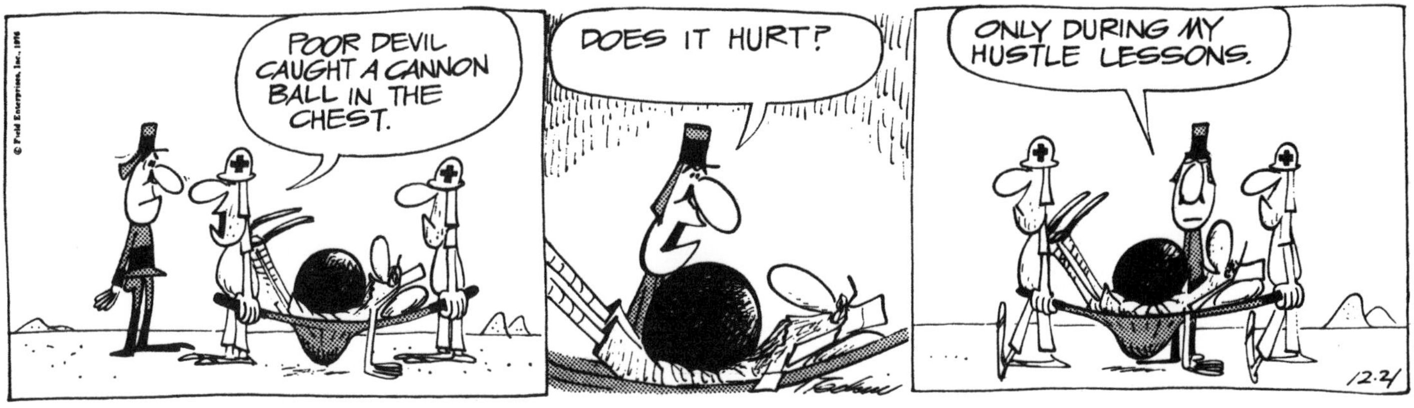
© Field Enterprises, Inc., 1976
POOR DEVIL CAUGHT A CANNON BALL IN THE CHEST.
DOES IT HURT?
Rechin
ONLY DURING MY HUSTLE LESSONS.
12·21

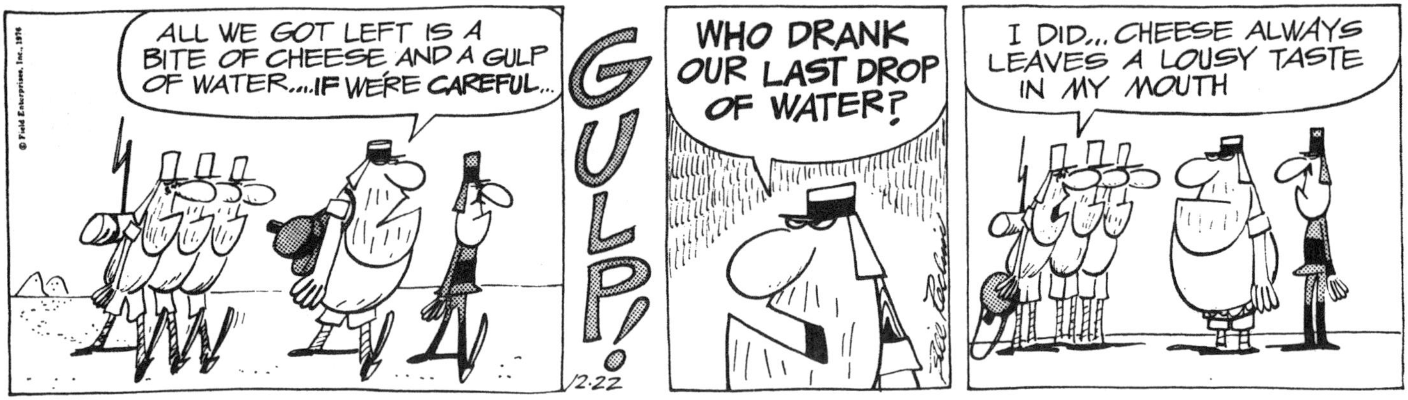
© Field Enterprises, Inc., 1976
ALL WE GOT LEFT IS A BITE OF CHEESE AND A GULP OF WATER....IF WE'RE CAREFUL...
GULP!
12·22
WHO DRANK OUR LAST DROP OF WATER?
I DID... CHEESE ALWAYS LEAVES A LOUSY TASTE IN MY MOUTH

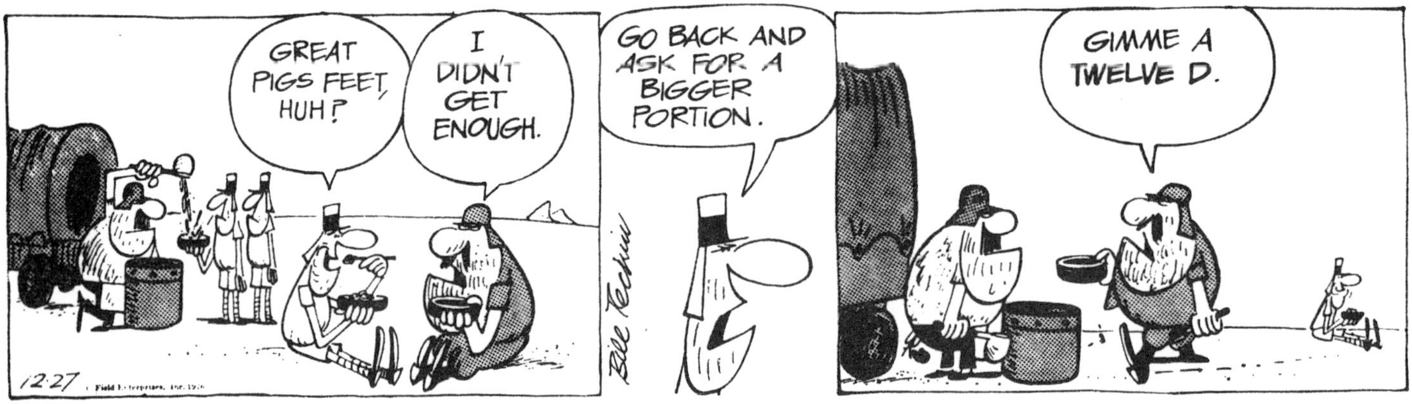
GREAT PIGS FEET, HUH?
I DIDN'T GET ENOUGH.
12·27
GO BACK AND ASK FOR A BIGGER PORTION.
GIMME A TWELVE D.

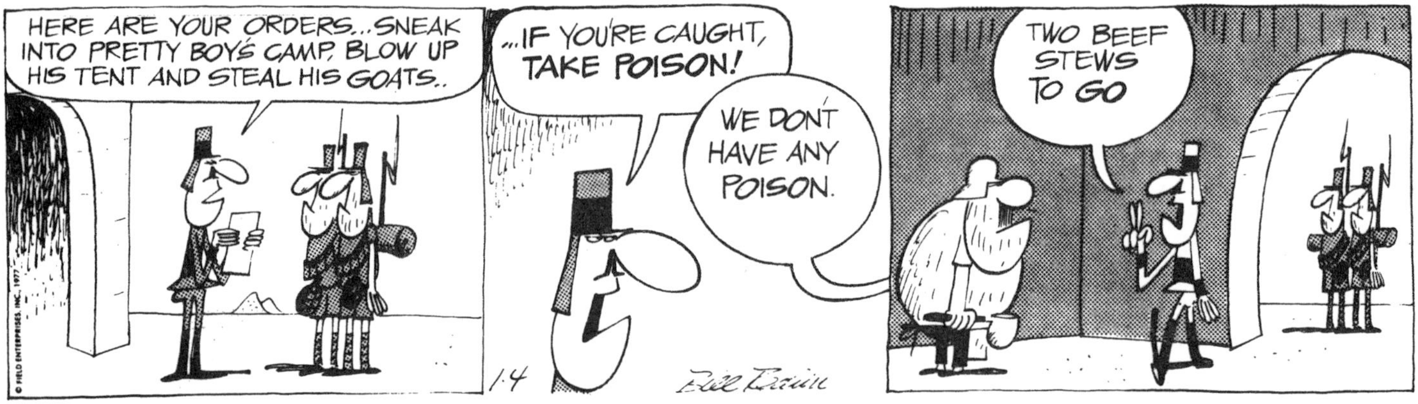
© FIELD ENTERPRISES, INC. 1977
HERE ARE YOUR ORDERS...SNEAK INTO PRETTY BOY'S CAMP, BLOW UP HIS TENT AND STEAL HIS GOATS..
...IF YOU'RE CAUGHT, TAKE POISON!
WE DON'T HAVE ANY POISON.
1·4
TWO BEEF STEWS TO GO

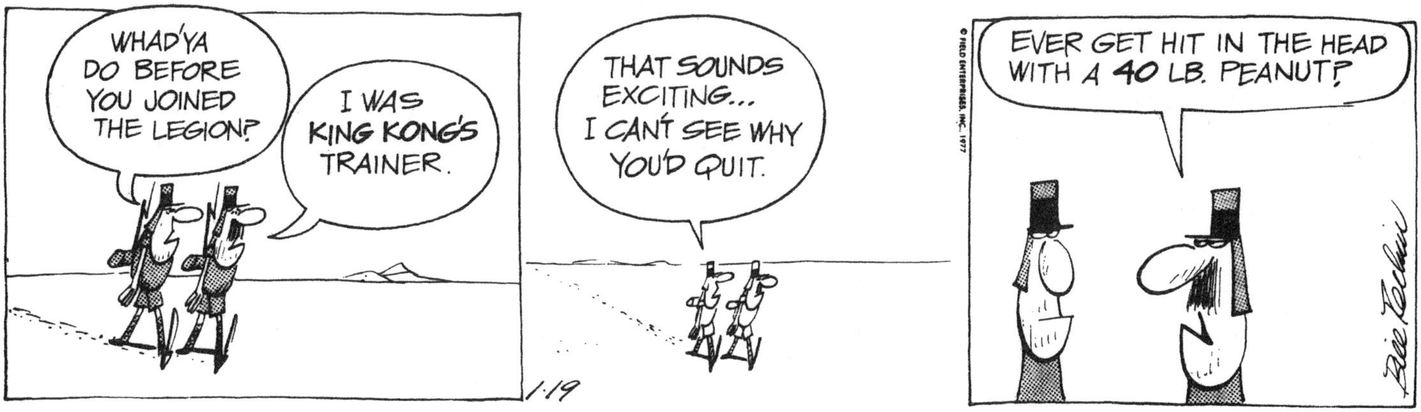
WHAD'YA DO BEFORE YOU JOINED THE LEGION?
I WAS KING KONG'S TRAINER.
THAT SOUNDS EXCITING... I CAN'T SEE WHY YOU'D QUIT.
EVER GET HIT IN THE HEAD WITH A 40 LB. PEANUT?
1·19
© FIELD ENTERPRISES, INC. 1977

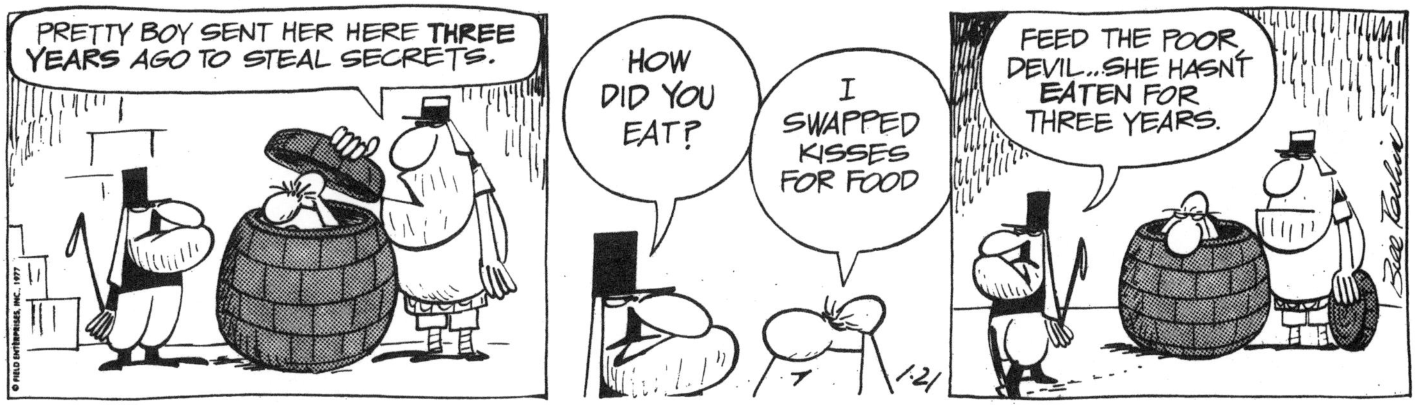
PRETTY BOY SENT HER HERE THREE YEARS AGO TO STEAL SECRETS.
HOW DID YOU EAT?
I SWAPPED KISSES FOR FOOD
1·21
FEED THE POOR DEVIL...SHE HASN'T EATEN FOR THREE YEARS.
© FIELD ENTERPRISES, INC. 1977

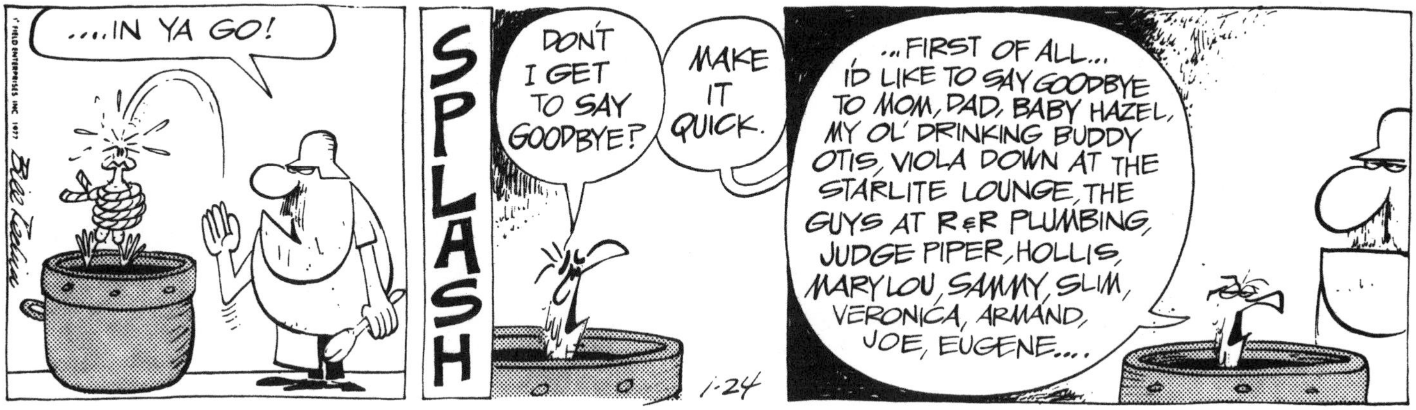
....IN YA GO!
SPLASH
DON'T I GET TO SAY GOODBYE?
MAKE IT QUICK.
...FIRST OF ALL... I'D LIKE TO SAY GOODBYE TO MOM, DAD, BABY HAZEL, MY OL' DRINKING BUDDY OTIS, VIOLA DOWN AT THE STARLITE LOUNGE, THE GUYS AT R&R PLUMBING, JUDGE PIPER, HOLLIS, MARYLOU, SAMMY, SLIM, VERONICA, ARMAND, JOE, EUGENE....
1·24
© FIELD ENTERPRISES INC 1977

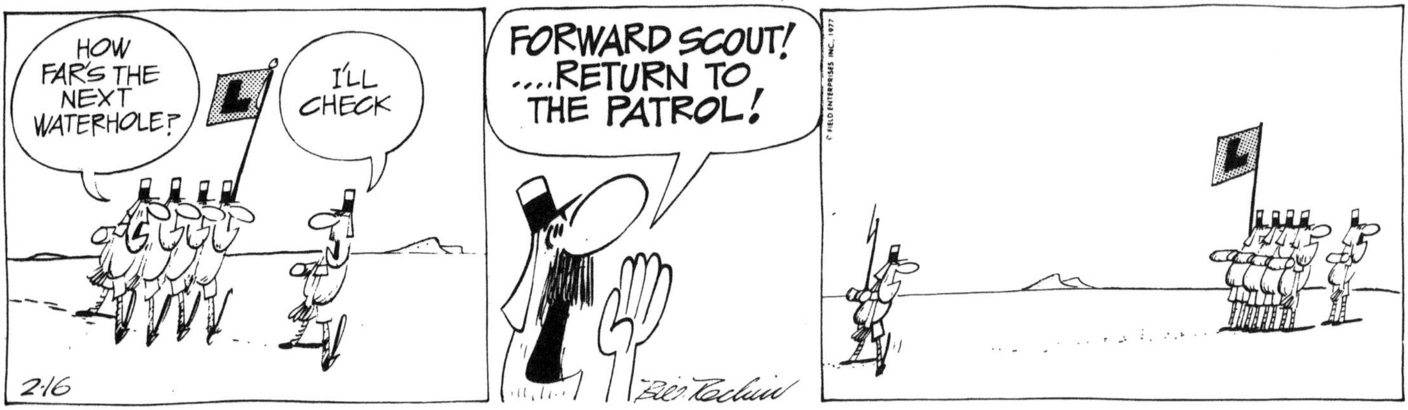
HOW FAR'S THE NEXT WATERHOLE?
I'LL CHECK
2·16
FORWARD SCOUT! ....RETURN TO THE PATROL!
Bill Rechin
© FIELD ENTERPRISES, INC. 1977

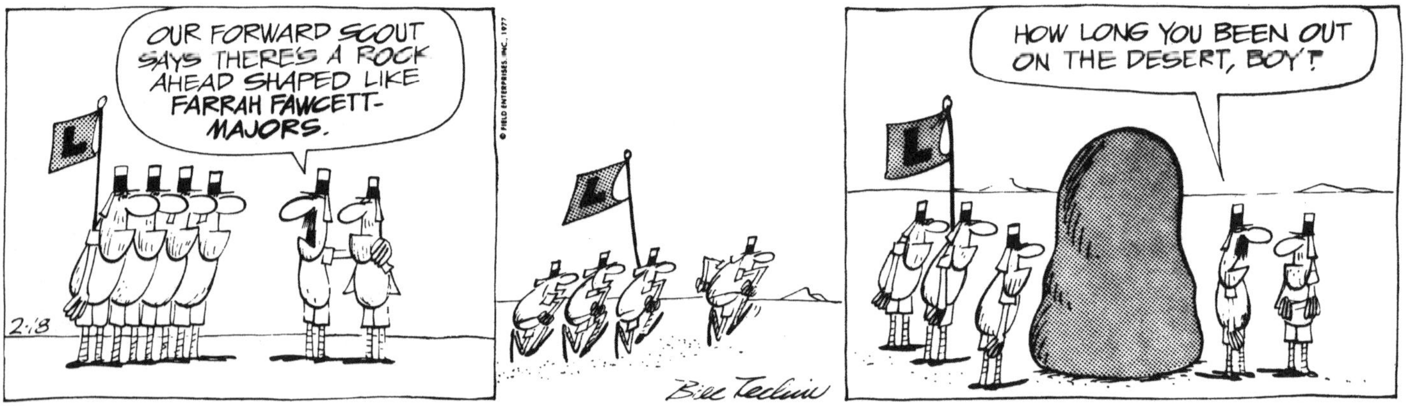
OUR FORWARD SCOUT SAYS THERE'S A ROCK AHEAD SHAPED LIKE FARRAH FAWCETT-MAJORS.
2·18
© FIELD ENTERPRISES, INC. 1977
Bill Rechin
HOW LONG YOU BEEN OUT ON THE DESERT, BOY?

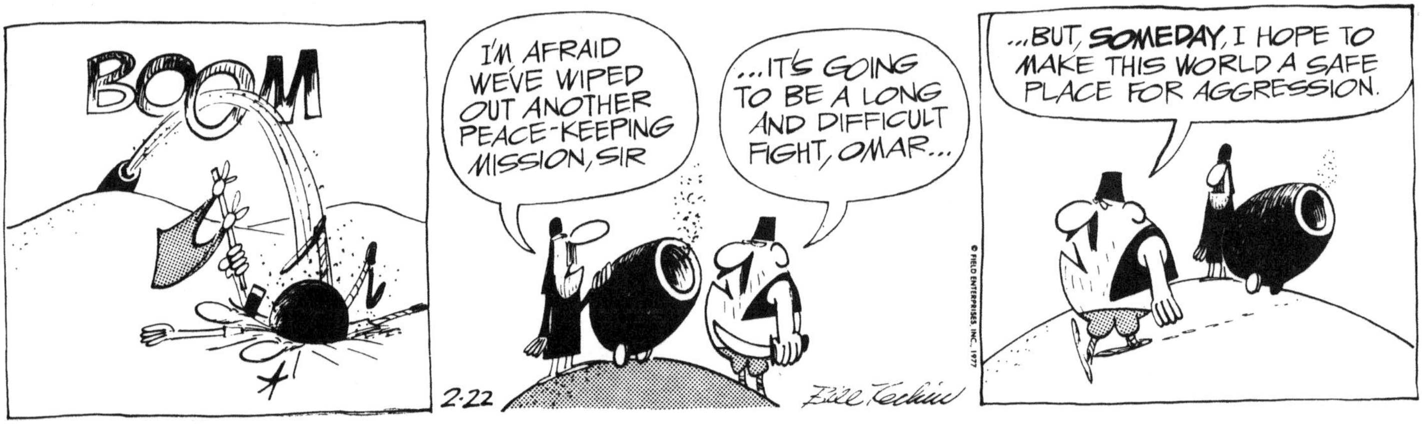
BOOM
I'M AFRAID WE'VE WIPED OUT ANOTHER PEACE-KEEPING MISSION, SIR
...IT'S GOING TO BE A LONG AND DIFFICULT FIGHT, OMAR...
2·22
Bill Rechin
© FIELD ENTERPRISES, INC. 1977
...BUT, SOMEDAY, I HOPE TO MAKE THIS WORLD A SAFE PLACE FOR AGGRESSION.

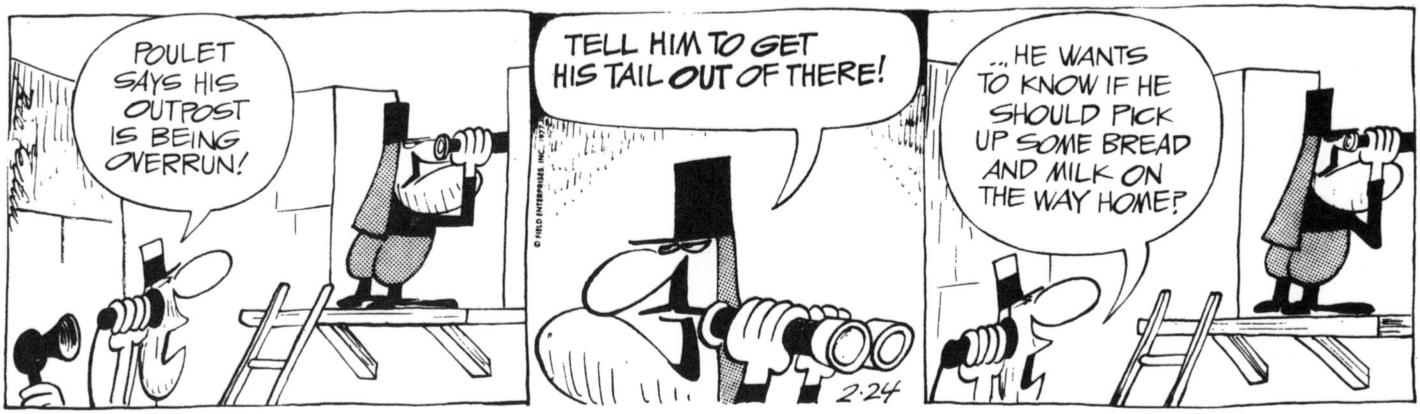
POULET SAYS HIS OUTPOST IS BEING OVERRUN!
© FIELD ENTERPRISES, INC. 1977
TELL HIM TO GET HIS TAIL OUT OF THERE!
2·24
... HE WANTS TO KNOW IF HE SHOULD PICK UP SOME BREAD AND MILK ON THE WAY HOME?

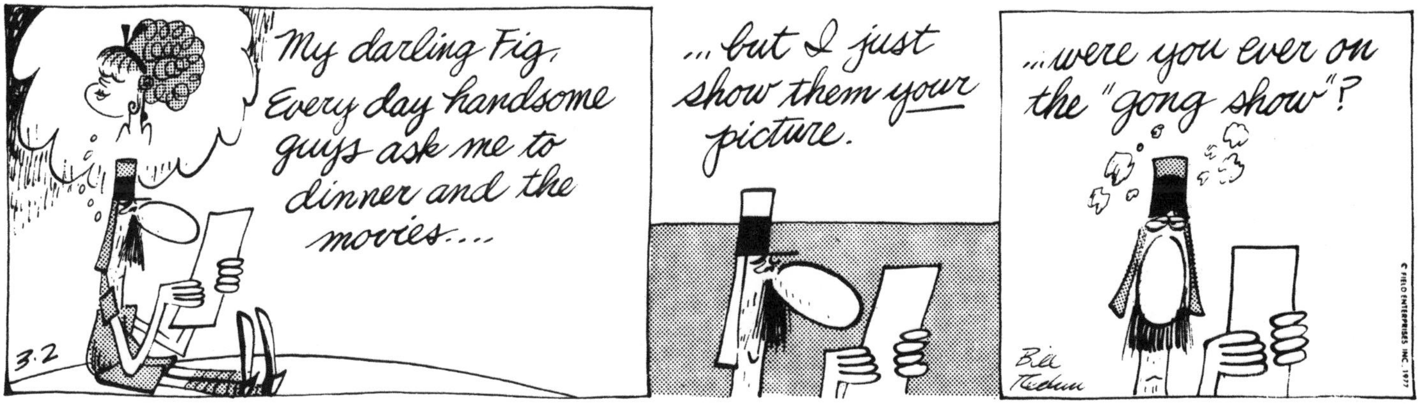
My darling Fig, Every day handsome guys ask me to dinner and the movies....
3·2
... but I just show them your picture.
... were you ever on the "gong show"?
© FIELD ENTERPRISES, INC. 1977

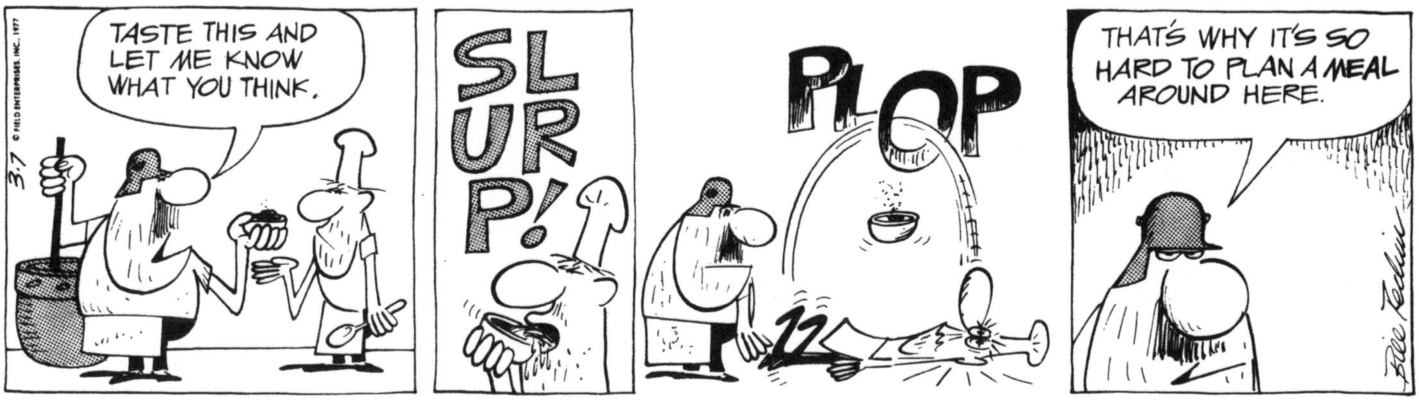
3·7
© FIELD ENTERPRISES, INC. 1977
TASTE THIS AND LET ME KNOW WHAT YOU THINK.
SLURP!
PLOP
THAT'S WHY IT'S SO HARD TO PLAN A MEAL AROUND HERE.

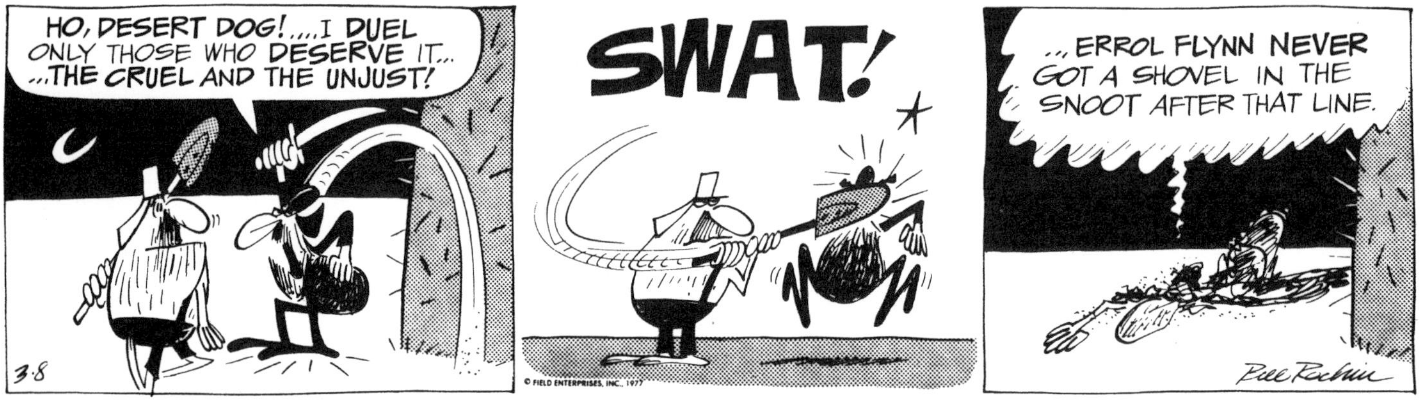
HO, DESERT DOG!....I DUEL ONLY THOSE WHO DESERVE IT... ...THE CRUEL AND THE UNJUST!
3·8
SWAT!
© FIELD ENTERPRISES, INC., 1977
...ERROL FLYNN NEVER GOT A SHOVEL IN THE SNOOT AFTER THAT LINE.

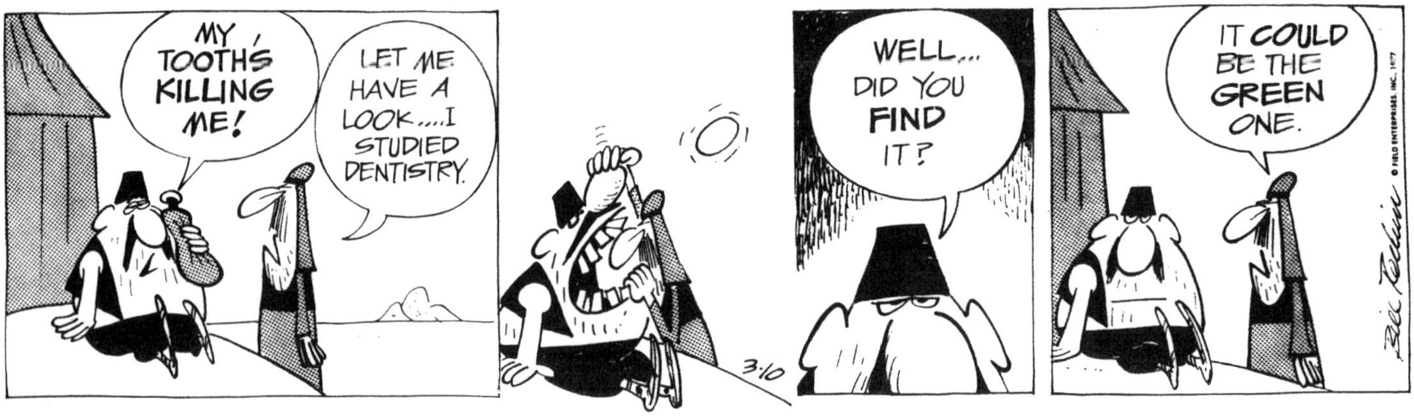
MY TOOTH'S KILLING ME!
LET ME HAVE A LOOK....I STUDIED DENTISTRY.
3·10
WELL... DID YOU FIND IT?
IT COULD BE THE GREEN ONE.
© FIELD ENTERPRISES, INC., 1977

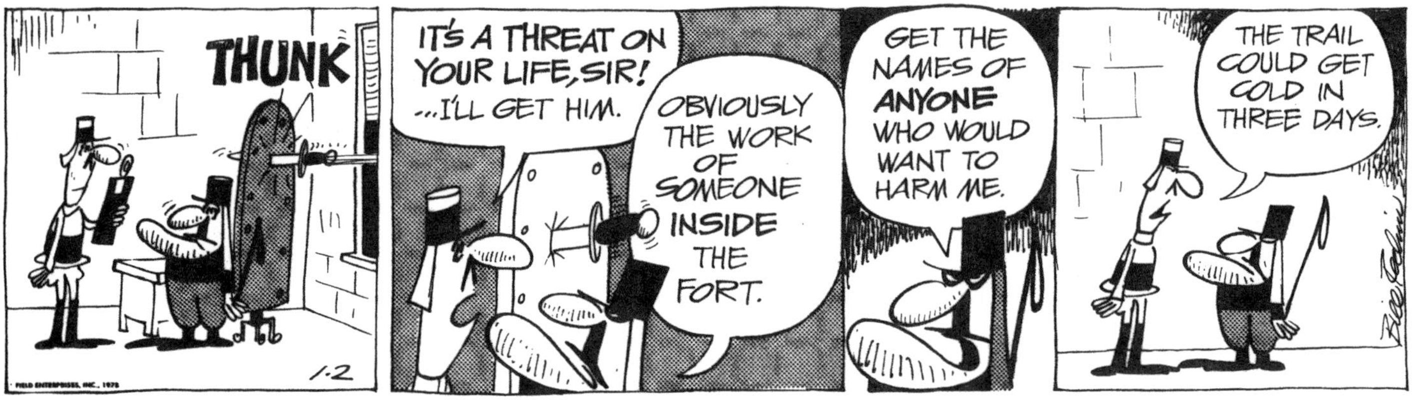
THUNK
1·2
IT'S A THREAT ON YOUR LIFE, SIR! ...I'LL GET HIM.
OBVIOUSLY THE WORK OF SOMEONE INSIDE THE FORT.
GET THE NAMES OF ANYONE WHO WOULD WANT TO HARM ME.
THE TRAIL COULD GET COLD IN THREE DAYS.

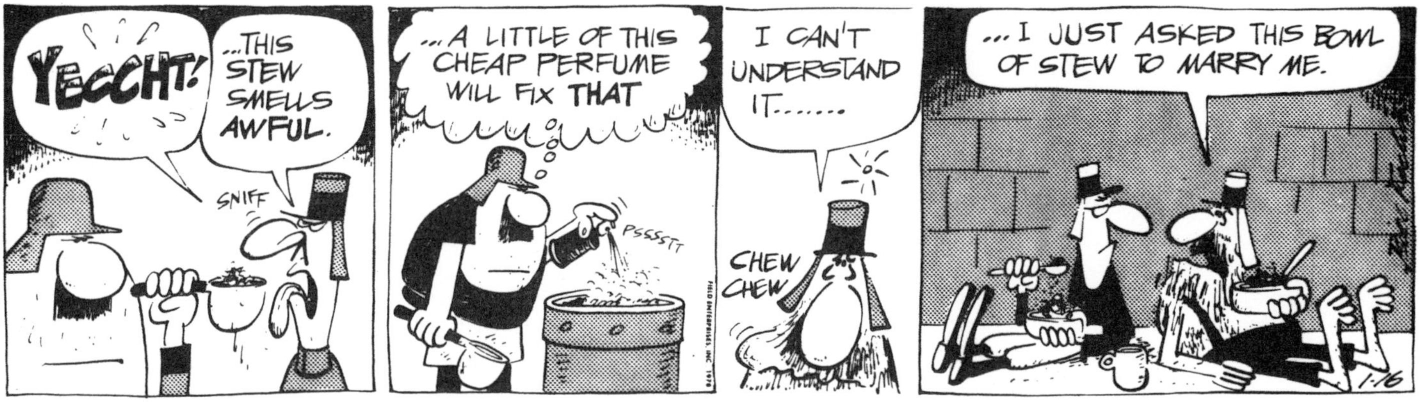
YECCHT!
...THIS STEW SMELLS AWFUL.
SNIFF
...A LITTLE OF THIS CHEAP PERFUME WILL FIX THAT
PSSSSTT
I CAN'T UNDERSTAND IT.......
CHEW CHEW
...I JUST ASKED THIS BOWL OF STEW TO MARRY ME.
1-16

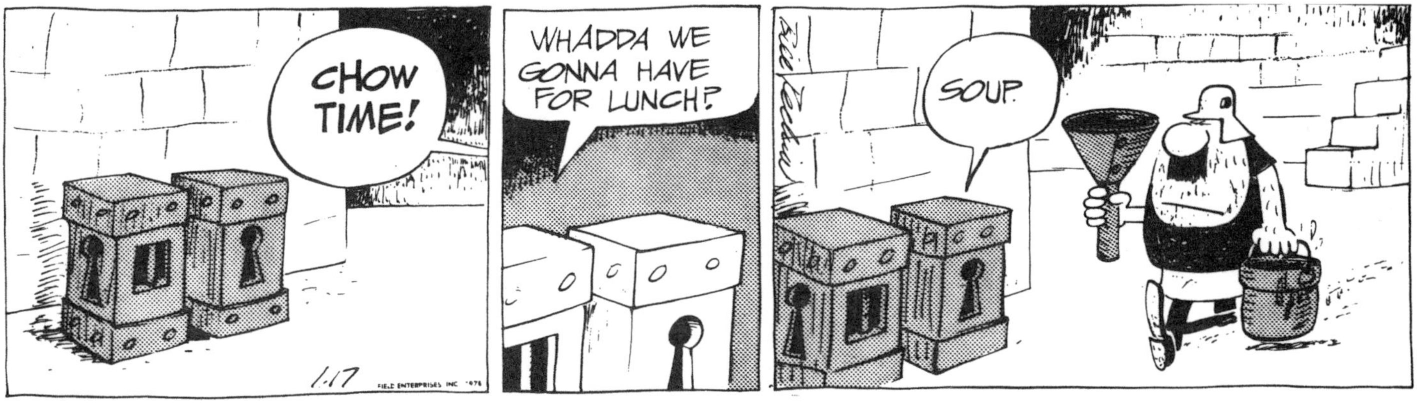
CHOW TIME!
1-17
WHADDA WE GONNA HAVE FOR LUNCH?
SOUP.

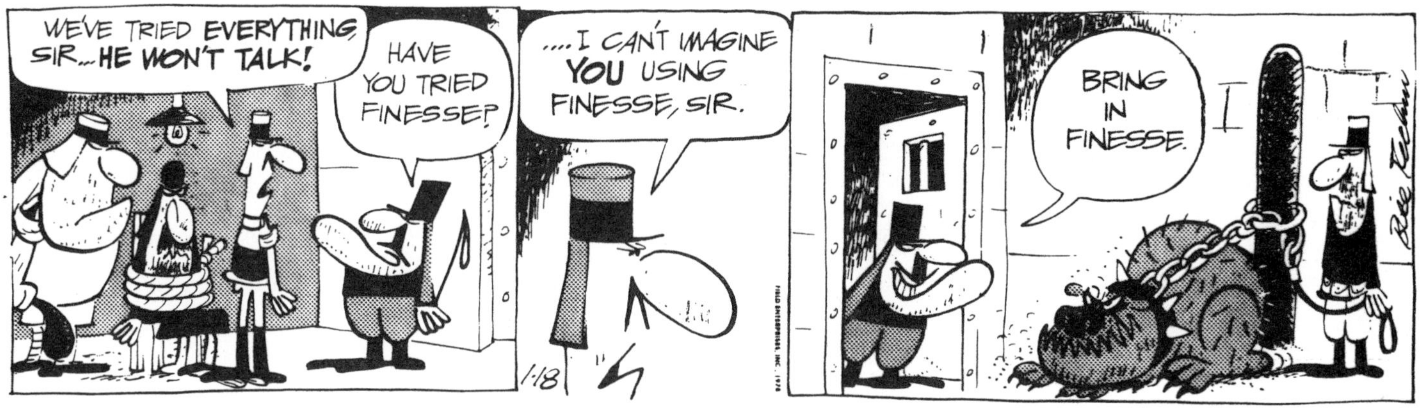
WE'VE TRIED EVERYTHING, SIR...HE WON'T TALK!
HAVE YOU TRIED FINESSE?
....I CAN'T IMAGINE YOU USING FINESSE, SIR.
1-18
BRING IN FINESSE.

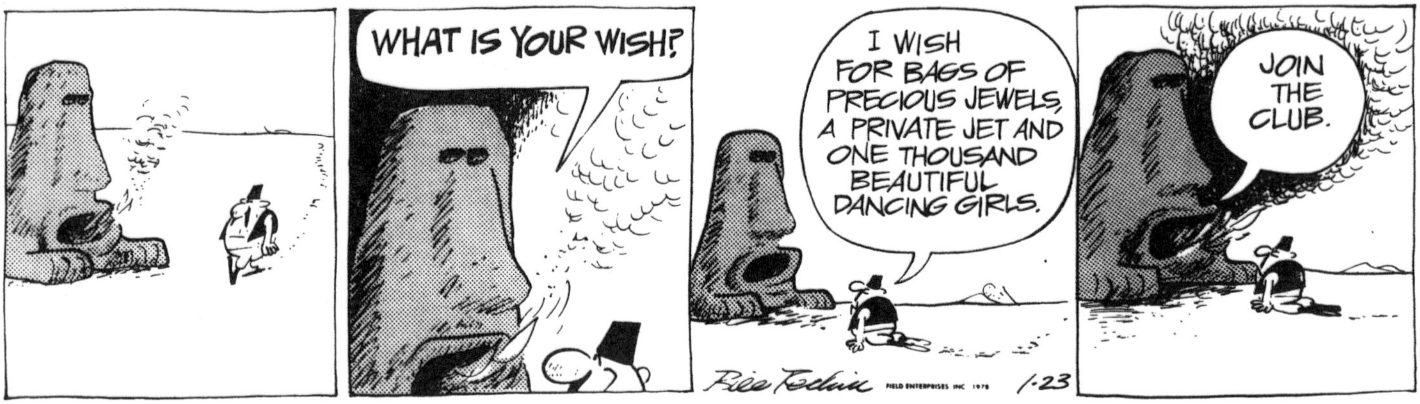
WHAT IS YOUR WISH?
I WISH FOR BAGS OF PRECIOUS JEWELS, A PRIVATE JET AND ONE THOUSAND BEAUTIFUL DANCING GIRLS.
JOIN THE CLUB.
1-23

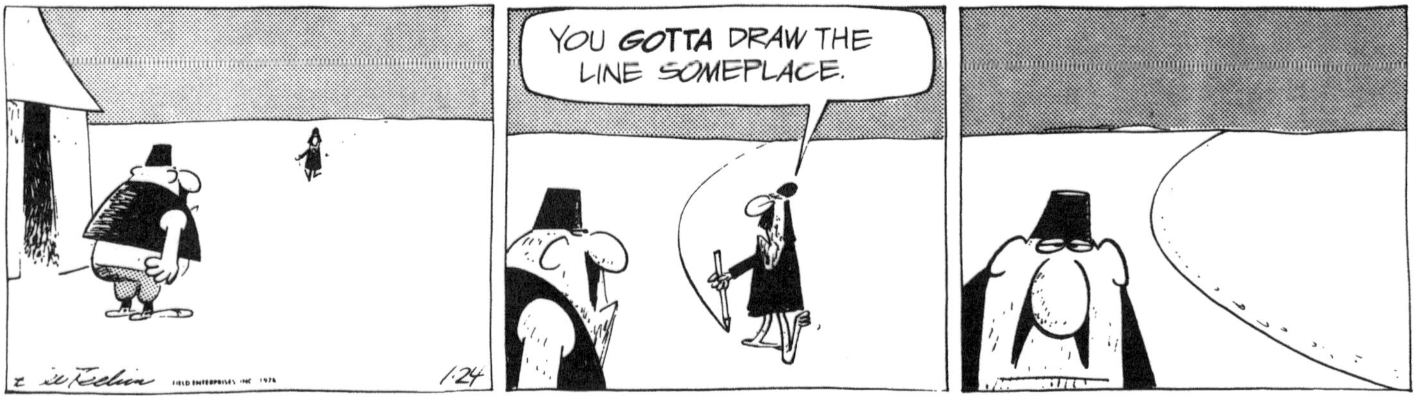
1-24
YOU GOTTA DRAW THE LINE SOMEPLACE.

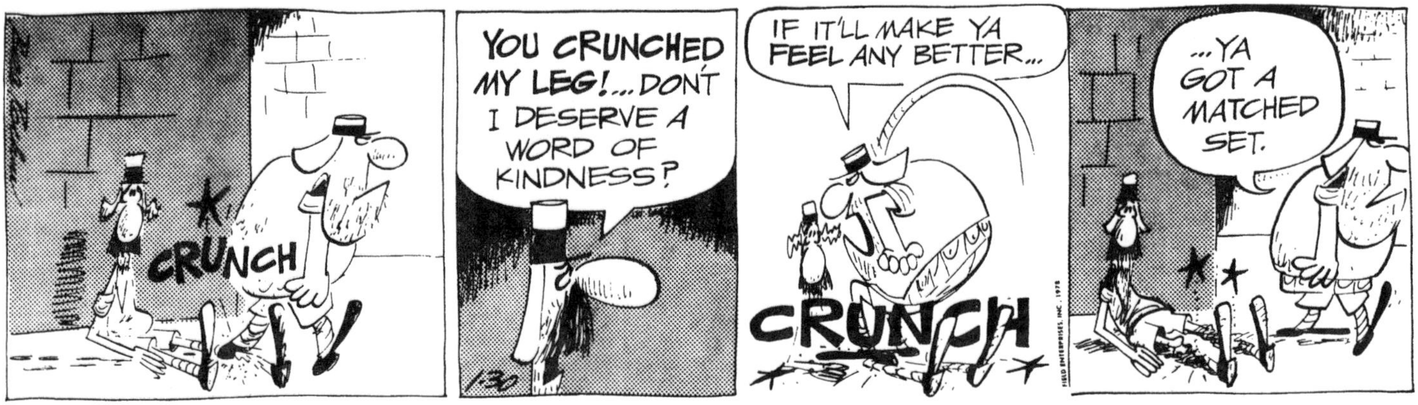
CRUNCH
YOU CRUNCHED MY LEG!...DON'T I DESERVE A WORD OF KINDNESS?
1-30
IF IT'LL MAKE YA FEEL ANY BETTER...
CRUNCH
...YA GOT A MATCHED SET.

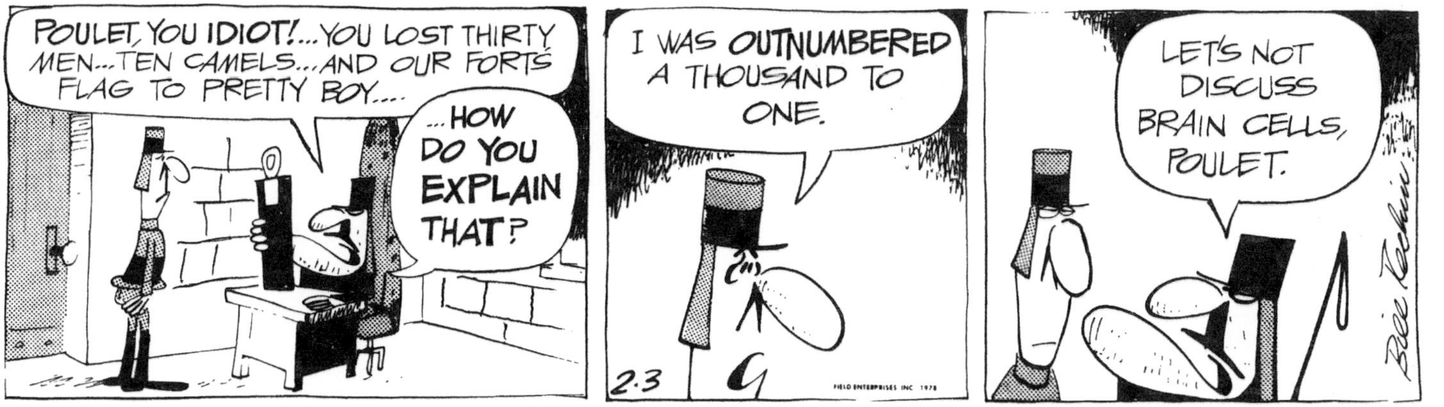
POULET, YOU IDIOT!... YOU LOST THIRTY MEN... TEN CAMELS... AND OUR FORT'S FLAG TO PRETTY BOY....
...HOW DO YOU EXPLAIN THAT?
I WAS OUTNUMBERED A THOUSAND TO ONE.
2·3
LET'S NOT DISCUSS BRAIN CELLS, POULET.
Bill Rechin

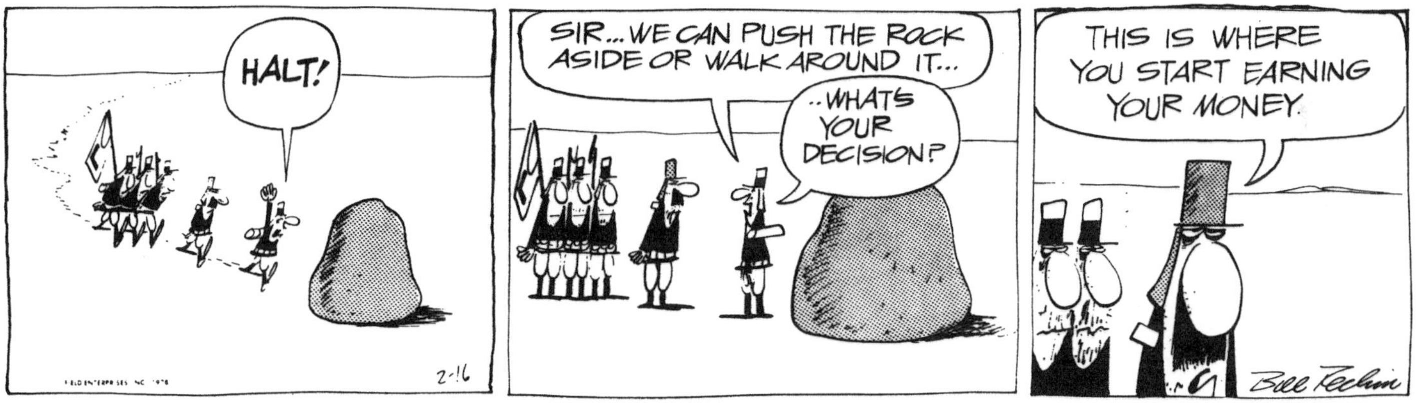
HALT!
2·16
SIR... WE CAN PUSH THE ROCK ASIDE OR WALK AROUND IT...
..WHAT'S YOUR DECISION?
THIS IS WHERE YOU START EARNING YOUR MONEY.
Bill Rechin

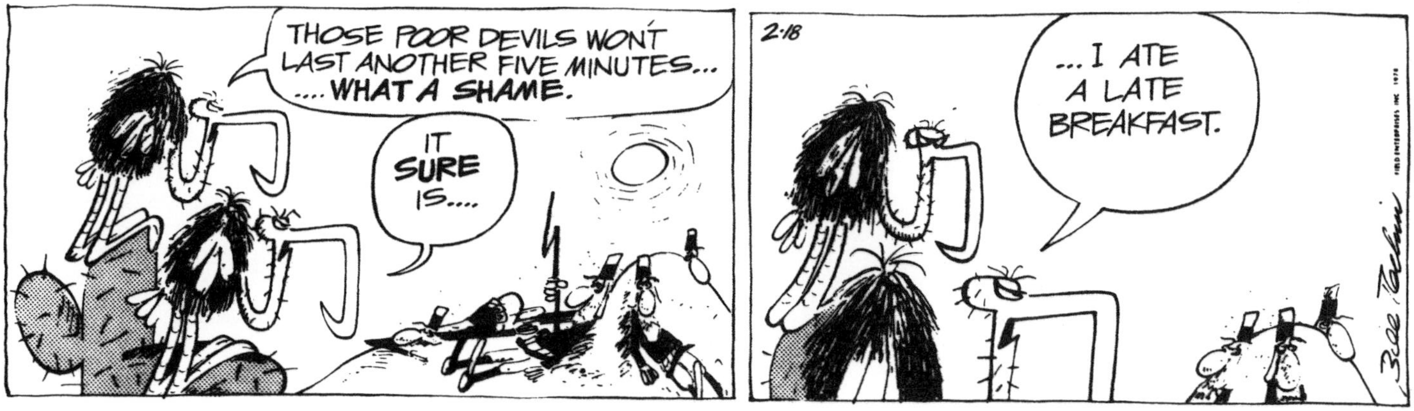
THOSE POOR DEVILS WON'T LAST ANOTHER FIVE MINUTES... ....WHAT A SHAME.
IT SURE IS....
2·18
...I ATE A LATE BREAKFAST.
Bill Rechin

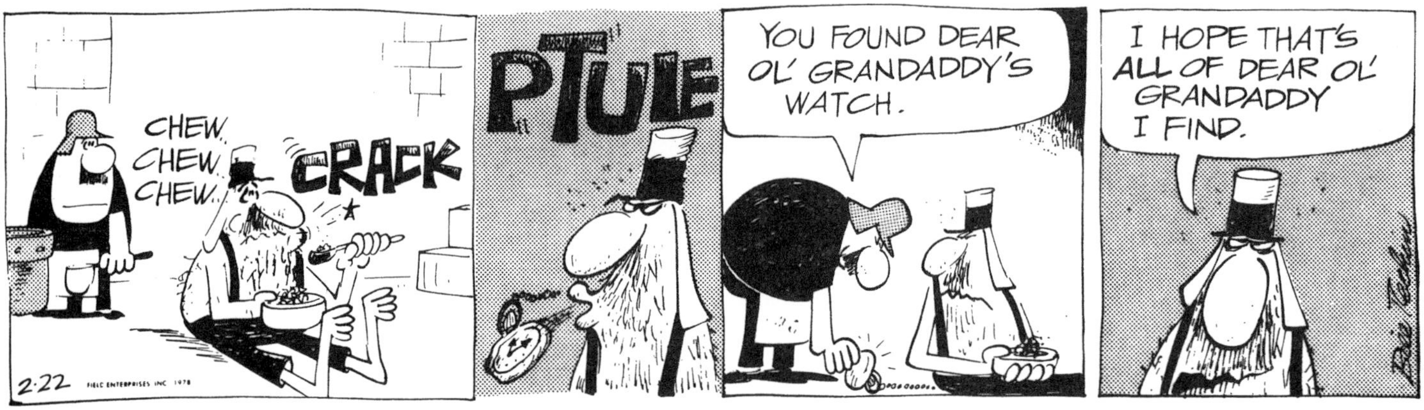
CHEW CHEW CHEW
CRACK
PTUIE
YOU FOUND DEAR OL' GRANDADDY'S WATCH.
I HOPE THAT'S **ALL** OF DEAR OL' GRANDADDY I FIND.
2-22
FIELD ENTERPRISES INC 1978

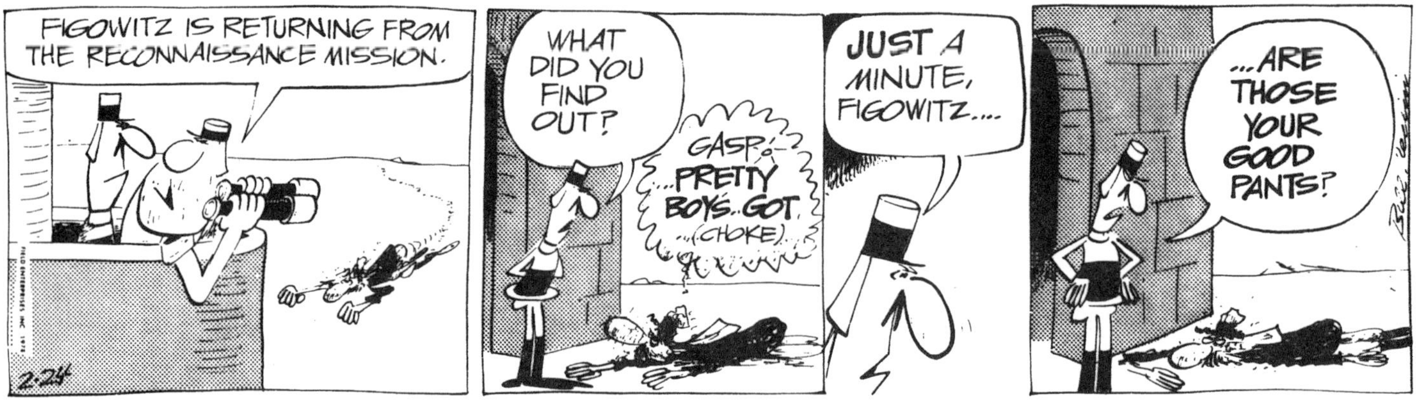
FIGOWITZ IS RETURNING FROM THE RECONNAISSANCE MISSION.
2-24
WHAT DID YOU FIND OUT?
GASP! ...PRETTY BOYS..GOT ...(CHOKE)
JUST A MINUTE, FIGOWITZ....
...ARE THOSE YOUR GOOD PANTS?

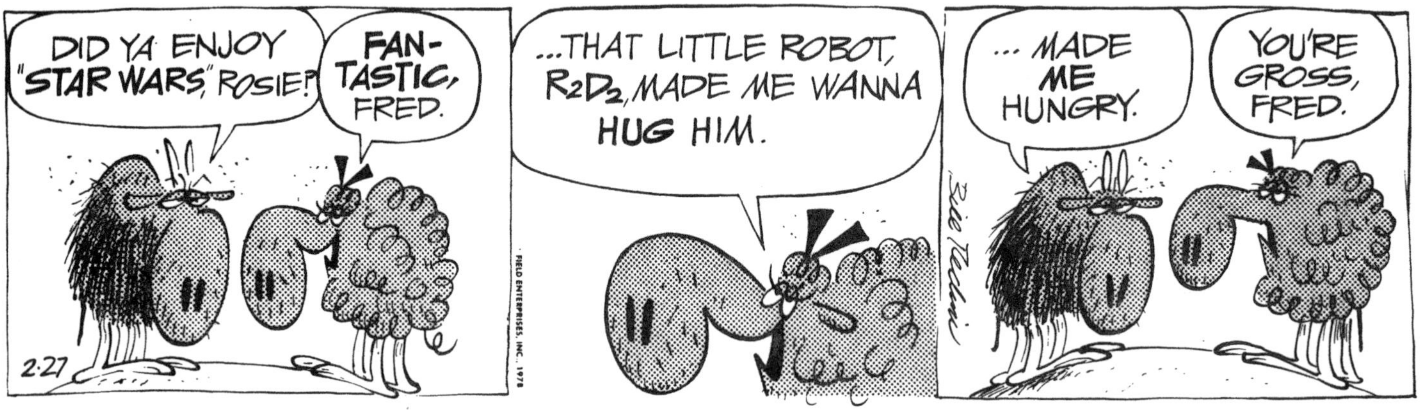
DID YA ENJOY "**STAR WARS**," ROSIE?
FAN-TASTIC, FRED.
2-27
...THAT LITTLE ROBOT, R2D2, MADE ME WANNA **HUG** HIM.
... MADE **ME** HUNGRY.
YOU'RE GROSS, FRED.

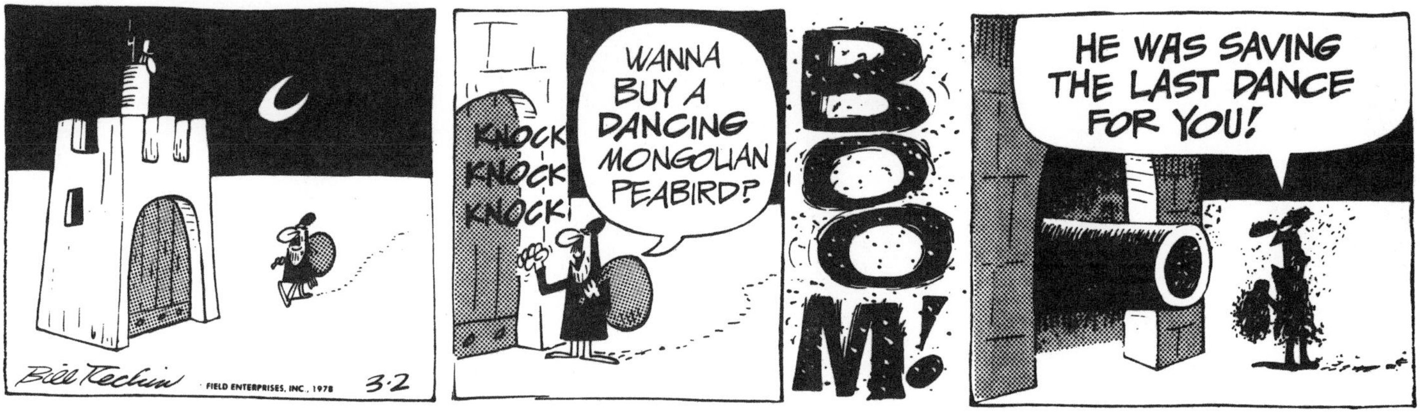
FIELD ENTERPRISES, INC., 1978
3-2
KNOCK KNOCK KNOCK
WANNA BUY A DANCING MONGOLIAN PEABIRD?
BOOM!
HE WAS SAVING THE LAST DANCE FOR YOU!

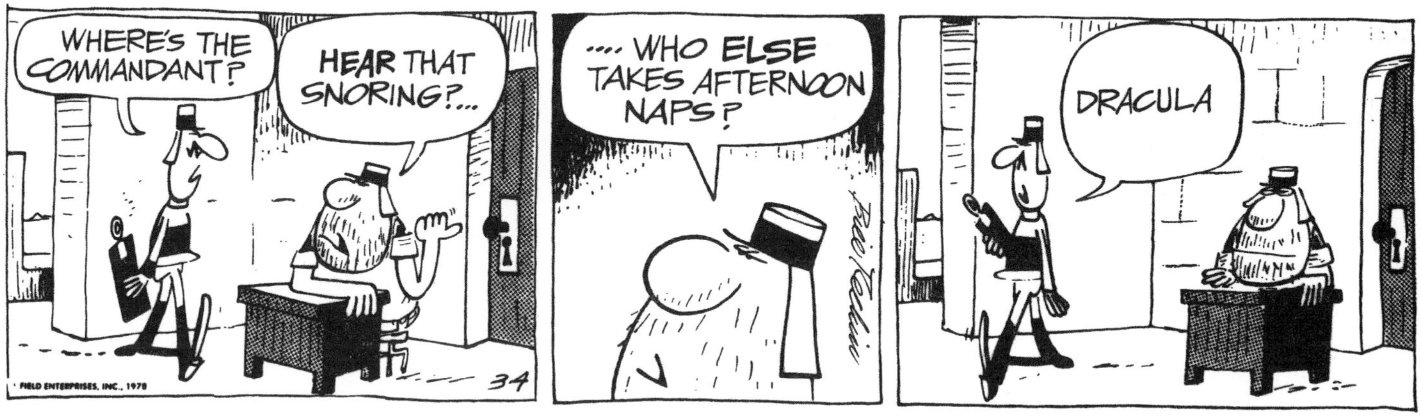
WHERE'S THE COMMANDANT?
HEAR THAT SNORING?...
FIELD ENTERPRISES, INC., 1978
3-4
.... WHO ELSE TAKES AFTERNOON NAPS?
DRACULA

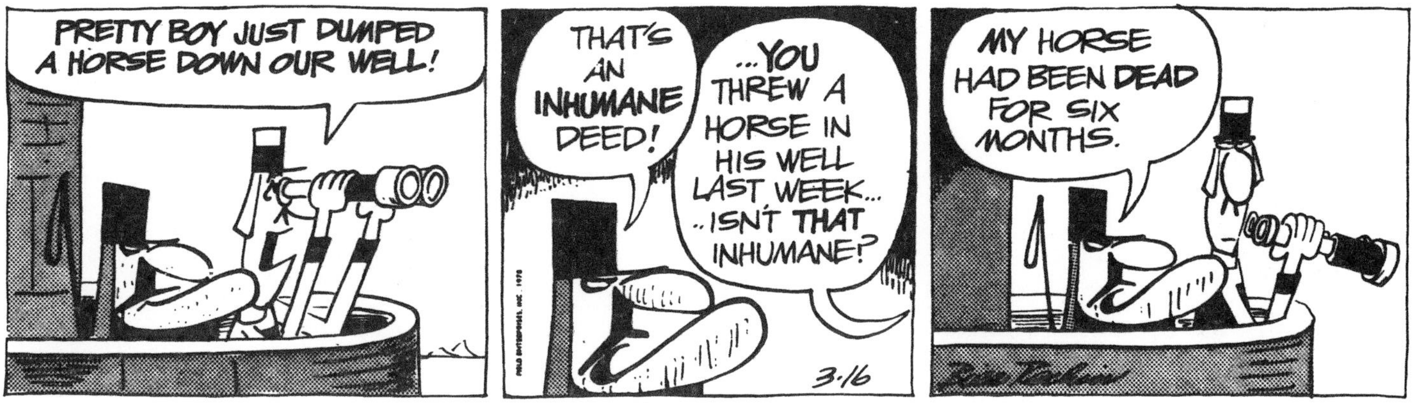
PRETTY BOY JUST DUMPED A HORSE DOWN OUR WELL!
THAT'S AN INHUMANE DEED!
...YOU THREW A HORSE IN HIS WELL LAST WEEK... ..ISN'T THAT INHUMANE?
3-16
MY HORSE HAD BEEN DEAD FOR SIX MONTHS.

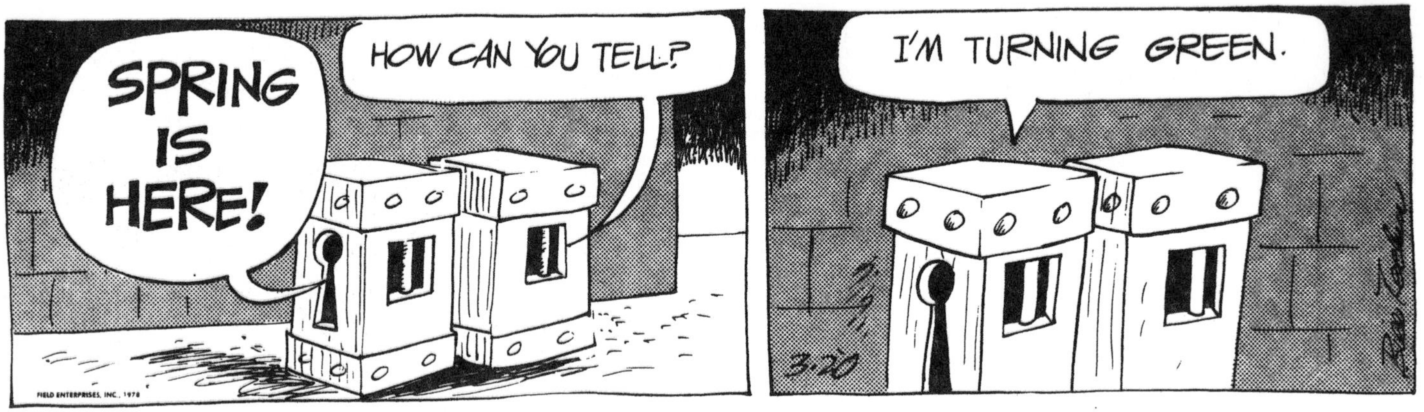
SPRING IS HERE!
HOW CAN YOU TELL?
I'M TURNING GREEN.
3·20
FIELD ENTERPRISES, INC., 1978

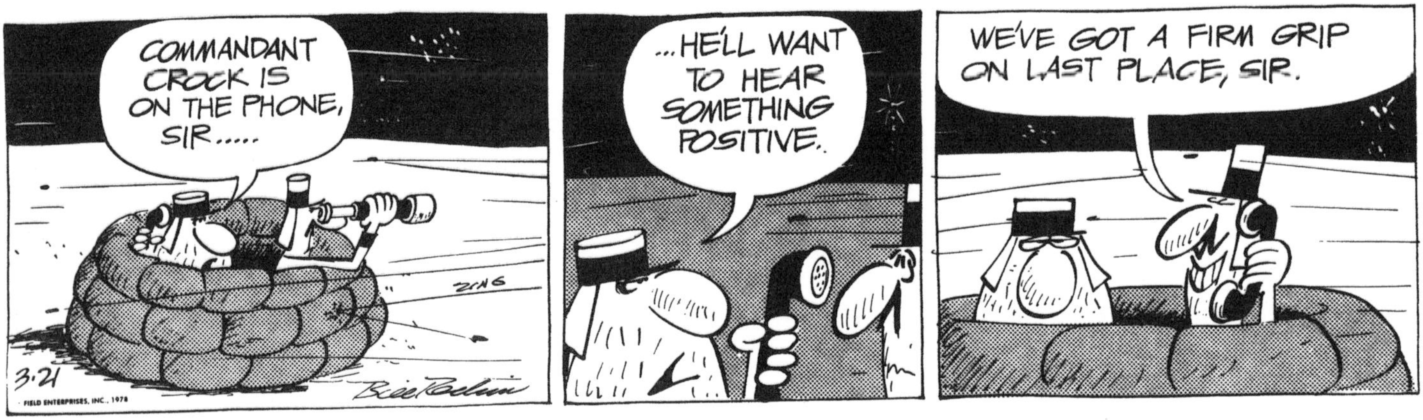
COMMANDANT CROCK IS ON THE PHONE, SIR.....
ZING
3·21
Bill Rechin
FIELD ENTERPRISES, INC., 1978
...HE'LL WANT TO HEAR SOMETHING POSITIVE.
WE'VE GOT A FIRM GRIP ON LAST PLACE, SIR.

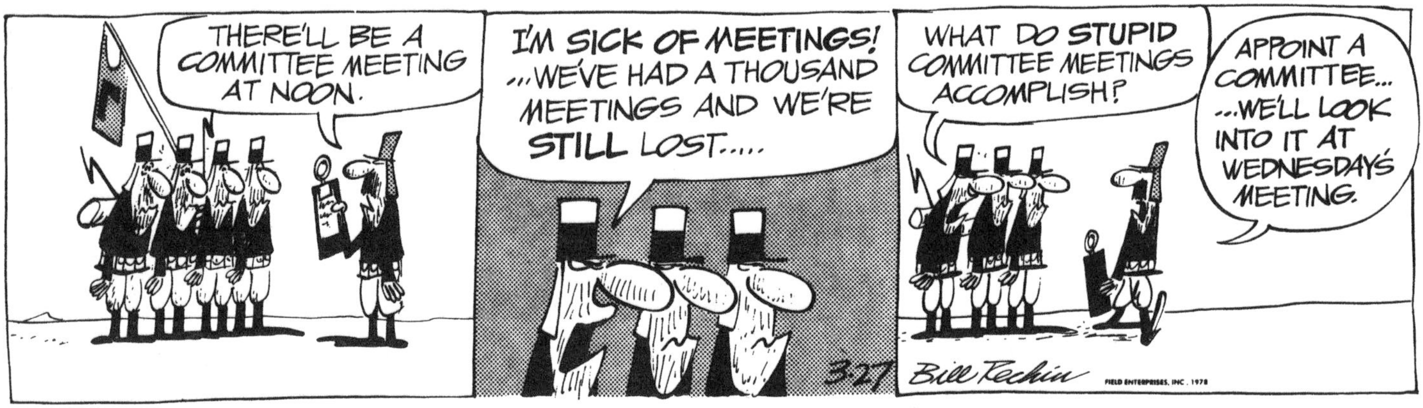
THERE'LL BE A COMMITTEE MEETING AT NOON.
I'M SICK OF MEETINGS! ...WE'VE HAD A THOUSAND MEETINGS AND WE'RE STILL LOST.....
WHAT DO STUPID COMMITTEE MEETINGS ACCOMPLISH?
APPOINT A COMMITTEE... ...WE'LL LOOK INTO IT AT WEDNESDAY'S MEETING.
3·27
Bill Rechin
FIELD ENTERPRISES, INC., 1978

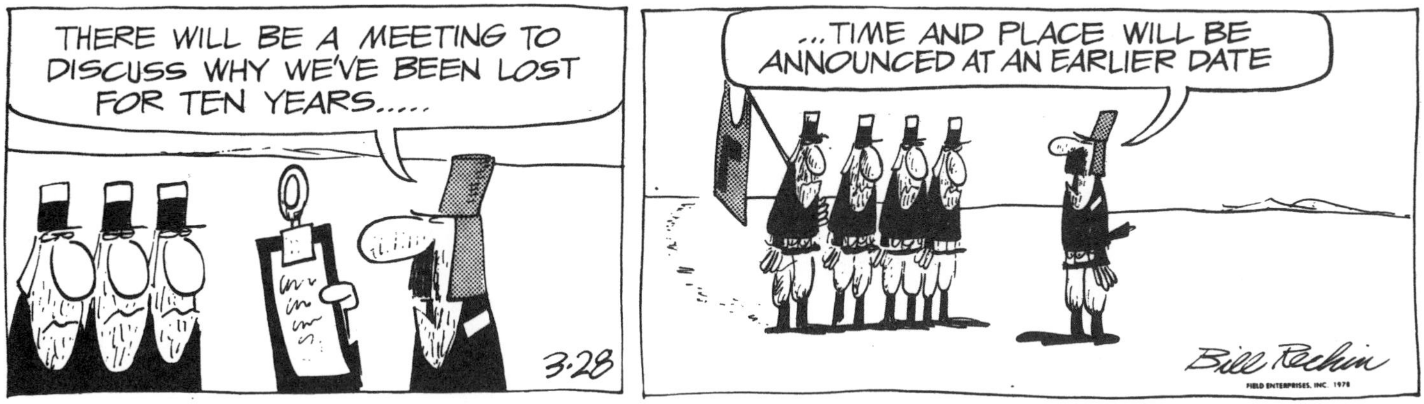
THERE WILL BE A MEETING TO DISCUSS WHY WE'VE BEEN LOST FOR TEN YEARS.....
3·28
...TIME AND PLACE WILL BE ANNOUNCED AT AN EARLIER DATE
Bill Rechin
FIELD ENTERPRISES, INC. 1978

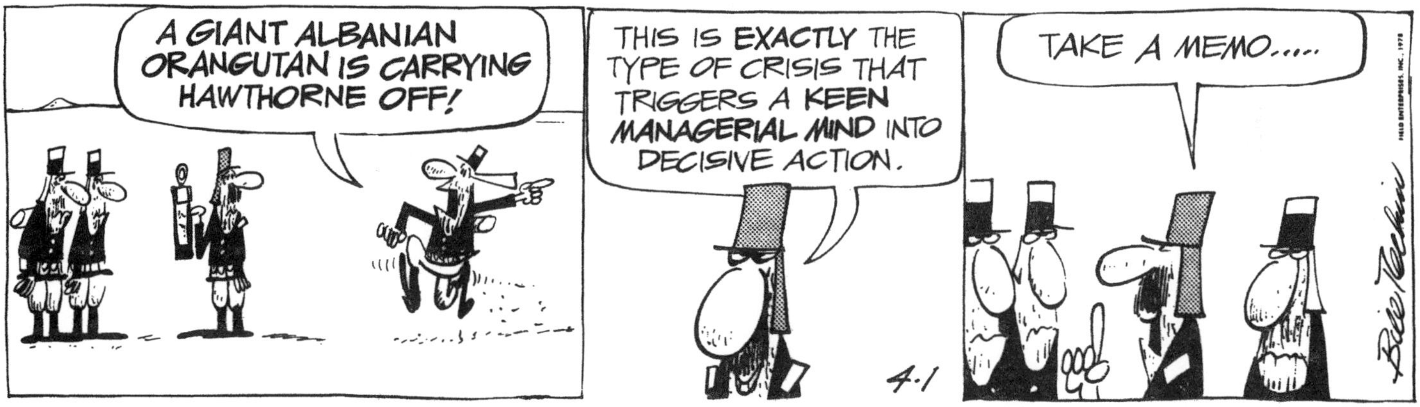
A GIANT ALBANIAN ORANGUTAN IS CARRYING HAWTHORNE OFF!
THIS IS EXACTLY THE TYPE OF CRISIS THAT TRIGGERS A KEEN MANAGERIAL MIND INTO DECISIVE ACTION.
4·1
TAKE A MEMO.....
FIELD ENTERPRISES, INC. 1978
Bill Rechin

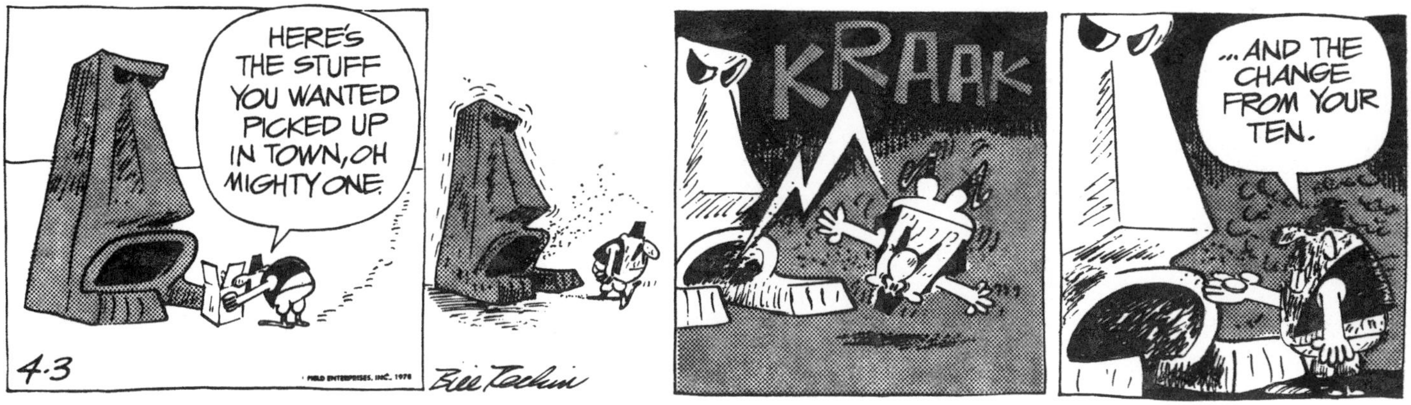
HERE'S THE STUFF YOU WANTED PICKED UP IN TOWN, OH MIGHTY ONE.
4·3
FIELD ENTERPRISES, INC. 1978
Bill Rechin
KRAAK
...AND THE CHANGE FROM YOUR TEN.

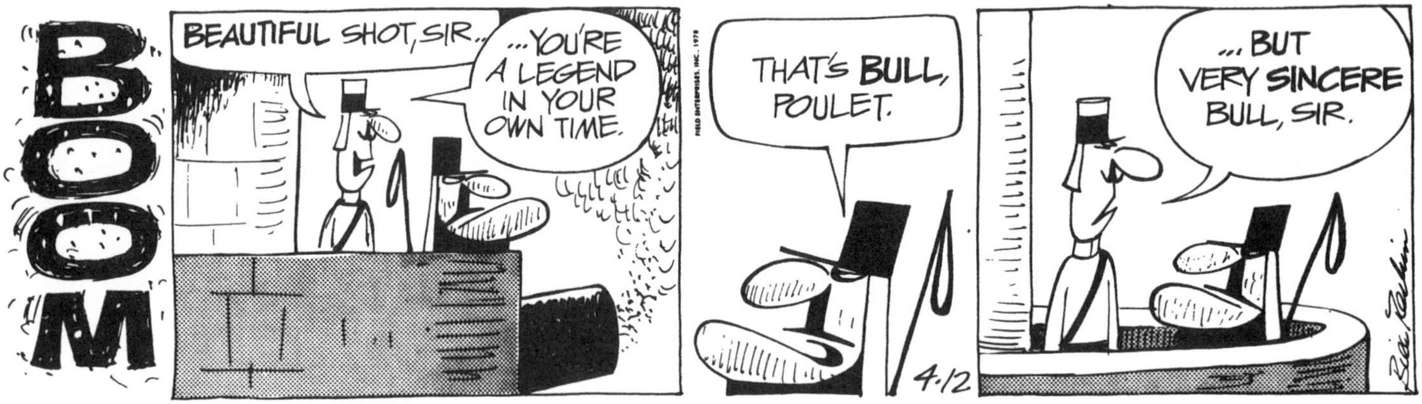
BOOM
BEAUTIFUL SHOT, SIR..
...YOU'RE A LEGEND IN YOUR OWN TIME.
FIELD ENTERPRISES, INC. 1978
THAT'S BULL, POULET.
4.12
...BUT VERY SINCERE BULL, SIR.
Bill Rechin

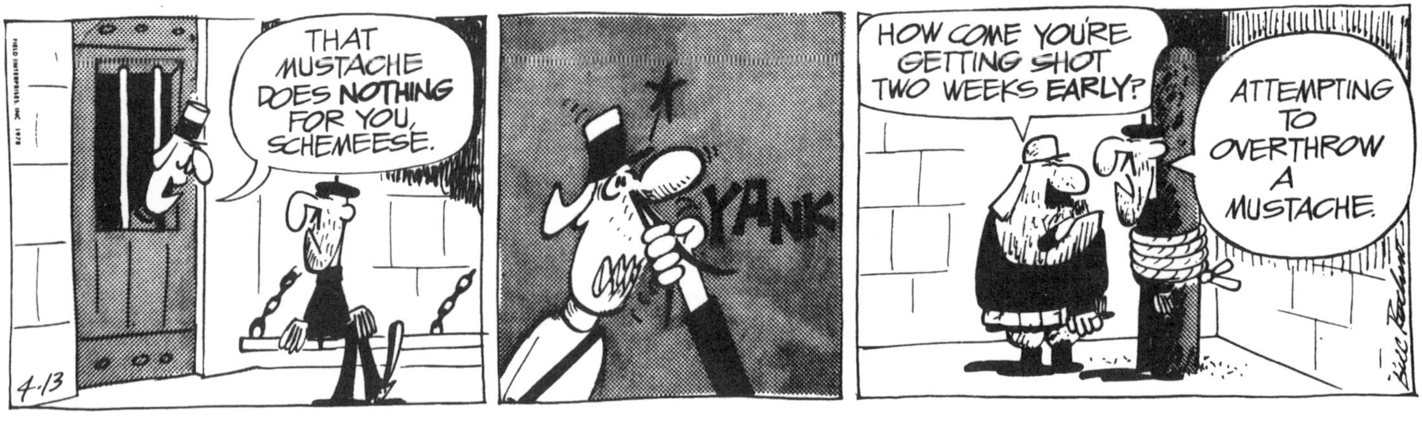
FIELD ENTERPRISES, INC. 1978
THAT MUSTACHE DOES NOTHING FOR YOU, SCHEMEESE.
4.13
YANK
HOW COME YOU'RE GETTING SHOT TWO WEEKS EARLY?
ATTEMPTING TO OVERTHROW A MUSTACHE.
Bill Rechin

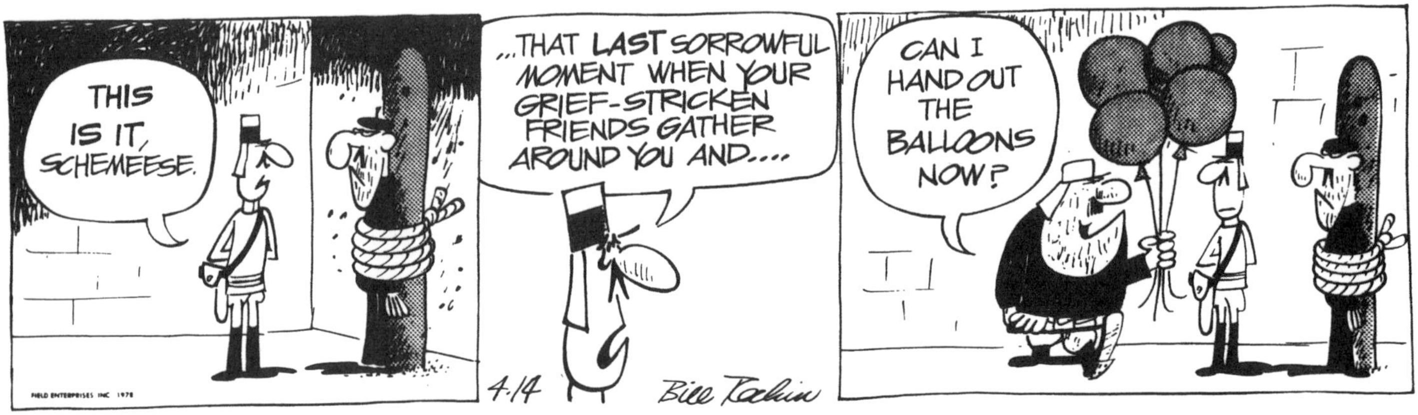
THIS IS IT, SCHEMEESE.
FIELD ENTERPRISES INC 1978
...THAT LAST SORROWFUL MOMENT WHEN YOUR GRIEF-STRICKEN FRIENDS GATHER AROUND YOU AND....
4.14
Bill Rechin
CAN I HAND OUT THE BALLOONS NOW?

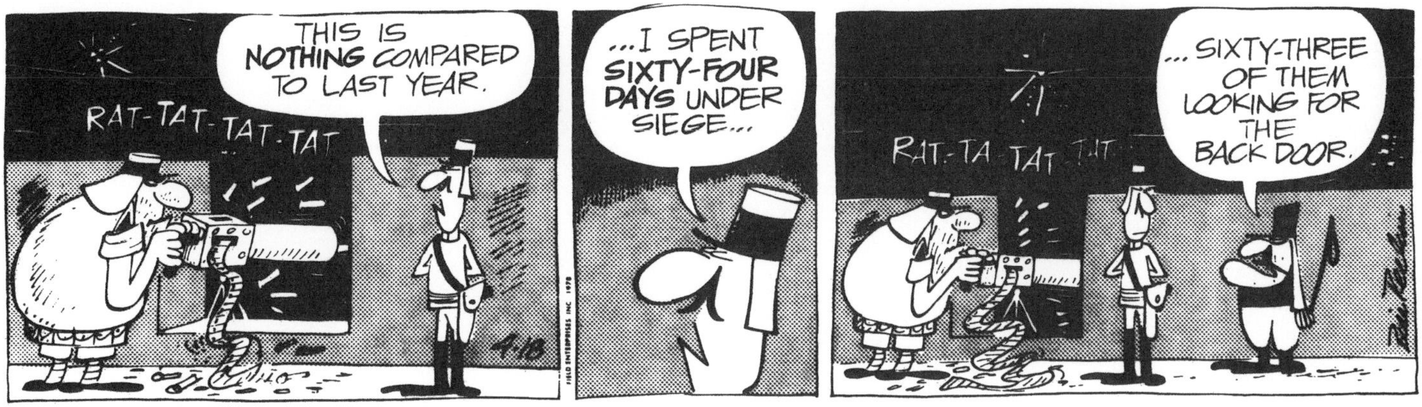
THIS IS NOTHING COMPARED TO LAST YEAR.
RAT-TAT-TAT-TAT
4-18
...I SPENT SIXTY-FOUR DAYS UNDER SIEGE...
RAT-TA-TAT TAT
...SIXTY-THREE OF THEM LOOKING FOR THE BACK DOOR.

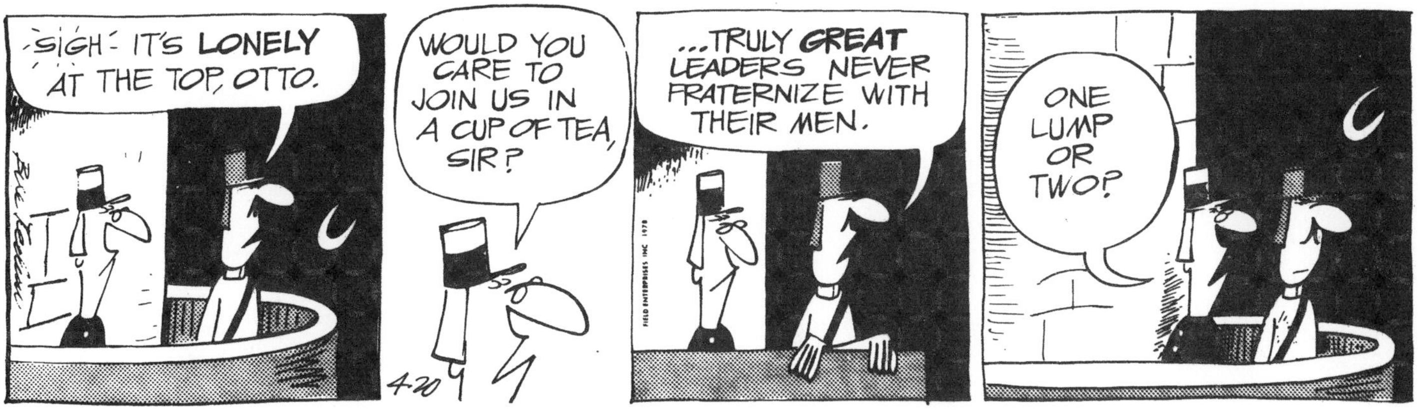
SIGH IT'S LONELY AT THE TOP, OTTO.
WOULD YOU CARE TO JOIN US IN A CUP OF TEA, SIR?
4-20
...TRULY GREAT LEADERS NEVER FRATERNIZE WITH THEIR MEN.
ONE LUMP OR TWO?

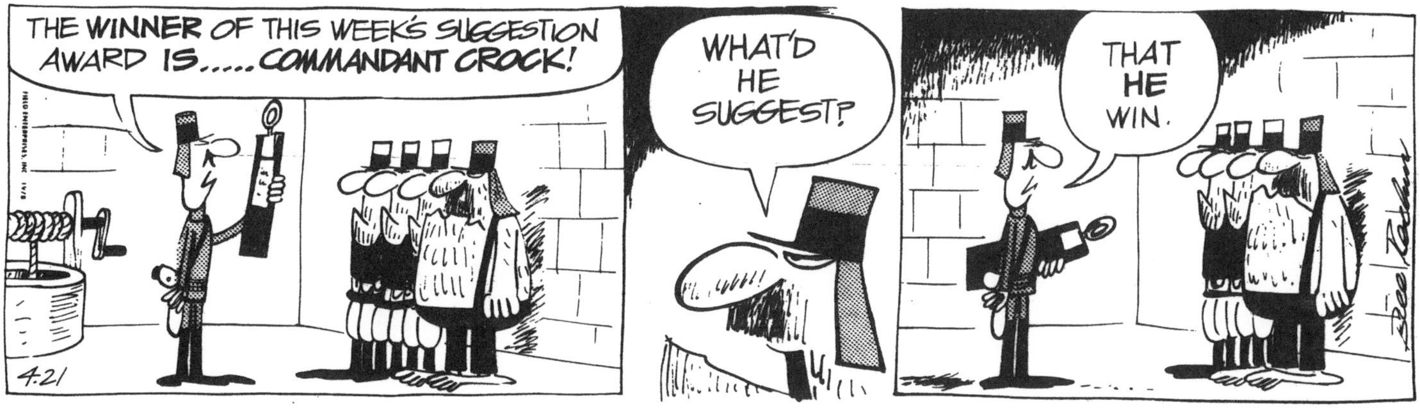
THE WINNER OF THIS WEEK'S SUGGESTION AWARD IS.....COMMANDANT CROCK!
4-21
WHAT'D HE SUGGEST?
THAT HE WIN.

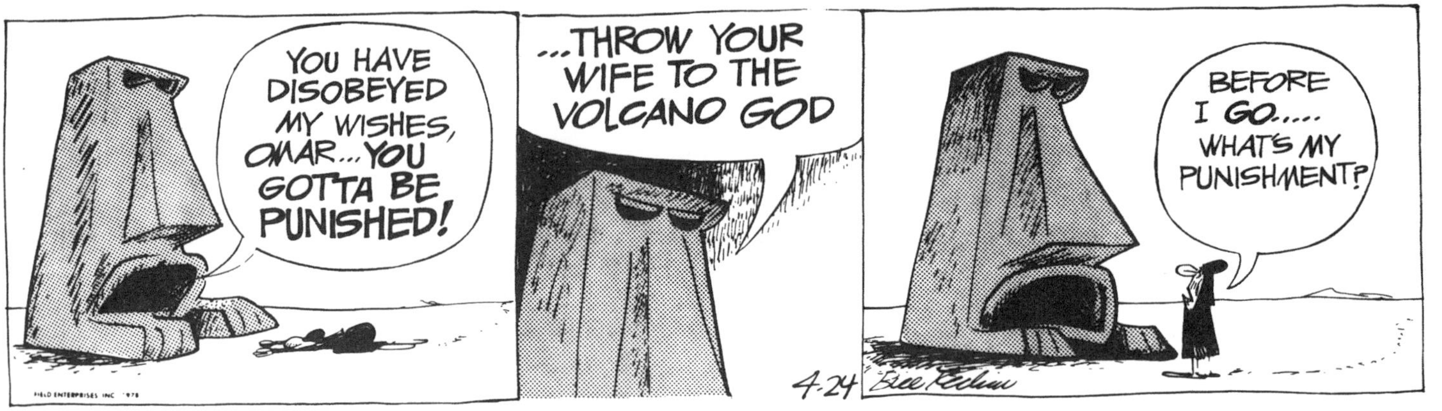
YOU HAVE DISOBEYED MY WISHES, OMAR... YOU GOTTA BE PUNISHED!
...THROW YOUR WIFE TO THE VOLCANO GOD
BEFORE I GO..... WHAT'S MY PUNISHMENT?
4-24

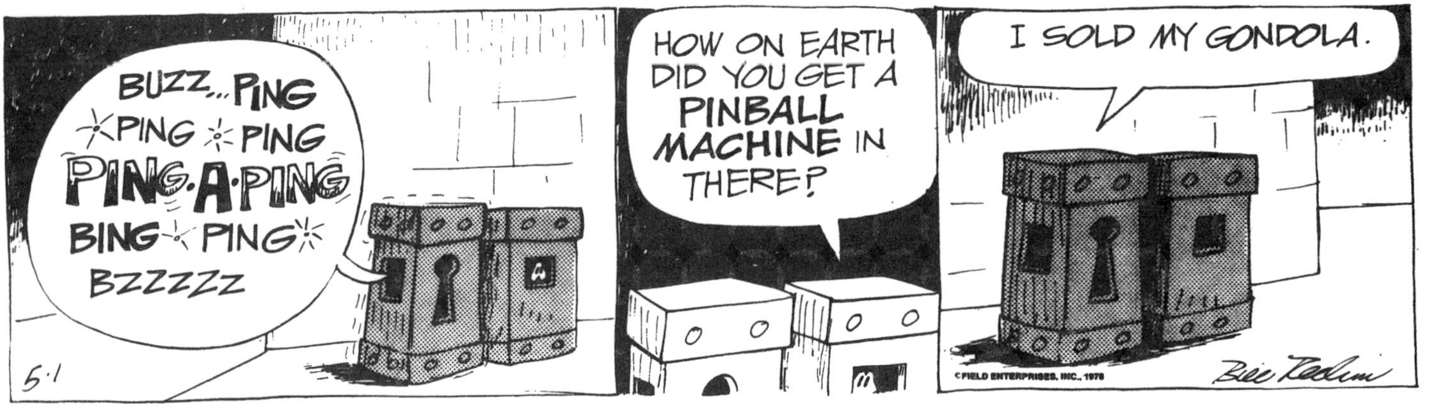
BUZZ...PING PING PING PING-A-PING BING PING BZZZZZ
HOW ON EARTH DID YOU GET A PINBALL MACHINE IN THERE?
I SOLD MY GONDOLA.
5-1
©FIELD ENTERPRISES, INC., 1978

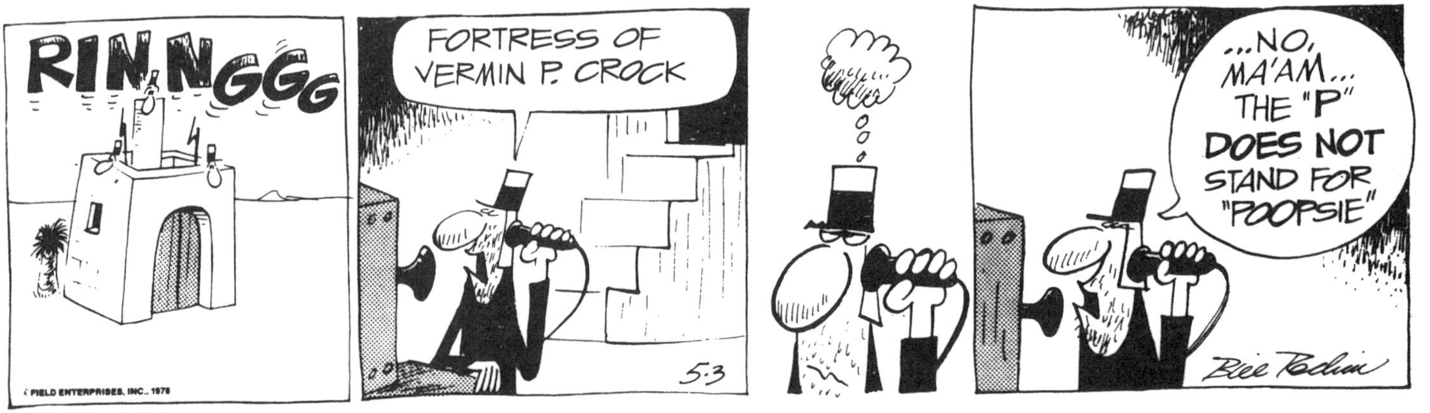
RIN,NGGG
FORTRESS OF VERMIN P. CROCK
...NO, MA'AM... THE "P" DOES NOT STAND FOR "POOPSIE"
5-3
©FIELD ENTERPRISES, INC., 1978

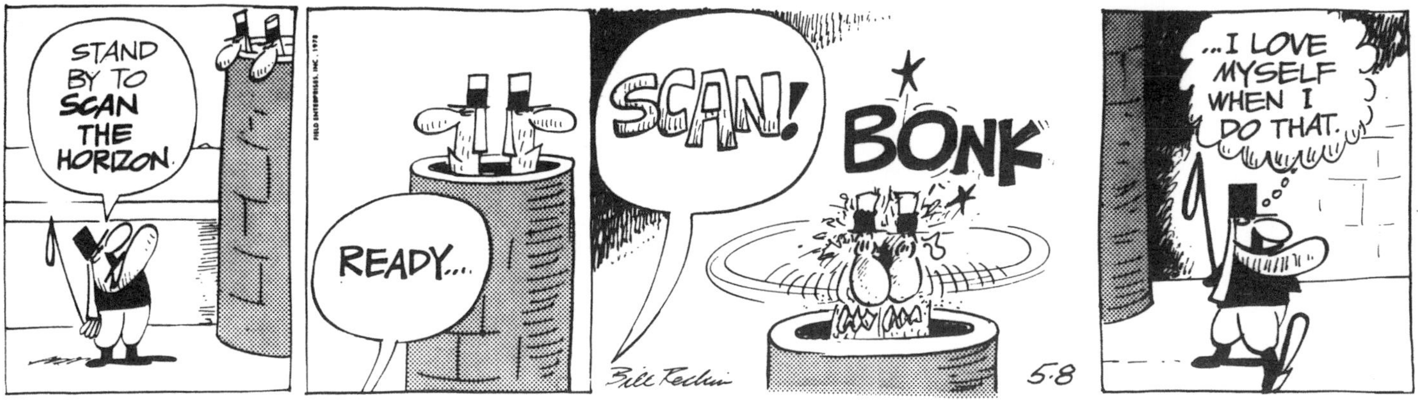
STAND BY TO SCAN THE HORIZON.
READY...
SCAN!
BONK
...I LOVE MYSELF WHEN I DO THAT.
5·8

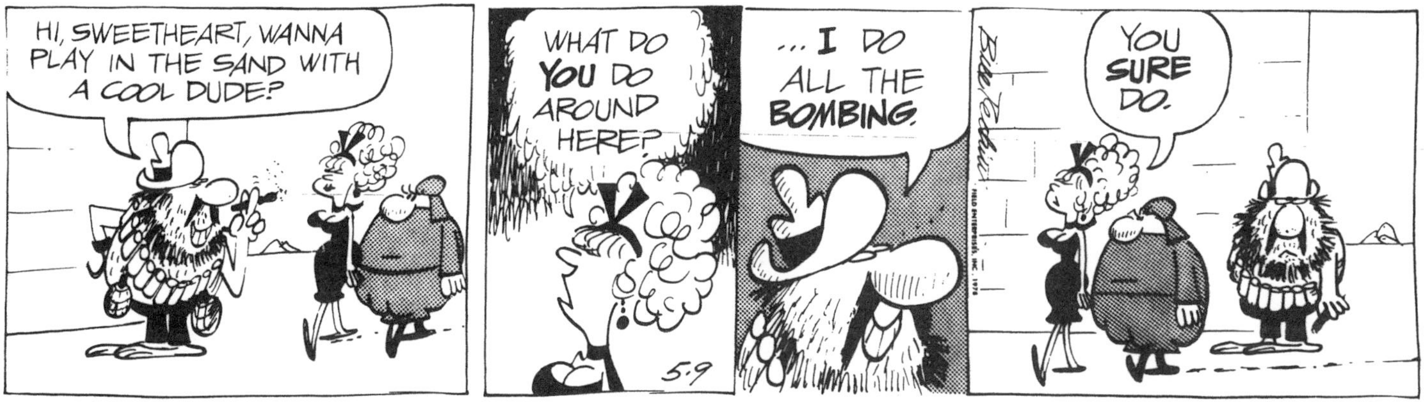
HI, SWEETHEART, WANNA PLAY IN THE SAND WITH A COOL DUDE?
WHAT DO YOU DO AROUND HERE?
...I DO ALL THE BOMBING.
YOU SURE DO.
5·9

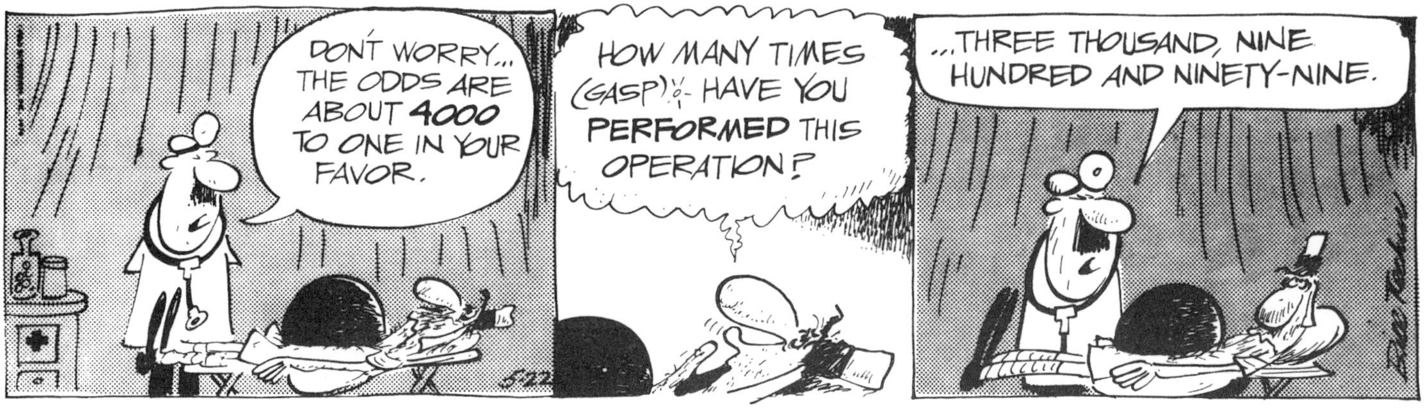
DON'T WORRY... THE ODDS ARE ABOUT 4000 TO ONE IN YOUR FAVOR.
HOW MANY TIMES (GASP) HAVE YOU PERFORMED THIS OPERATION?
...THREE THOUSAND, NINE HUNDRED AND NINETY-NINE.
5·22

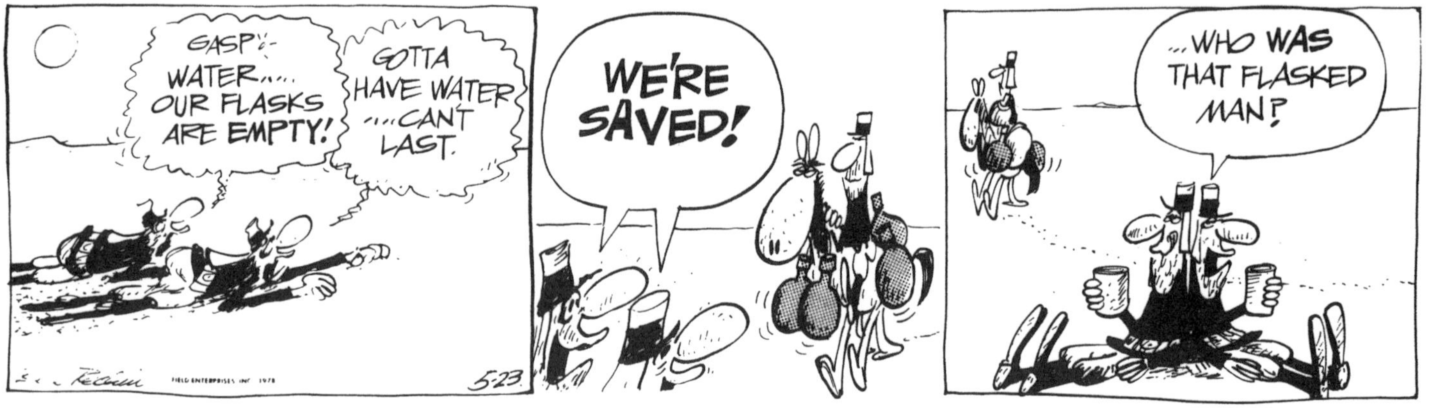
GASP!.. WATER.... OUR FLASKS ARE EMPTY!
GOTTA HAVE WATER ....CAN'T LAST.
5-23
WE'RE SAVED!
...WHO WAS THAT FLASKED MAN?

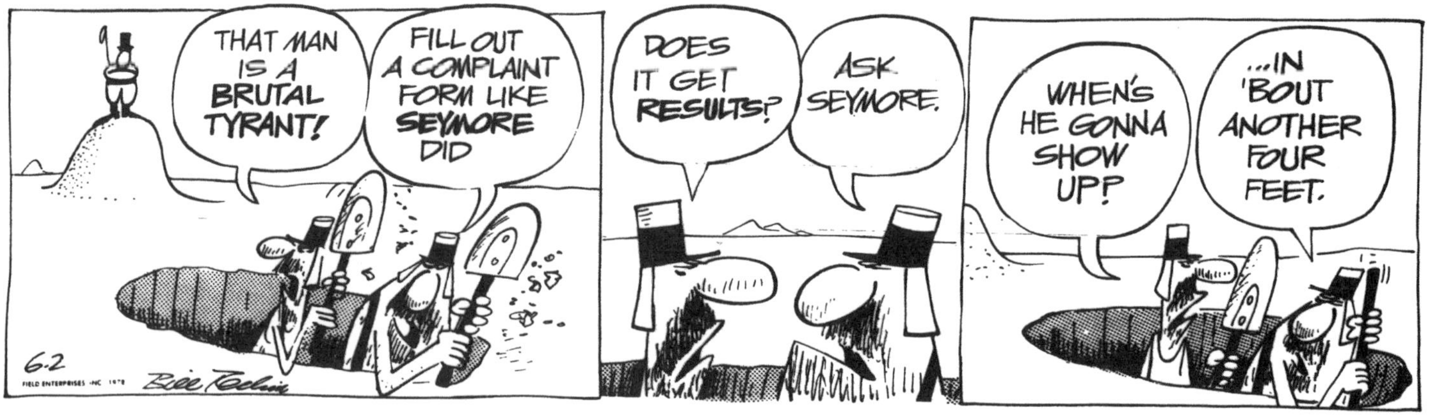
THAT MAN IS A BRUTAL TYRANT!
FILL OUT A COMPLAINT FORM LIKE SEYMORE DID
6-2
DOES IT GET RESULTS?
ASK SEYMORE.
WHEN'S HE GONNA SHOW UP?
...IN 'BOUT ANOTHER FOUR FEET.

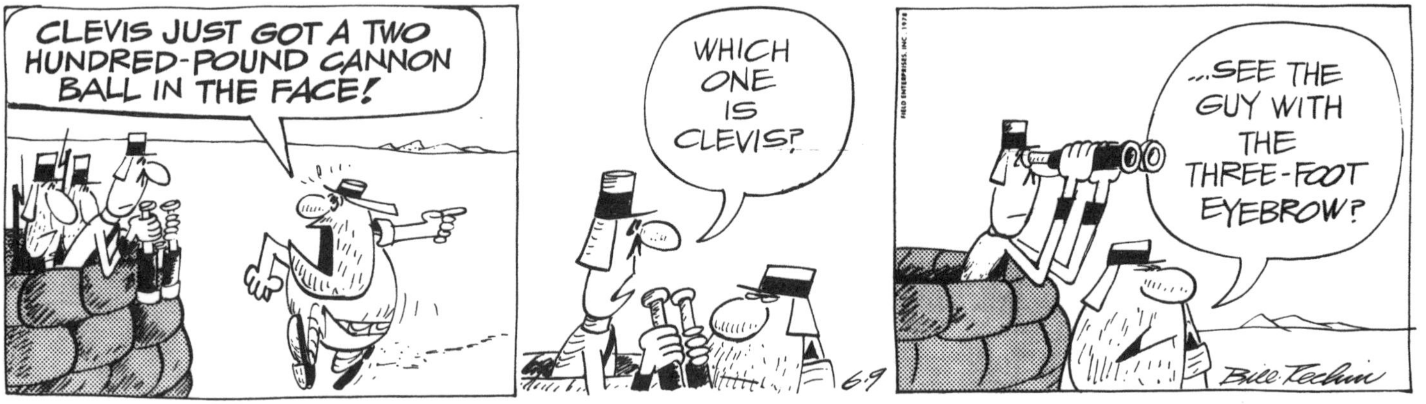
CLEVIS JUST GOT A TWO HUNDRED-POUND CANNON BALL IN THE FACE!
WHICH ONE IS CLEVIS?
6-9
...SEE THE GUY WITH THE THREE-FOOT EYEBROW?

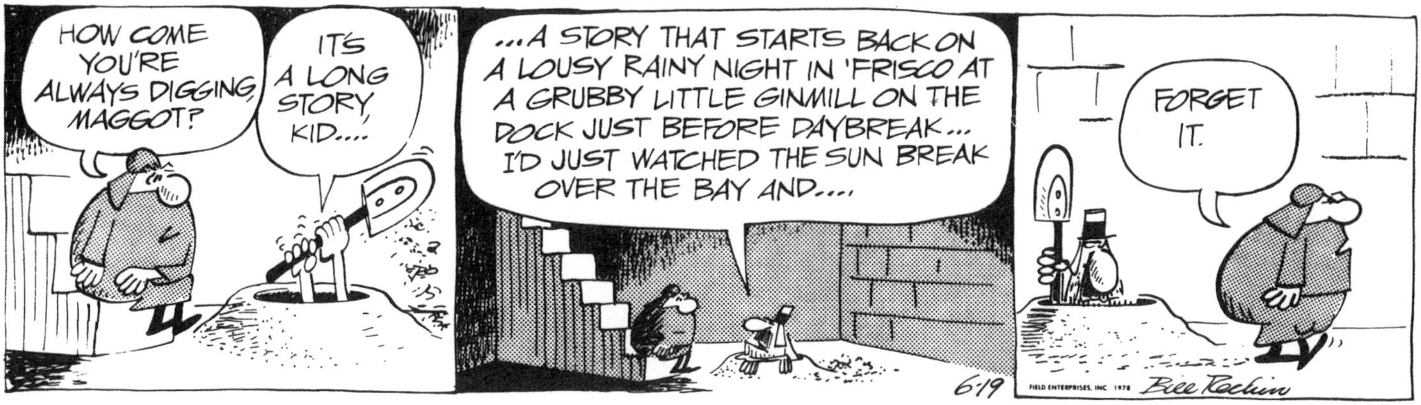
HOW COME YOU'RE ALWAYS DIGGING, MAGGOT?
IT'S A LONG STORY, KID....
...A STORY THAT STARTS BACK ON A LOUSY RAINY NIGHT IN 'FRISCO AT A GRUBBY LITTLE GINMILL ON THE DOCK JUST BEFORE DAYBREAK... I'D JUST WATCHED THE SUN BREAK OVER THE BAY AND....
FORGET IT.
6-19

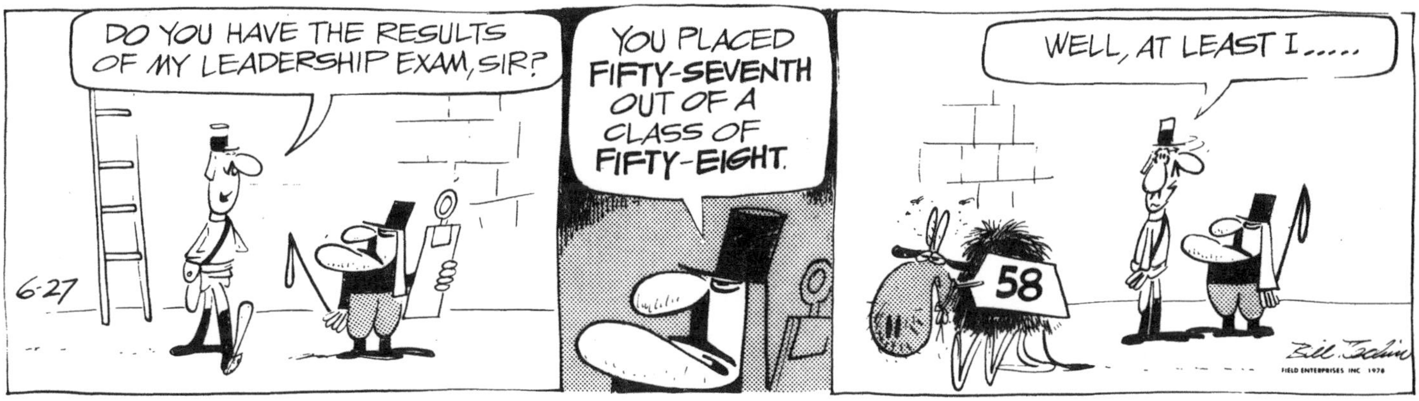
DO YOU HAVE THE RESULTS OF MY LEADERSHIP EXAM, SIR?
6-27
YOU PLACED FIFTY-SEVENTH OUT OF A CLASS OF FIFTY-EIGHT.
WELL, AT LEAST I.....
58

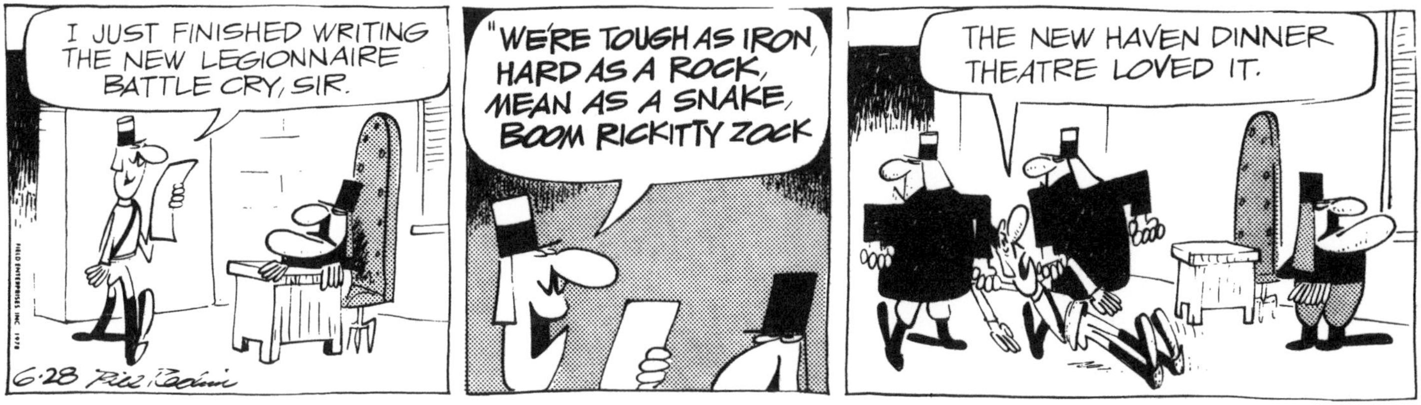
I JUST FINISHED WRITING THE NEW LEGIONNAIRE BATTLE CRY, SIR.
6-28
"WE'RE TOUGH AS IRON, HARD AS A ROCK, MEAN AS A SNAKE, BOOM RICKITTY ZOCK
THE NEW HAVEN DINNER THEATRE LOVED IT.

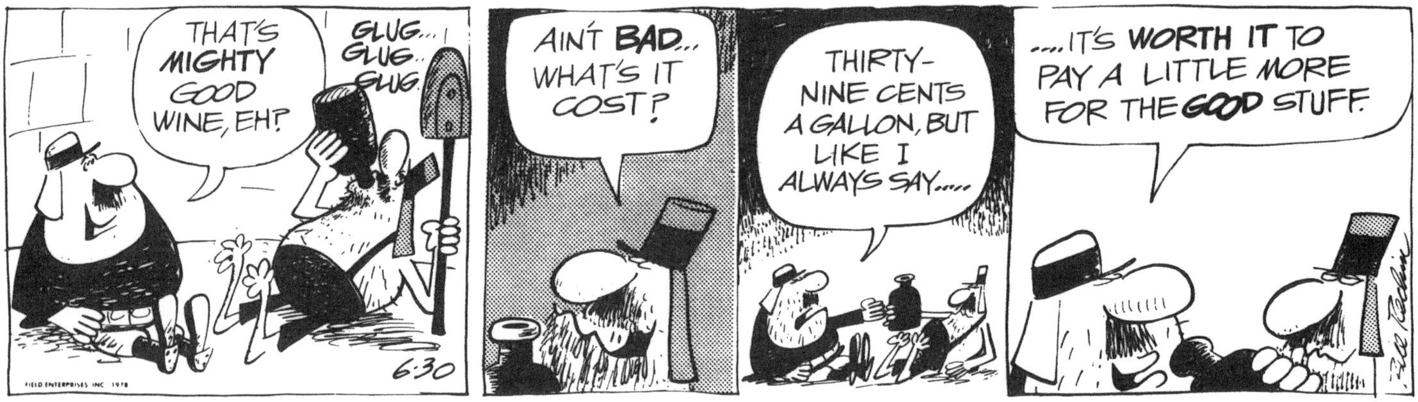
THAT'S MIGHTY GOOD WINE, EH?
GLUG... GLUG... GLUG
6·30
FIELD ENTERPRISES INC 1978
AIN'T BAD... WHAT'S IT COST?
THIRTY-NINE CENTS A GALLON, BUT LIKE I ALWAYS SAY.....
....IT'S WORTH IT TO PAY A LITTLE MORE FOR THE GOOD STUFF.

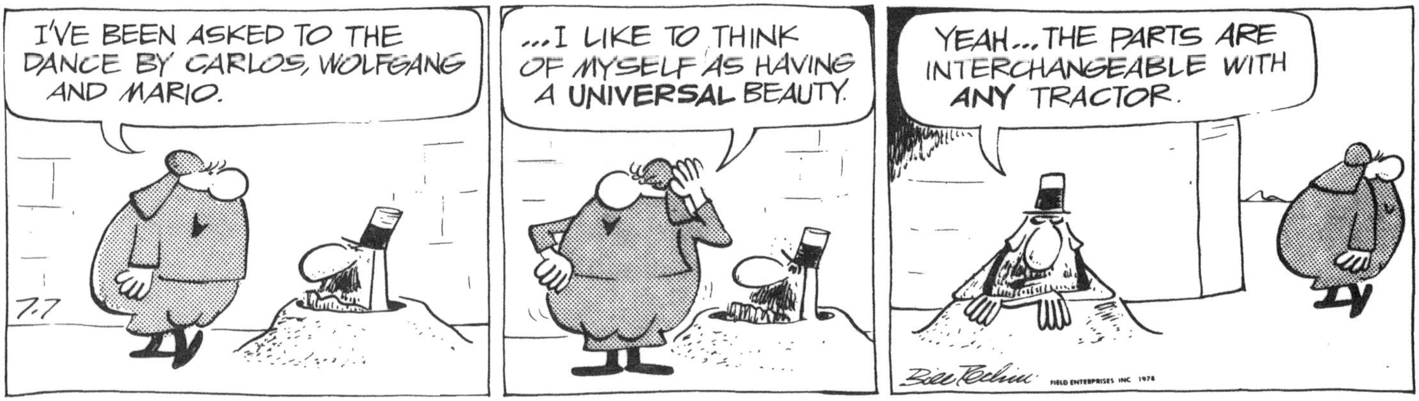
I'VE BEEN ASKED TO THE DANCE BY CARLOS, WOLFGANG AND MARIO.
7·7
...I LIKE TO THINK OF MYSELF AS HAVING A UNIVERSAL BEAUTY.
YEAH... THE PARTS ARE INTERCHANGEABLE WITH ANY TRACTOR.
FIELD ENTERPRISES INC 1978

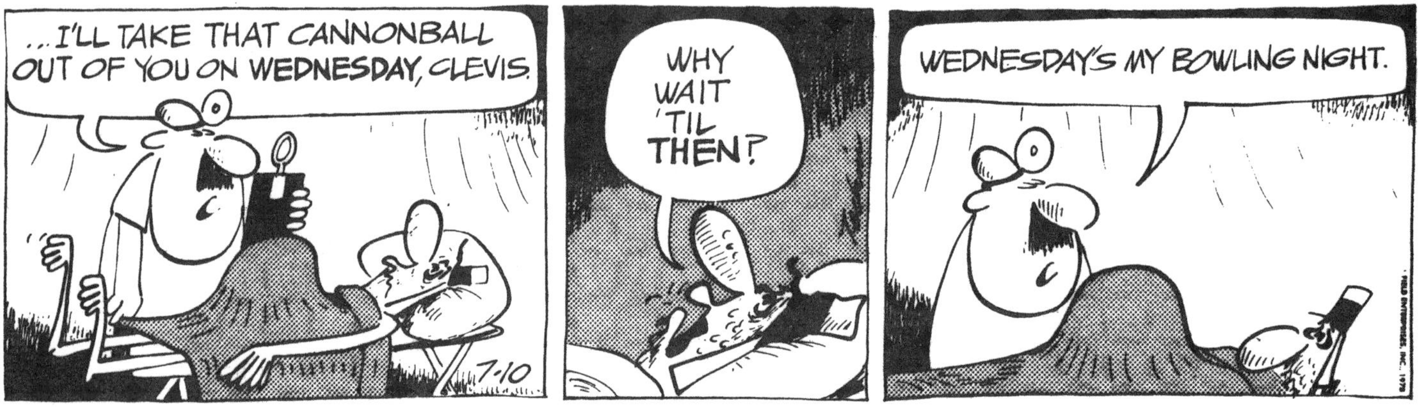
...I'LL TAKE THAT CANNONBALL OUT OF YOU ON WEDNESDAY, CLEVIS.
7·10
WHY WAIT 'TIL THEN?
WEDNESDAY'S MY BOWLING NIGHT.

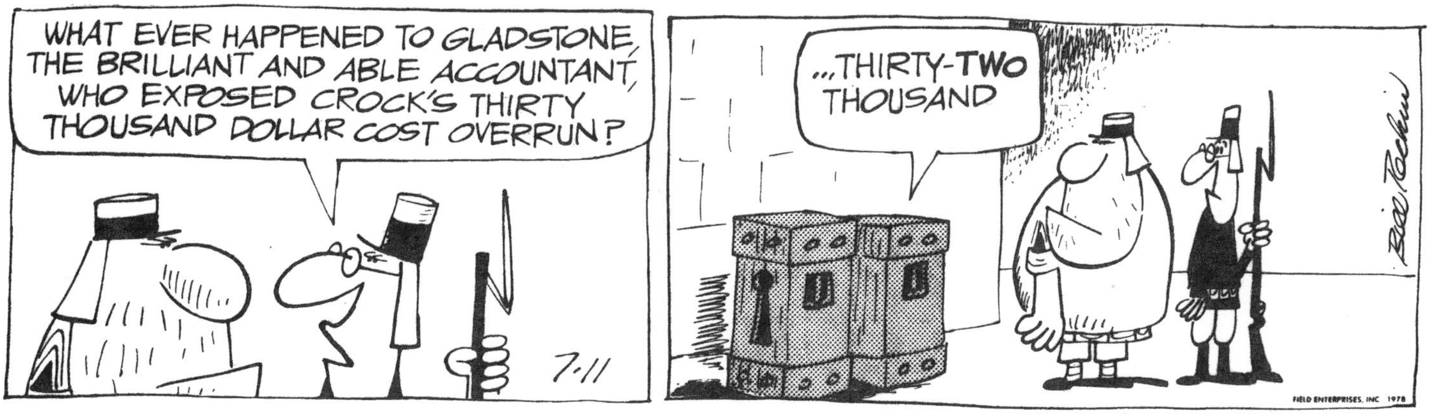
WHAT EVER HAPPENED TO GLADSTONE, THE BRILLIANT AND ABLE ACCOUNTANT, WHO EXPOSED CROCK'S THIRTY THOUSAND DOLLAR COST OVERRUN?
7-11
...THIRTY-TWO THOUSAND
FIELD ENTERPRISES, INC 1978

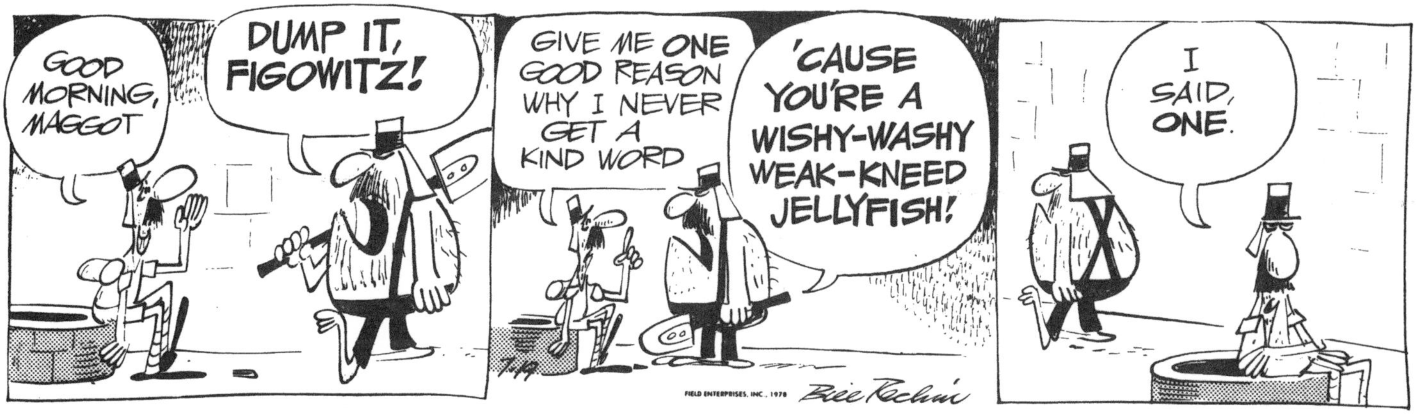
GOOD MORNING, MAGGOT
DUMP IT, FIGOWITZ!
GIVE ME ONE GOOD REASON WHY I NEVER GET A KIND WORD
'CAUSE YOU'RE A WISHY-WASHY WEAK-KNEED JELLYFISH!
7-19
FIELD ENTERPRISES, INC., 1978
I SAID, ONE.

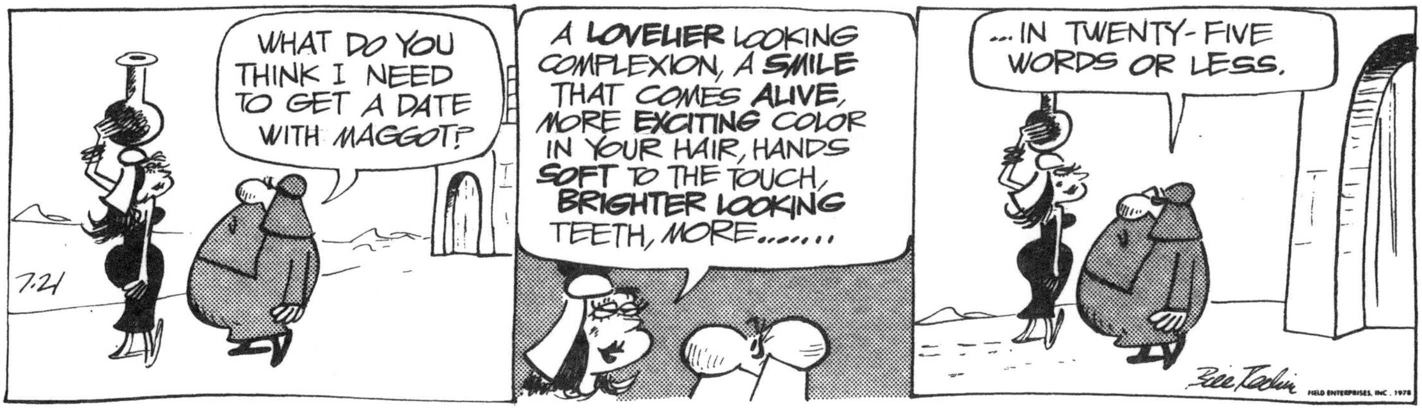
WHAT DO YOU THINK I NEED TO GET A DATE WITH MAGGOT?
7-21
A LOVELIER LOOKING COMPLEXION, A SMILE THAT COMES ALIVE, MORE EXCITING COLOR IN YOUR HAIR, HANDS SOFT TO THE TOUCH, BRIGHTER LOOKING TEETH, MORE......
...IN TWENTY-FIVE WORDS OR LESS.
FIELD ENTERPRISES, INC. 1978

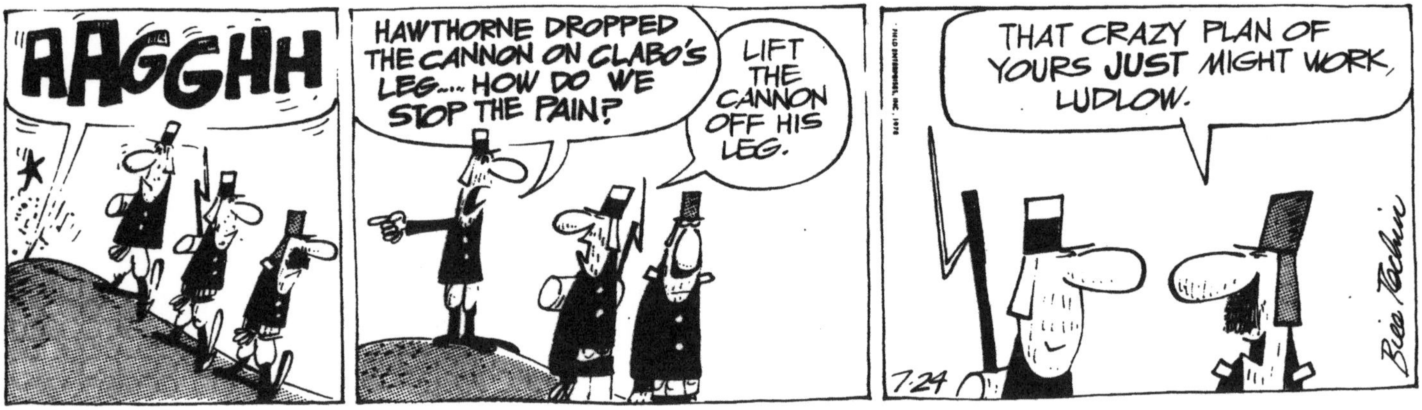
AAGGHH
HAWTHORNE DROPPED THE CANNON ON CLABO'S LEG.... HOW DO WE STOP THE PAIN?
LIFT THE CANNON OFF HIS LEG.
THAT CRAZY PLAN OF YOURS JUST MIGHT WORK, LUDLOW.
7·24

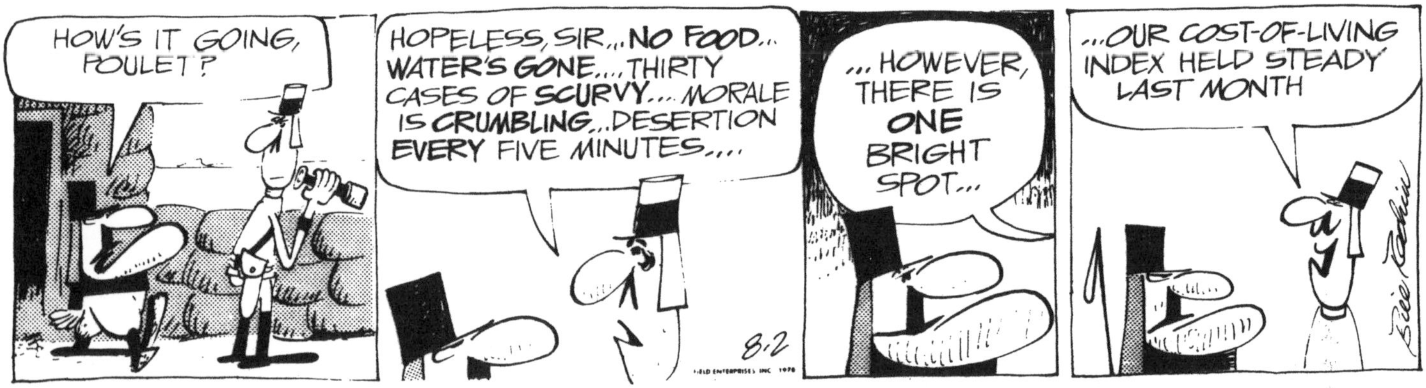
HOW'S IT GOING, POULET?
HOPELESS, SIR... NO FOOD.. WATER'S GONE.... THIRTY CASES OF SCURVY... MORALE IS CRUMBLING.. DESERTION EVERY FIVE MINUTES....
8·2
... HOWEVER, THERE IS ONE BRIGHT SPOT...
...OUR COST-OF-LIVING INDEX HELD STEADY LAST MONTH

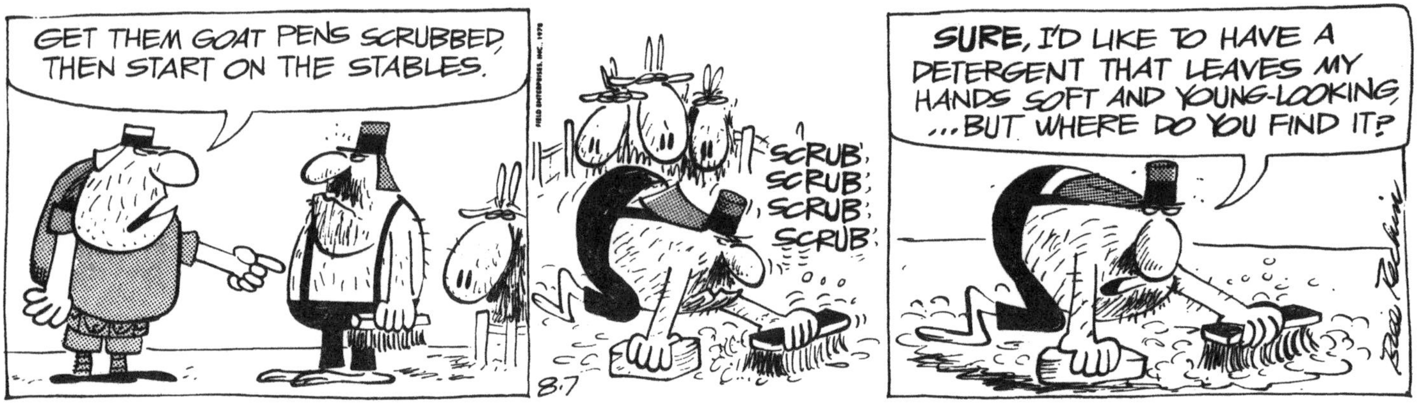
GET THEM GOAT PENS SCRUBBED, THEN START ON THE STABLES.
SCRUB, SCRUB, SCRUB, SCRUB
8·7
SURE, I'D LIKE TO HAVE A DETERGENT THAT LEAVES MY HANDS SOFT AND YOUNG-LOOKING, ... BUT WHERE DO YOU FIND IT?

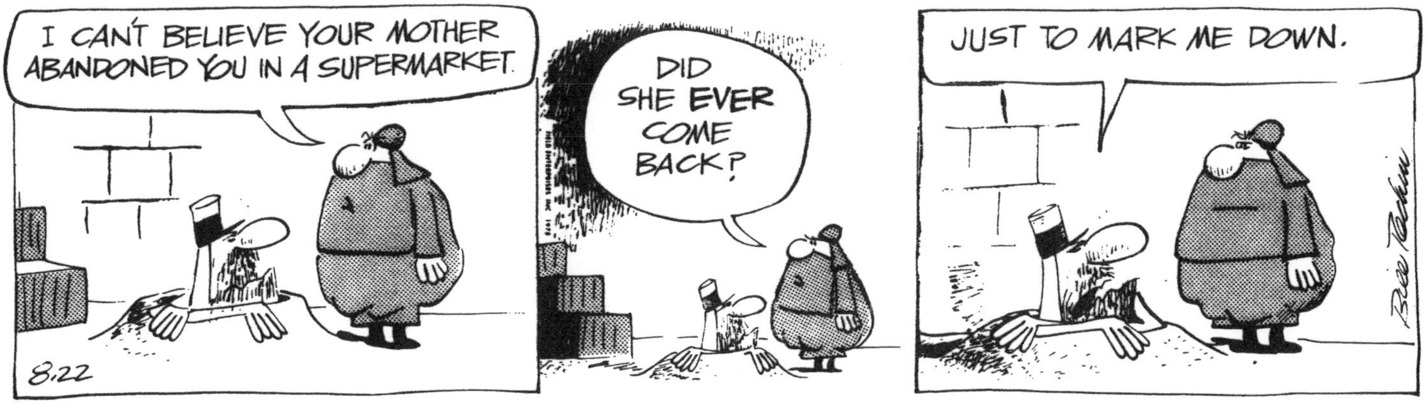
I CAN'T BELIEVE YOUR MOTHER ABANDONED YOU IN A SUPERMARKET.
8.22
DID SHE EVER COME BACK?
JUST TO MARK ME DOWN.

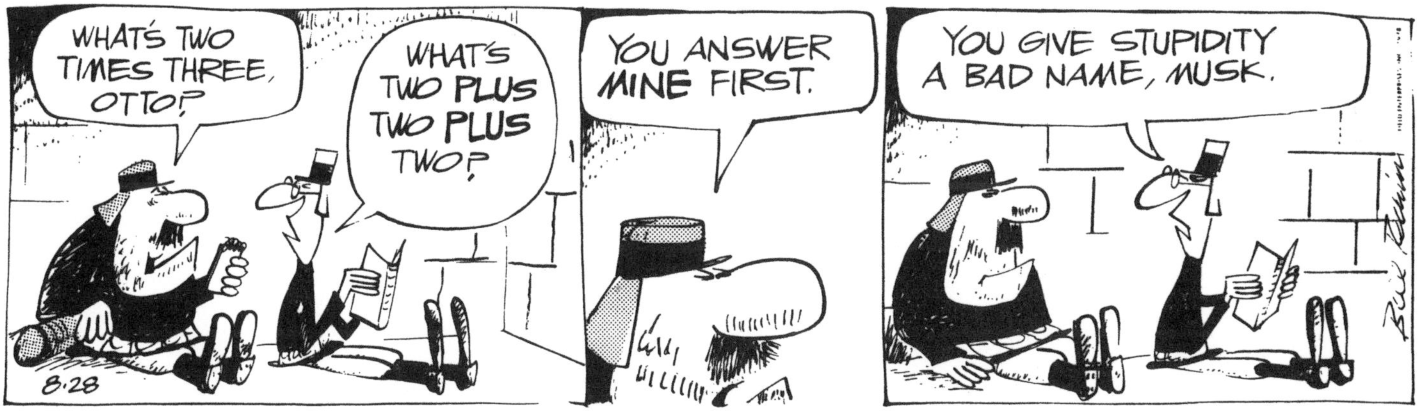
WHAT'S TWO TIMES THREE, OTTO?
WHAT'S TWO PLUS TWO PLUS TWO?
8.28
YOU ANSWER MINE FIRST.
YOU GIVE STUPIDITY A BAD NAME, MUSK.

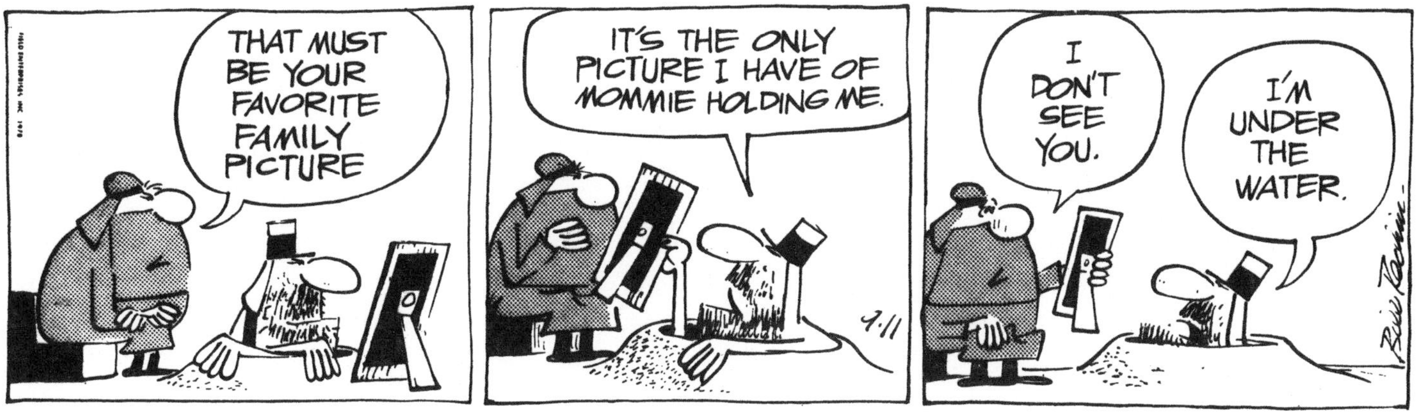
THAT MUST BE YOUR FAVORITE FAMILY PICTURE
IT'S THE ONLY PICTURE I HAVE OF MOMMIE HOLDING ME.
9.11
I DON'T SEE YOU.
I'M UNDER THE WATER.

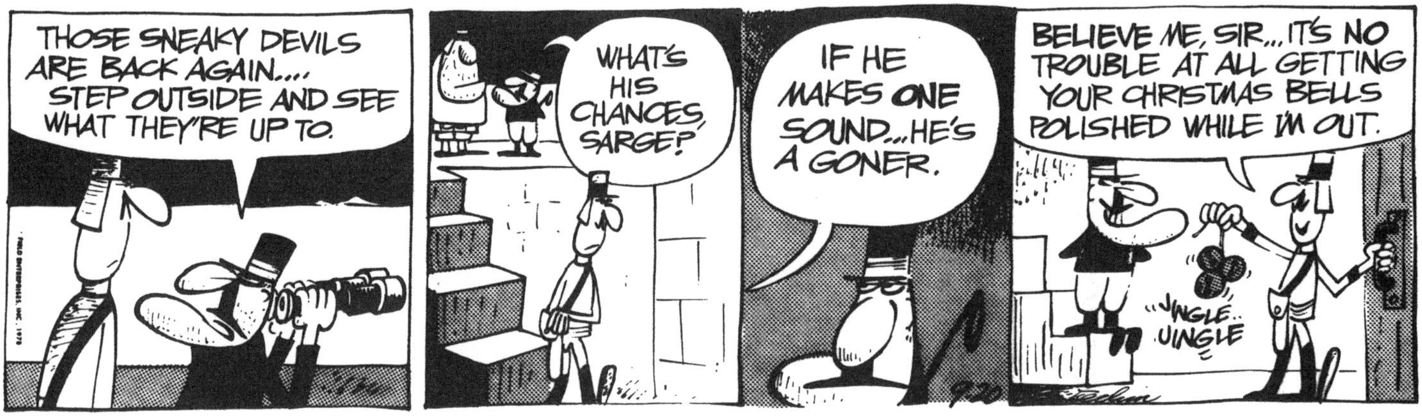
THOSE SNEAKY DEVILS ARE BACK AGAIN.... STEP OUTSIDE AND SEE WHAT THEY'RE UP TO.
WHAT'S HIS CHANCES, SARGE?
IF HE MAKES ONE SOUND... HE'S A GONER.
BELIEVE ME, SIR... IT'S NO TROUBLE AT ALL GETTING YOUR CHRISTMAS BELLS POLISHED WHILE I'M OUT.
JINGLE.. JINGLE

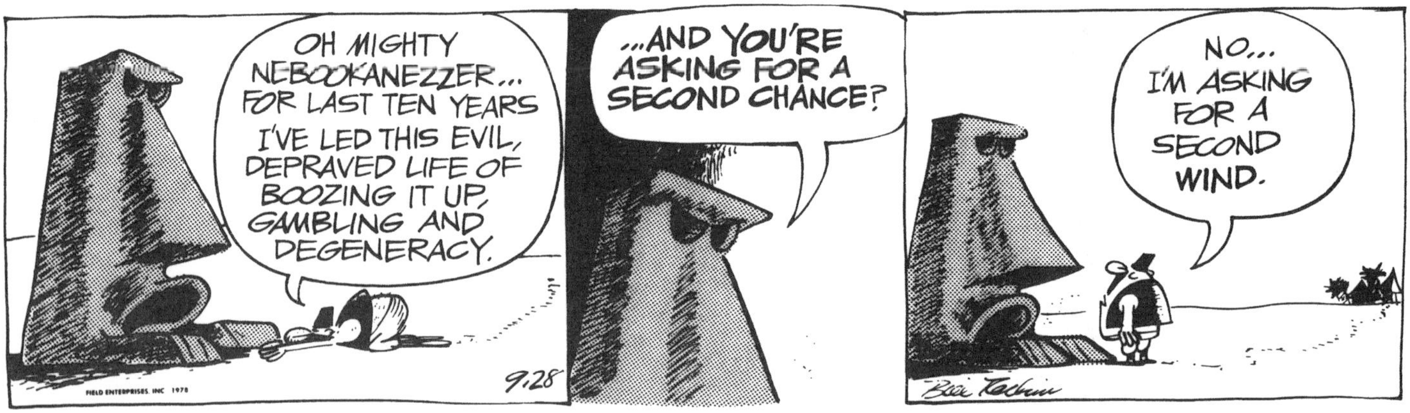
OH MIGHTY NEBOOKANEZZER... FOR LAST TEN YEARS I'VE LED THIS EVIL, DEPRAVED LIFE OF BOOZING IT UP, GAMBLING AND DEGENERACY.
FIELD ENTERPRISES, INC 1978
9.28
...AND YOU'RE ASKING FOR A SECOND CHANCE?
NO... I'M ASKING FOR A SECOND WIND.

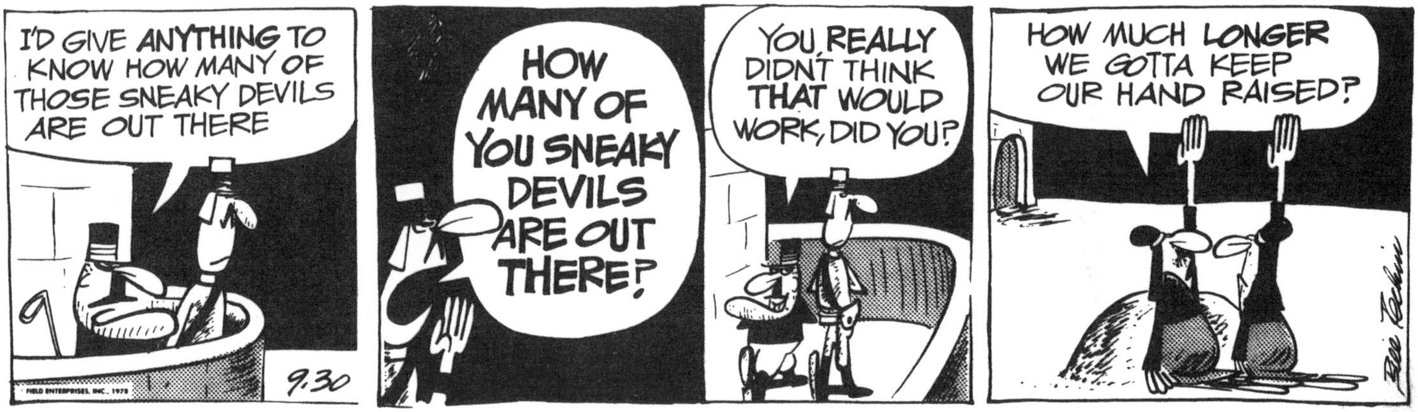
I'D GIVE ANYTHING TO KNOW HOW MANY OF THOSE SNEAKY DEVILS ARE OUT THERE
FIELD ENTERPRISES, INC., 1978
9.30
HOW MANY OF YOU SNEAKY DEVILS ARE OUT THERE?
YOU REALLY DIDN'T THINK THAT WOULD WORK, DID YOU?
HOW MUCH LONGER WE GOTTA KEEP OUR HAND RAISED?

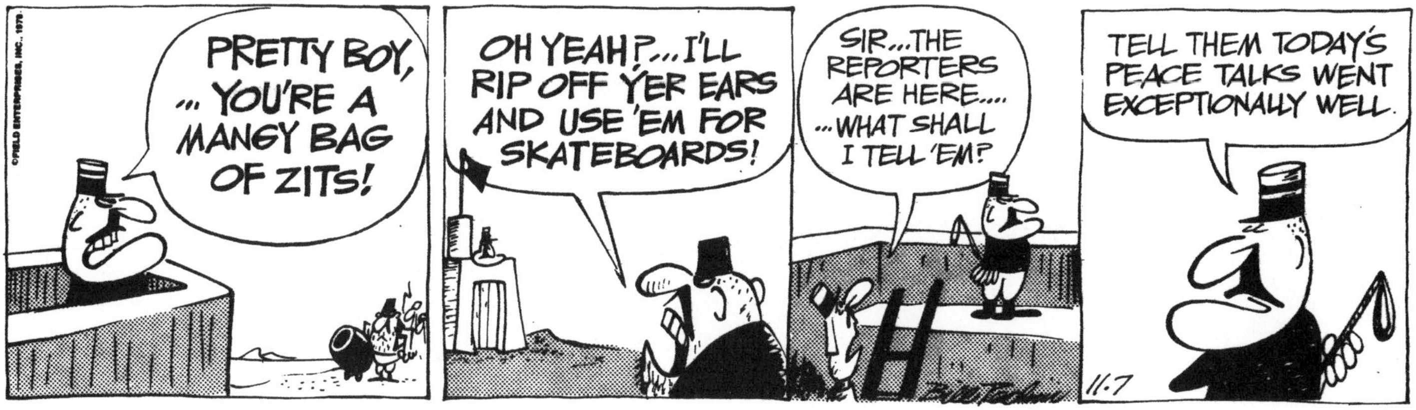
©FIELD ENTERPRISES, INC. 1979.
PRETTY BOY, ... YOU'RE A MANGY BAG OF ZITS!
OH YEAH?... I'LL RIP OFF YER EARS AND USE 'EM FOR SKATEBOARDS!
SIR... THE REPORTERS ARE HERE.... ...WHAT SHALL I TELL 'EM?
TELL THEM TODAY'S PEACE TALKS WENT EXCEPTIONALLY WELL.
11·7

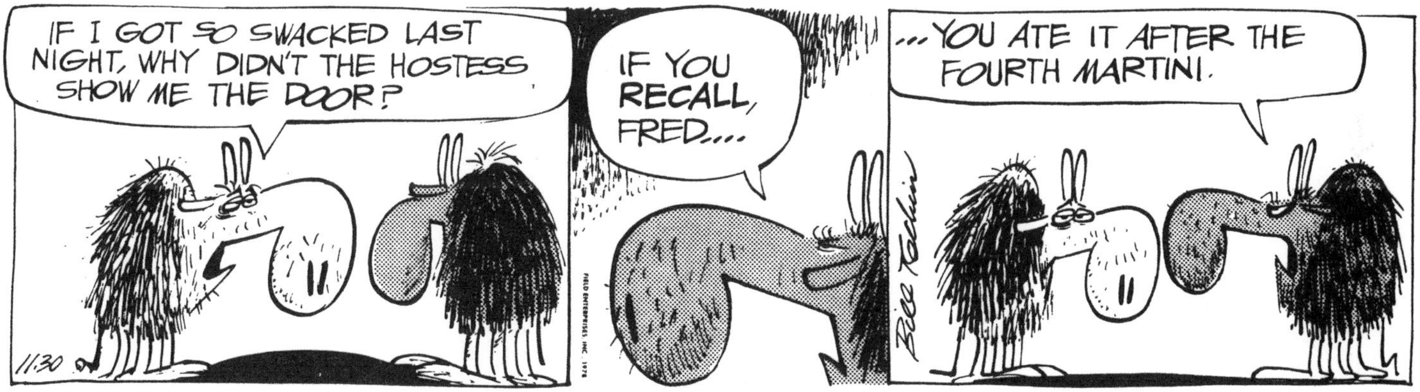
IF I GOT SO SWACKED LAST NIGHT, WHY DIDN'T THE HOSTESS SHOW ME THE DOOR?
11·30
IF YOU RECALL, FRED....
FIELD ENTERPRISES, INC. 1978
...YOU ATE IT AFTER THE FOURTH MARTINI.

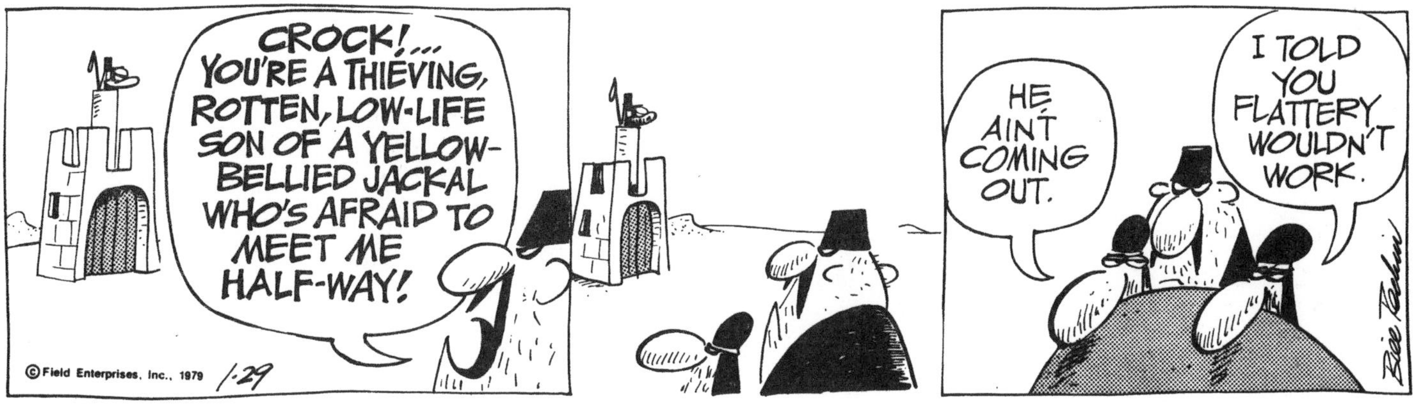
CROCK!... YOU'RE A THIEVING, ROTTEN, LOW-LIFE SON OF A YELLOW-BELLIED JACKAL WHO'S AFRAID TO MEET ME HALF-WAY!
© Field Enterprises, Inc., 1979
1·29
HE AIN'T COMING OUT.
I TOLD YOU FLATTERY WOULDN'T WORK.

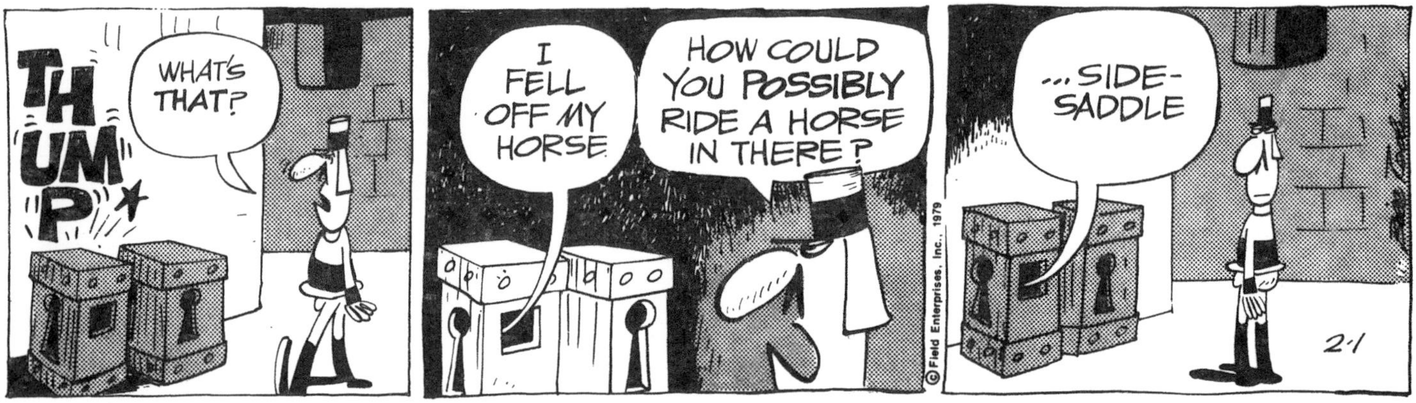
THUMP
WHAT'S THAT?
I FELL OFF MY HORSE
HOW COULD YOU POSSIBLY RIDE A HORSE IN THERE?
© Field Enterprises, Inc., 1979
...SIDE-SADDLE
2·1

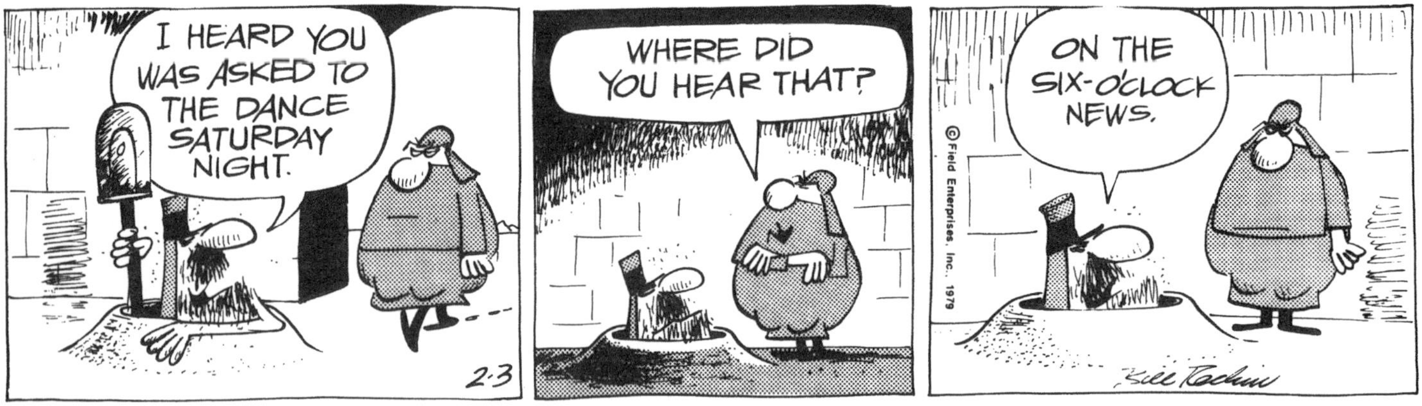
I HEARD YOU WAS ASKED TO THE DANCE SATURDAY NIGHT.
2·3
WHERE DID YOU HEAR THAT?
© Field Enterprises, Inc., 1979
ON THE SIX-O'CLOCK NEWS.

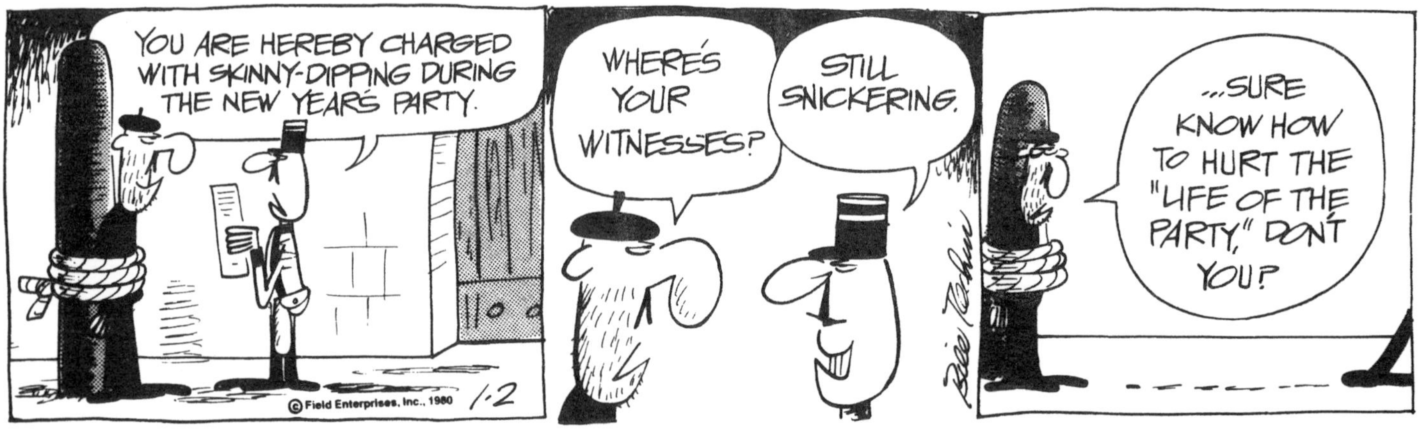
YOU ARE HEREBY CHARGED WITH SKINNY-DIPPING DURING THE NEW YEAR'S PARTY.
© Field Enterprises, Inc., 1980
1·2
WHERE'S YOUR WITNESSES?
STILL SNICKERING.
...SURE KNOW HOW TO HURT THE "LIFE OF THE PARTY," DON'T YOU?

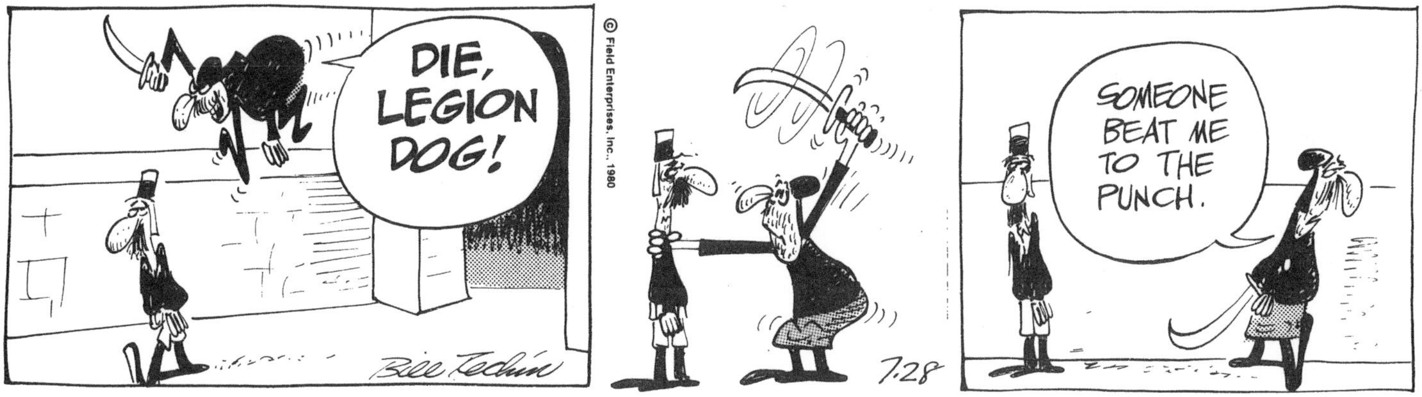
DIE, LEGION DOG!
© Field Enterprises, Inc., 1980
Bill Rechin
7·28
SOMEONE BEAT ME TO THE PUNCH.

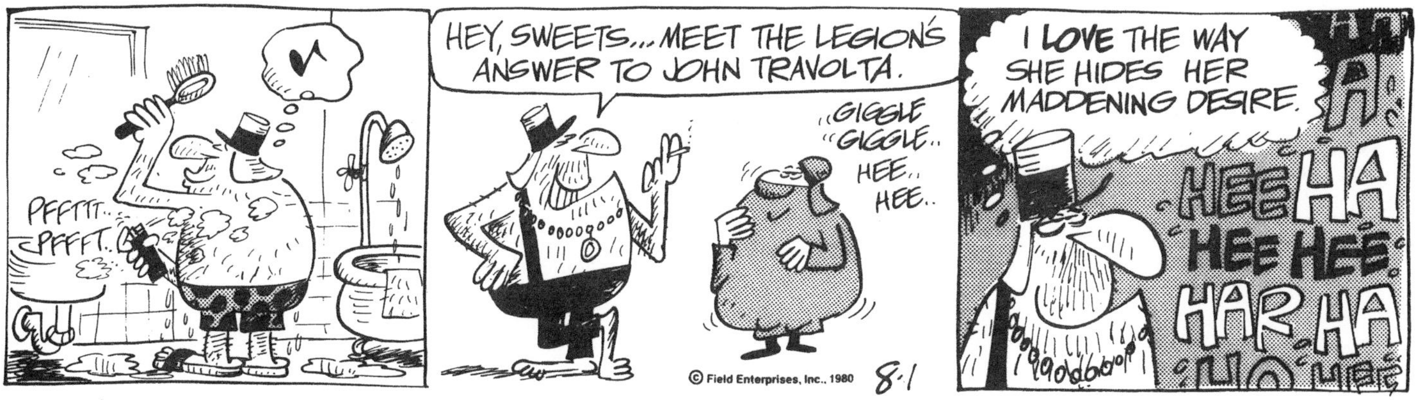
PFFTTT..
PFFFT..
HEY, SWEETS... MEET THE LEGION'S ANSWER TO JOHN TRAVOLTA.
GIGGLE
GIGGLE..
HEE..
HEE..
© Field Enterprises, Inc., 1980
8·1
I LOVE THE WAY SHE HIDES HER MADDENING DESIRE.
HEE HA
HEE HEE
HAR HA

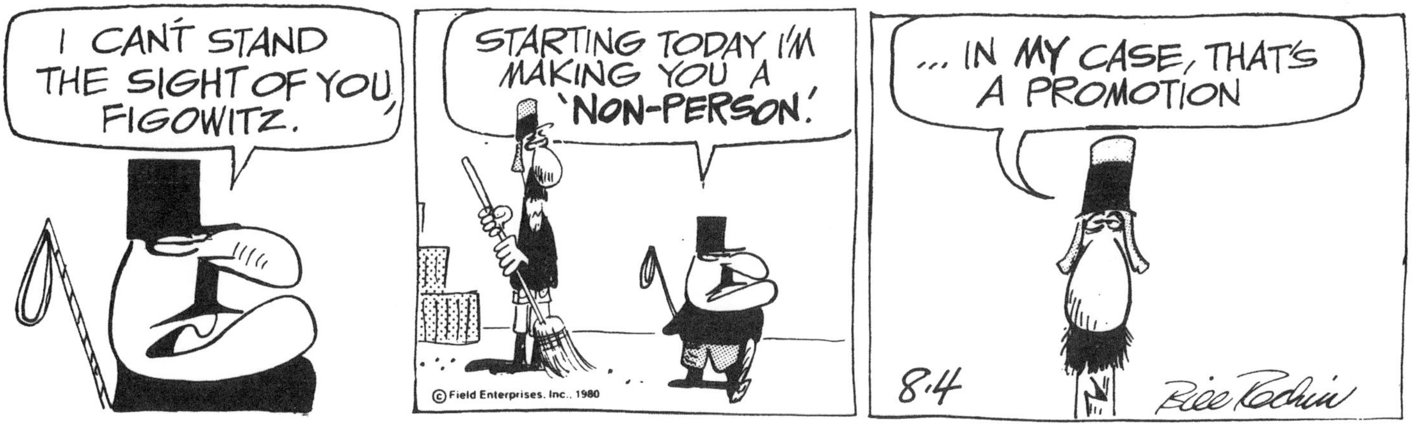
I CAN'T STAND THE SIGHT OF YOU, FIGOWITZ.
STARTING TODAY I'M MAKING YOU A 'NON-PERSON.'
© Field Enterprises, Inc., 1980
... IN MY CASE, THAT'S A PROMOTION
8·4
Bill Rechin

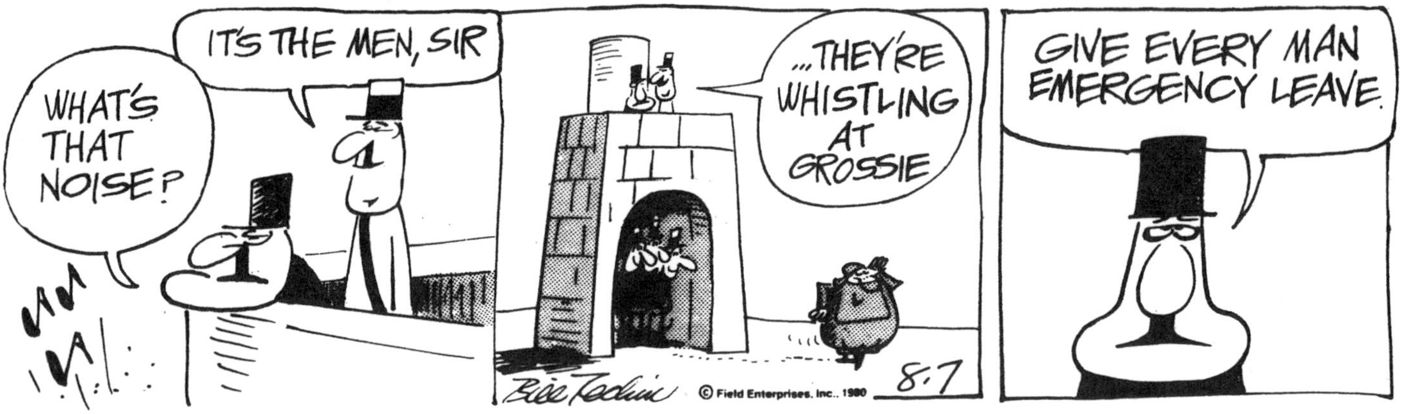
WHAT'S THAT NOISE?
IT'S THE MEN, SIR
...THEY'RE WHISTLING AT GROSSIE
GIVE EVERY MAN EMERGENCY LEAVE.
© Field Enterprises, Inc., 1980
8·7

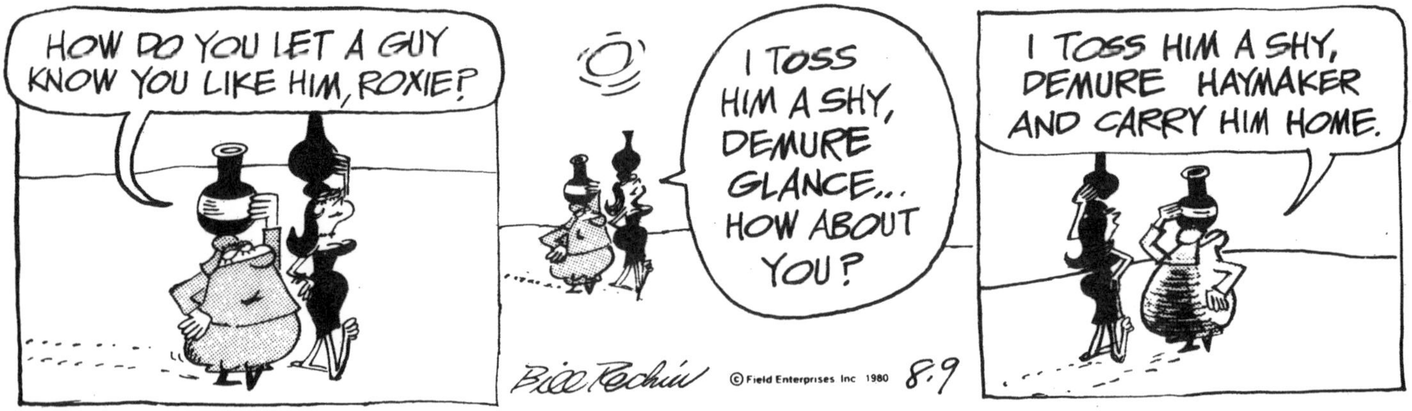
HOW DO YOU LET A GUY KNOW YOU LIKE HIM, ROXIE?
I TOSS HIM A SHY, DEMURE GLANCE... HOW ABOUT YOU?
I TOSS HIM A SHY, DEMURE HAYMAKER AND CARRY HIM HOME.
© Field Enterprises Inc 1980
8·9

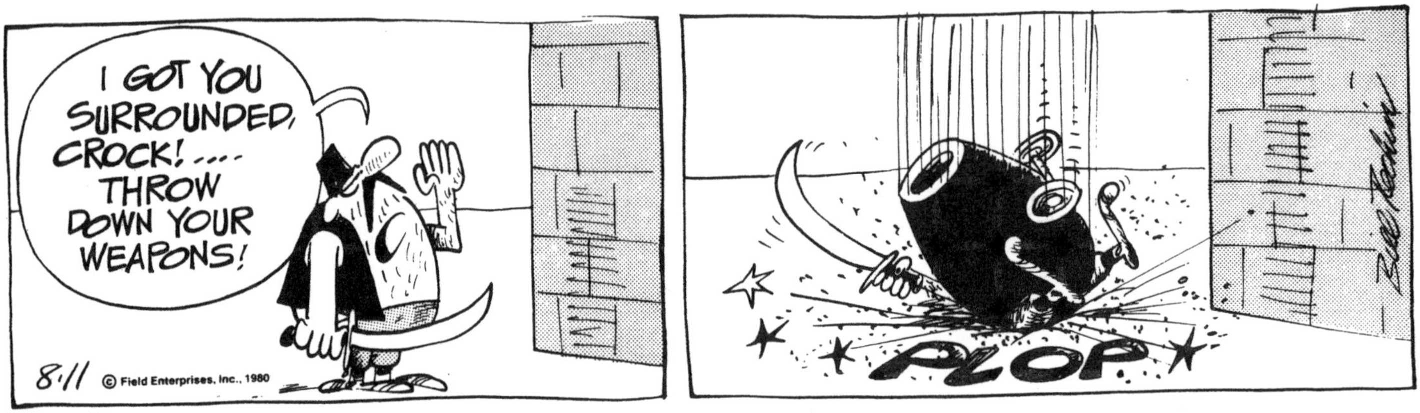
I GOT YOU SURROUNDED, CROCK! .... THROW DOWN YOUR WEAPONS!
8·11
© Field Enterprises, Inc., 1980
PLOP

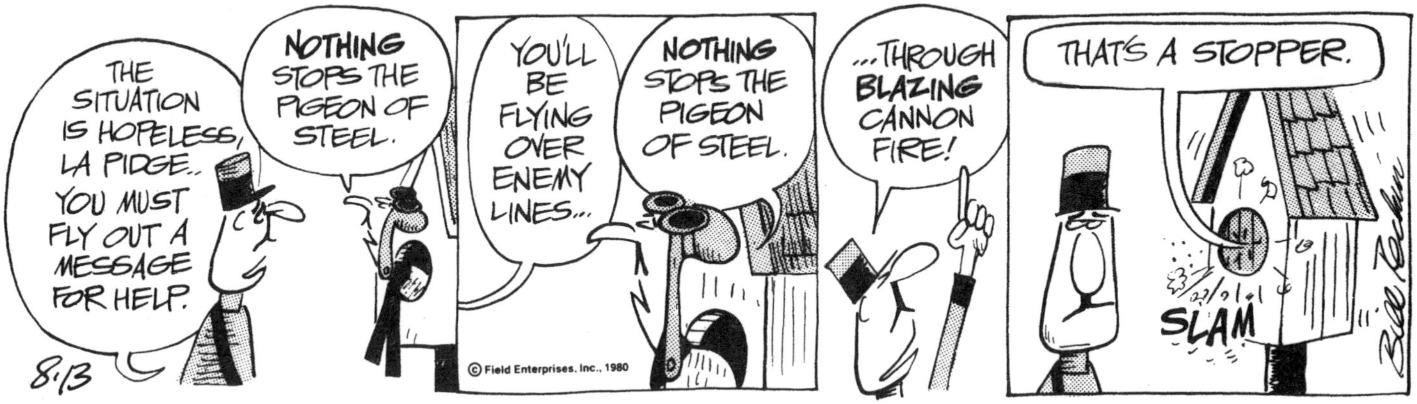

THE SITUATION IS HOPELESS, LA PIDGE.. YOU MUST FLY OUT A MESSAGE FOR HELP.
8.13
NOTHING STOPS THE PIGEON OF STEEL.
YOU'LL BE FLYING OVER ENEMY LINES...
NOTHING STOPS THE PIGEON OF STEEL.
© Field Enterprises, Inc., 1980
...THROUGH BLAZING CANNON FIRE!
THAT'S A STOPPER.
SLAM

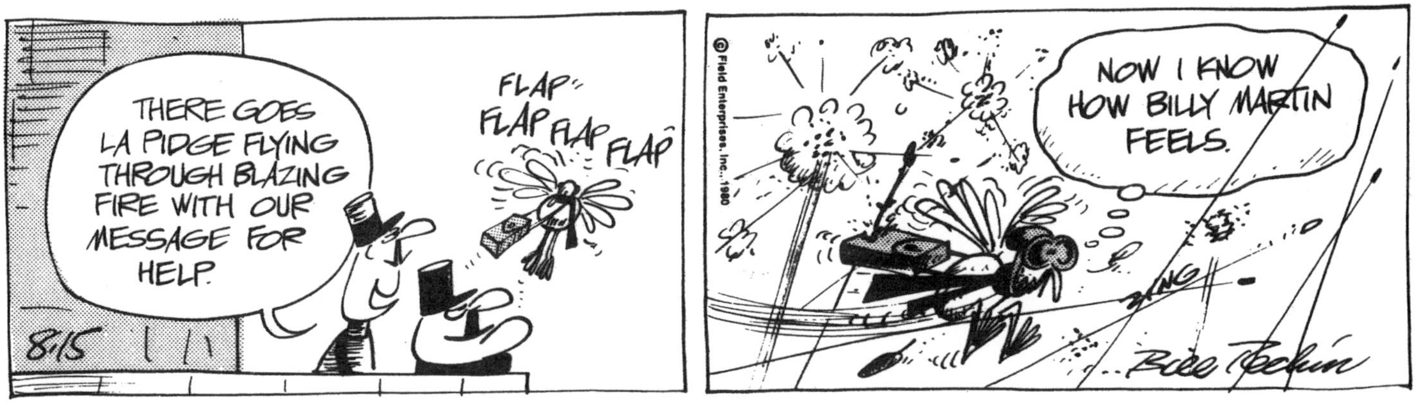

THERE GOES LA PIDGE FLYING THROUGH BLAZING FIRE WITH OUR MESSAGE FOR HELP.
FLAP FLAP FLAP FLAP
8.15
© Field Enterprises, Inc., 1980
NOW I KNOW HOW BILLY MARTIN FEELS.
ZANG

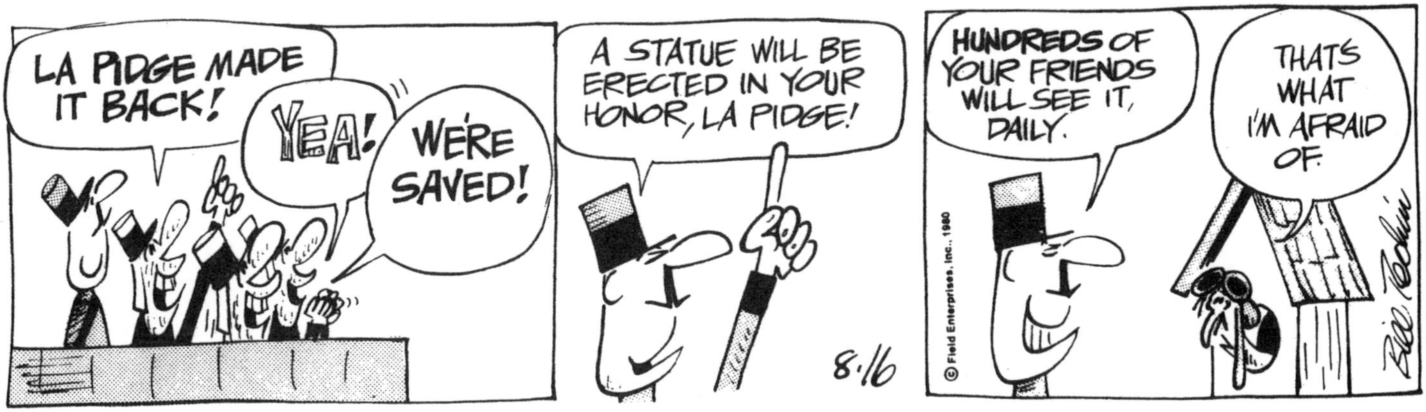

LA PIDGE MADE IT BACK!
YEA!
WE'RE SAVED!
A STATUE WILL BE ERECTED IN YOUR HONOR, LA PIDGE!
8.16
HUNDREDS OF YOUR FRIENDS WILL SEE IT, DAILY.
THAT'S WHAT I'M AFRAID OF.
© Field Enterprises, Inc., 1980

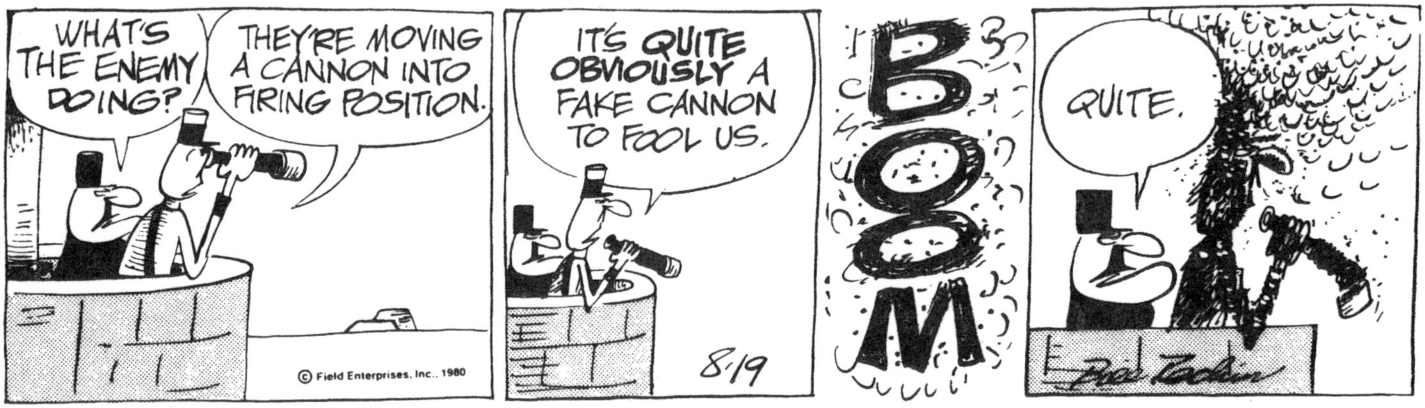
WHAT'S THE ENEMY DOING?
THEY'RE MOVING A CANNON INTO FIRING POSITION.
© Field Enterprises, Inc., 1980
IT'S **QUITE OBVIOUSLY** A FAKE CANNON TO FOOL US.
8.19
BOOM
QUITE.

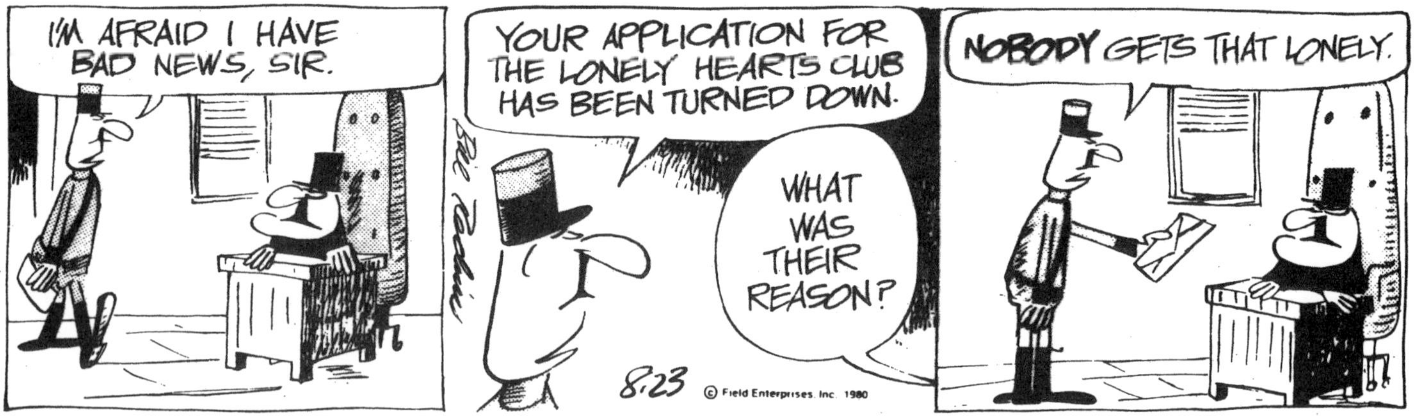
I'M AFRAID I HAVE BAD NEWS, SIR.
Bill Rechin
YOUR APPLICATION FOR THE LONELY HEARTS CLUB HAS BEEN TURNED DOWN.
WHAT WAS THEIR REASON?
8.23
© Field Enterprises, Inc. 1980
NOBODY GETS THAT LONELY.

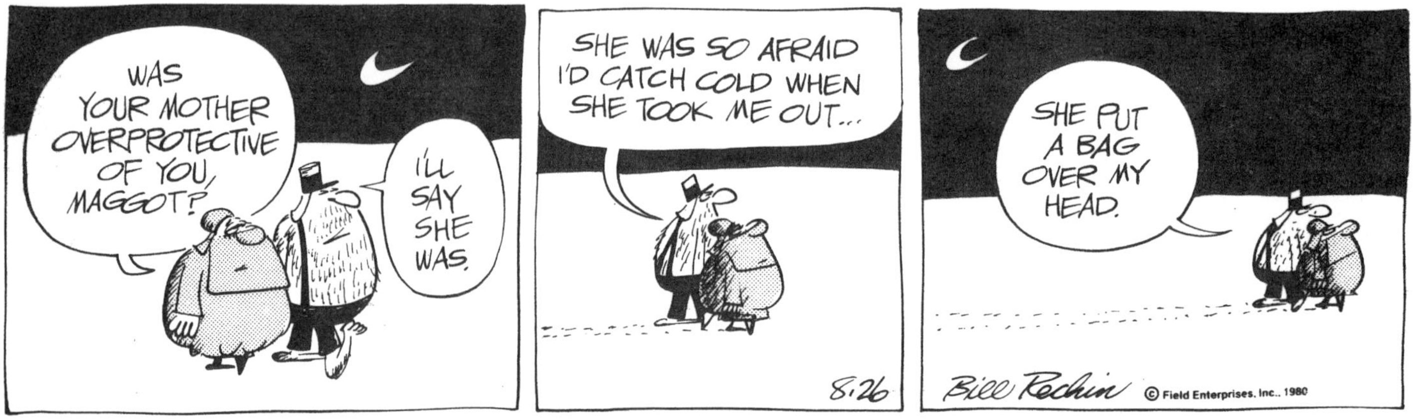
WAS YOUR MOTHER OVERPROTECTIVE OF YOU, MAGGOT?
I'LL SAY SHE WAS.
SHE WAS SO AFRAID I'D CATCH COLD WHEN SHE TOOK ME OUT...
8.26
SHE PUT A BAG OVER MY HEAD.
Bill Rechin
© Field Enterprises, Inc., 1980

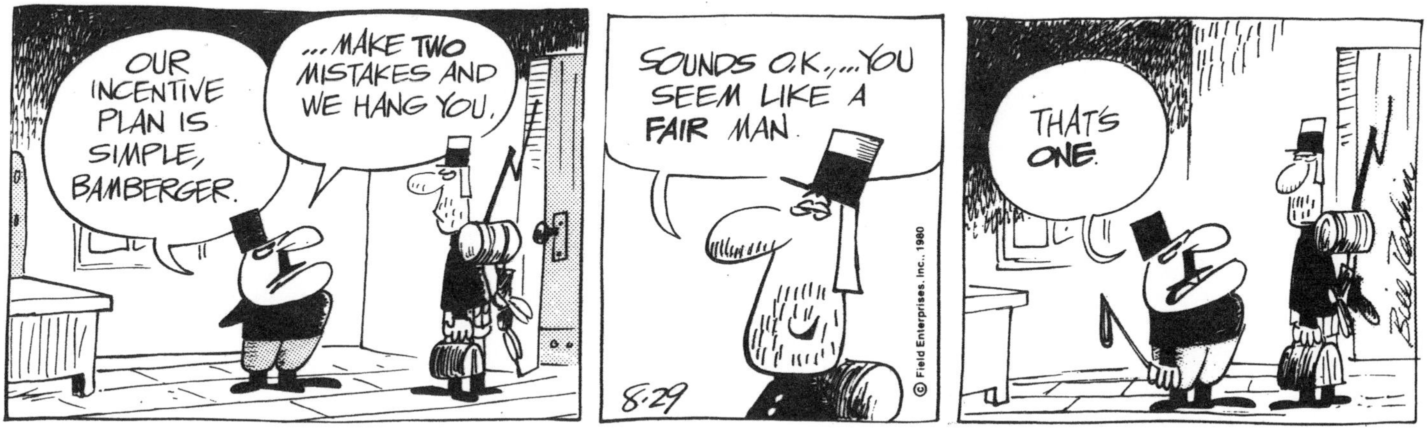
OUR INCENTIVE PLAN IS SIMPLE, BAMBERGER.
...MAKE TWO MISTAKES AND WE HANG YOU.
SOUNDS O.K.,...YOU SEEM LIKE A FAIR MAN.
8·29
© Field Enterprises, Inc., 1980
THAT'S ONE.
Bill Rechin

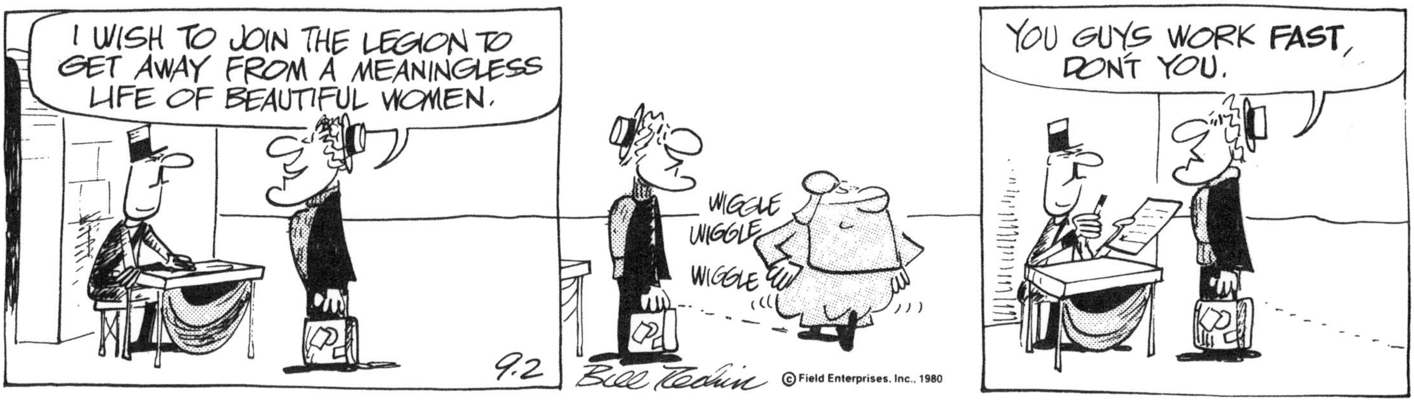
I WISH TO JOIN THE LEGION TO GET AWAY FROM A MEANINGLESS LIFE OF BEAUTIFUL WOMEN.
9·2
WIGGLE
WIGGLE
WIGGLE
Bill Rechin
© Field Enterprises, Inc., 1980
YOU GUYS WORK FAST, DON'T YOU.

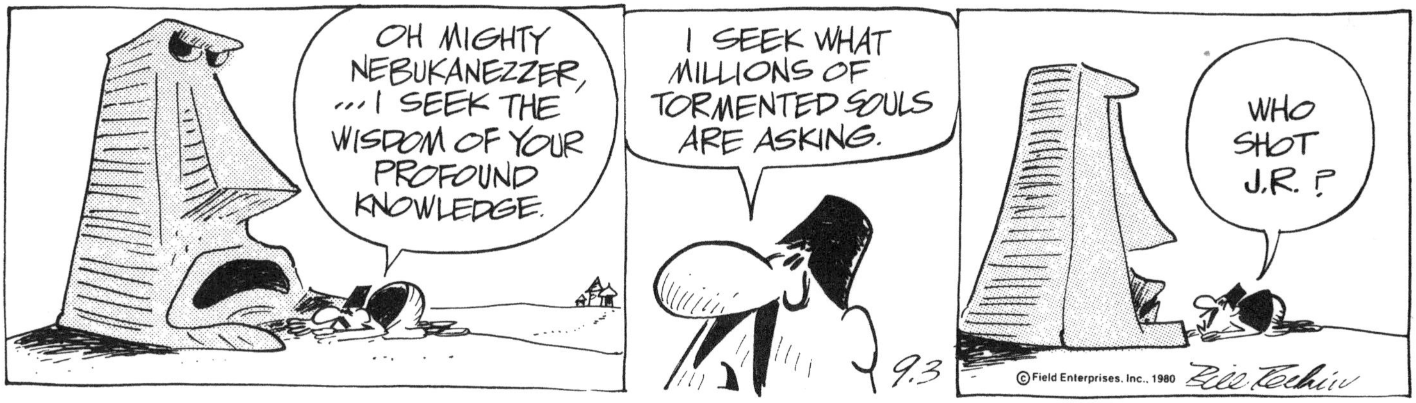
OH MIGHTY NEBUKANEZZER, ...I SEEK THE WISDOM OF YOUR PROFOUND KNOWLEDGE.
I SEEK WHAT MILLIONS OF TORMENTED SOULS ARE ASKING.
9·3
WHO SHOT J.R. ?
© Field Enterprises, Inc., 1980
Bill Rechin

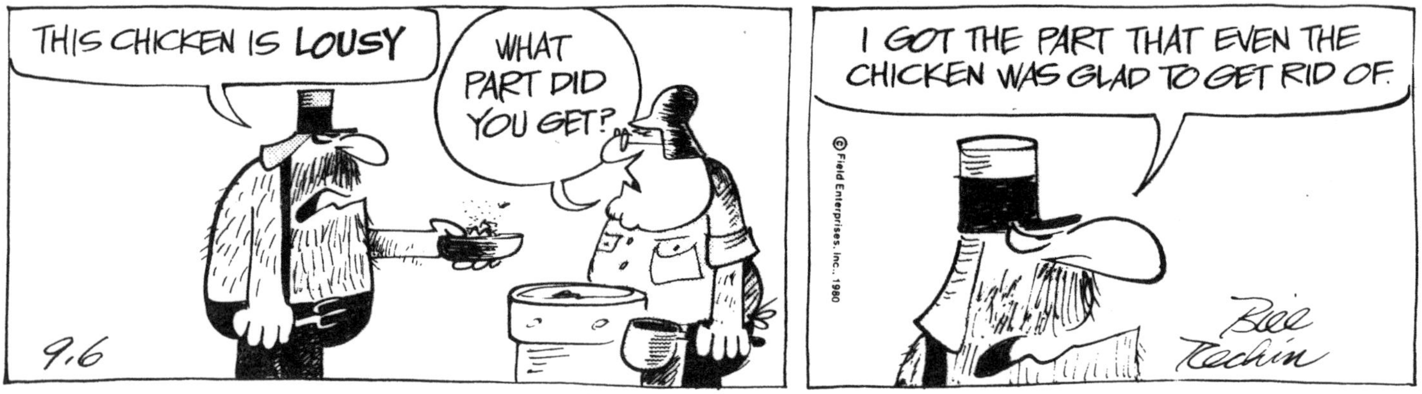
THIS CHICKEN IS **LOUSY**
WHAT PART DID YOU GET?
9.6
I GOT THE PART THAT EVEN THE CHICKEN WAS GLAD TO GET RID OF.
© Field Enterprises, Inc., 1980
Bill Rechin

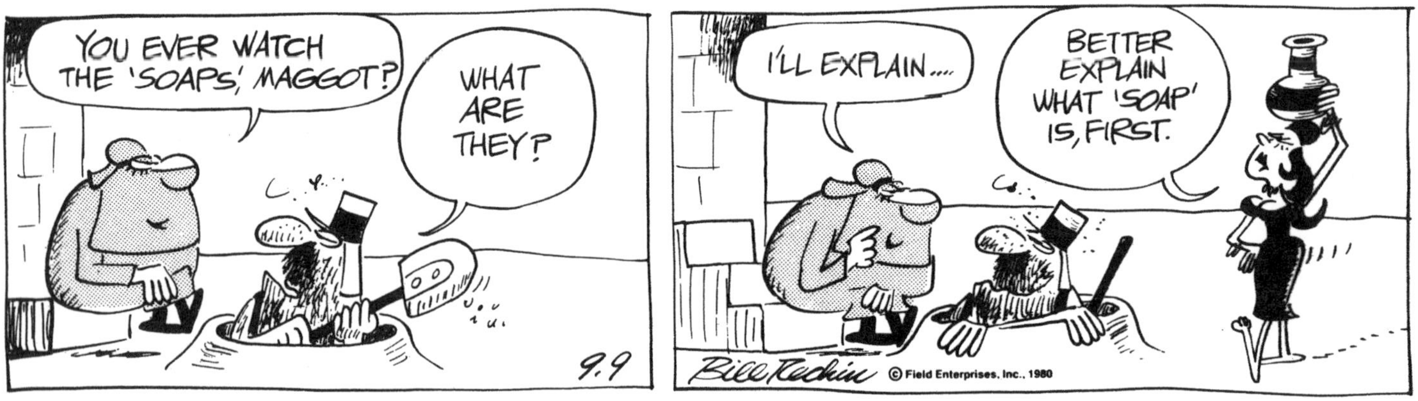
YOU EVER WATCH THE 'SOAPS,' MAGGOT?
WHAT ARE THEY?
9.9
I'LL EXPLAIN....
BETTER EXPLAIN WHAT 'SOAP' IS, FIRST.
Bill Rechin
© Field Enterprises, Inc., 1980

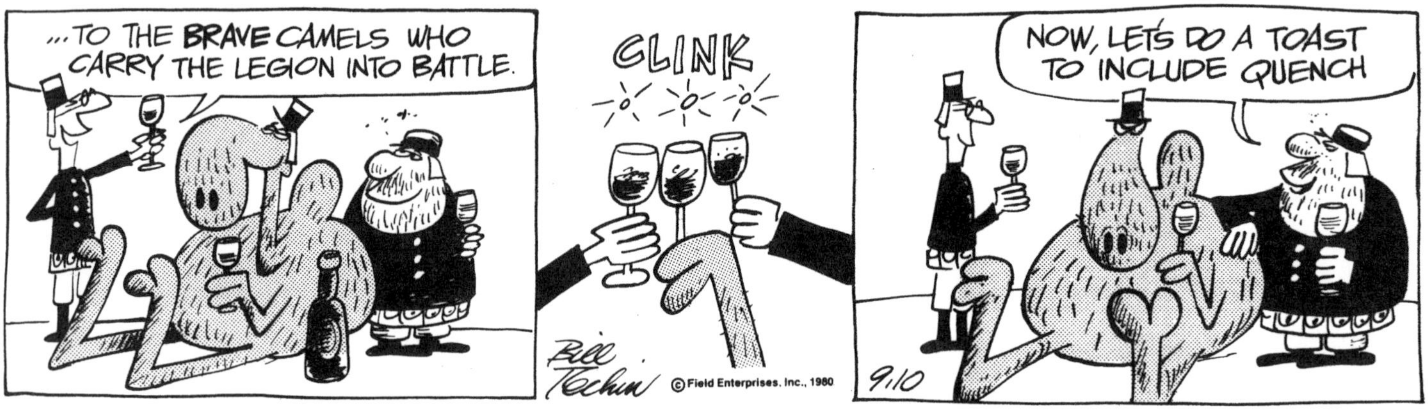
...TO THE **BRAVE** CAMELS WHO CARRY THE LEGION INTO BATTLE.
CLINK
Bill Rechin
© Field Enterprises, Inc., 1980
NOW, LET'S DO A TOAST TO INCLUDE QUENCH
9.10

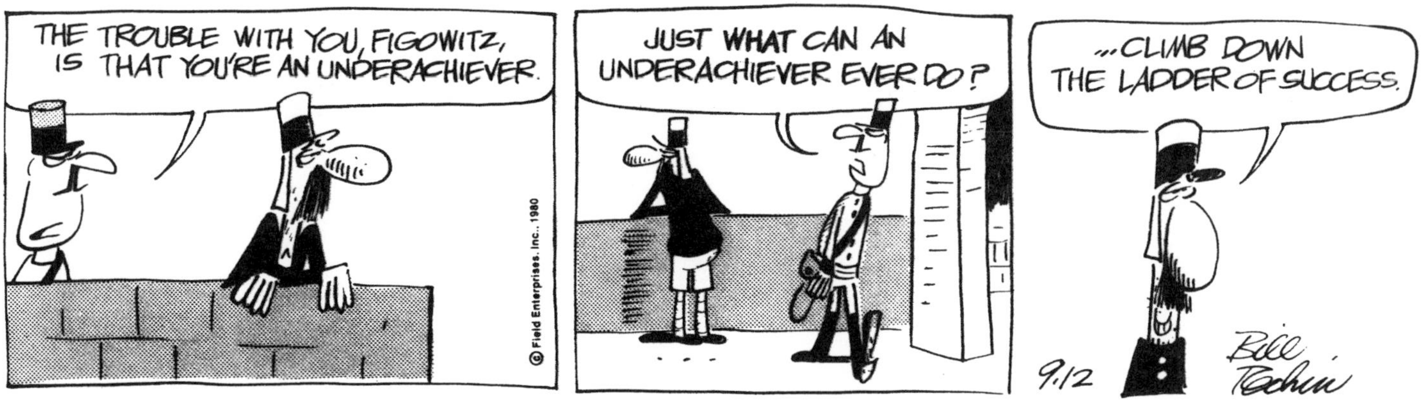
THE TROUBLE WITH YOU, FIGOWITZ, IS THAT YOU'RE AN UNDERACHIEVER.
JUST WHAT CAN AN UNDERACHIEVER EVER DO?
...CLIMB DOWN THE LADDER OF SUCCESS.
© Field Enterprises, Inc., 1980
9.12

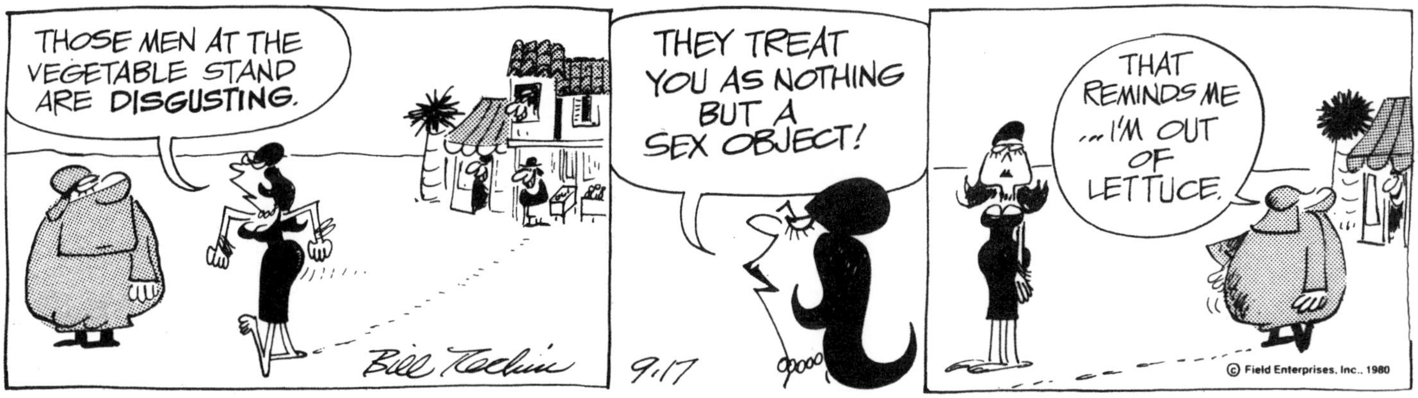
THOSE MEN AT THE VEGETABLE STAND ARE DISGUSTING.
THEY TREAT YOU AS NOTHING BUT A SEX OBJECT!
THAT REMINDS ME ...I'M OUT OF LETTUCE.
9.17
© Field Enterprises, Inc., 1980

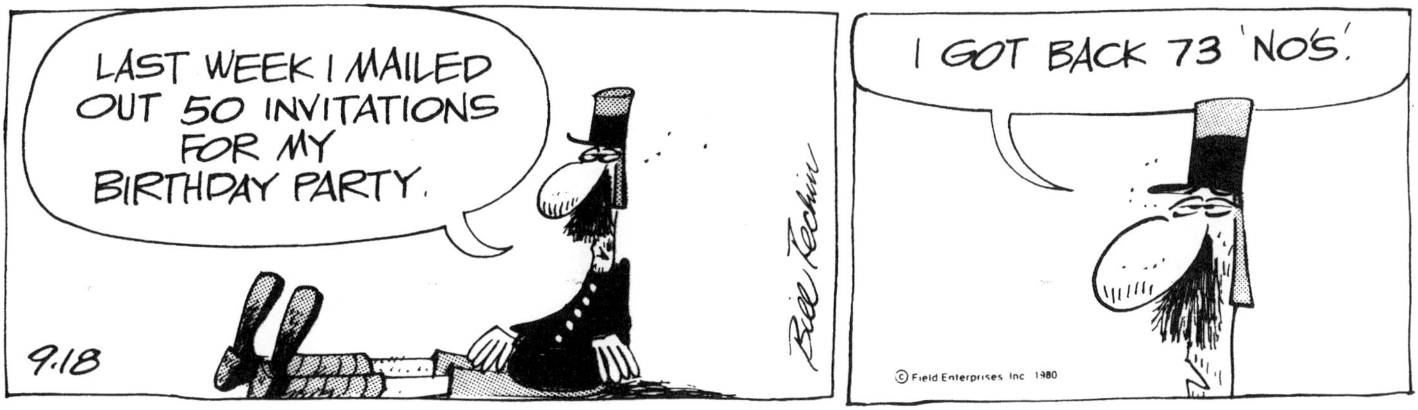
LAST WEEK I MAILED OUT 50 INVITATIONS FOR MY BIRTHDAY PARTY.
I GOT BACK 73 'NO'S'.
9.18
© Field Enterprises Inc 1980

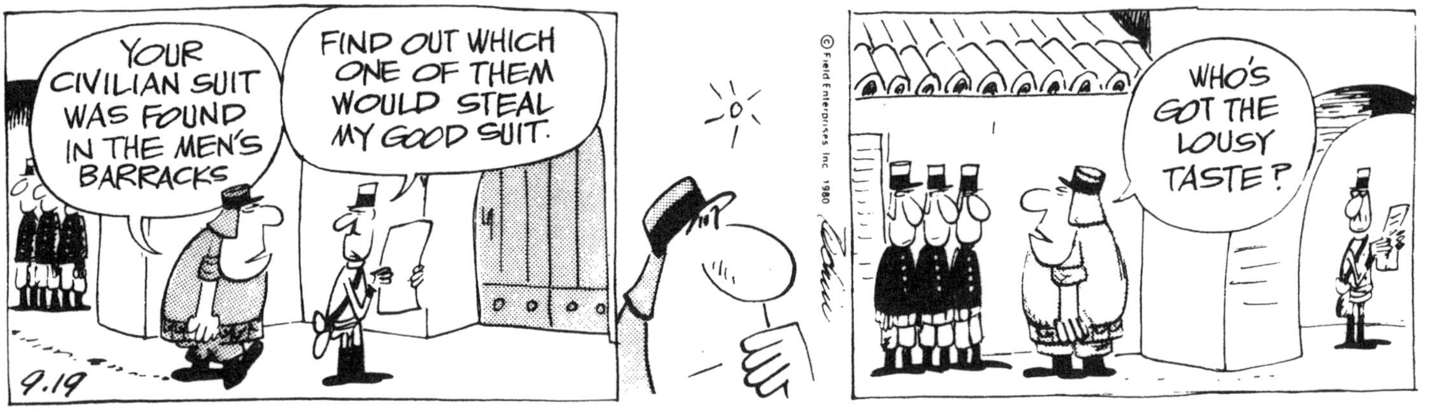
YOUR CIVILIAN SUIT WAS FOUND IN THE MEN'S BARRACKS
FIND OUT WHICH ONE OF THEM WOULD STEAL MY GOOD SUIT.
WHO'S GOT THE LOUSY TASTE?
9.19
© Field Enterprises Inc. 1980

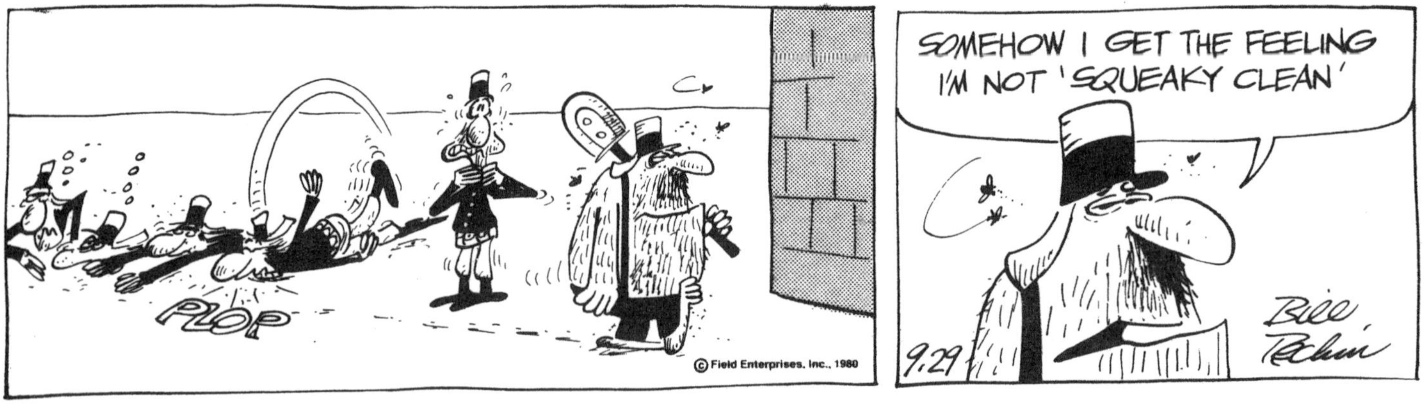
PLOP
© Field Enterprises, Inc., 1980
SOMEHOW I GET THE FEELING I'M NOT 'SQUEAKY CLEAN'
9.29
Bill Rechin

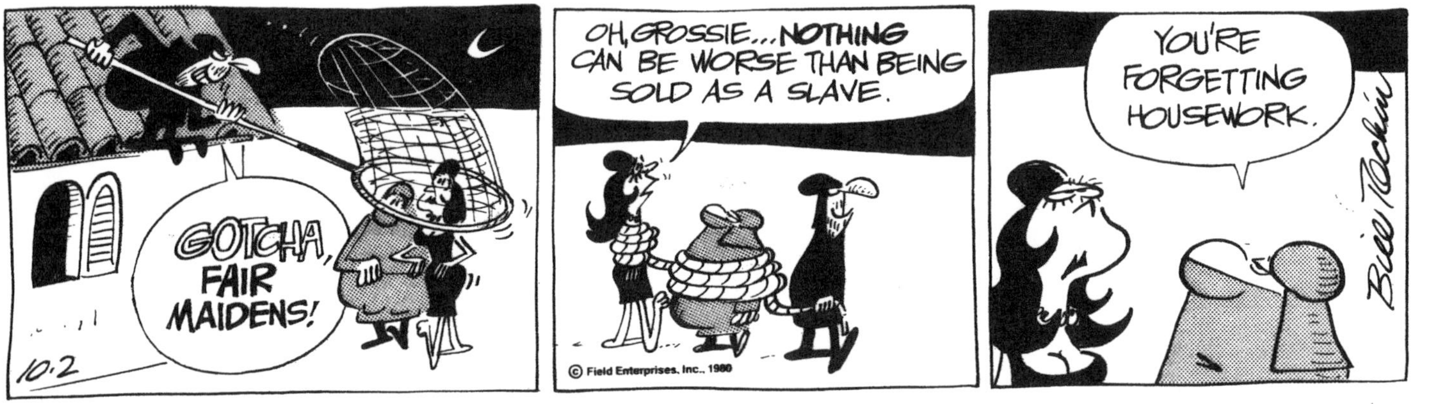
GOTCHA, FAIR MAIDENS!
10.2
OH, GROSSIE... NOTHING CAN BE WORSE THAN BEING SOLD AS A SLAVE.
© Field Enterprises, Inc., 1980
YOU'RE FORGETTING HOUSEWORK.
Bill Rechin

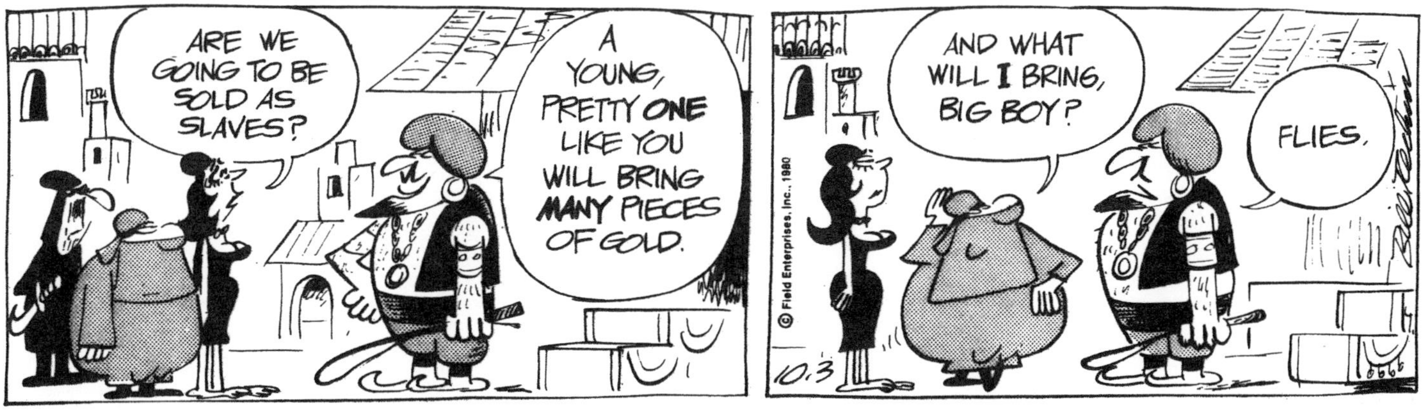

ARE WE GOING TO BE SOLD AS SLAVES?
A YOUNG, PRETTY ONE LIKE YOU WILL BRING MANY PIECES OF GOLD.
AND WHAT WILL I BRING, BIG BOY?
FLIES.
© Field Enterprises, Inc., 1980
10.3

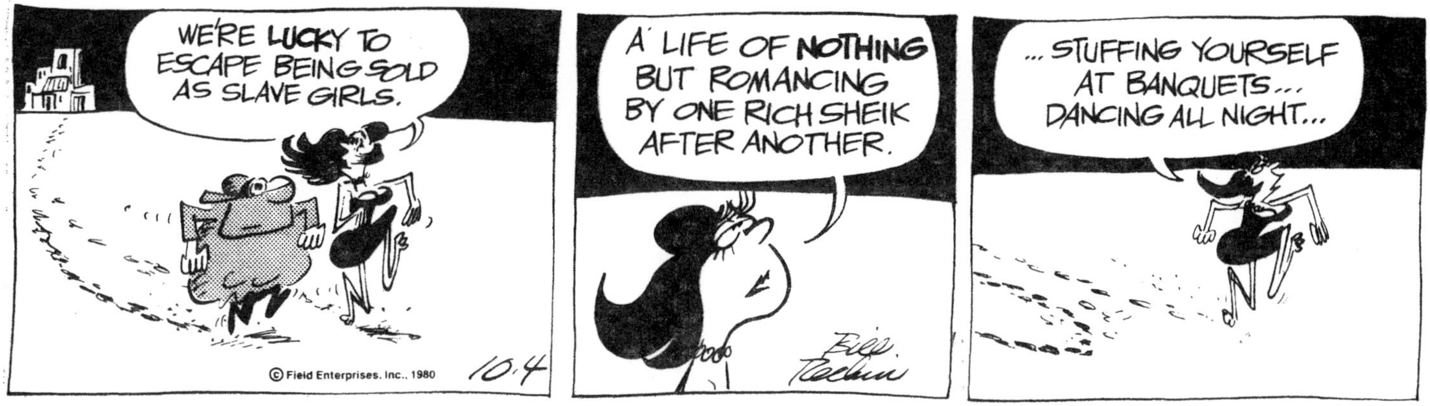

WE'RE LUCKY TO ESCAPE BEING SOLD AS SLAVE GIRLS.
© Field Enterprises, Inc., 1980
10.4
A LIFE OF NOTHING BUT ROMANCING BY ONE RICH SHEIK AFTER ANOTHER.
...STUFFING YOURSELF AT BANQUETS... DANCING ALL NIGHT...

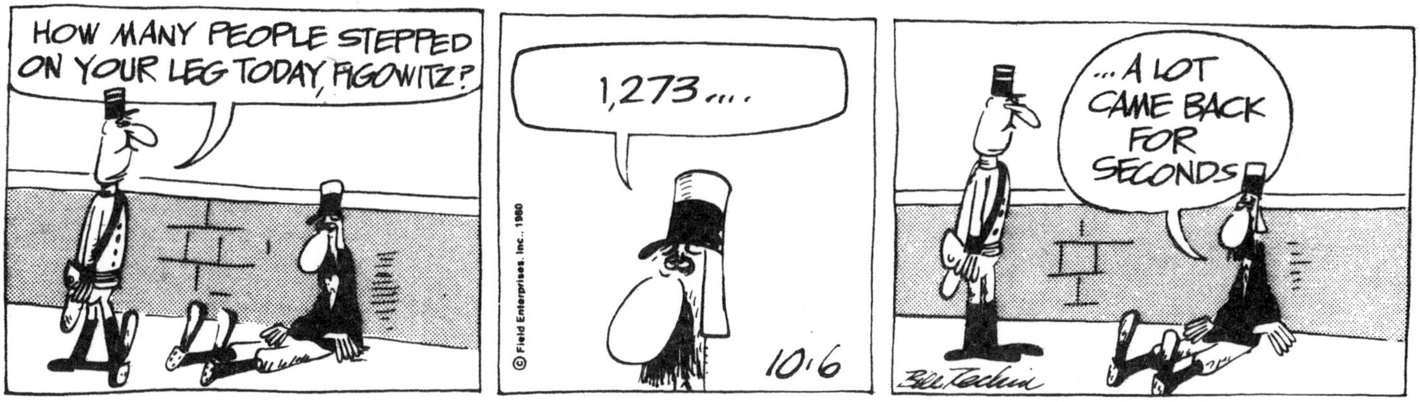

HOW MANY PEOPLE STEPPED ON YOUR LEG TODAY, FIGOWITZ?
1,273....
© Field Enterprises, Inc., 1980
10.6
...A LOT CAME BACK FOR SECONDS

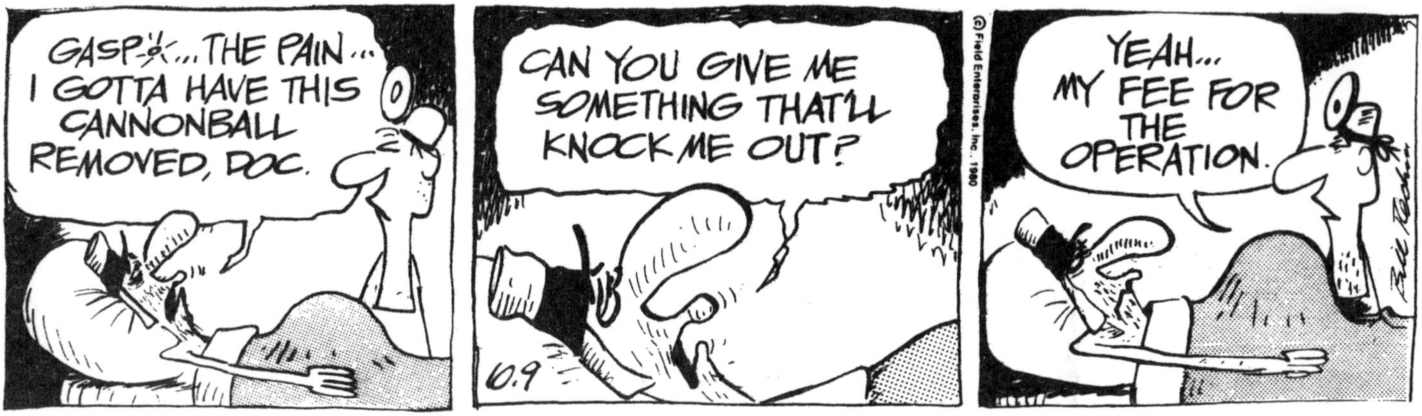
GASP!... THE PAIN... I GOTTA HAVE THIS CANNONBALL REMOVED, DOC.
CAN YOU GIVE ME SOMETHING THAT'LL KNOCK ME OUT?
10.9
© Field Enterprises, Inc., 1980
YEAH... MY FEE FOR THE OPERATION.

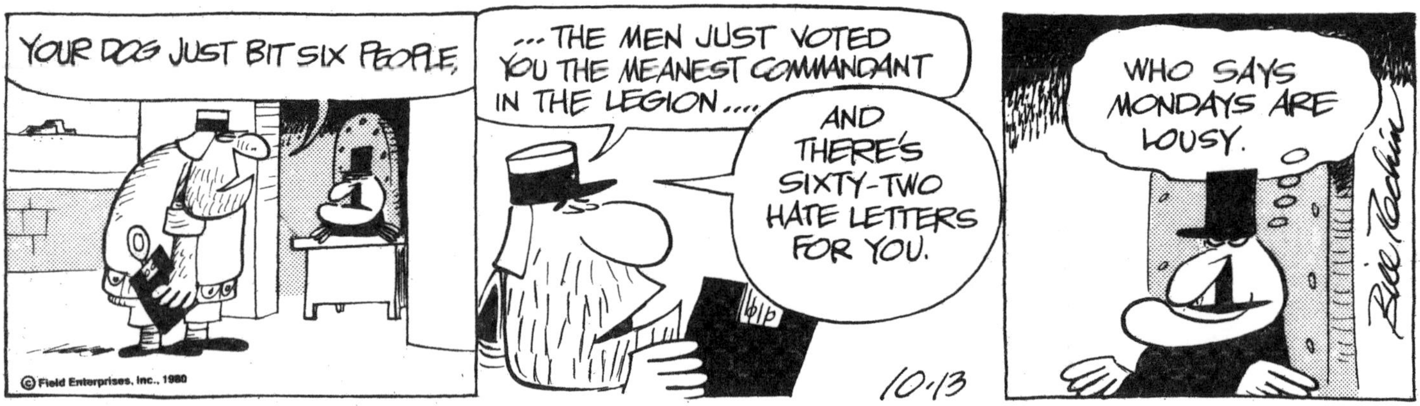
YOUR DOG JUST BIT SIX PEOPLE.
© Field Enterprises, Inc., 1980
...THE MEN JUST VOTED YOU THE MEANEST COMMANDANT IN THE LEGION....
AND THERE'S SIXTY-TWO HATE LETTERS FOR YOU.
10.13
WHO SAYS MONDAYS ARE LOUSY.

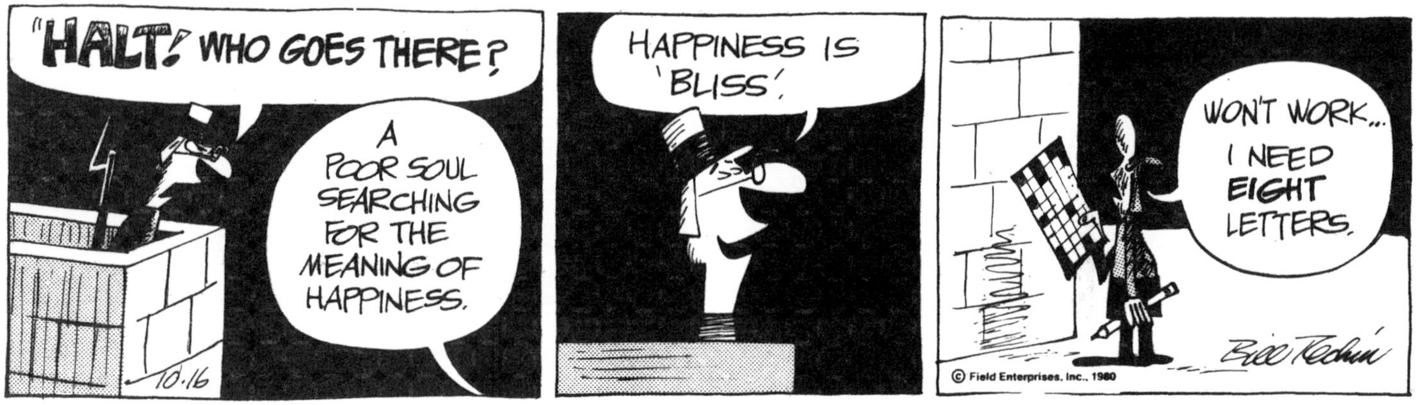
"HALT! WHO GOES THERE?
A POOR SOUL SEARCHING FOR THE MEANING OF HAPPINESS.
10.16
HAPPINESS IS 'BLISS'.
WON'T WORK... I NEED EIGHT LETTERS.
© Field Enterprises, Inc., 1980

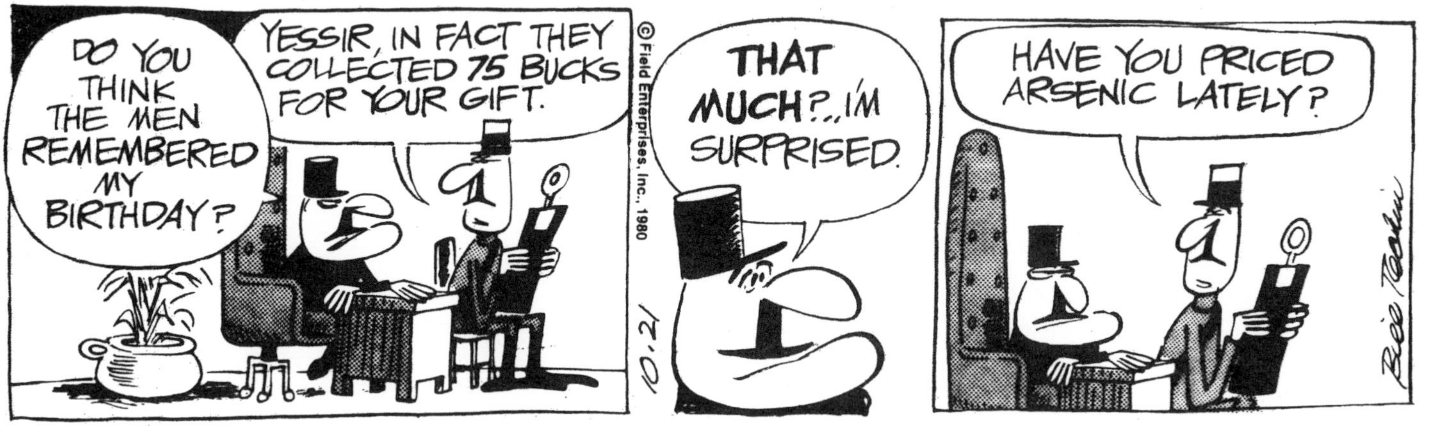
DO YOU THINK THE MEN REMEMBERED MY BIRTHDAY?
YESSIR, IN FACT THEY COLLECTED 75 BUCKS FOR YOUR GIFT.
© Field Enterprises, Inc., 1980
10.21
THAT MUCH?..I'M SURPRISED.
HAVE YOU PRICED ARSENIC LATELY?

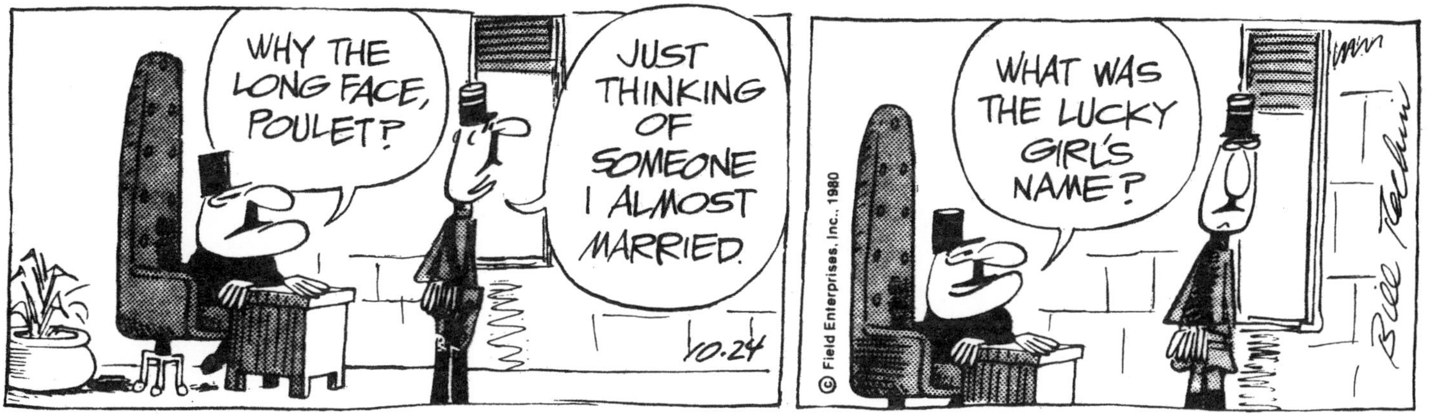
WHY THE LONG FACE, POULET?
JUST THINKING OF SOMEONE I ALMOST MARRIED.
10.24
© Field Enterprises, Inc., 1980
WHAT WAS THE LUCKY GIRL'S NAME?

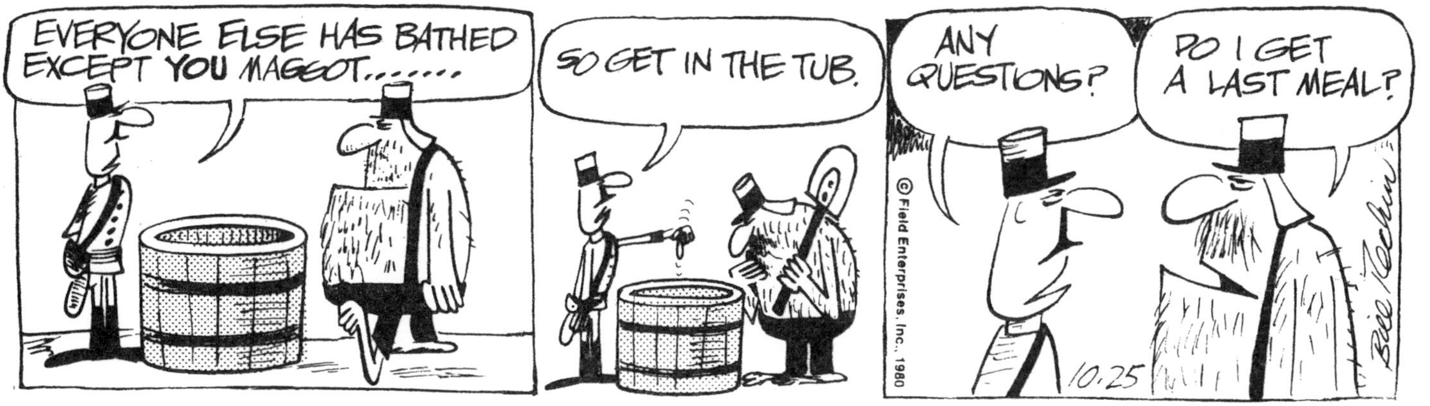
EVERYONE ELSE HAS BATHED EXCEPT YOU MAGGOT.......
SO GET IN THE TUB.
ANY QUESTIONS?
DO I GET A LAST MEAL?
© Field Enterprises, Inc., 1980
10.25

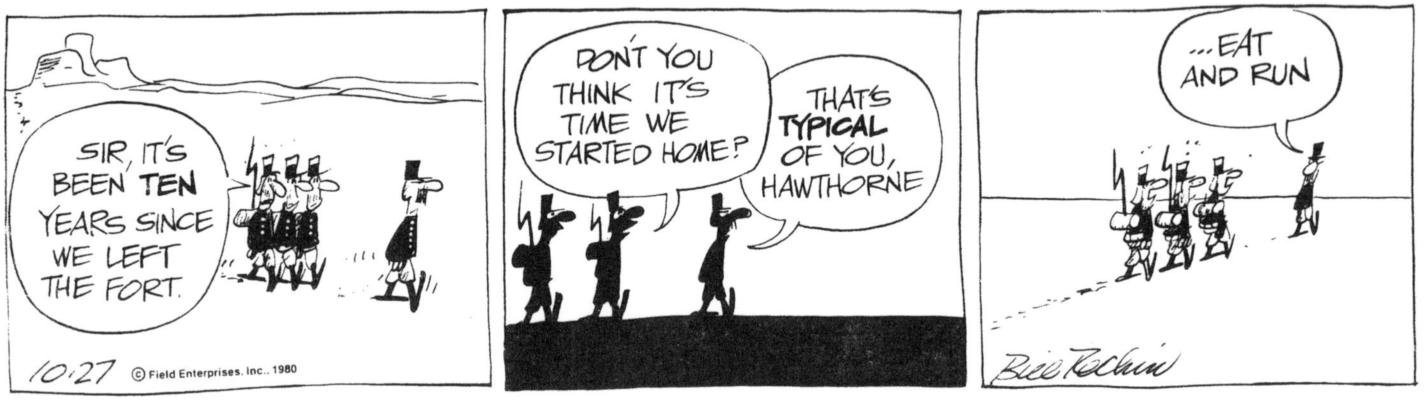
SIR, IT'S BEEN **TEN** YEARS SINCE WE LEFT THE FORT.
10·27
© Field Enterprises, Inc., 1980
DON'T YOU THINK IT'S TIME WE STARTED HOME?
THAT'S **TYPICAL** OF YOU, HAWTHORNE
...EAT AND RUN

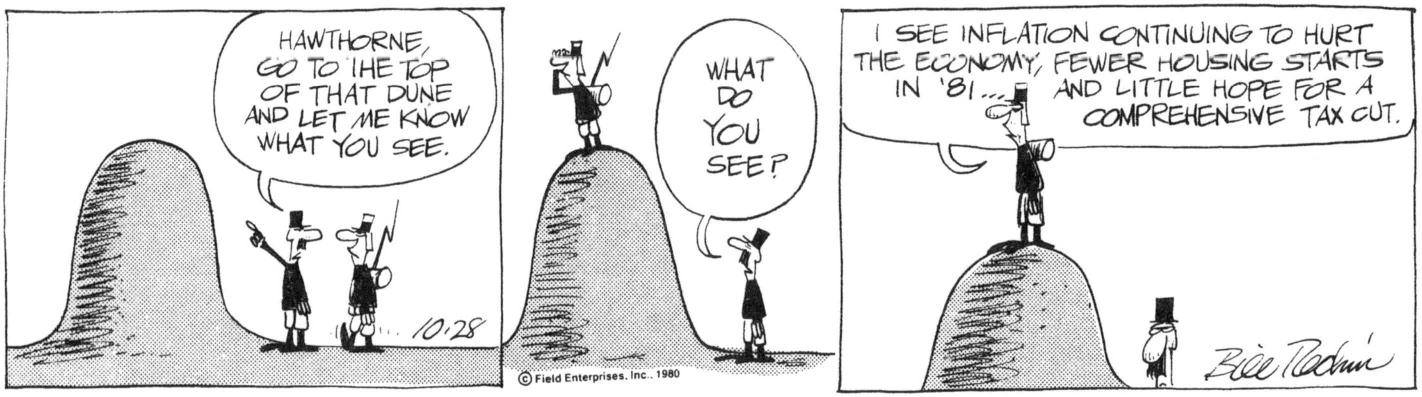
HAWTHORNE, GO TO THE TOP OF THAT DUNE AND LET ME KNOW WHAT YOU SEE.
10·28
WHAT DO YOU SEE?
© Field Enterprises, Inc., 1980
I SEE INFLATION CONTINUING TO HURT THE ECONOMY, FEWER HOUSING STARTS IN '81... AND LITTLE HOPE FOR A COMPREHENSIVE TAX CUT.

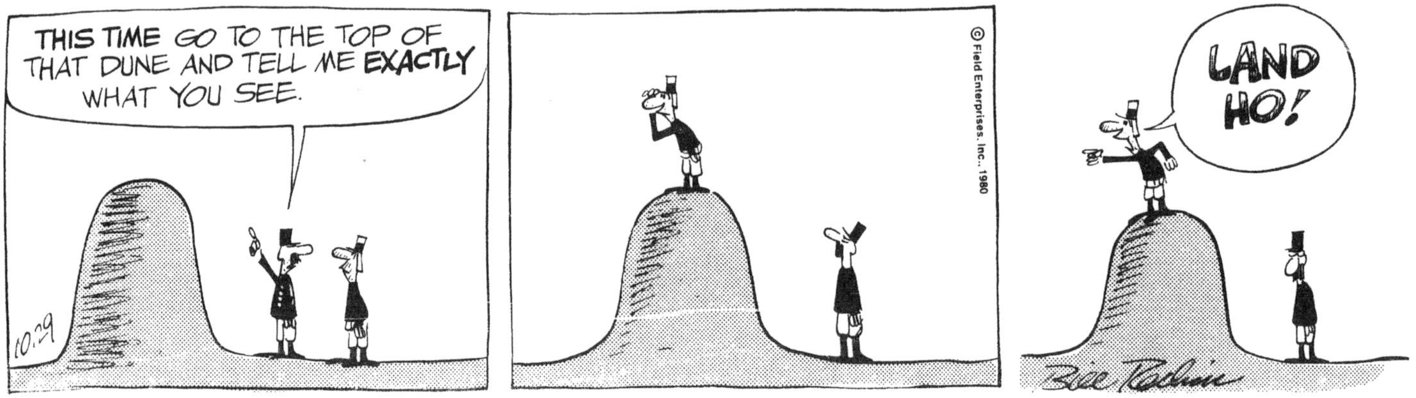
THIS TIME GO TO THE TOP OF THAT DUNE AND TELL ME **EXACTLY** WHAT YOU SEE.
10·29
© Field Enterprises, Inc., 1980
LAND HO!

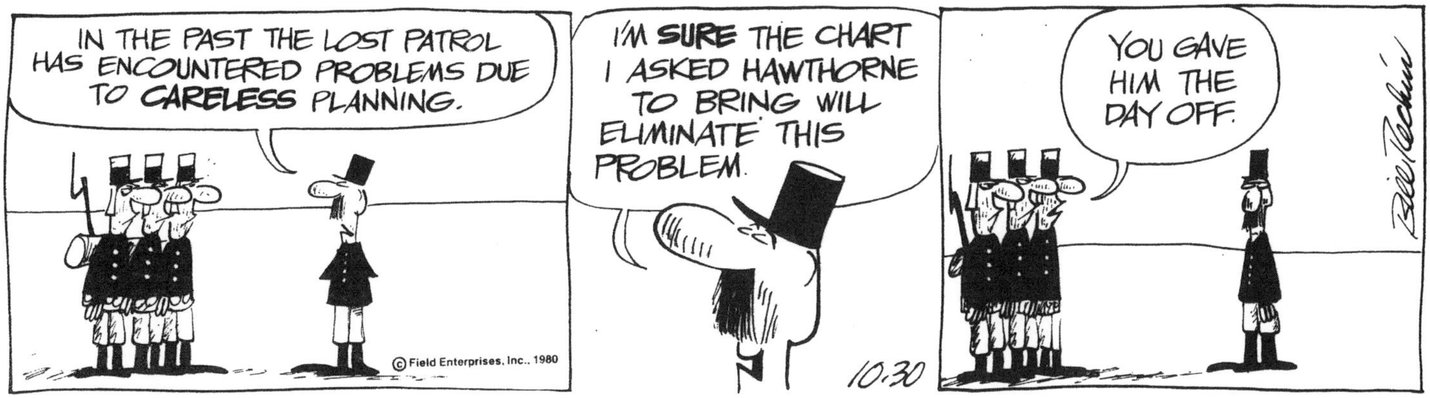
IN THE PAST THE LOST PATROL HAS ENCOUNTERED PROBLEMS DUE TO **CARELESS** PLANNING.
© Field Enterprises, Inc., 1980
I'M **SURE** THE CHART I ASKED HAWTHORNE TO BRING WILL ELIMINATE THIS PROBLEM.
10-30
YOU GAVE HIM THE DAY OFF.

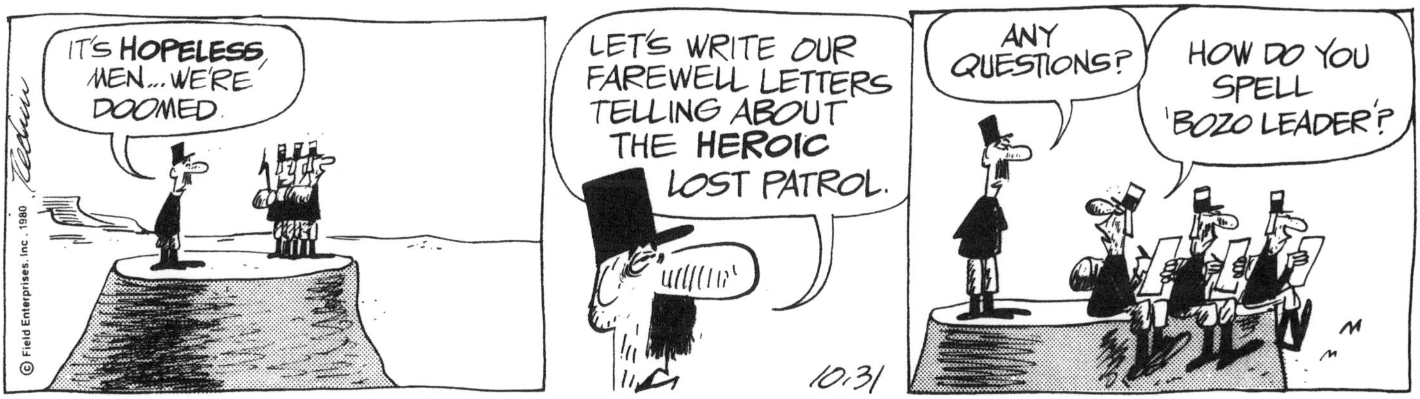
IT'S **HOPELESS**, MEN... WE'RE DOOMED.
© Field Enterprises, Inc. 1980
LET'S WRITE OUR FAREWELL LETTERS TELLING ABOUT THE **HEROIC** LOST PATROL.
10-31
ANY QUESTIONS?
HOW DO YOU SPELL 'BOZO LEADER'?

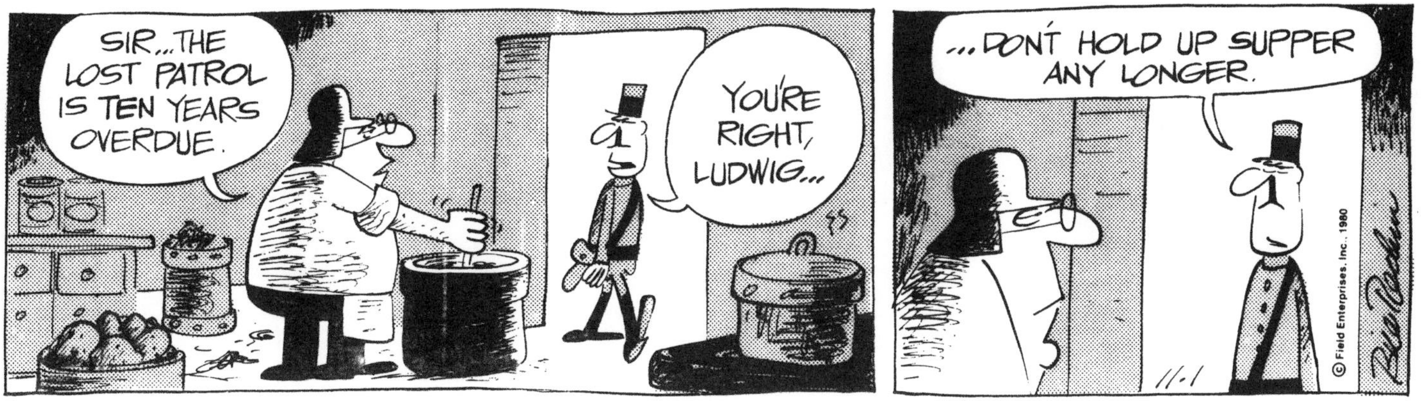
SIR... THE LOST PATROL IS **TEN** YEARS OVERDUE.
YOU'RE RIGHT, LUDWIG...
...DON'T HOLD UP SUPPER ANY LONGER.
11-1
© Field Enterprises, Inc. 1980

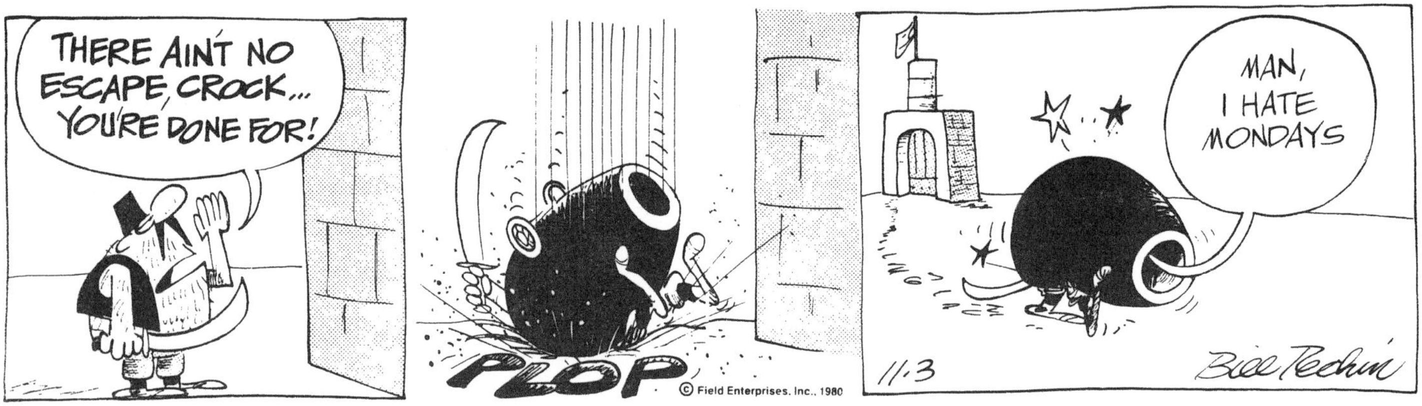
THERE AIN'T NO ESCAPE, CROCK,... YOU'RE DONE FOR!
PLOP
© Field Enterprises, Inc., 1980
MAN, I HATE MONDAYS
11·3
Bill Rechin

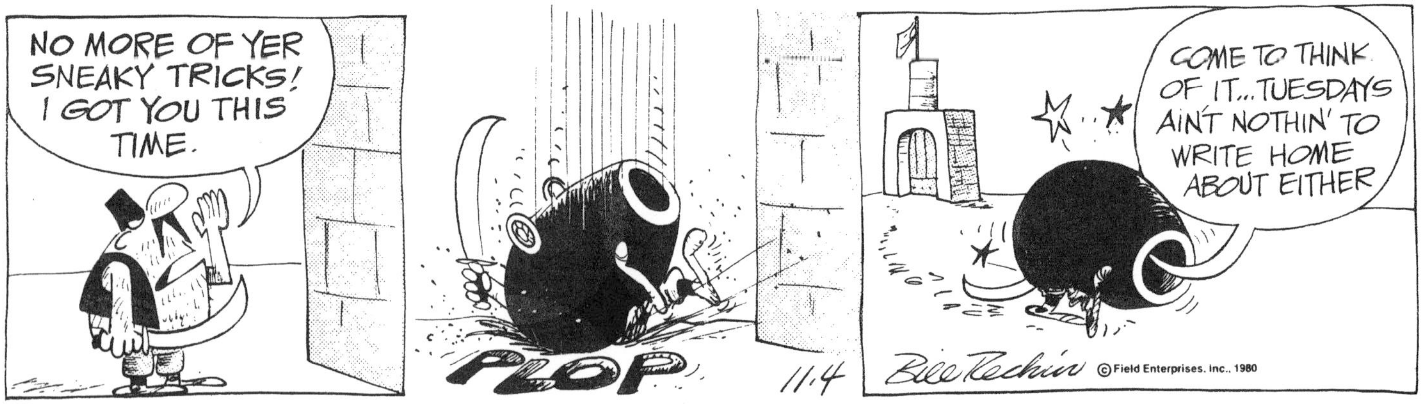
NO MORE OF YER SNEAKY TRICKS! I GOT YOU THIS TIME.
PLOP
11·4
COME TO THINK OF IT...TUESDAYS AIN'T NOTHIN' TO WRITE HOME ABOUT EITHER
Bill Rechin
© Field Enterprises, Inc., 1980

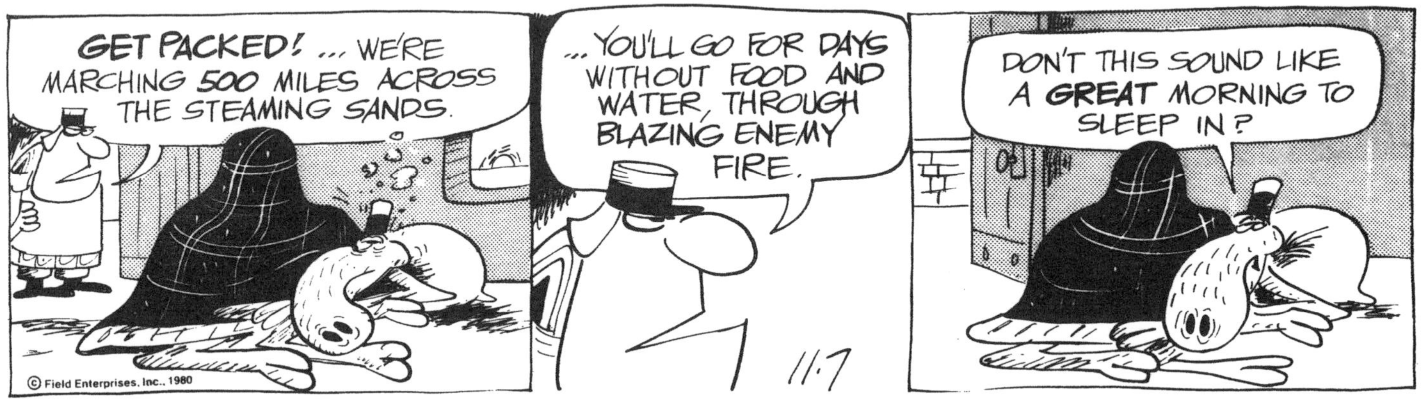
GET PACKED! ... WE'RE MARCHING 500 MILES ACROSS THE STEAMING SANDS.
© Field Enterprises, Inc., 1980
... YOU'LL GO FOR DAYS WITHOUT FOOD AND WATER, THROUGH BLAZING ENEMY FIRE.
11·7
DON'T THIS SOUND LIKE A GREAT MORNING TO SLEEP IN?

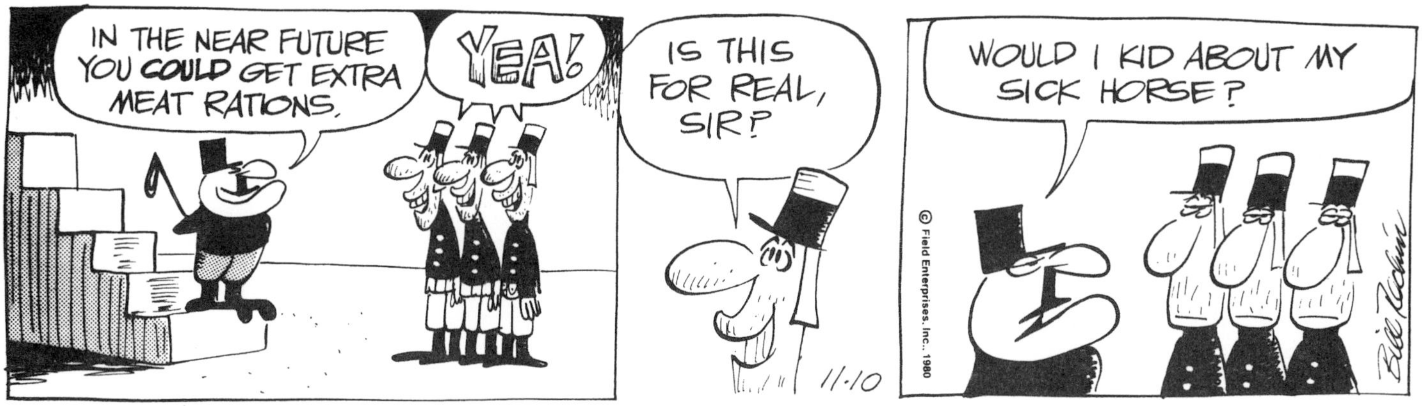
IN THE NEAR FUTURE YOU **COULD** GET EXTRA MEAT RATIONS.
YEA!
IS THIS FOR REAL, SIR?
11·10
WOULD I KID ABOUT MY SICK HORSE?
© Field Enterprises, Inc., 1980

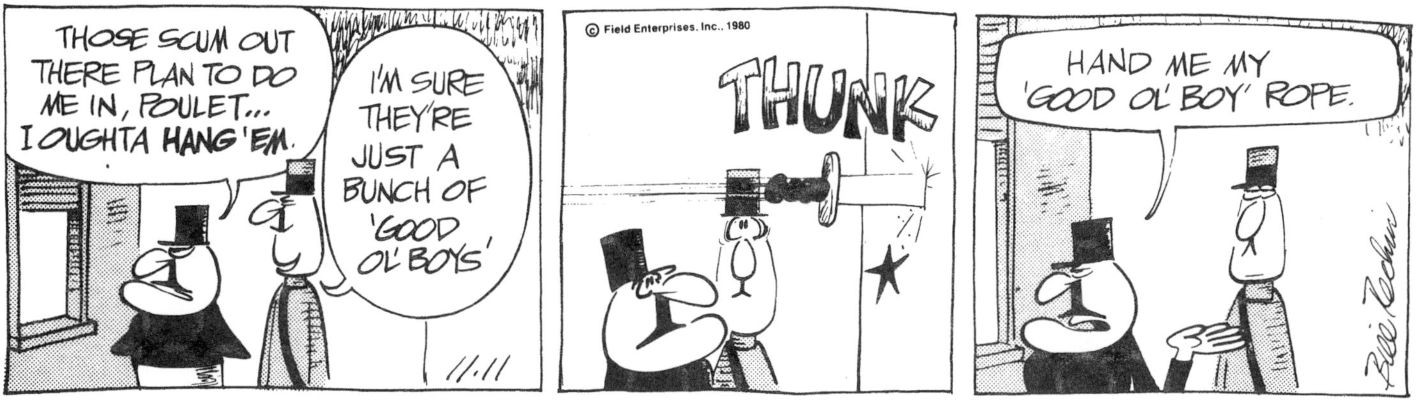
THOSE SCUM OUT THERE PLAN TO DO ME IN, POULET... I OUGHTA **HANG** 'EM.
I'M SURE THEY'RE JUST A BUNCH OF 'GOOD OL' BOYS'
11·11
© Field Enterprises, Inc., 1980
THUNK
HAND ME MY 'GOOD OL' BOY' ROPE.

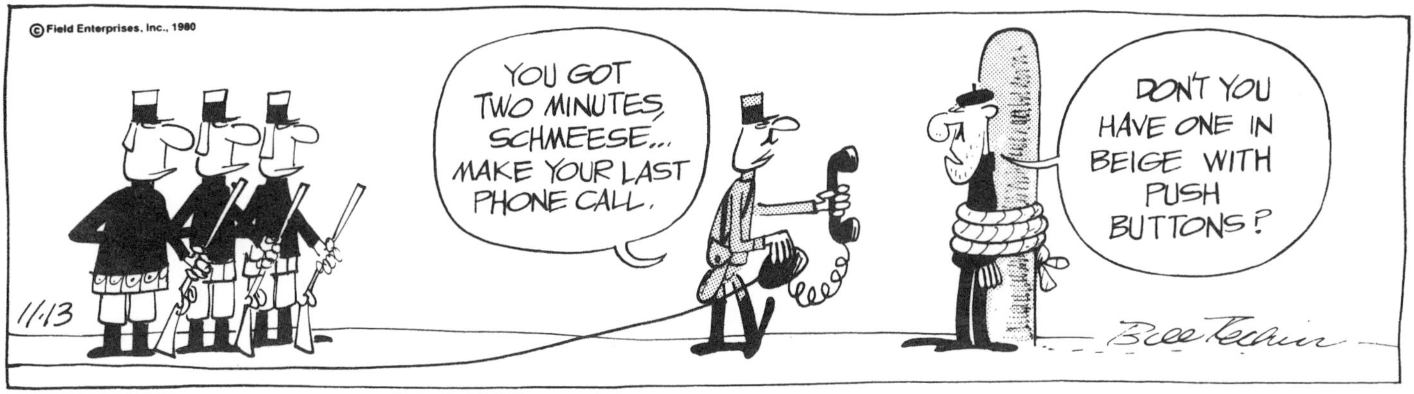
© Field Enterprises, Inc., 1980
11·13
YOU GOT TWO MINUTES, SCHMEESE... MAKE YOUR LAST PHONE CALL.
DON'T YOU HAVE ONE IN BEIGE WITH PUSH BUTTONS?

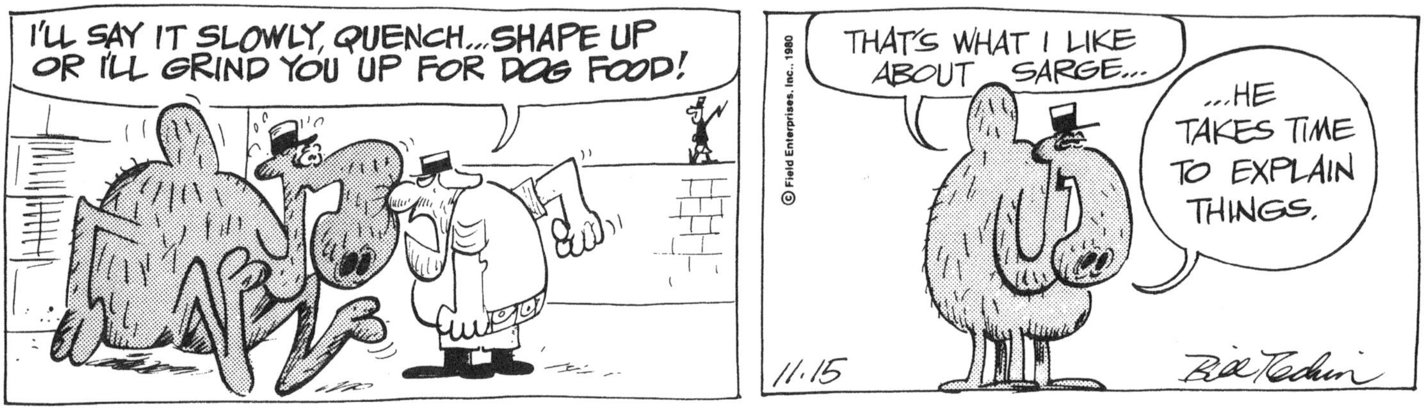
I'LL SAY IT SLOWLY, QUENCH... SHAPE UP OR I'LL GRIND YOU UP FOR DOG FOOD!
THAT'S WHAT I LIKE ABOUT SARGE...
...HE TAKES TIME TO EXPLAIN THINGS.
© Field Enterprises, Inc., 1980
11.15

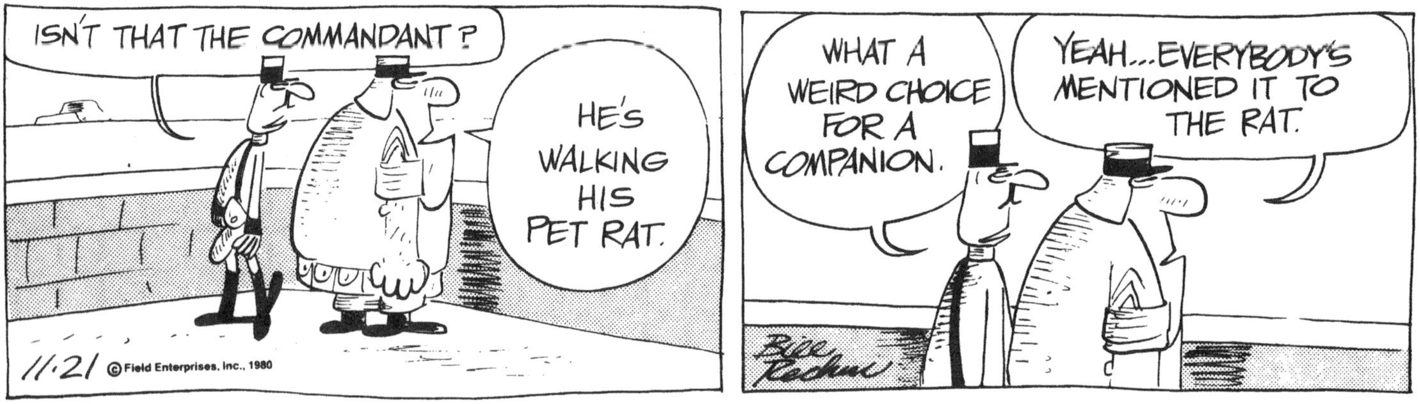
ISN'T THAT THE COMMANDANT?
HE'S WALKING HIS PET RAT.
11.21
© Field Enterprises, Inc., 1980
WHAT A WEIRD CHOICE FOR A COMPANION.
YEAH... EVERYBODY'S MENTIONED IT TO THE RAT.

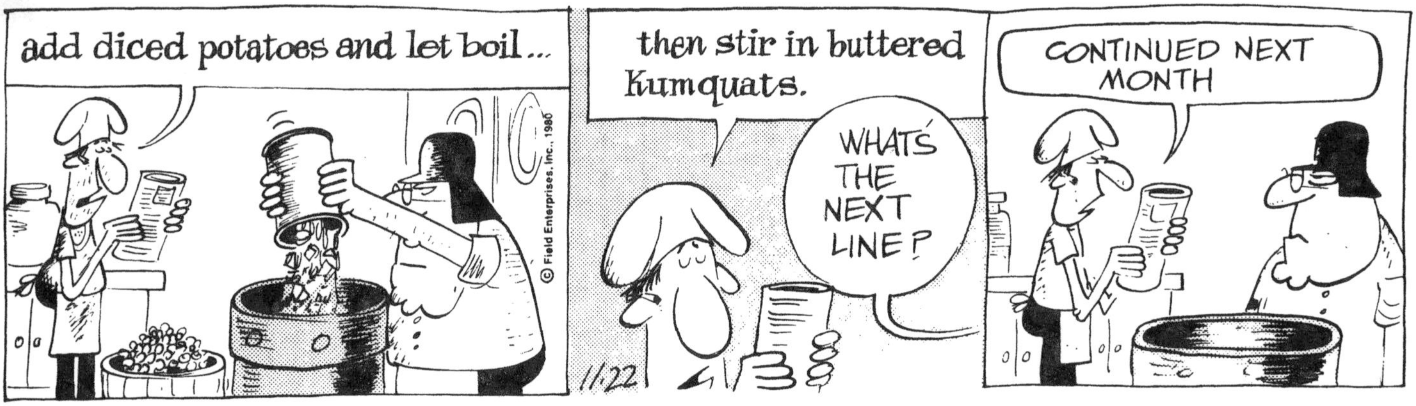
add diced potatoes and let boil...
© Field Enterprises, Inc., 1980
then stir in buttered Kumquats.
WHAT'S THE NEXT LINE?
11.22
CONTINUED NEXT MONTH

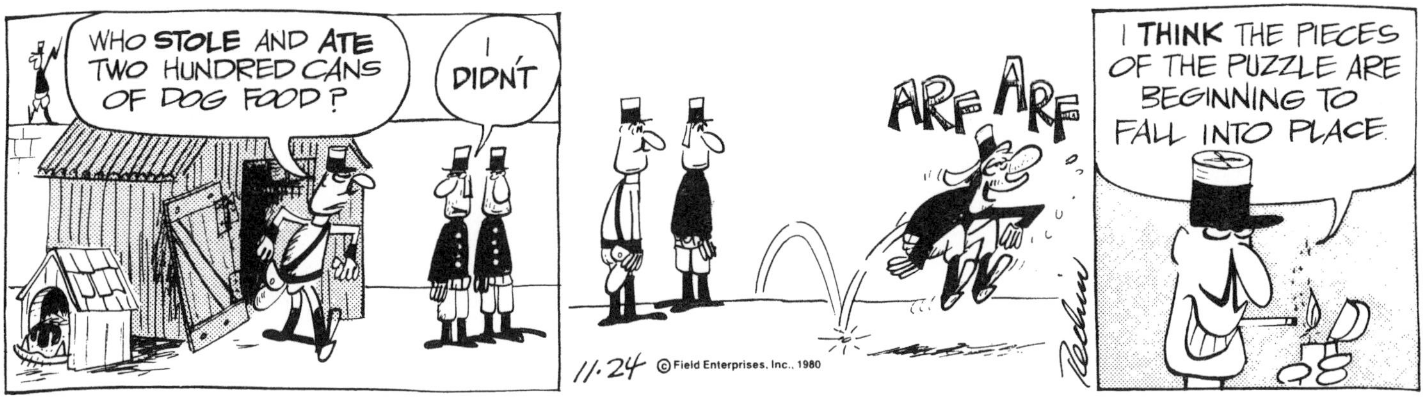
WHO STOLE AND ATE TWO HUNDRED CANS OF DOG FOOD?
I DIDN'T
ARF ARF
I THINK THE PIECES OF THE PUZZLE ARE BEGINNING TO FALL INTO PLACE
11·24
© Field Enterprises, Inc., 1980
Rechin

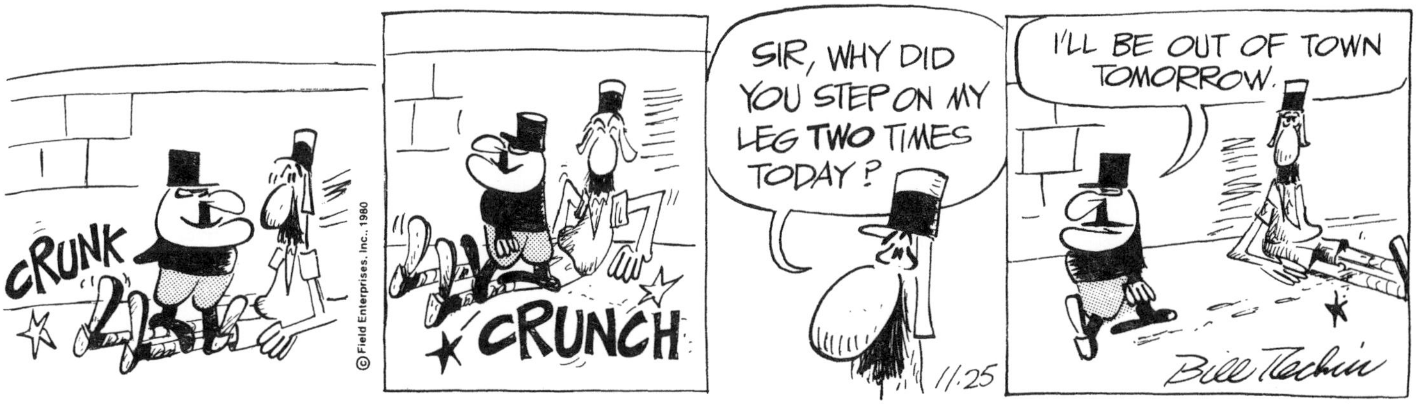
CRUNK
© Field Enterprises, Inc., 1980
CRUNCH
SIR, WHY DID YOU STEP ON MY LEG TWO TIMES TODAY?
11·25
I'LL BE OUT OF TOWN TOMORROW.
Bill Rechin

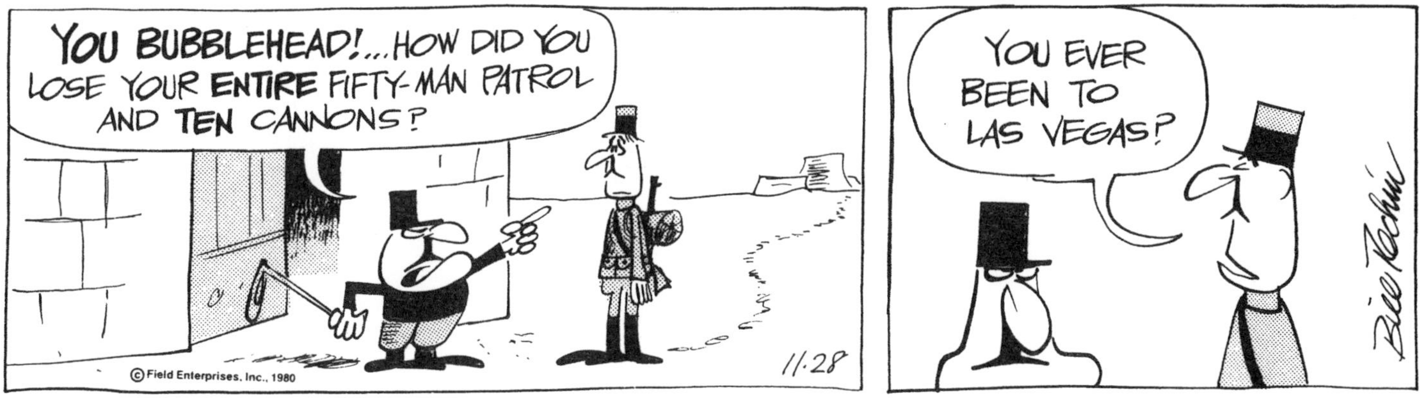
YOU BUBBLEHEAD!...HOW DID YOU LOSE YOUR ENTIRE FIFTY-MAN PATROL AND TEN CANNONS?
11·28
© Field Enterprises, Inc., 1980
YOU EVER BEEN TO LAS VEGAS?
Bill Rechin

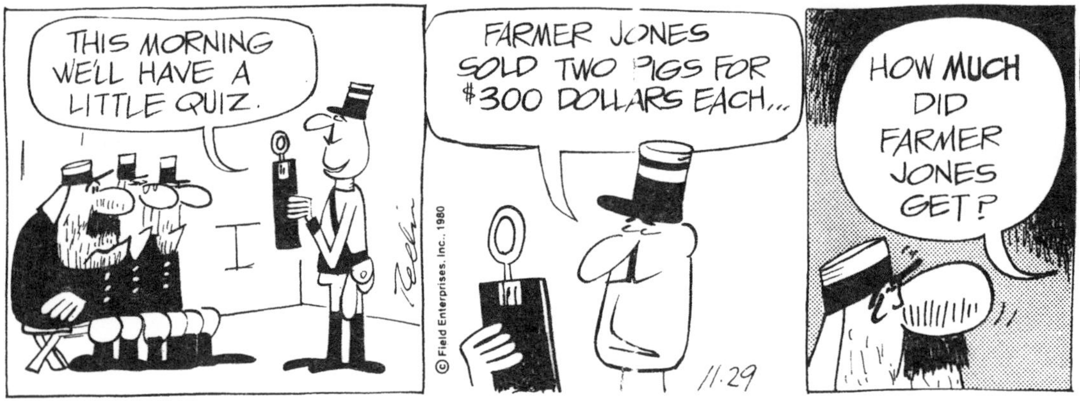
THIS MORNING WE'LL HAVE A LITTLE QUIZ.
FARMER JONES SOLD TWO PIGS FOR $300 DOLLARS EACH...
© Field Enterprises, Inc., 1980
11·29
HOW MUCH DID FARMER JONES GET?
THREE TO FIVE YEARS IF THE PIGS AIN'T HIS.

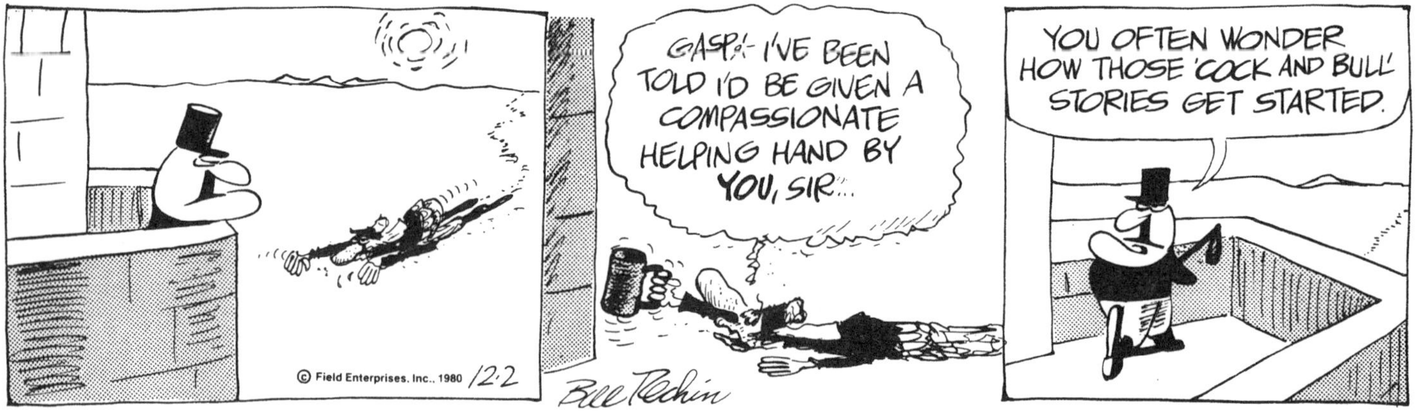
© Field Enterprises, Inc., 1980
12·2
GASP!- I'VE BEEN TOLD I'D BE GIVEN A COMPASSIONATE HELPING HAND BY YOU, SIR...
YOU OFTEN WONDER HOW THOSE 'COCK AND BULL' STORIES GET STARTED.

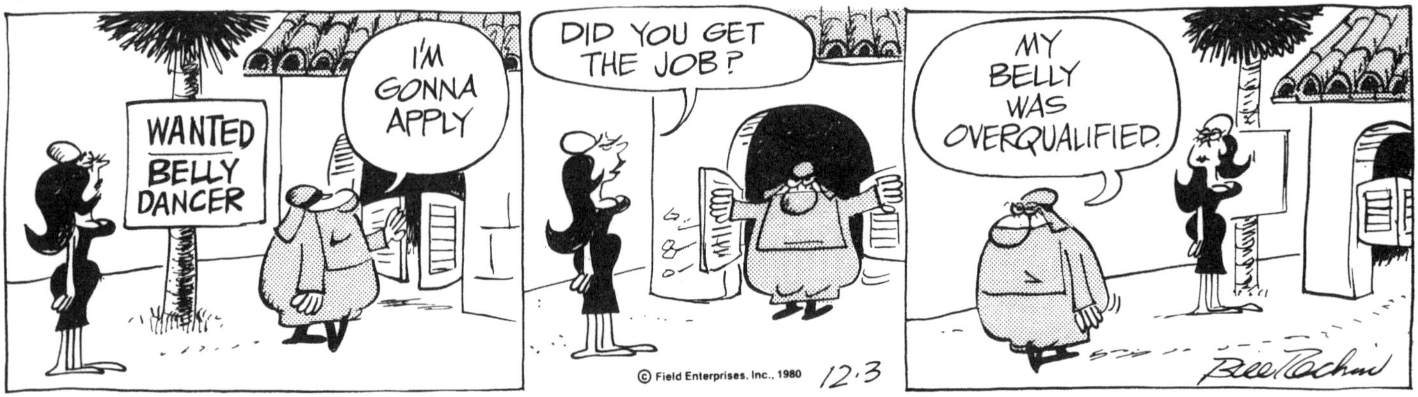
WANTED BELLY DANCER
I'M GONNA APPLY
DID YOU GET THE JOB?
© Field Enterprises, Inc., 1980
12·3
MY BELLY WAS OVERQUALIFIED.

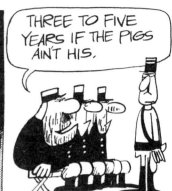

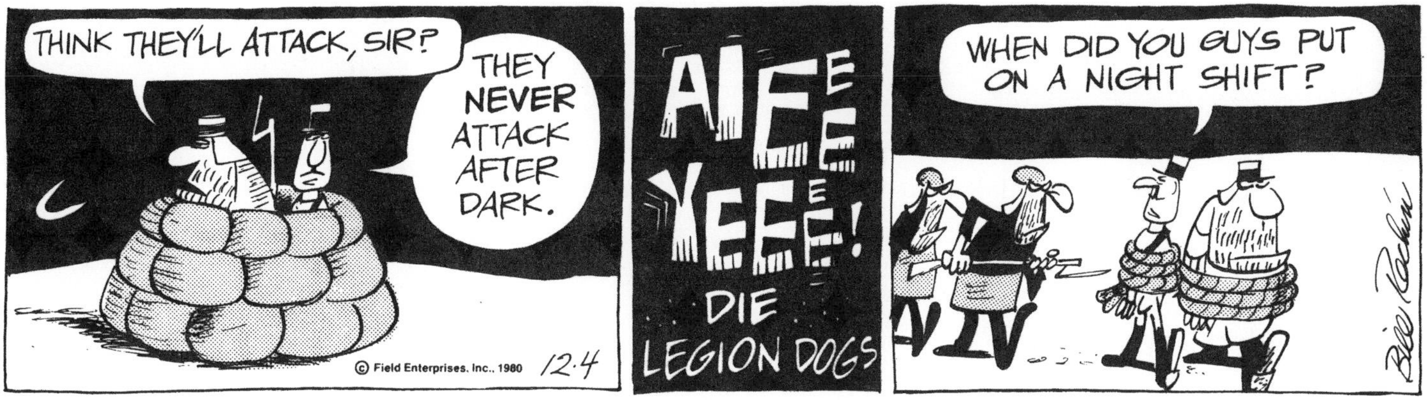
THINK THEY'LL ATTACK, SIR?
THEY NEVER ATTACK AFTER DARK.
© Field Enterprises, Inc., 1980
12·4
AIEEE YEEEE! DIE LEGION DOGS
WHEN DID YOU GUYS PUT ON A NIGHT SHIFT?
Bill Rechin

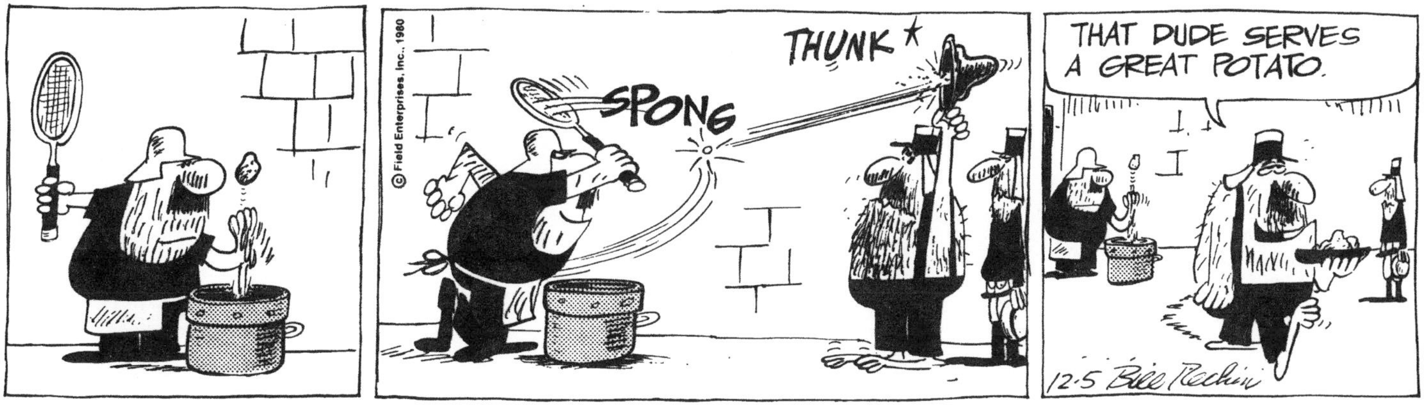
© Field Enterprises, Inc., 1980
SPONG
THUNK
THAT DUDE SERVES A GREAT POTATO.
12·5 Bill Rechin

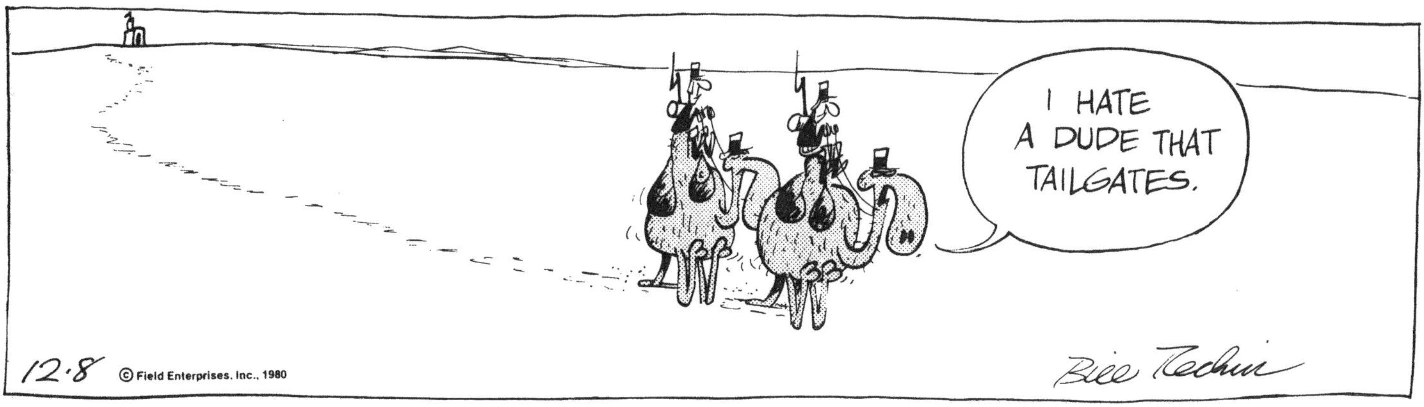
I HATE A DUDE THAT TAILGATES.
12·8
© Field Enterprises, Inc., 1980
Bill Rechin

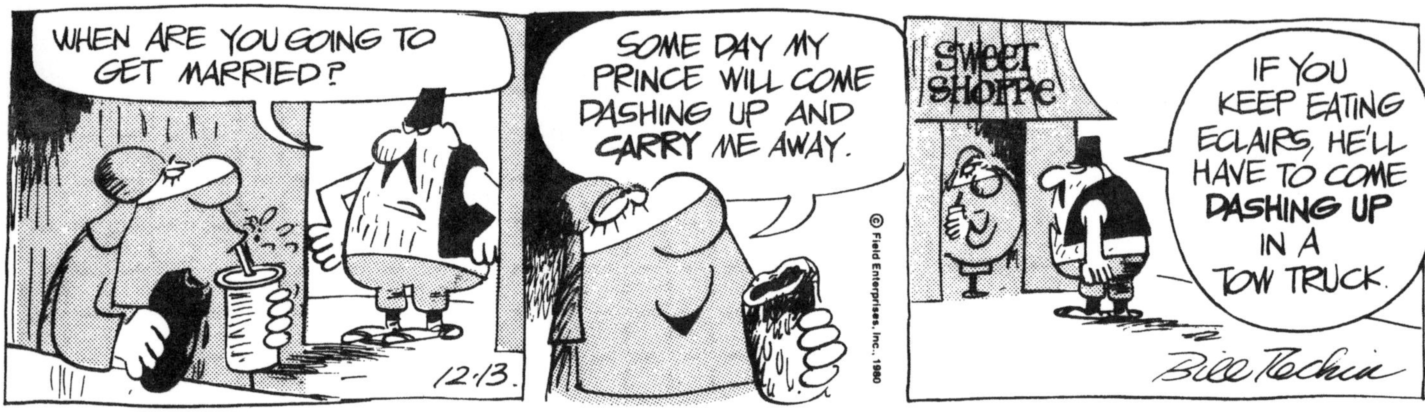
WHEN ARE YOU GOING TO GET MARRIED?
12·13.
SOME DAY MY PRINCE WILL COME DASHING UP AND CARRY ME AWAY.
© Field Enterprises, Inc., 1980
SWEET SHOPPE
IF YOU KEEP EATING ECLAIRS, HE'LL HAVE TO COME DASHING UP IN A TOW TRUCK.
Bill Rechin

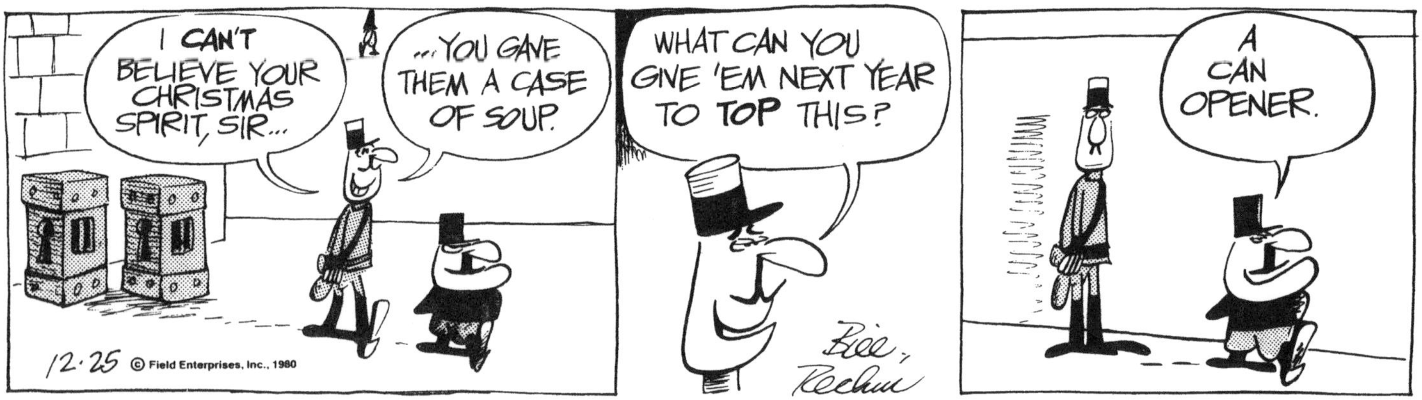
I CAN'T BELIEVE YOUR CHRISTMAS SPIRIT, SIR...
...YOU GAVE THEM A CASE OF SOUP.
12·25 © Field Enterprises, Inc., 1980
WHAT CAN YOU GIVE 'EM NEXT YEAR TO TOP THIS?
Bill, Rechin
A CAN OPENER.

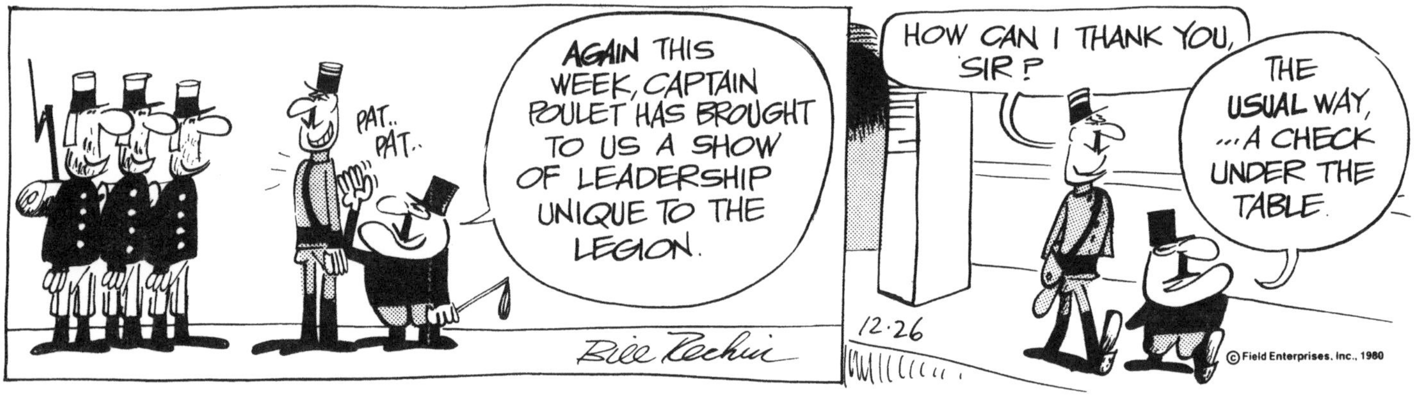
PAT.. PAT..
AGAIN THIS WEEK, CAPTAIN POULET HAS BROUGHT TO US A SHOW OF LEADERSHIP UNIQUE TO THE LEGION.
Bill Rechin
HOW CAN I THANK YOU, SIR?
THE USUAL WAY, ...A CHECK UNDER THE TABLE.
12·26
© Field Enterprises, Inc., 1980

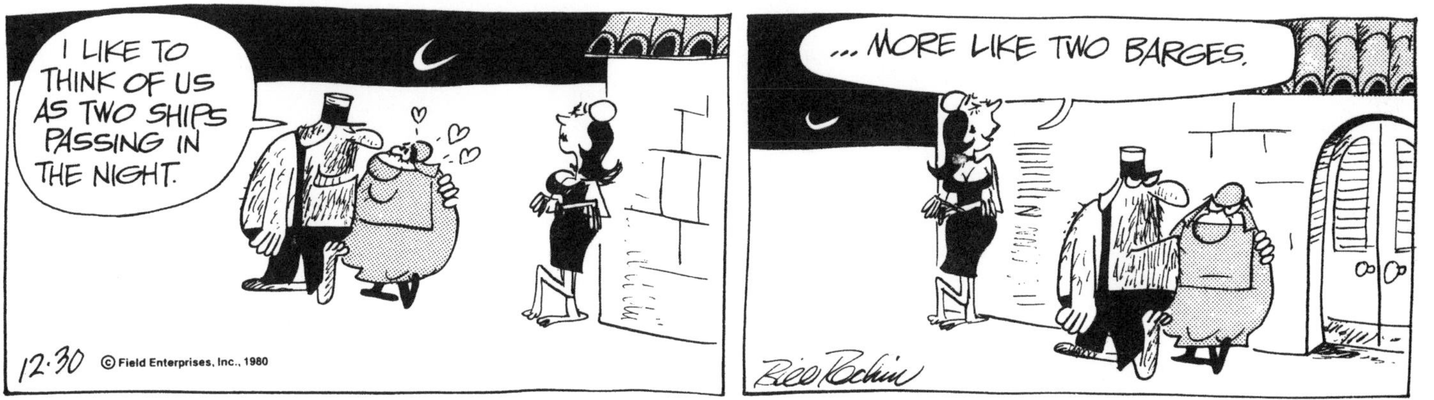
I LIKE TO THINK OF US AS TWO SHIPS PASSING IN THE NIGHT.
12·30
© Field Enterprises, Inc., 1980
... MORE LIKE TWO BARGES.
Bill Rechin

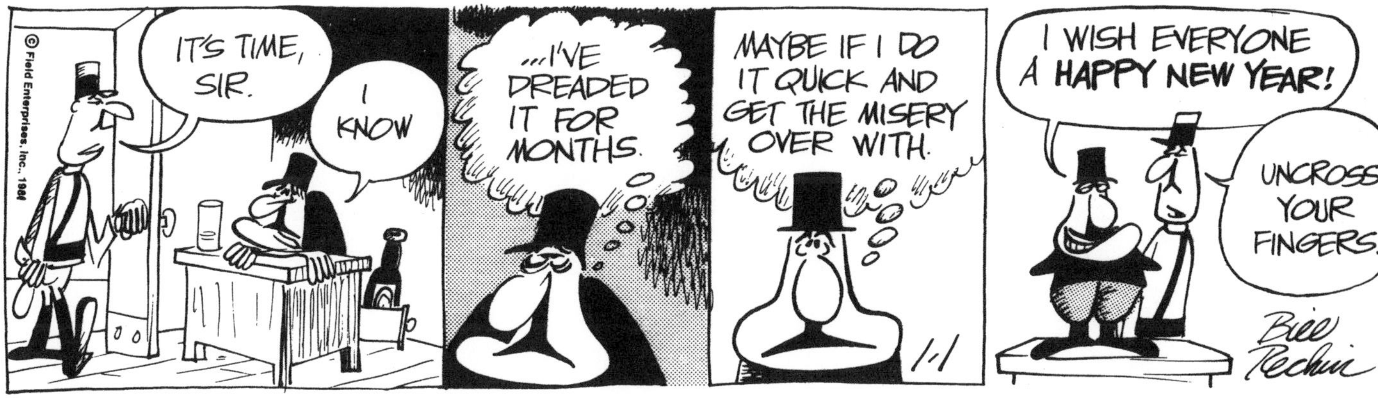
© Field Enterprises, Inc., 1981
IT'S TIME, SIR.
I KNOW
...I'VE DREADED IT FOR MONTHS.
MAYBE IF I DO IT QUICK AND GET THE MISERY OVER WITH.
1·1
I WISH EVERYONE A **HAPPY NEW YEAR!**
UNCROSS YOUR FINGERS.
Bill Rechin

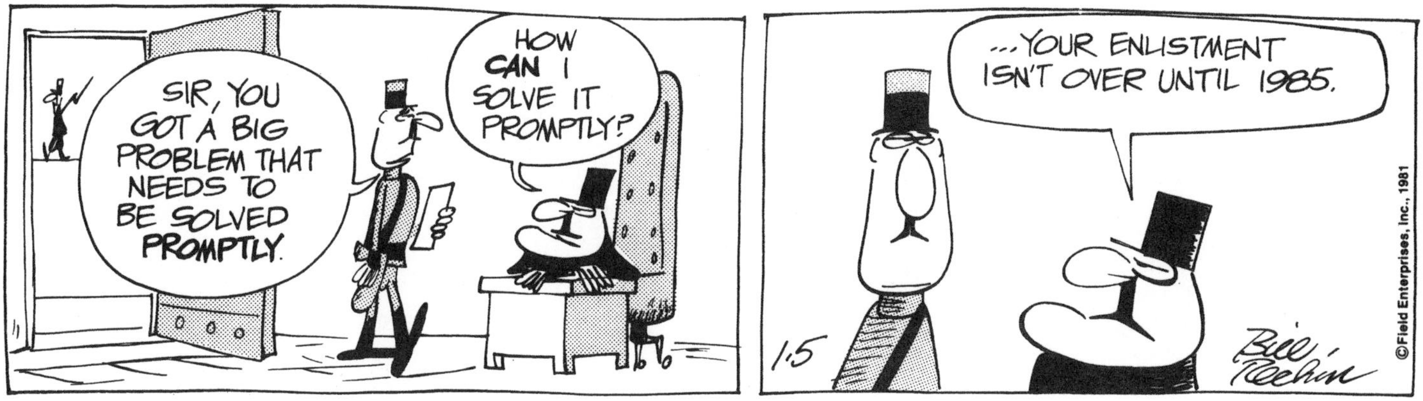
SIR, YOU GOT A BIG PROBLEM THAT NEEDS TO BE SOLVED **PROMPTLY**.
HOW **CAN** I SOLVE IT PROMPTLY?
...YOUR ENLISTMENT ISN'T OVER UNTIL 1985.
1·5
Bill Rechin
©Field Enterprises, Inc., 1981

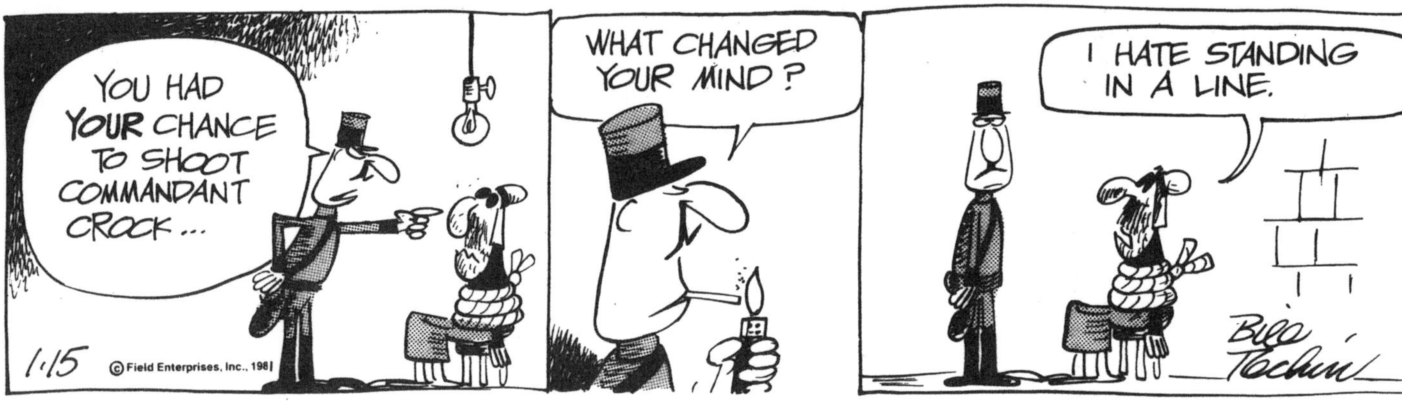
YOU HAD YOUR CHANCE TO SHOOT COMMANDANT CROCK...
1·15
© Field Enterprises, Inc., 1981
WHAT CHANGED YOUR MIND?
I HATE STANDING IN A LINE.
Bill Rechin

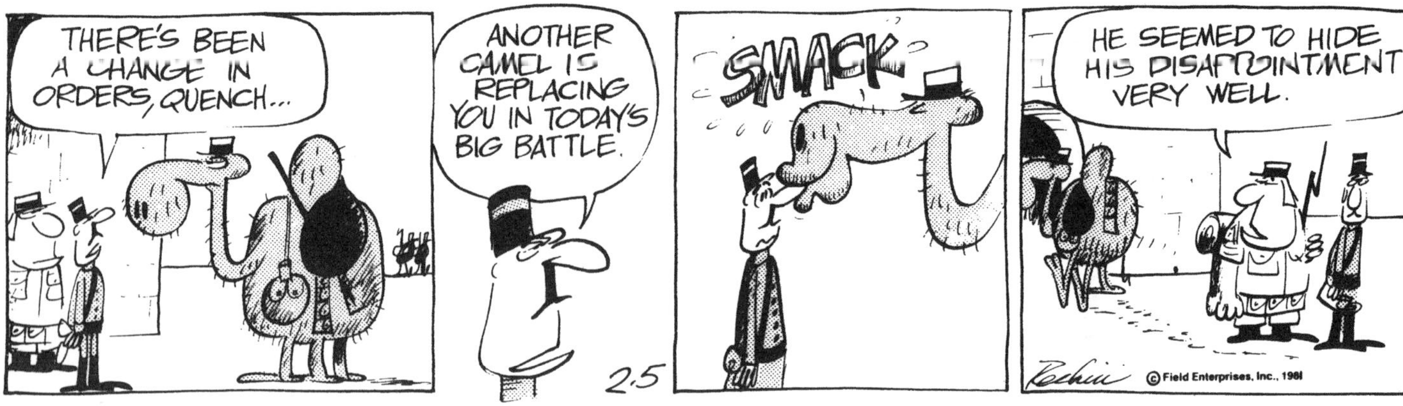
THERE'S BEEN A CHANGE IN ORDERS, QUENCH...
ANOTHER CAMEL IS REPLACING YOU IN TODAY'S BIG BATTLE.
2·5
SMACK
HE SEEMED TO HIDE HIS DISAPPOINTMENT VERY WELL.
Rechin
© Field Enterprises, Inc., 1981

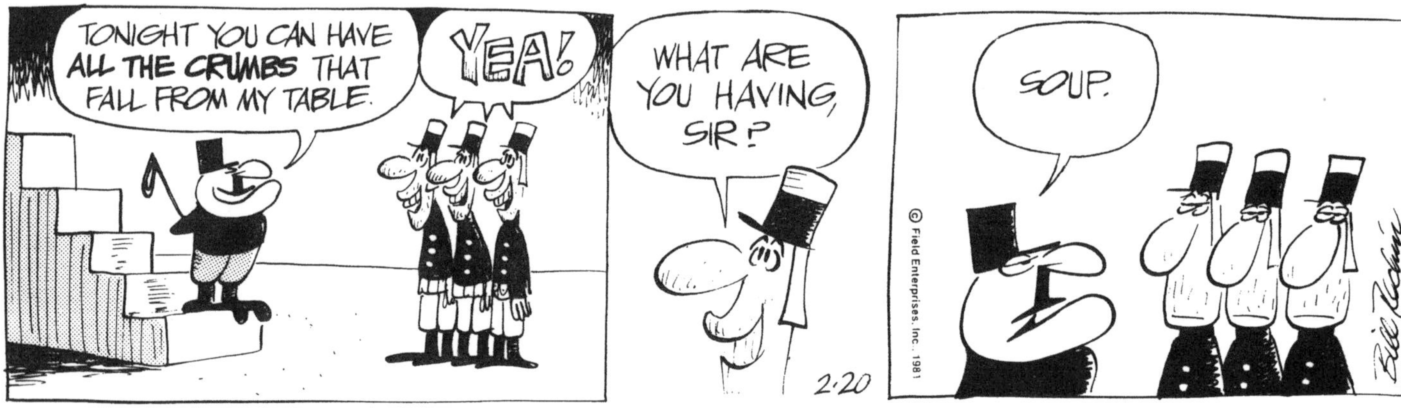
TONIGHT YOU CAN HAVE ALL THE CRUMBS THAT FALL FROM MY TABLE.
YEA!
WHAT ARE YOU HAVING, SIR?
2·20
SOUP.
© Field Enterprises, Inc., 1981
Bill Rechin

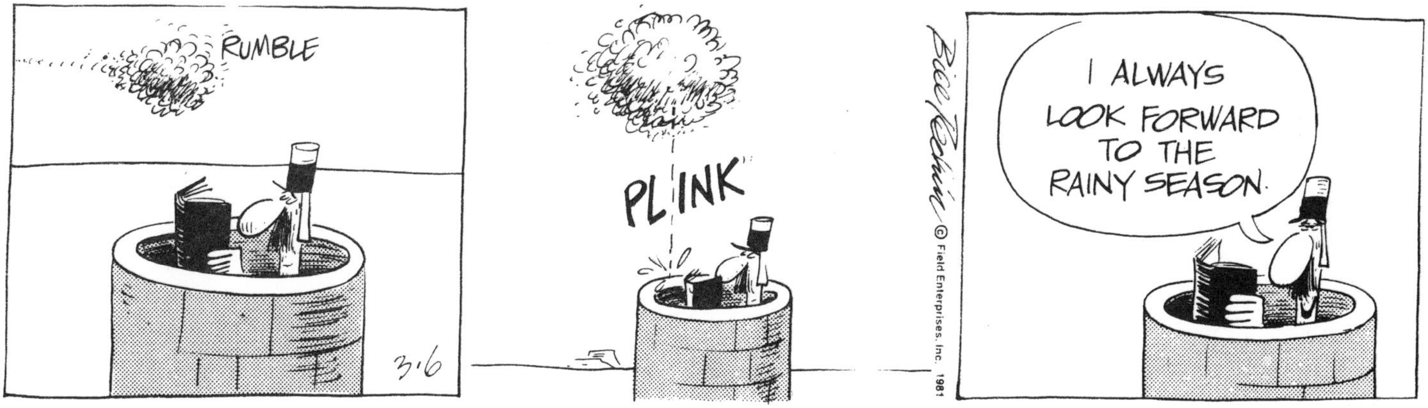
RUMBLE
3·6
PLINK
I ALWAYS LOOK FORWARD TO THE RAINY SEASON.
Bill Rechin
© Field Enterprises, Inc. 1981

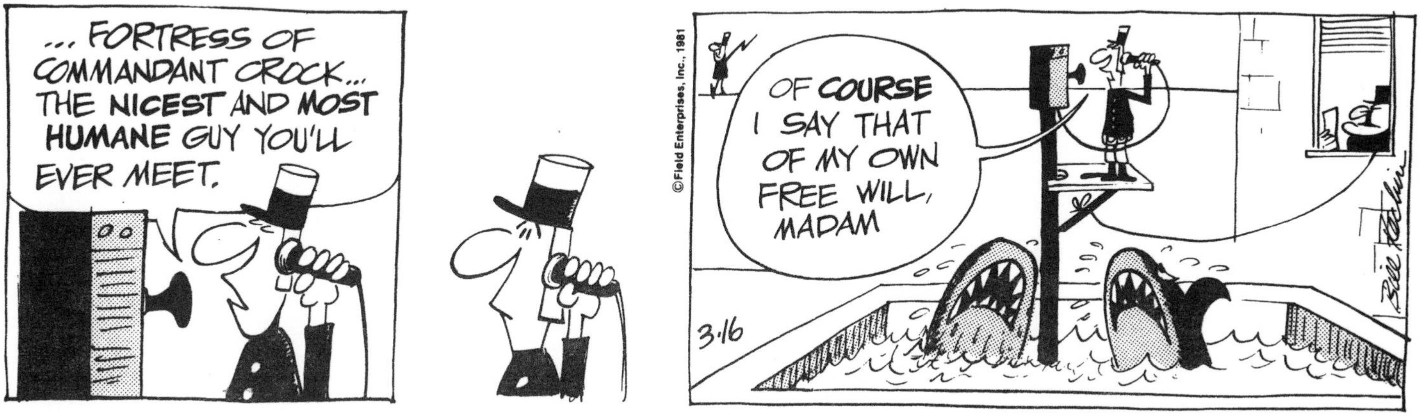
... FORTRESS OF COMMANDANT CROCK... THE **NICEST** AND **MOST HUMANE** GUY YOU'LL EVER MEET.
©Field Enterprises, Inc., 1981
OF **COURSE** I SAY THAT OF MY OWN FREE WILL, MADAM
3·16
Bill Rechin

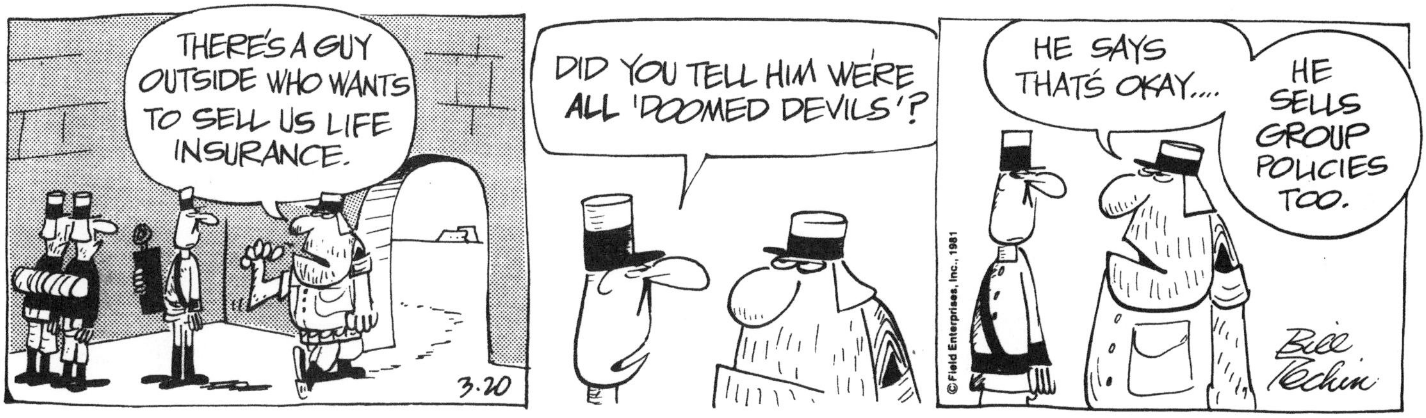
THERE'S A GUY OUTSIDE WHO WANTS TO SELL US LIFE INSURANCE.
3·20
DID YOU TELL HIM WE'RE **ALL** 'DOOMED DEVILS'?
HE SAYS THAT'S OKAY....
HE SELLS GROUP POLICIES TOO.
©Field Enterprises, Inc., 1981
Bill Rechin

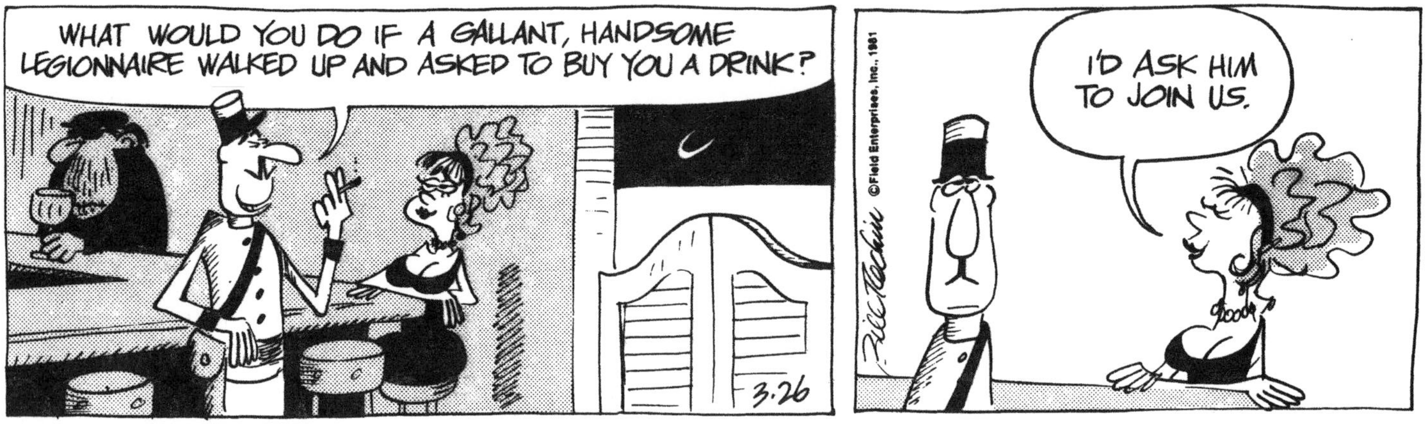
WHAT WOULD YOU DO IF A GALLANT, HANDSOME LEGIONNAIRE WALKED UP AND ASKED TO BUY YOU A DRINK?
3.26
©Field Enterprises, Inc., 1981
I'D ASK HIM TO JOIN US.

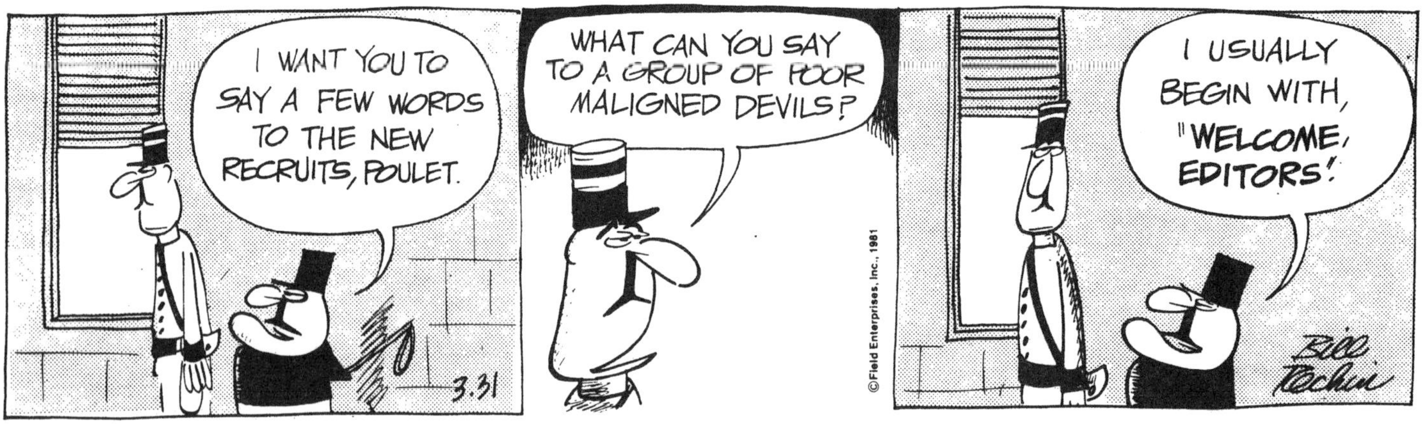
I WANT YOU TO SAY A FEW WORDS TO THE NEW RECRUITS, POULET.
3.31
WHAT CAN YOU SAY TO A GROUP OF POOR MALIGNED DEVILS?
©Field Enterprises, Inc., 1981
I USUALLY BEGIN WITH, "WELCOME, EDITORS!"

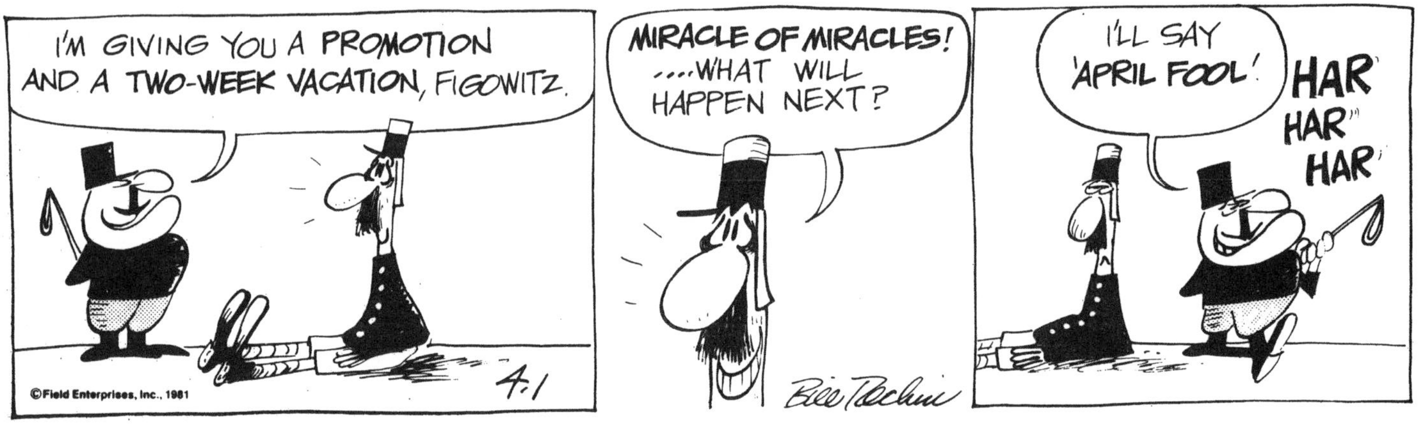
I'M GIVING YOU A PROMOTION AND A TWO-WEEK VACATION, FIGOWITZ.
©Field Enterprises, Inc., 1981
4.1
MIRACLE OF MIRACLES! ....WHAT WILL HAPPEN NEXT?
I'LL SAY 'APRIL FOOL'!
HAR HAR HAR

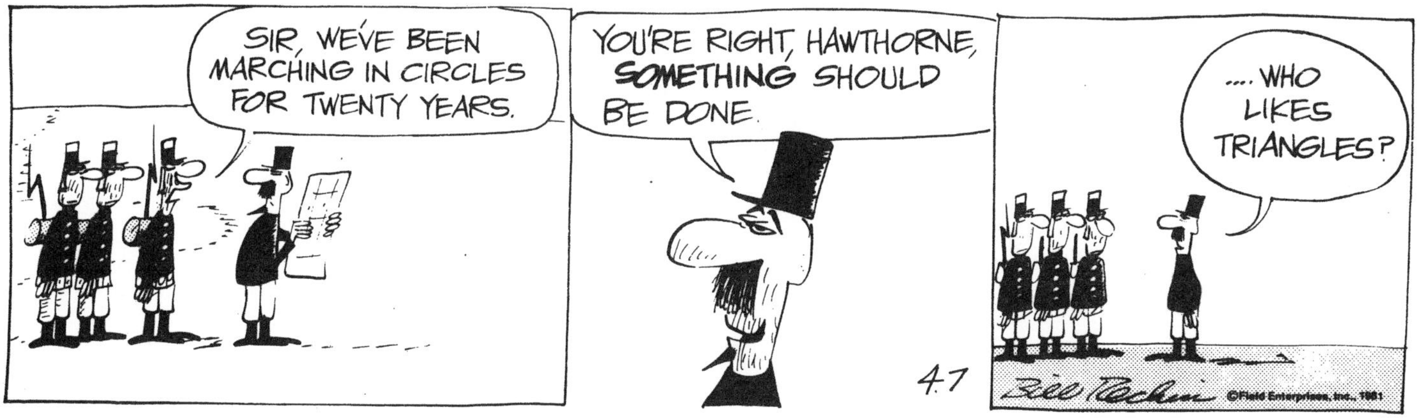
SIR, WE'VE BEEN MARCHING IN CIRCLES FOR TWENTY YEARS.
YOU'RE RIGHT, HAWTHORNE, SOMETHING SHOULD BE DONE.
.... WHO LIKES TRIANGLES?
4.7
©Field Enterprises, Inc., 1981

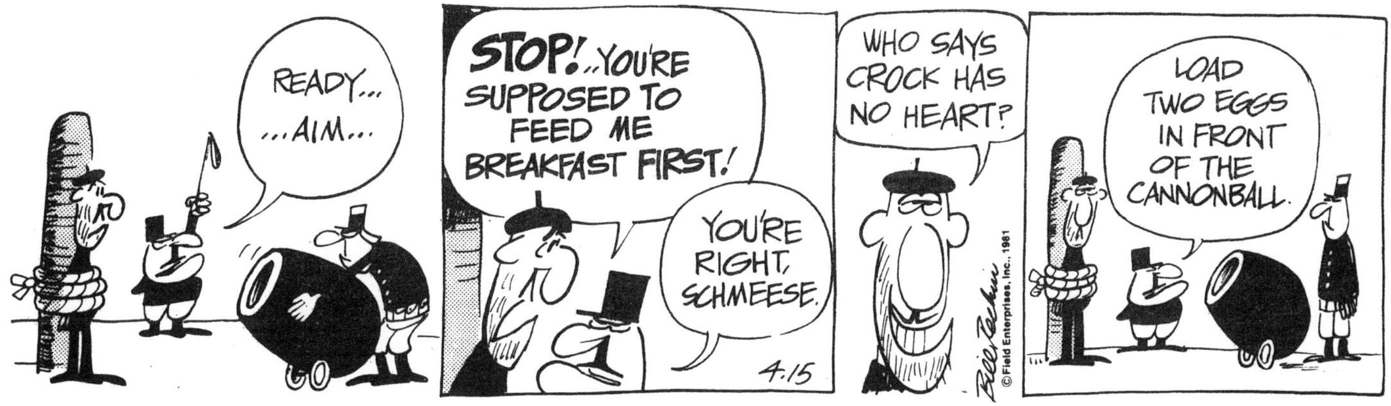
READY... ...AIM...
STOP!...YOU'RE SUPPOSED TO FEED ME BREAKFAST FIRST!
YOU'RE RIGHT, SCHMEESE.
4.15
WHO SAYS CROCK HAS NO HEART?
©Field Enterprises, Inc., 1981
LOAD TWO EGGS IN FRONT OF THE CANNONBALL.

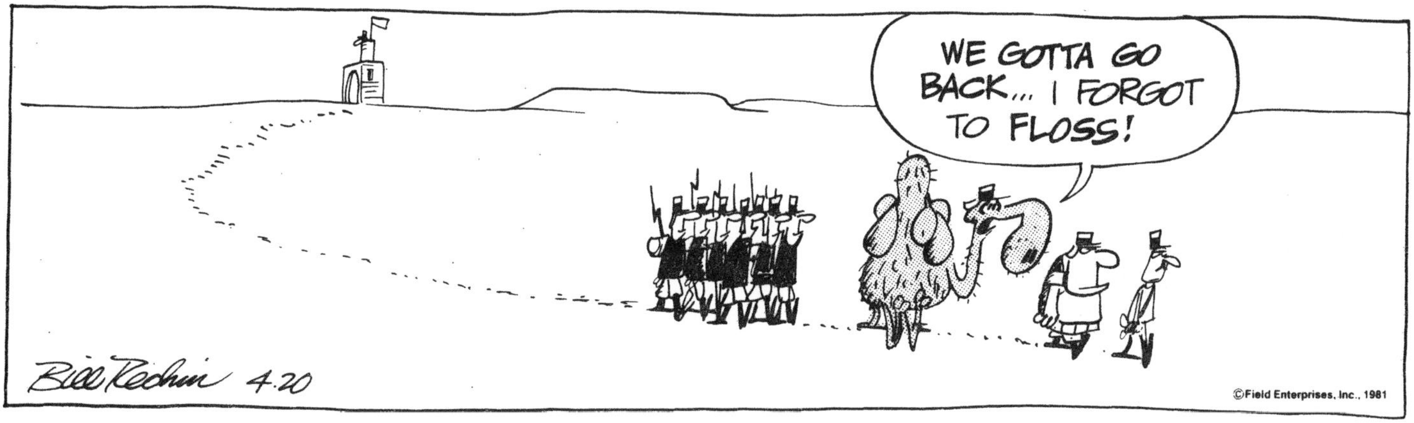
WE GOTTA GO BACK... I FORGOT TO FLOSS!
4.20
©Field Enterprises, Inc., 1981

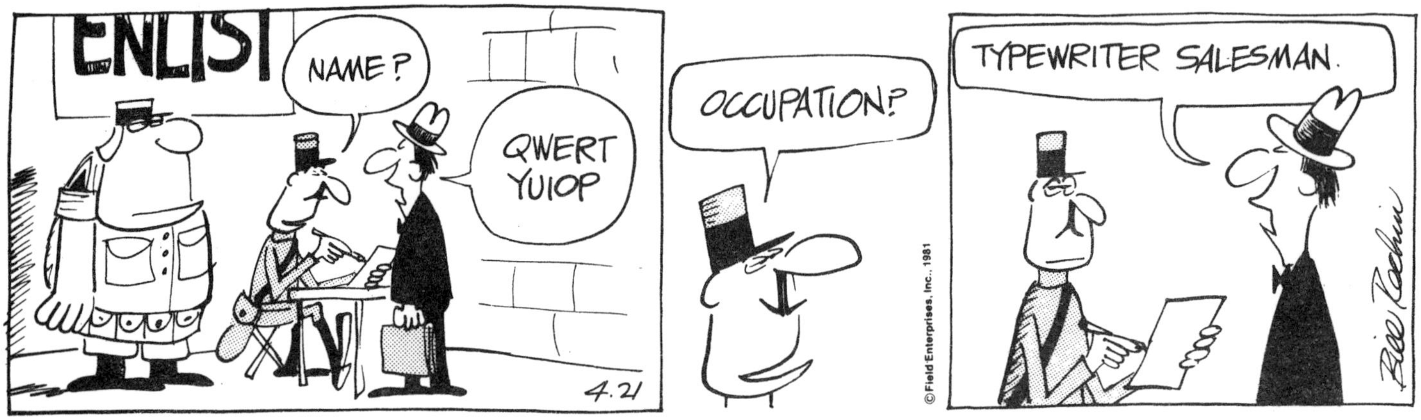
ENLIST
NAME?
QWERT YUIOP
4.21
OCCUPATION?
©Field Enterprises, Inc., 1981
TYPEWRITER SALESMAN.

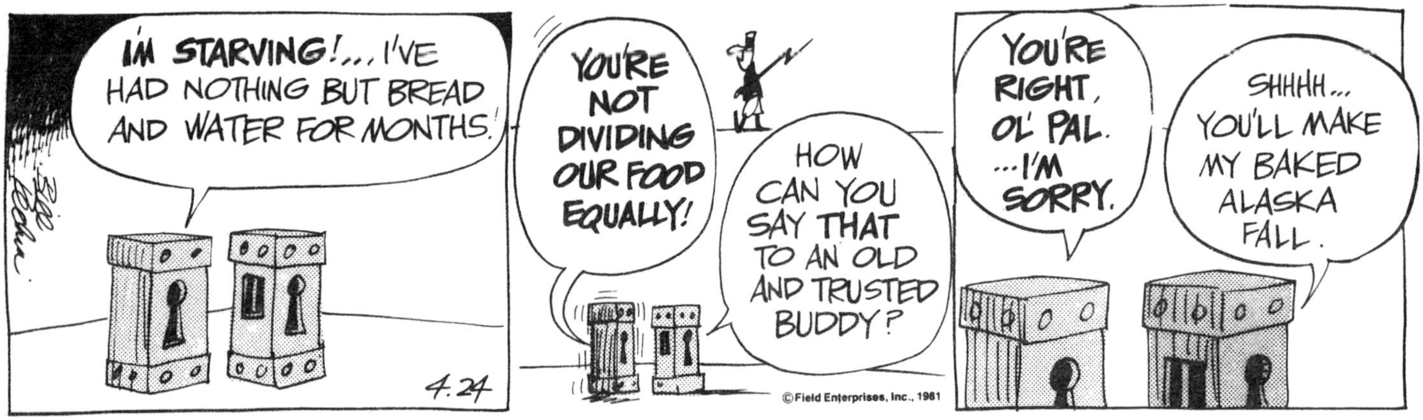
I'M STARVING!... I'VE HAD NOTHING BUT BREAD AND WATER FOR MONTHS!
4.24
YOU'RE NOT DIVIDING OUR FOOD EQUALLY!
HOW CAN YOU SAY THAT TO AN OLD AND TRUSTED BUDDY?
©Field Enterprises, Inc., 1981
YOU'RE RIGHT, OL' PAL. ...I'M SORRY.
SHHHH... YOU'LL MAKE MY BAKED ALASKA FALL.

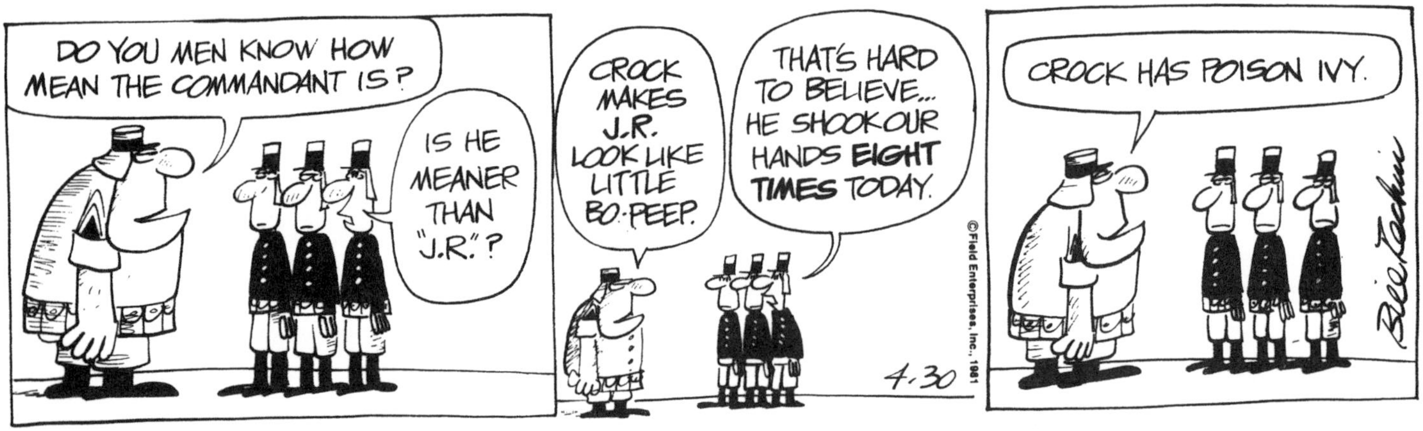
DO YOU MEN KNOW HOW MEAN THE COMMANDANT IS?
IS HE MEANER THAN "J.R."?
CROCK MAKES J.R. LOOK LIKE LITTLE BO-PEEP.
THAT'S HARD TO BELIEVE... HE SHOOK OUR HANDS EIGHT TIMES TODAY.
©Field Enterprises, Inc., 1981
4.30
CROCK HAS POISON IVY.

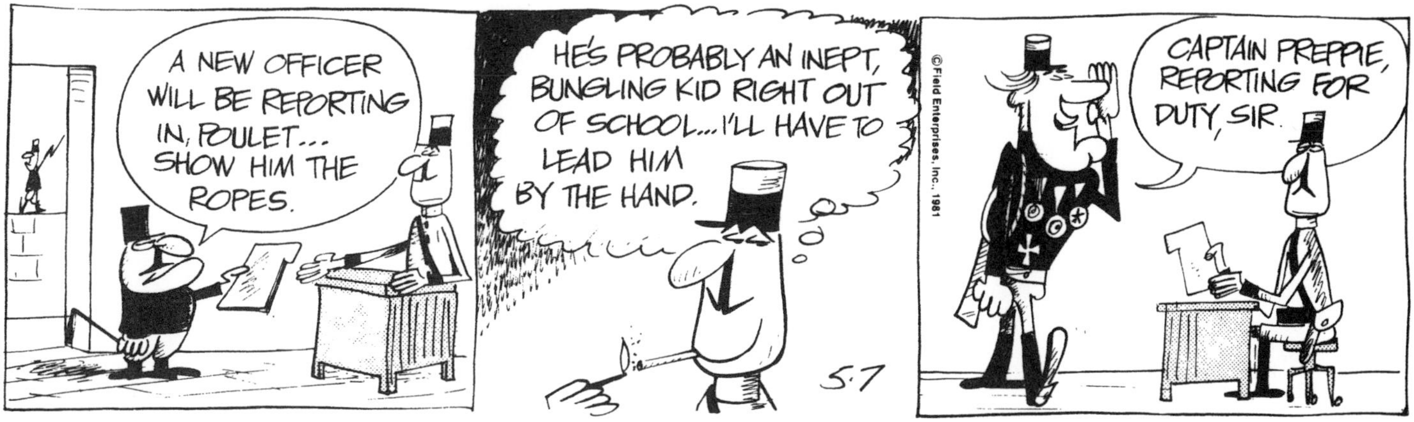
A NEW OFFICER WILL BE REPORTING IN, POULET... SHOW HIM THE ROPES.
HE'S PROBABLY AN INEPT, BUNGLING KID RIGHT OUT OF SCHOOL...I'LL HAVE TO LEAD HIM BY THE HAND.
5-7
© Field Enterprises, Inc., 1981
CAPTAIN PREPPIE, REPORTING FOR DUTY, SIR.

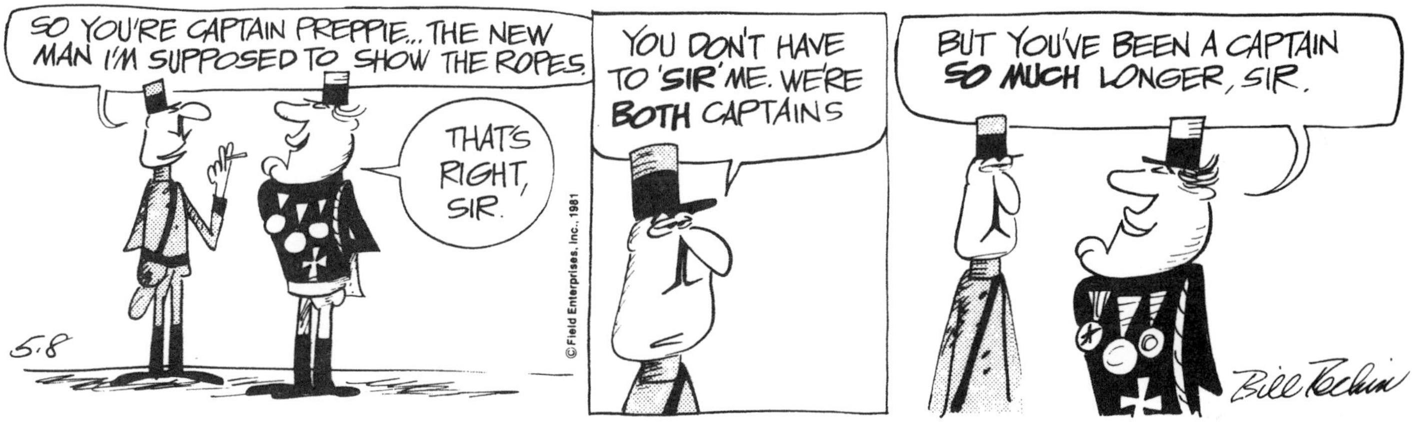
SO YOU'RE CAPTAIN PREPPIE... THE NEW MAN I'M SUPPOSED TO SHOW THE ROPES.
THAT'S RIGHT, SIR.
5-8
© Field Enterprises, Inc., 1981
YOU DON'T HAVE TO 'SIR' ME. WE'RE BOTH CAPTAINS
BUT YOU'VE BEEN A CAPTAIN SO MUCH LONGER, SIR.

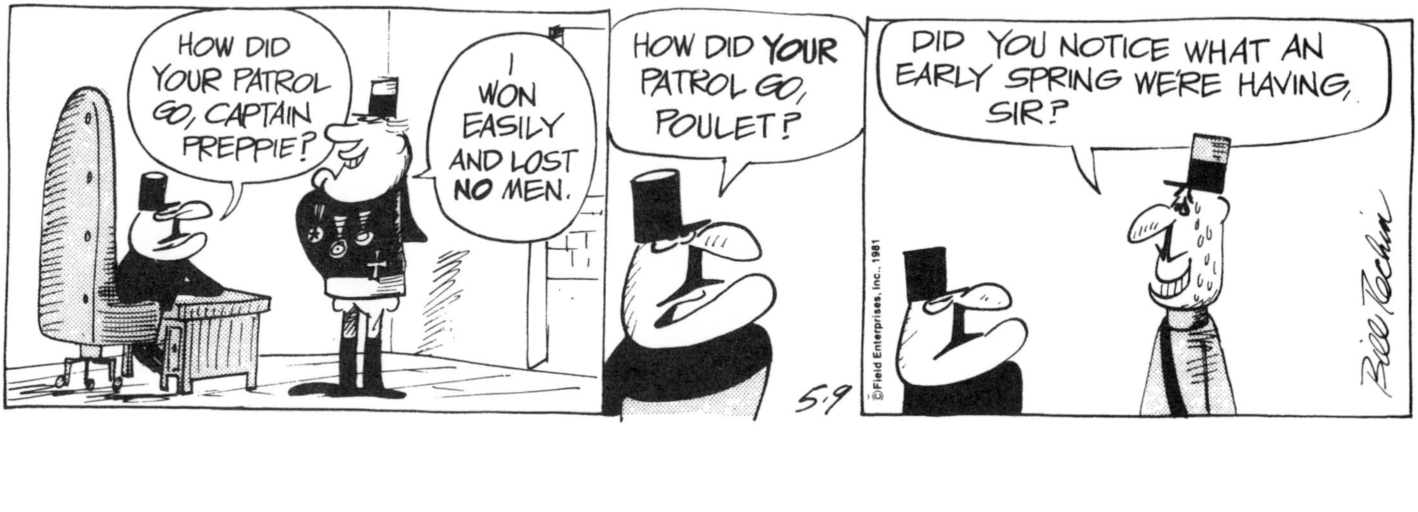
HOW DID YOUR PATROL GO, CAPTAIN PREPPIE?
I WON EASILY AND LOST NO MEN.
HOW DID YOUR PATROL GO, POULET?
5-9
© Field Enterprises, Inc., 1981
DID YOU NOTICE WHAT AN EARLY SPRING WE'RE HAVING, SIR?

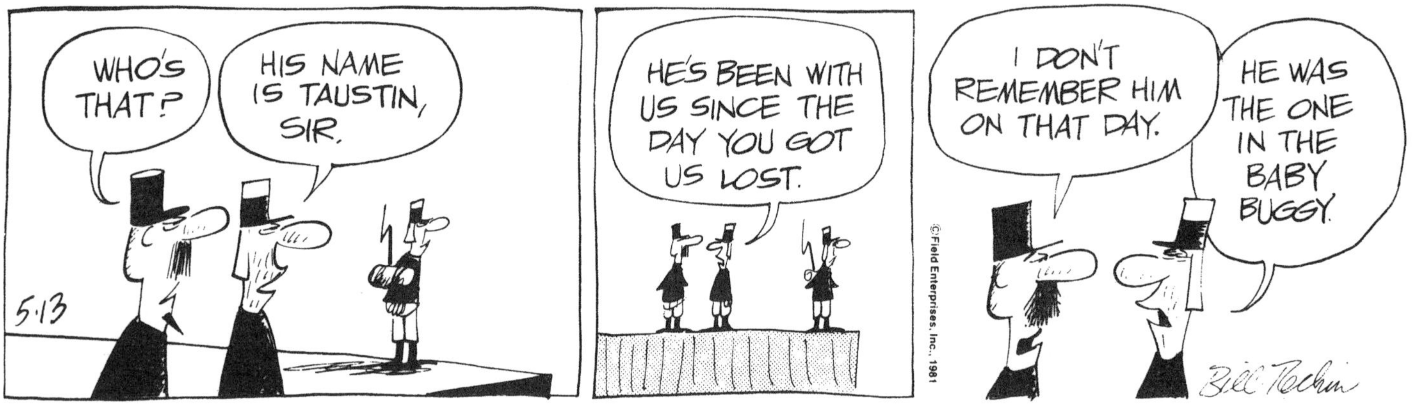

WHO'S THAT?
HIS NAME IS TAUSTIN, SIR.
5·13
HE'S BEEN WITH US SINCE THE DAY YOU GOT US LOST.
©Field Enterprises, Inc., 1981
I DON'T REMEMBER HIM ON THAT DAY.
HE WAS THE ONE IN THE BABY BUGGY.
Bill Rechin

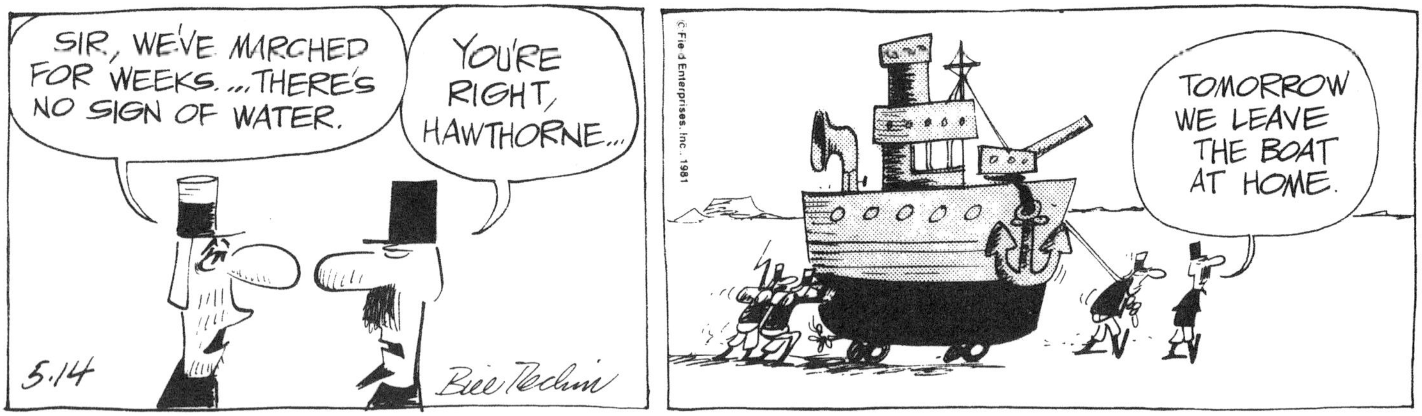

SIR, WE'VE MARCHED FOR WEEKS.....THERE'S NO SIGN OF WATER.
YOU'RE RIGHT, HAWTHORNE...
5·14
Bill Rechin
©Field Enterprises, Inc., 1981
TOMORROW WE LEAVE THE BOAT AT HOME.

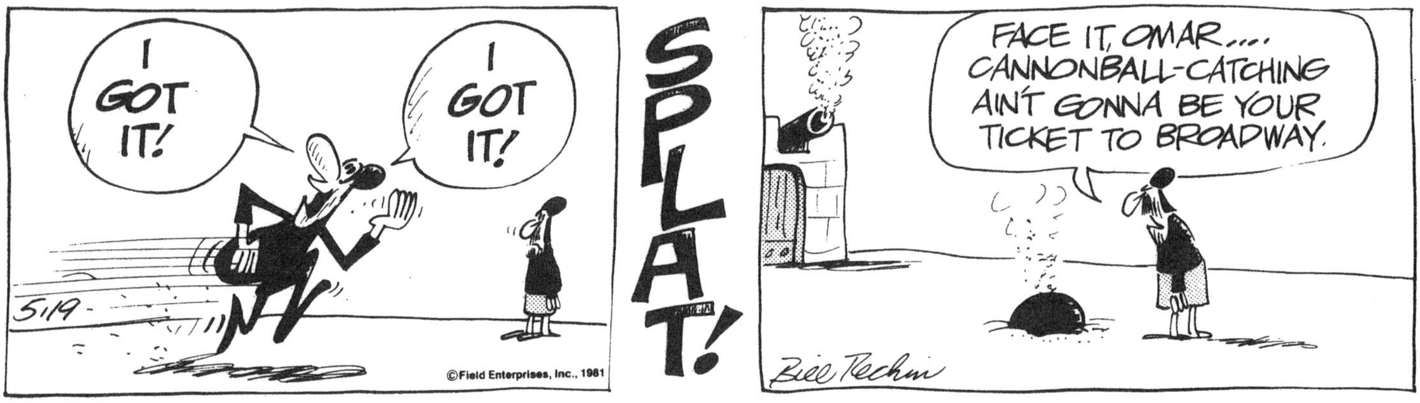

I GOT IT!
I GOT IT!
5·19
©Field Enterprises, Inc., 1981
SPLAT!
FACE IT, OMAR.... CANNONBALL-CATCHING AIN'T GONNA BE YOUR TICKET TO BROADWAY.
Bill Rechin

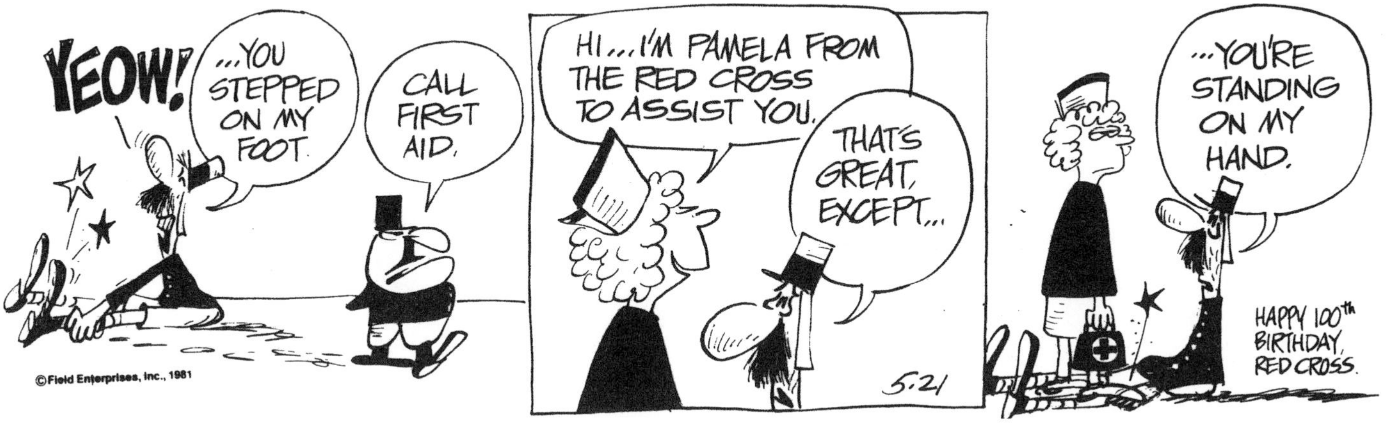
YEOW!
...YOU STEPPED ON MY FOOT.
CALL FIRST AID.
HI... I'M PAMELA FROM THE RED CROSS TO ASSIST YOU.
THAT'S GREAT, EXCEPT...
...YOU'RE STANDING ON MY HAND.
HAPPY 100th BIRTHDAY, RED CROSS.
5·21
©Field Enterprises, Inc., 1981

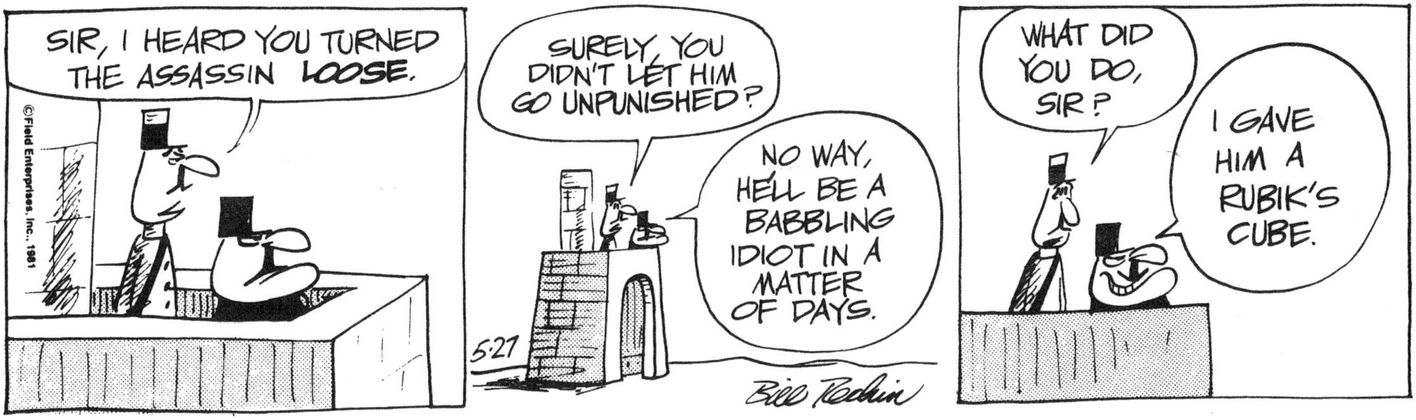
SIR, I HEARD YOU TURNED THE ASSASSIN LOOSE.
SURELY, YOU DIDN'T LET HIM GO UNPUNISHED?
NO WAY, HE'LL BE A BABBLING IDIOT IN A MATTER OF DAYS.
WHAT DID YOU DO, SIR?
I GAVE HIM A RUBIK'S CUBE.
5·27
Bill Rechin
©Field Enterprises, Inc., 1981

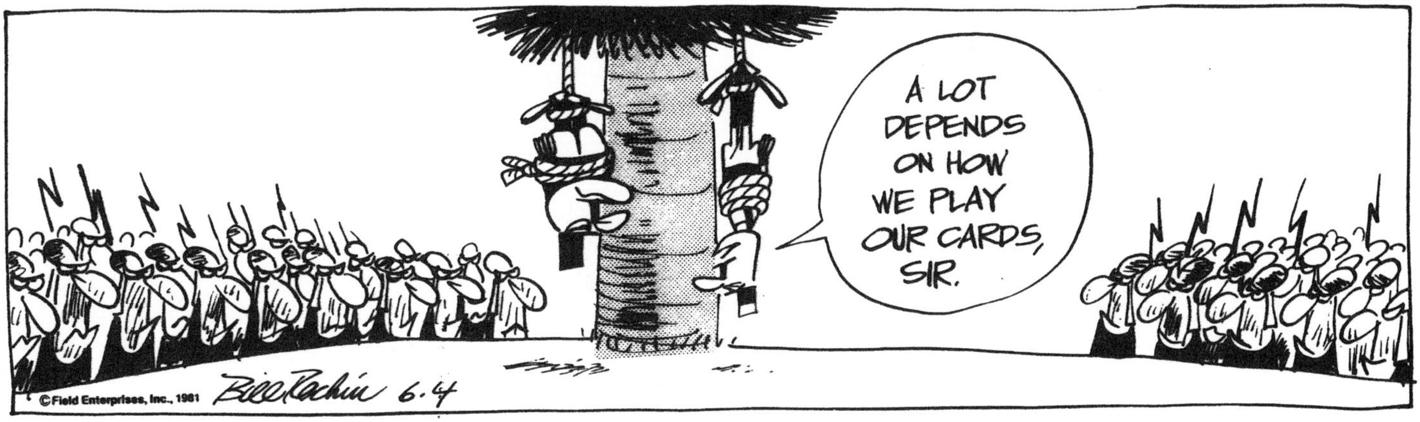
A LOT DEPENDS ON HOW WE PLAY OUR CARDS, SIR.
Bill Rechin 6·4
©Field Enterprises, Inc., 1981

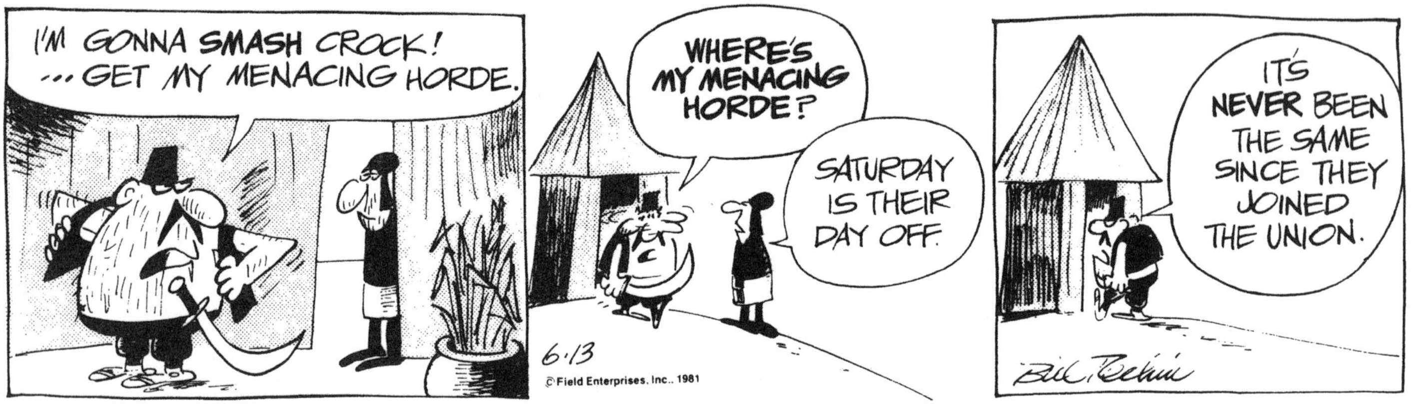
I'M GONNA SMASH CROCK! ... GET MY MENACING HORDE.
WHERE'S MY MENACING HORDE?
SATURDAY IS THEIR DAY OFF.
IT'S NEVER BEEN THE SAME SINCE THEY JOINED THE UNION.
6.13
© Field Enterprises, Inc., 1981
Bill Rechin

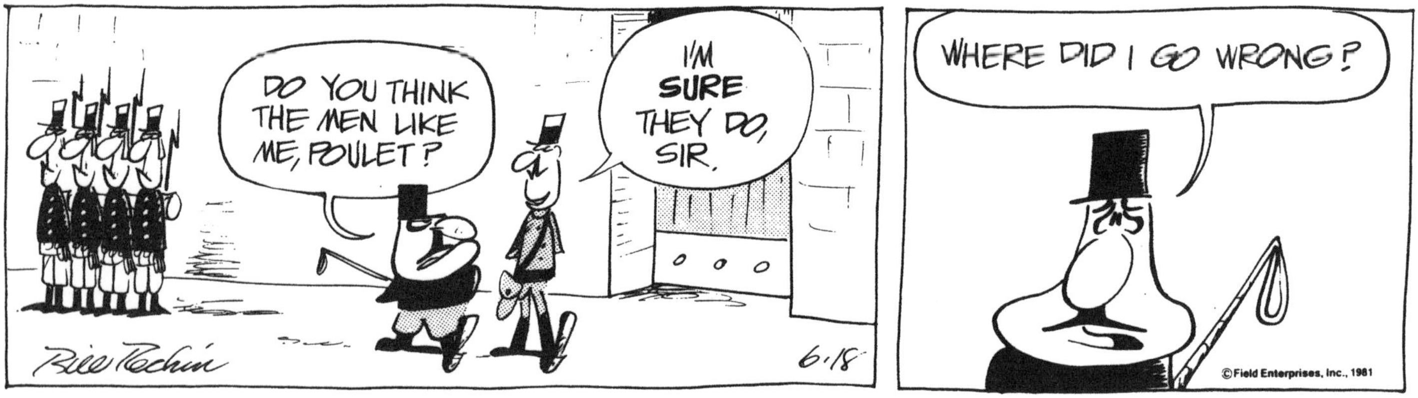
DO YOU THINK THE MEN LIKE ME, POULET?
I'M SURE THEY DO, SIR.
WHERE DID I GO WRONG?
Bill Rechin
6.18
© Field Enterprises, Inc., 1981

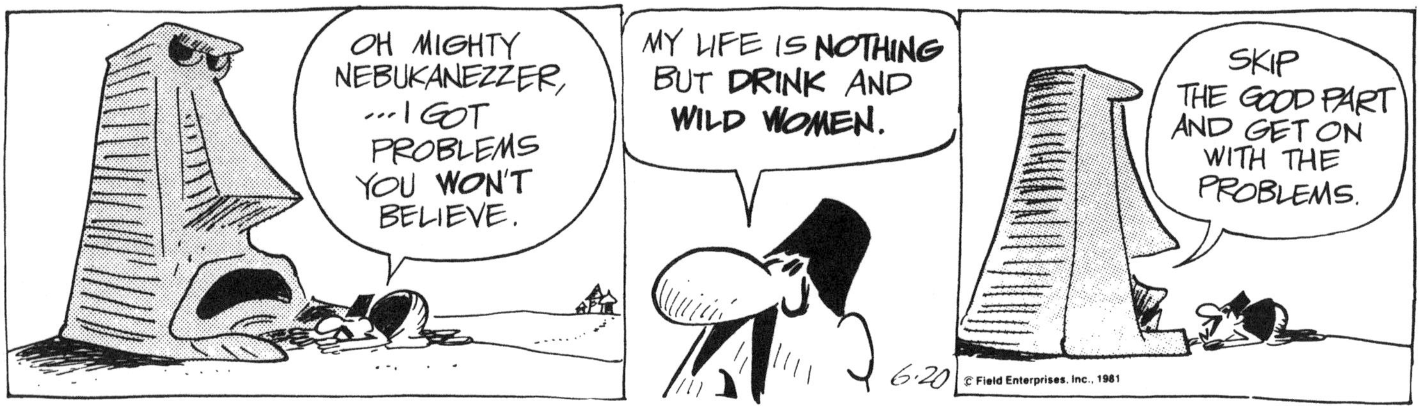
OH MIGHTY NEBUKANEZZER, ... I GOT PROBLEMS YOU WON'T BELIEVE.
MY LIFE IS NOTHING BUT DRINK AND WILD WOMEN.
SKIP THE GOOD PART AND GET ON WITH THE PROBLEMS.
6.20
© Field Enterprises, Inc., 1981

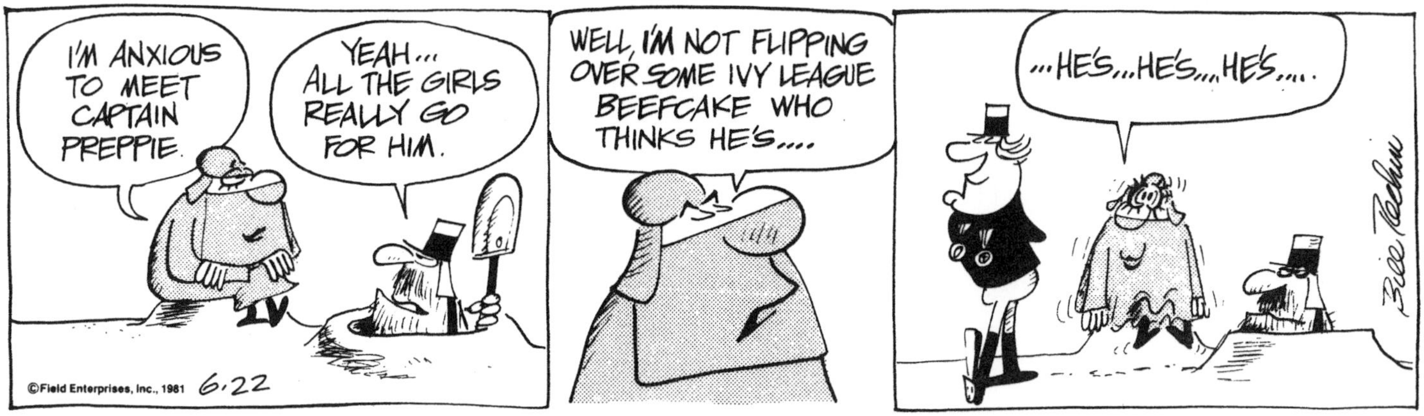
I'M ANXIOUS TO MEET CAPTAIN PREPPIE.
YEAH... ALL THE GIRLS REALLY GO FOR HIM.
©Field Enterprises, Inc., 1981
6.22
WELL, I'M NOT FLIPPING OVER SOME IVY LEAGUE BEEFCAKE WHO THINKS HE'S....
...HE'S...HE'S...HE'S.....
Bill Rechin

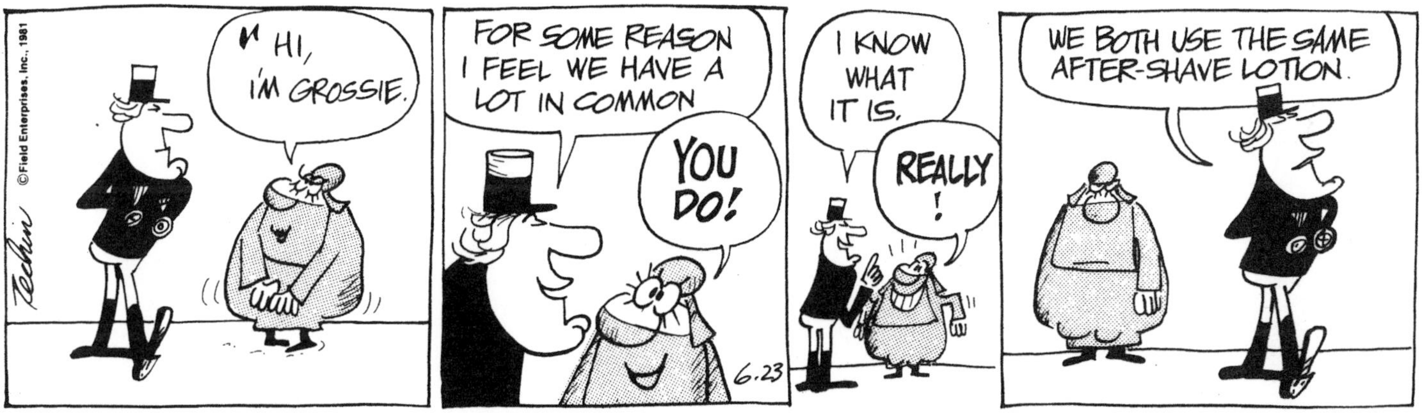
©Field Enterprises, Inc., 1981
Rechin
" HI, I'M GROSSIE.
FOR SOME REASON I FEEL WE HAVE A LOT IN COMMON
YOU DO!
6.23
I KNOW WHAT IT IS,
REALLY!
WE BOTH USE THE SAME AFTER-SHAVE LOTION.

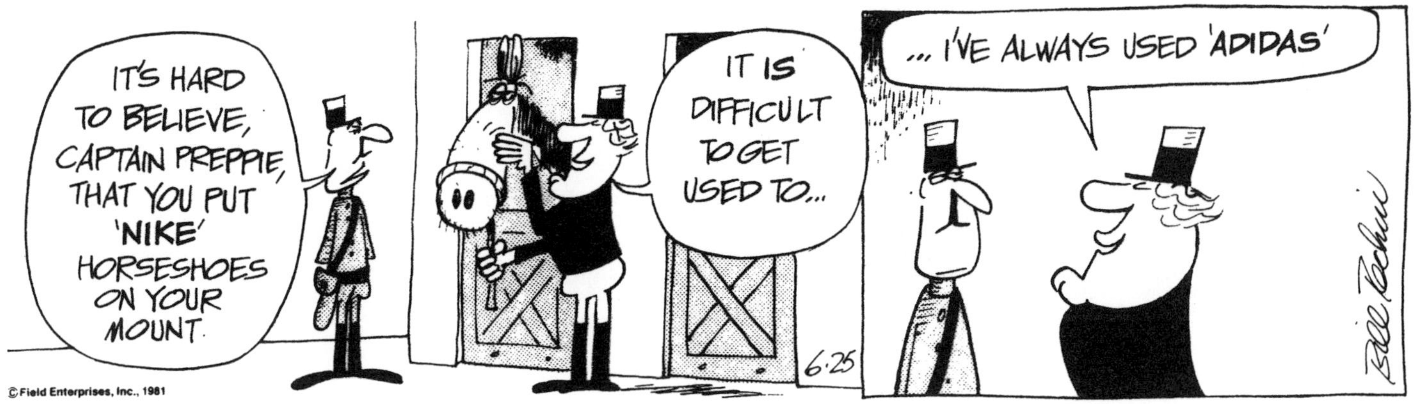
IT'S HARD TO BELIEVE, CAPTAIN PREPPIE, THAT YOU PUT 'NIKE' HORSESHOES ON YOUR MOUNT.
©Field Enterprises, Inc., 1981
IT IS DIFFICULT TO GET USED TO...
6.25
... I'VE ALWAYS USED 'ADIDAS'
Bill Rechin

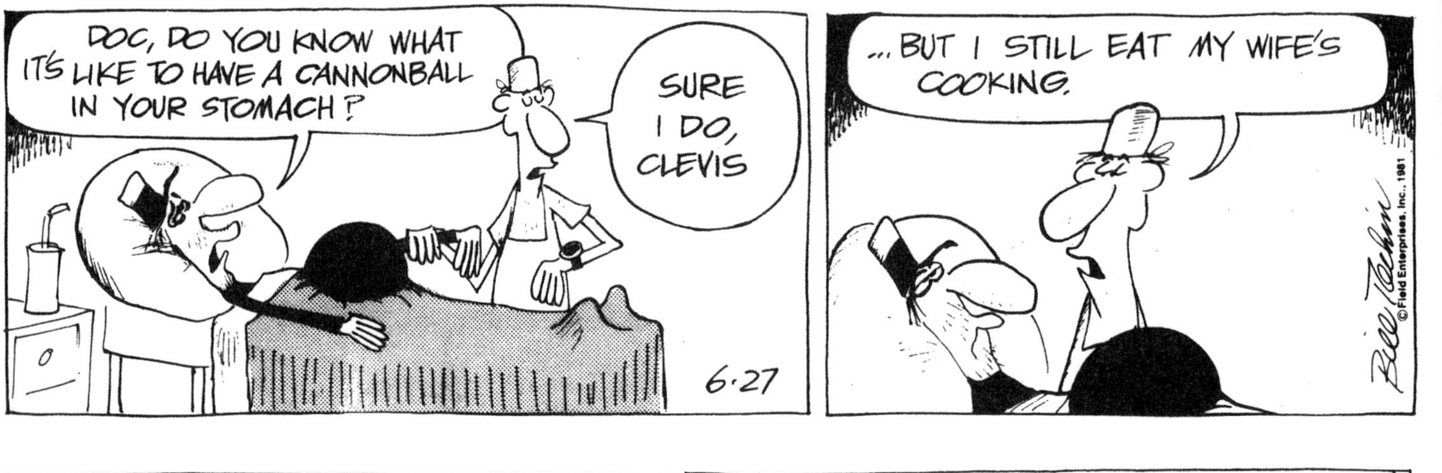
DOC, DO YOU KNOW WHAT IT'S LIKE TO HAVE A CANNONBALL IN YOUR STOMACH?
SURE I DO, CLEVIS
6·27
...BUT I STILL EAT MY WIFE'S COOKING.
©Field Enterprises, Inc., 1981
Bill Rechin

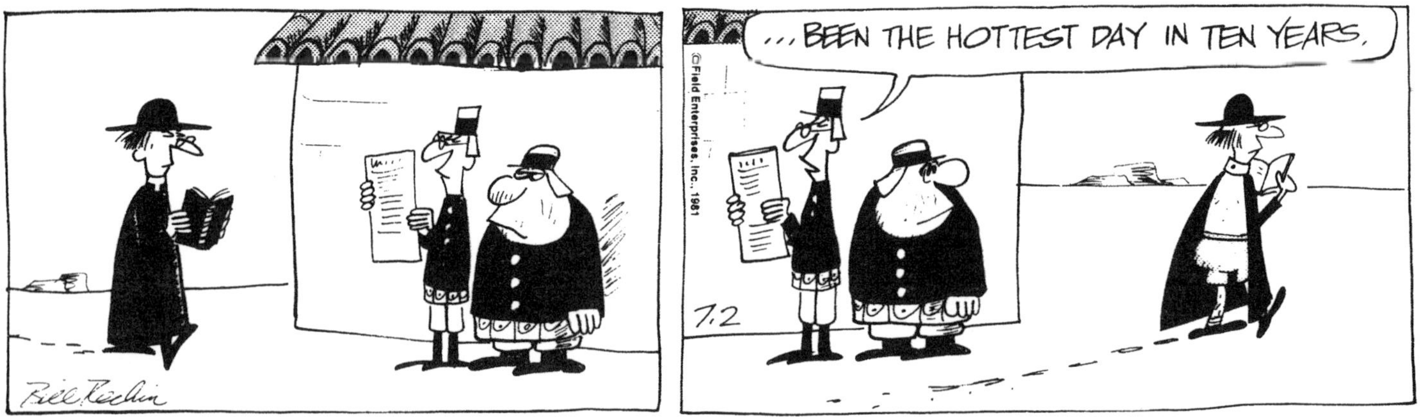
Bill Rechin
©Field Enterprises, Inc., 1981
7·2
...BEEN THE HOTTEST DAY IN TEN YEARS.

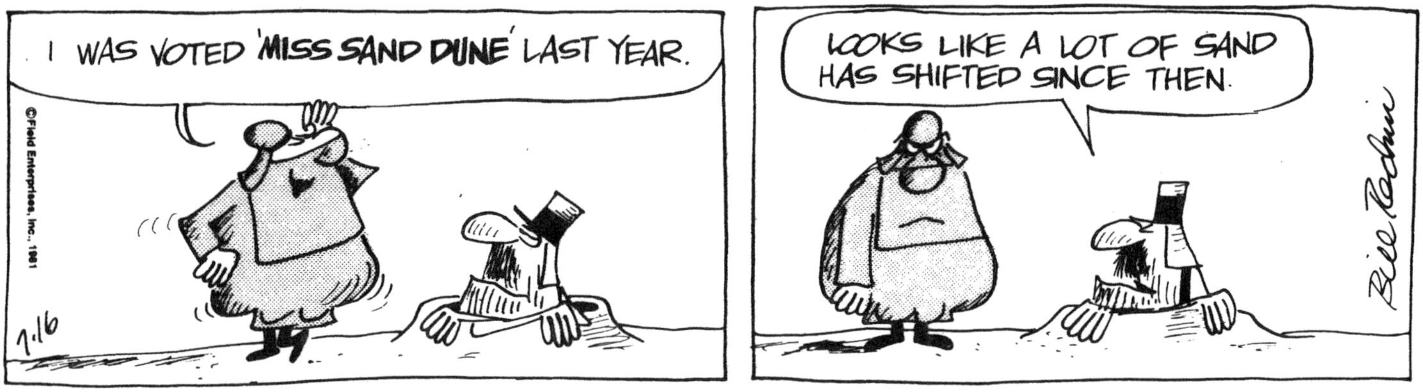
I WAS VOTED 'MISS SAND DUNE' LAST YEAR.
©Field Enterprises, Inc., 1981
7·16
LOOKS LIKE A LOT OF SAND HAS SHIFTED SINCE THEN.
Bill Rechin

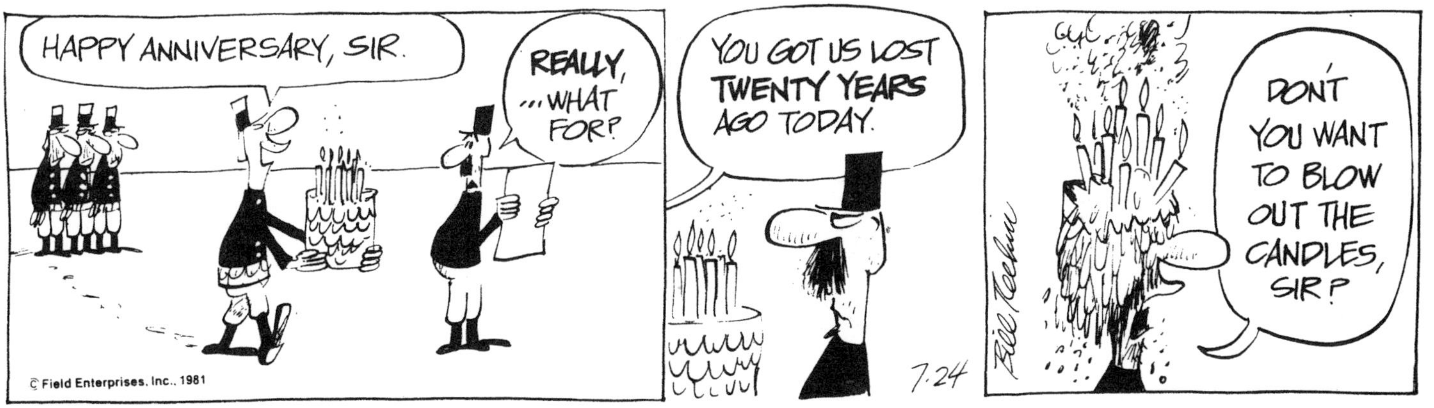
HAPPY ANNIVERSARY, SIR.
REALLY, ...WHAT FOR?
YOU GOT US LOST TWENTY YEARS AGO TODAY.
DON'T YOU WANT TO BLOW OUT THE CANDLES, SIR?
© Field Enterprises, Inc., 1981
Bill Rechin
7.24

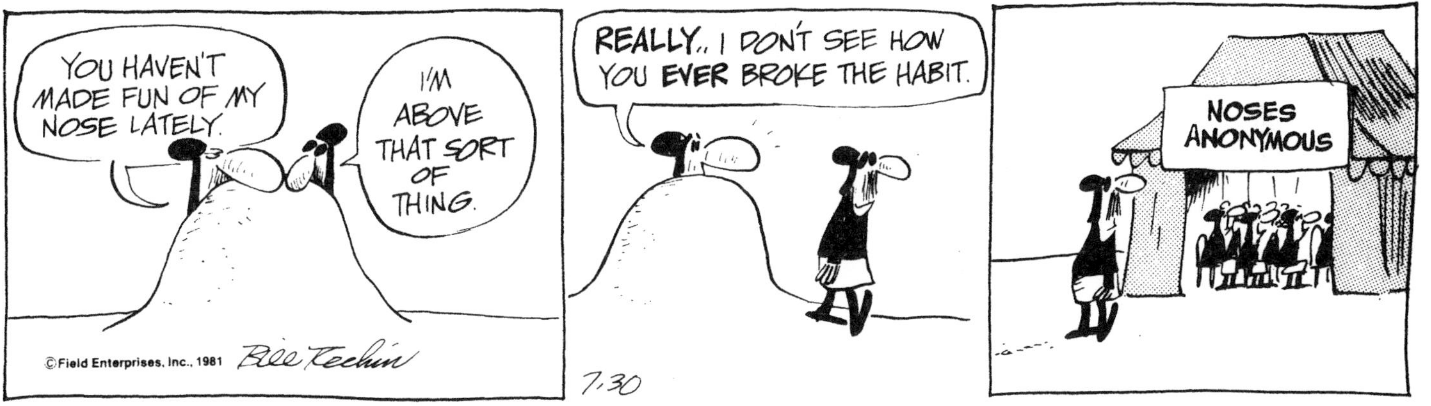
YOU HAVEN'T MADE FUN OF MY NOSE LATELY.
I'M ABOVE THAT SORT OF THING.
REALLY.. I DON'T SEE HOW YOU EVER BROKE THE HABIT.
NOSES ANONYMOUS
© Field Enterprises, Inc., 1981
Bill Rechin
7.30

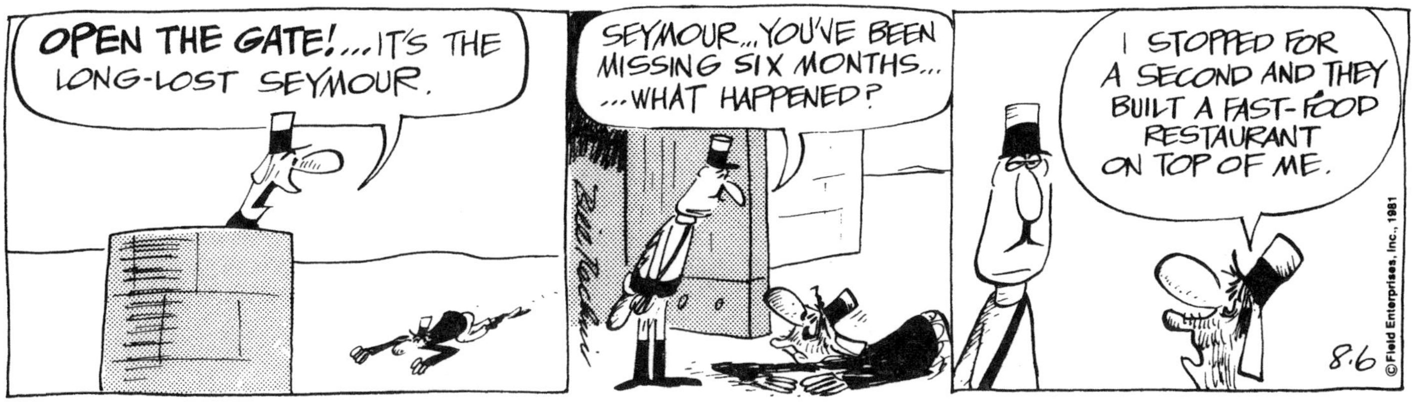
OPEN THE GATE!...IT'S THE LONG-LOST SEYMOUR.
SEYMOUR...YOU'VE BEEN MISSING SIX MONTHS... ...WHAT HAPPENED?
I STOPPED FOR A SECOND AND THEY BUILT A FAST-FOOD RESTAURANT ON TOP OF ME.
Bill Rechin
© Field Enterprises, Inc., 1981
8.6

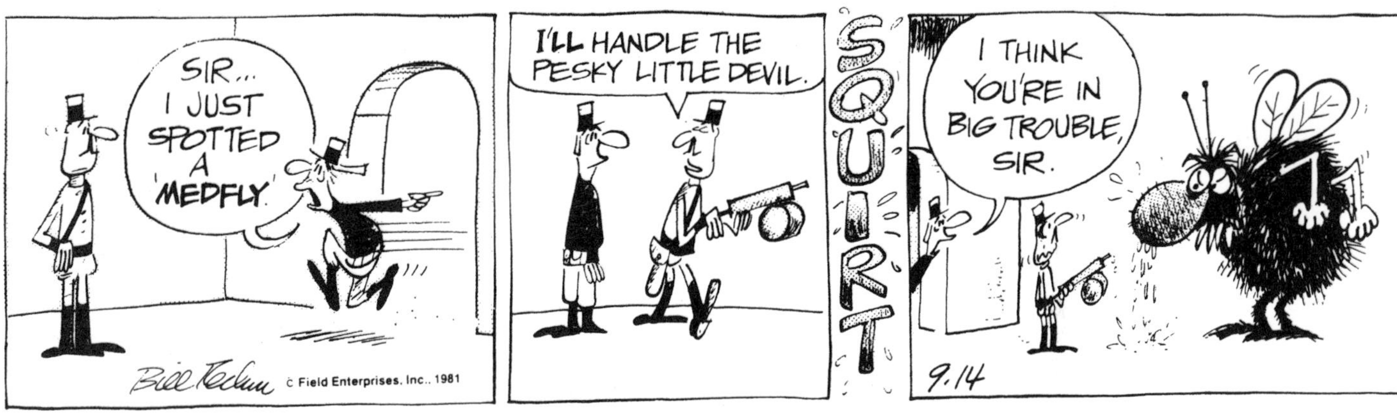
SIR... I JUST SPOTTED A MEDFLY.
Bill Rechin
© Field Enterprises, Inc., 1981
I'LL HANDLE THE PESKY LITTLE DEVIL.
SQUIRT
I THINK YOU'RE IN BIG TROUBLE, SIR.
9.14

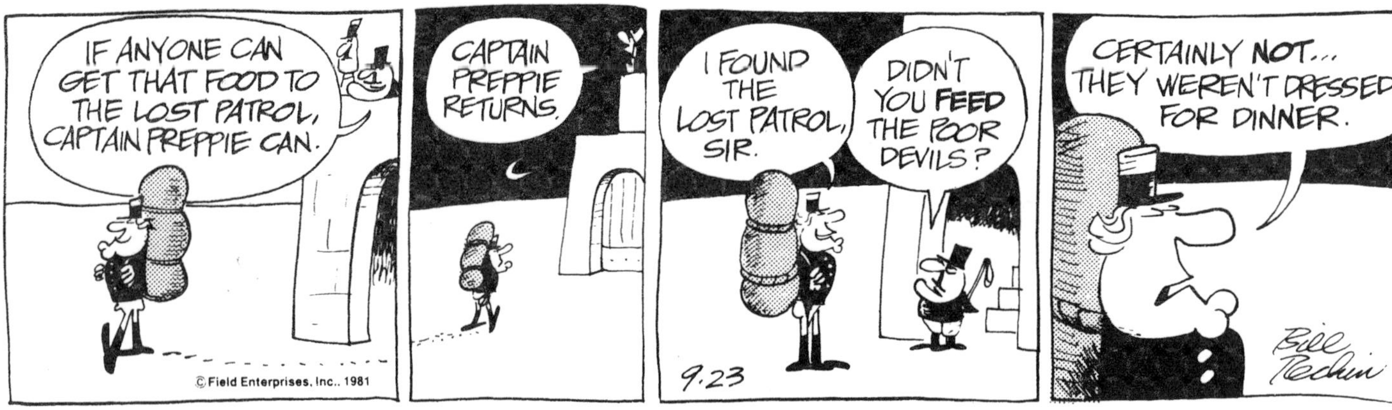
IF ANYONE CAN GET THAT FOOD TO THE LOST PATROL, CAPTAIN PREPPIE CAN.
© Field Enterprises, Inc., 1981
CAPTAIN PREPPIE RETURNS.
I FOUND THE LOST PATROL, SIR.
DIDN'T YOU FEED THE POOR DEVILS?
9.23
CERTAINLY NOT... THEY WEREN'T DRESSED FOR DINNER.
Bill Rechin

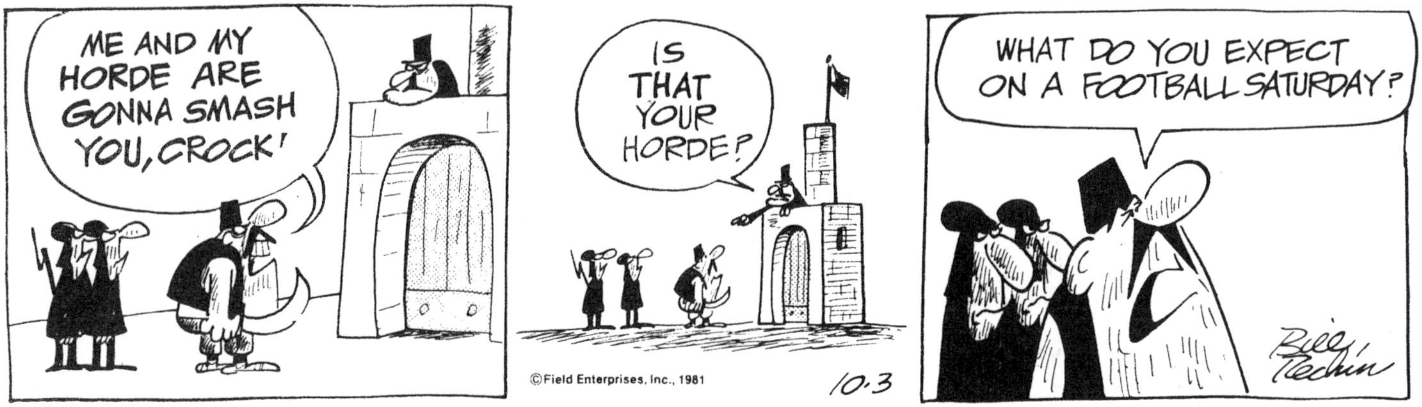
ME AND MY HORDE ARE GONNA SMASH YOU, CROCK!
IS THAT YOUR HORDE?
© Field Enterprises, Inc., 1981
10.3
WHAT DO YOU EXPECT ON A FOOTBALL SATURDAY?
Bill Rechin

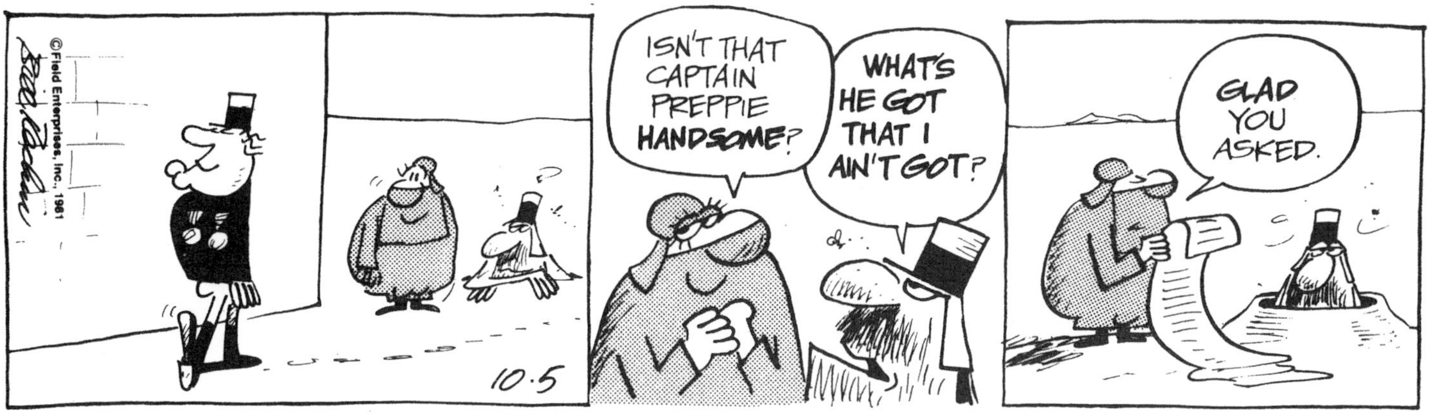
©Field Enterprises, Inc., 1981
ISN'T THAT CAPTAIN PREPPIE HANDSOME?
WHAT'S HE GOT THAT I AIN'T GOT?
GLAD YOU ASKED.
10·5

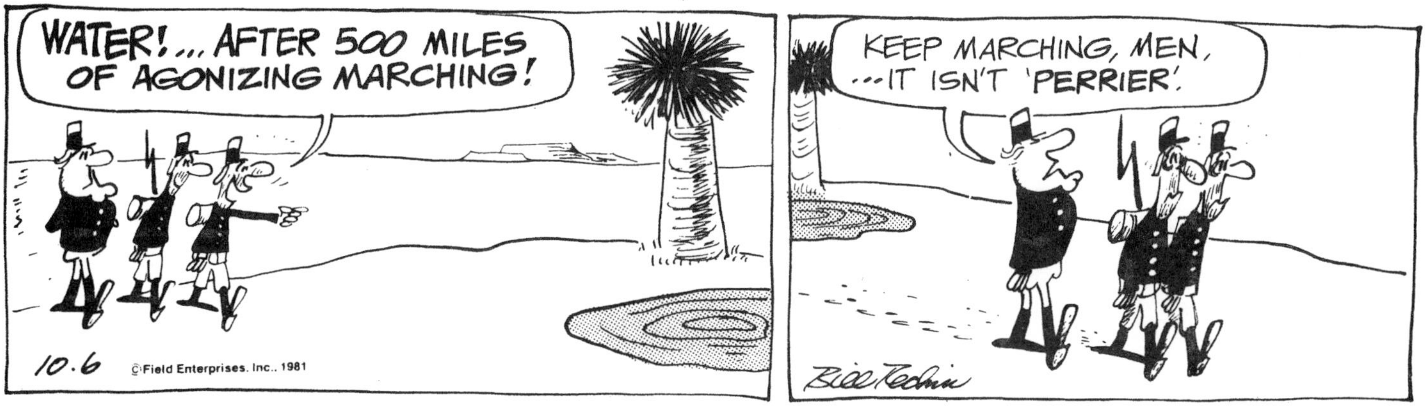
WATER! ... AFTER 500 MILES OF AGONIZING MARCHING!
10·6
©Field Enterprises, Inc., 1981
KEEP MARCHING, MEN, ... IT ISN'T 'PERRIER'.

Release Wednesday

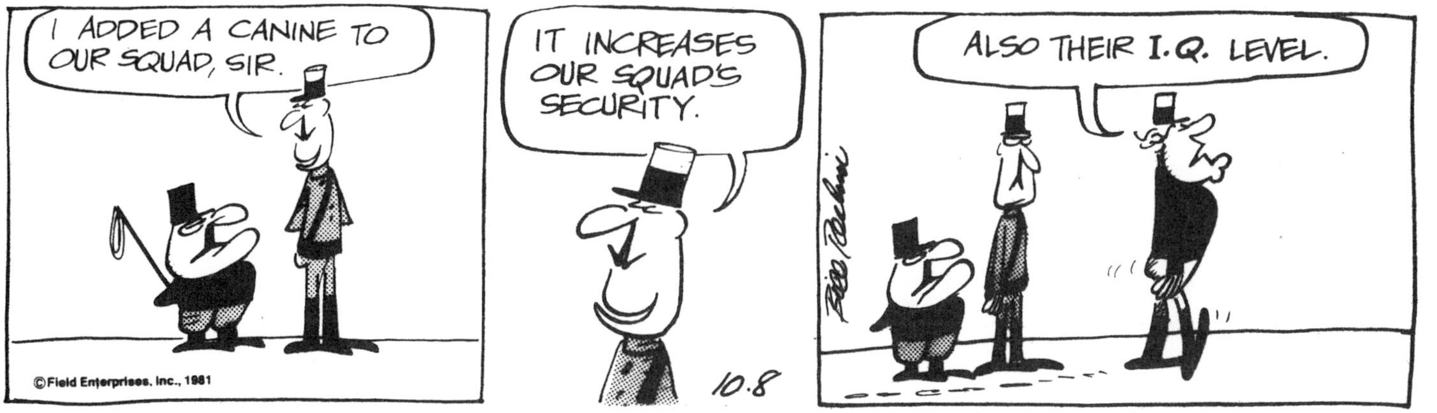
I ADDED A CANINE TO OUR SQUAD, SIR.
©Field Enterprises, Inc., 1981
IT INCREASES OUR SQUAD'S SECURITY.
10·8
ALSO THEIR I.Q. LEVEL.

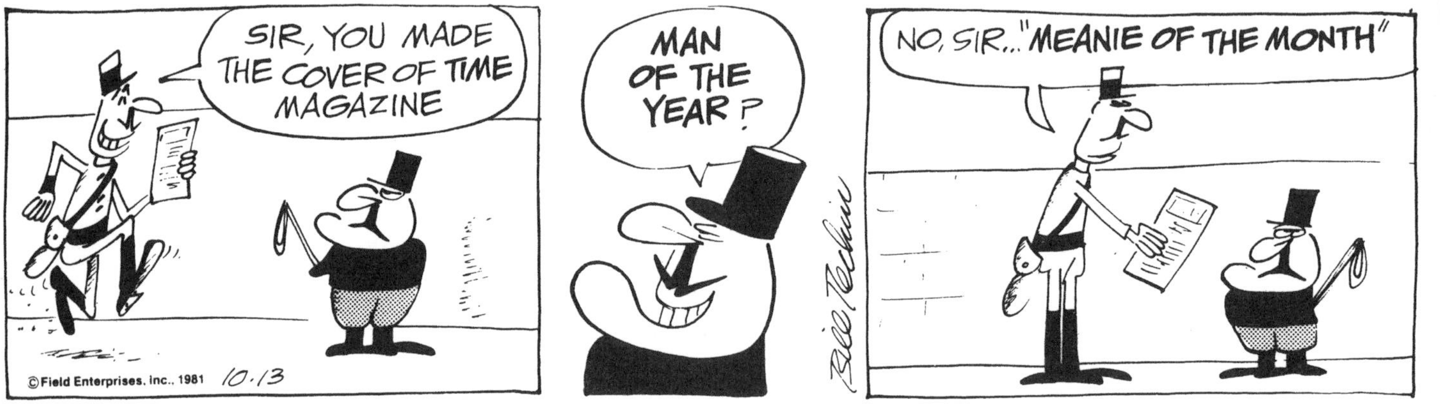
SIR, YOU MADE THE COVER OF TIME MAGAZINE
©Field Enterprises, Inc., 1981 10·13
MAN OF THE YEAR?
NO, SIR... "MEANIE OF THE MONTH"

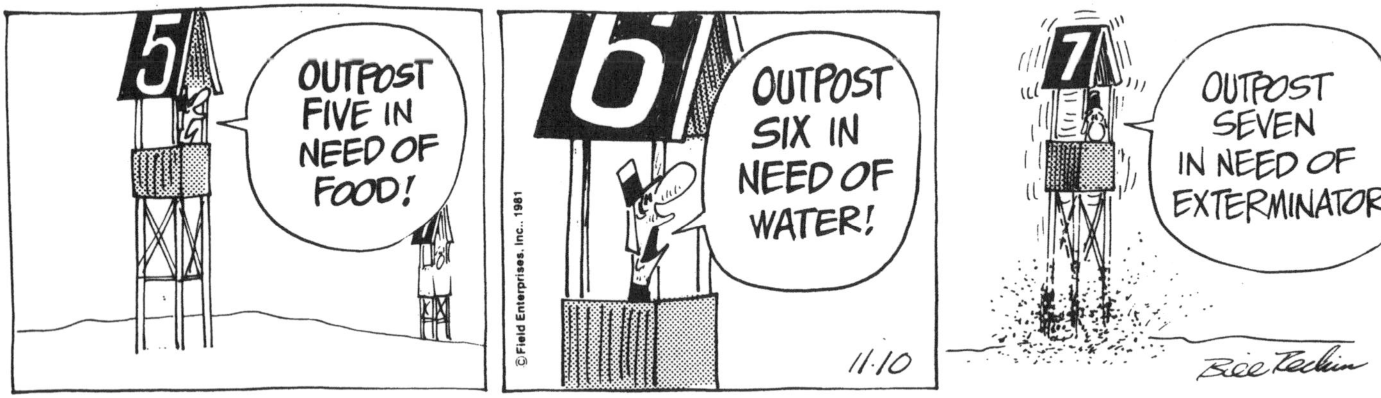
OUTPOST FIVE IN NEED OF FOOD!
OUTPOST SIX IN NEED OF WATER!
©Field Enterprises, Inc., 1981
11·10
OUTPOST SEVEN IN NEED OF EXTERMINATOR.

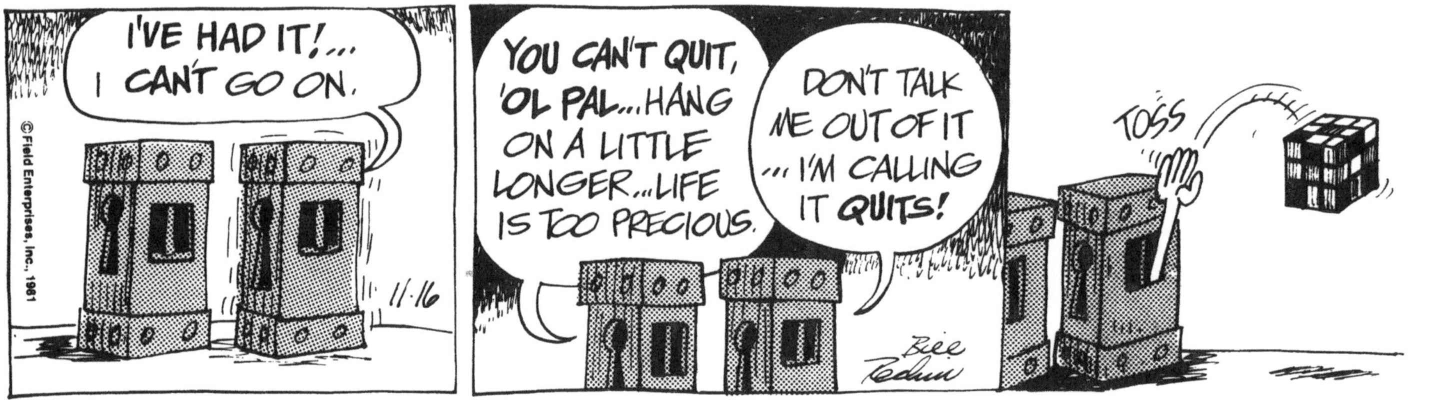
I'VE HAD IT!... I CAN'T GO ON.
©Field Enterprises, Inc., 1981
11·16
YOU CAN'T QUIT, 'OL PAL... HANG ON A LITTLE LONGER... LIFE IS TOO PRECIOUS.
DON'T TALK ME OUT OF IT ... I'M CALLING IT QUITS!
TOSS

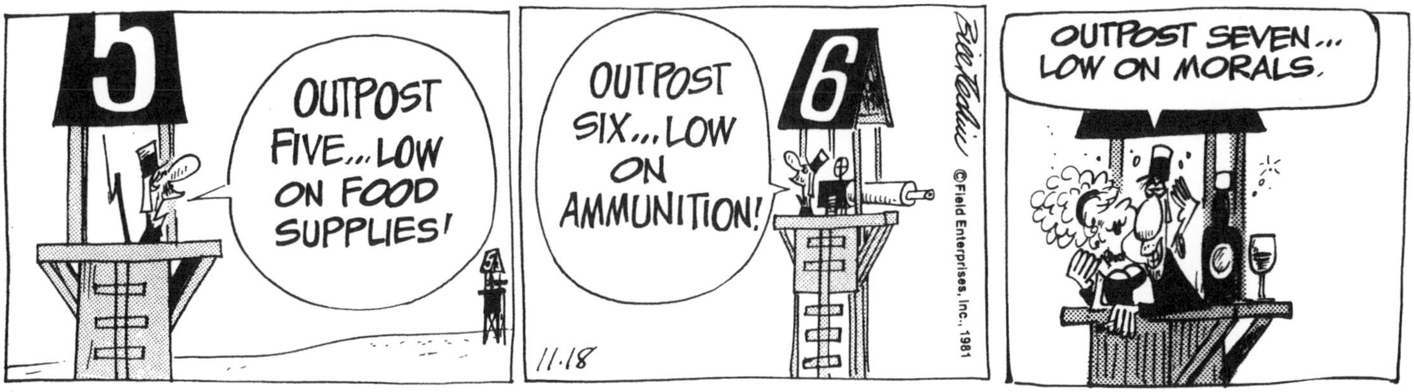
5
OUTPOST FIVE... LOW ON FOOD SUPPLIES!
OUTPOST SIX... LOW ON AMMUNITION!
6
11.18
Bill Rechin
©Field Enterprises, Inc., 1981
OUTPOST SEVEN... LOW ON MORALS.

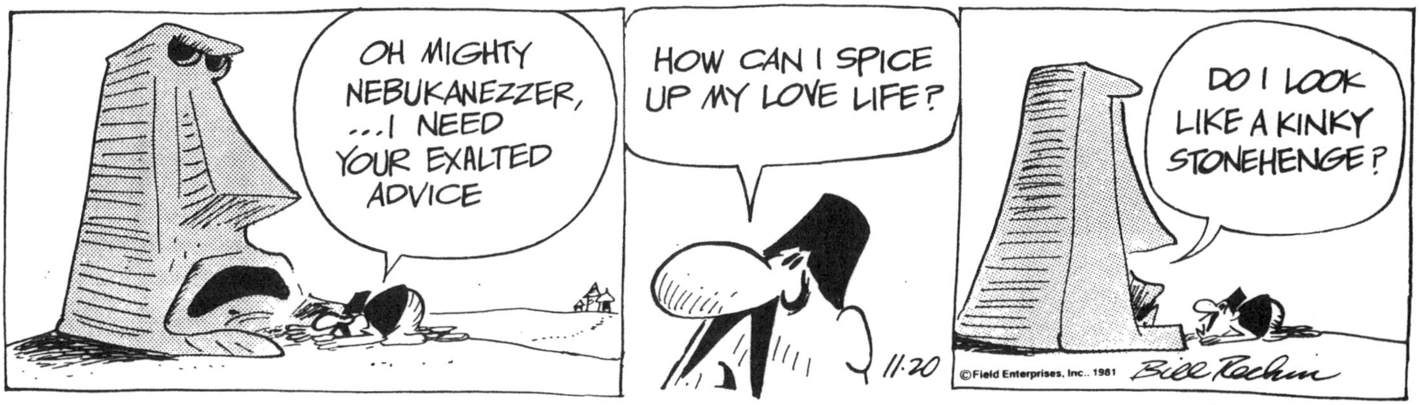
OH MIGHTY NEBUKANEZZER, ...I NEED YOUR EXALTED ADVICE
HOW CAN I SPICE UP MY LOVE LIFE?
11.20
DO I LOOK LIKE A KINKY STONEHENGE?
©Field Enterprises, Inc., 1981
Bill Rechin

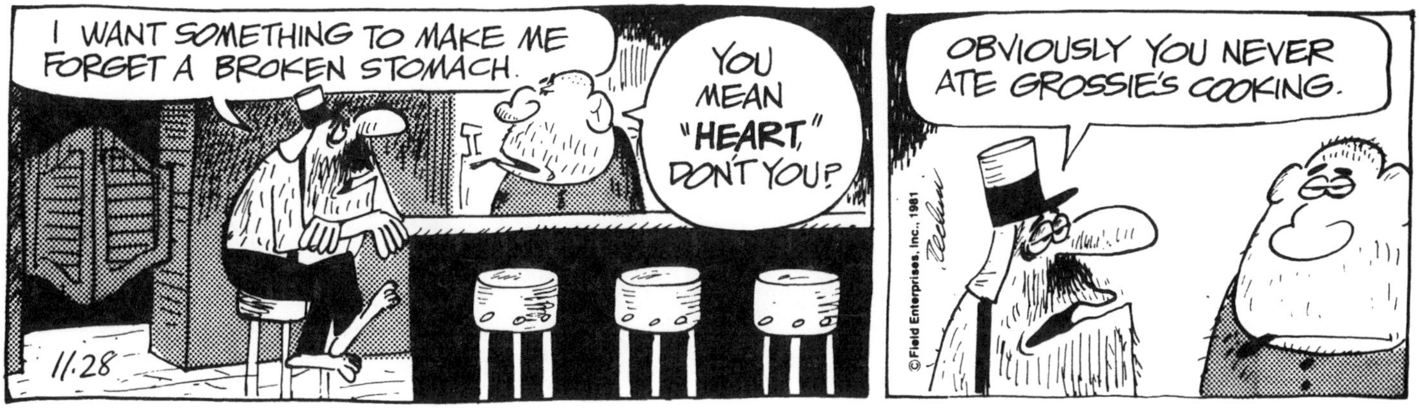
I WANT SOMETHING TO MAKE ME FORGET A BROKEN STOMACH.
YOU MEAN "HEART," DON'T YOU?
11.28
OBVIOUSLY YOU NEVER ATE GROSSIE'S COOKING.
©Field Enterprises, Inc., 1981
Rechin

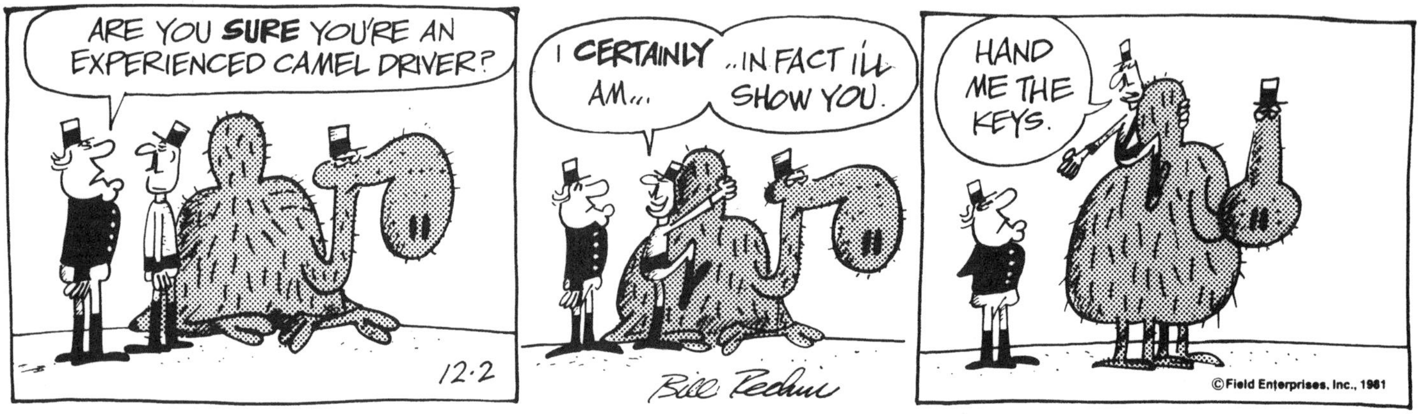
ARE YOU SURE YOU'RE AN EXPERIENCED CAMEL DRIVER?
12·2
I CERTAINLY AM...
..IN FACT I'LL SHOW YOU.
HAND ME THE KEYS.
©Field Enterprises, Inc., 1981

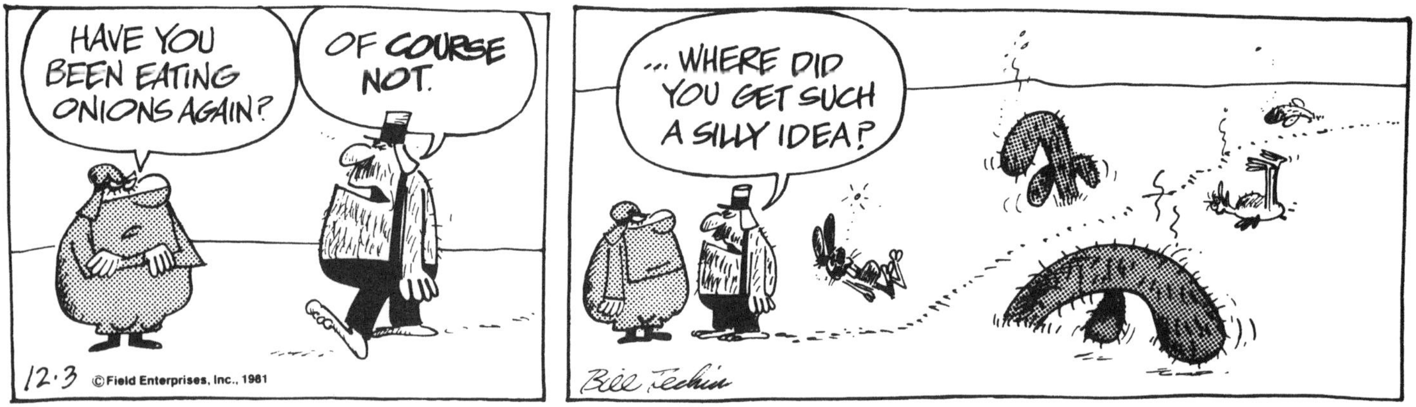
HAVE YOU BEEN EATING ONIONS AGAIN?
OF COURSE NOT.
12·3
©Field Enterprises, Inc., 1981
... WHERE DID YOU GET SUCH A SILLY IDEA?

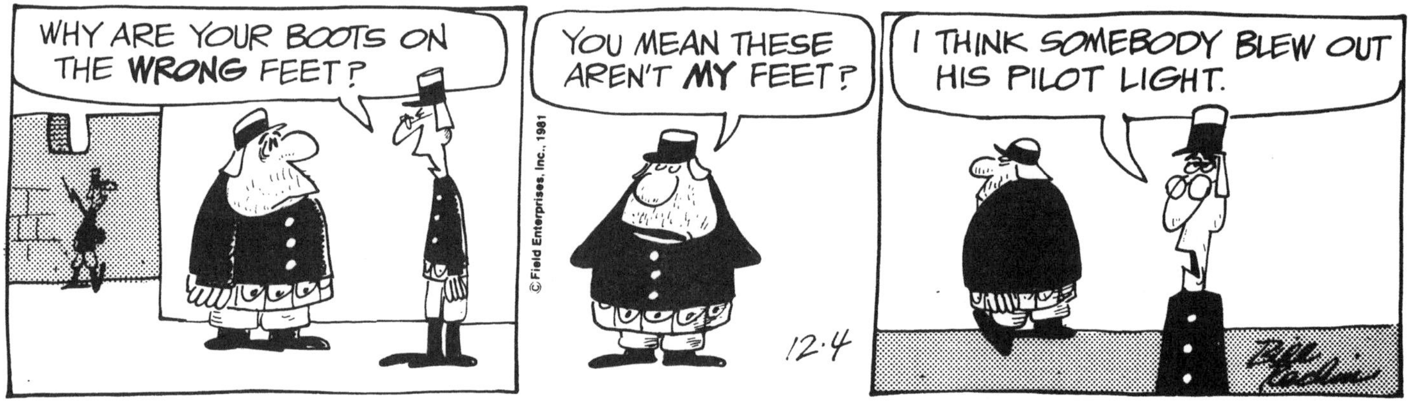
WHY ARE YOUR BOOTS ON THE WRONG FEET?
YOU MEAN THESE AREN'T MY FEET?
© Field Enterprises, Inc., 1981
12·4
I THINK SOMEBODY BLEW OUT HIS PILOT LIGHT.

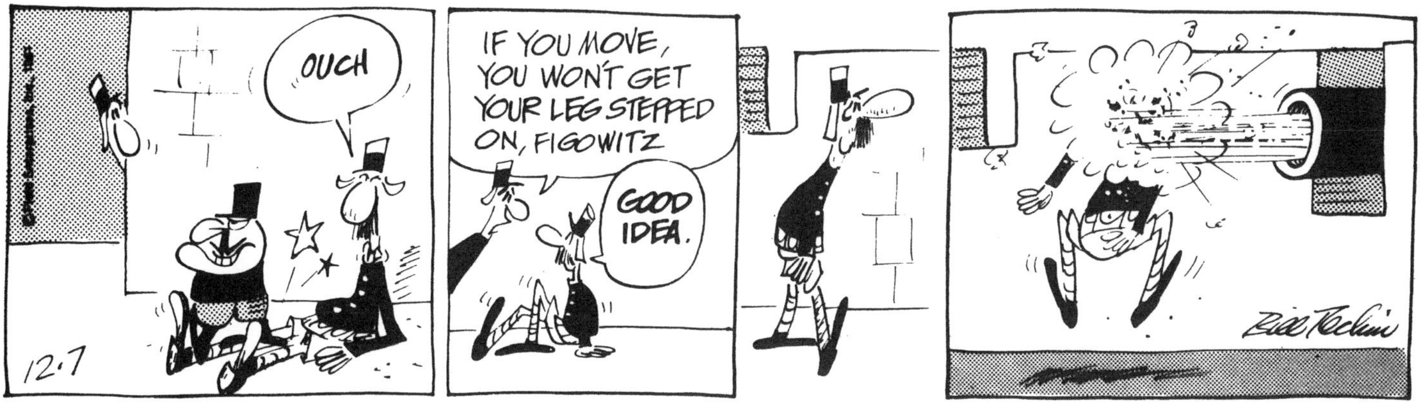
OUCH
IF YOU MOVE, YOU WON'T GET YOUR LEG STEPPED ON, FIGOWITZ
GOOD IDEA.
12·7
Bill Rechin

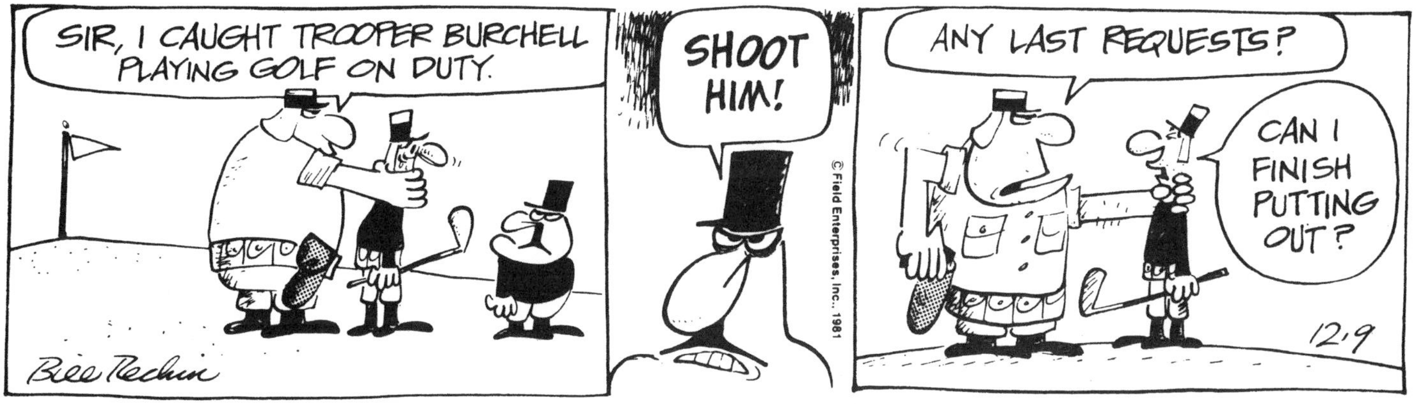
SIR, I CAUGHT TROOPER BURCHELL PLAYING GOLF ON DUTY.
Bill Rechin
SHOOT HIM!
© Field Enterprises, Inc., 1981
ANY LAST REQUESTS?
CAN I FINISH PUTTING OUT?
12·9

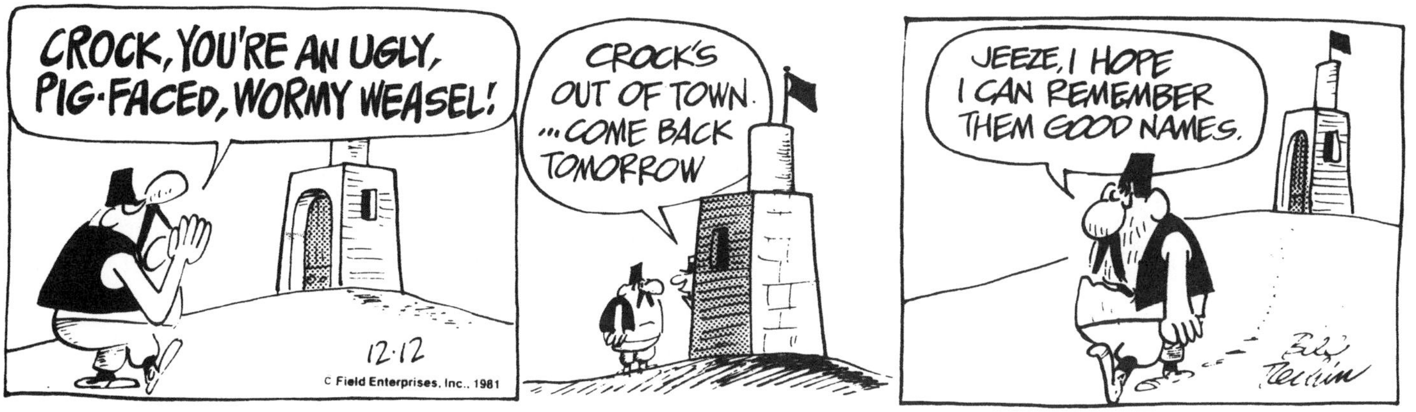
CROCK, YOU'RE AN UGLY, PIG-FACED, WORMY WEASEL!
12·12
© Field Enterprises, Inc., 1981
CROCK'S OUT OF TOWN. ...COME BACK TOMORROW
JEEZE, I HOPE I CAN REMEMBER THEM GOOD NAMES.
Bill Rechin

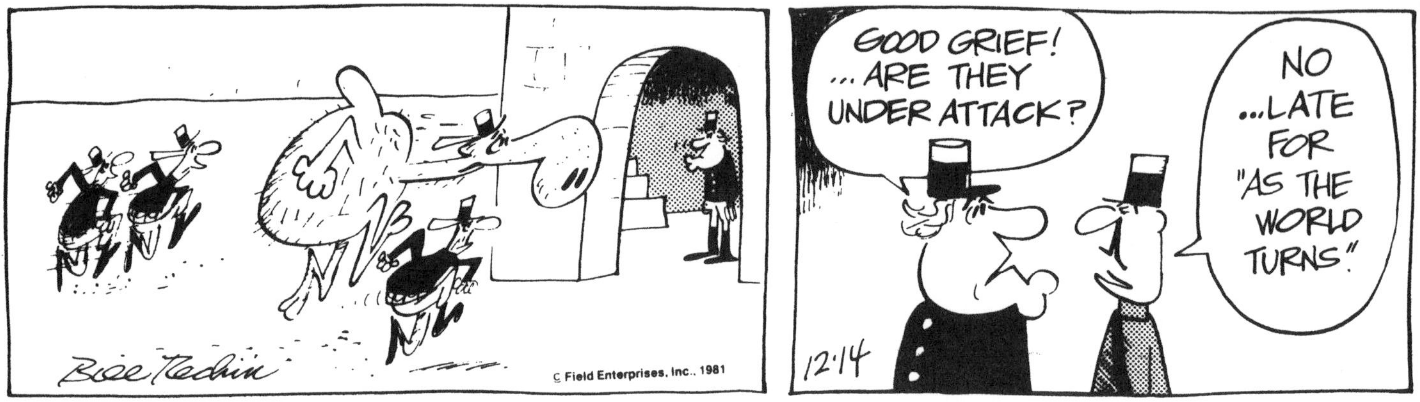
© Field Enterprises, Inc., 1981
GOOD GRIEF! ...ARE THEY UNDER ATTACK?
NO ...LATE FOR "AS THE WORLD TURNS."
12·14

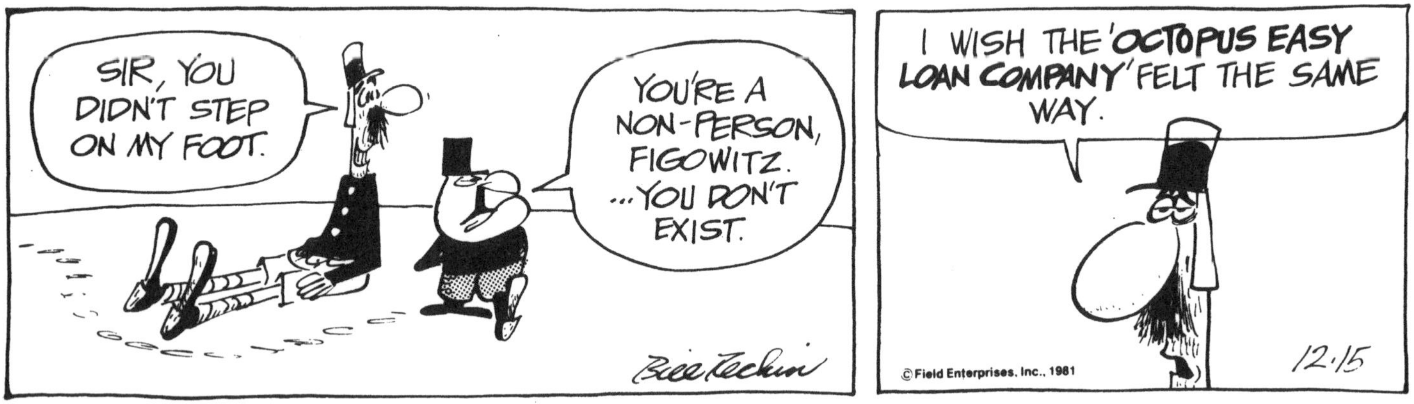
SIR, YOU DIDN'T STEP ON MY FOOT.
YOU'RE A NON-PERSON, FIGOWITZ. ...YOU DON'T EXIST.
I WISH THE 'OCTOPUS EASY LOAN COMPANY' FELT THE SAME WAY.
© Field Enterprises, Inc., 1981
12·15

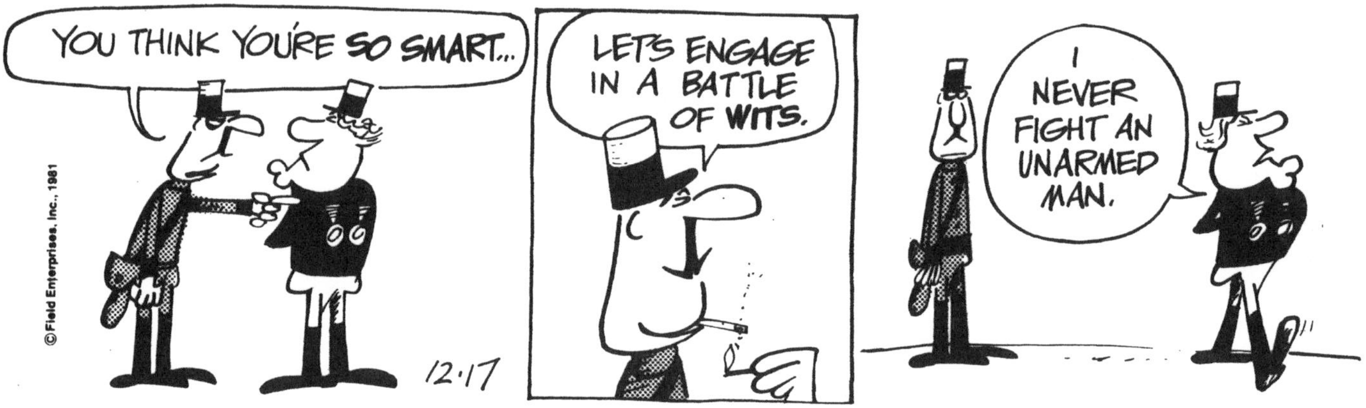
© Field Enterprises, Inc., 1981
YOU THINK YOU'RE SO SMART...
12·17
LET'S ENGAGE IN A BATTLE OF WITS.
I NEVER FIGHT AN UNARMED MAN.

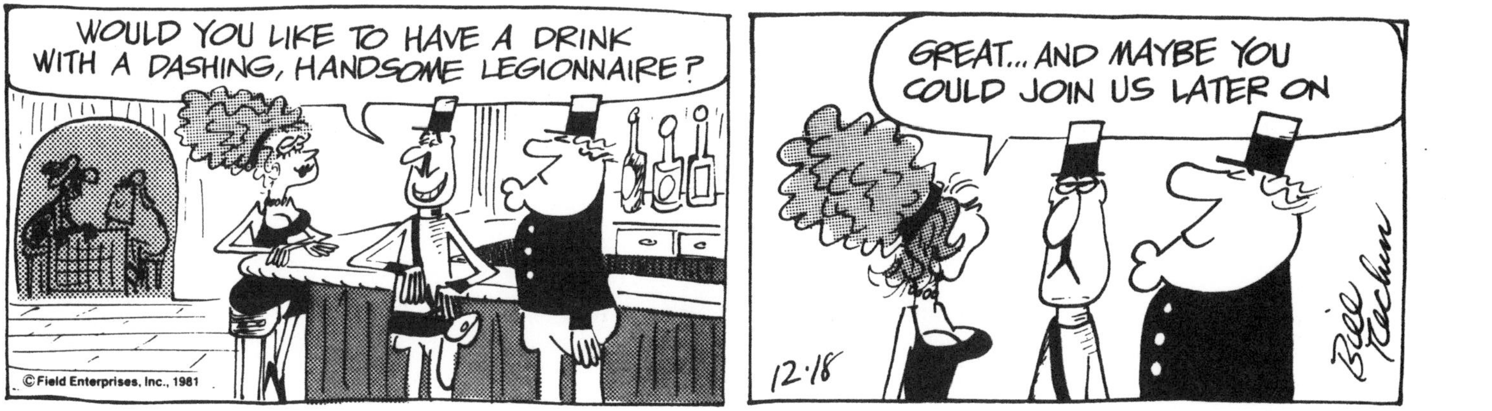
WOULD YOU LIKE TO HAVE A DRINK WITH A DASHING, HANDSOME LEGIONNAIRE?
© Field Enterprises, Inc., 1981
GREAT... AND MAYBE YOU COULD JOIN US LATER ON
12·18
Bill Rechin

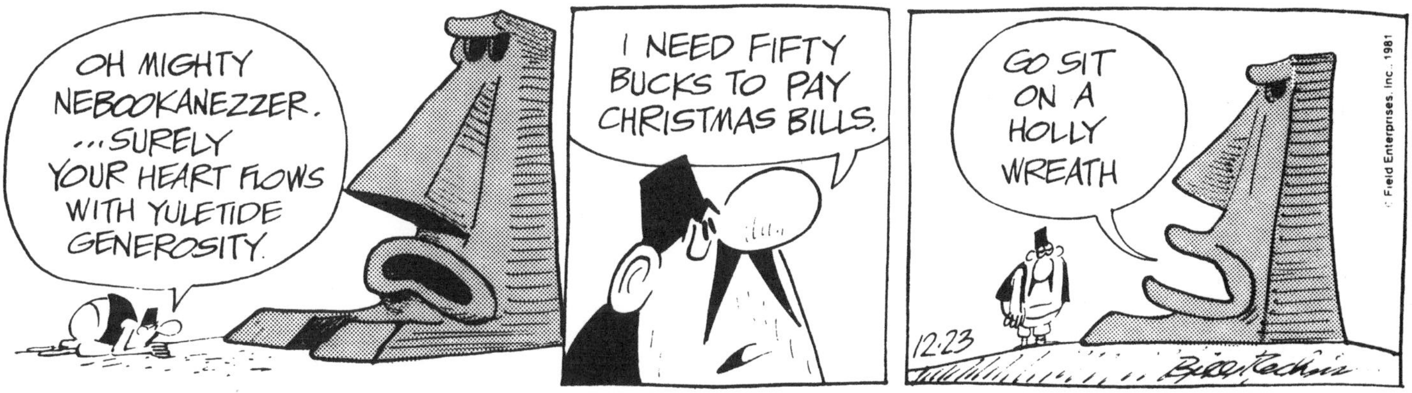
OH MIGHTY NEBOOKANEZZER. ...SURELY YOUR HEART FLOWS WITH YULETIDE GENEROSITY.
I NEED FIFTY BUCKS TO PAY CHRISTMAS BILLS.
GO SIT ON A HOLLY WREATH
© Field Enterprises, Inc. 1981
12·23
Bill Rechin

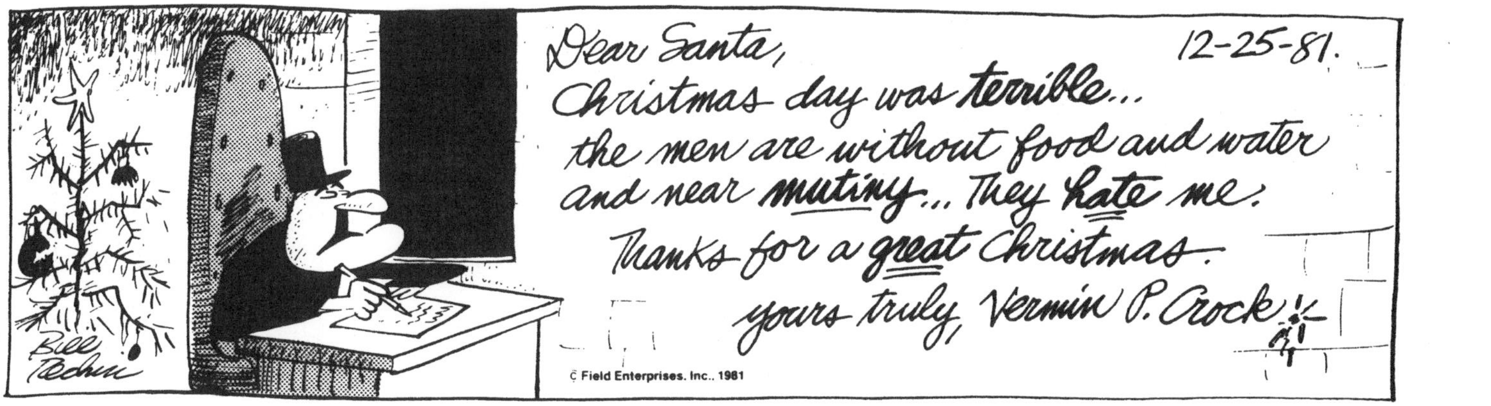
Dear Santa, 12-25-81.
Christmas day was terrible...
the men are without food and water
and near mutiny... They hate me.
Thanks for a great Christmas.
yours truly, Vermin P. Crock
Bill Rechin
© Field Enterprises, Inc., 1981

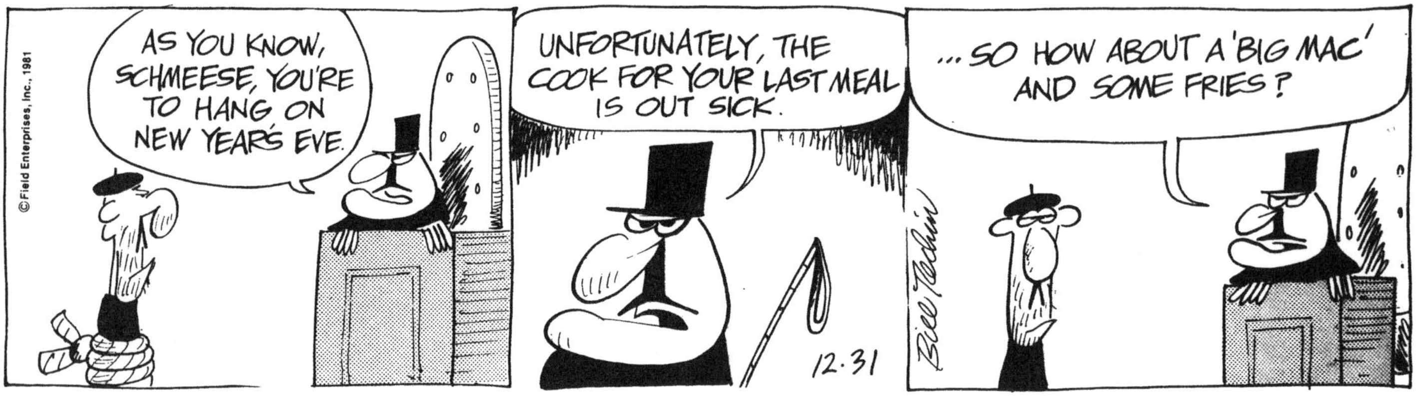
© Field Enterprises, Inc., 1981
AS YOU KNOW, SCHMEESE, YOU'RE TO HANG ON NEW YEAR'S EVE.
UNFORTUNATELY, THE COOK FOR YOUR LAST MEAL IS OUT SICK.
12·31
...SO HOW ABOUT A 'BIG MAC' AND SOME FRIES?

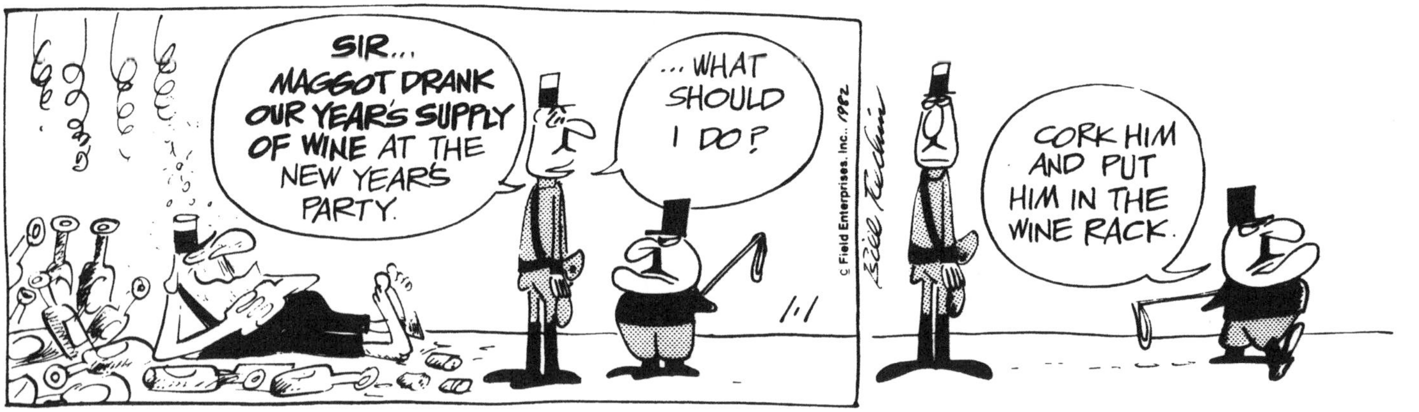
SIR... MAGGOT DRANK OUR YEAR'S SUPPLY OF WINE AT THE NEW YEAR'S PARTY.
...WHAT SHOULD I DO?
1·1
© Field Enterprises, Inc. 1982
CORK HIM AND PUT HIM IN THE WINE RACK.

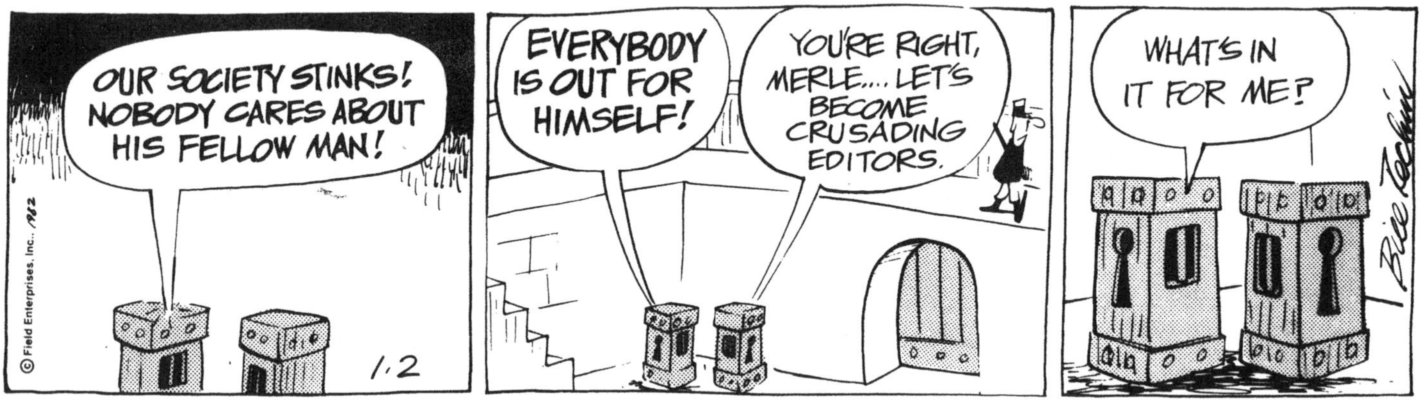
© Field Enterprises, Inc., 1982
OUR SOCIETY STINKS! NOBODY CARES ABOUT HIS FELLOW MAN!
1·2
EVERYBODY IS OUT FOR HIMSELF!
YOU'RE RIGHT, MERLE.... LET'S BECOME CRUSADING EDITORS.
WHAT'S IN IT FOR ME?

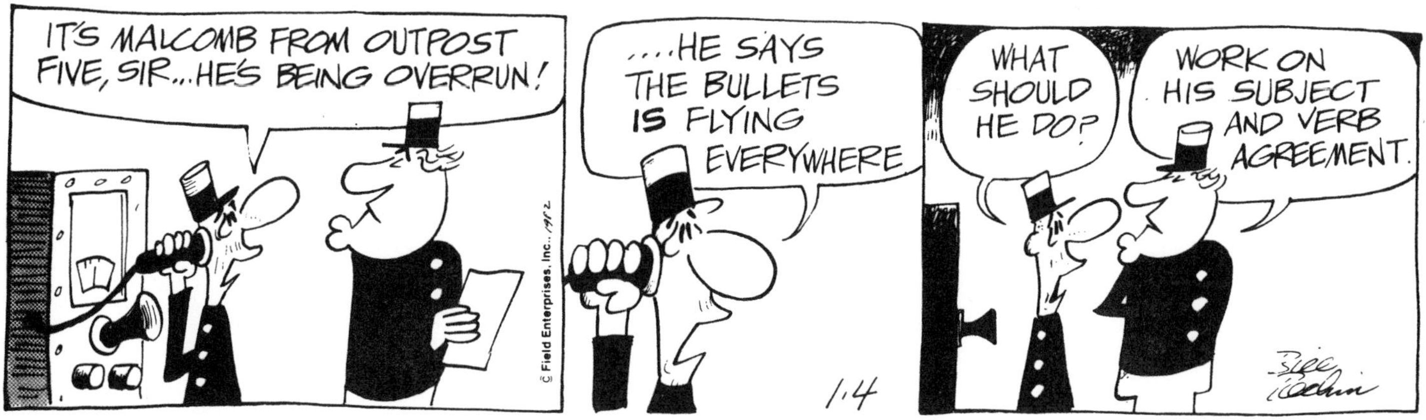
IT'S MALCOMB FROM OUTPOST FIVE, SIR... HE'S BEING OVERRUN!
© Field Enterprises, Inc., 1982
....HE SAYS THE BULLETS **IS** FLYING EVERYWHERE
1·4
WHAT SHOULD HE DO?
WORK ON HIS SUBJECT AND VERB AGREEMENT.

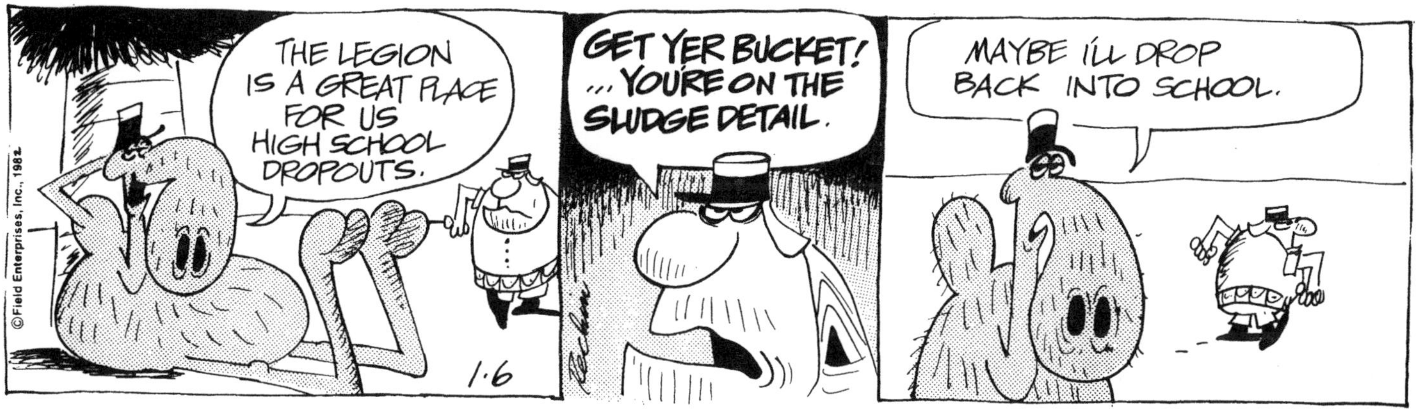
THE LEGION IS A GREAT PLACE FOR US HIGH SCHOOL DROPOUTS.
©Field Enterprises, Inc., 1982
1·6
GET YER BUCKET! ...YOU'RE ON THE SLUDGE DETAIL.
MAYBE I'LL DROP BACK INTO SCHOOL.

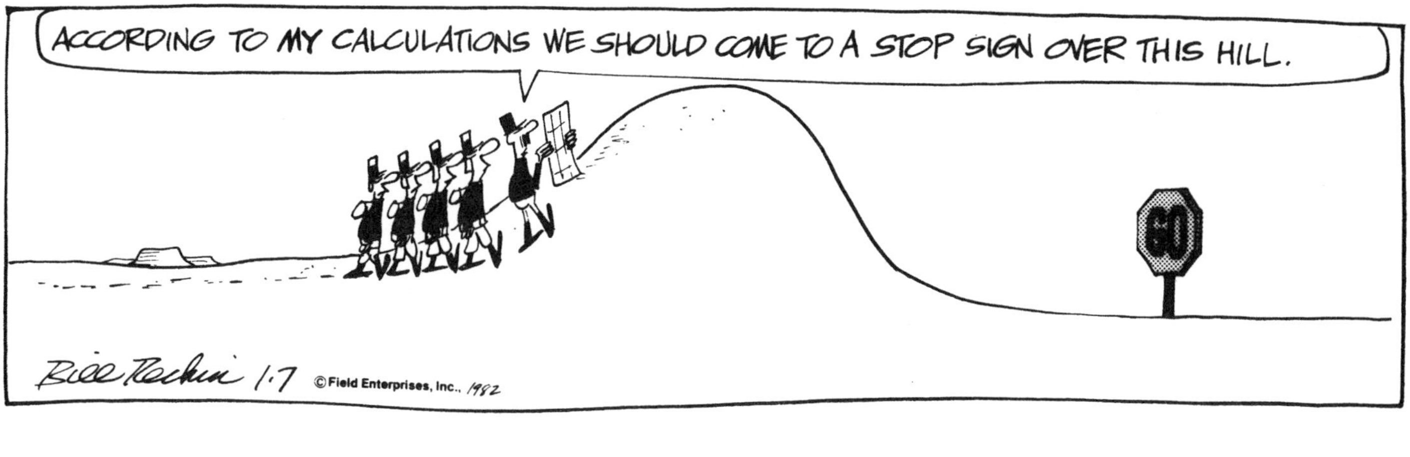
ACCORDING TO **MY** CALCULATIONS WE SHOULD COME TO A STOP SIGN OVER THIS HILL.
60
1·7 ©Field Enterprises, Inc., 1982

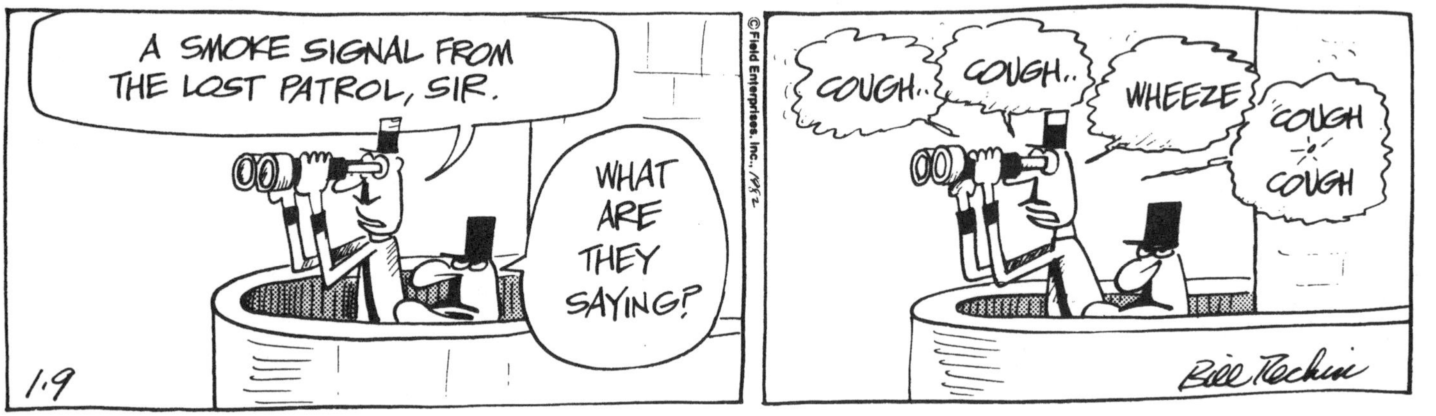
A SMOKE SIGNAL FROM THE LOST PATROL, SIR.
WHAT ARE THEY SAYING?
1.9
©Field Enterprises, Inc., 1982
COUGH..
COUGH..
WHEEZE
COUGH COUGH
Bill Rechin

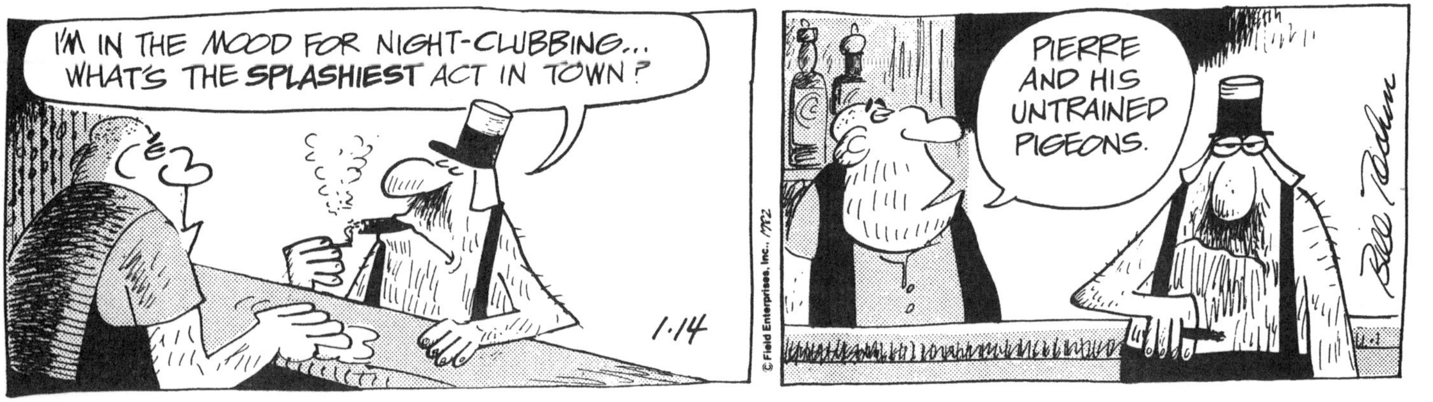
I'M IN THE MOOD FOR NIGHT-CLUBBING... WHAT'S THE **SPLASHIEST** ACT IN TOWN?
1.14
©Field Enterprises, Inc., 1982
PIERRE AND HIS UNTRAINED PIGEONS.
Bill Rechin

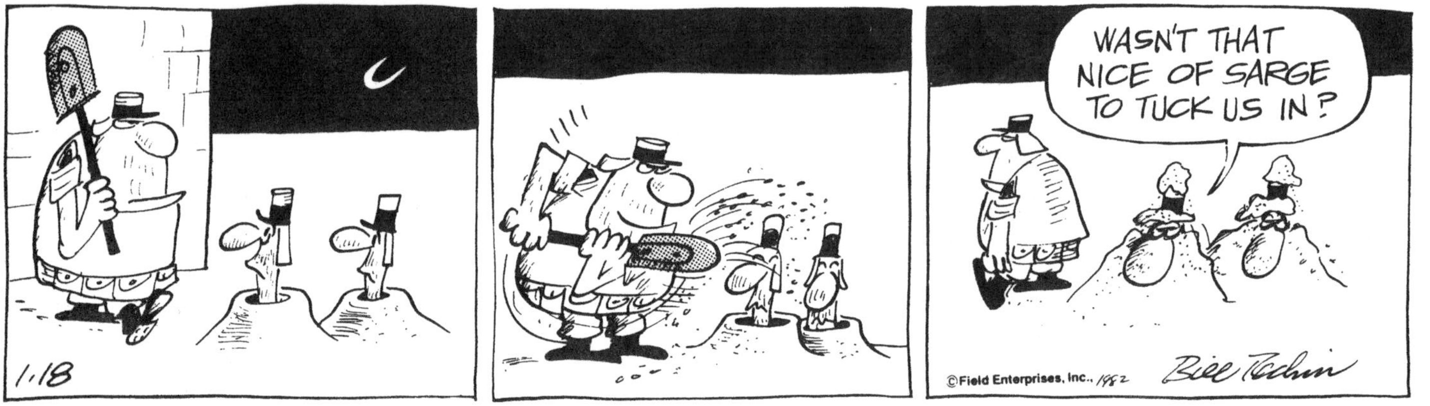
1.18
WASN'T THAT NICE OF SARGE TO TUCK US IN?
©Field Enterprises, Inc., 1982
Bill Rechin

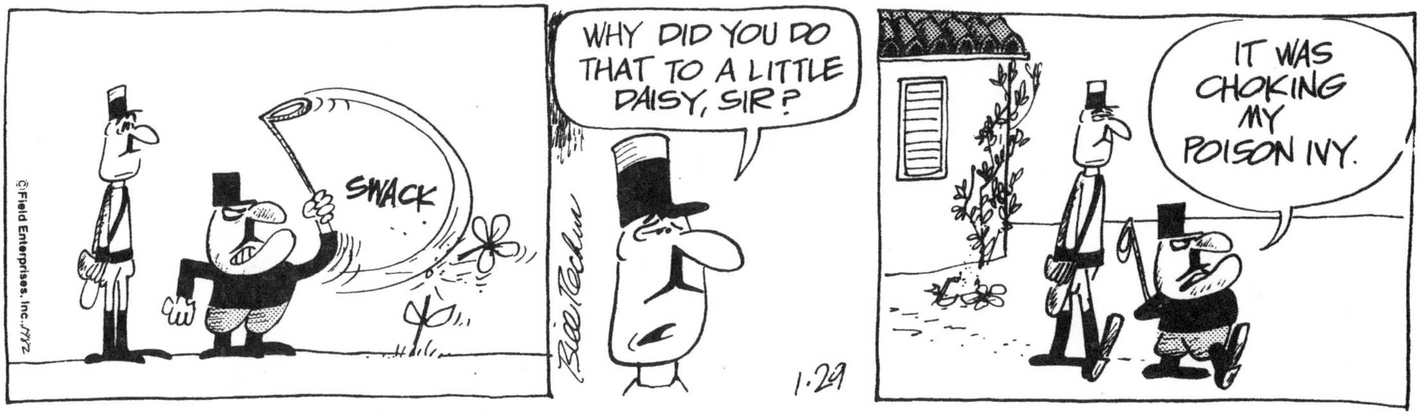
©Field Enterprises, Inc. 1982
SWACK
WHY DID YOU DO THAT TO A LITTLE DAISY, SIR?
Bill Rechin
1·29
IT WAS CHOKING MY POISON IVY.

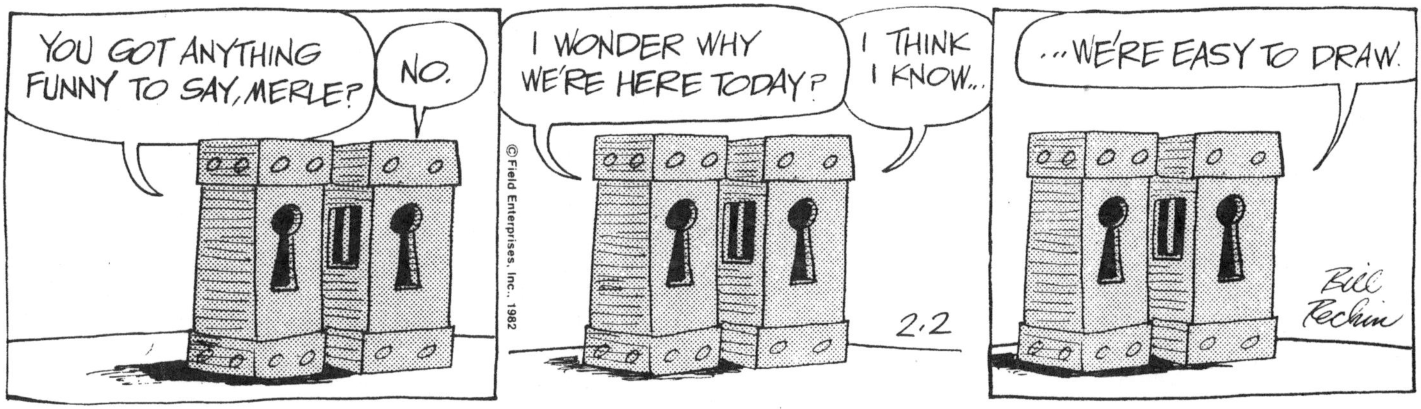
YOU GOT ANYTHING FUNNY TO SAY, MERLE?
NO.
© Field Enterprises, Inc. 1982
I WONDER WHY WE'RE HERE TODAY?
I THINK I KNOW...
2·2
...WE'RE EASY TO DRAW.
Bill Rechin

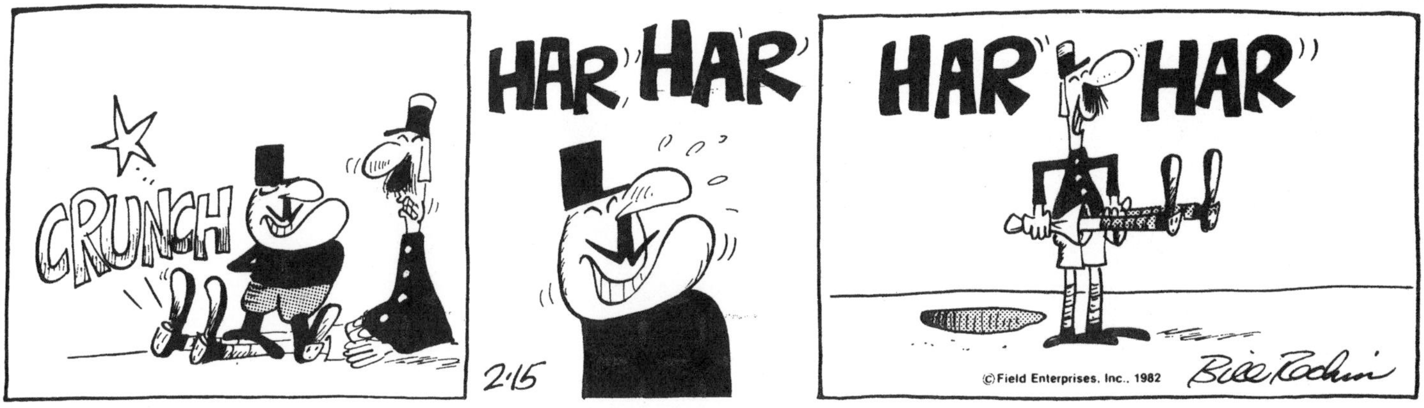
CRUNCH
2·15
HAR HAR
HAR HAR
©Field Enterprises, Inc., 1982
Bill Rechin

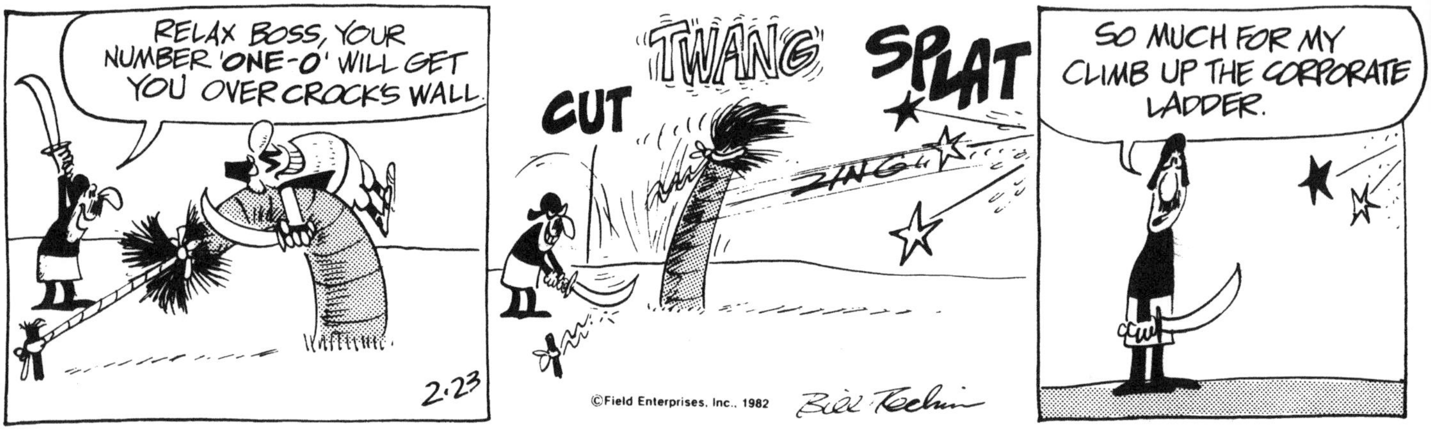
RELAX BOSS, YOUR NUMBER 'ONE-O' WILL GET YOU OVER CROCK'S WALL.
2·23
CUT
TWANG
ZING
SPLAT
©Field Enterprises, Inc., 1982
Bill Rechin
SO MUCH FOR MY CLIMB UP THE CORPORATE LADDER.

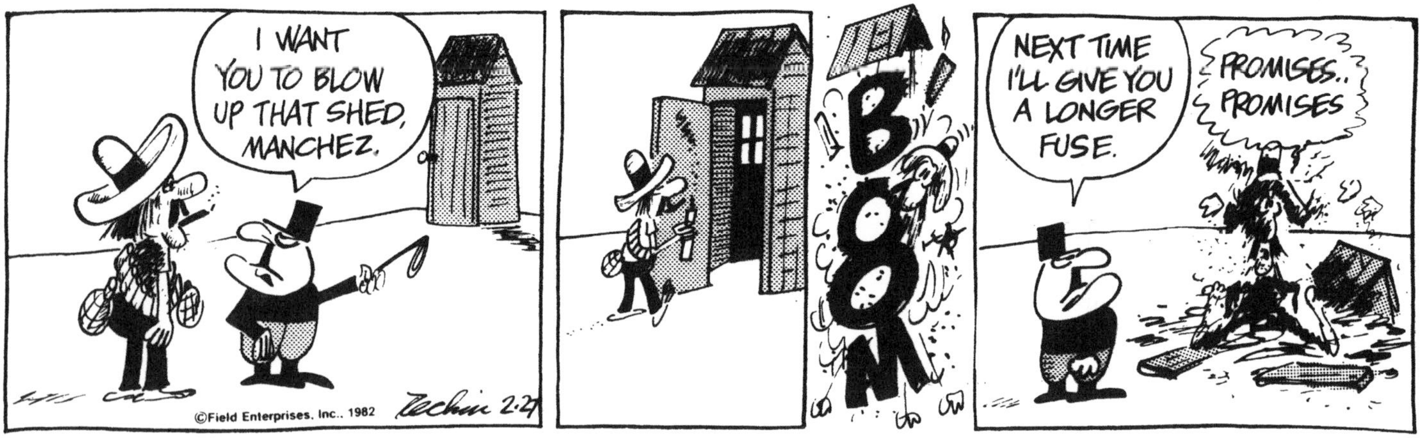
I WANT YOU TO BLOW UP THAT SHED, MANCHEZ.
©Field Enterprises, Inc., 1982
Rechin 2·27
BOOM
NEXT TIME I'LL GIVE YOU A LONGER FUSE.
PROMISES.. PROMISES

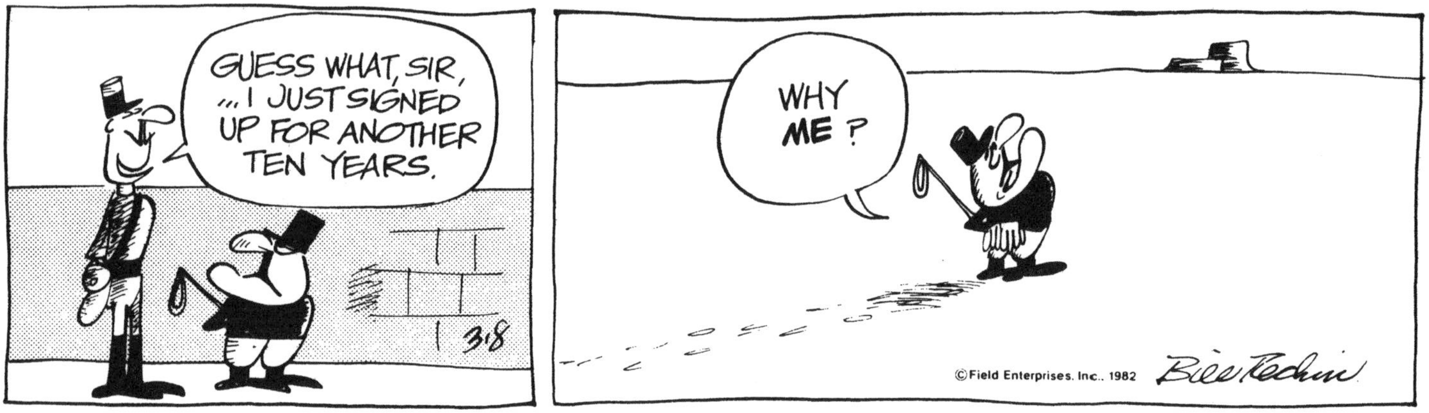
GUESS WHAT, SIR, ...I JUST SIGNED UP FOR ANOTHER TEN YEARS.
3·8
WHY ME?
©Field Enterprises, Inc., 1982
Bill Rechin

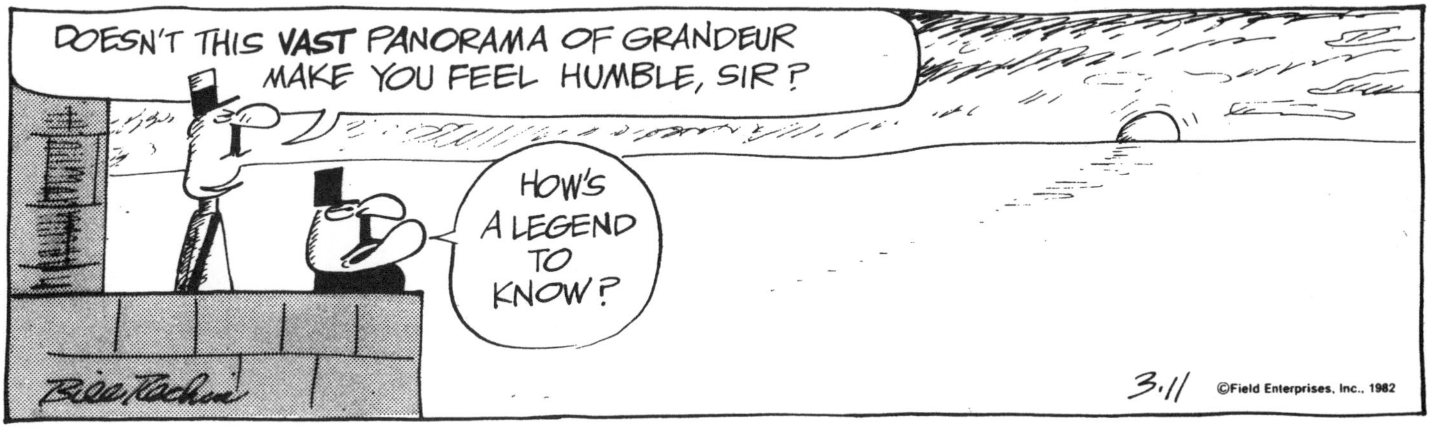
DOESN'T THIS VAST PANORAMA OF GRANDEUR MAKE YOU FEEL HUMBLE, SIR?
HOW'S A LEGEND TO KNOW?
3.11
©Field Enterprises, Inc., 1982

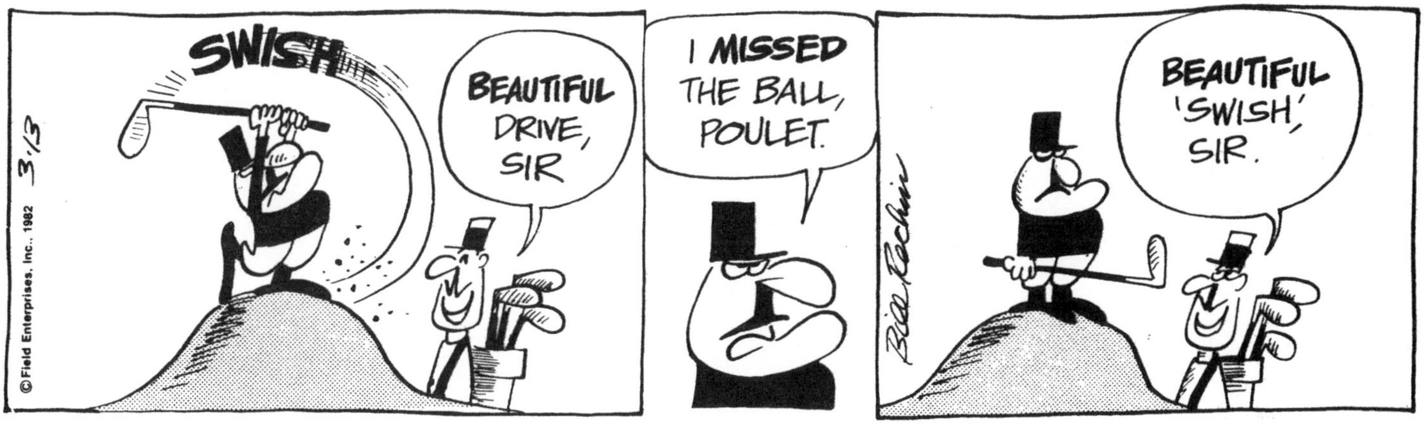
SWISH
BEAUTIFUL DRIVE, SIR
I MISSED THE BALL, POULET.
BEAUTIFUL 'SWISH,' SIR.
3.13
©Field Enterprises, Inc., 1982

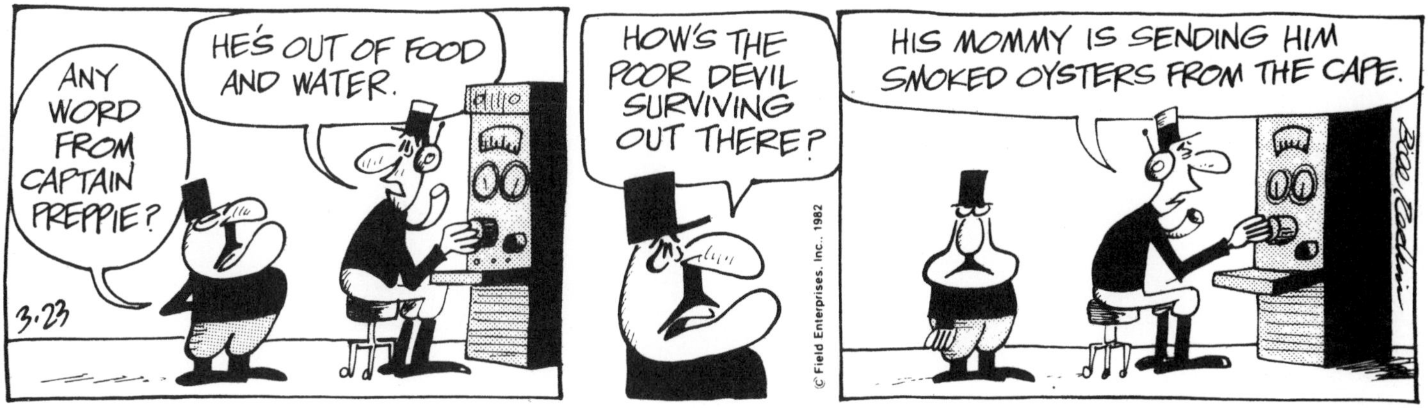
ANY WORD FROM CAPTAIN PREPPIE?
HE'S OUT OF FOOD AND WATER.
HOW'S THE POOR DEVIL SURVIVING OUT THERE?
HIS MOMMY IS SENDING HIM SMOKED OYSTERS FROM THE CAPE.
3.23
© Field Enterprises, Inc., 1982

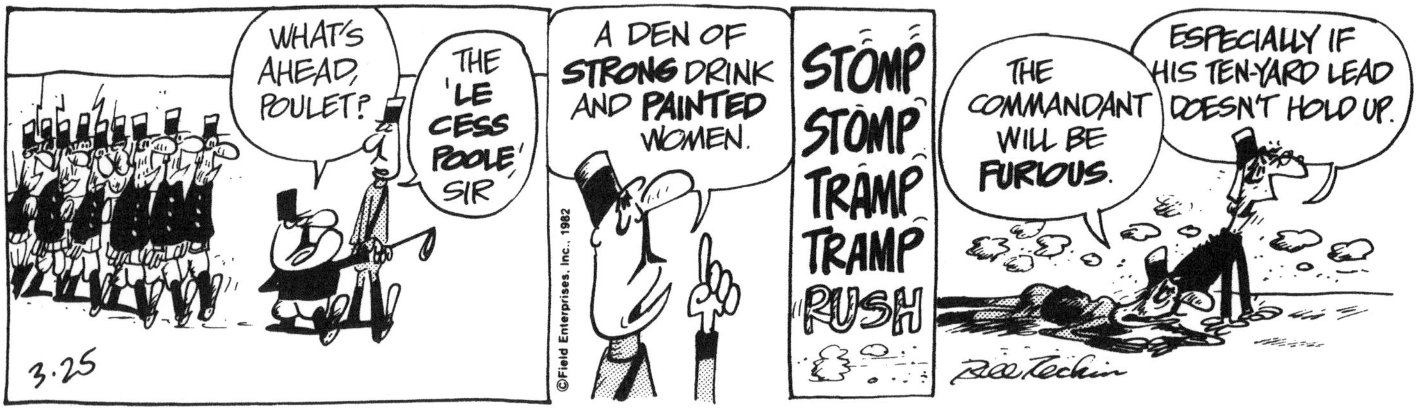
WHAT'S AHEAD, POULET?
THE 'LE CESS POOLE' SIR
A DEN OF STRONG DRINK AND PAINTED WOMEN.
STOMP STOMP TRAMP TRAMP RUSH
THE COMMANDANT WILL BE FURIOUS.
ESPECIALLY IF HIS TEN-YARD LEAD DOESN'T HOLD UP.
3.25
©Field Enterprises, Inc., 1982
Bill Rechin

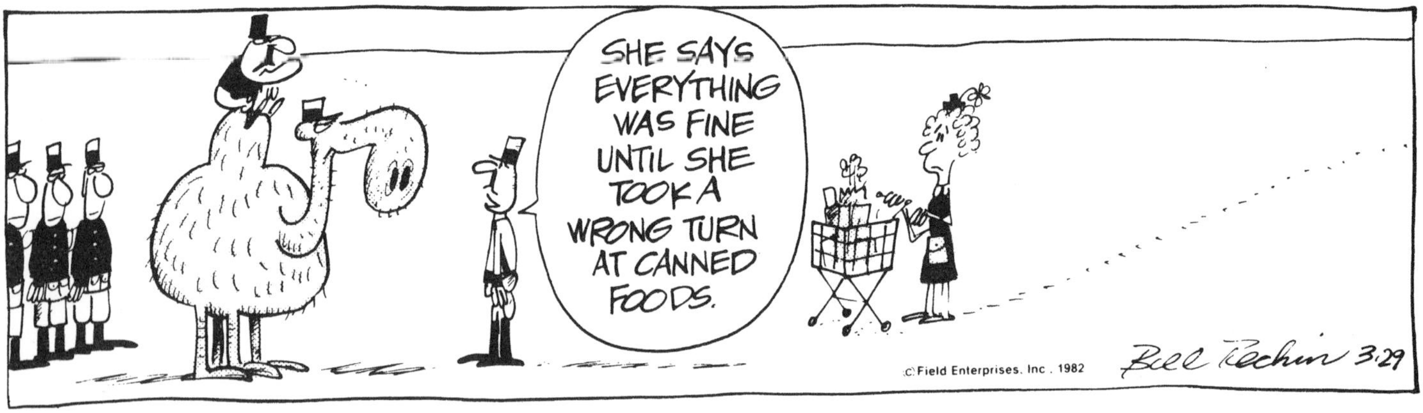
SHE SAYS EVERYTHING WAS FINE UNTIL SHE TOOK A WRONG TURN AT CANNED FOODS.
©Field Enterprises, Inc. 1982
Bill Rechin 3.29

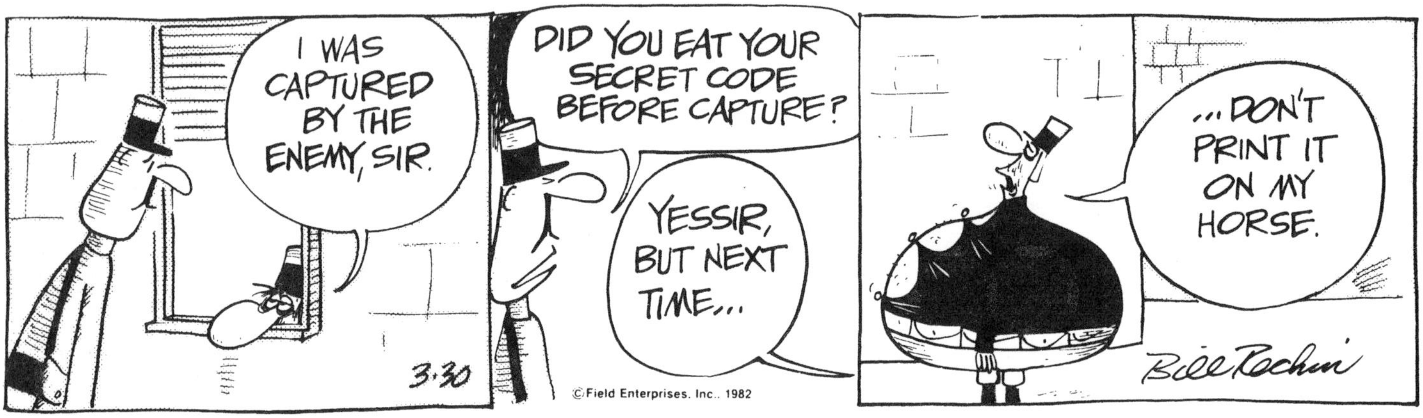
I WAS CAPTURED BY THE ENEMY, SIR.
3.30
DID YOU EAT YOUR SECRET CODE BEFORE CAPTURE?
YESSIR, BUT NEXT TIME...
©Field Enterprises, Inc., 1982
...DON'T PRINT IT ON MY HORSE.
Bill Rechin

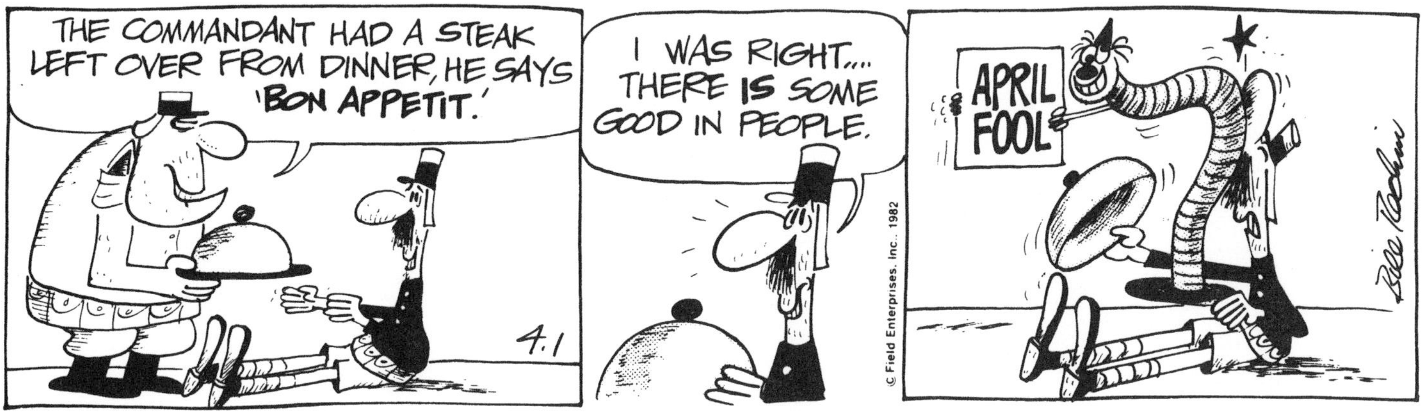
THE COMMANDANT HAD A STEAK LEFT OVER FROM DINNER, HE SAYS 'BON APPETIT.'
4.1
I WAS RIGHT.... THERE IS SOME GOOD IN PEOPLE.
© Field Enterprises, Inc., 1982
APRIL FOOL
Bill Rechin

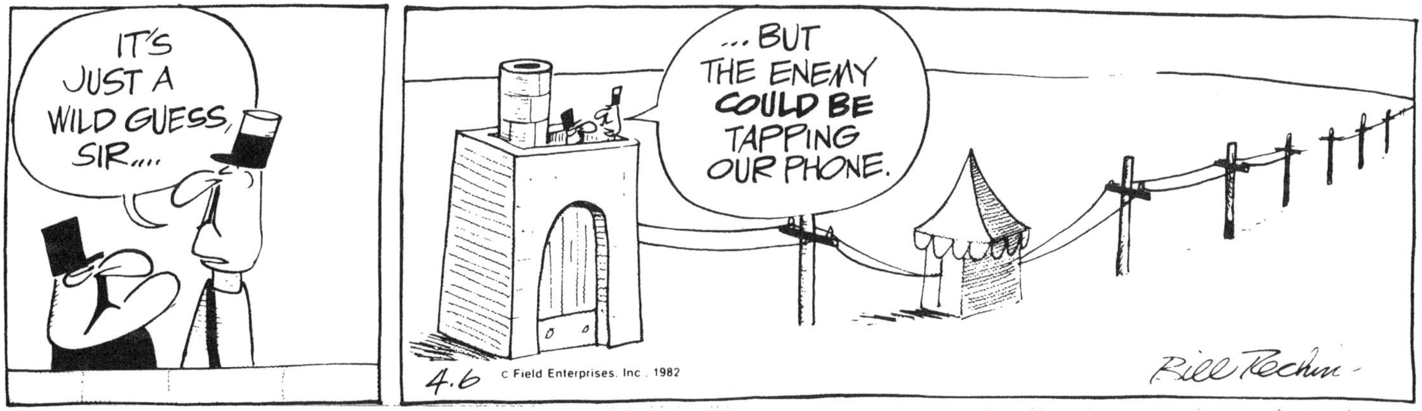
IT'S JUST A WILD GUESS, SIR....
...BUT THE ENEMY COULD BE TAPPING OUR PHONE.
4.6
© Field Enterprises, Inc . 1982
Bill Rechin

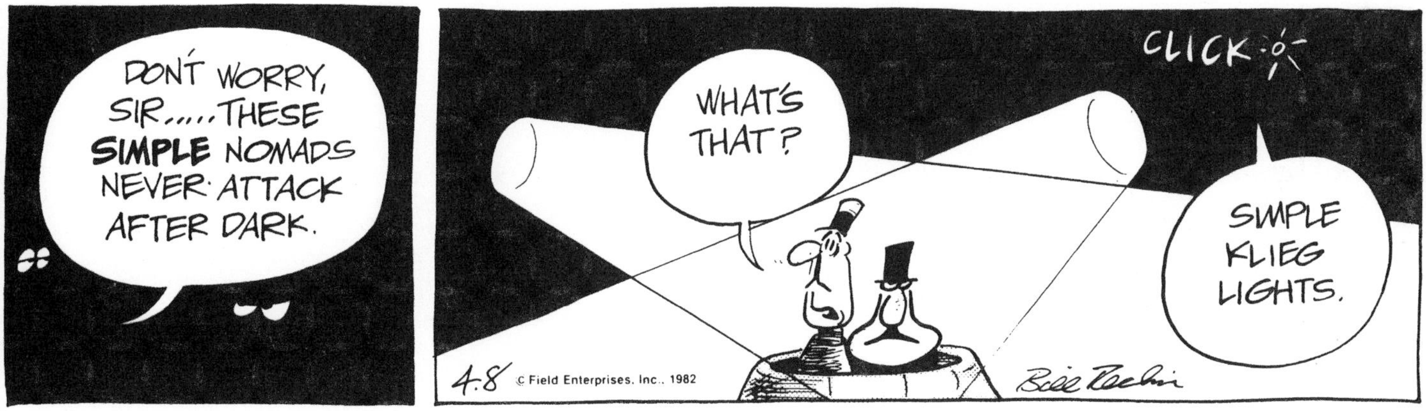
DON'T WORRY, SIR..... THESE SIMPLE NOMADS NEVER ATTACK AFTER DARK.
CLICK
WHAT'S THAT?
SIMPLE KLIEG LIGHTS.
4.8
© Field Enterprises, Inc., 1982
Bill Rechin

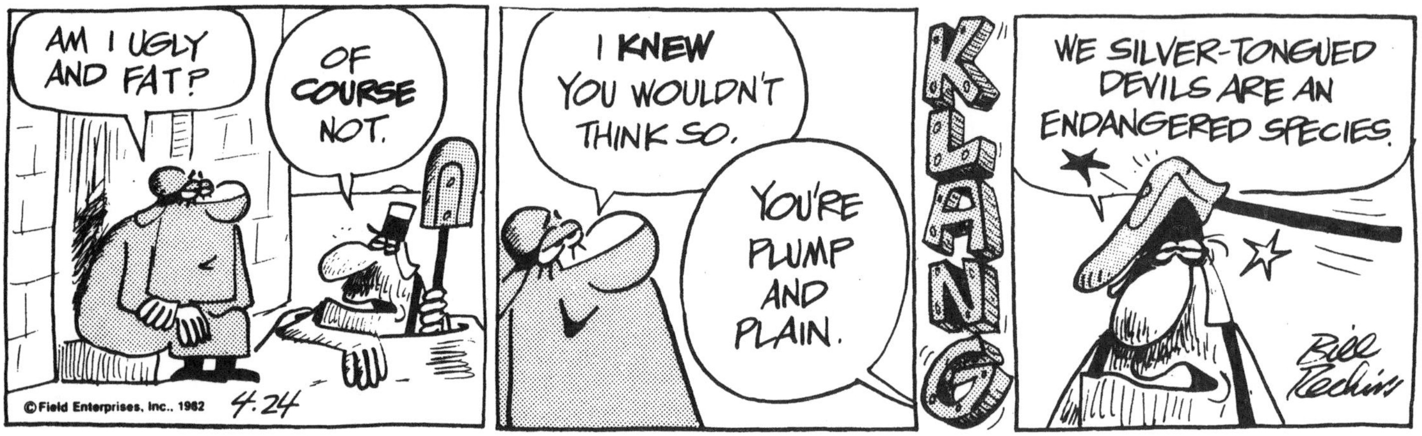
AM I UGLY AND FAT?
OF COURSE NOT.
© Field Enterprises, Inc., 1982
4·24
I KNEW YOU WOULDN'T THINK SO.
YOU'RE PLUMP AND PLAIN.
KLANG
WE SILVER-TONGUED DEVILS ARE AN ENDANGERED SPECIES.
Bill Rechin

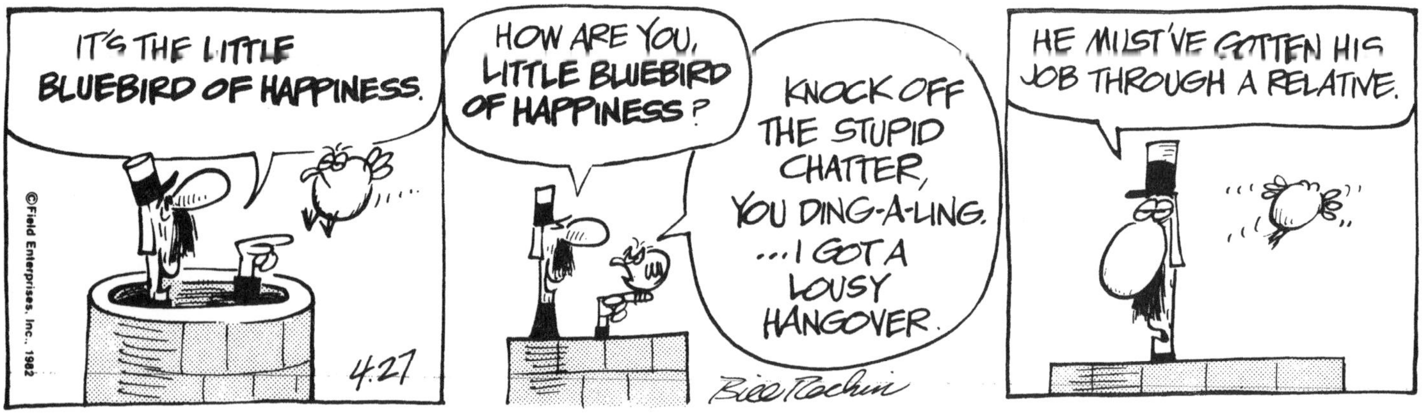
IT'S THE LITTLE BLUEBIRD OF HAPPINESS.
©Field Enterprises, Inc., 1982
4·27
HOW ARE YOU, LITTLE BLUEBIRD OF HAPPINESS?
KNOCK OFF THE STUPID CHATTER, YOU DING-A-LING. ...I GOT A LOUSY HANGOVER.
Bill Rechin
HE MUST'VE GOTTEN HIS JOB THROUGH A RELATIVE.

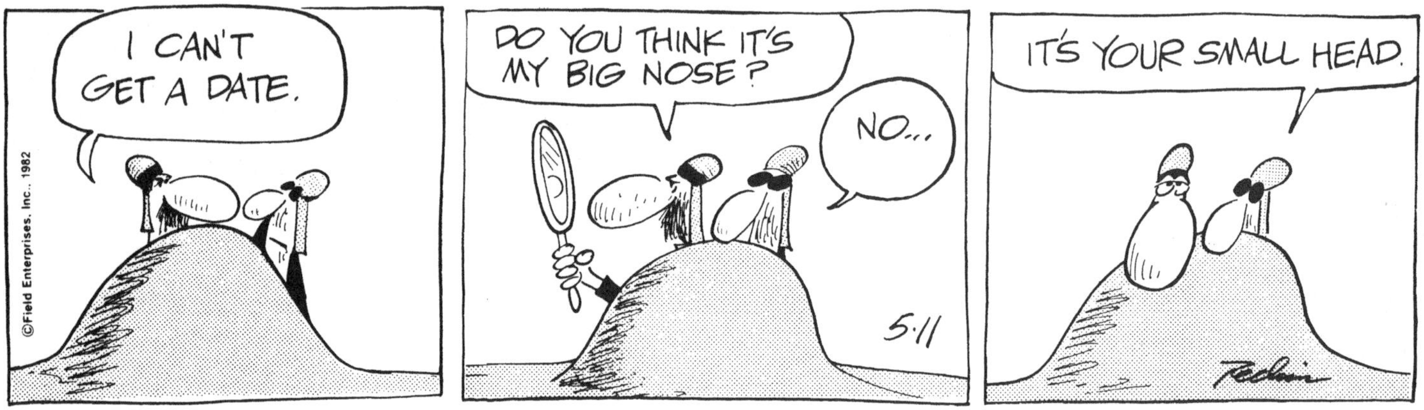
I CAN'T GET A DATE.
©Field Enterprises, Inc., 1982
DO YOU THINK IT'S MY BIG NOSE?
NO...
5·11
IT'S YOUR SMALL HEAD.
Rechin

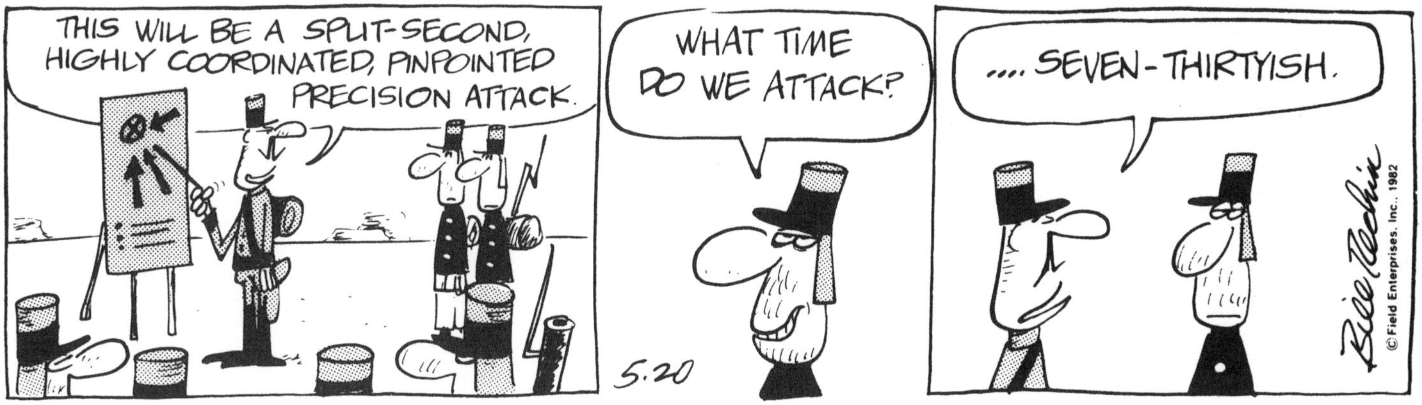
THIS WILL BE A SPLIT-SECOND, HIGHLY COORDINATED, PINPOINTED PRECISION ATTACK.
WHAT TIME DO WE ATTACK?
5.20
.... SEVEN-THIRTYISH.
©Field Enterprises, Inc., 1982

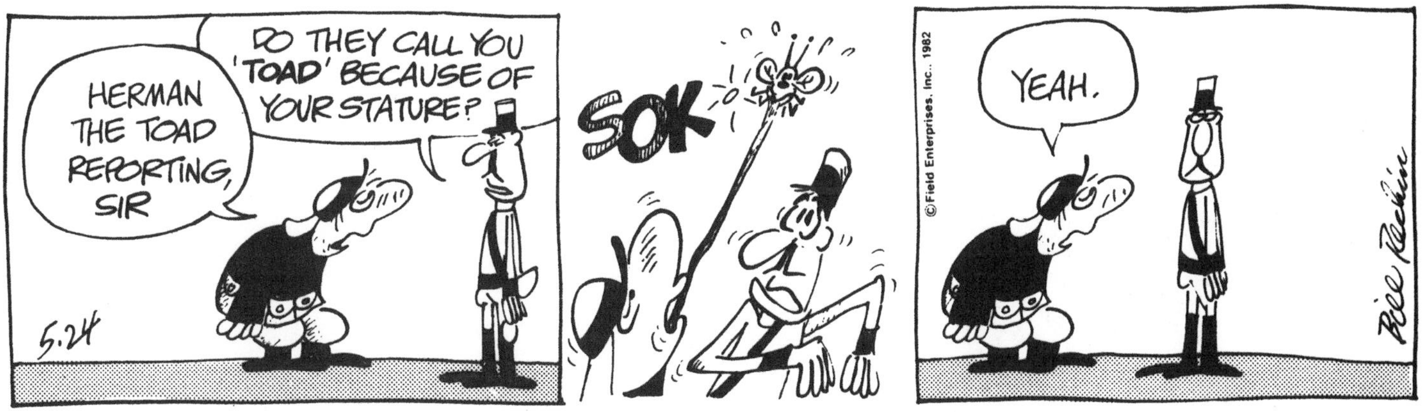
HERMAN THE TOAD REPORTING, SIR
DO THEY CALL YOU 'TOAD' BECAUSE OF YOUR STATURE?
5.24
SOK
©Field Enterprises, Inc., 1982
YEAH.

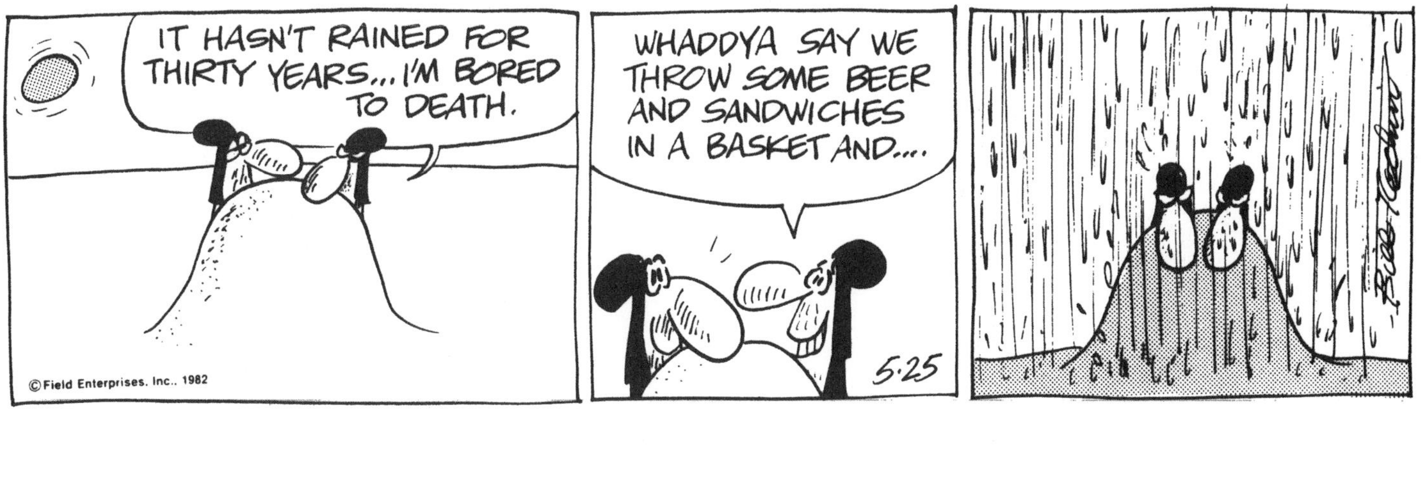
IT HASN'T RAINED FOR THIRTY YEARS... I'M BORED TO DEATH.
©Field Enterprises, Inc., 1982
WHADDYA SAY WE THROW SOME BEER AND SANDWICHES IN A BASKET AND....
5.25

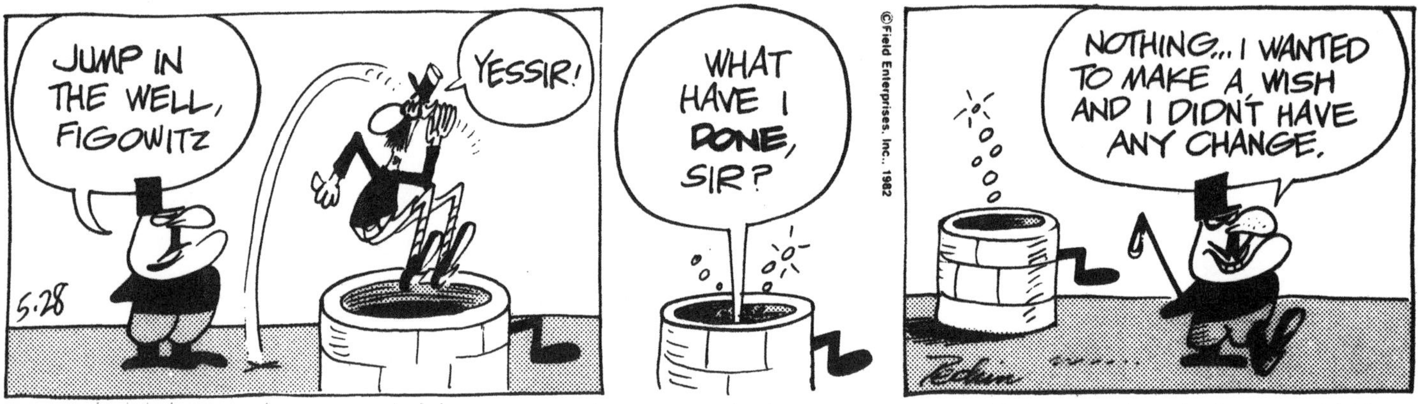
JUMP IN THE WELL, FIGOWITZ
YESSIR!
5·28
WHAT HAVE I DONE, SIR?
©Field Enterprises, Inc., 1982
NOTHING... I WANTED TO MAKE A WISH AND I DIDN'T HAVE ANY CHANGE.
Pechin

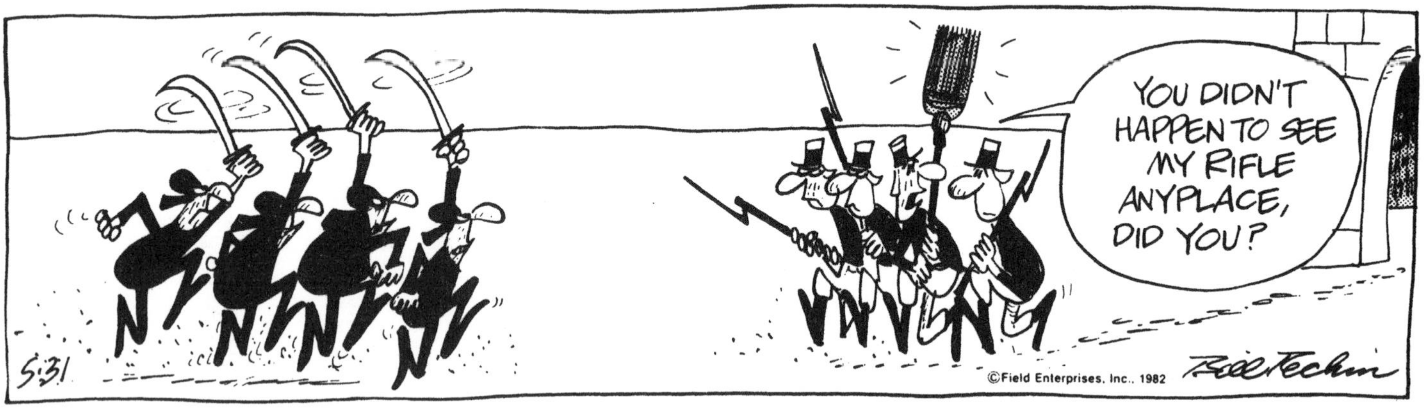
YOU DIDN'T HAPPEN TO SEE MY RIFLE ANYPLACE, DID YOU?
5·31
©Field Enterprises, Inc., 1982
Bill Rechin

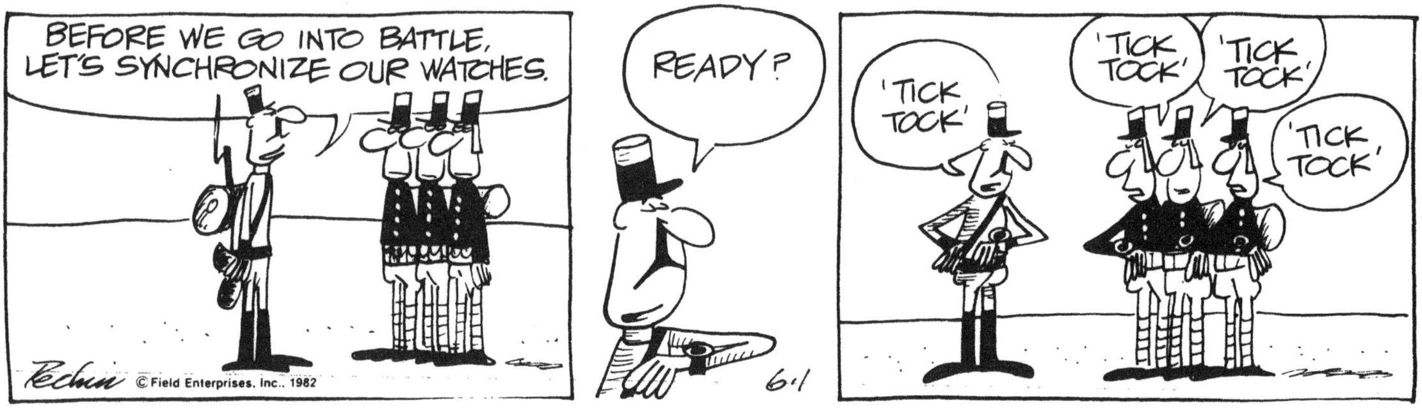
BEFORE WE GO INTO BATTLE, LET'S SYNCHRONIZE OUR WATCHES.
Rechin ©Field Enterprises, Inc., 1982
READY?
6·1
'TICK TOCK'
'TICK TOCK'
'TICK TOCK'
'TICK TOCK'

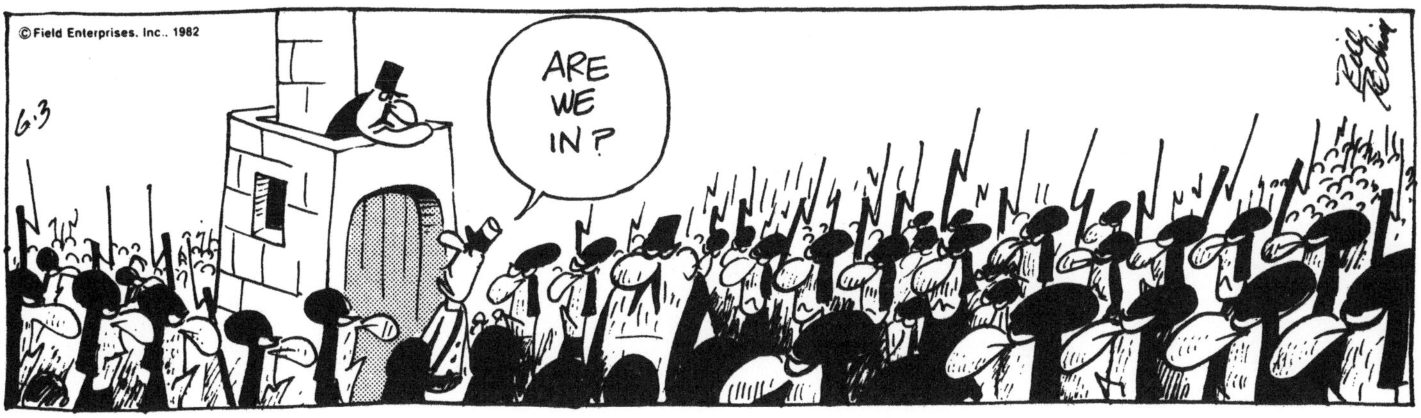
©Field Enterprises, Inc., 1982
6.3
ARE WE IN?

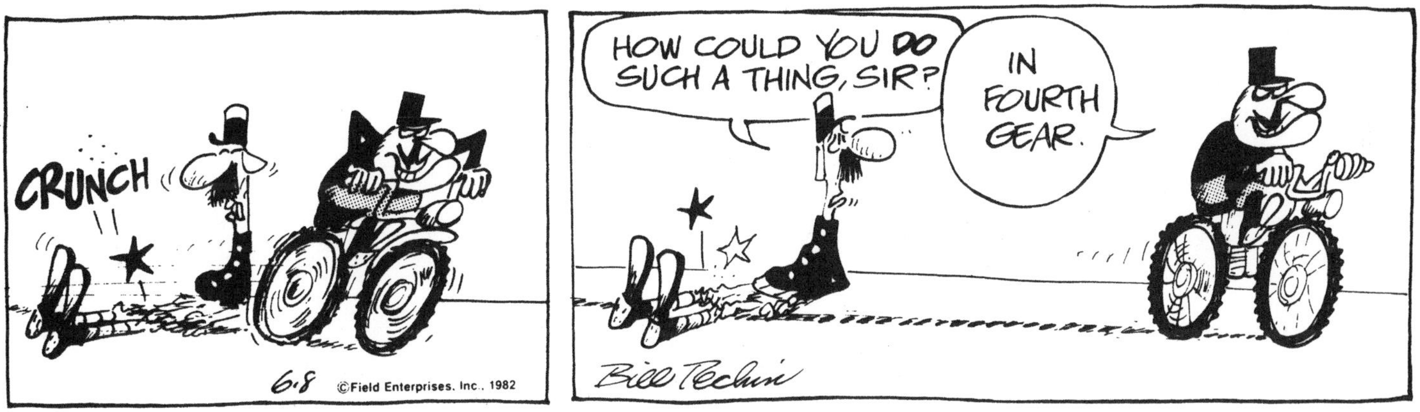
CRUNCH
6.8
©Field Enterprises, Inc., 1982
HOW COULD YOU DO SUCH A THING, SIR?
IN FOURTH GEAR.
Bill Rechin

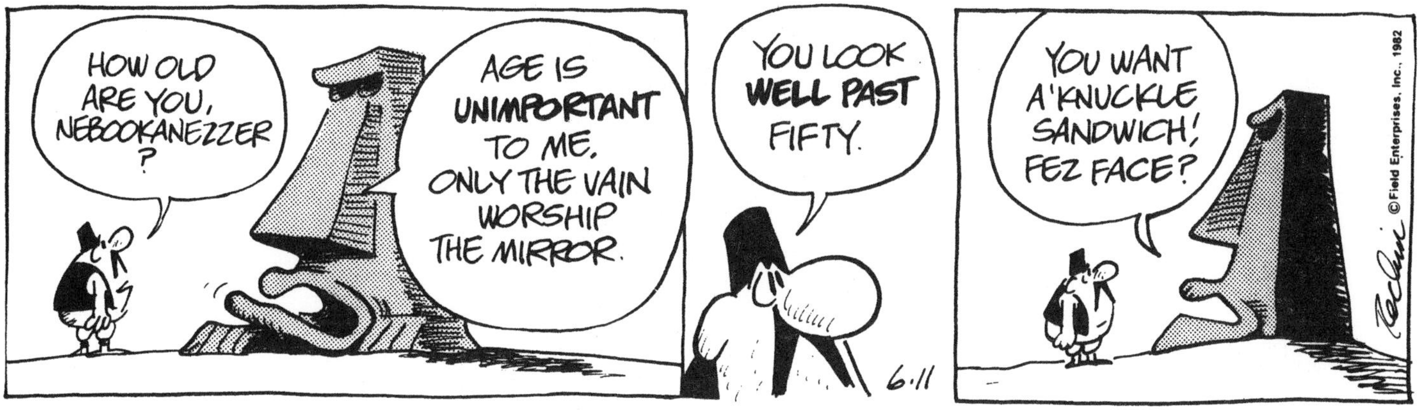
HOW OLD ARE YOU, NEBOOKANEZZER?
AGE IS UNIMPORTANT TO ME. ONLY THE VAIN WORSHIP THE MIRROR.
YOU LOOK WELL PAST FIFTY.
6.11
YOU WANT A 'KNUCKLE SANDWICH,' FEZ FACE?
©Field Enterprises, Inc., 1982
Rechin

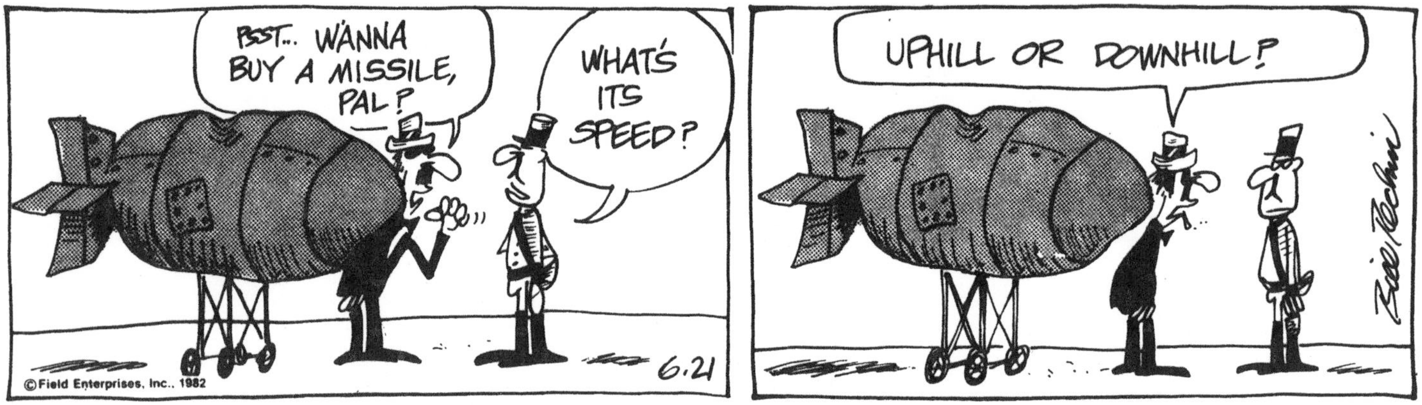
PSST... WANNA BUY A MISSILE, PAL?
WHAT'S ITS SPEED?
UPHILL OR DOWNHILL?
6.21
©Field Enterprises, Inc., 1982

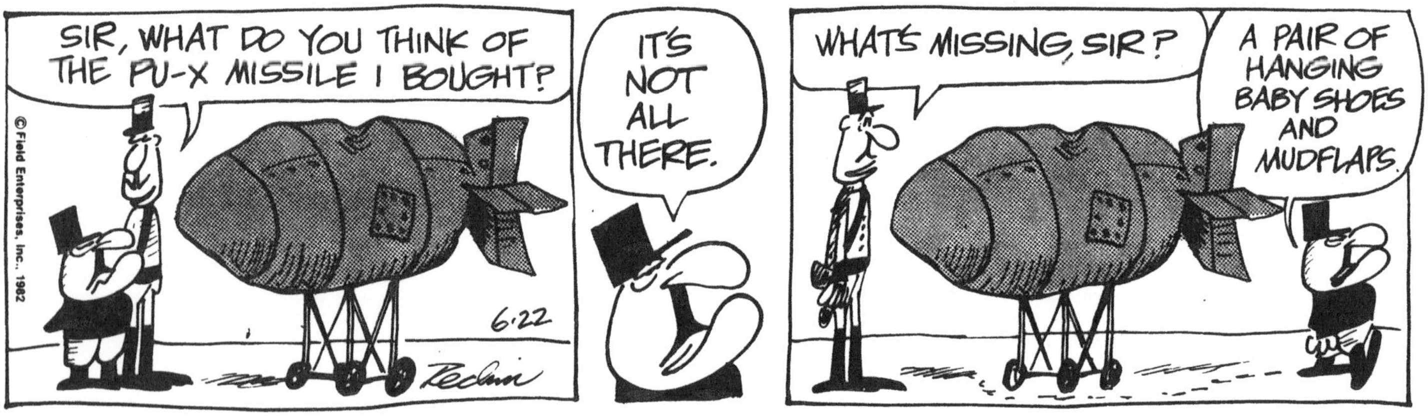
SIR, WHAT DO YOU THINK OF THE PU-X MISSILE I BOUGHT?
IT'S NOT ALL THERE.
WHAT'S MISSING, SIR?
A PAIR OF HANGING BABY SHOES AND MUDFLAPS.
6.22
© Field Enterprises, Inc., 1982

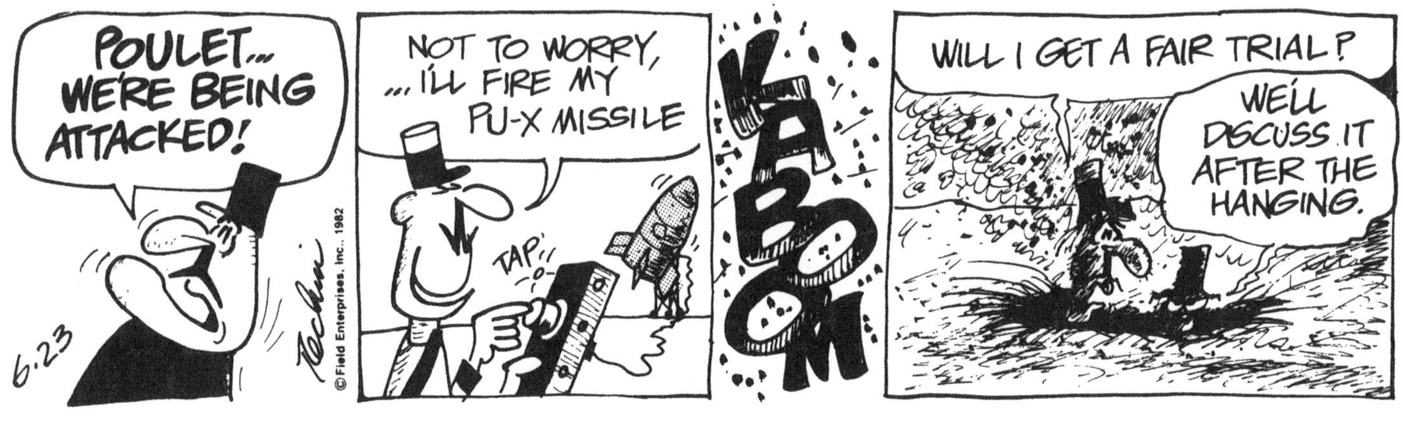
POULET... WE'RE BEING ATTACKED!
NOT TO WORRY, ...I'LL FIRE MY PU-X MISSILE
TAP
KABOOM
WILL I GET A FAIR TRIAL?
WE'LL DISCUSS IT AFTER THE HANGING.
6.23
© Field Enterprises, Inc., 1982

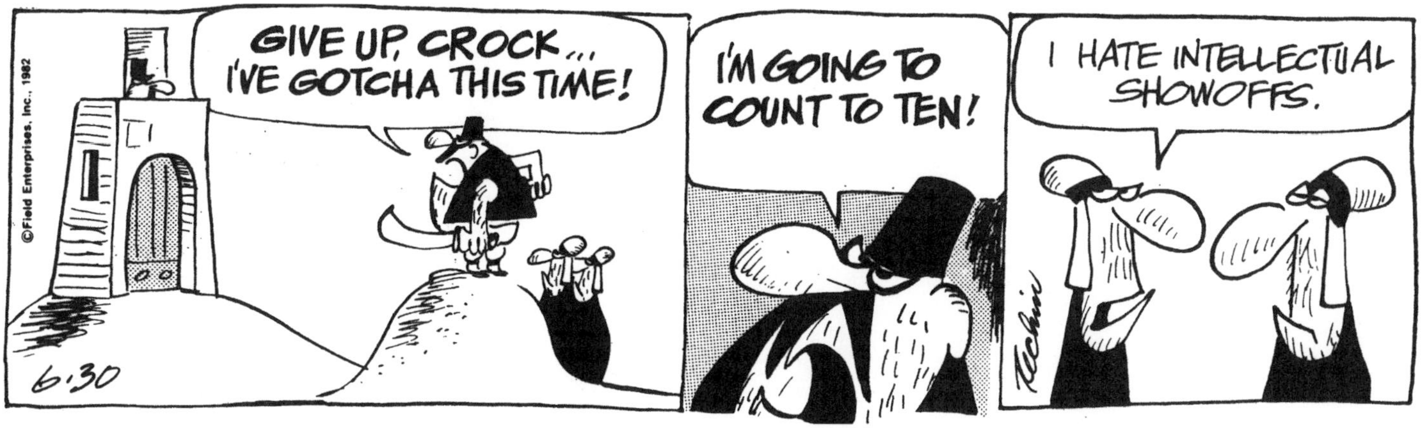

©Field Enterprises, Inc., 1982
6·30
GIVE UP, CROCK... I'VE GOTCHA THIS TIME!
I'M GOING TO COUNT TO TEN!
I HATE INTELLECTUAL SHOWOFFS.
Rechin

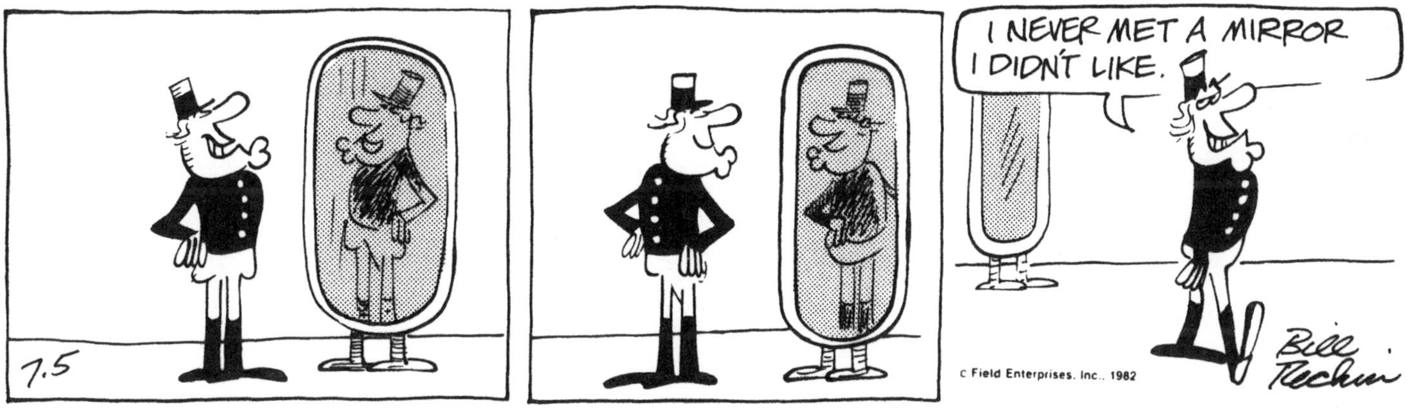

7.5
I NEVER MET A MIRROR I DIDN'T LIKE.
© Field Enterprises, Inc., 1982
Bill Rechin

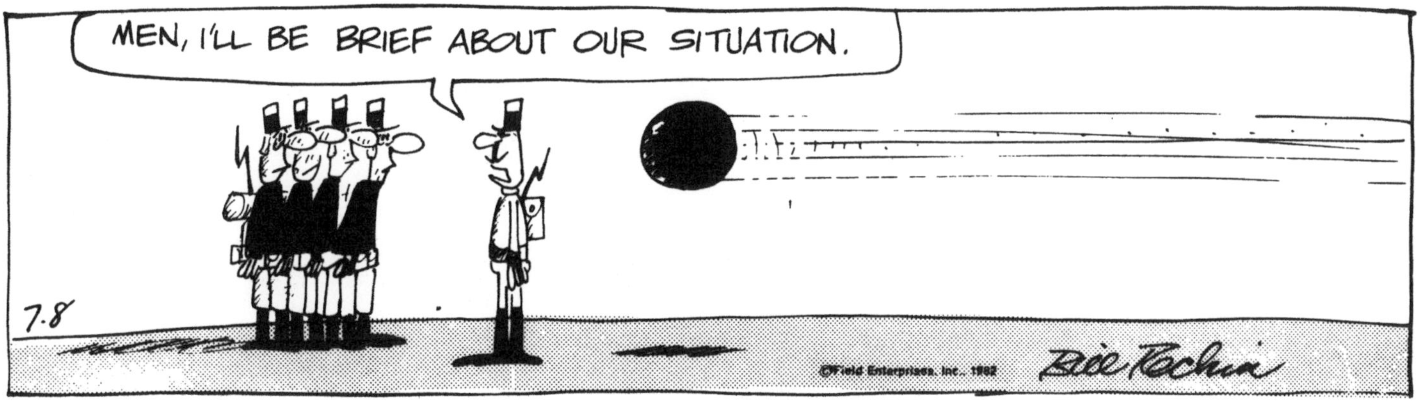

MEN, I'LL BE BRIEF ABOUT OUR SITUATION.
7·8
©Field Enterprises, Inc., 1982
Bill Rechin

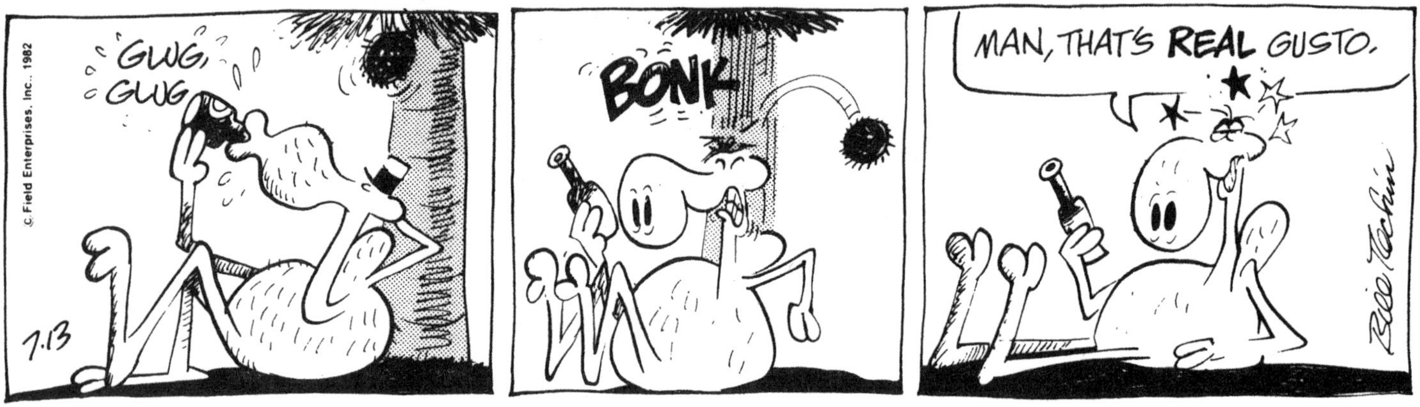

© Field Enterprises, Inc., 1982
GLUG, GLUG
7.13
BONK
MAN, THAT'S **REAL** GUSTO.

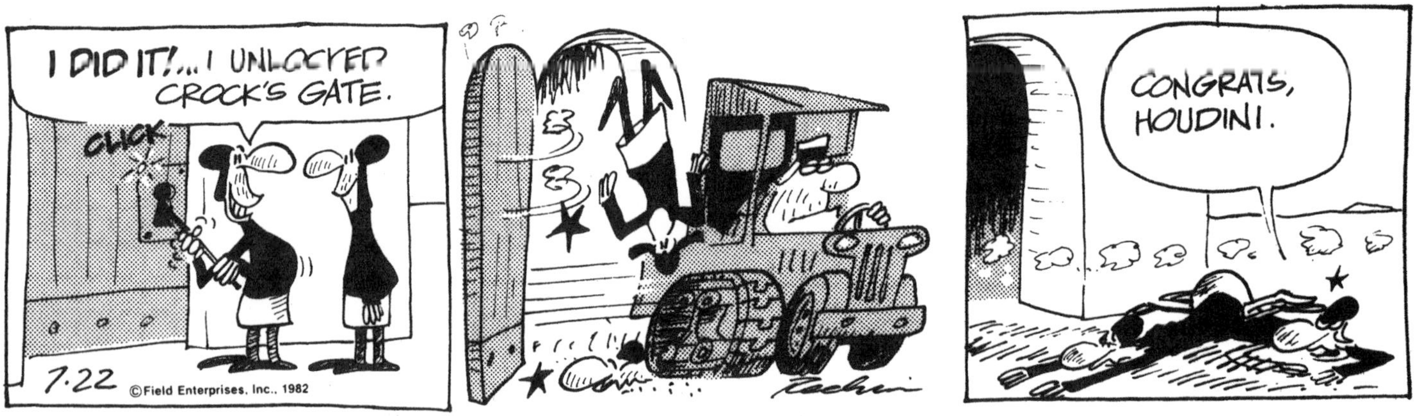

I DID IT!... I UNLOCKED CROCK'S GATE.
CLICK
7·22
©Field Enterprises, Inc., 1982
CONGRATS, HOUDINI.

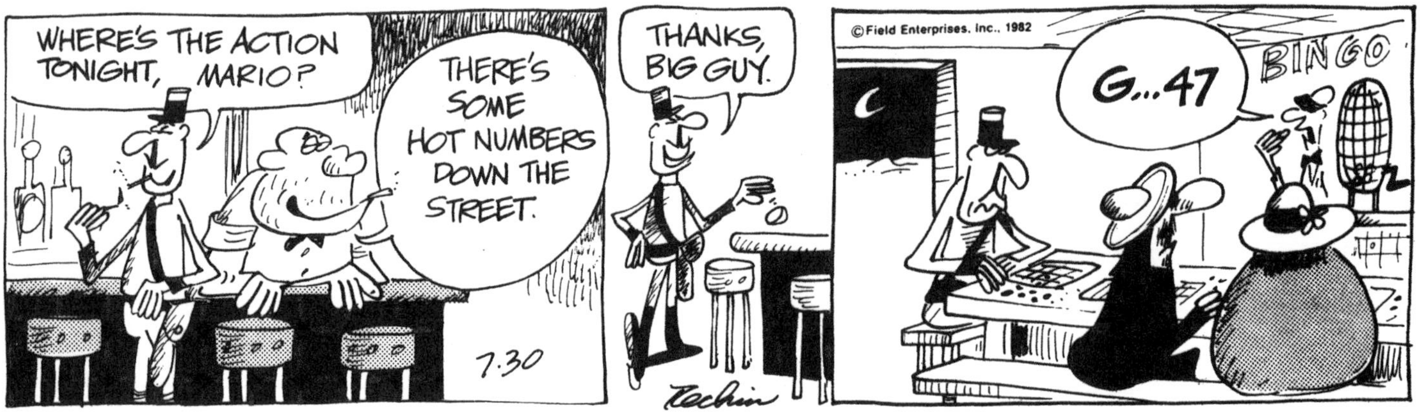

WHERE'S THE ACTION TONIGHT, MARIO?
THERE'S SOME HOT NUMBERS DOWN THE STREET.
7·30
THANKS, BIG GUY.
©Field Enterprises, Inc., 1982
BINGO
G...47

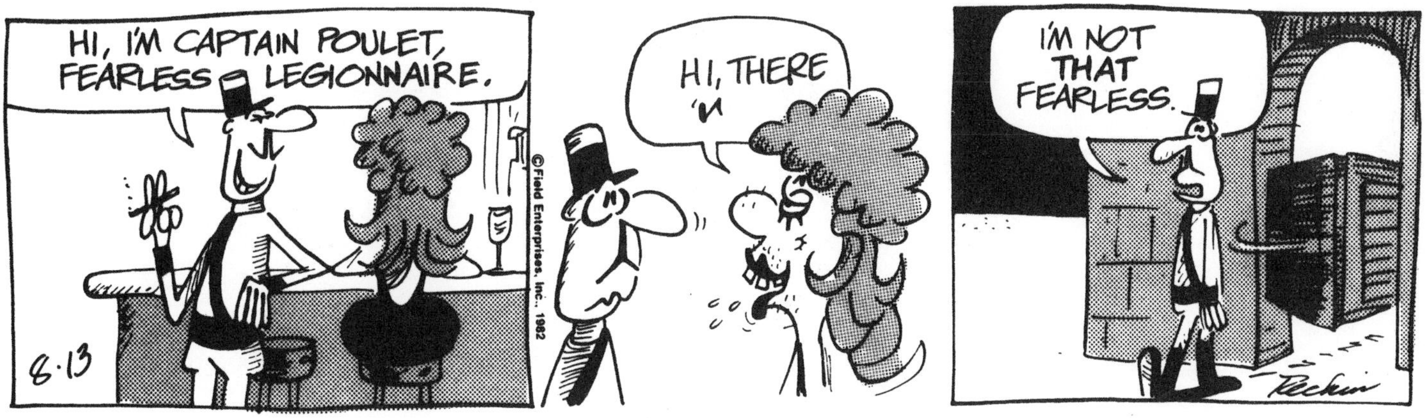
HI, I'M CAPTAIN POULET, FEARLESS LEGIONNAIRE.
8·13
©Field Enterprises, Inc., 1982
HI, THERE
I'M NOT THAT FEARLESS.

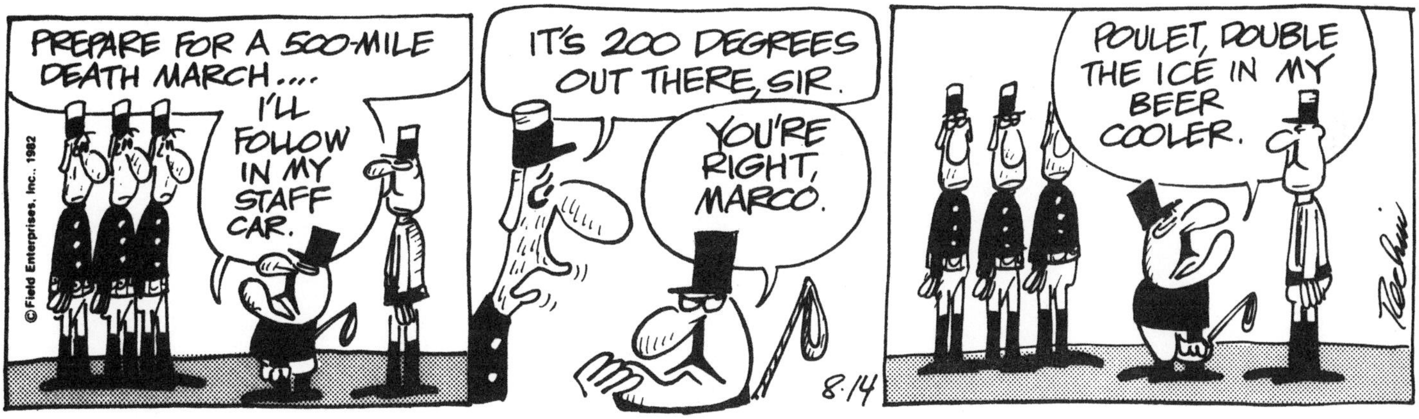
PREPARE FOR A 500-MILE DEATH MARCH....
I'LL FOLLOW IN MY STAFF CAR.
©Field Enterprises, Inc., 1982
IT'S 200 DEGREES OUT THERE, SIR.
YOU'RE RIGHT, MARCO.
8·14
POULET, DOUBLE THE ICE IN MY BEER COOLER.

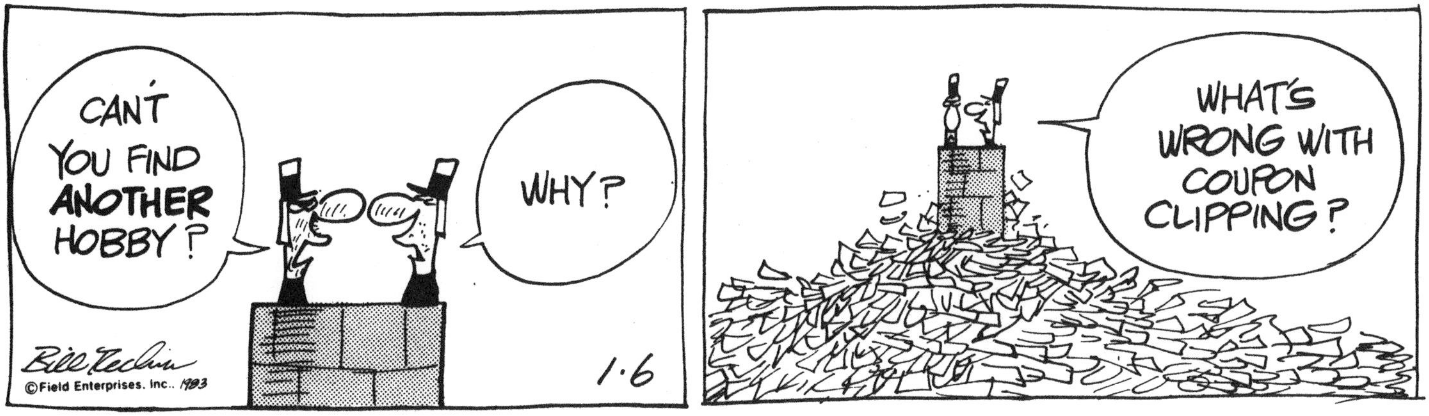
CAN'T YOU FIND ANOTHER HOBBY?
WHY?
©Field Enterprises, Inc., 1983
1·6
WHAT'S WRONG WITH COUPON CLIPPING?

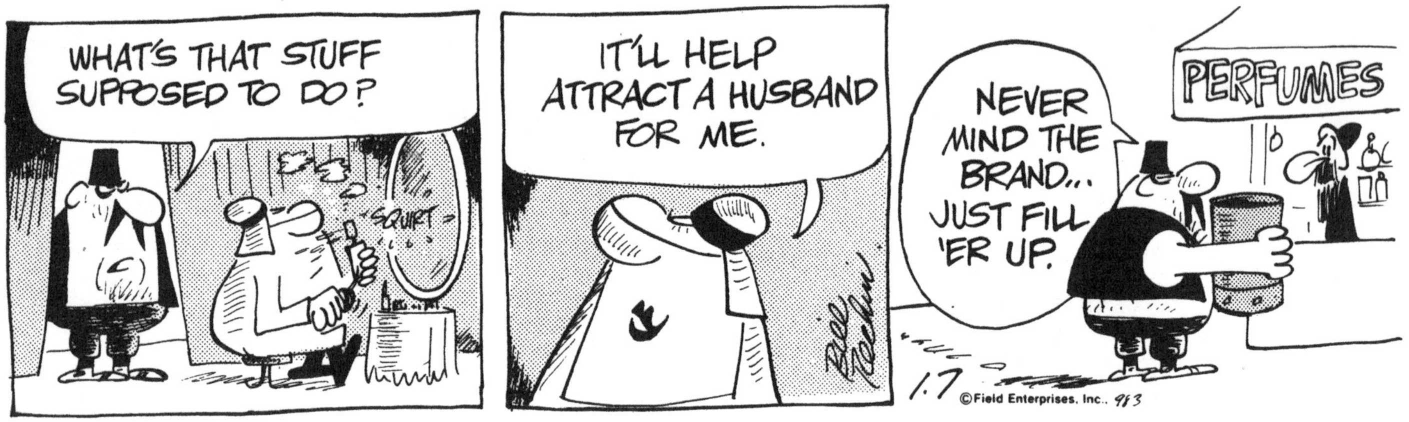
WHAT'S THAT STUFF SUPPOSED TO DO?
SQUIRT
IT'LL HELP ATTRACT A HUSBAND FOR ME.
PERFUMES
NEVER MIND THE BRAND... JUST FILL 'ER UP.
1-7
©Field Enterprises, Inc., 1983

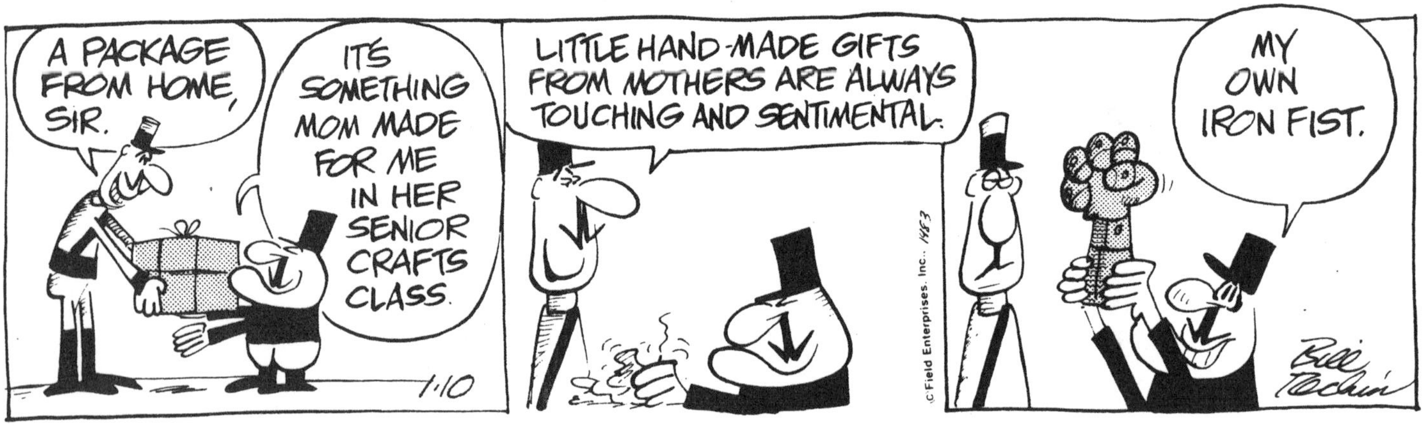
A PACKAGE FROM HOME, SIR.
IT'S SOMETHING MOM MADE FOR ME IN HER SENIOR CRAFTS CLASS.
1-10
LITTLE HAND-MADE GIFTS FROM MOTHERS ARE ALWAYS TOUCHING AND SENTIMENTAL.
©Field Enterprises, Inc., 1983
MY OWN IRON FIST.

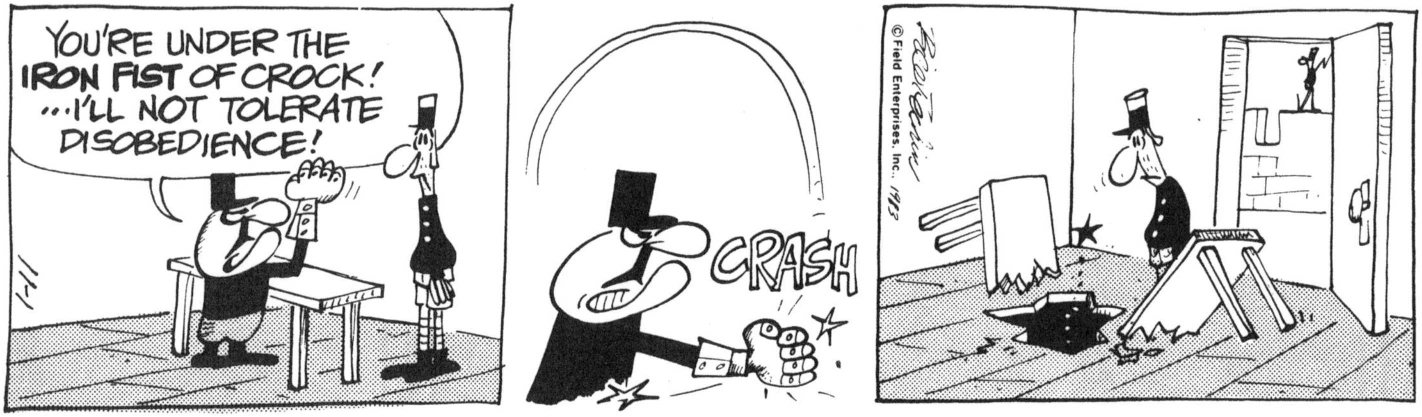
YOU'RE UNDER THE IRON FIST OF CROCK! ...I'LL NOT TOLERATE DISOBEDIENCE!
1-11
CRASH
©Field Enterprises, Inc., 1983

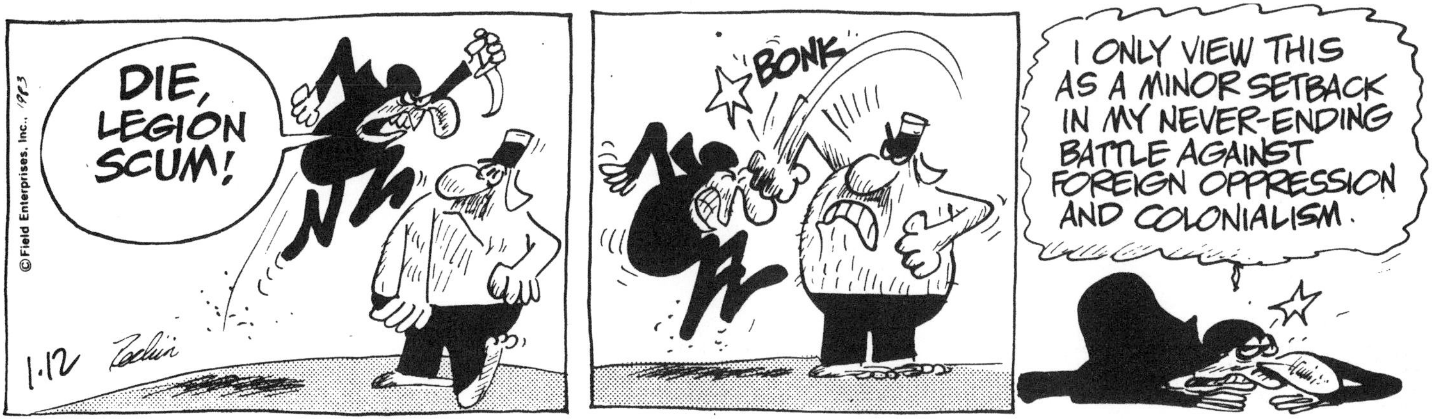
©Field Enterprises, Inc., 1983
DIE, LEGION SCUM!
1·12
BONK
I ONLY VIEW THIS AS A MINOR SETBACK IN MY NEVER-ENDING BATTLE AGAINST FOREIGN OPPRESSION AND COLONIALISM.

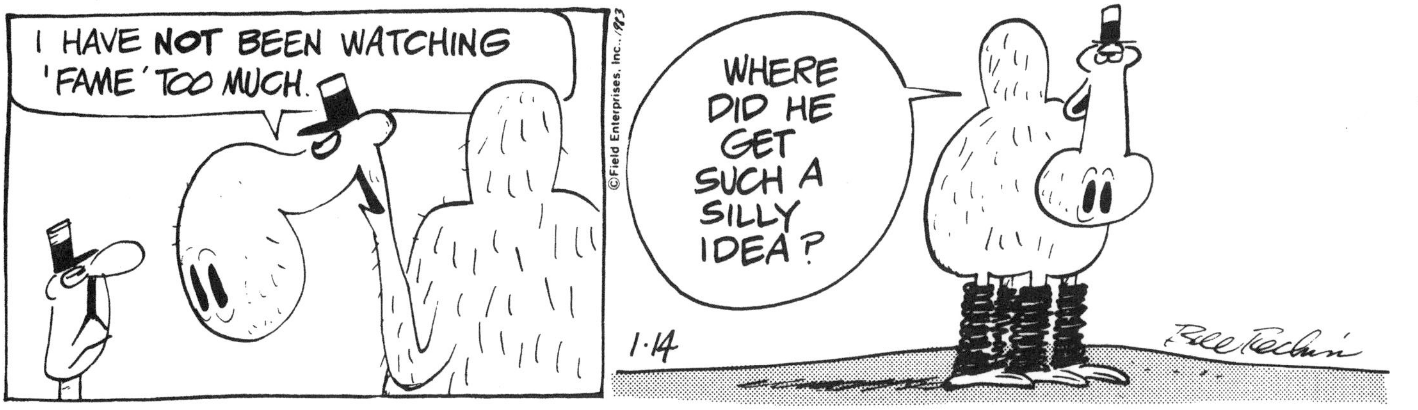
I HAVE NOT BEEN WATCHING 'FAME' TOO MUCH.
©Field Enterprises, Inc., 1983
WHERE DID HE GET SUCH A SILLY IDEA?
1·14

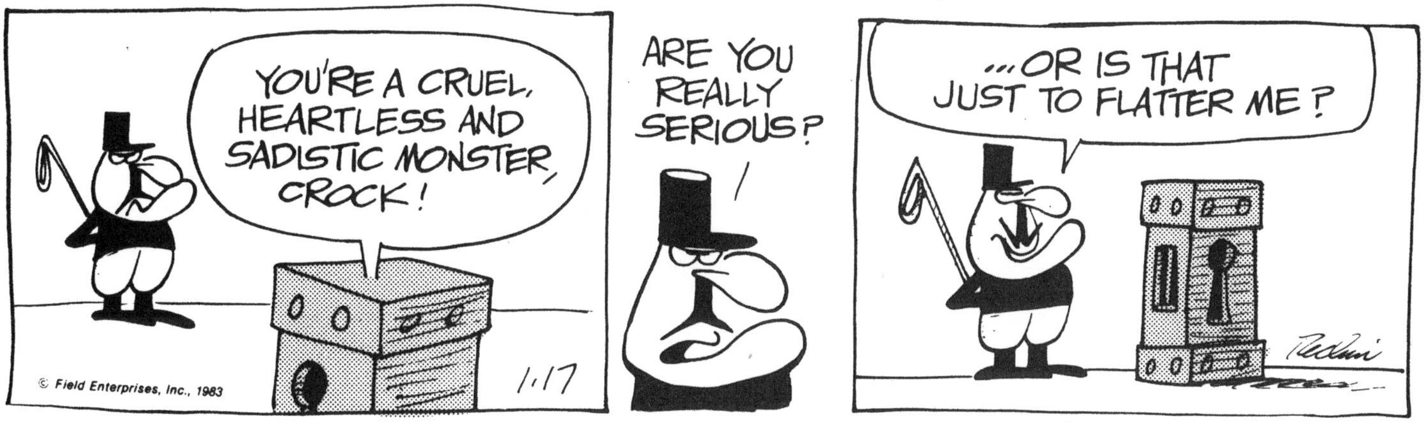
YOU'RE A CRUEL, HEARTLESS AND SADISTIC MONSTER, CROCK!
© Field Enterprises, Inc., 1983
1·17
ARE YOU REALLY SERIOUS?
...OR IS THAT JUST TO FLATTER ME?

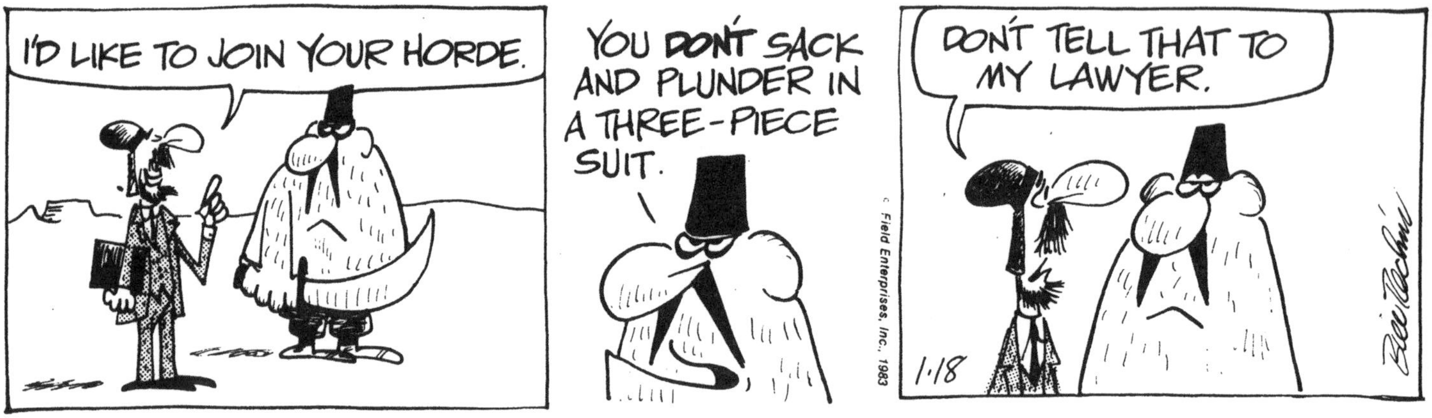
I'D LIKE TO JOIN YOUR HORDE.
YOU DON'T SACK AND PLUNDER IN A THREE-PIECE SUIT.
© Field Enterprises, Inc. 1983
DON'T TELL THAT TO MY LAWYER.
1.18

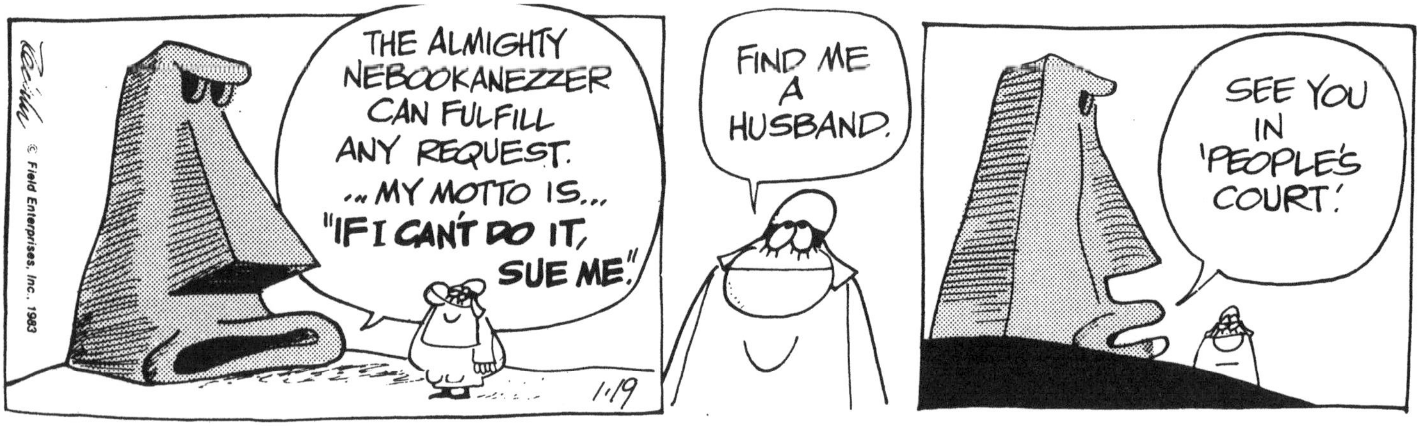
© Field Enterprises, Inc. 1983
THE ALMIGHTY NEBOOKANEZZER CAN FULFILL ANY REQUEST. ... MY MOTTO IS... "IF I CAN'T DO IT, SUE ME."
1.19
FIND ME A HUSBAND.
SEE YOU IN 'PEOPLE'S COURT.'

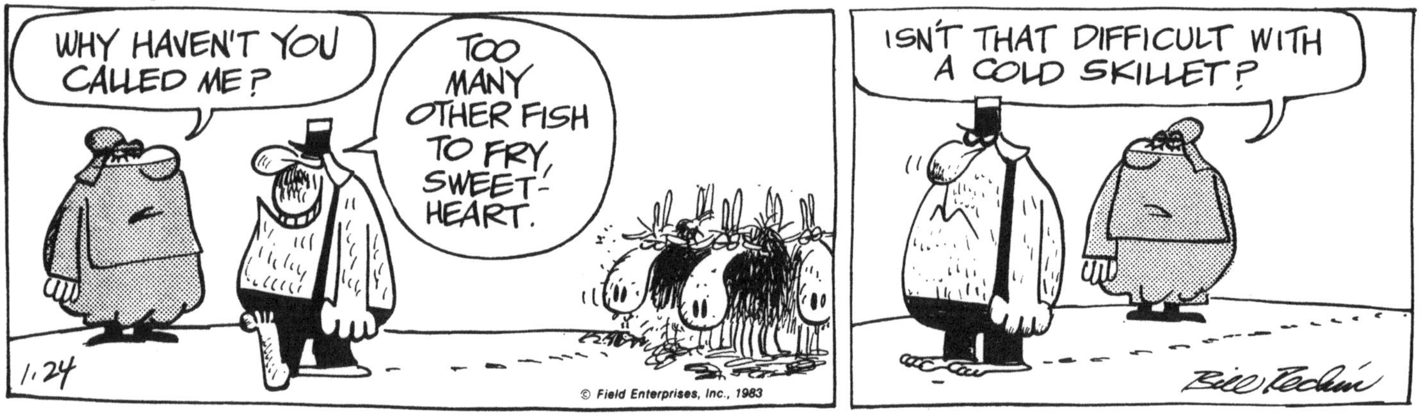
WHY HAVEN'T YOU CALLED ME?
TOO MANY OTHER FISH TO FRY, SWEET-HEART.
1.24
© Field Enterprises, Inc., 1983
ISN'T THAT DIFFICULT WITH A COLD SKILLET?

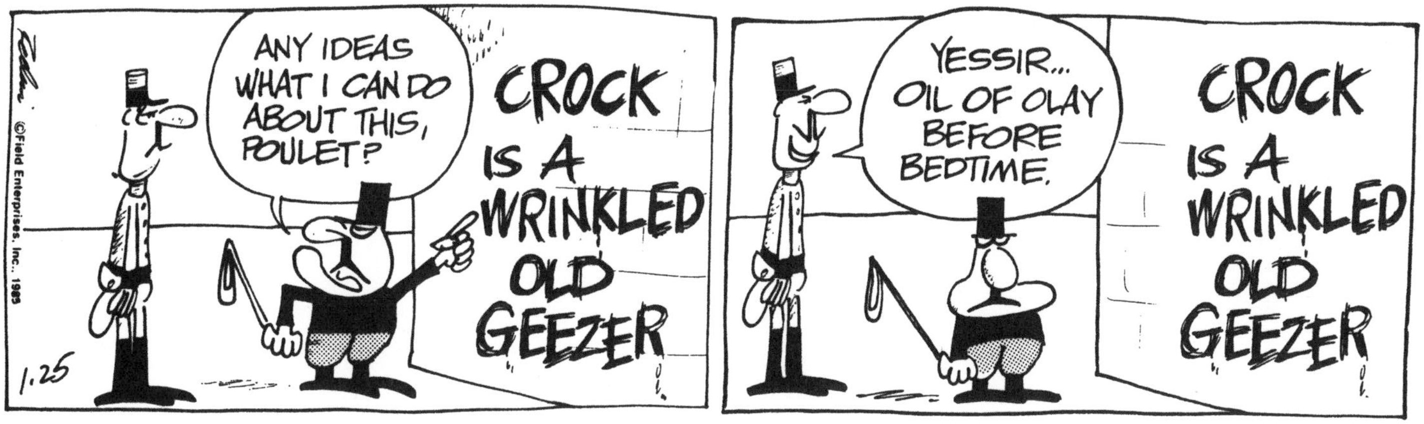
©Field Enterprises, Inc. 1983
1.25
ANY IDEAS WHAT I CAN DO ABOUT THIS, POULET?
CROCK IS A WRINKLED OLD GEEZER
YESSIR... OIL OF OLAY BEFORE BEDTIME.
CROCK IS A WRINKLED OLD GEEZER

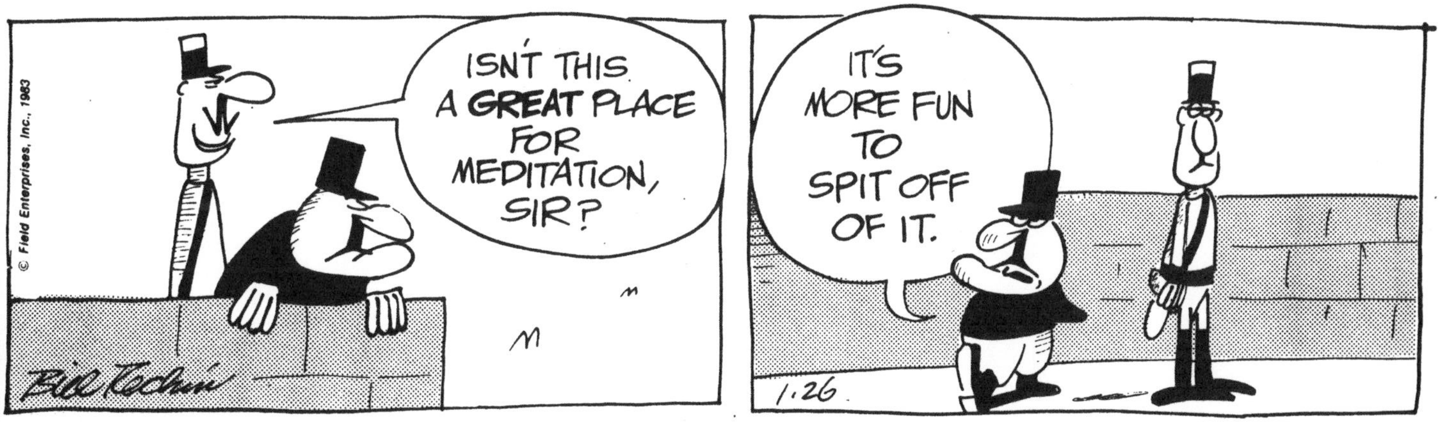
© Field Enterprises, Inc., 1983
ISN'T THIS A **GREAT** PLACE FOR MEDITATION, SIR?
IT'S MORE FUN TO SPIT OFF OF IT.
1.26

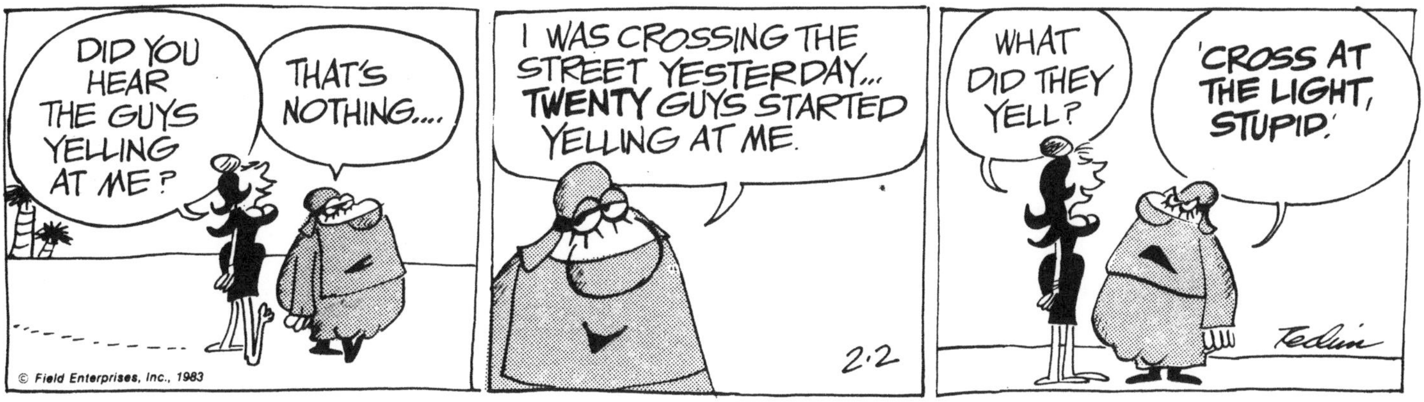
DID YOU HEAR THE GUYS YELLING AT ME?
THAT'S NOTHING....
© Field Enterprises, Inc., 1983
I WAS CROSSING THE STREET YESTERDAY... **TWENTY** GUYS STARTED YELLING AT ME.
2.2
WHAT DID THEY YELL?
'CROSS AT THE LIGHT, STUPID.'

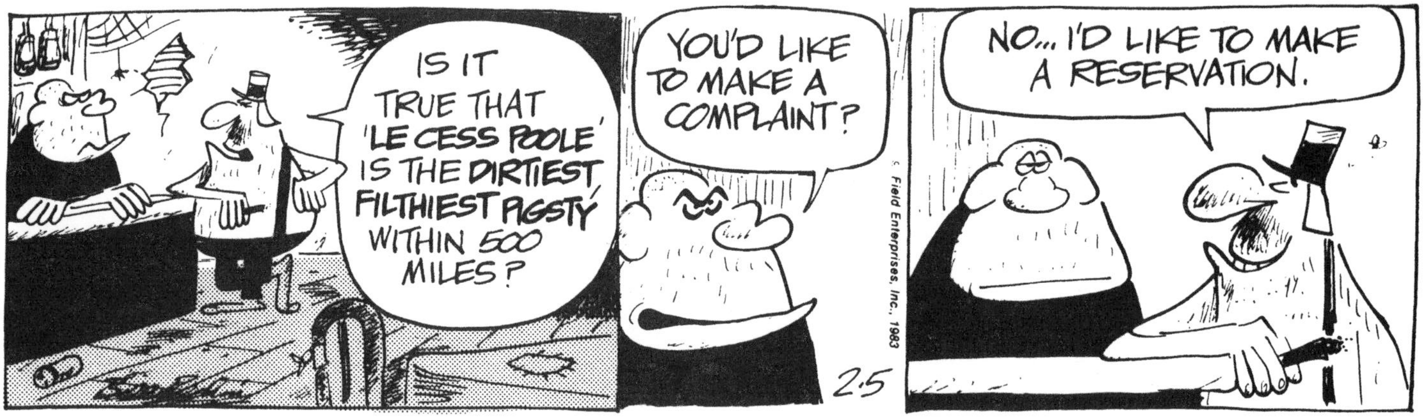
IS IT TRUE THAT 'LE CESS POOLE' IS THE DIRTIEST FILTHIEST PIGSTY WITHIN 500 MILES?
YOU'D LIKE TO MAKE A COMPLAINT?
© Field Enterprises, Inc., 1983
2·5
NO... I'D LIKE TO MAKE A RESERVATION.

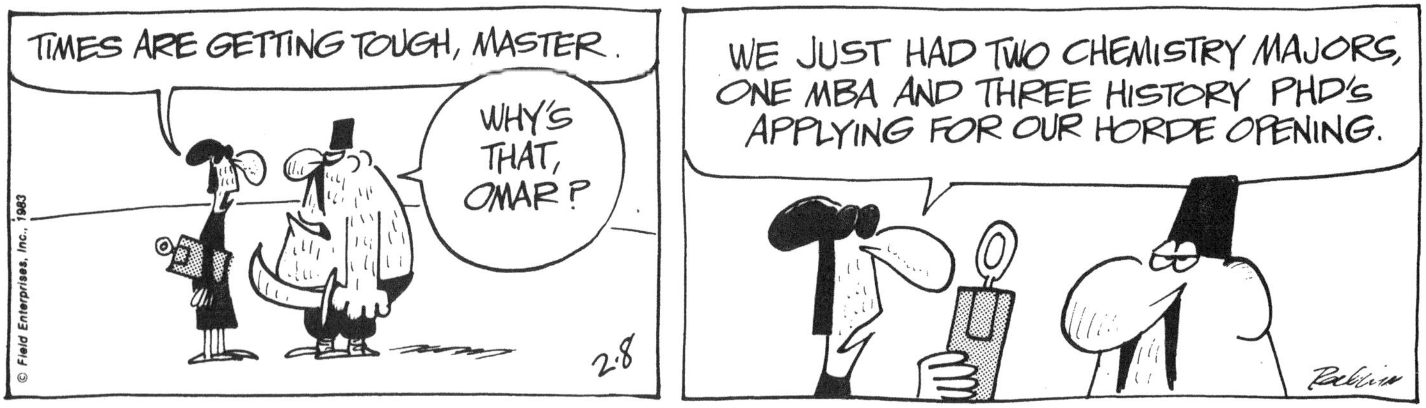
TIMES ARE GETTING TOUGH, MASTER.
WHY'S THAT, OMAR?
© Field Enterprises, Inc., 1983
2·8
WE JUST HAD TWO CHEMISTRY MAJORS, ONE MBA AND THREE HISTORY PHD's APPLYING FOR OUR HORDE OPENING.

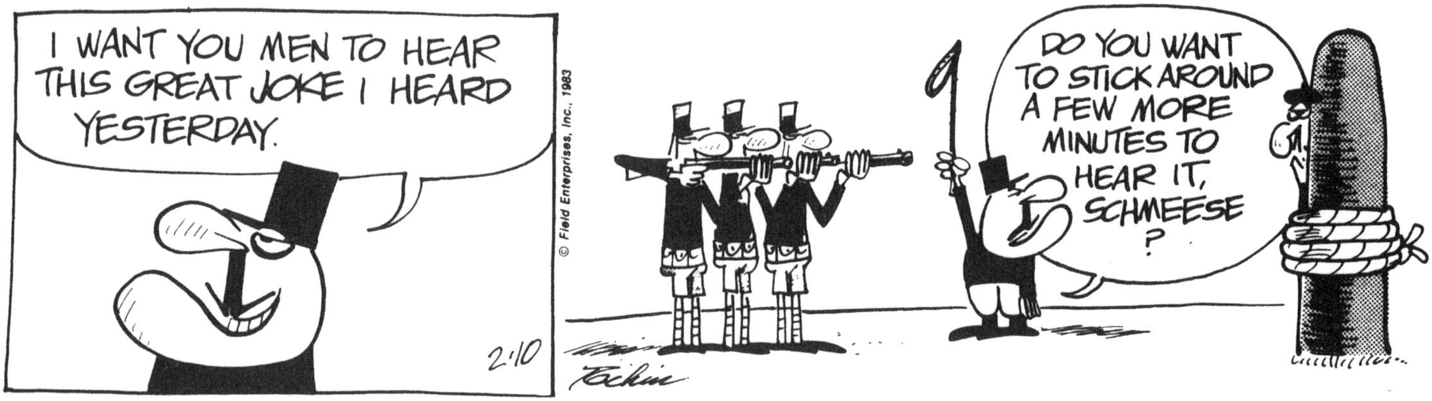
I WANT YOU MEN TO HEAR THIS GREAT JOKE I HEARD YESTERDAY.
2·10
© Field Enterprises, Inc., 1983
DO YOU WANT TO STICK AROUND A FEW MORE MINUTES TO HEAR IT, SCHMEESE?

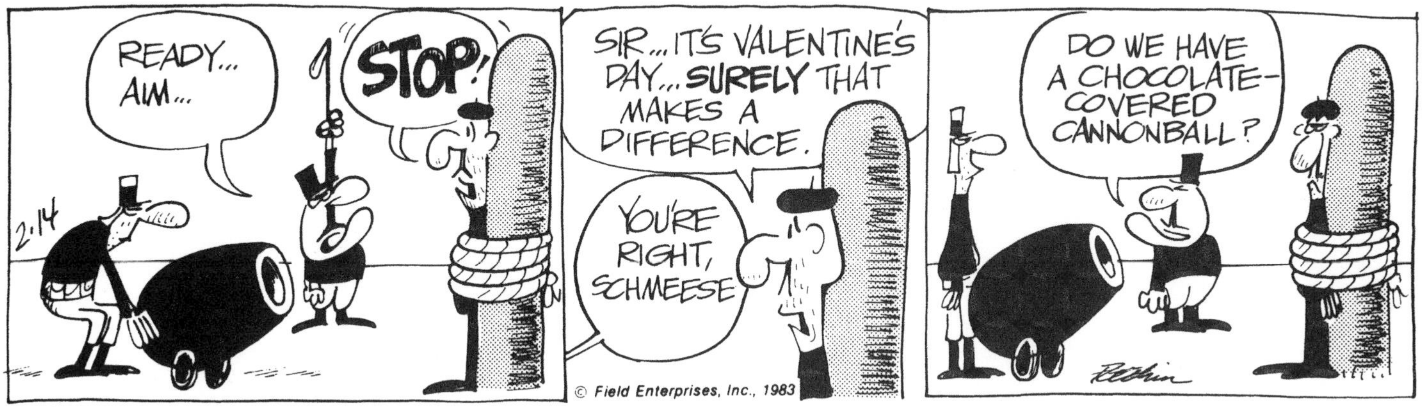
READY... AIM...
STOP!
2·14
SIR... IT'S VALENTINE'S DAY... SURELY THAT MAKES A DIFFERENCE.
YOU'RE RIGHT, SCHMEESE
© Field Enterprises, Inc., 1983
DO WE HAVE A CHOCOLATE-COVERED CANNONBALL?

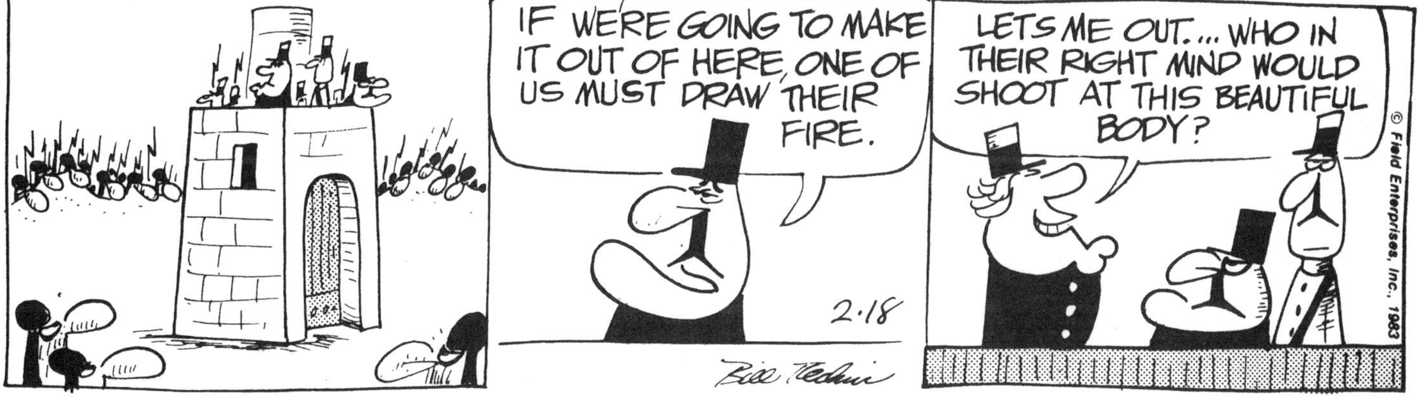
IF WE'RE GOING TO MAKE IT OUT OF HERE, ONE OF US MUST DRAW THEIR FIRE.
2·18
LETS ME OUT.... WHO IN THEIR RIGHT MIND WOULD SHOOT AT THIS BEAUTIFUL BODY?
© Field Enterprises, Inc., 1983

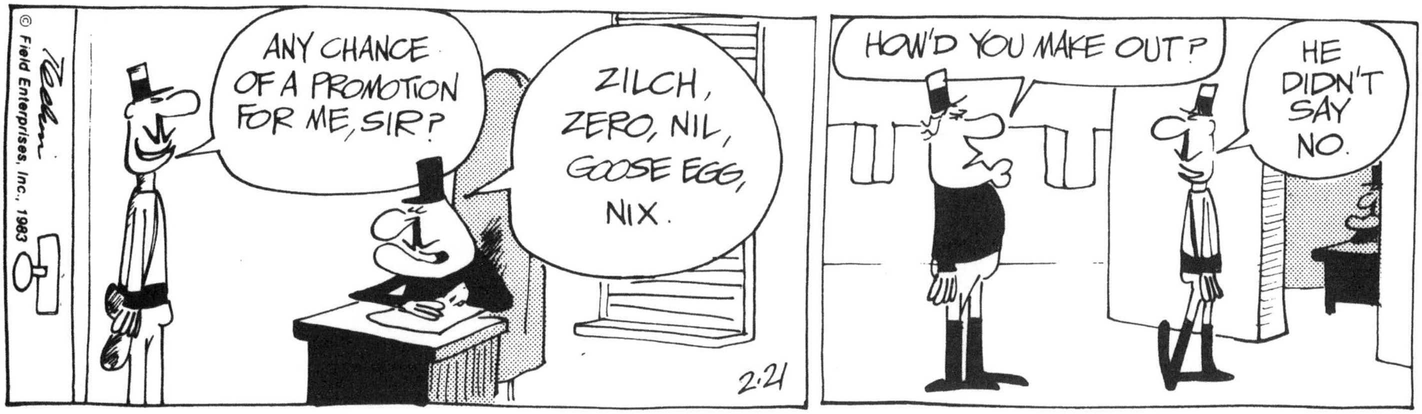
© Field Enterprises, Inc., 1983
ANY CHANCE OF A PROMOTION FOR ME, SIR?
ZILCH, ZERO, NIL, GOOSE EGG, NIX.
2·21
HOW'D YOU MAKE OUT?
HE DIDN'T SAY NO.

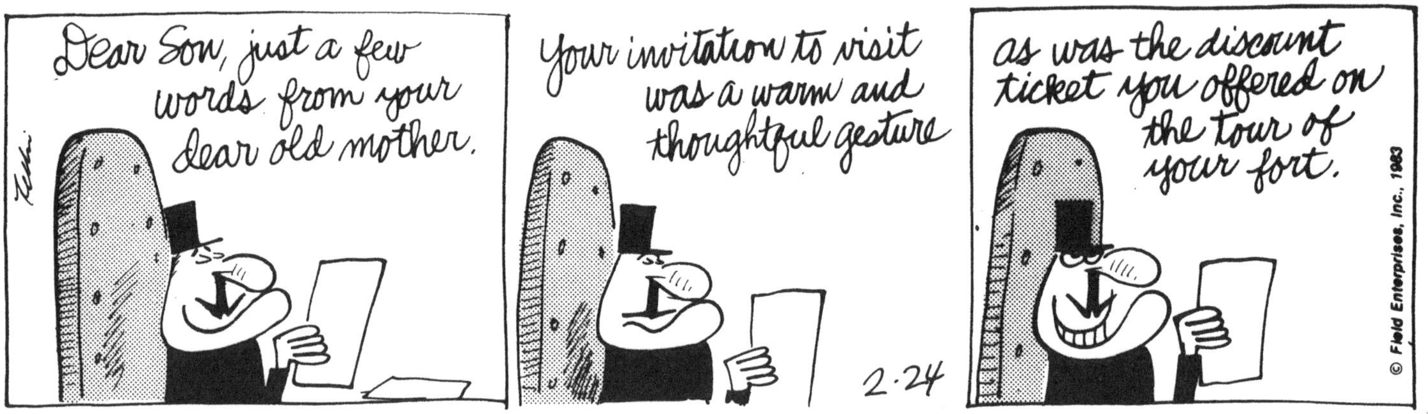
Dear Son, just a few words from your dear old mother.
Your invitation to visit was a warm and thoughtful gesture
2·24
as was the discount ticket you offered on the tour of your fort.
© Field Enterprises, Inc., 1983

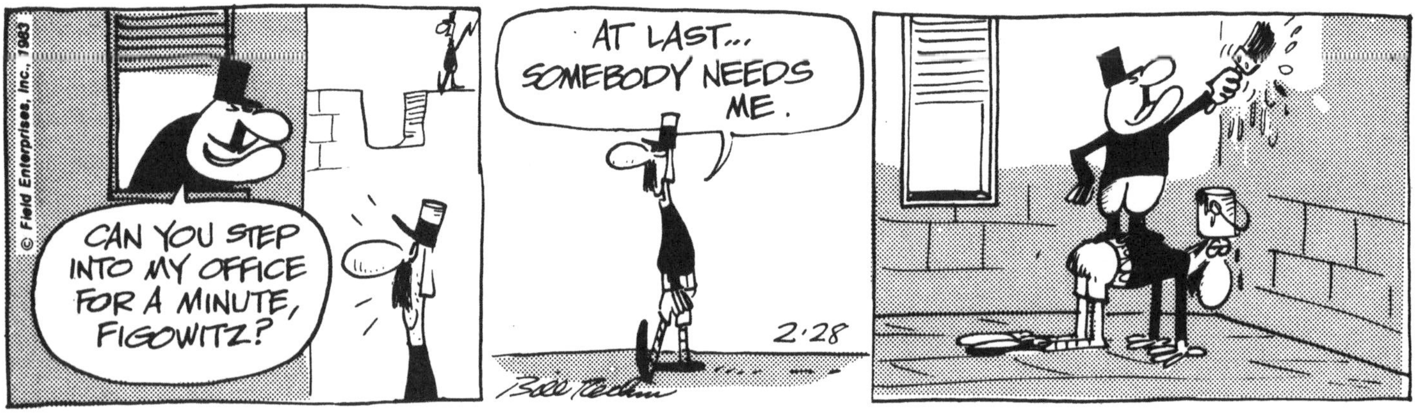
© Field Enterprises, Inc., 1983
CAN YOU STEP INTO MY OFFICE FOR A MINUTE, FIGOWITZ?
AT LAST... SOMEBODY NEEDS ME.
2·28

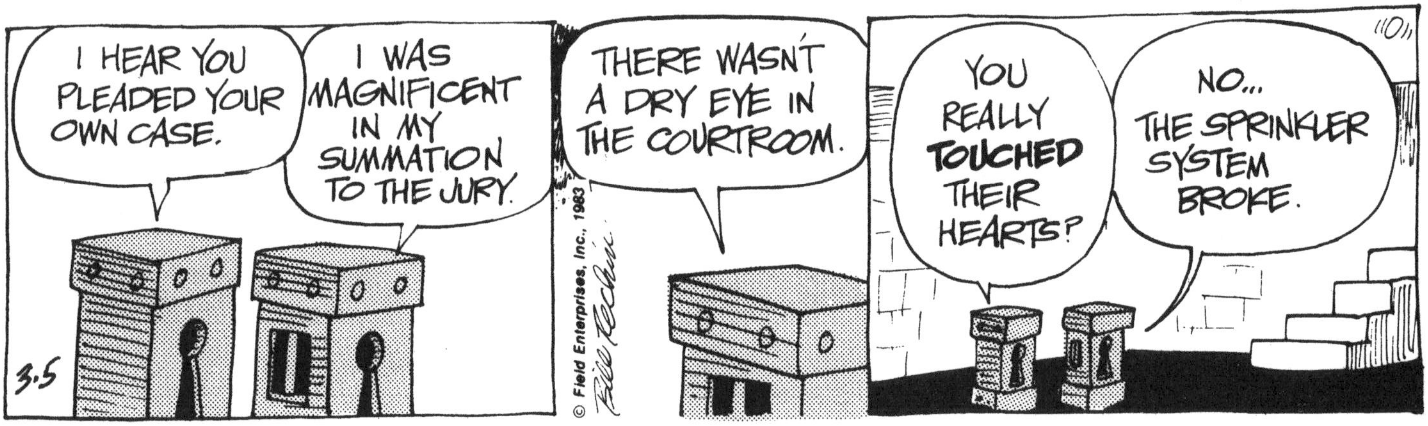
I HEAR YOU PLEADED YOUR OWN CASE.
I WAS MAGNIFICENT IN MY SUMMATION TO THE JURY.
3·5
© Field Enterprises, Inc., 1983
THERE WASN'T A DRY EYE IN THE COURTROOM.
YOU REALLY **TOUCHED** THEIR HEARTS?
NO... THE SPRINKLER SYSTEM BROKE.

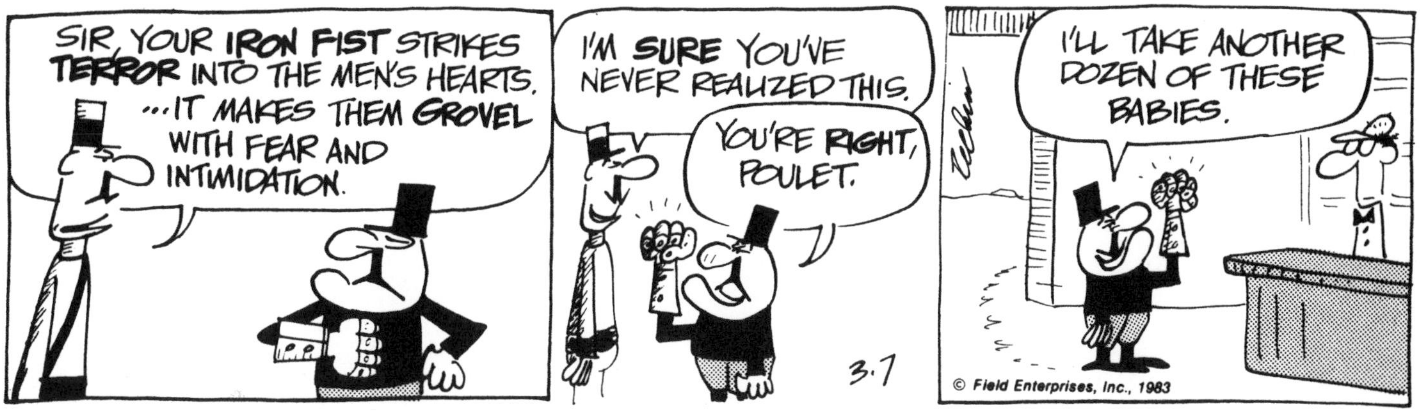
SIR, YOUR **IRON FIST** STRIKES **TERROR** INTO THE MEN'S HEARTS. ...IT MAKES THEM **GROVEL** WITH FEAR AND INTIMIDATION.
I'M **SURE** YOU'VE NEVER REALIZED THIS.
YOU'RE **RIGHT**, POULET.
3.7
I'LL TAKE ANOTHER DOZEN OF THESE BABIES.
© Field Enterprises, Inc., 1983

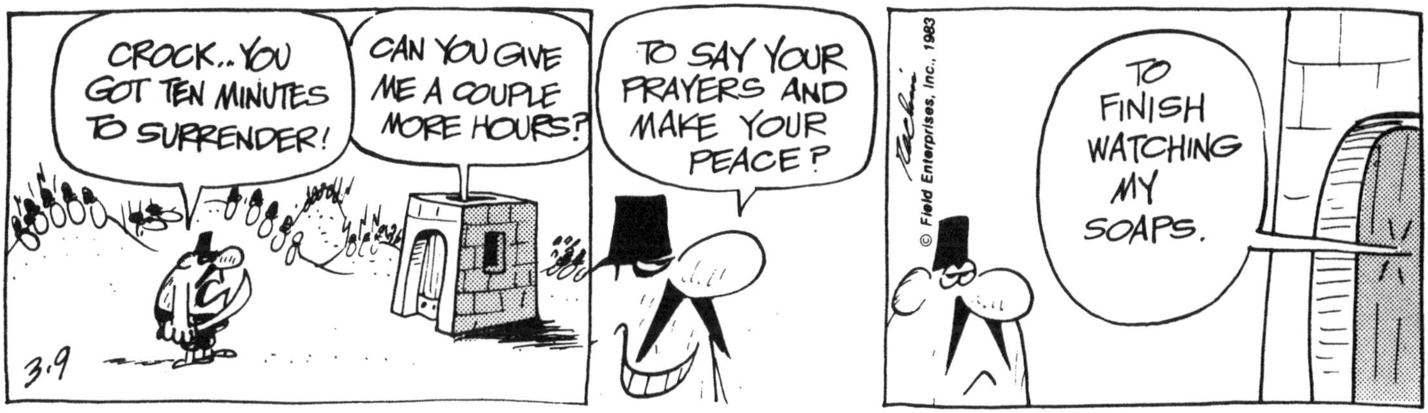
CROCK... YOU GOT TEN MINUTES TO SURRENDER!
CAN YOU GIVE ME A COUPLE MORE HOURS?
3.9
TO SAY YOUR PRAYERS AND MAKE YOUR PEACE?
© Field Enterprises, Inc., 1983
TO FINISH WATCHING MY SOAPS.

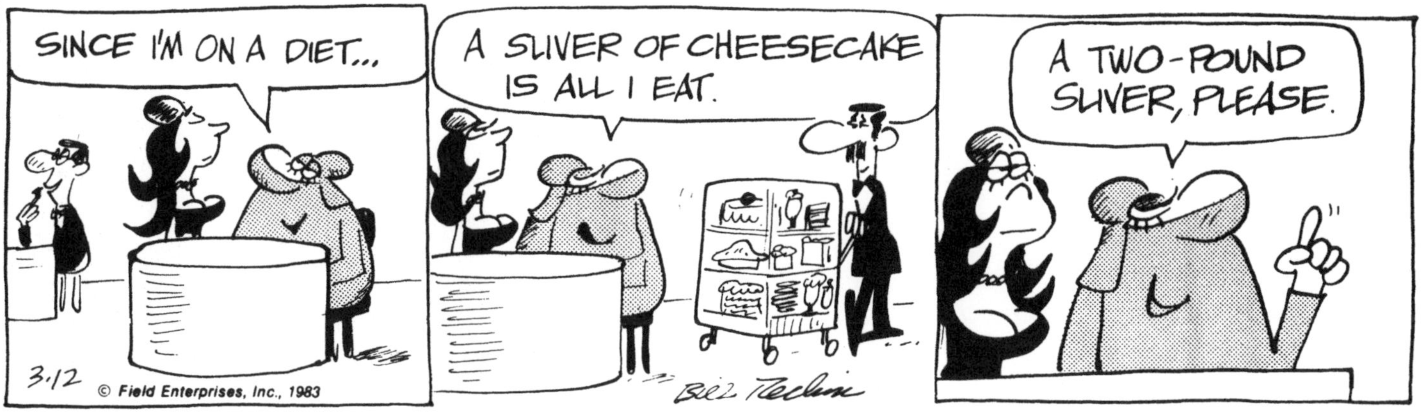
SINCE I'M ON A DIET...
3.12
© Field Enterprises, Inc., 1983
A SLIVER OF CHEESECAKE IS ALL I EAT.
A TWO-POUND SLIVER, PLEASE.

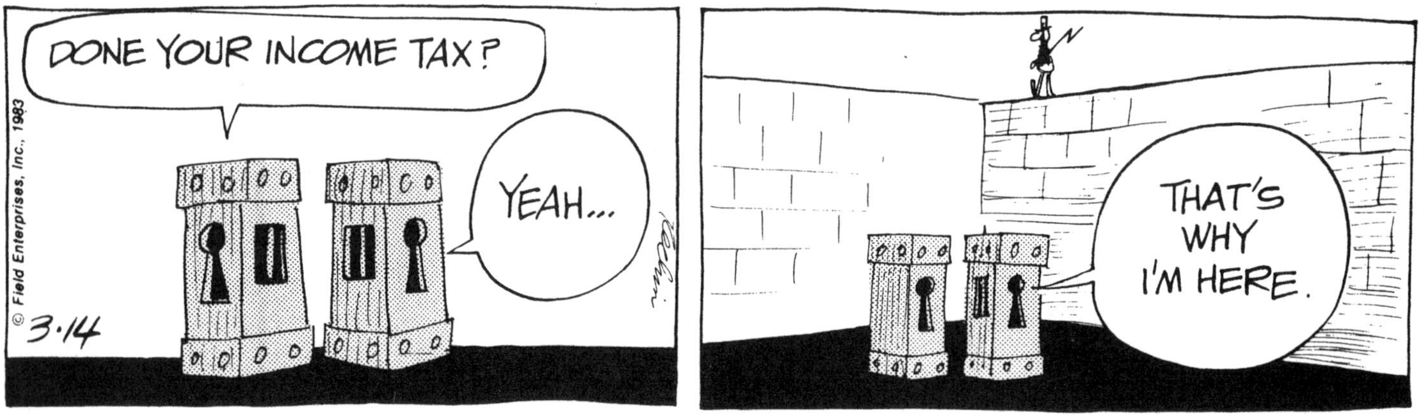
© Field Enterprises, Inc., 1983
3·14
DONE YOUR INCOME TAX?
YEAH...
THAT'S WHY I'M HERE.

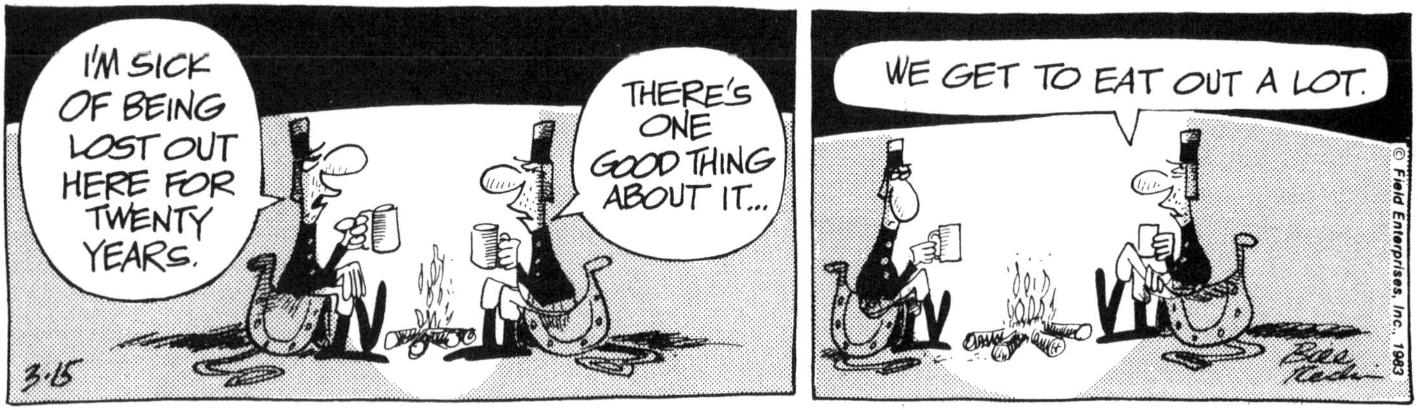
I'M SICK OF BEING LOST OUT HERE FOR TWENTY YEARS.
THERE'S ONE GOOD THING ABOUT IT...
WE GET TO EAT OUT A LOT.
3·15
© Field Enterprises, Inc., 1983

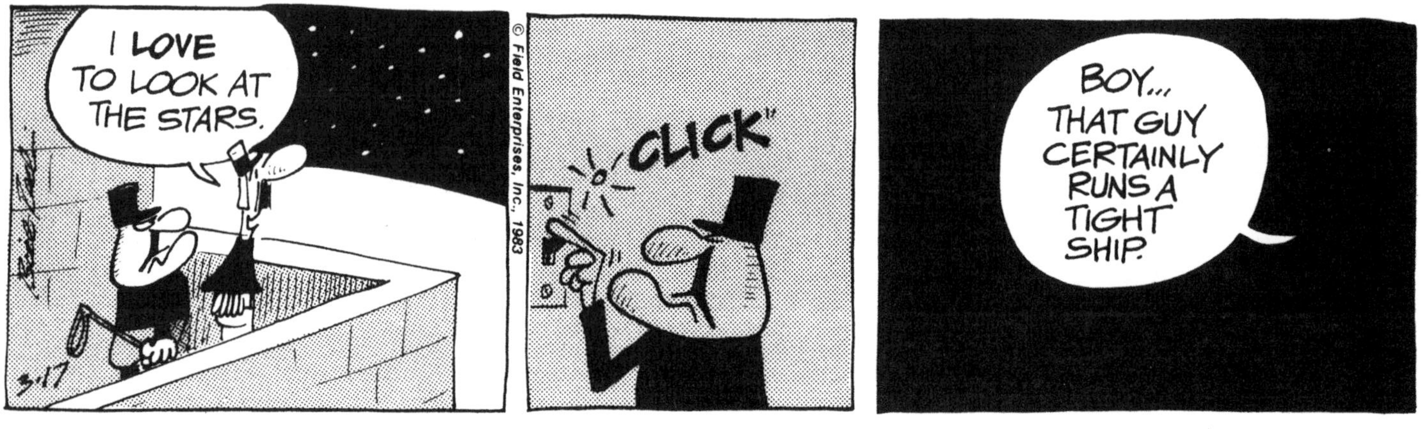
I **LOVE** TO LOOK AT THE STARS.
3·17
© Field Enterprises, Inc., 1983
CLICK
BOY... THAT GUY CERTAINLY RUNS A TIGHT SHIP.

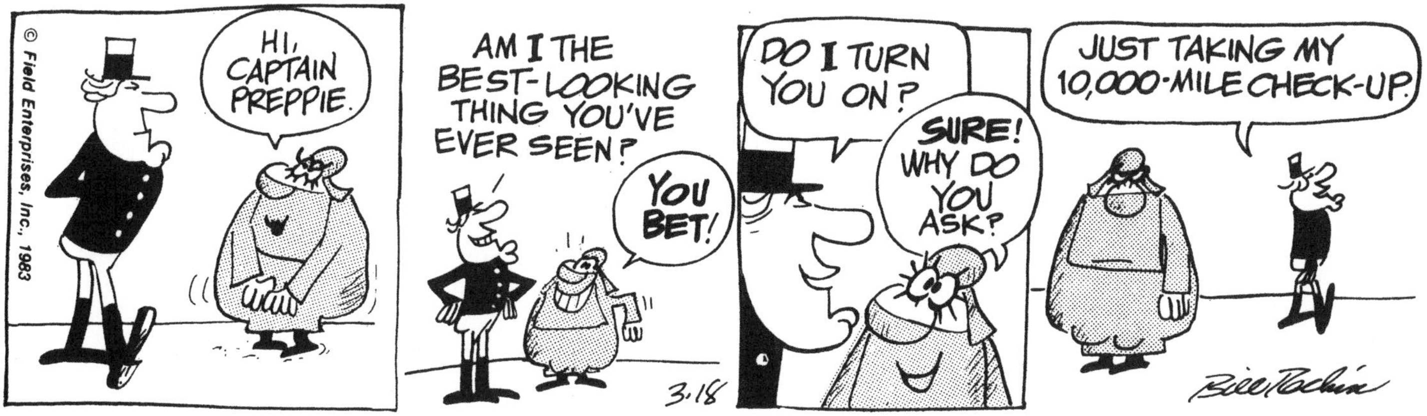
© Field Enterprises, Inc. 1983
HI, CAPTAIN PREPPIE.
AM I THE BEST-LOOKING THING YOU'VE EVER SEEN?
YOU BET!
3.18
DO I TURN YOU ON?
SURE! WHY DO YOU ASK?
JUST TAKING MY 10,000-MILE CHECK-UP.
Bill Rechin

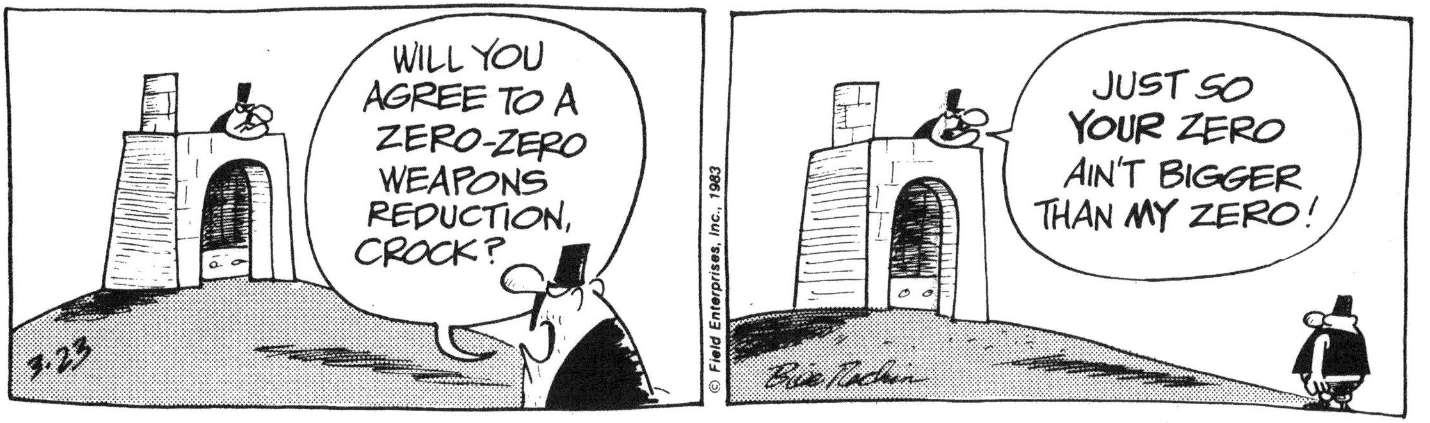
WILL YOU AGREE TO A ZERO-ZERO WEAPONS REDUCTION, CROCK?
3.23
© Field Enterprises, Inc., 1983
JUST SO YOUR ZERO AIN'T BIGGER THAN MY ZERO!
Bill Rechin

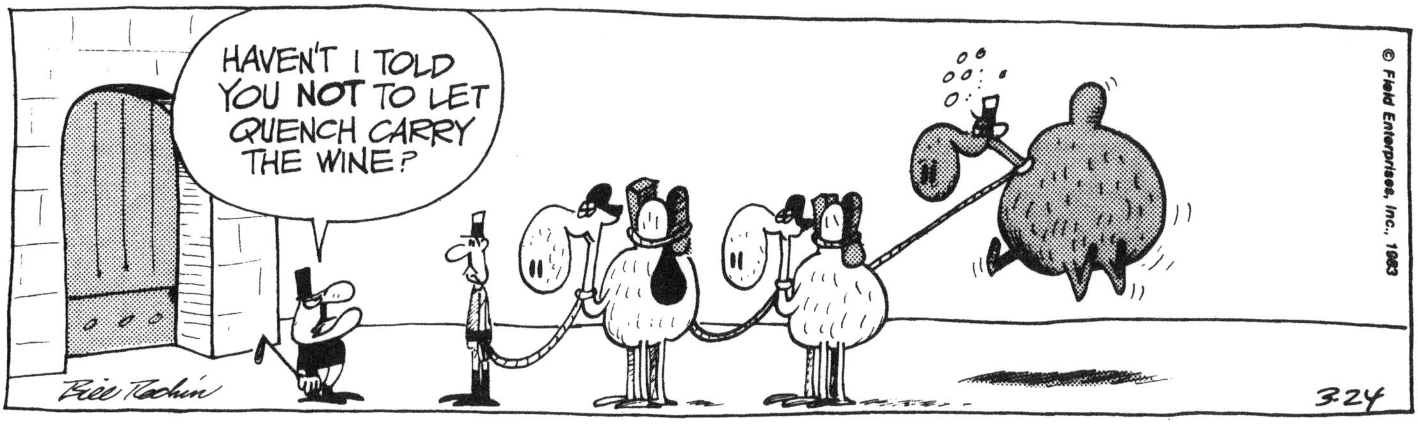
HAVEN'T I TOLD YOU NOT TO LET QUENCH CARRY THE WINE?
© Field Enterprises, Inc., 1983
Bill Rechin
3.24

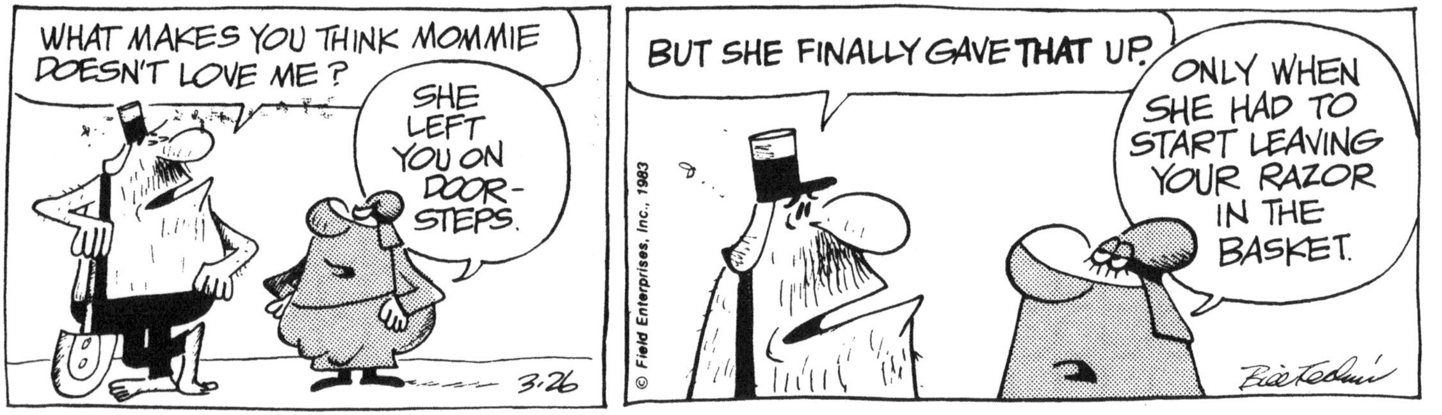
WHAT MAKES YOU THINK MOMMIE DOESN'T LOVE ME?
SHE LEFT YOU ON DOOR-STEPS.
3.26
BUT SHE FINALLY GAVE **THAT** UP.
ONLY WHEN SHE HAD TO START LEAVING YOUR RAZOR IN THE BASKET.
© Field Enterprises, Inc., 1983
Bill Rechin

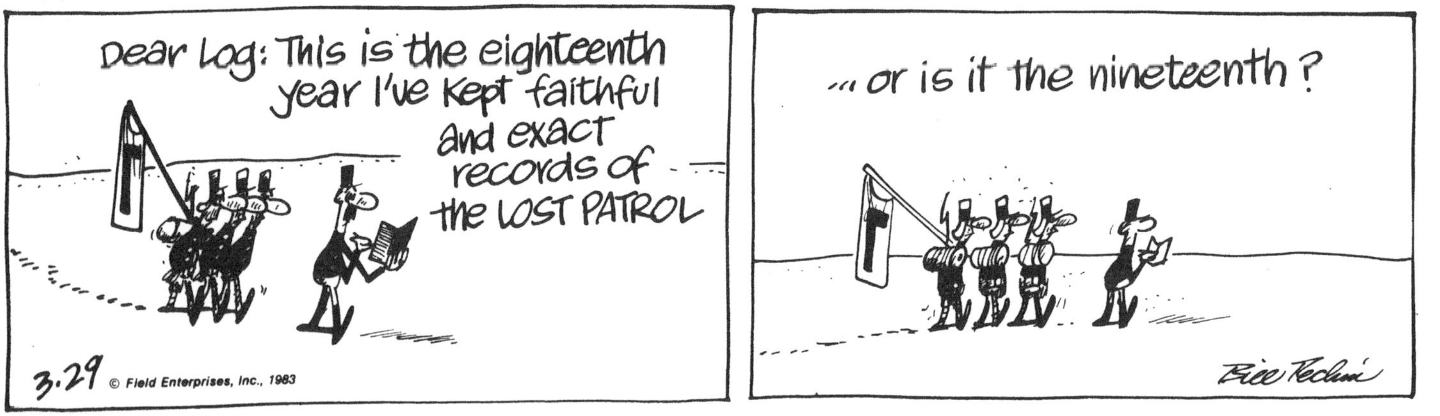
Dear Log: This is the eighteenth year I've kept faithful and exact records of the LOST PATROL
3.29 © Field Enterprises, Inc., 1983
... or is it the nineteenth?
Bill Rechin

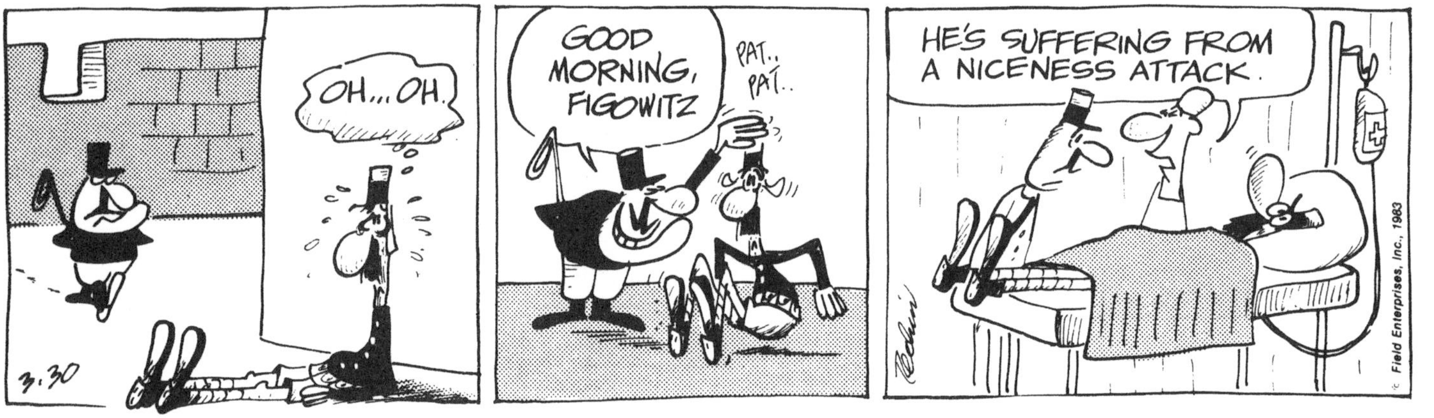
OH... OH.
3.30
GOOD MORNING, FIGOWITZ
PAT.. PAT..
HE'S SUFFERING FROM A NICENESS ATTACK.
Rechin
© Field Enterprises, Inc., 1983

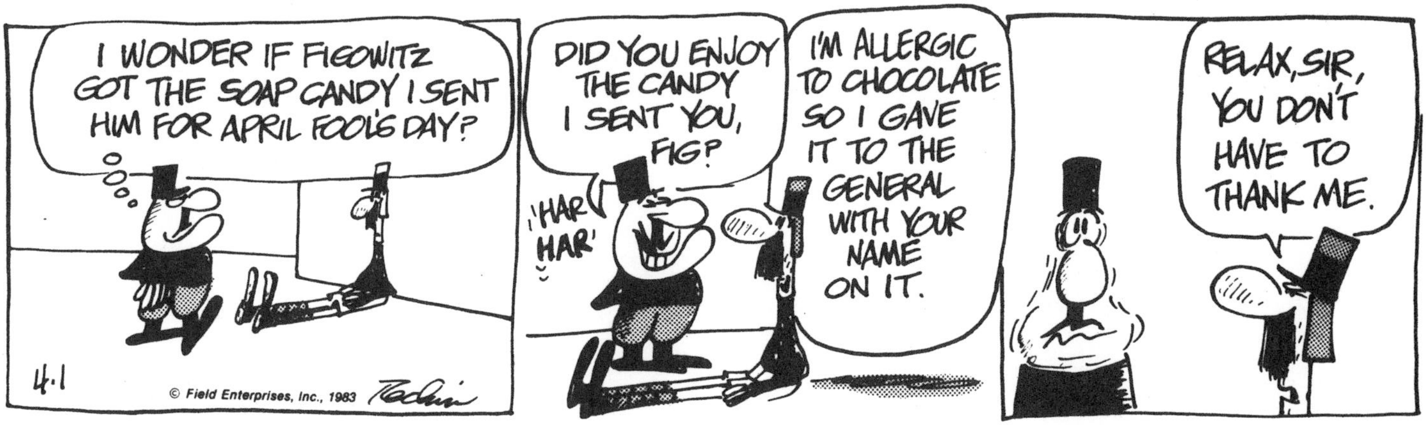
I WONDER IF FIGOWITZ GOT THE SOAP CANDY I SENT HIM FOR APRIL FOOL'S DAY?
4.1
© Field Enterprises, Inc., 1983
DID YOU ENJOY THE CANDY I SENT YOU, FIG?
HAR HAR
I'M ALLERGIC TO CHOCOLATE SO I GAVE IT TO THE GENERAL WITH YOUR NAME ON IT.
RELAX, SIR, YOU DON'T HAVE TO THANK ME.

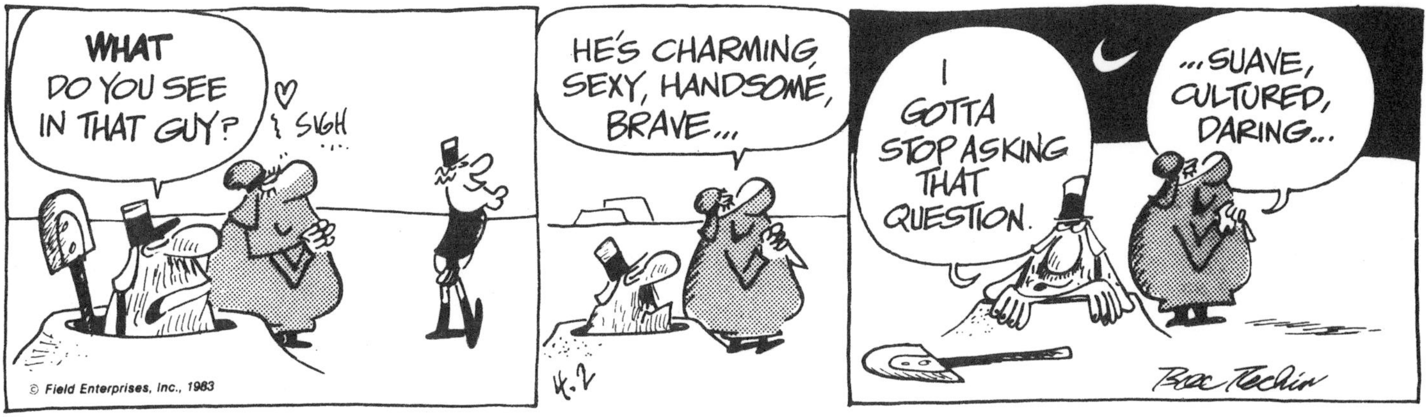
WHAT DO YOU SEE IN THAT GUY?
SIGH
© Field Enterprises, Inc., 1983
HE'S CHARMING, SEXY, HANDSOME, BRAVE...
4.2
I GOTTA STOP ASKING THAT QUESTION.
...SUAVE, CULTURED, DARING...

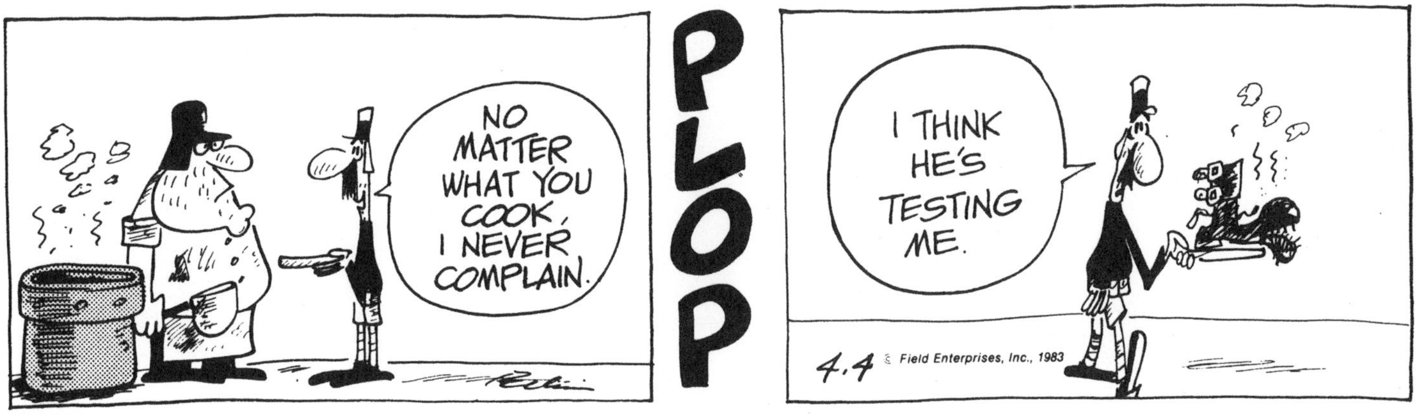
NO MATTER WHAT YOU COOK, I NEVER COMPLAIN.
PLOP
I THINK HE'S TESTING ME.
4.4
© Field Enterprises, Inc., 1983

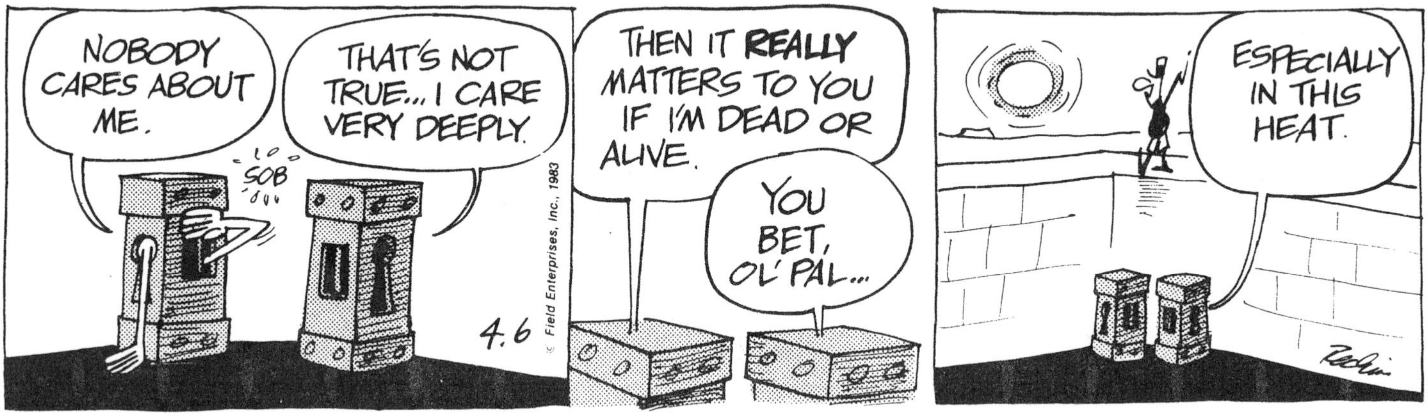
NOBODY CARES ABOUT ME.
SOB
THAT'S NOT TRUE... I CARE VERY DEEPLY.
4.6
© Field Enterprises, Inc., 1983
THEN IT **REALLY** MATTERS TO YOU IF I'M DEAD OR ALIVE.
YOU BET, OL' PAL...
ESPECIALLY IN THIS HEAT.

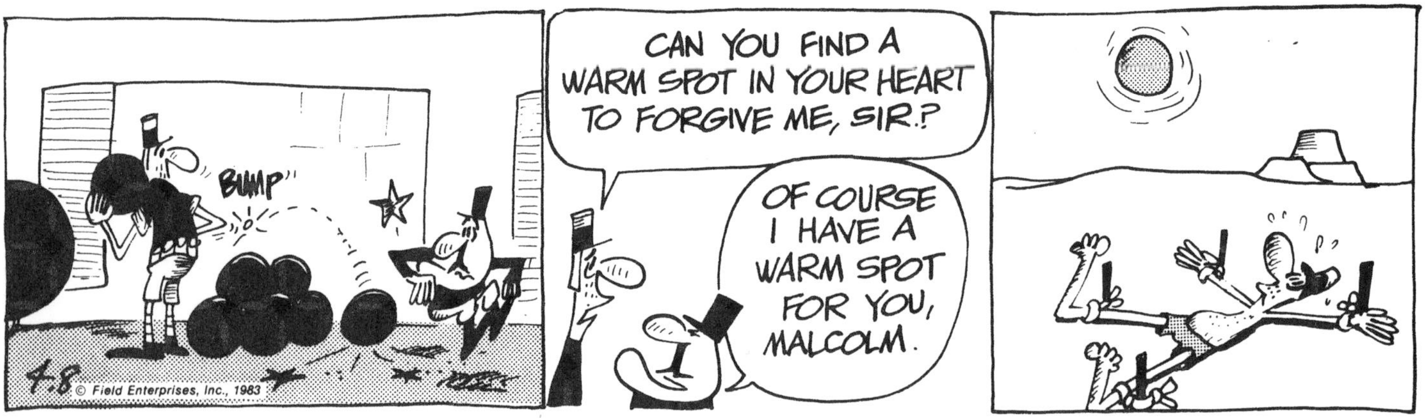
BUMP
4.8
© Field Enterprises, Inc., 1983
CAN YOU FIND A WARM SPOT IN YOUR HEART TO FORGIVE ME, SIR.?
OF COURSE I HAVE A WARM SPOT FOR YOU, MALCOLM.

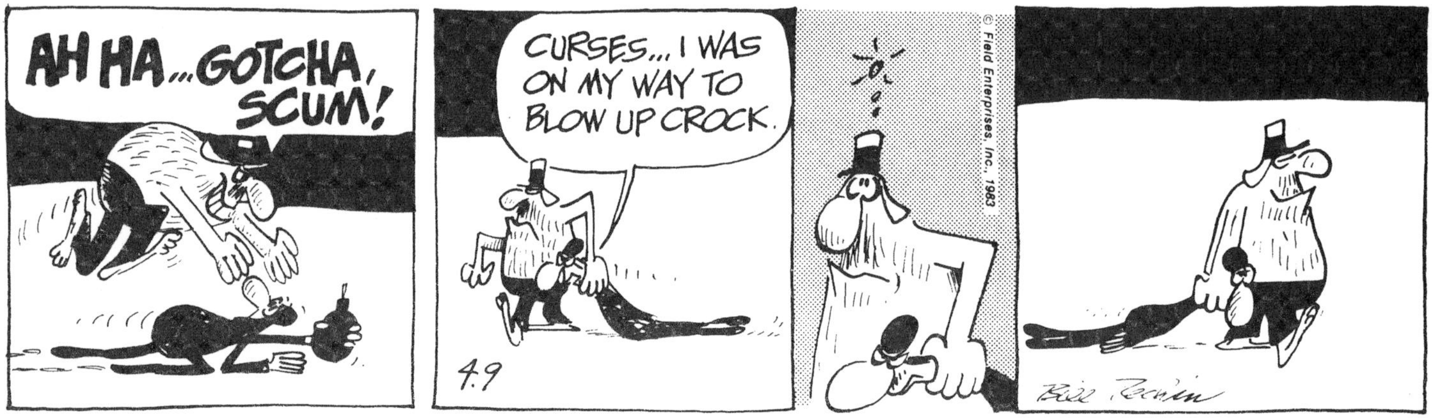
AH HA...GOTCHA, SCUM!
CURSES... I WAS ON MY WAY TO BLOW UP CROCK.
4.9
© Field Enterprises, Inc., 1983

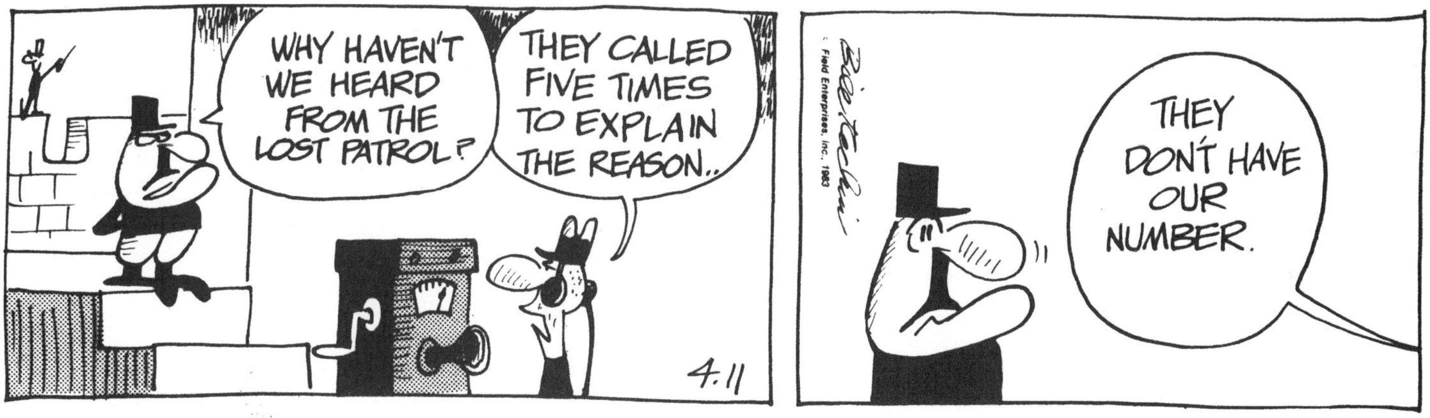
WHY HAVEN'T WE HEARD FROM THE LOST PATROL?
THEY CALLED FIVE TIMES TO EXPLAIN THE REASON...
4.11
© Field Enterprises, Inc., 1983
THEY DON'T HAVE OUR NUMBER.

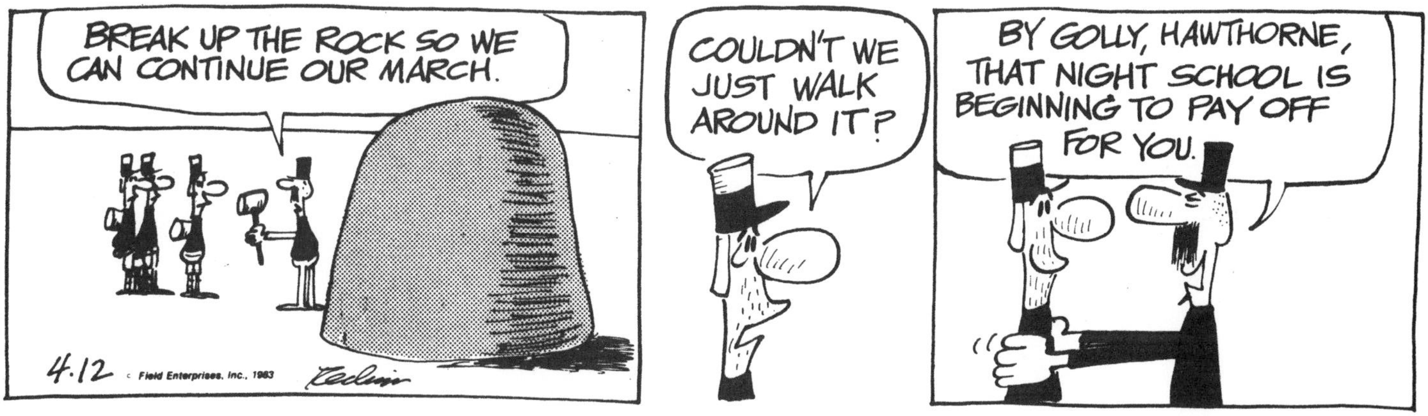
BREAK UP THE ROCK SO WE CAN CONTINUE OUR MARCH.
4.12
© Field Enterprises, Inc., 1983
COULDN'T WE JUST WALK AROUND IT?
BY GOLLY, HAWTHORNE, THAT NIGHT SCHOOL IS BEGINNING TO PAY OFF FOR YOU.

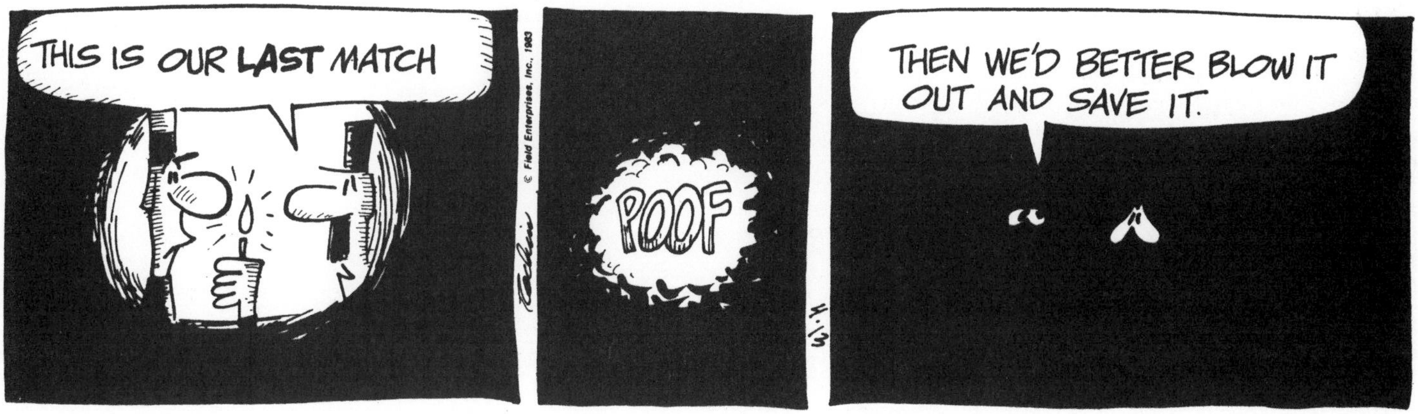
THIS IS OUR **LAST** MATCH
© Field Enterprises, Inc., 1983
POOF
4.13
THEN WE'D BETTER BLOW IT OUT AND SAVE IT.

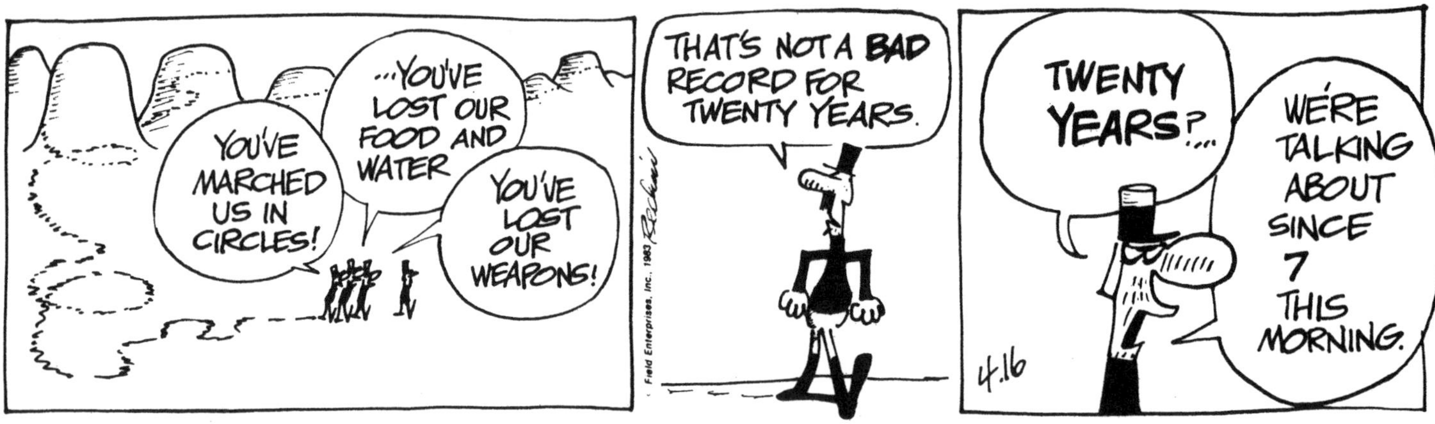
YOU'VE MARCHED US IN CIRCLES!
...YOU'VE LOST OUR FOOD AND WATER
YOU'VE LOST OUR WEAPONS!
© Field Enterprises, Inc., 1983
Rechin
THAT'S NOT A **BAD** RECORD FOR TWENTY YEARS.
TWENTY YEARS?...
WE'RE TALKING ABOUT SINCE 7 THIS MORNING.
4.16

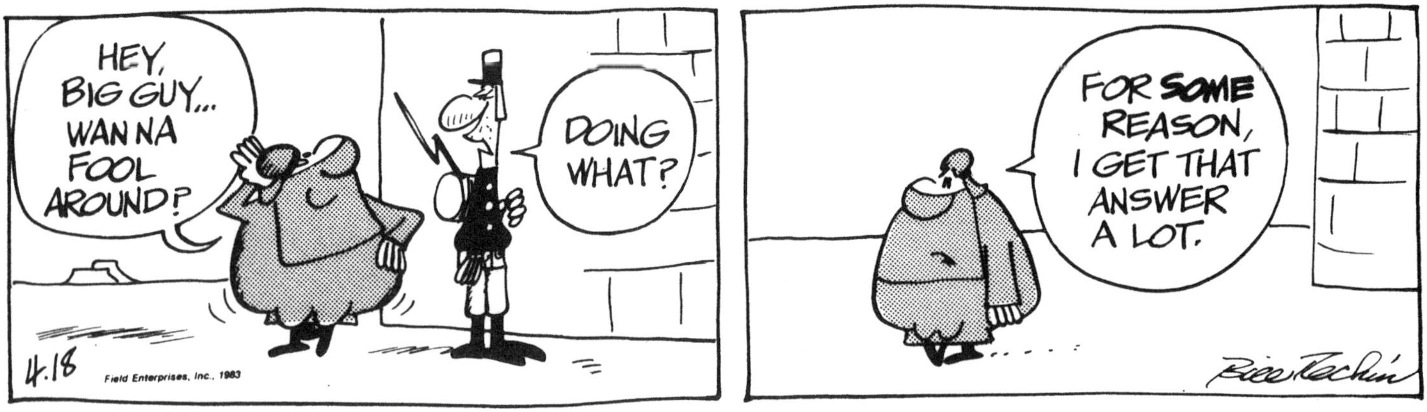
HEY, BIG GUY... WAN NA FOOL AROUND?
DOING WHAT?
4.18
Field Enterprises, Inc., 1983
FOR **SOME** REASON, I GET THAT ANSWER A LOT.
Bill Rechin

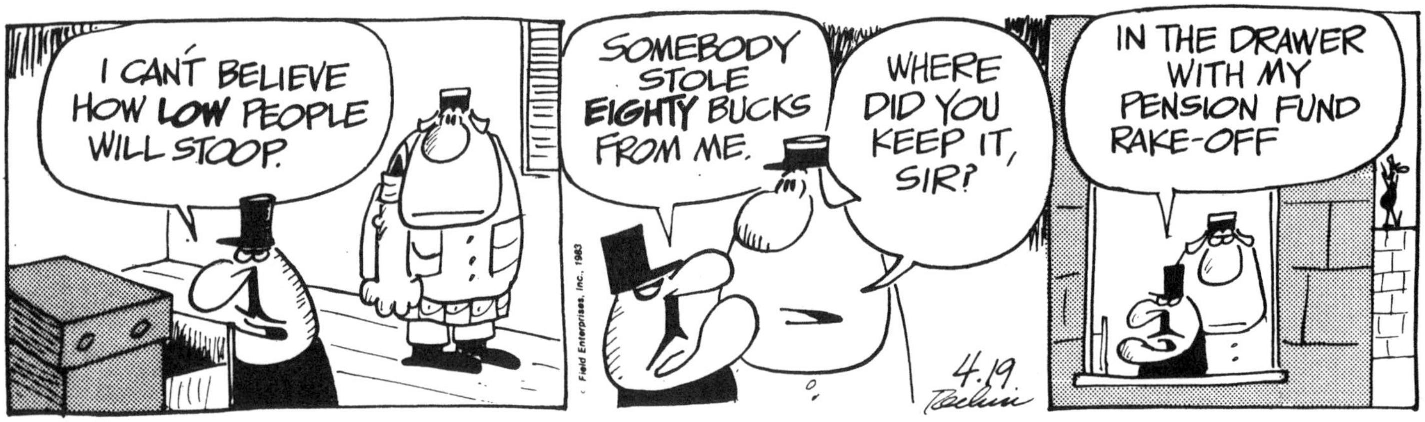
I CAN'T BELIEVE HOW **LOW** PEOPLE WILL STOOP.
SOMEBODY STOLE **EIGHTY** BUCKS FROM ME.
WHERE DID YOU KEEP IT, SIR?
© Field Enterprises, Inc., 1983
4.19
Rechin
IN THE DRAWER WITH MY PENSION FUND RAKE-OFF

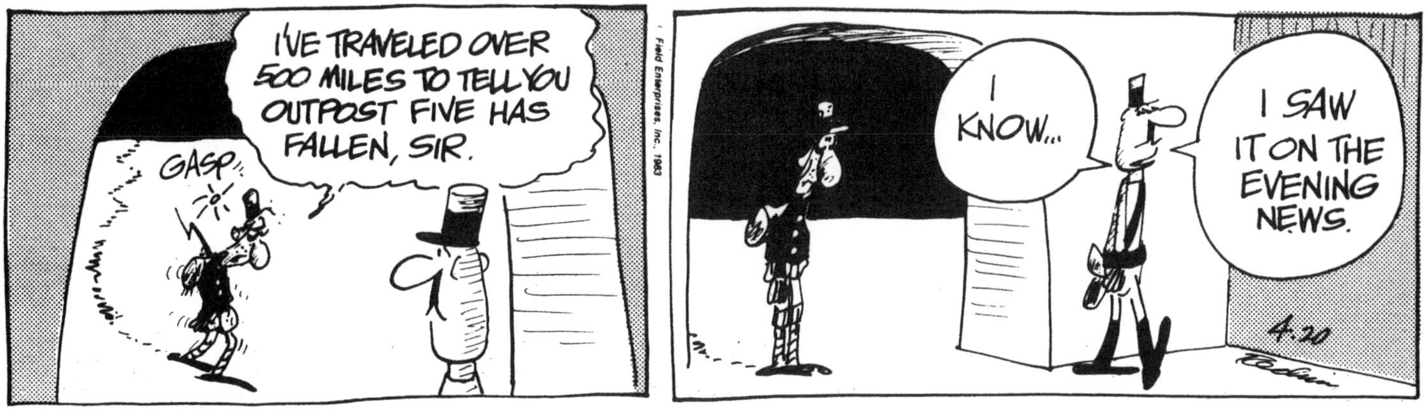
I'VE TRAVELED OVER 500 MILES TO TELL YOU OUTPOST FIVE HAS FALLEN, SIR.
GASP
I KNOW...
I SAW IT ON THE EVENING NEWS.
4·20
© Field Enterprises, Inc., 1983

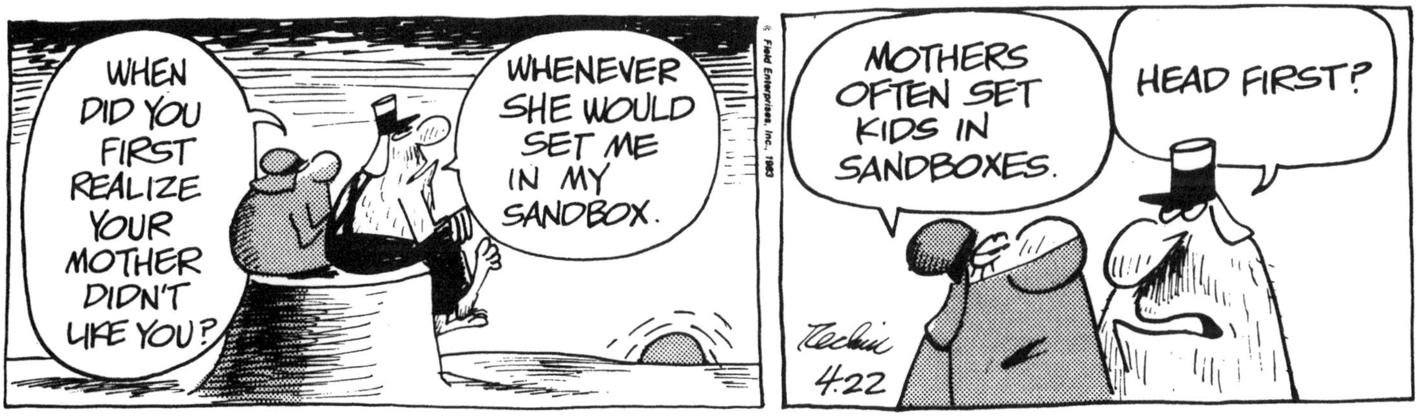
WHEN DID YOU FIRST REALIZE YOUR MOTHER DIDN'T LIKE YOU?
WHENEVER SHE WOULD SET ME IN MY SANDBOX.
MOTHERS OFTEN SET KIDS IN SANDBOXES.
HEAD FIRST?
4·22
© Field Enterprises, Inc., 1983

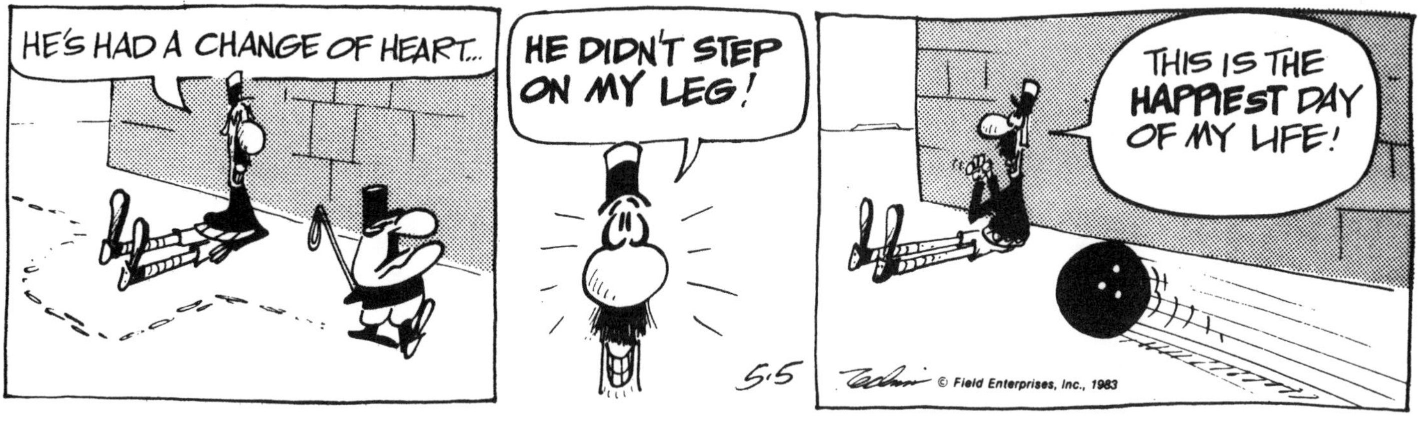
HE'S HAD A CHANGE OF HEART...
HE DIDN'T STEP ON MY LEG!
THIS IS THE HAPPIEST DAY OF MY LIFE!
5·5
© Field Enterprises, Inc., 1983

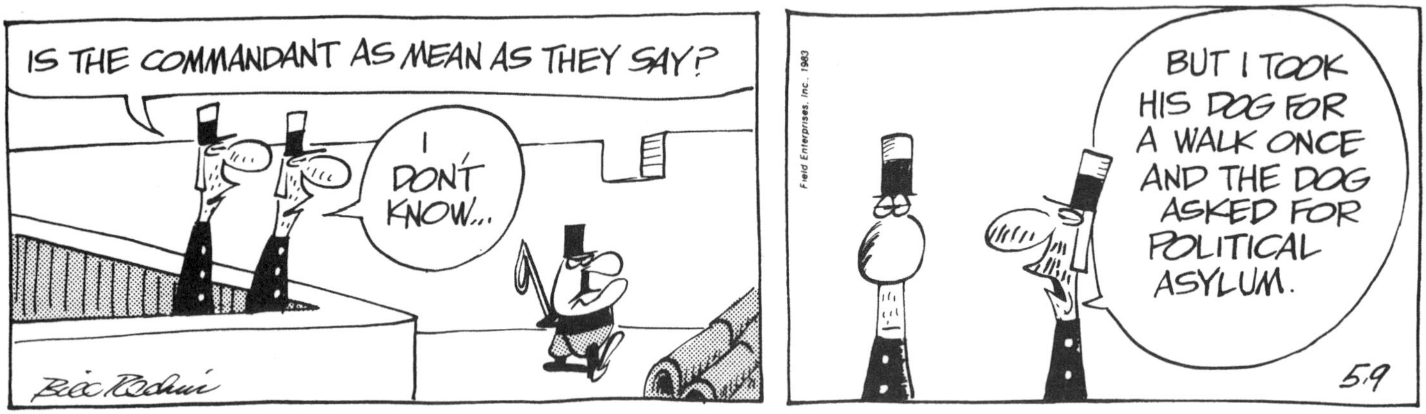
IS THE COMMANDANT AS MEAN AS THEY SAY?
I DON'T KNOW...
BUT I TOOK HIS DOG FOR A WALK ONCE AND THE DOG ASKED FOR POLITICAL ASYLUM.
Field Enterprises, Inc. 1983
5.9

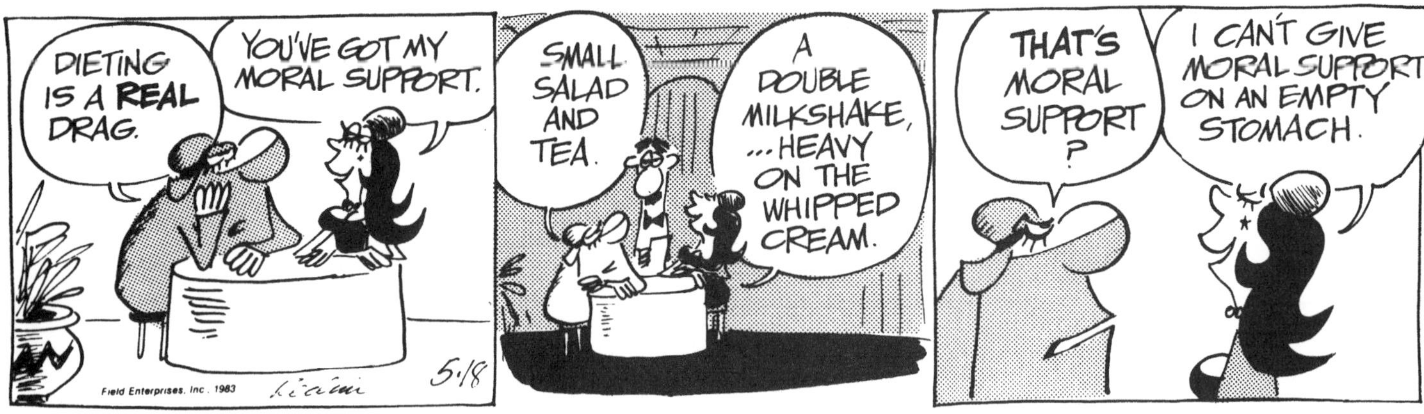
DIETING IS A **REAL** DRAG.
YOU'VE GOT MY MORAL SUPPORT.
Field Enterprises, Inc. 1983
5.18
SMALL SALAD AND TEA.
A DOUBLE MILKSHAKE, ...HEAVY ON THE WHIPPED CREAM.
THAT'S MORAL SUPPORT?
I CAN'T GIVE MORAL SUPPORT ON AN EMPTY STOMACH.

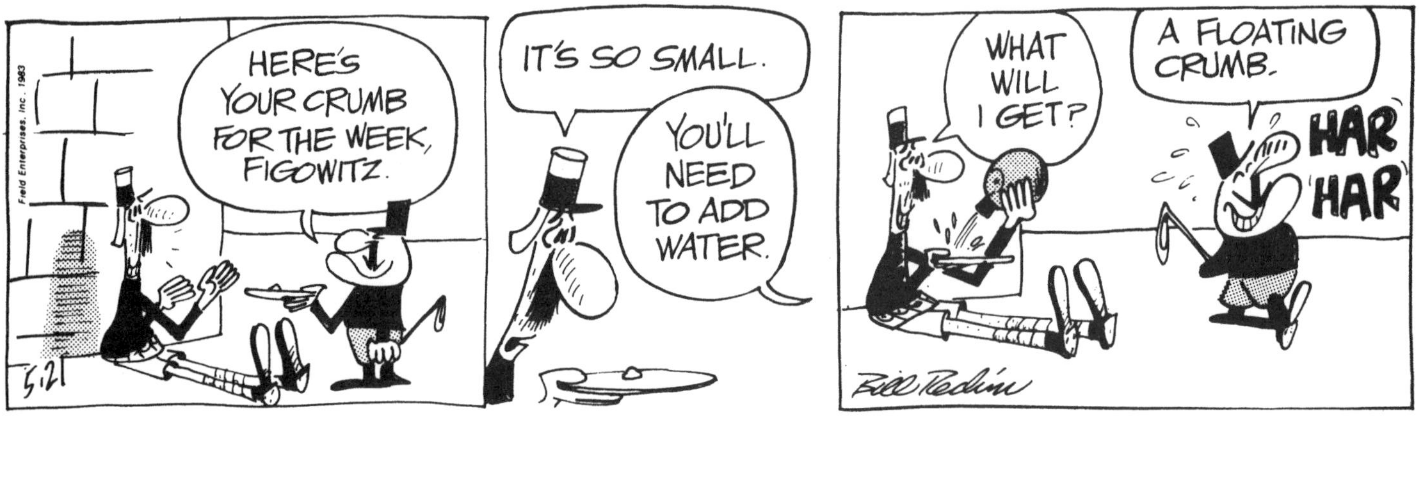
Field Enterprises, Inc. 1983
HERE'S YOUR CRUMB FOR THE WEEK, FIGOWITZ.
5.21
IT'S SO SMALL.
YOU'LL NEED TO ADD WATER.
WHAT WILL I GET?
A FLOATING CRUMB.
HAR HAR

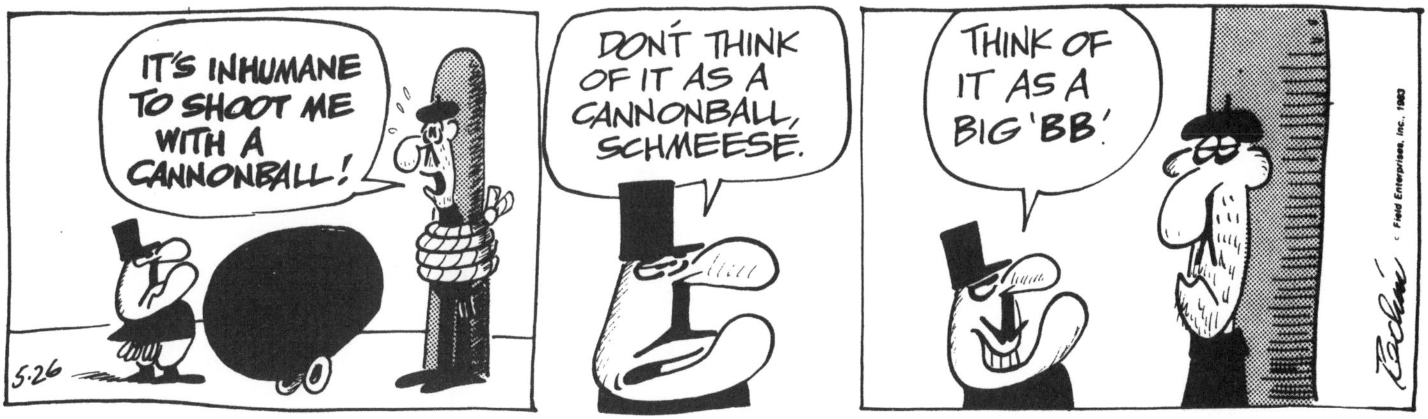
IT'S INHUMANE TO SHOOT ME WITH A CANNONBALL!
5.26
DON'T THINK OF IT AS A CANNONBALL, SCHMEESE.
THINK OF IT AS A BIG 'BB'.
© Field Enterprises, Inc., 1983

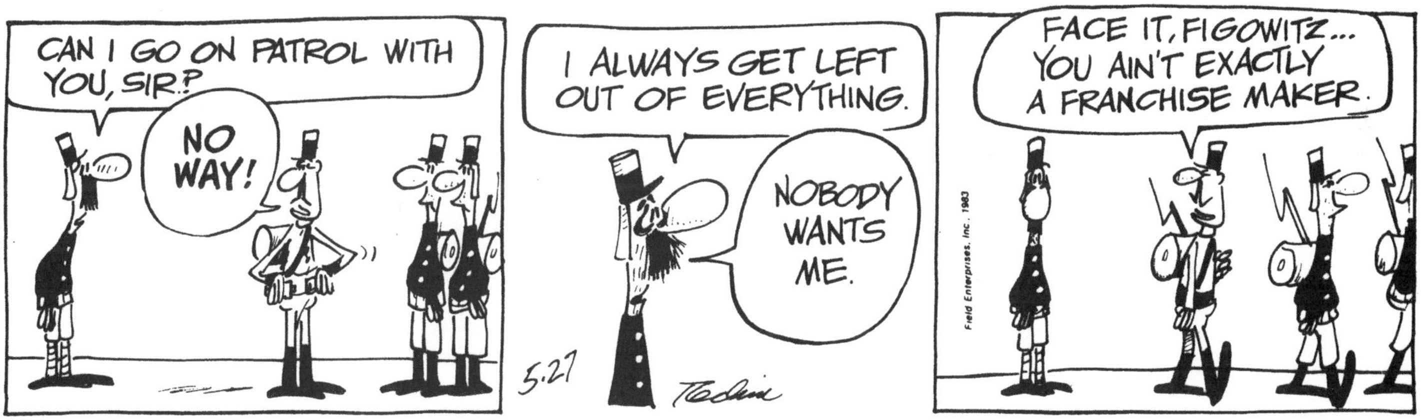
CAN I GO ON PATROL WITH YOU, SIR?
NO WAY!
I ALWAYS GET LEFT OUT OF EVERYTHING.
NOBODY WANTS ME.
5.27
FACE IT, FIGOWITZ... YOU AIN'T EXACTLY A FRANCHISE MAKER.
Field Enterprises, Inc., 1983

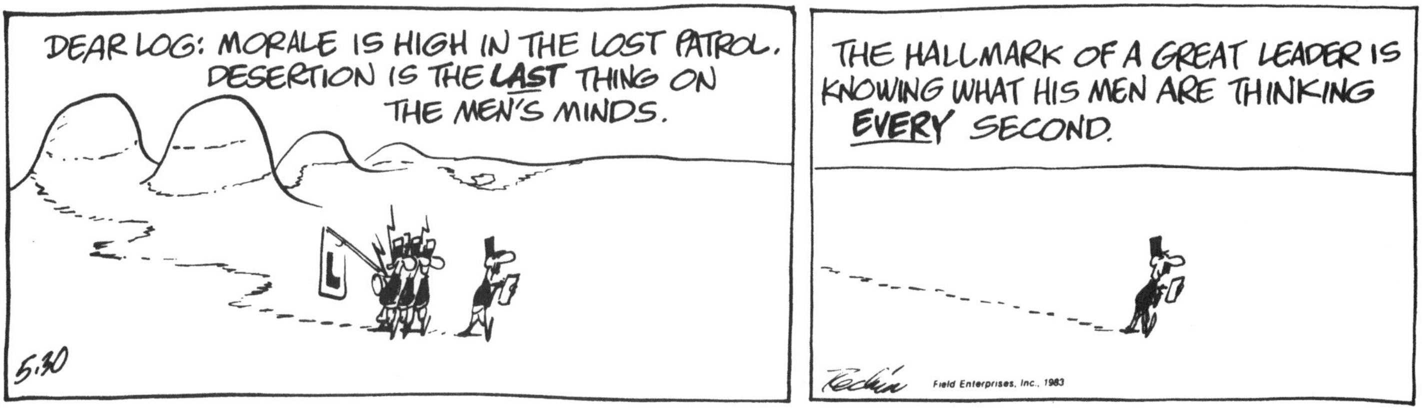
DEAR LOG: MORALE IS HIGH IN THE LOST PATROL. DESERTION IS THE LAST THING ON THE MEN'S MINDS.
L
5.30
THE HALLMARK OF A GREAT LEADER IS KNOWING WHAT HIS MEN ARE THINKING EVERY SECOND.
Field Enterprises, Inc., 1983

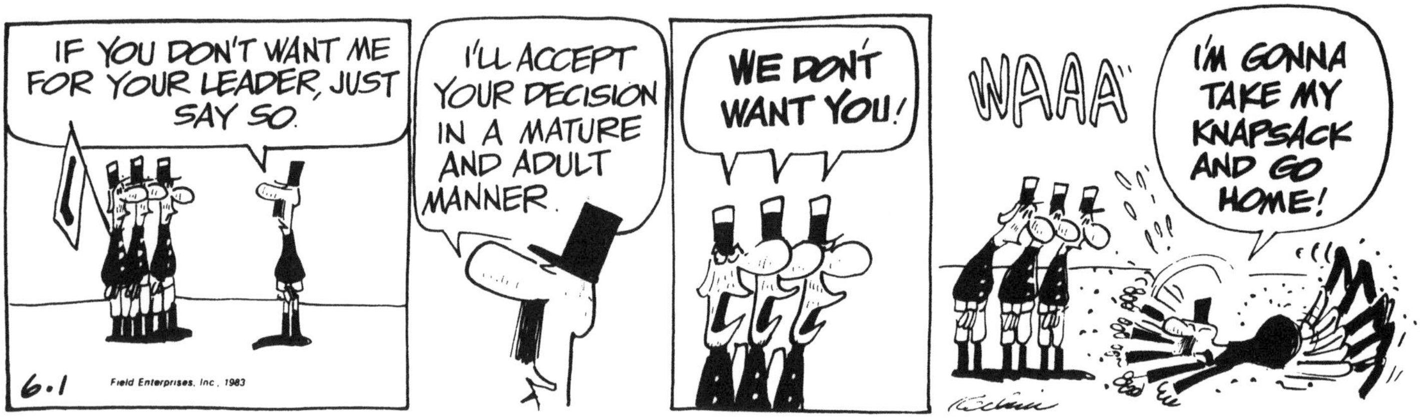
IF YOU DON'T WANT ME FOR YOUR LEADER, JUST SAY SO.
6·1
© Field Enterprises, Inc., 1983
I'LL ACCEPT YOUR DECISION IN A MATURE AND ADULT MANNER.
WE DON'T WANT YOU!
WAAA
I'M GONNA TAKE MY KNAPSACK AND GO HOME!

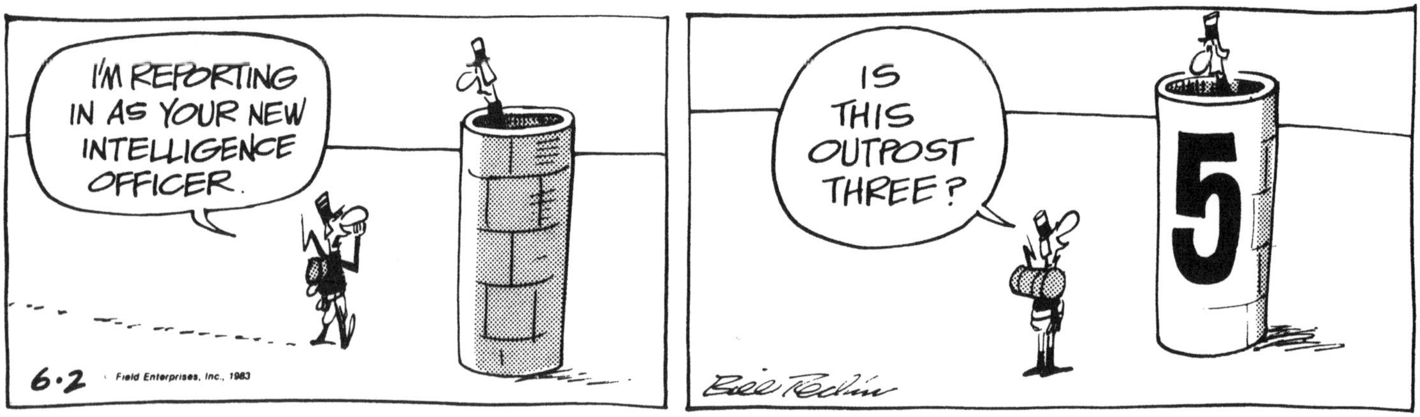
I'M REPORTING IN AS YOUR NEW INTELLIGENCE OFFICER.
6·2
© Field Enterprises, Inc., 1983
IS THIS OUTPOST THREE?
5
Bill Rechin

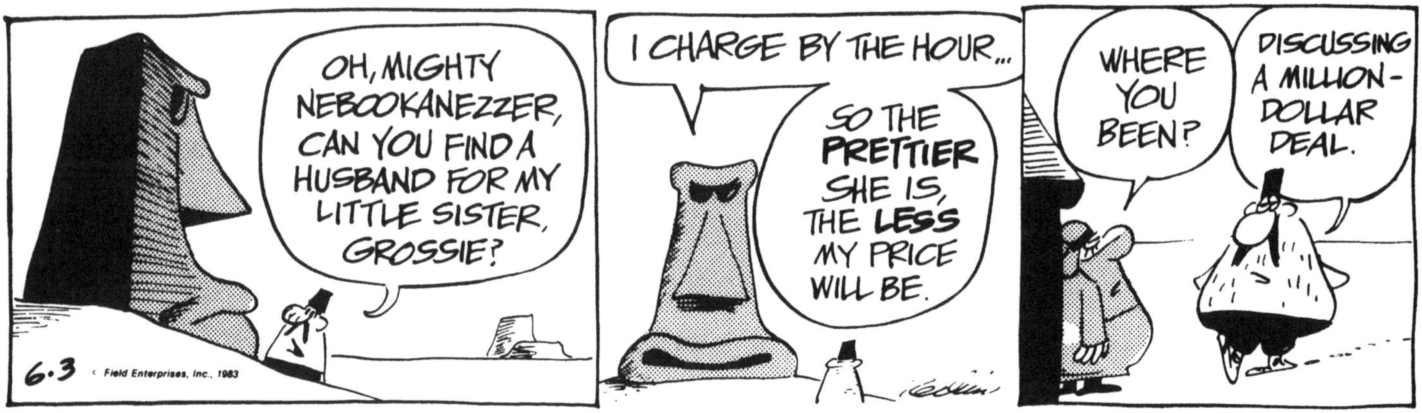
OH, MIGHTY NEBOOKANEZZER, CAN YOU FIND A HUSBAND FOR MY LITTLE SISTER, GROSSIE?
6·3
© Field Enterprises, Inc., 1983
I CHARGE BY THE HOUR...
SO THE PRETTIER SHE IS, THE LESS MY PRICE WILL BE.
WHERE YOU BEEN?
DISCUSSING A MILLION-DOLLAR DEAL.

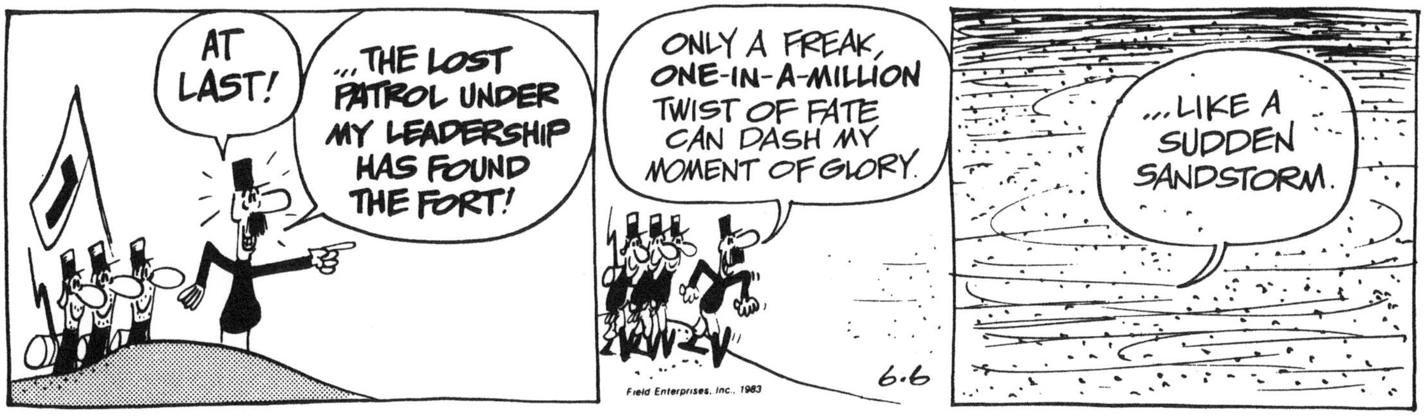
AT LAST!
...THE LOST PATROL UNDER MY LEADERSHIP HAS FOUND THE FORT!
ONLY A FREAK, ONE-IN-A-MILLION TWIST OF FATE CAN DASH MY MOMENT OF GLORY.
Field Enterprises, Inc., 1983
6·6
...LIKE A SUDDEN SANDSTORM.

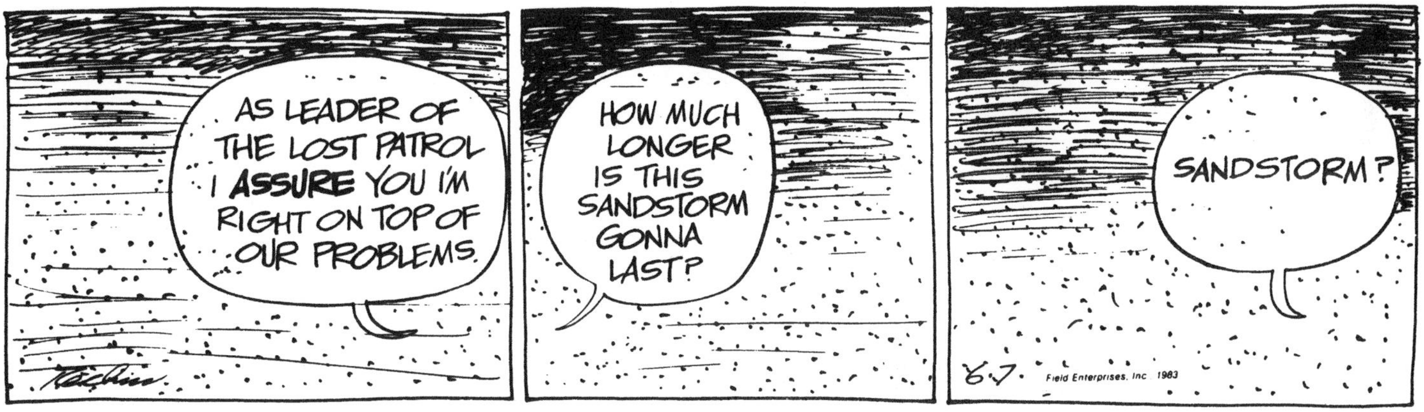
AS LEADER OF THE LOST PATROL I ASSURE YOU I'M RIGHT ON TOP OF OUR PROBLEMS.
HOW MUCH LONGER IS THIS SANDSTORM GONNA LAST?
SANDSTORM?
6·7
Field Enterprises, Inc 1983

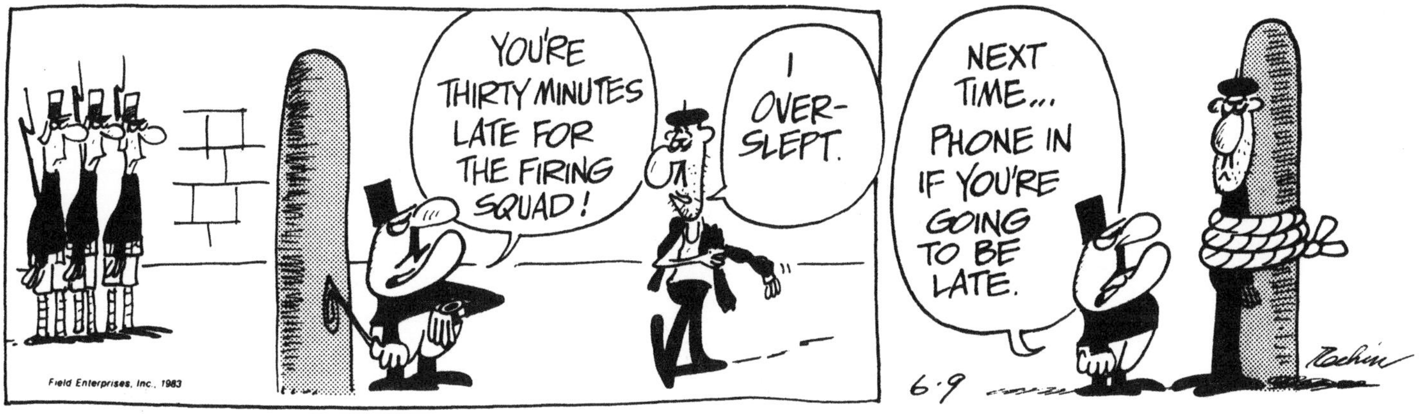
YOU'RE THIRTY MINUTES LATE FOR THE FIRING SQUAD!
I OVER-SLEPT.
Field Enterprises, Inc., 1983
NEXT TIME... PHONE IN IF YOU'RE GOING TO BE LATE.
6·9

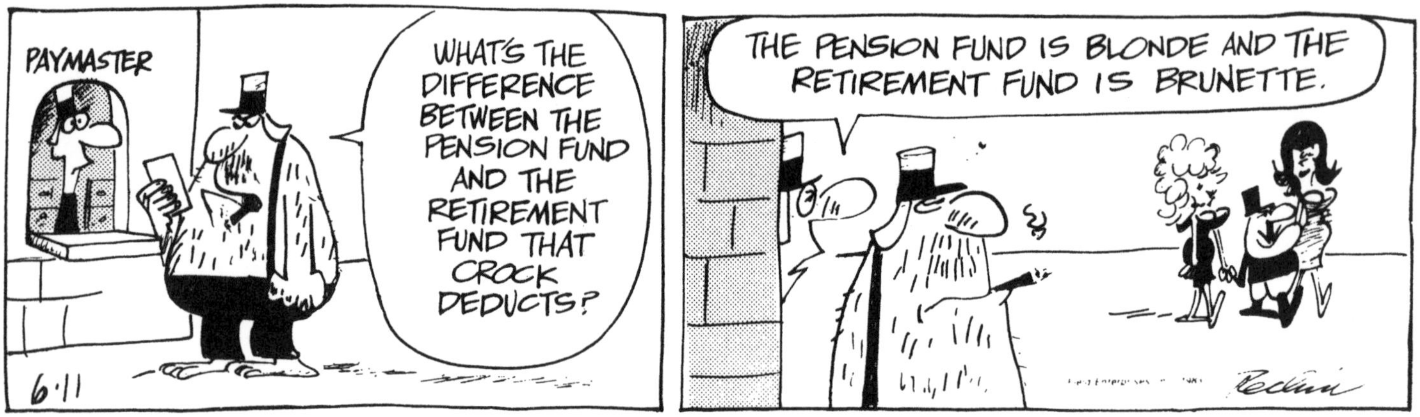
PAYMASTER
WHAT'S THE DIFFERENCE BETWEEN THE PENSION FUND AND THE RETIREMENT FUND THAT CROCK DEDUCTS?
THE PENSION FUND IS BLONDE AND THE RETIREMENT FUND IS BRUNETTE.
6·11

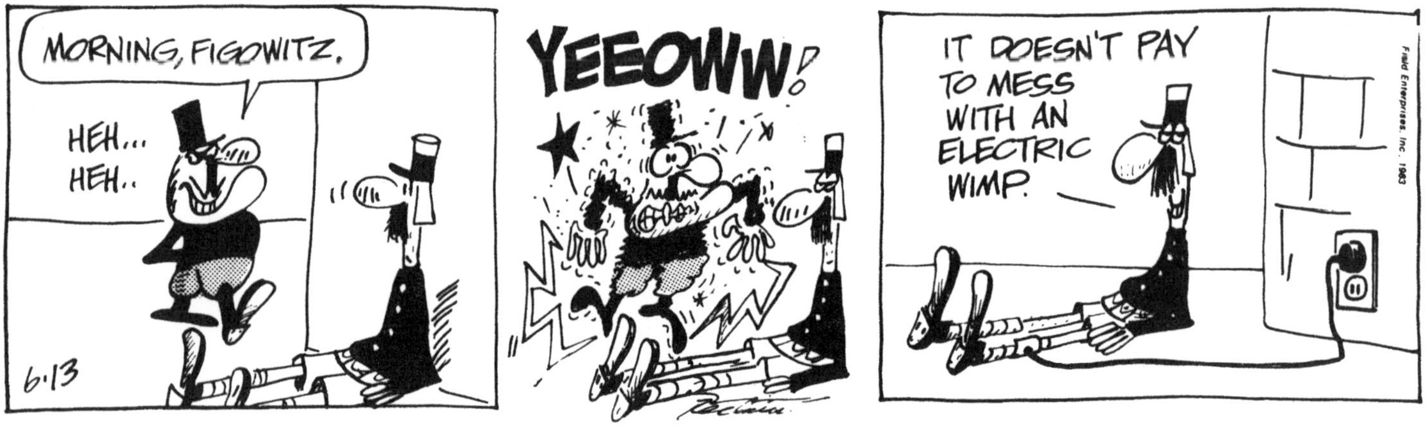
MORNING, FIGOWITZ.
HEH... HEH..
6·13
YEEOWW!
IT DOESN'T PAY TO MESS WITH AN ELECTRIC WIMP.
Field Enterprises, Inc. 1983

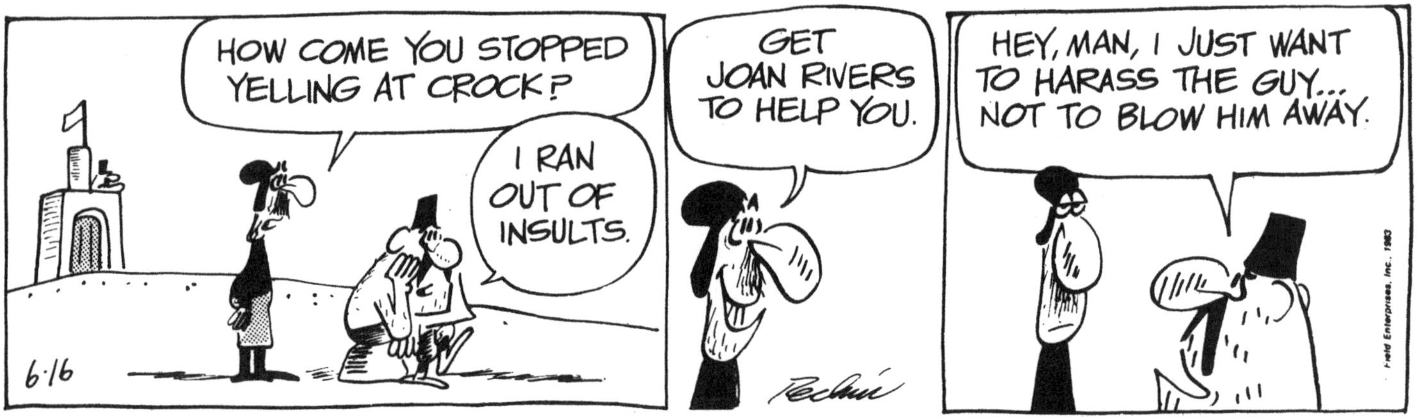
HOW COME YOU STOPPED YELLING AT CROCK?
I RAN OUT OF INSULTS.
6·16
GET JOAN RIVERS TO HELP YOU.
HEY, MAN, I JUST WANT TO HARASS THE GUY... NOT TO BLOW HIM AWAY.
Field Enterprises, Inc. 1983

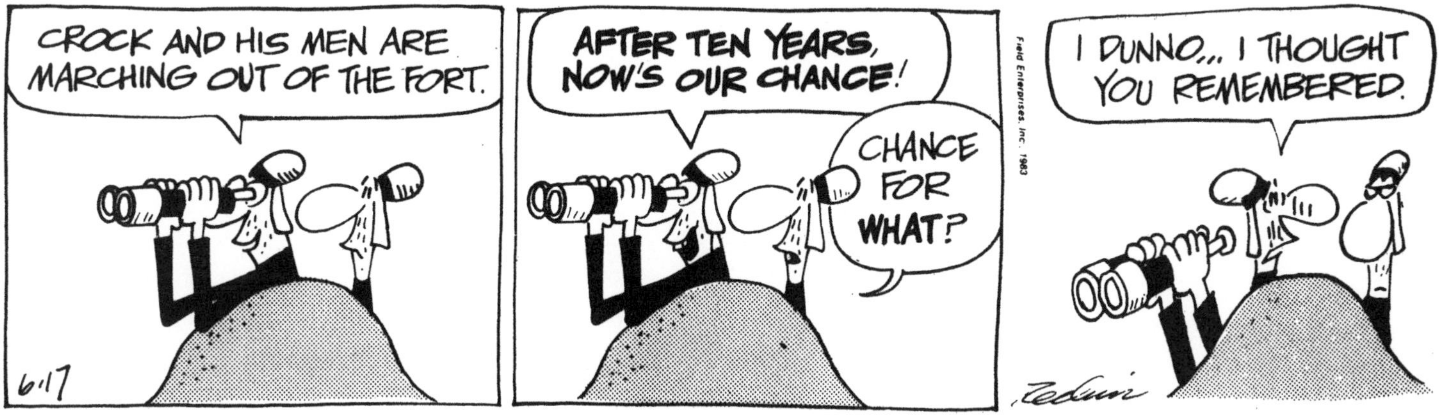
CROCK AND HIS MEN ARE MARCHING OUT OF THE FORT.
6·17
AFTER TEN YEARS, NOW'S OUR CHANCE!
CHANCE FOR WHAT?
Field Enterprises, Inc. 1983
I DUNNO... I THOUGHT YOU REMEMBERED.

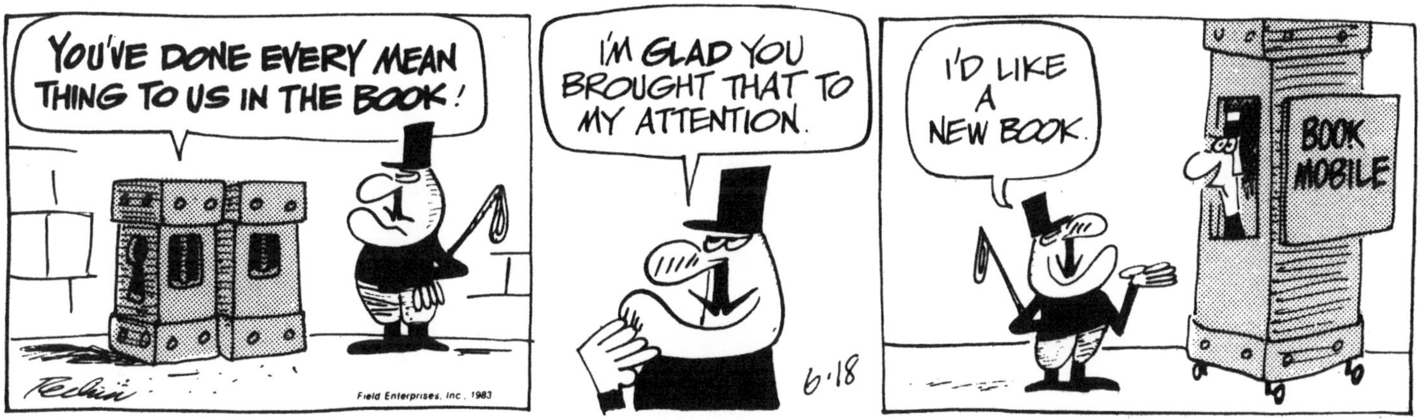
YOU'VE DONE EVERY MEAN THING TO US IN THE BOOK!
Field Enterprises, Inc. 1983
I'M GLAD YOU BROUGHT THAT TO MY ATTENTION.
6·18
I'D LIKE A NEW BOOK.
BOOK MOBILE

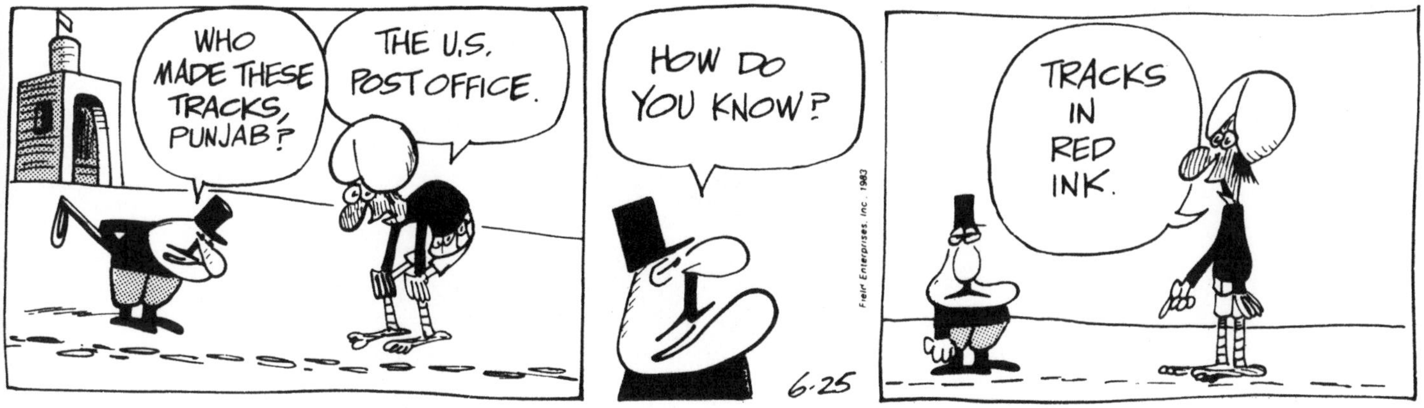
WHO MADE THESE TRACKS, PUNJAB?
THE U.S. POST OFFICE.
HOW DO YOU KNOW?
6·25
Field Enterprises, Inc. 1983
TRACKS IN RED INK.

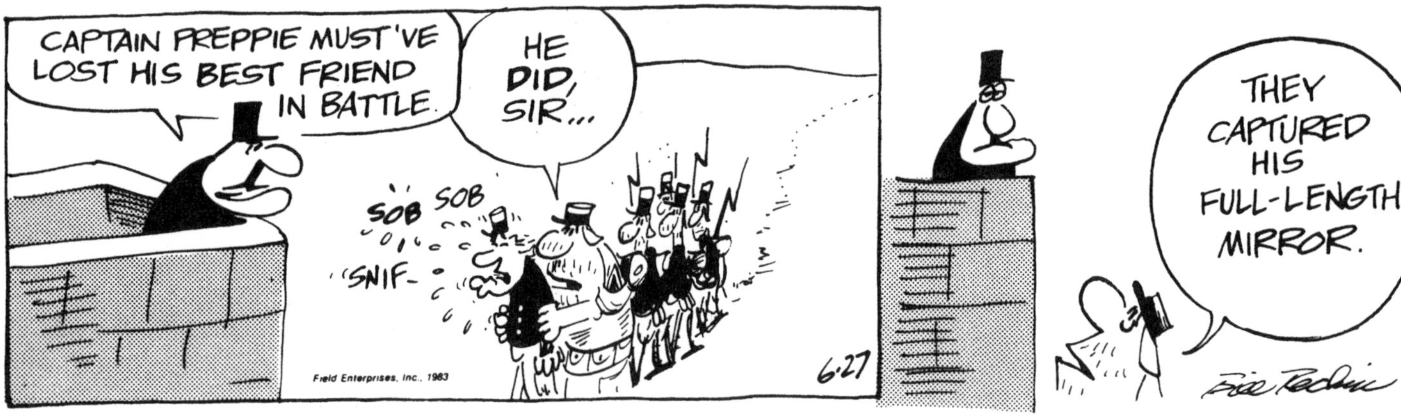
CAPTAIN PREPPIE MUST'VE LOST HIS BEST FRIEND IN BATTLE.
HE DID, SIR...
SOB SOB
SNIF
Field Enterprises, Inc., 1983
6·27
THEY CAPTURED HIS FULL-LENGTH MIRROR.
Bill Rechin

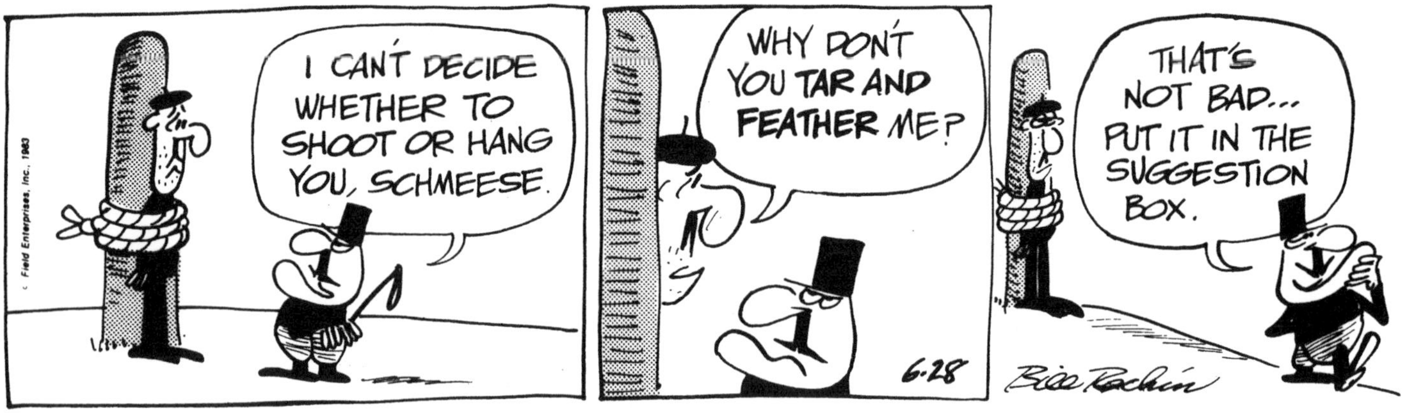
© Field Enterprises, Inc., 1983
I CAN'T DECIDE WHETHER TO SHOOT OR HANG YOU, SCHMEESE.
WHY DON'T YOU TAR AND FEATHER ME?
6·28
THAT'S NOT BAD... PUT IT IN THE SUGGESTION BOX.
Bill Rechin

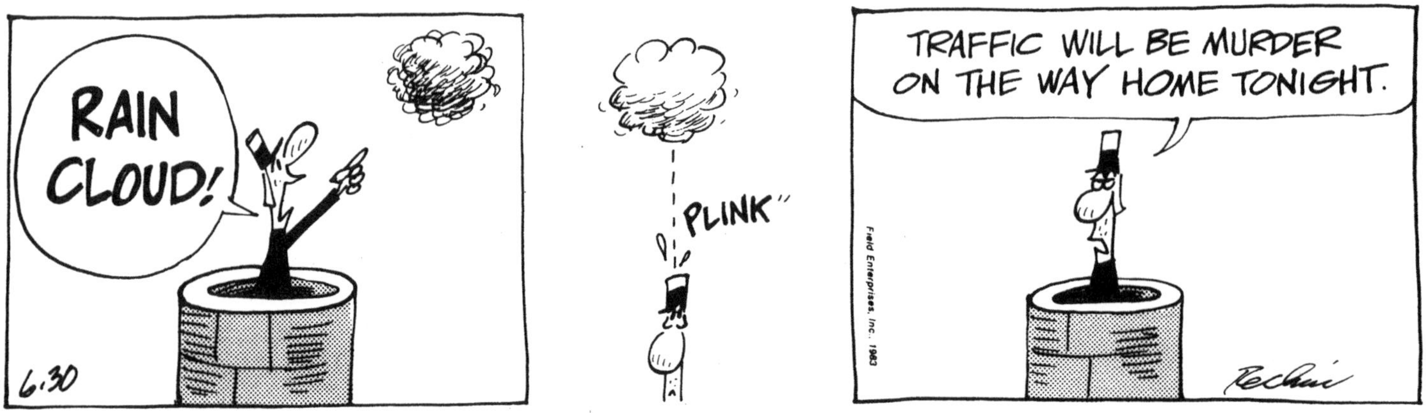
RAIN CLOUD!
6·30
PLINK
TRAFFIC WILL BE MURDER ON THE WAY HOME TONIGHT.
Field Enterprises, Inc., 1983
Rechin

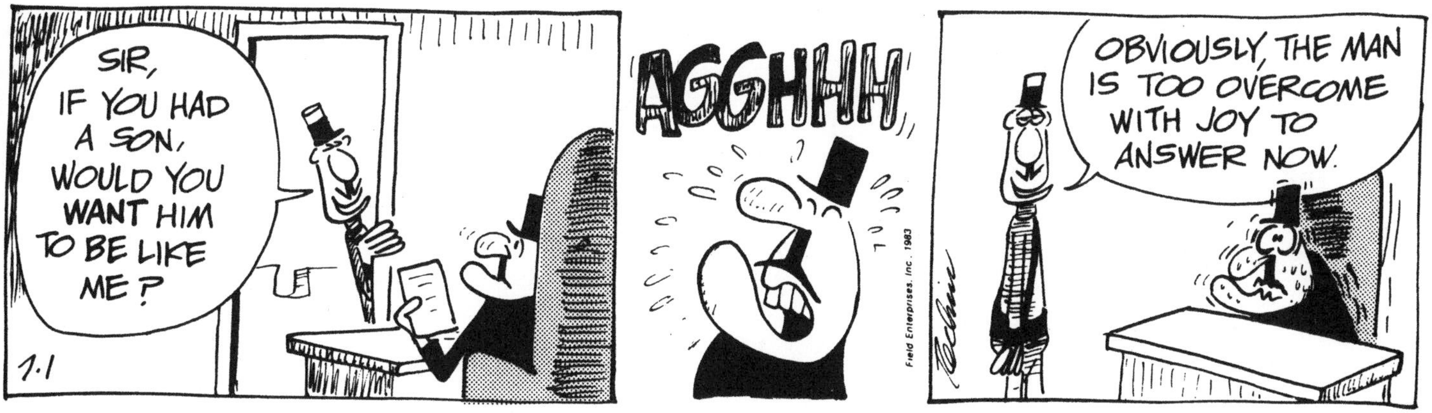
SIR, IF YOU HAD A SON, WOULD YOU WANT HIM TO BE LIKE ME?
7.1
AGGHHH
Field Enterprises, Inc. 1983
OBVIOUSLY, THE MAN IS TOO OVERCOME WITH JOY TO ANSWER NOW.

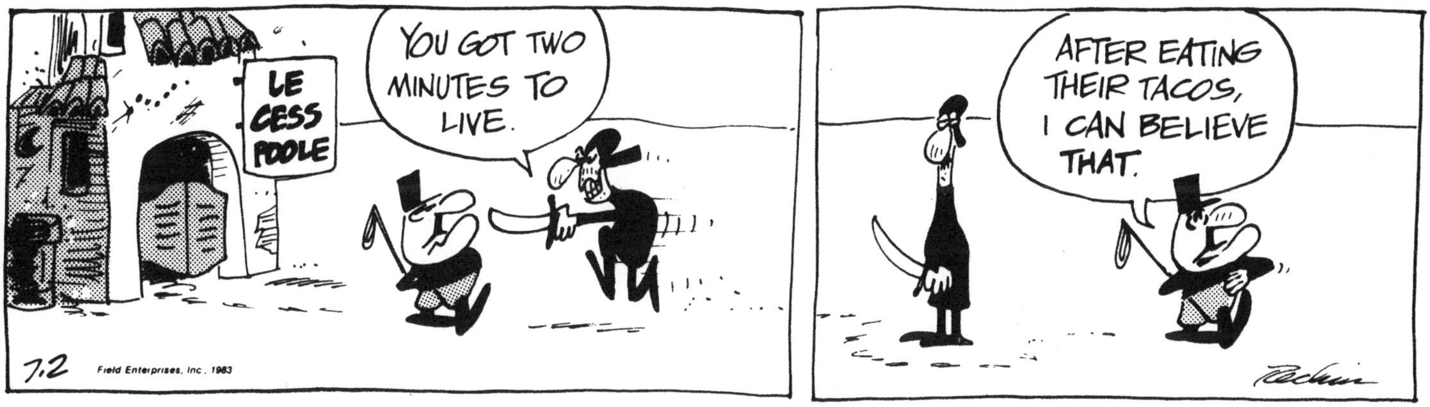
LE CESS POOLE
YOU GOT TWO MINUTES TO LIVE.
7.2
Field Enterprises, Inc. 1983
AFTER EATING THEIR TACOS, I CAN BELIEVE THAT.

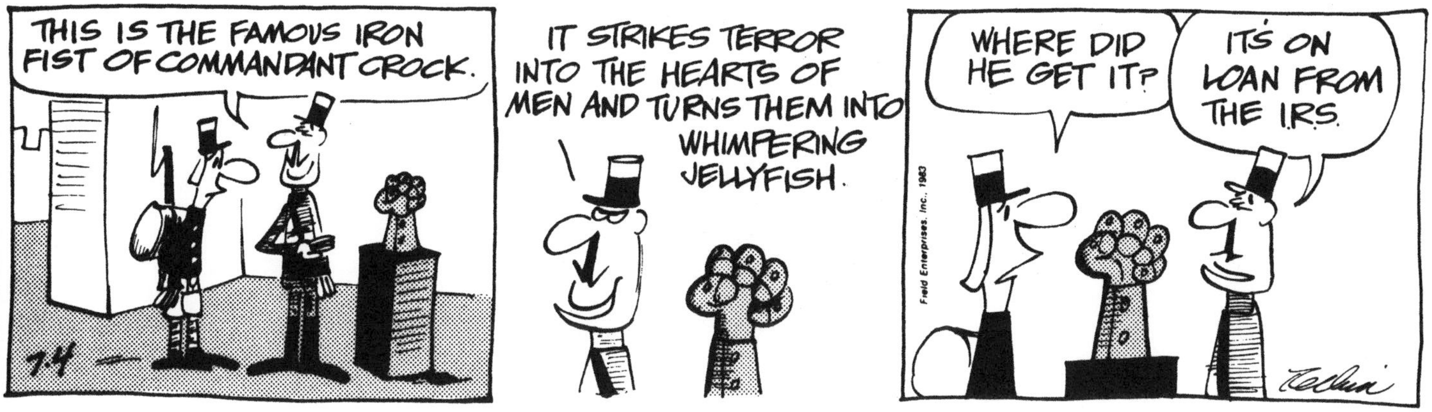
THIS IS THE FAMOUS IRON FIST OF COMMANDANT CROCK.
7.4
IT STRIKES TERROR INTO THE HEARTS OF MEN AND TURNS THEM INTO WHIMPERING JELLYFISH.
Field Enterprises, Inc., 1983
WHERE DID HE GET IT?
IT'S ON LOAN FROM THE I.R.S.

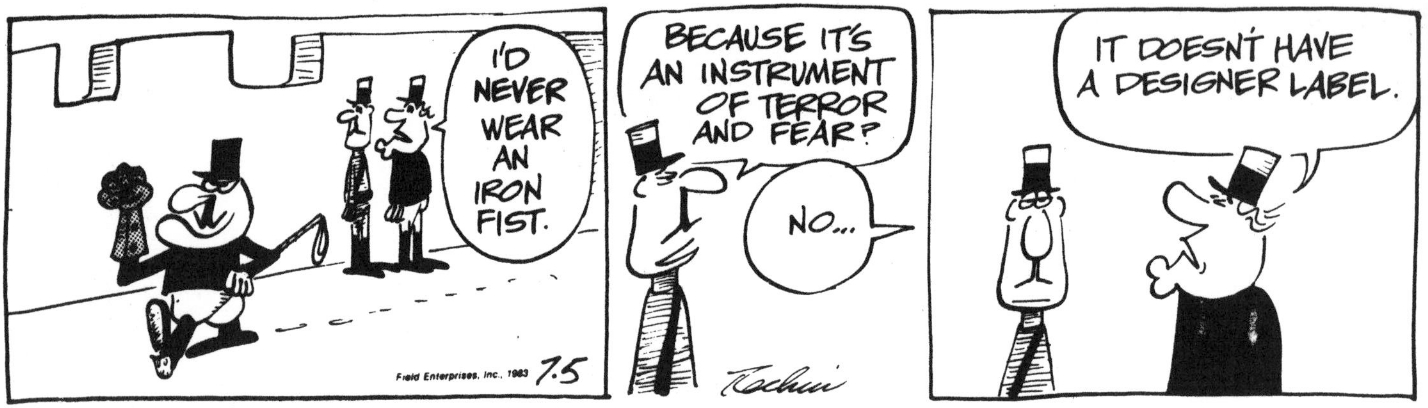
I'D NEVER WEAR AN IRON FIST.
Field Enterprises, Inc., 1983 7.5
BECAUSE IT'S AN INSTRUMENT OF TERROR AND FEAR?
NO...
IT DOESN'T HAVE A DESIGNER LABEL.

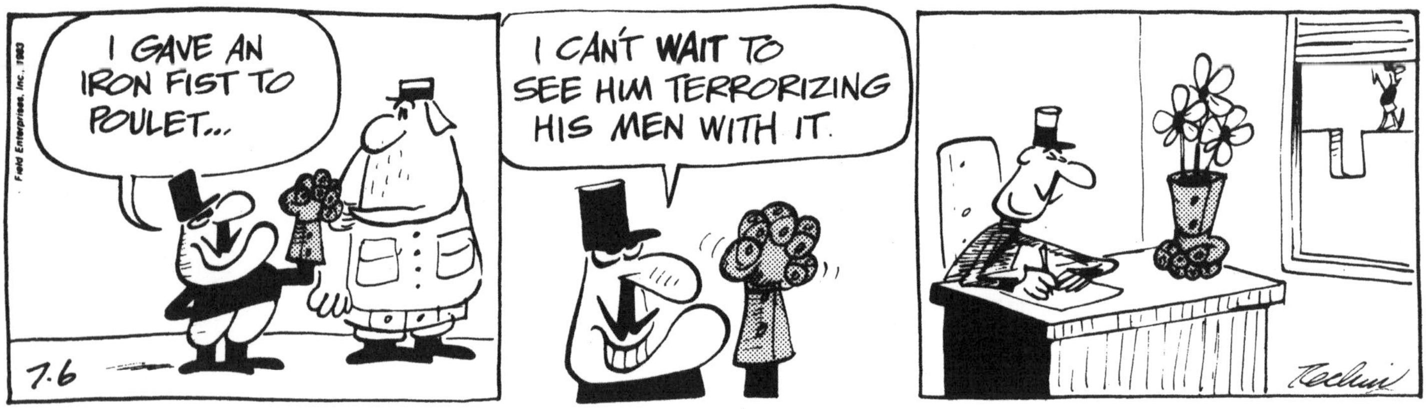
Field Enterprises, Inc., 1983
I GAVE AN IRON FIST TO POULET...
7.6
I CAN'T WAIT TO SEE HIM TERRORIZING HIS MEN WITH IT.

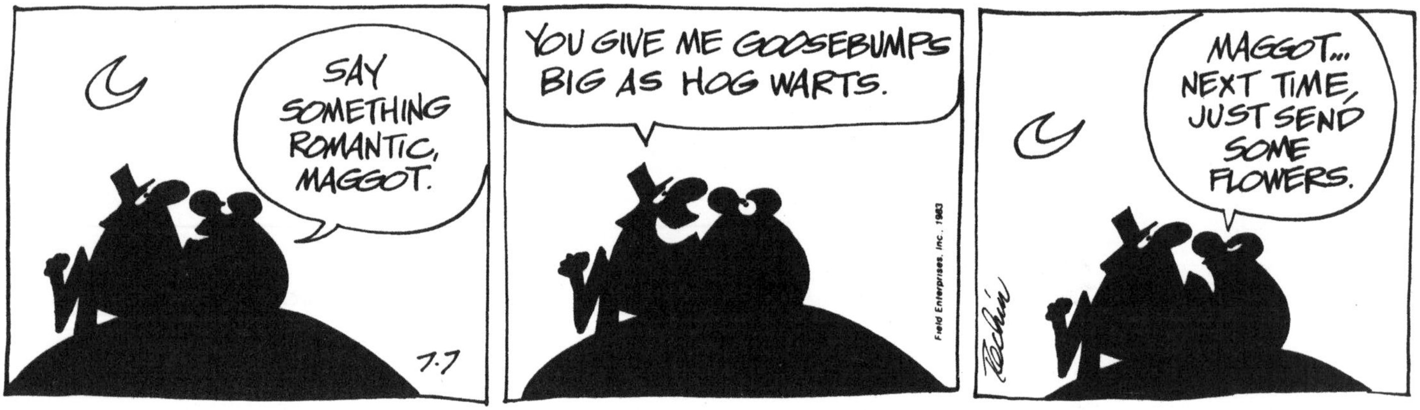
SAY SOMETHING ROMANTIC, MAGGOT.
7.7
YOU GIVE ME GOOSEBUMPS BIG AS HOG WARTS.
Field Enterprises, Inc., 1983
MAGGOT... NEXT TIME, JUST SEND SOME FLOWERS.

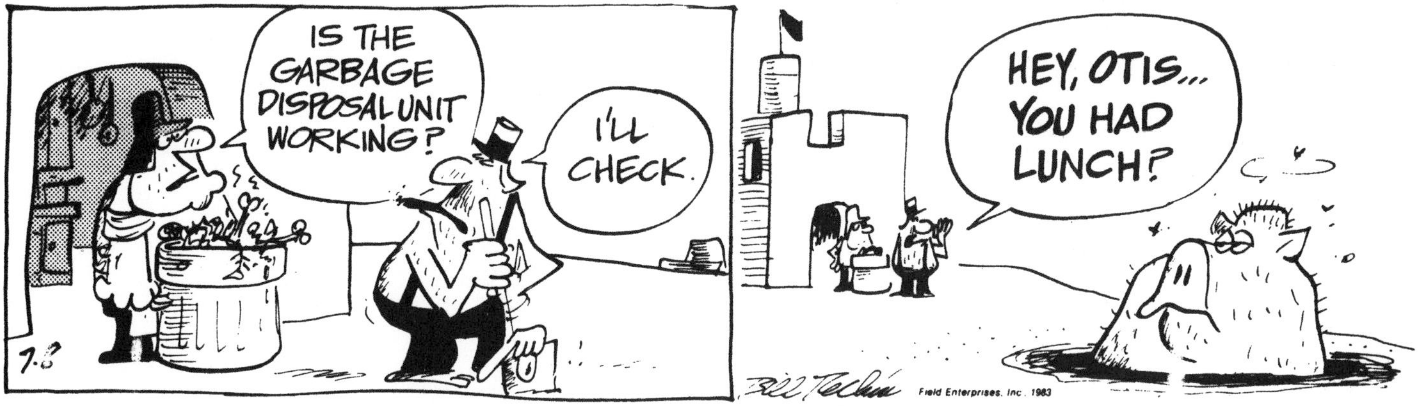
IS THE GARBAGE DISPOSAL UNIT WORKING?
I'LL CHECK.
HEY, OTIS... YOU HAD LUNCH?
Field Enterprises, Inc. 1983

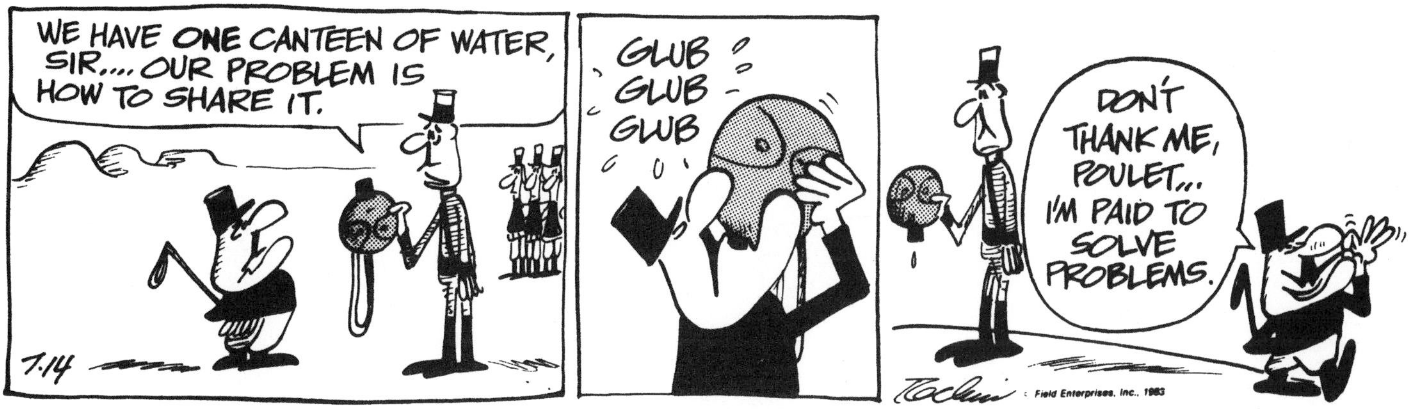
WE HAVE ONE CANTEEN OF WATER, SIR.... OUR PROBLEM IS HOW TO SHARE IT.
7.14
GLUB GLUB GLUB
DON'T THANK ME, POULET... I'M PAID TO SOLVE PROBLEMS.
Field Enterprises, Inc., 1983

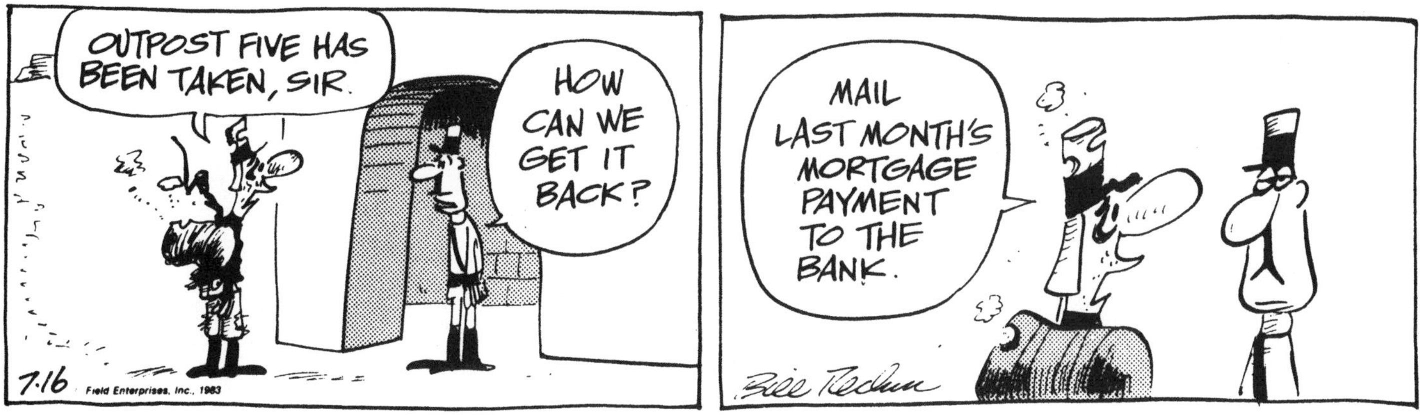
OUTPOST FIVE HAS BEEN TAKEN, SIR.
HOW CAN WE GET IT BACK?
7.16
Field Enterprises, Inc., 1983
MAIL LAST MONTH'S MORTGAGE PAYMENT TO THE BANK.

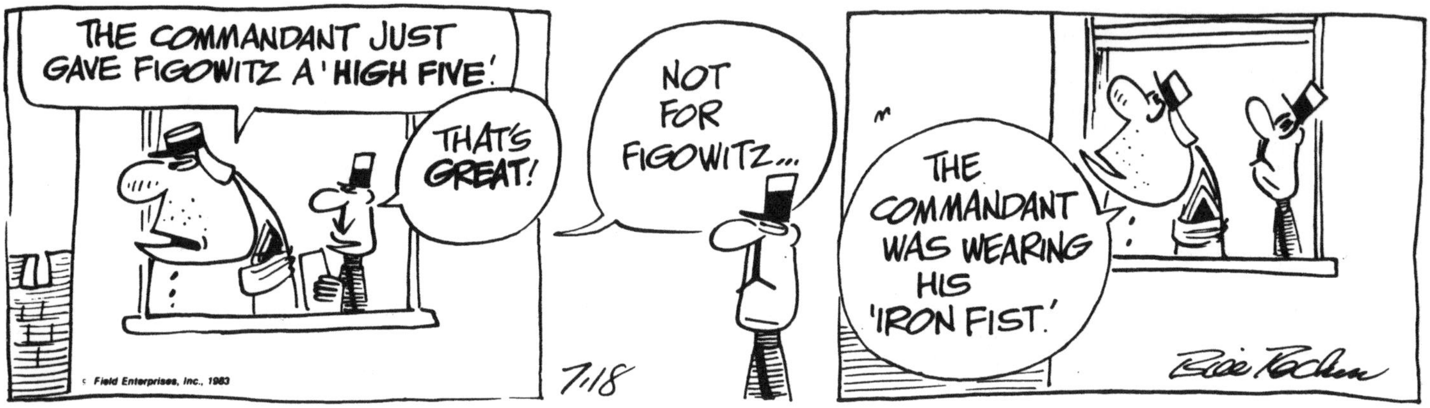
THE COMMANDANT JUST GAVE FIGOWITZ A 'HIGH FIVE'.
THAT'S GREAT!
NOT FOR FIGOWITZ...
THE COMMANDANT WAS WEARING HIS 'IRON FIST.'
© Field Enterprises, Inc., 1983
7.18

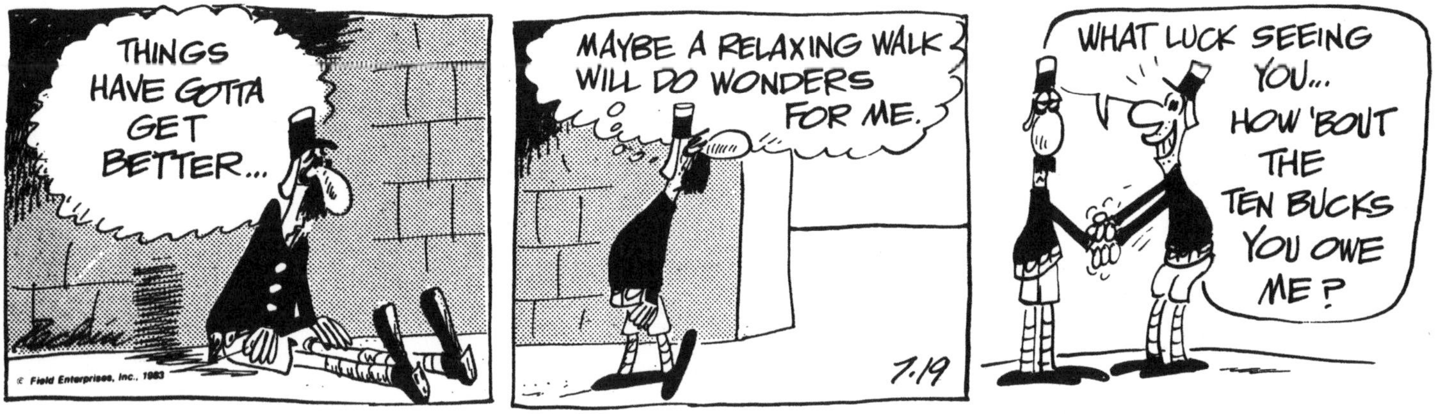
THINGS HAVE GOTTA GET BETTER...
MAYBE A RELAXING WALK WILL DO WONDERS FOR ME.
WHAT LUCK SEEING YOU... HOW 'BOUT THE TEN BUCKS YOU OWE ME?
© Field Enterprises, Inc., 1983
7.19

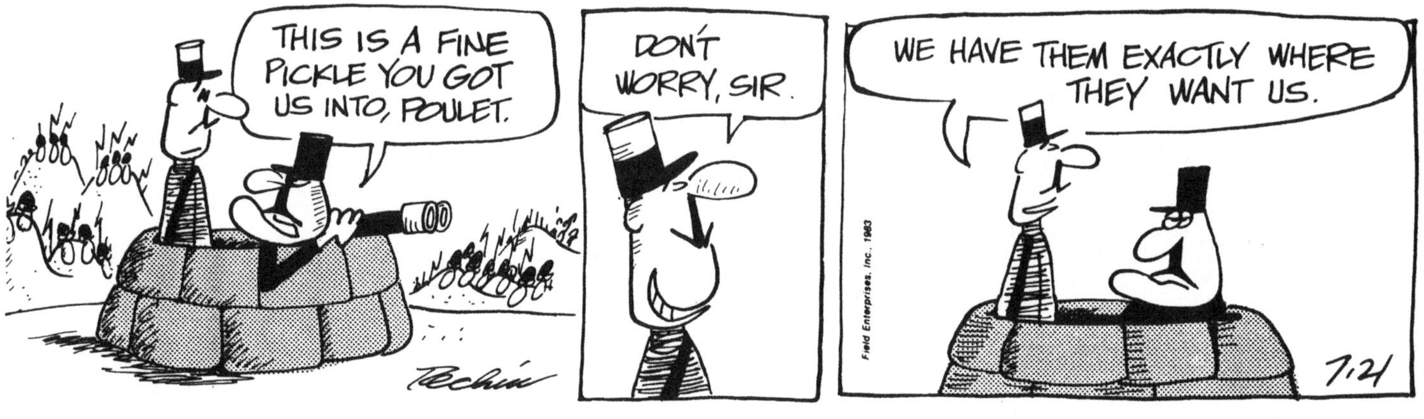
THIS IS A FINE PICKLE YOU GOT US INTO, POULET.
DON'T WORRY, SIR.
WE HAVE THEM EXACTLY WHERE THEY WANT US.
Field Enterprises, Inc., 1983
7.21

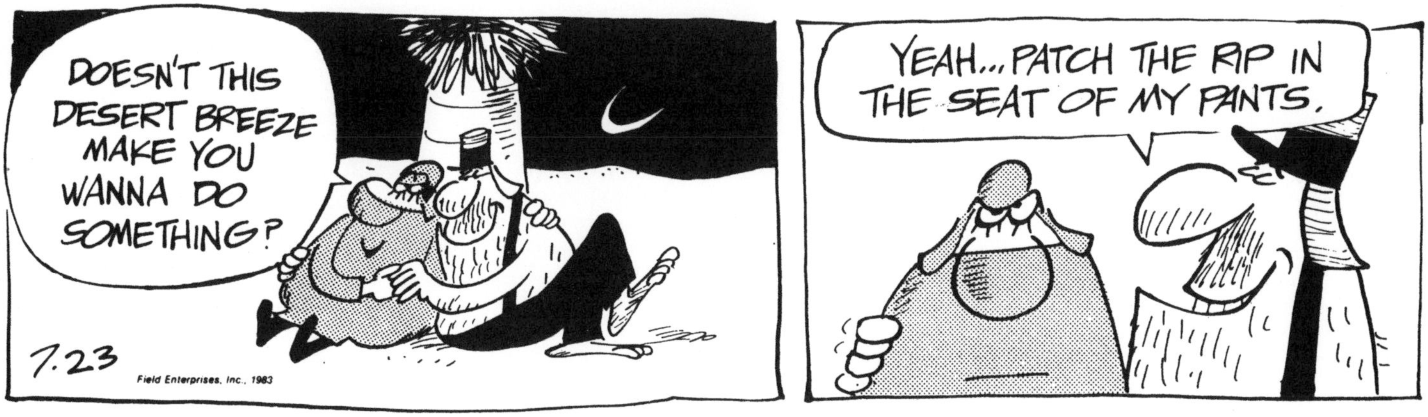
DOESN'T THIS DESERT BREEZE MAKE YOU WANNA DO SOMETHING?
YEAH... PATCH THE RIP IN THE SEAT OF MY PANTS.
7.23
Field Enterprises, Inc., 1983

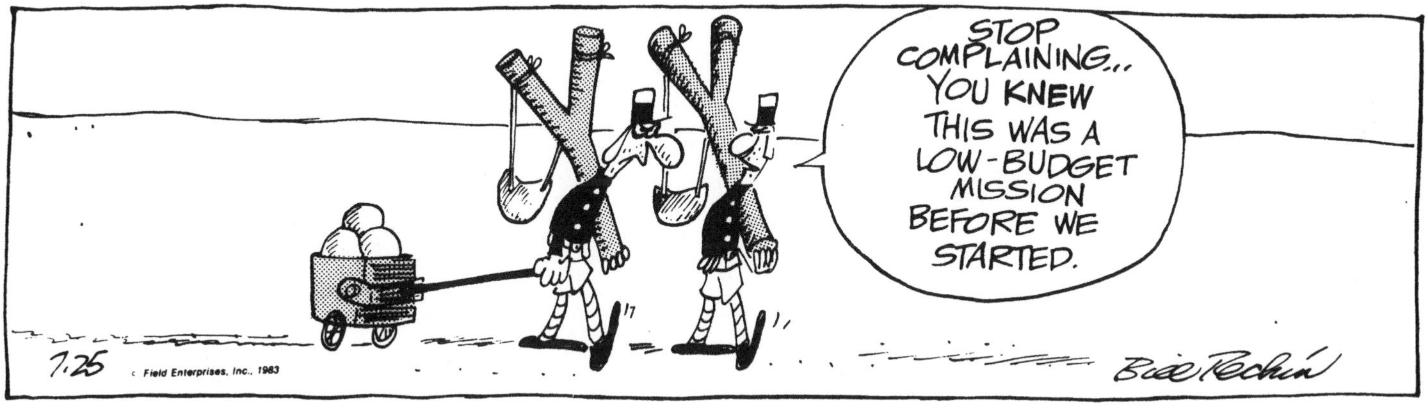
STOP COMPLAINING... YOU KNEW THIS WAS A LOW-BUDGET MISSION BEFORE WE STARTED.
7.25
Field Enterprises, Inc., 1983

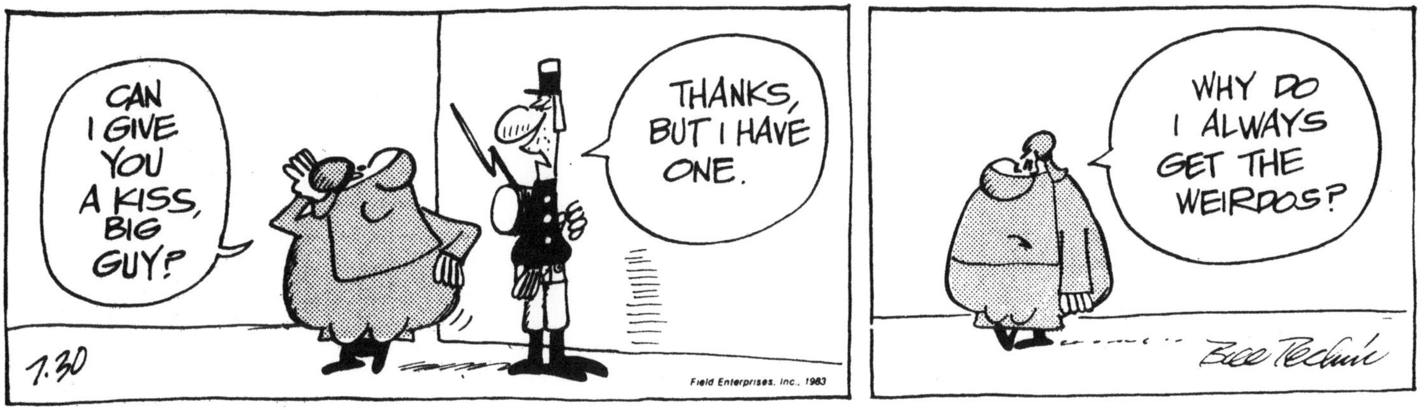
CAN I GIVE YOU A KISS, BIG GUY?
THANKS, BUT I HAVE ONE.
WHY DO I ALWAYS GET THE WEIRDOS?
7.30
Field Enterprises, Inc., 1983

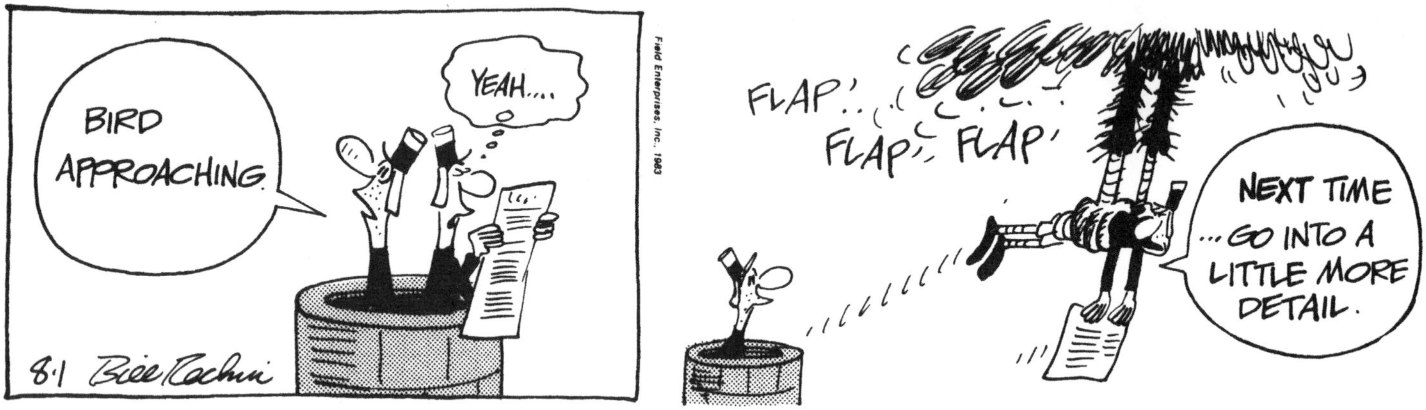
BIRD APPROACHING.
YEAH....
8·1 Bill Rechin
Field Enterprises, Inc., 1983
FLAP
FLAP FLAP
NEXT TIME ...GO INTO A LITTLE MORE DETAIL.

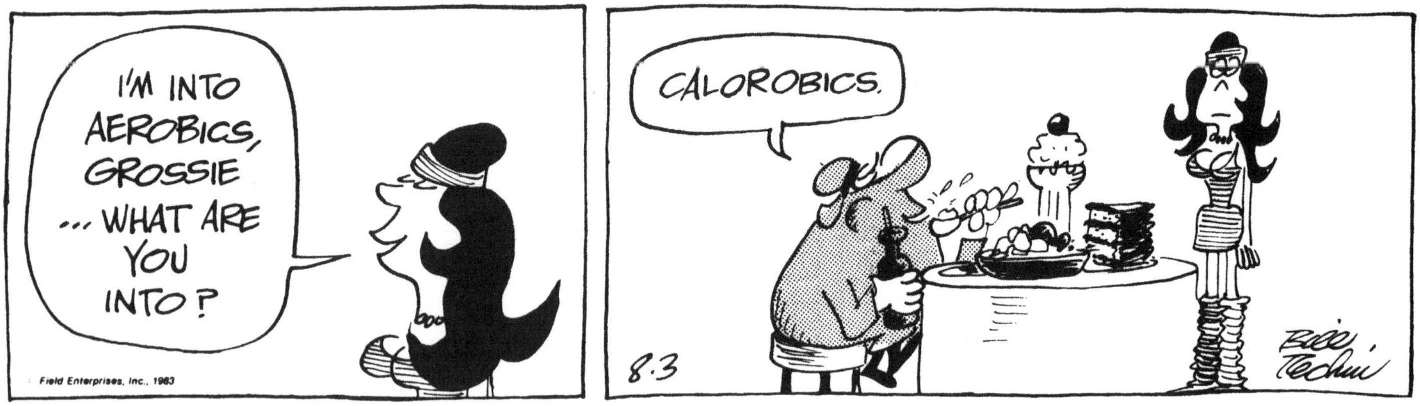
I'M INTO AEROBICS, GROSSIE ... WHAT ARE YOU INTO?
Field Enterprises, Inc., 1983
CALOROBICS.
8·3
Bill Rechin

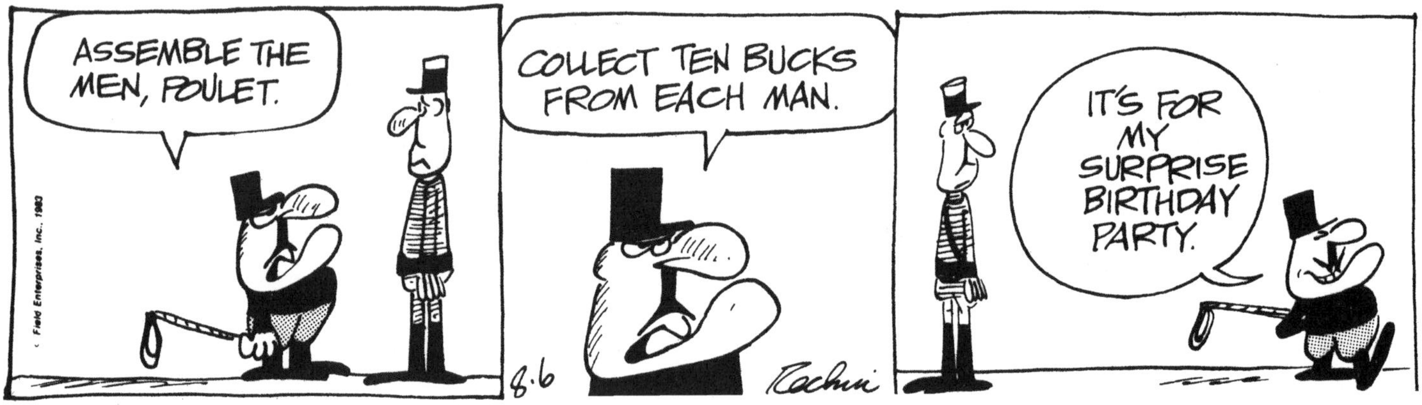
ASSEMBLE THE MEN, POULET.
Field Enterprises, Inc., 1983
COLLECT TEN BUCKS FROM EACH MAN.
8·6
Rechin
IT'S FOR MY SURPRISE BIRTHDAY PARTY.

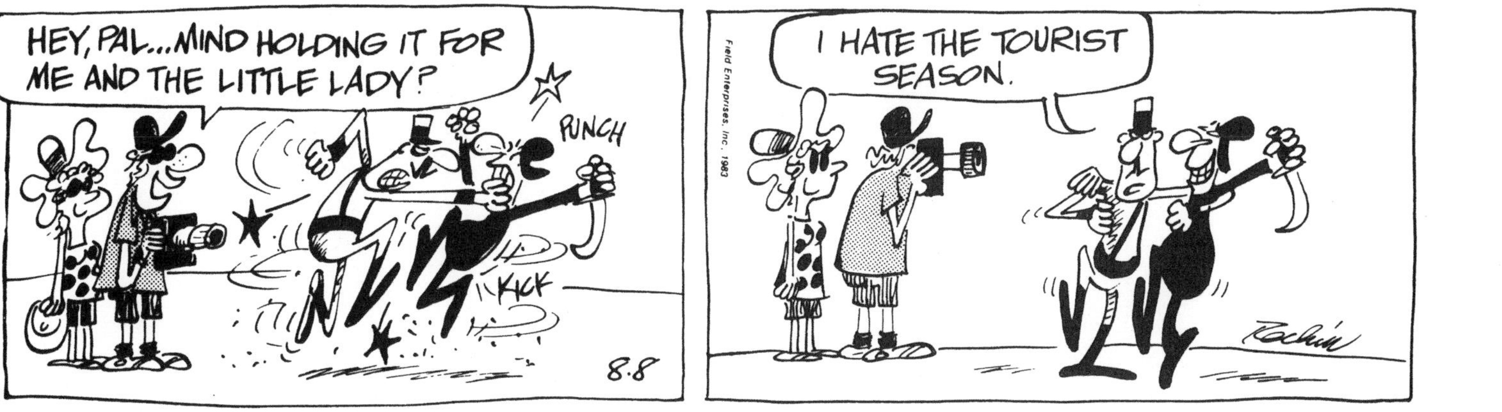
HEY, PAL...MIND HOLDING IT FOR ME AND THE LITTLE LADY?
PUNCH
KICK
8.8
Field Enterprises, Inc. 1983
I HATE THE TOURIST SEASON.

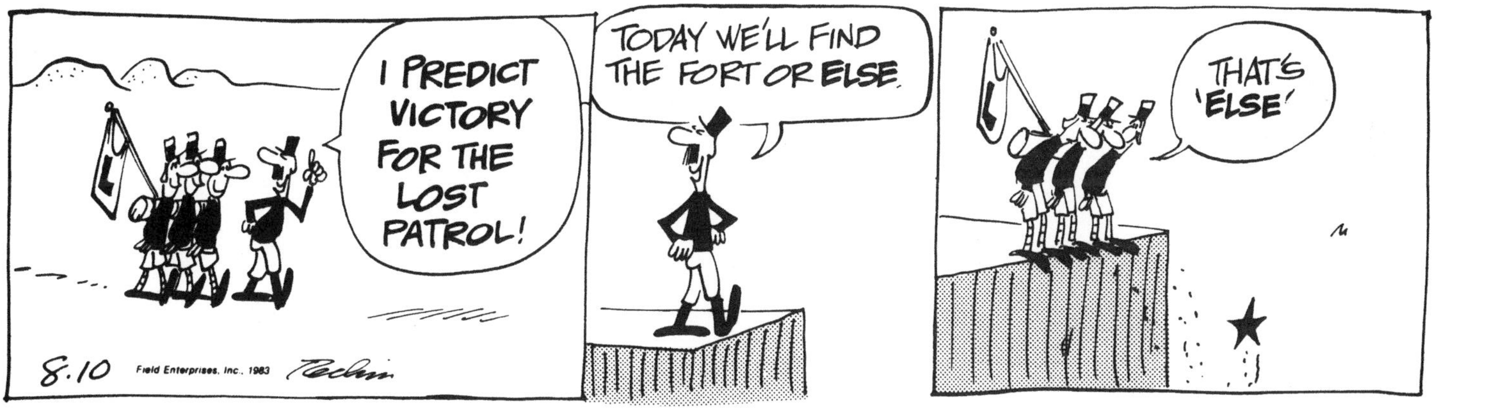
I PREDICT VICTORY FOR THE LOST PATROL!
8.10
Field Enterprises, Inc., 1983
TODAY WE'LL FIND THE FORT OR ELSE.
THAT'S 'ELSE'

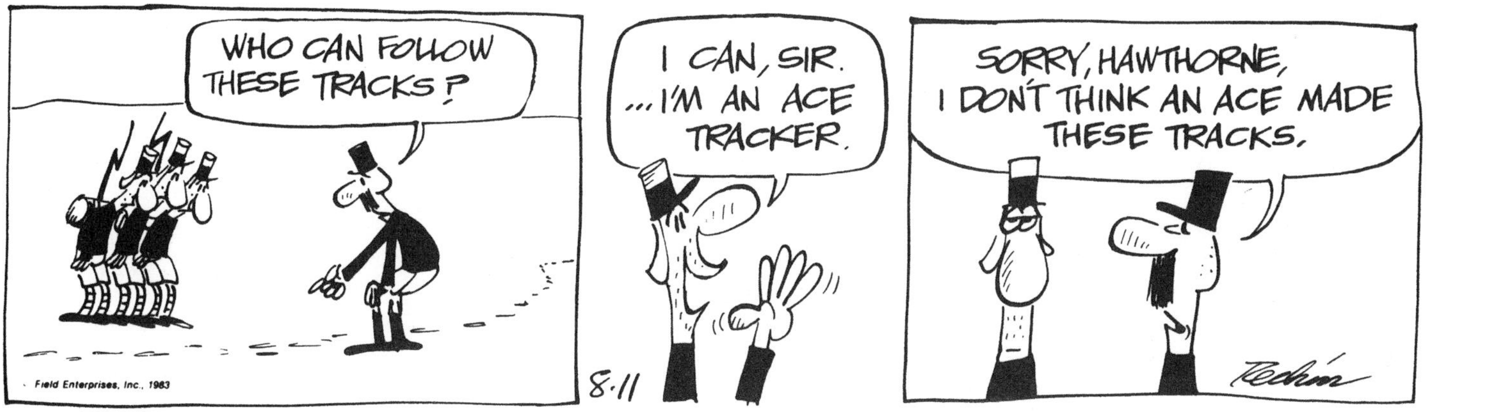
WHO CAN FOLLOW THESE TRACKS?
Field Enterprises, Inc., 1983
I CAN, SIR. ...I'M AN ACE TRACKER.
8.11
SORRY, HAWTHORNE, I DON'T THINK AN ACE MADE THESE TRACKS.

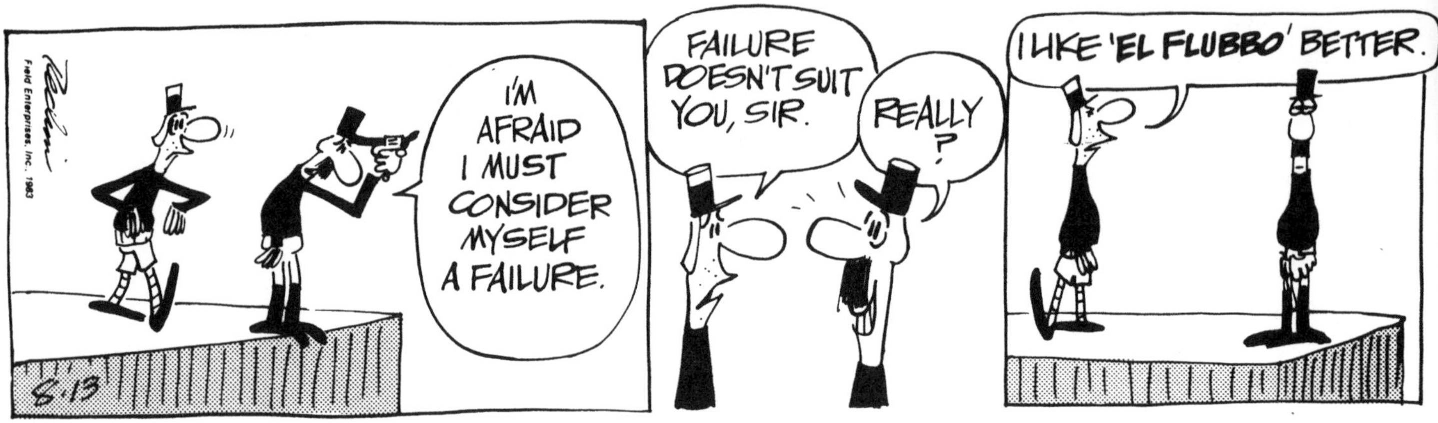
Field Enterprises, Inc. 1983
8.13
I'M AFRAID I MUST CONSIDER MYSELF A FAILURE.
FAILURE DOESN'T SUIT YOU, SIR.
REALLY?
I LIKE '**EL FLUBBO**' BETTER.

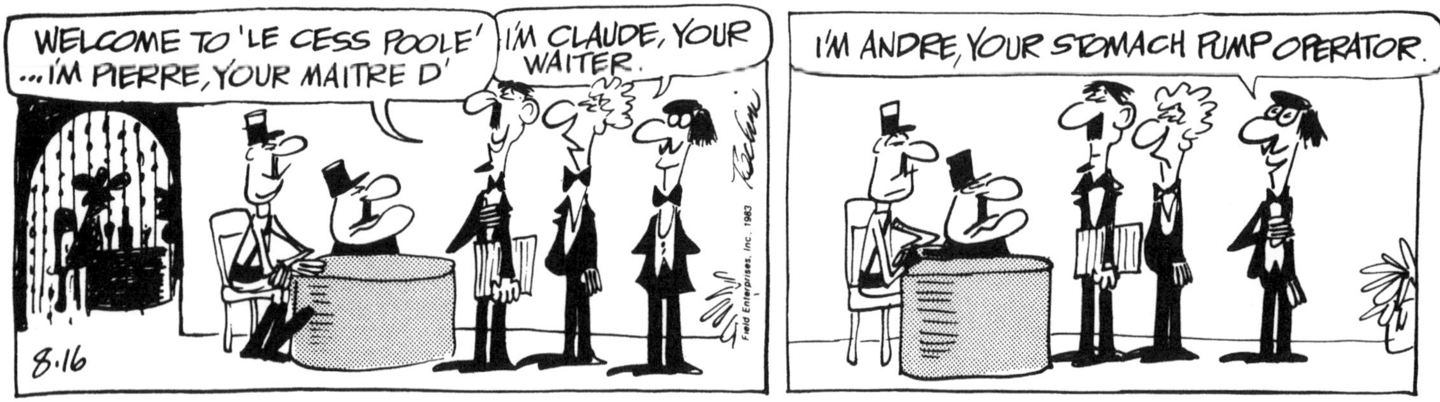
WELCOME TO 'LE CESS POOLE' ...I'M PIERRE, YOUR MAITRE D'
I'M CLAUDE, YOUR WAITER.
Field Enterprises, Inc. 1983
8.16
I'M ANDRE, YOUR STOMACH PUMP OPERATOR.

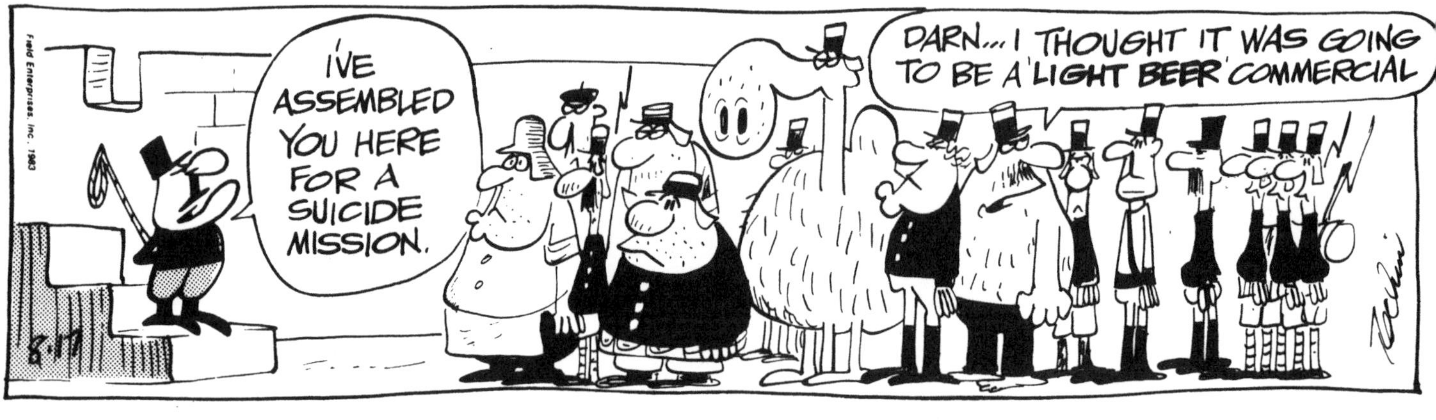
Field Enterprises, Inc. 1983
I'VE ASSEMBLED YOU HERE FOR A SUICIDE MISSION.
DARN... I THOUGHT IT WAS GOING TO BE A '**LIGHT BEER**' COMMERCIAL
8.17

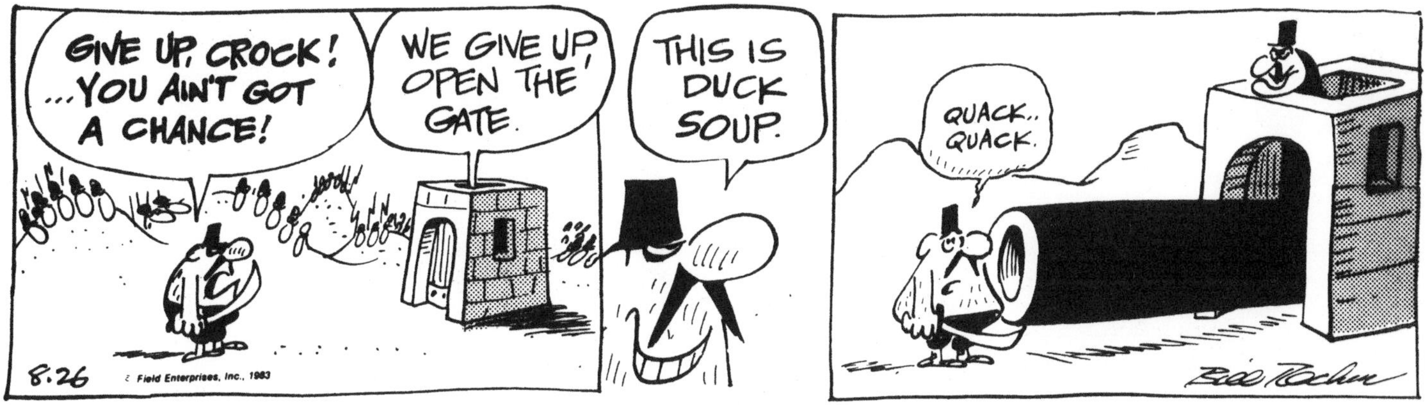
GIVE UP, CROCK! ...YOU AIN'T GOT A CHANCE!
WE GIVE UP, OPEN THE GATE.
THIS IS DUCK SOUP.
QUACK.. QUACK.
8.26
© Field Enterprises, Inc., 1983
Bill Rechin

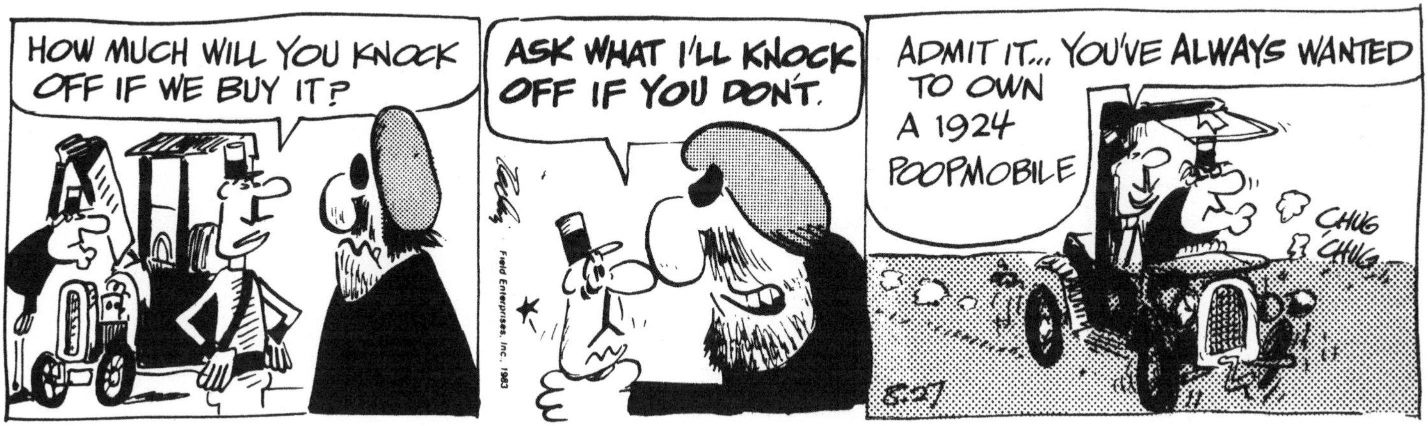
HOW MUCH WILL YOU KNOCK OFF IF WE BUY IT?
ASK WHAT I'LL KNOCK OFF IF YOU DON'T.
Field Enterprises, Inc., 1983
ADMIT IT... YOU'VE ALWAYS WANTED TO OWN A 1924 POOPMOBILE
CHUG CHUG
8.27

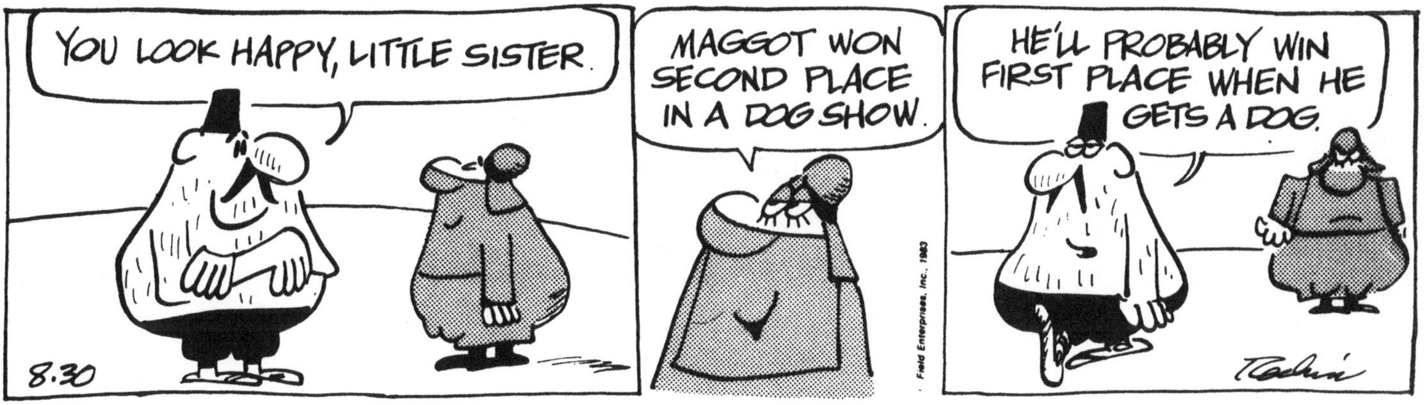
YOU LOOK HAPPY, LITTLE SISTER.
8.30
MAGGOT WON SECOND PLACE IN A DOG SHOW.
Field Enterprises, Inc., 1983
HE'LL PROBABLY WIN FIRST PLACE WHEN HE GETS A DOG.
Rechin

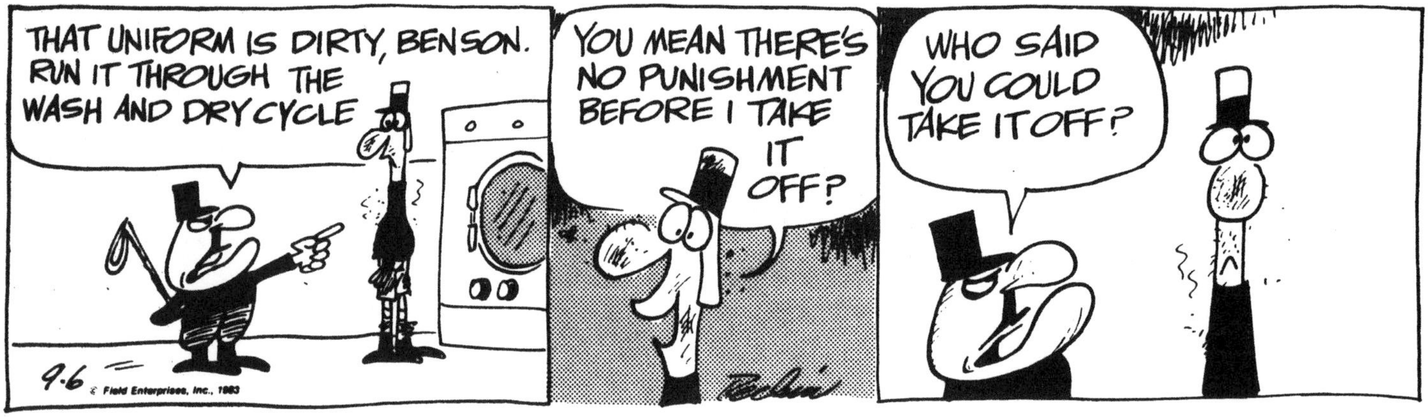
THAT UNIFORM IS DIRTY, BENSON. RUN IT THROUGH THE WASH AND DRY CYCLE
9·6
© Field Enterprises, Inc., 1983
YOU MEAN THERE'S NO PUNISHMENT BEFORE I TAKE IT OFF?
Rechin
WHO SAID YOU COULD TAKE IT OFF?

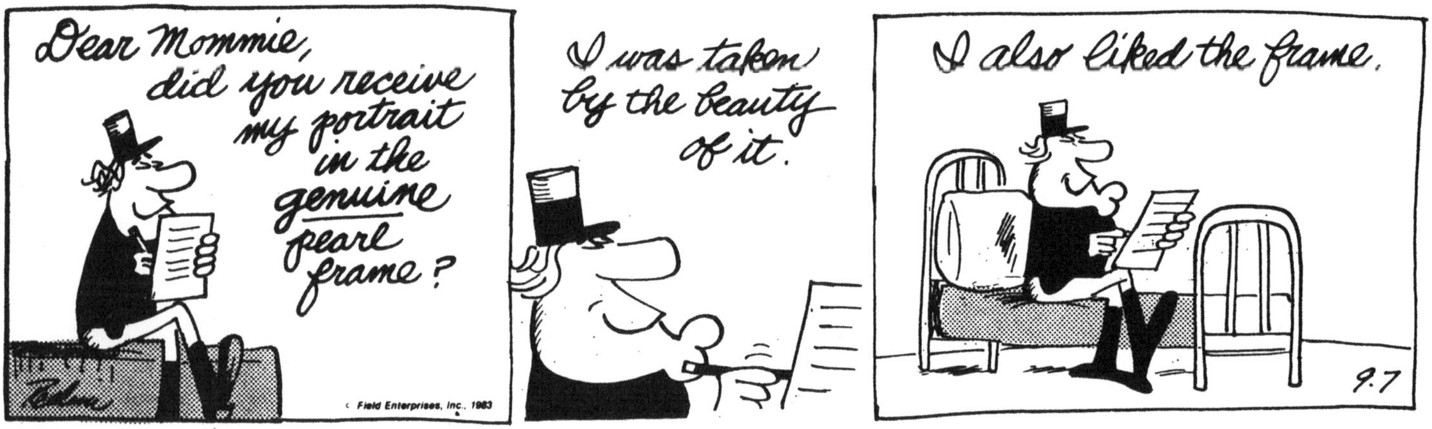
Dear Mommie, did you receive my portrait in the genuine pearl frame?
Rechin
© Field Enterprises, Inc., 1983
I was taken by the beauty of it.
I also liked the frame.
9·7

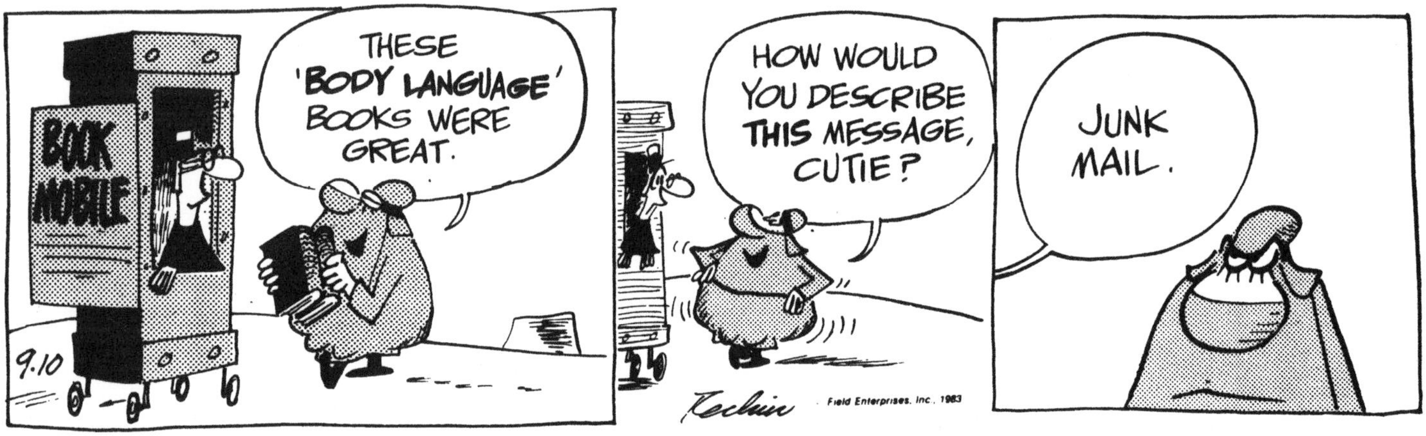
BOOK MOBILE
THESE 'BODY LANGUAGE' BOOKS WERE GREAT.
9·10
HOW WOULD YOU DESCRIBE THIS MESSAGE, CUTIE?
Rechin
Field Enterprises, Inc., 1983
JUNK MAIL.

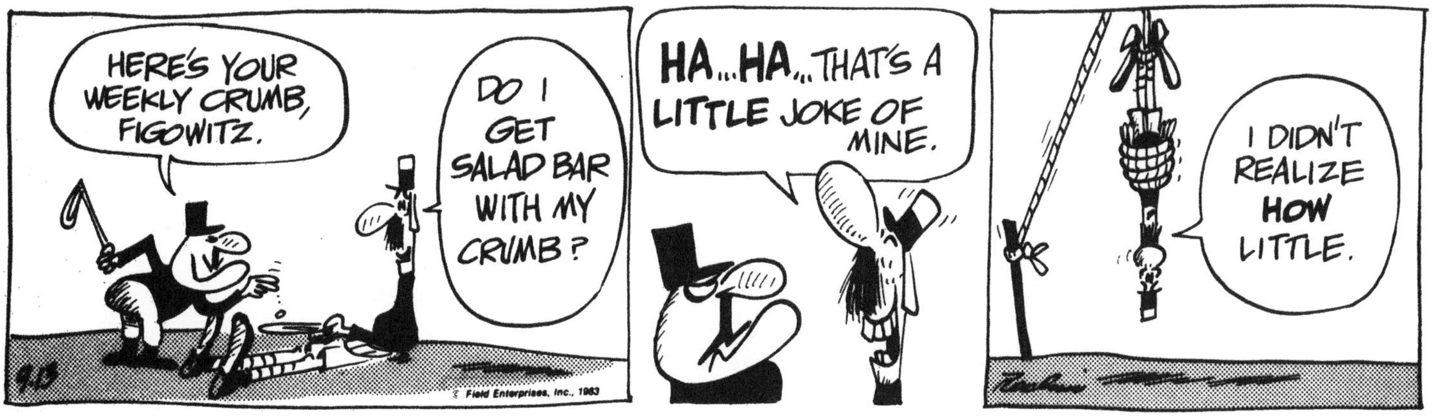
HERE'S YOUR WEEKLY CRUMB, FIGOWITZ.
DO I GET SALAD BAR WITH MY CRUMB?
HA...HA... THAT'S A LITTLE JOKE OF MINE.
I DIDN'T REALIZE HOW LITTLE.
9.13
© Field Enterprises, Inc., 1983

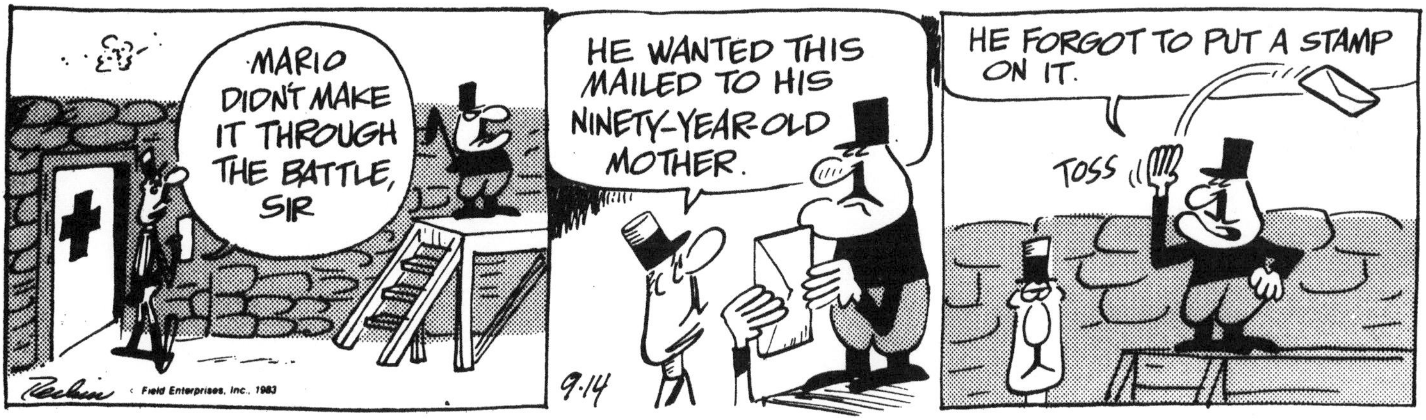
MARIO DIDN'T MAKE IT THROUGH THE BATTLE, SIR
HE WANTED THIS MAILED TO HIS NINETY-YEAR-OLD MOTHER.
HE FORGOT TO PUT A STAMP ON IT.
TOSS
9.14
© Field Enterprises, Inc., 1983

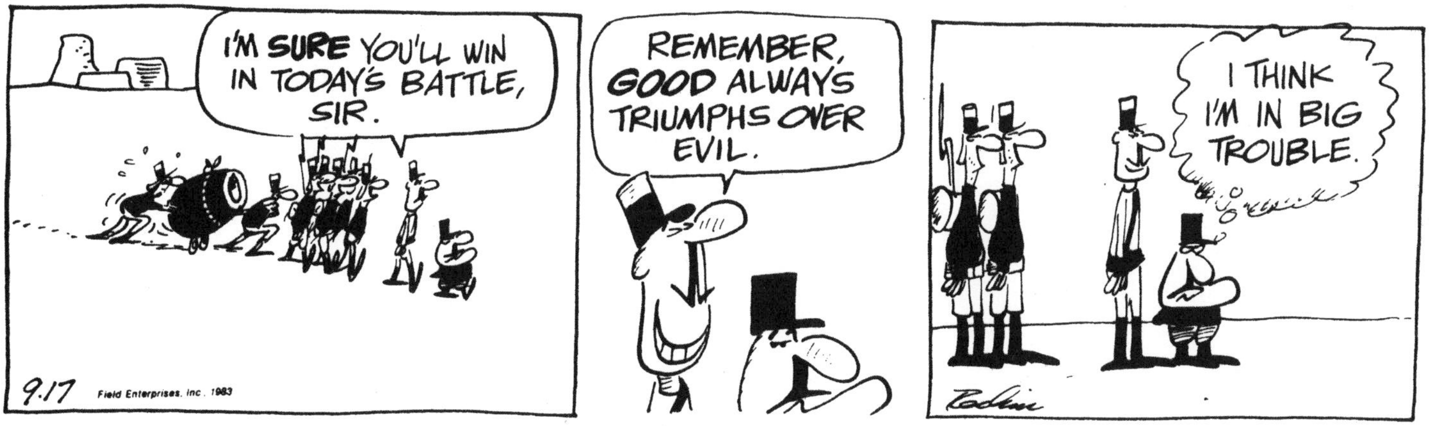
I'M SURE YOU'LL WIN IN TODAY'S BATTLE, SIR.
REMEMBER, GOOD ALWAYS TRIUMPHS OVER EVIL.
I THINK I'M IN BIG TROUBLE.
9.17
Field Enterprises, Inc. 1983

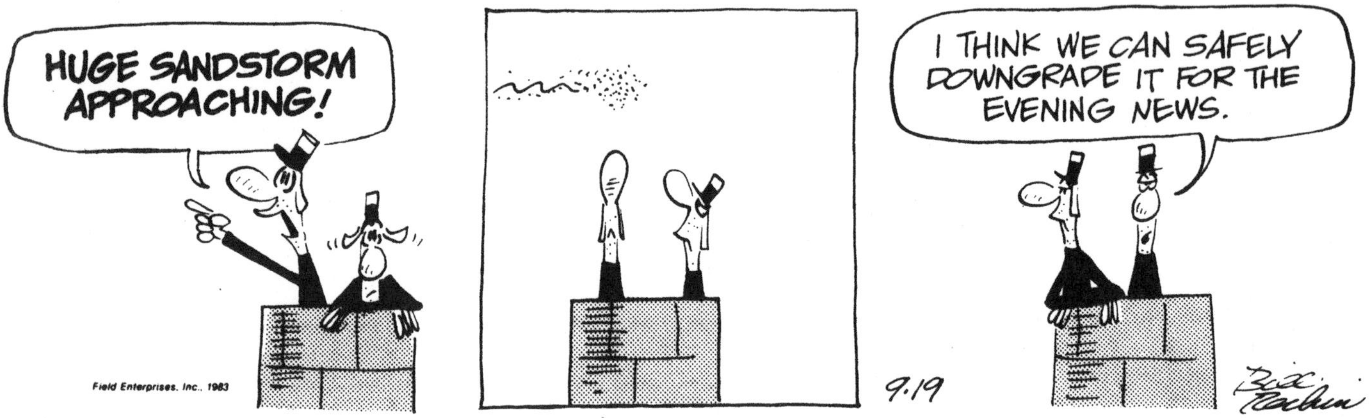
HUGE SANDSTORM APPROACHING!
I THINK WE CAN SAFELY DOWNGRADE IT FOR THE EVENING NEWS.
Field Enterprises, Inc., 1983
9.19

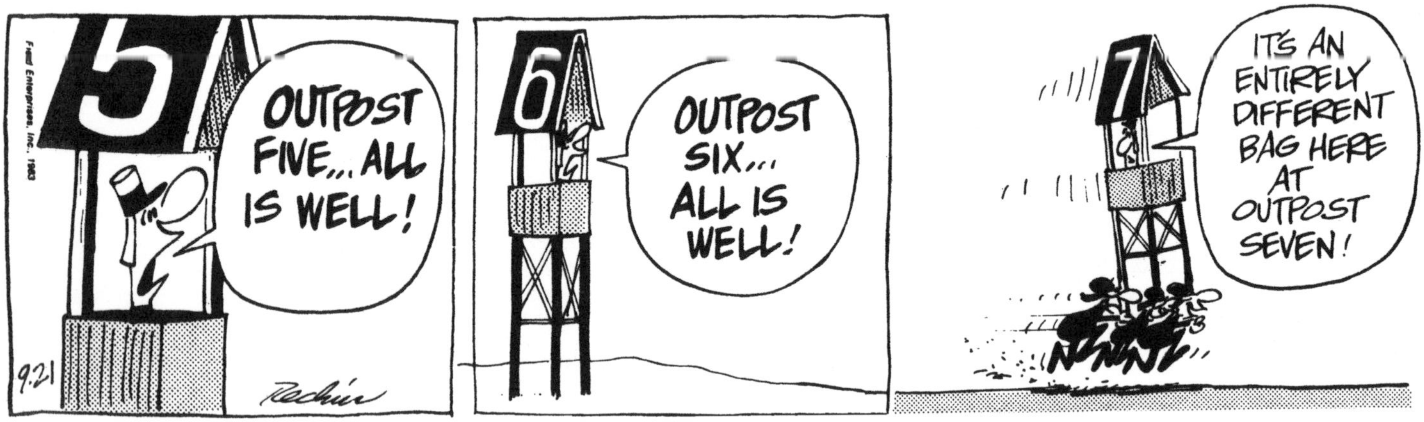
5
OUTPOST FIVE... ALL IS WELL!
6
OUTPOST SIX... ALL IS WELL!
7
IT'S AN ENTIRELY DIFFERENT BAG HERE AT OUTPOST SEVEN!
Field Enterprises, Inc., 1983
9.21

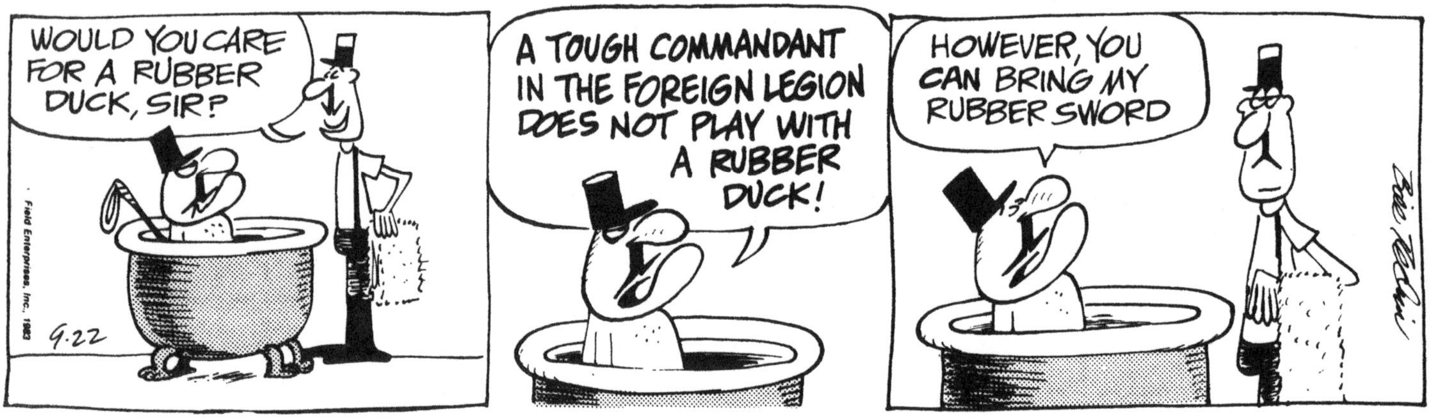
WOULD YOU CARE FOR A RUBBER DUCK, SIR?
A TOUGH COMMANDANT IN THE FOREIGN LEGION DOES NOT PLAY WITH A RUBBER DUCK!
HOWEVER, YOU CAN BRING MY RUBBER SWORD
Field Enterprises, Inc., 1983
9.22

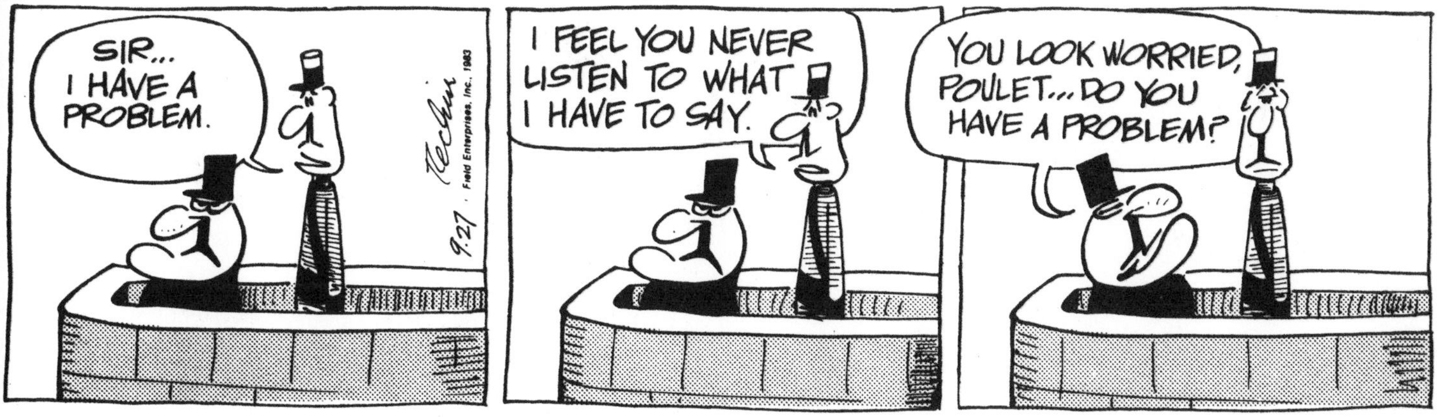
SIR... I HAVE A PROBLEM.
I FEEL YOU NEVER LISTEN TO WHAT I HAVE TO SAY.
YOU LOOK WORRIED, POULET... DO YOU HAVE A PROBLEM?
9.27 · Field Enterprises, Inc., 1983

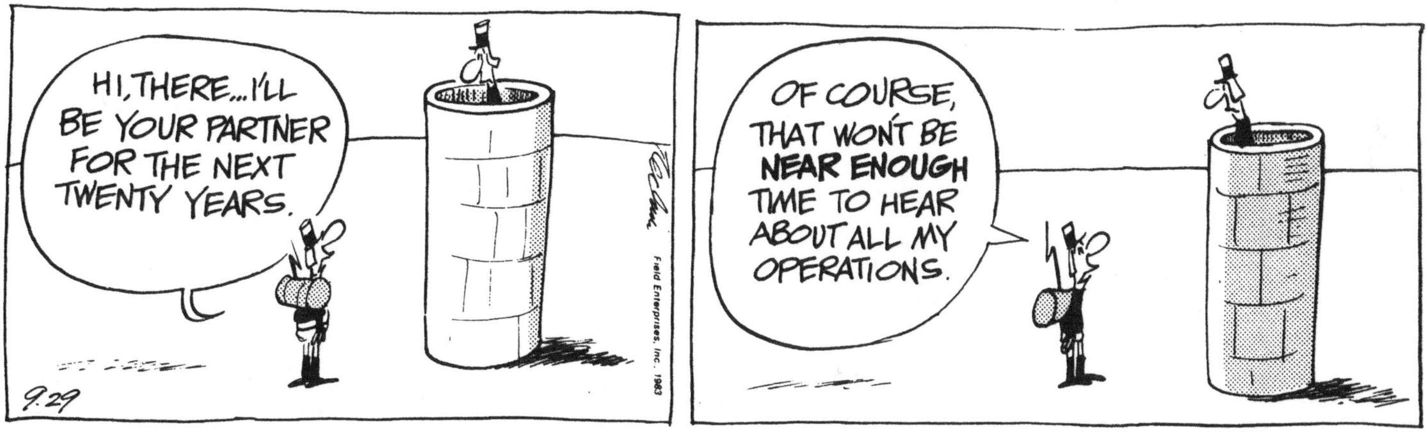
HI, THERE... I'LL BE YOUR PARTNER FOR THE NEXT TWENTY YEARS.
OF COURSE, THAT WON'T BE NEAR ENOUGH TIME TO HEAR ABOUT ALL MY OPERATIONS.
9.29
Field Enterprises, Inc. 1983

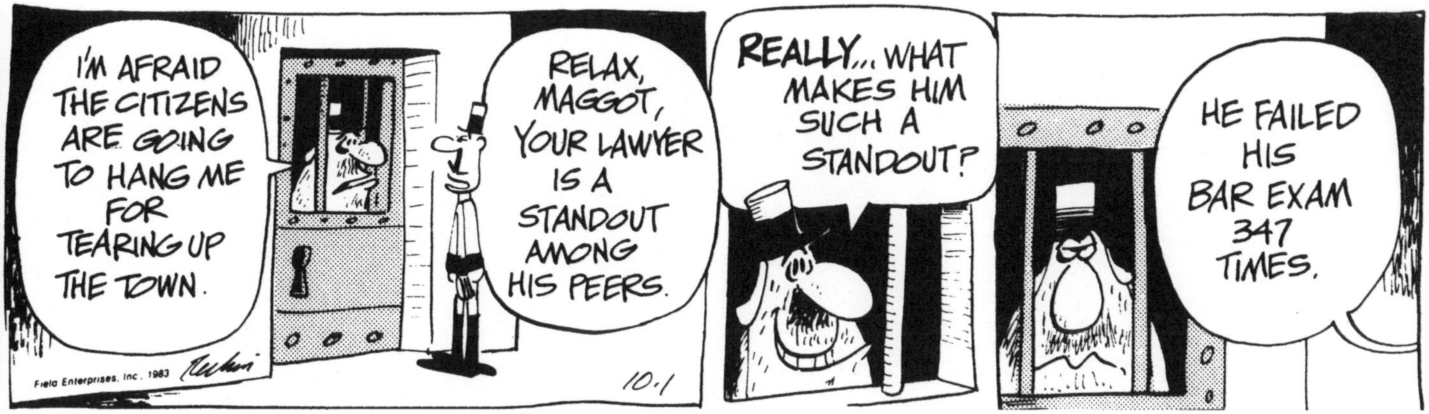
I'M AFRAID THE CITIZENS ARE GOING TO HANG ME FOR TEARING UP THE TOWN.
RELAX, MAGGOT, YOUR LAWYER IS A STANDOUT AMONG HIS PEERS.
REALLY... WHAT MAKES HIM SUCH A STANDOUT?
HE FAILED HIS BAR EXAM 347 TIMES.
Field Enterprises, Inc. 1983
10.1

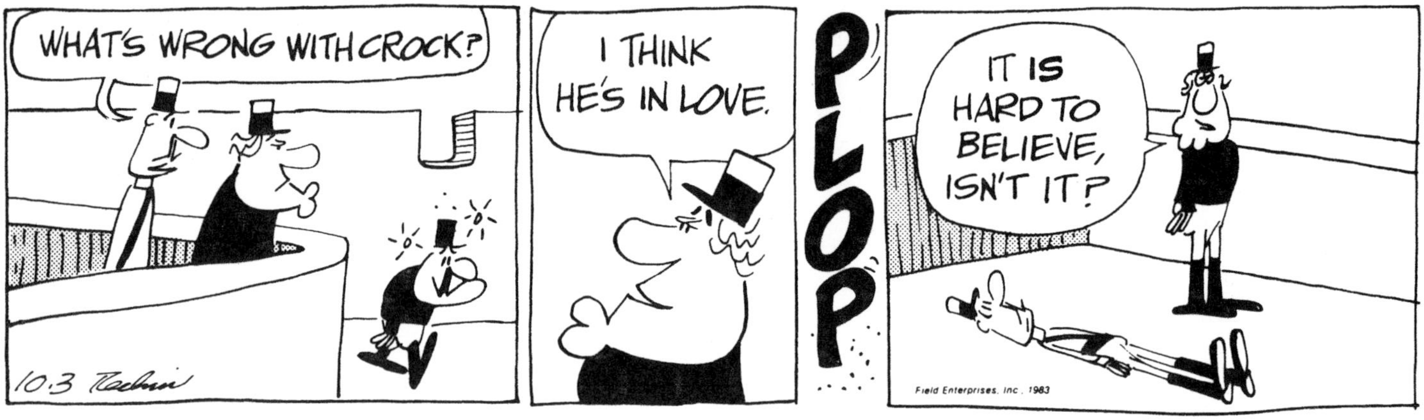
WHAT'S WRONG WITH CROCK?
I THINK HE'S IN LOVE.
PLOP
IT IS HARD TO BELIEVE, ISN'T IT?
10.3
Field Enterprises, Inc., 1983

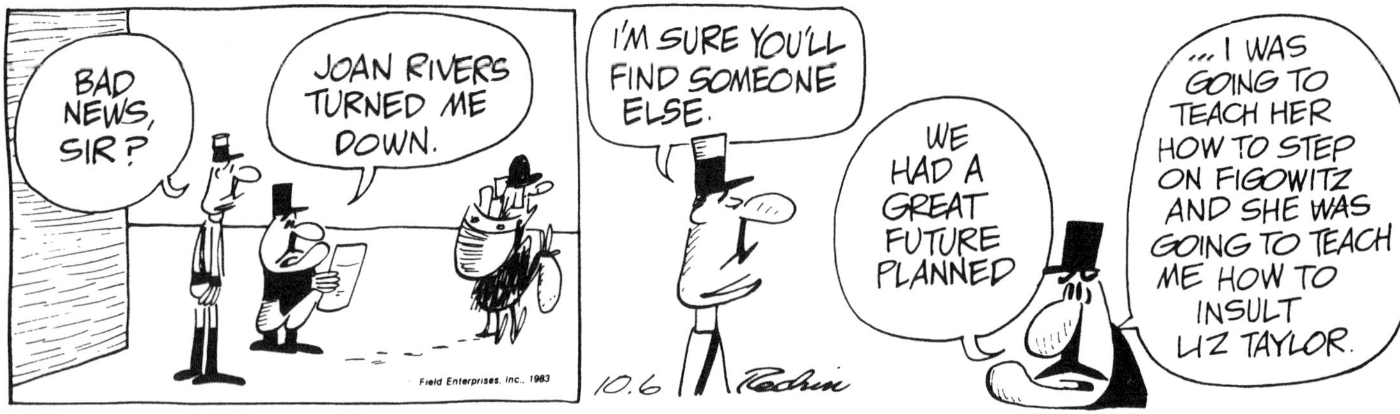
BAD NEWS, SIR?
JOAN RIVERS TURNED ME DOWN.
Field Enterprises, Inc., 1983
I'M SURE YOU'LL FIND SOMEONE ELSE.
WE HAD A GREAT FUTURE PLANNED
...I WAS GOING TO TEACH HER HOW TO STEP ON FIGOWITZ AND SHE WAS GOING TO TEACH ME HOW TO INSULT LIZ TAYLOR.
10.6

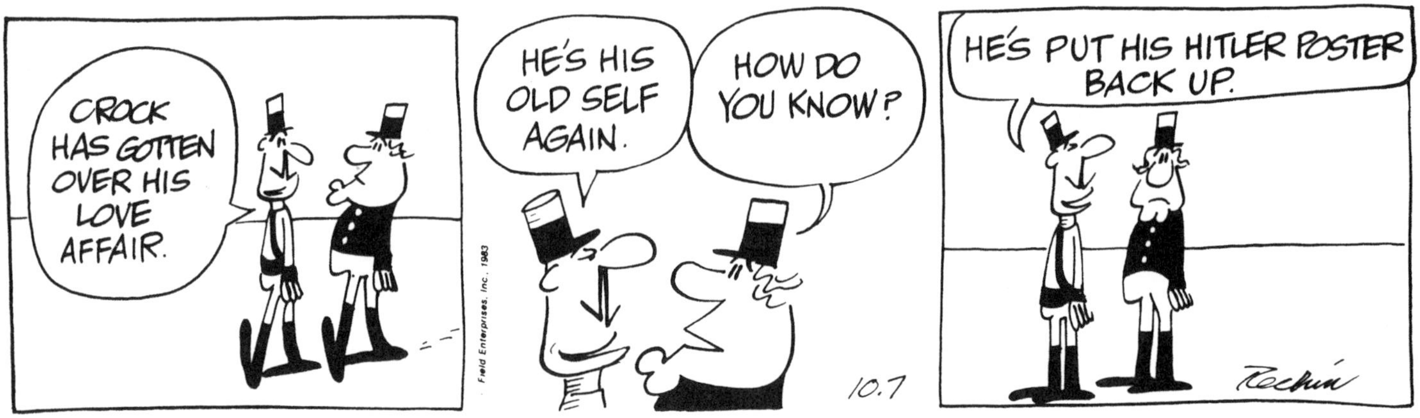
CROCK HAS GOTTEN OVER HIS LOVE AFFAIR.
Field Enterprises, Inc., 1983
HE'S HIS OLD SELF AGAIN.
HOW DO YOU KNOW?
HE'S PUT HIS HITLER POSTER BACK UP.
10.7

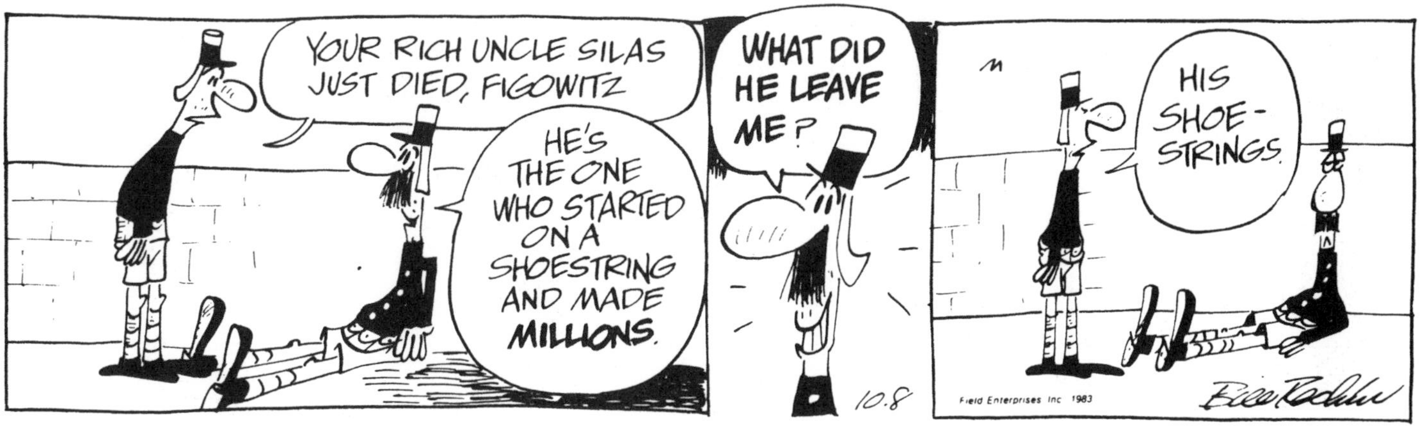
YOUR RICH UNCLE SILAS JUST DIED, FIGOWITZ
HE'S THE ONE WHO STARTED ON A SHOESTRING AND MADE **MILLIONS**.
WHAT DID HE LEAVE ME?
10.8
HIS SHOE-STRINGS.
Field Enterprises Inc 1983

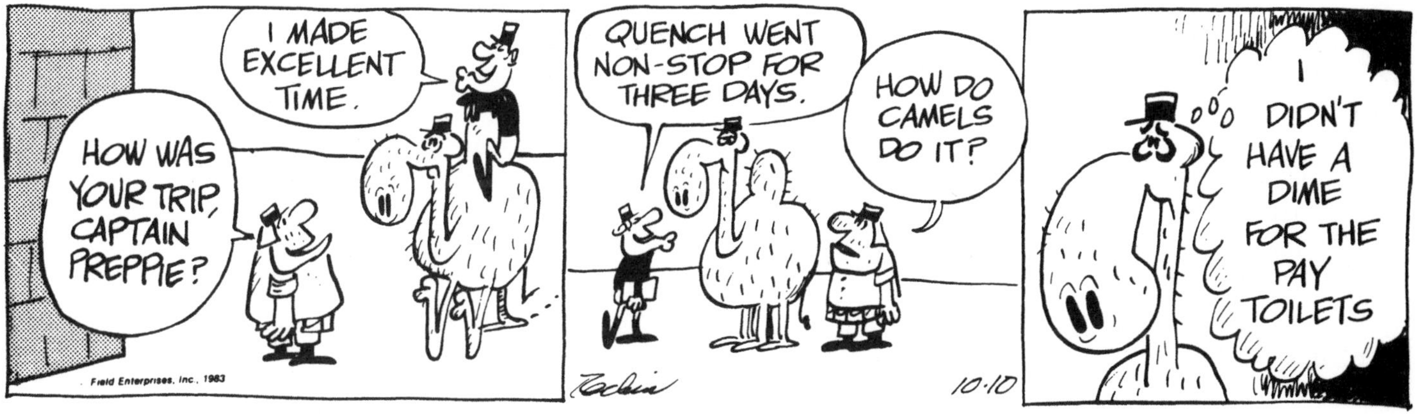
HOW WAS YOUR TRIP, CAPTAIN PREPPIE?
I MADE EXCELLENT TIME.
Field Enterprises, Inc., 1983
QUENCH WENT NON-STOP FOR THREE DAYS.
HOW DO CAMELS DO IT?
10.10
I DIDN'T HAVE A DIME FOR THE PAY TOILETS

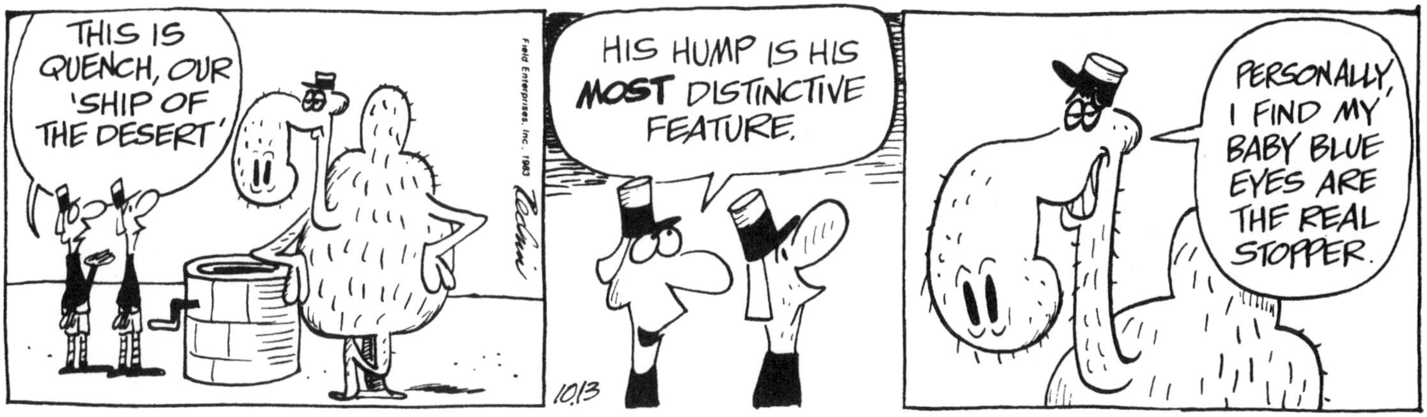
THIS IS QUENCH, OUR 'SHIP OF THE DESERT'
Field Enterprises, Inc. 1983
HIS HUMP IS HIS **MOST** DISTINCTIVE FEATURE.
10.13
PERSONALLY, I FIND MY BABY BLUE EYES ARE THE REAL STOPPER.

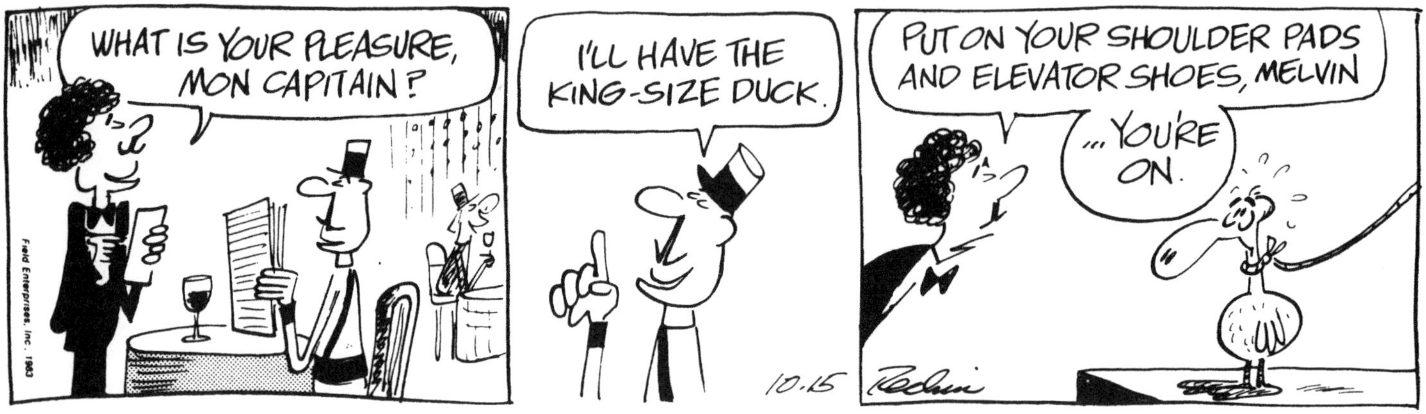
WHAT IS YOUR PLEASURE, MON CAPITAIN?
Field Enterprises, Inc. 1983
I'LL HAVE THE KING-SIZE DUCK.
10.15
PUT ON YOUR SHOULDER PADS AND ELEVATOR SHOES, MELVIN
... YOU'RE ON.

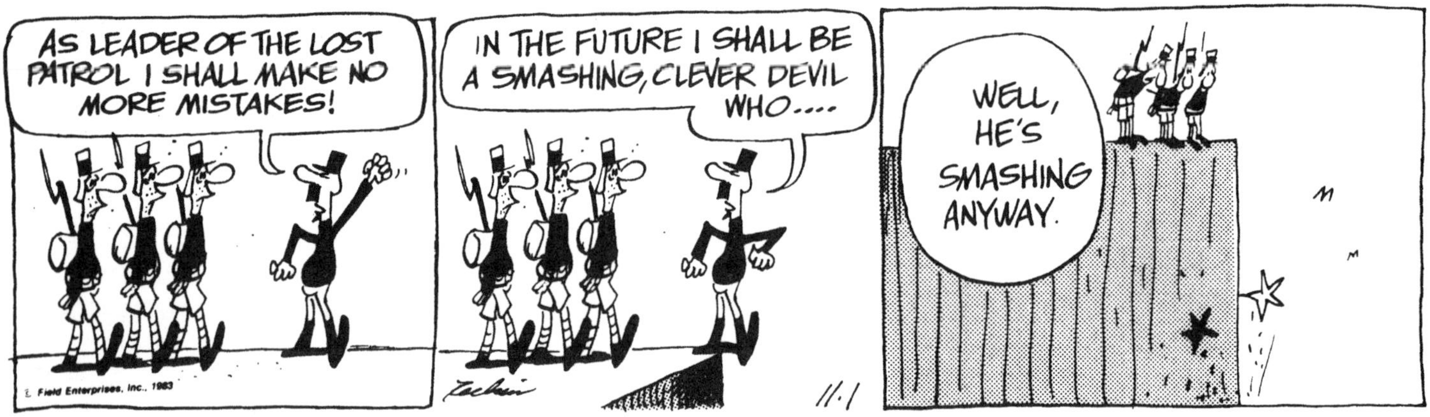
AS LEADER OF THE LOST PATROL I SHALL MAKE NO MORE MISTAKES!
Field Enterprises, Inc., 1983
IN THE FUTURE I SHALL BE A SMASHING, CLEVER DEVIL WHO....
11.1
WELL, HE'S SMASHING ANYWAY.

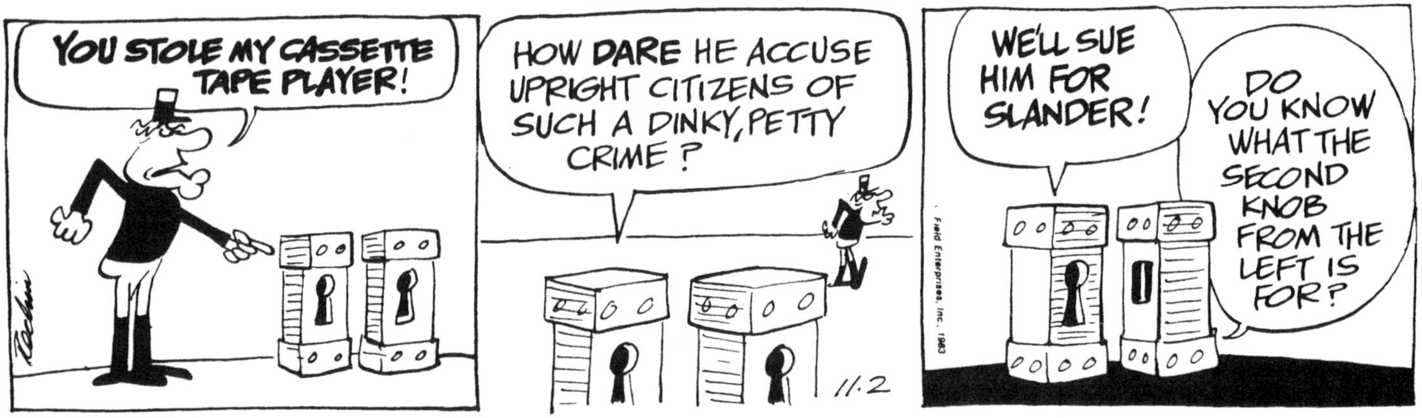
YOU STOLE MY CASSETTE TAPE PLAYER!
HOW DARE HE ACCUSE UPRIGHT CITIZENS OF SUCH A DINKY, PETTY CRIME?
11.2
WE'LL SUE HIM FOR SLANDER!
DO YOU KNOW WHAT THE SECOND KNOB FROM THE LEFT IS FOR?
Field Enterprises, Inc. 1983

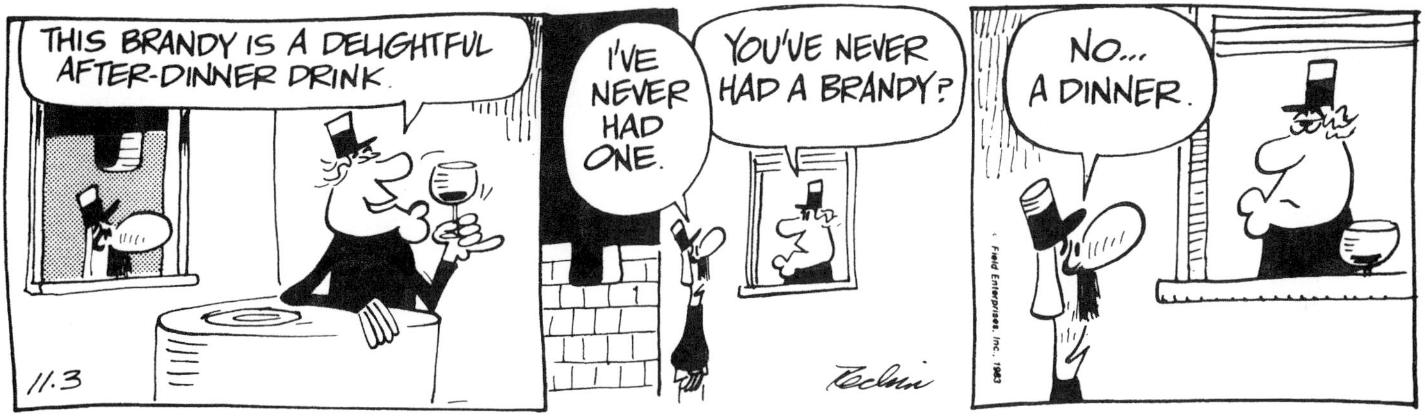
THIS BRANDY IS A DELIGHTFUL AFTER-DINNER DRINK.
11.3
I'VE NEVER HAD ONE.
YOU'VE NEVER HAD A BRANDY?
NO... A DINNER.
© Field Enterprises, Inc. 1983

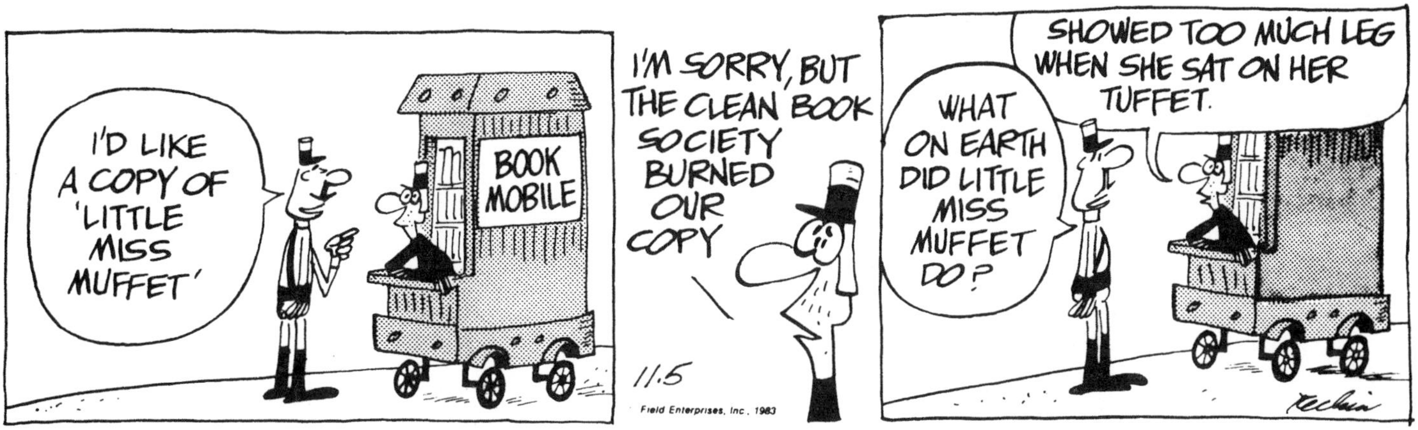
I'D LIKE A COPY OF 'LITTLE MISS MUFFET'
BOOK MOBILE
I'M SORRY, BUT THE CLEAN BOOK SOCIETY BURNED OUR COPY
11.5
Field Enterprises, Inc., 1983
WHAT ON EARTH DID LITTLE MISS MUFFET DO?
SHOWED TOO MUCH LEG WHEN SHE SAT ON HER TUFFET.

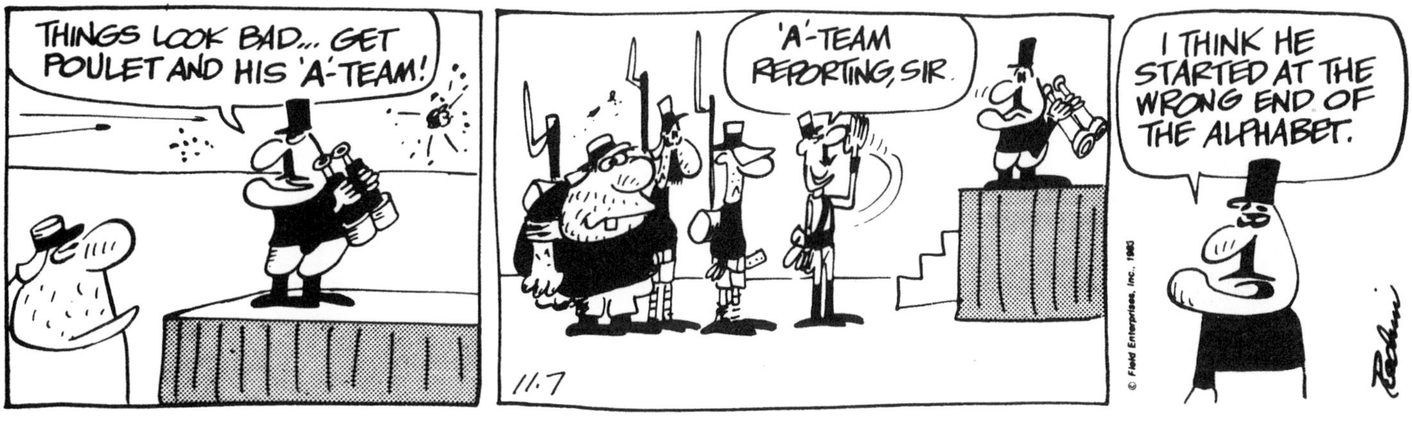
THINGS LOOK BAD... GET POULET AND HIS 'A'-TEAM!
'A'-TEAM REPORTING, SIR.
11.7
© Field Enterprises, Inc., 1983
I THINK HE STARTED AT THE WRONG END OF THE ALPHABET.

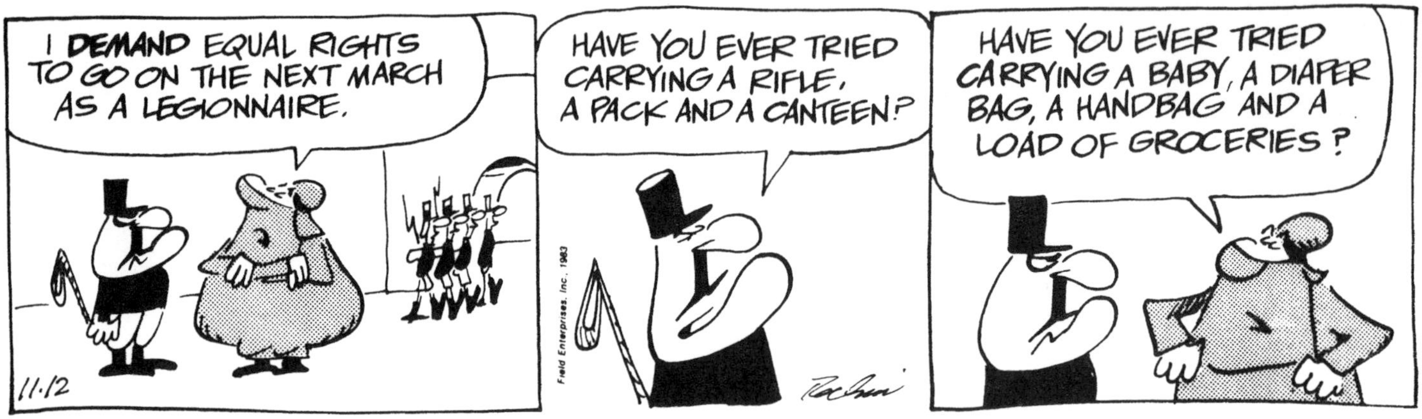
I DEMAND EQUAL RIGHTS TO GO ON THE NEXT MARCH AS A LEGIONNAIRE.
11.12
Field Enterprises, Inc. 1983
HAVE YOU EVER TRIED CARRYING A RIFLE, A PACK AND A CANTEEN?
HAVE YOU EVER TRIED CARRYING A BABY, A DIAPER BAG, A HANDBAG AND A LOAD OF GROCERIES?

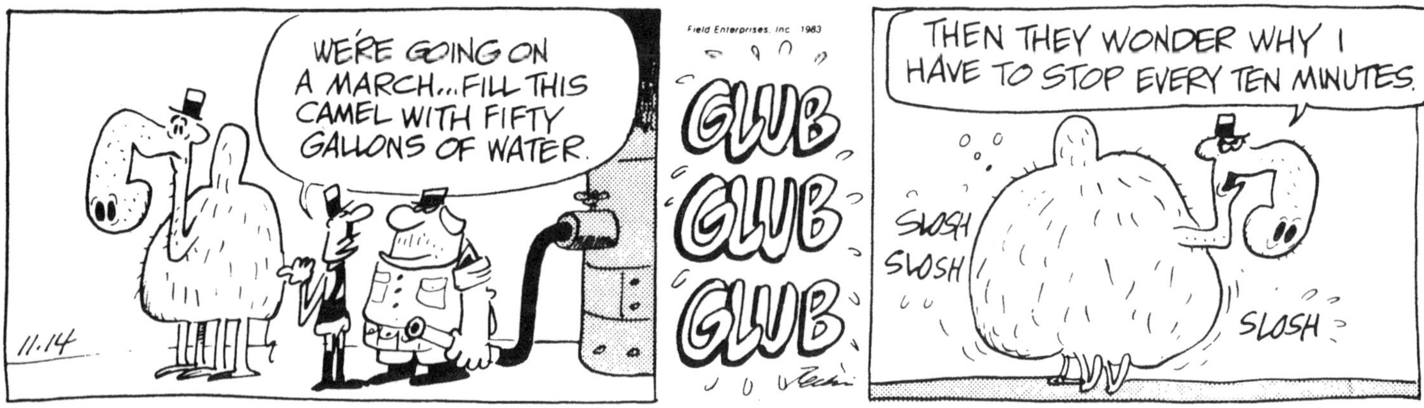
WE'RE GOING ON A MARCH... FILL THIS CAMEL WITH FIFTY GALLONS OF WATER.
11.14
Field Enterprises, Inc. 1983
GLUB
GLUB
GLUB
THEN THEY WONDER WHY I HAVE TO STOP EVERY TEN MINUTES.
SLOSH
SLOSH
SLOSH

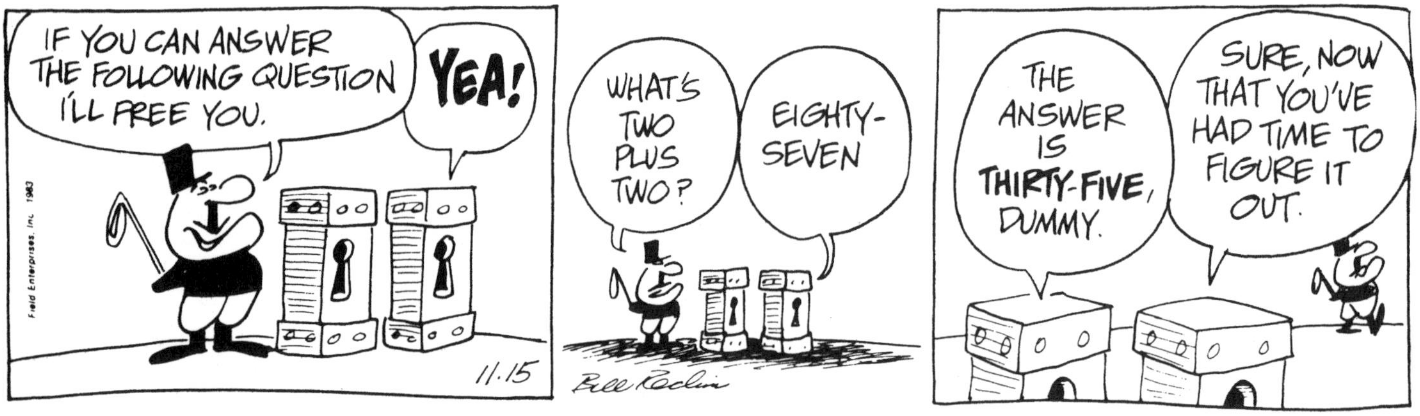
IF YOU CAN ANSWER THE FOLLOWING QUESTION I'LL FREE YOU.
YEA!
Field Enterprises, Inc. 1983
11.15
WHAT'S TWO PLUS TWO?
EIGHTY-SEVEN
Bill Rechin
THE ANSWER IS THIRTY-FIVE, DUMMY.
SURE, NOW THAT YOU'VE HAD TIME TO FIGURE IT OUT.

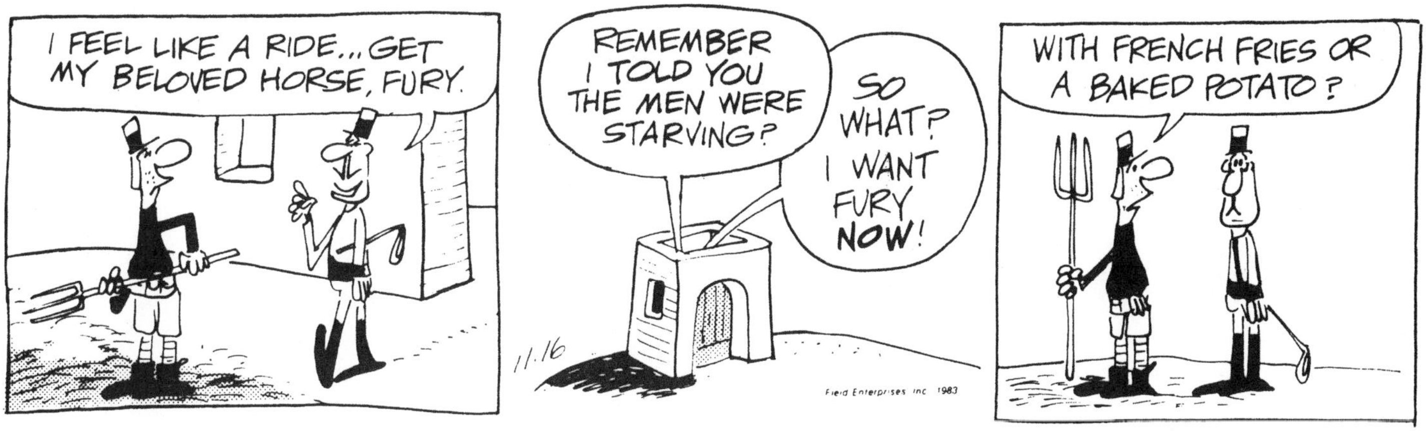
I FEEL LIKE A RIDE... GET MY BELOVED HORSE, FURY.
REMEMBER I TOLD YOU THE MEN WERE STARVING?
SO WHAT? I WANT FURY NOW!
11.16
Field Enterprises Inc 1983
WITH FRENCH FRIES OR A BAKED POTATO?

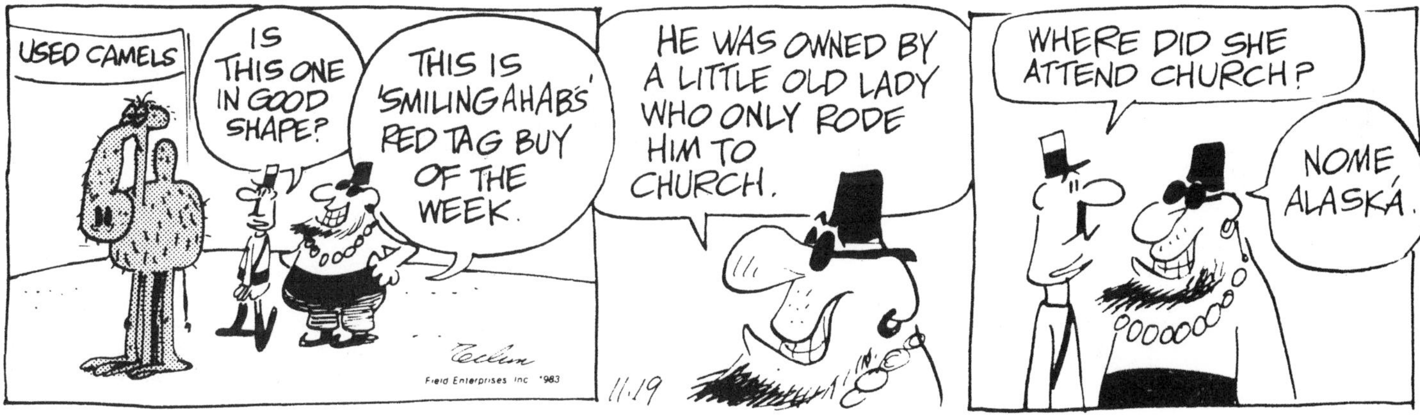
USED CAMELS
IS THIS ONE IN GOOD SHAPE?
THIS IS 'SMILING AHAB'S' RED TAG BUY OF THE WEEK.
Field Enterprises Inc 1983
HE WAS OWNED BY A LITTLE OLD LADY WHO ONLY RODE HIM TO CHURCH.
11.19
WHERE DID SHE ATTEND CHURCH?
NOME, ALASKA.

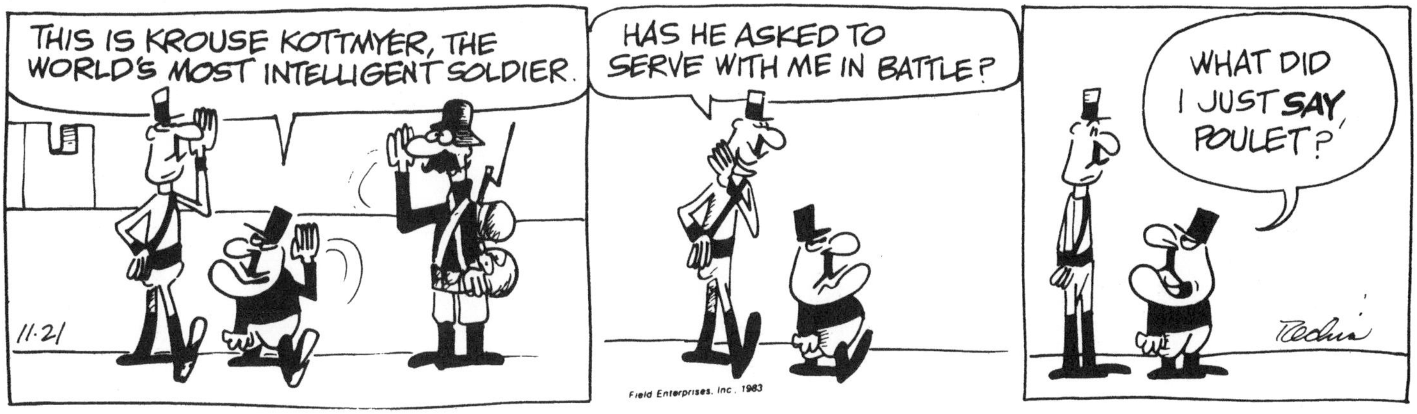
THIS IS KROUSE KOTTMYER, THE WORLD'S MOST INTELLIGENT SOLDIER.
11.21
HAS HE ASKED TO SERVE WITH ME IN BATTLE?
Field Enterprises, Inc. 1983
WHAT DID I JUST SAY, POULET?

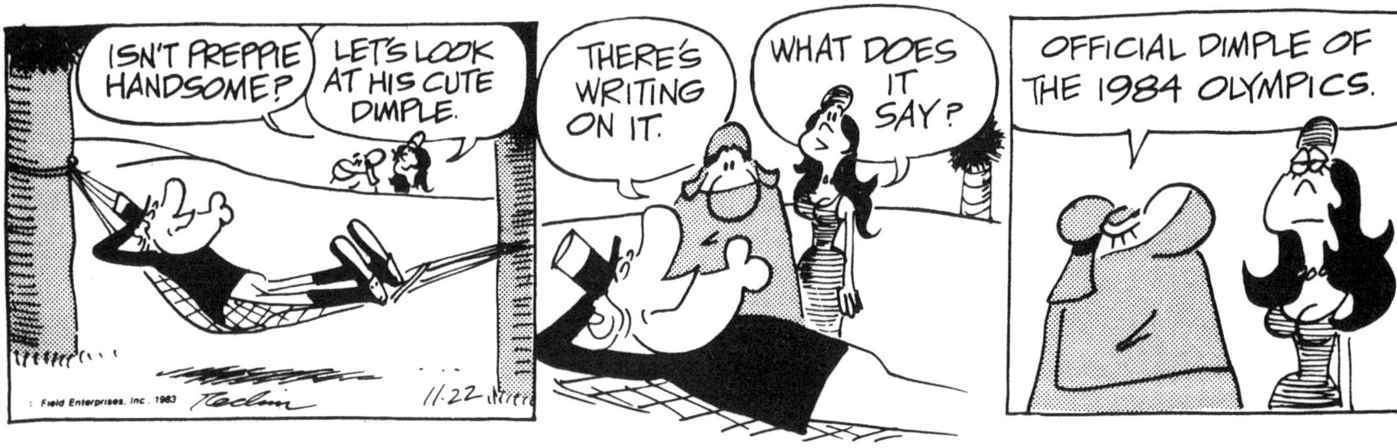
ISN'T PREPPIE HANDSOME?
LET'S LOOK AT HIS CUTE DIMPLE.
THERE'S WRITING ON IT.
WHAT DOES IT SAY?
OFFICIAL DIMPLE OF THE 1984 OLYMPICS.
© Field Enterprises, Inc. 1983
11.22

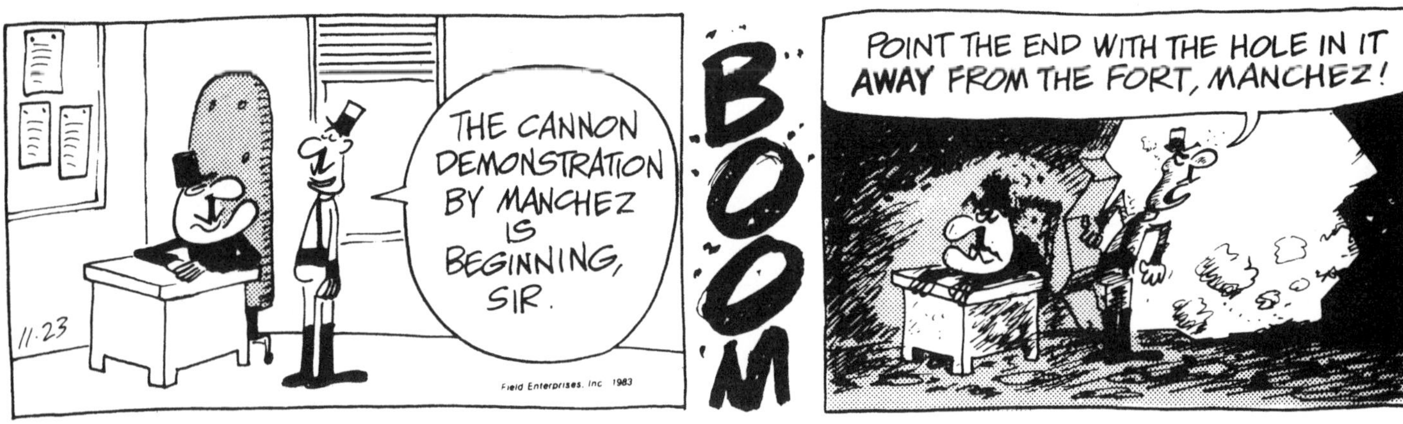
THE CANNON DEMONSTRATION BY MANCHEZ IS BEGINNING, SIR.
11.23
Field Enterprises, Inc. 1983
BOOOM
POINT THE END WITH THE HOLE IN IT AWAY FROM THE FORT, MANCHEZ!

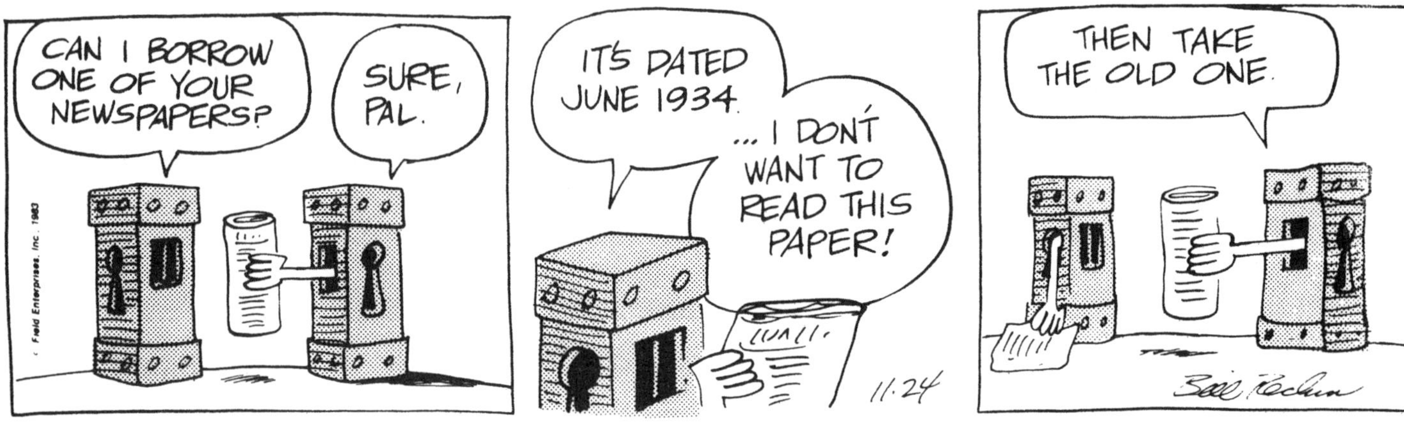
CAN I BORROW ONE OF YOUR NEWSPAPERS?
SURE, PAL.
© Field Enterprises, Inc. 1983
IT'S DATED JUNE 1934.
... I DON'T WANT TO READ THIS PAPER!
11.24
THEN TAKE THE OLD ONE.

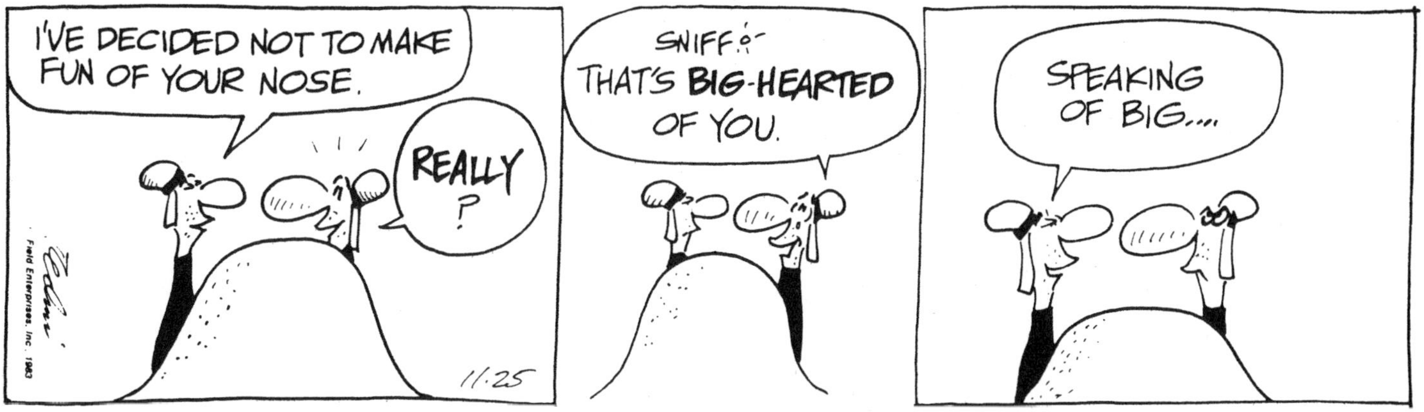
I'VE DECIDED NOT TO MAKE FUN OF YOUR NOSE.
REALLY ?
SNIFF
THAT'S **BIG-HEARTED** OF YOU.
SPEAKING OF BIG....
11·25
Field Enterprises, Inc. 1983

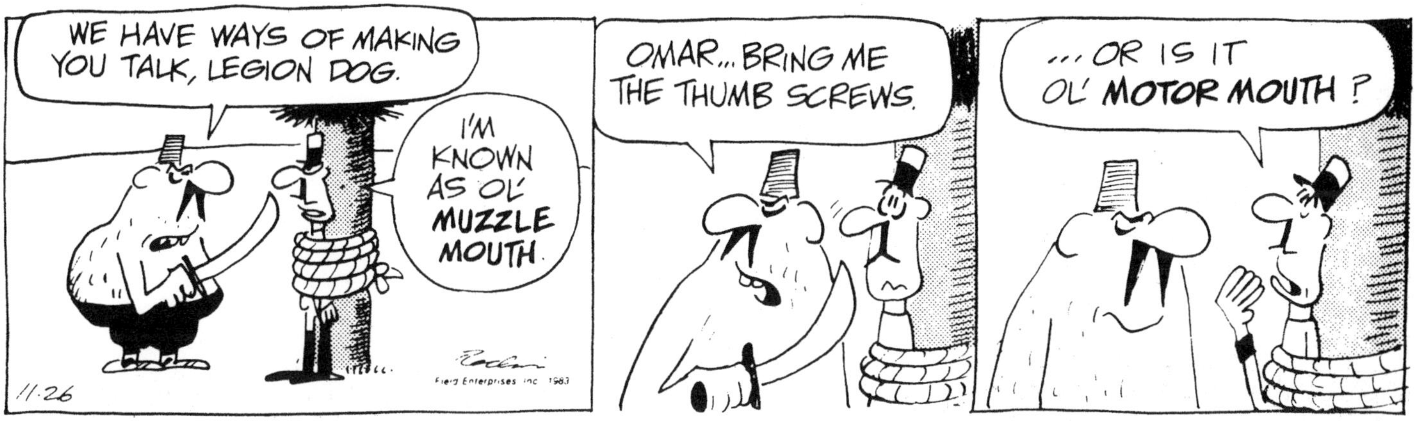
WE HAVE WAYS OF MAKING YOU TALK, LEGION DOG.
I'M KNOWN AS OL' **MUZZLE MOUTH**.
OMAR... BRING ME THE THUMB SCREWS.
...OR IS IT OL' **MOTOR MOUTH** ?
11·26
Field Enterprises, Inc. 1983

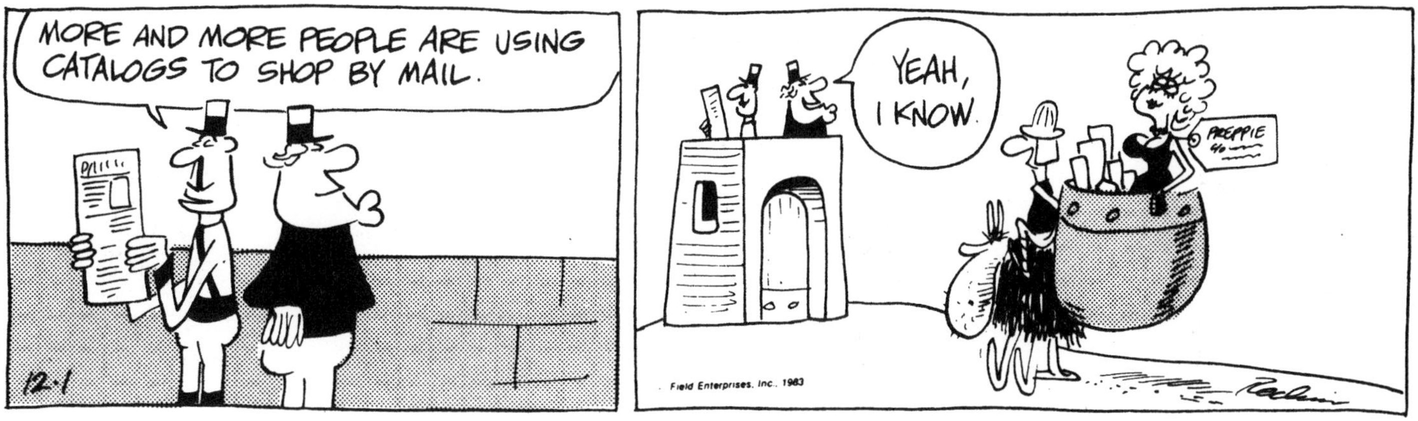
MORE AND MORE PEOPLE ARE USING CATALOGS TO SHOP BY MAIL.
YEAH, I KNOW.
PREPPIE
12·1
Field Enterprises, Inc., 1983

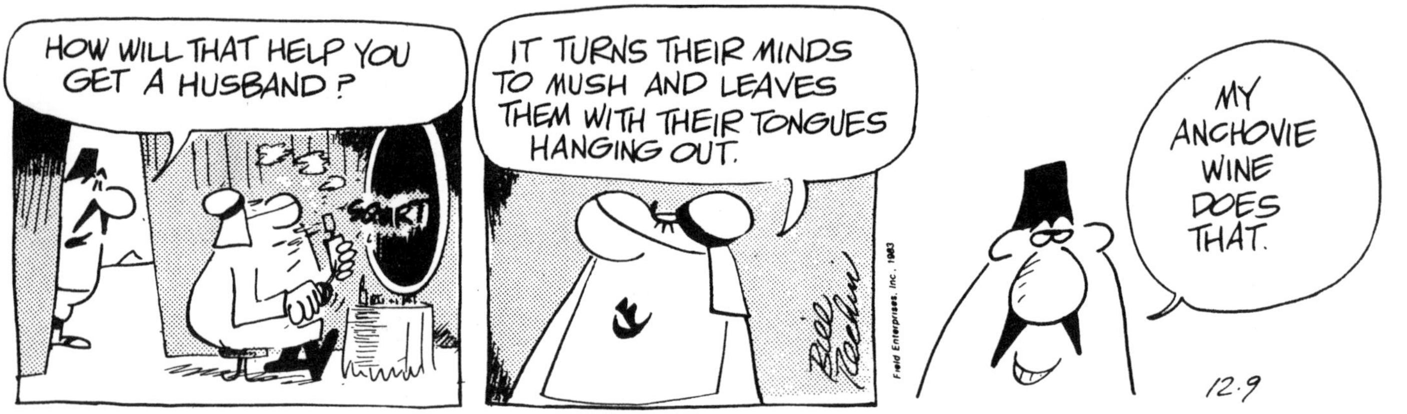
HOW WILL THAT HELP YOU GET A HUSBAND?
SQUIRT
IT TURNS THEIR MINDS TO MUSH AND LEAVES THEM WITH THEIR TONGUES HANGING OUT.
Field Enterprises, Inc., 1983
MY ANCHOVIE WINE DOES THAT.
12·9

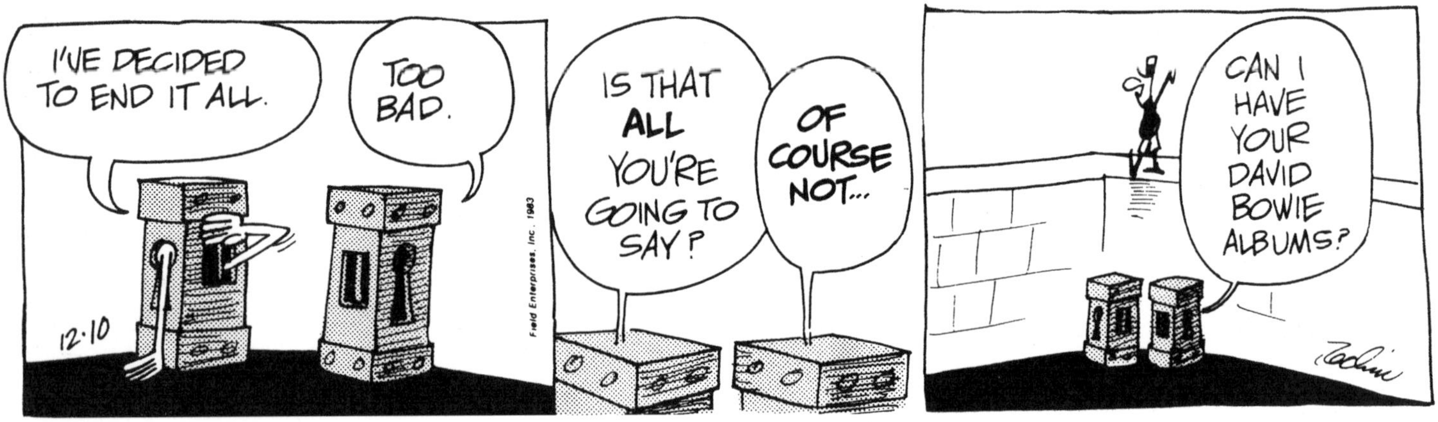
I'VE DECIDED TO END IT ALL.
TOO BAD.
12·10
Field Enterprises, Inc., 1983
IS THAT **ALL** YOU'RE GOING TO SAY?
OF COURSE NOT...
CAN I HAVE YOUR DAVID BOWIE ALBUMS?

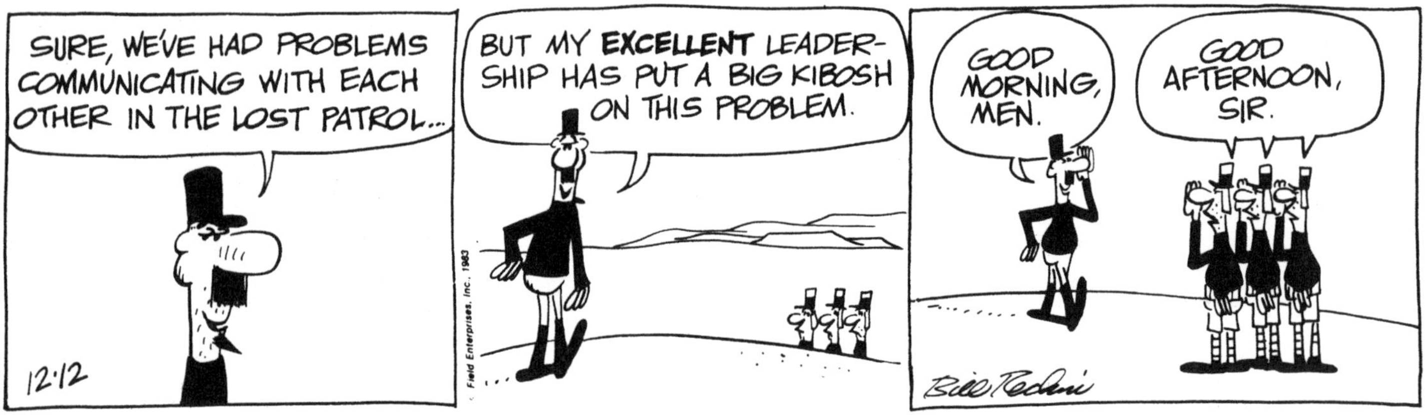
SURE, WE'VE HAD PROBLEMS COMMUNICATING WITH EACH OTHER IN THE LOST PATROL...
12·12
BUT MY **EXCELLENT** LEADERSHIP HAS PUT A BIG KIBOSH ON THIS PROBLEM.
Field Enterprises, Inc., 1983
GOOD MORNING, MEN.
GOOD AFTERNOON, SIR.

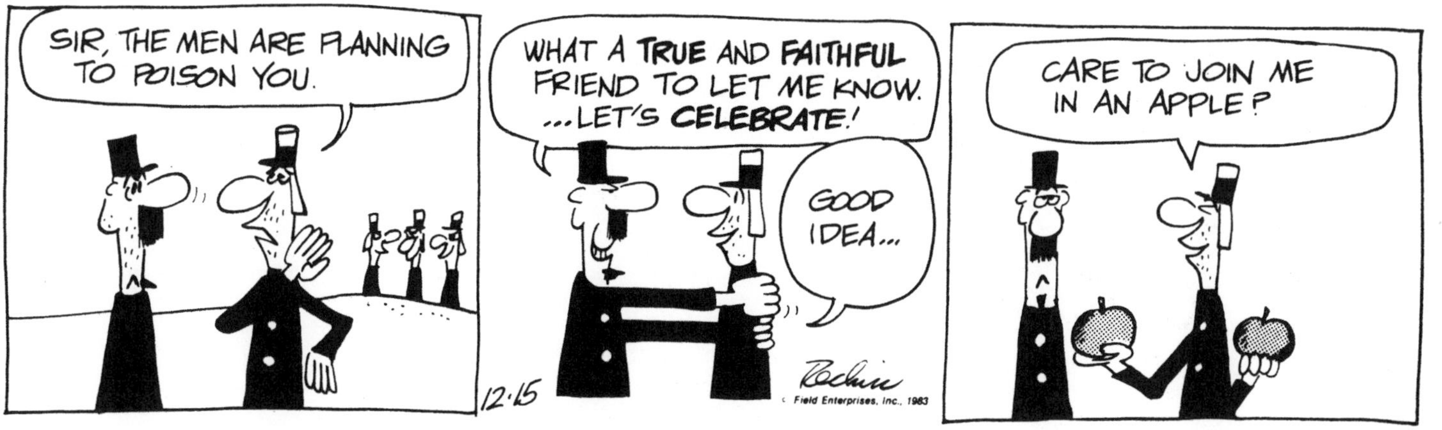
SIR, THE MEN ARE PLANNING TO POISON YOU.
WHAT A **TRUE** AND **FAITHFUL** FRIEND TO LET ME KNOW. ...LET'S **CELEBRATE**!
GOOD IDEA...
CARE TO JOIN ME IN AN APPLE?
12·15
© Field Enterprises, Inc., 1983

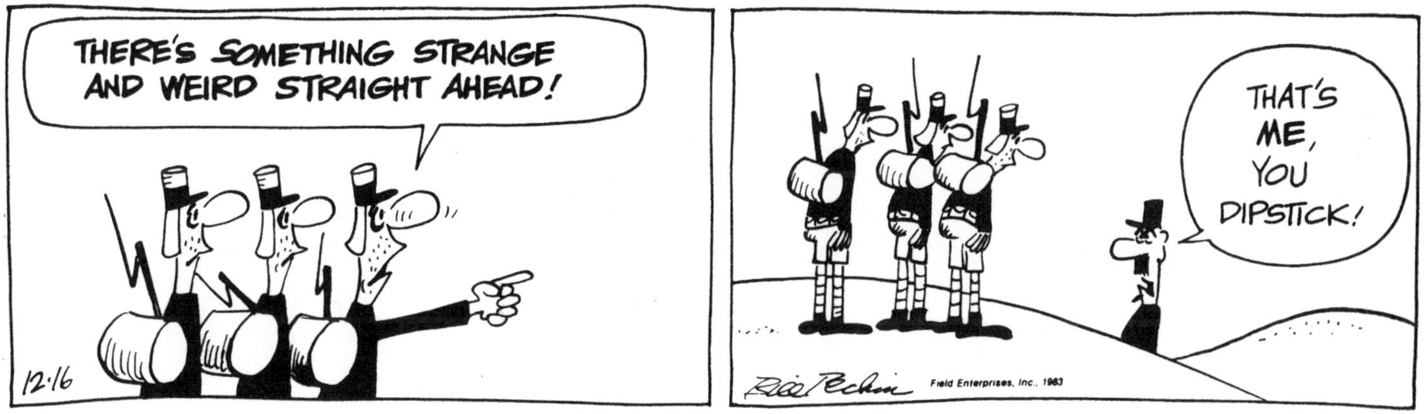
THERE'S *SOMETHING* STRANGE AND WEIRD STRAIGHT AHEAD!
THAT'S **ME**, YOU DIPSTICK!
12·16
Field Enterprises, Inc., 1983

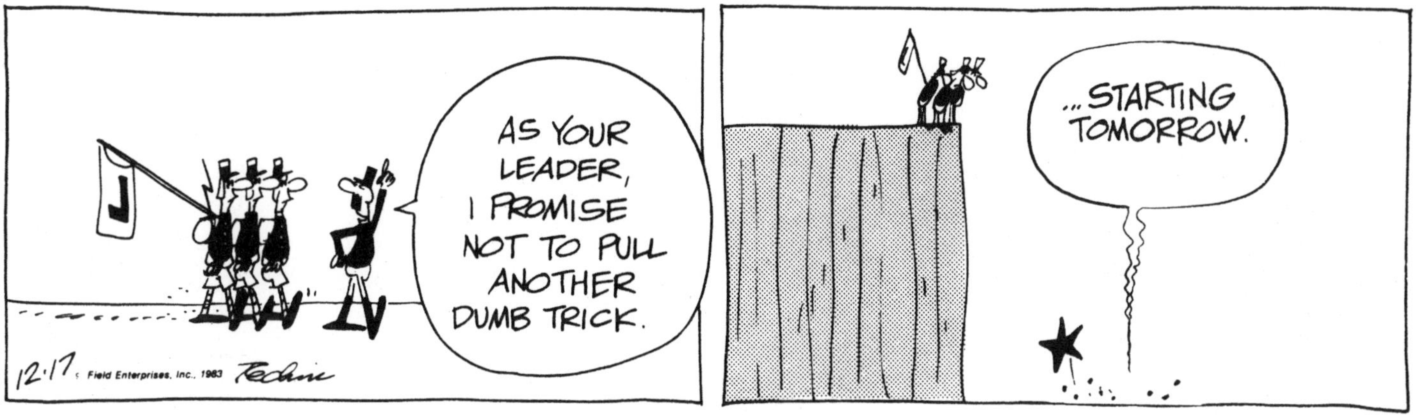
J
AS YOUR LEADER, I PROMISE NOT TO PULL ANOTHER DUMB TRICK.
...STARTING TOMORROW.
12·17
© Field Enterprises, Inc., 1983

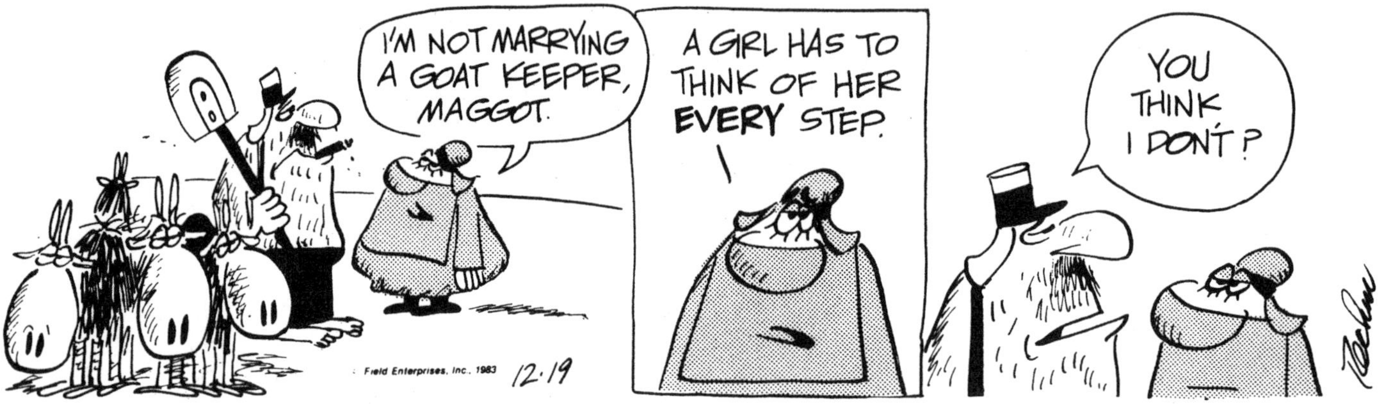
I'M NOT MARRYING A GOAT KEEPER, MAGGOT.
© Field Enterprises, Inc., 1983
12·19
A GIRL HAS TO THINK OF HER **EVERY** STEP.
YOU THINK I DON'T?

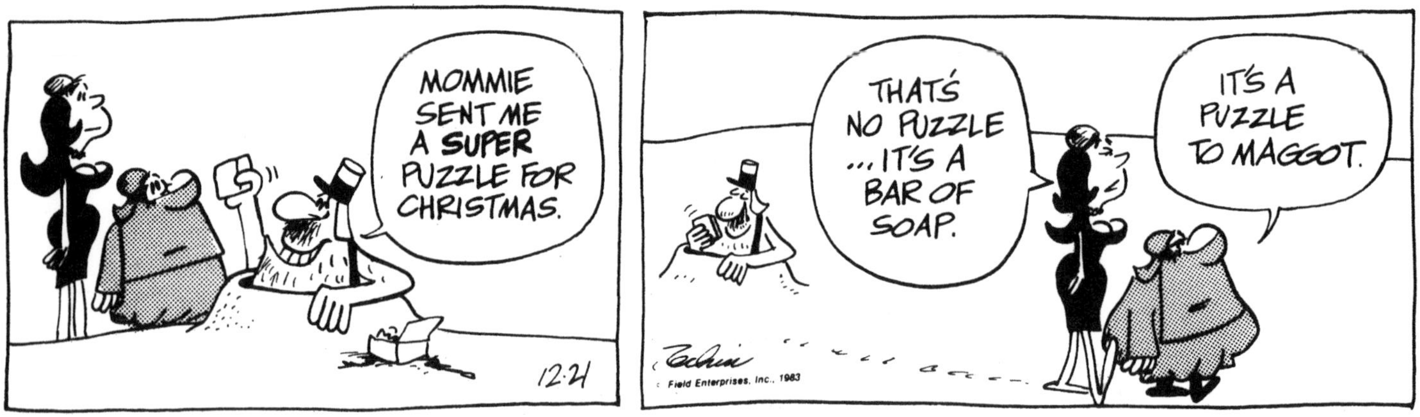
MOMMIE SENT ME A **SUPER** PUZZLE FOR CHRISTMAS.
12·21
THAT'S NO PUZZLE ...IT'S A BAR OF SOAP.
IT'S A PUZZLE TO MAGGOT.
© Field Enterprises, Inc., 1983

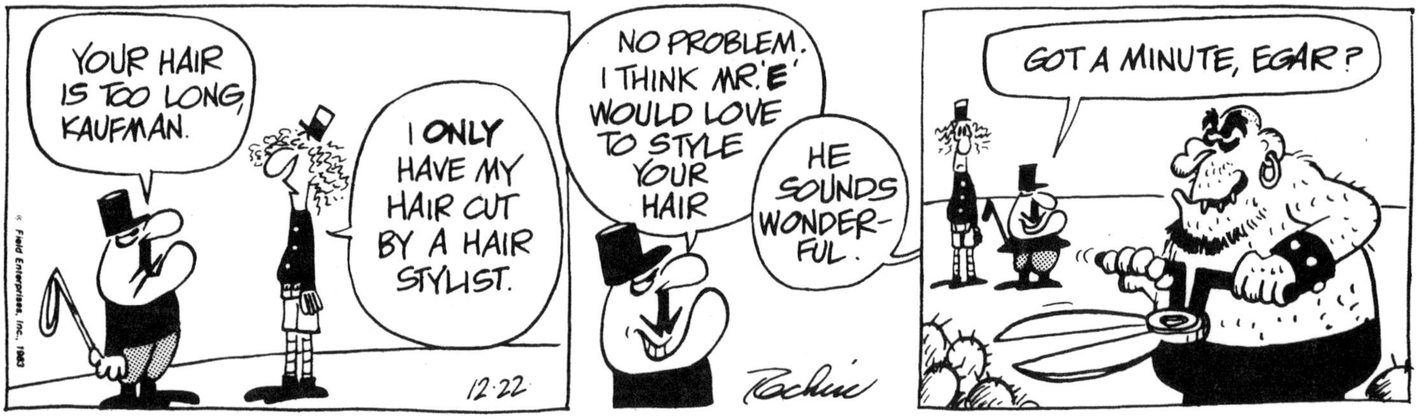
© Field Enterprises, Inc., 1983
YOUR HAIR IS TOO LONG, KAUFMAN.
I **ONLY** HAVE MY HAIR CUT BY A HAIR STYLIST.
12·22
NO PROBLEM. I THINK MR. '**E**' WOULD LOVE TO STYLE YOUR HAIR
HE SOUNDS WONDER-FUL.
GOT A MINUTE, EGAR?

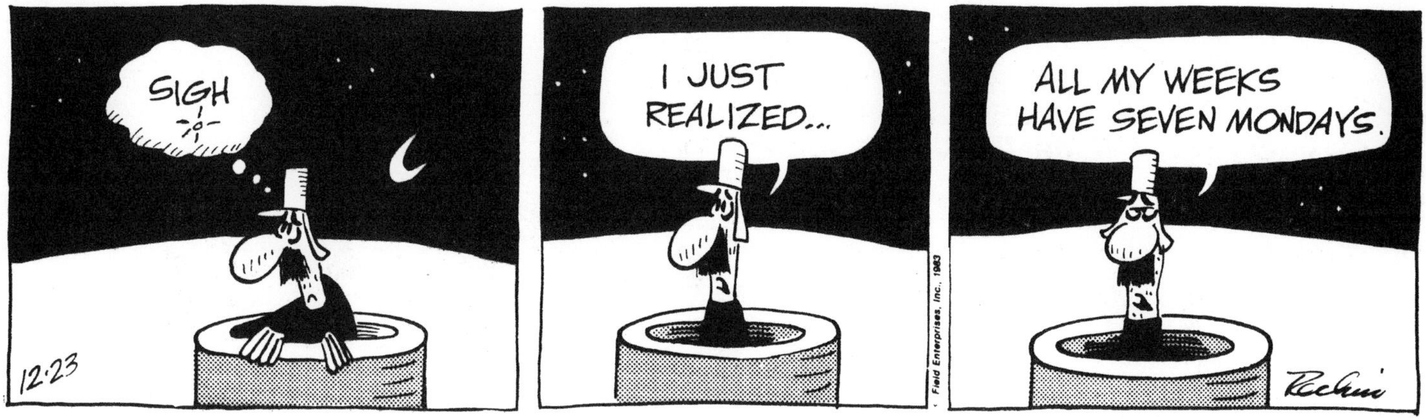
SIGH
I JUST REALIZED...
ALL MY WEEKS HAVE SEVEN MONDAYS.
12·23
Field Enterprises, Inc., 1983

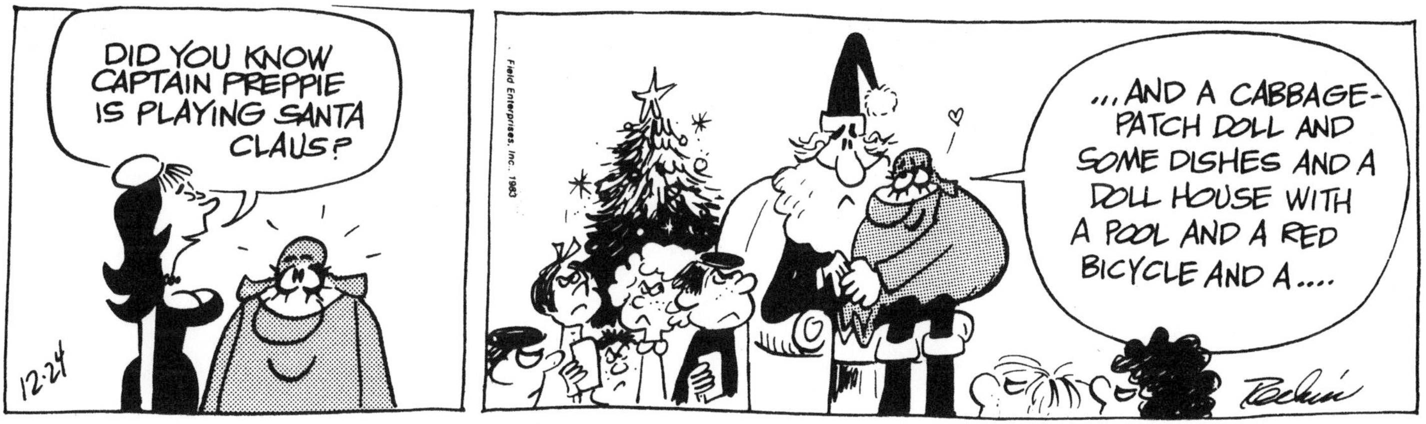
DID YOU KNOW CAPTAIN PREPPIE IS PLAYING SANTA CLAUS?
...AND A CABBAGE-PATCH DOLL AND SOME DISHES AND A DOLL HOUSE WITH A POOL AND A RED BICYCLE AND A....
12·24
Field Enterprises, Inc., 1983

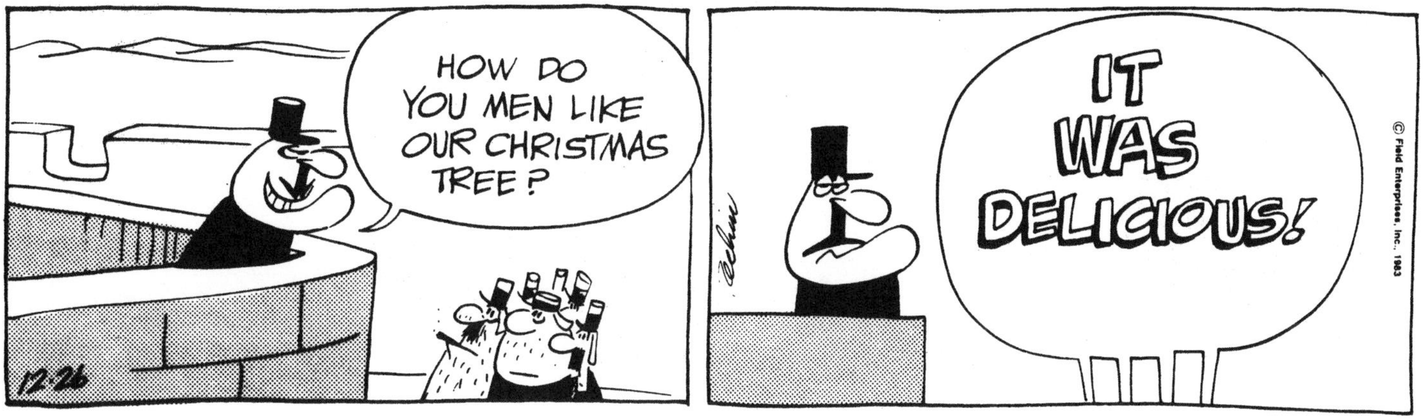
HOW DO YOU MEN LIKE OUR CHRISTMAS TREE?
IT WAS DELICIOUS!
12·26
© Field Enterprises, Inc., 1983

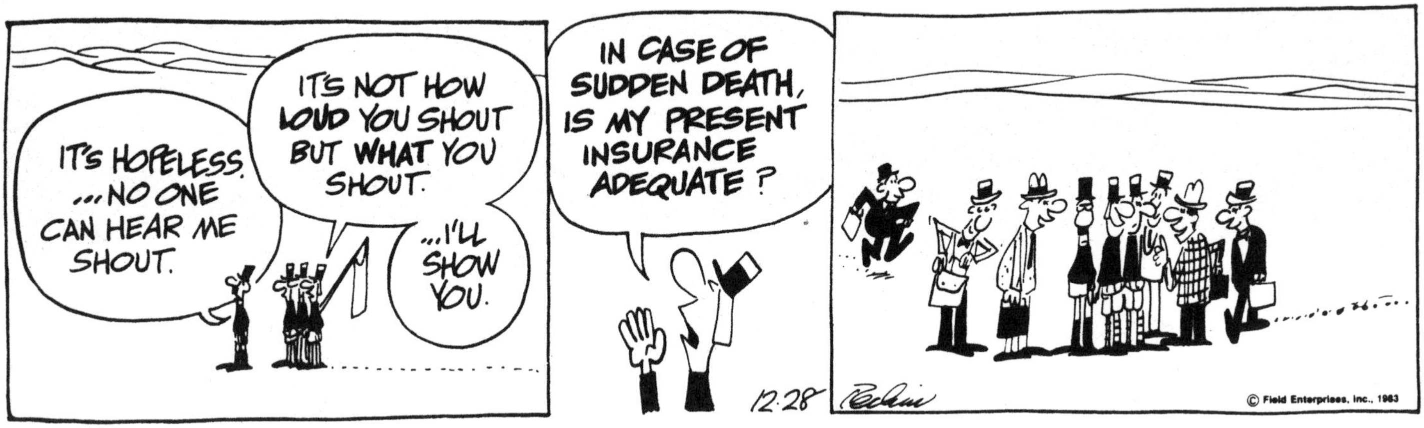
IT'S HOPELESS. ...NO ONE CAN HEAR ME SHOUT.
IT'S NOT HOW LOUD YOU SHOUT BUT WHAT YOU SHOUT.
...I'LL SHOW YOU.
IN CASE OF SUDDEN DEATH, IS MY PRESENT INSURANCE ADEQUATE ?
12·28
© Field Enterprises, Inc., 1983

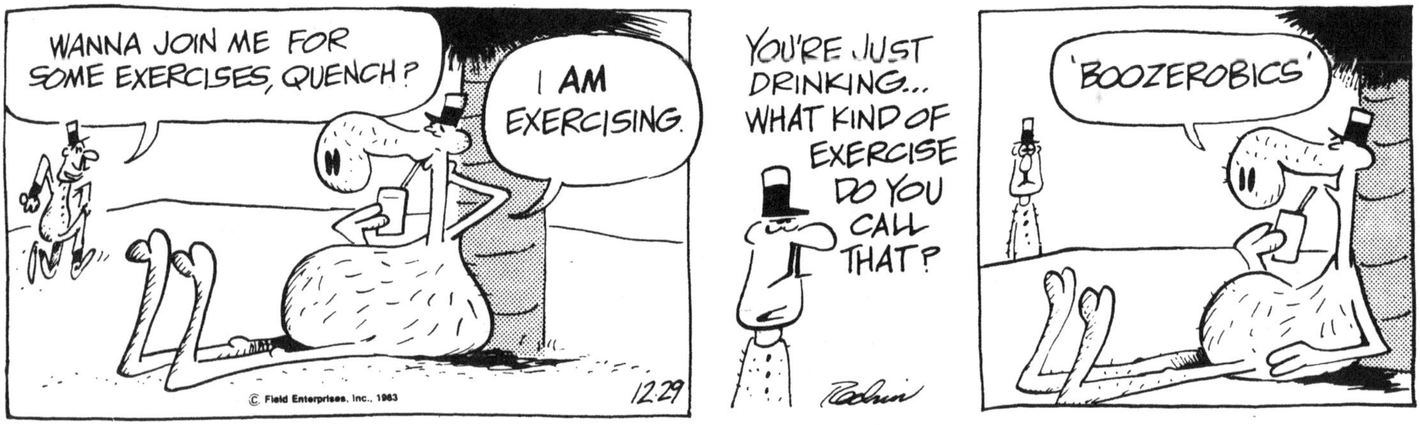
WANNA JOIN ME FOR SOME EXERCISES, QUENCH ?
I AM EXERCISING.
© Field Enterprises, Inc., 1983
12·29
YOU'RE JUST DRINKING... WHAT KIND OF EXERCISE DO YOU CALL THAT?
'BOOZEROBICS'

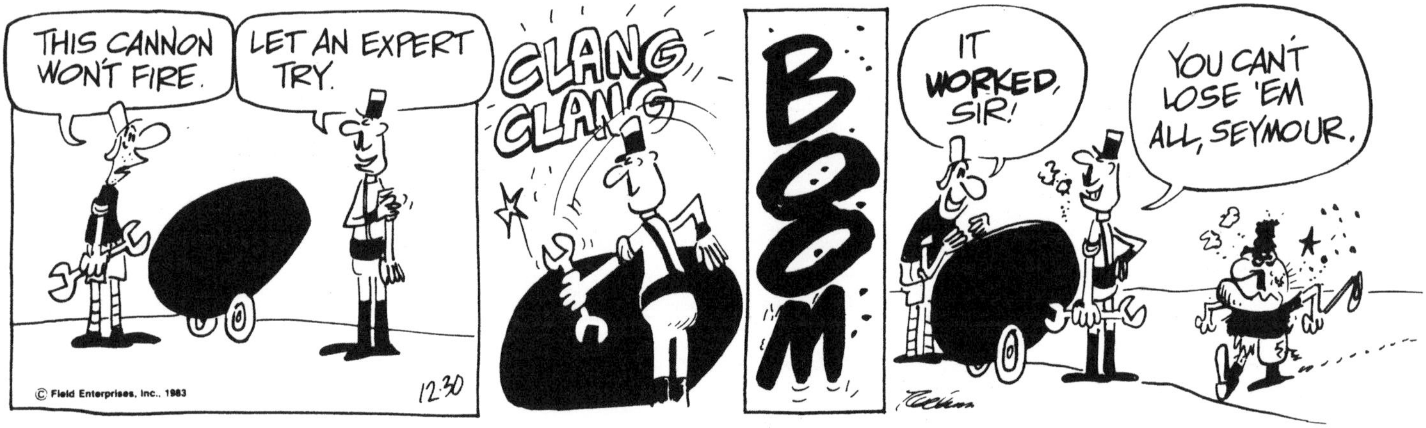
THIS CANNON WON'T FIRE.
LET AN EXPERT TRY.
© Field Enterprises, Inc., 1983
12·30
CLANG CLANG
BOOM
IT WORKED, SIR!
YOU CAN'T LOSE 'EM ALL, SEYMOUR.

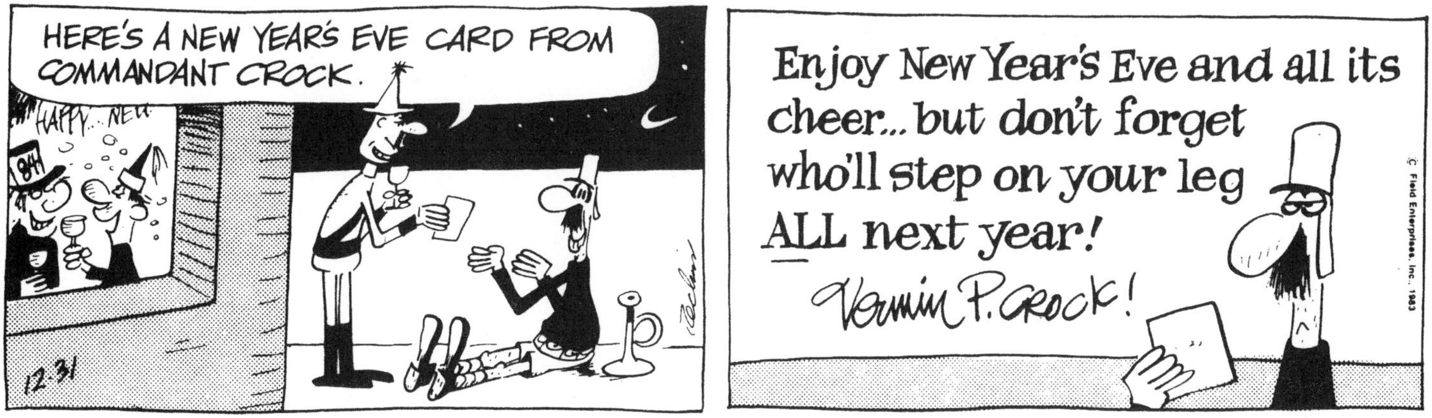
HERE'S A NEW YEAR'S EVE CARD FROM COMMANDANT CROCK.
HAPPY... NEW
84
12·31
Enjoy New Year's Eve and all its cheer... but don't forget who'll step on your leg ALL next year!
Vermin P. Crock!
© Field Enterprises, Inc., 1983

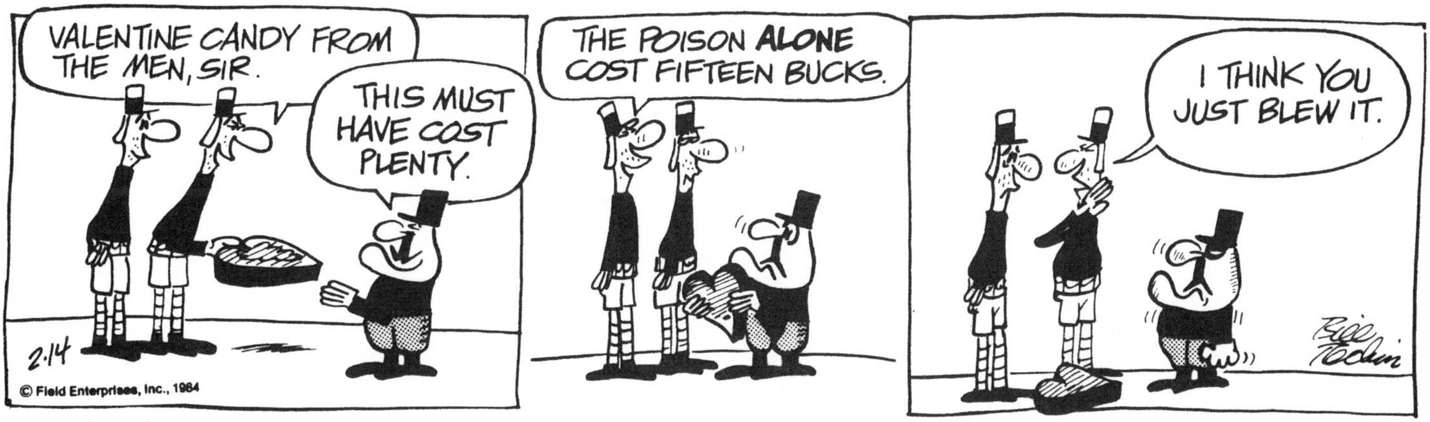
VALENTINE CANDY FROM THE MEN, SIR.
THIS MUST HAVE COST PLENTY.
2·14
© Field Enterprises, Inc., 1984
THE POISON ALONE COST FIFTEEN BUCKS.
I THINK YOU JUST BLEW IT.

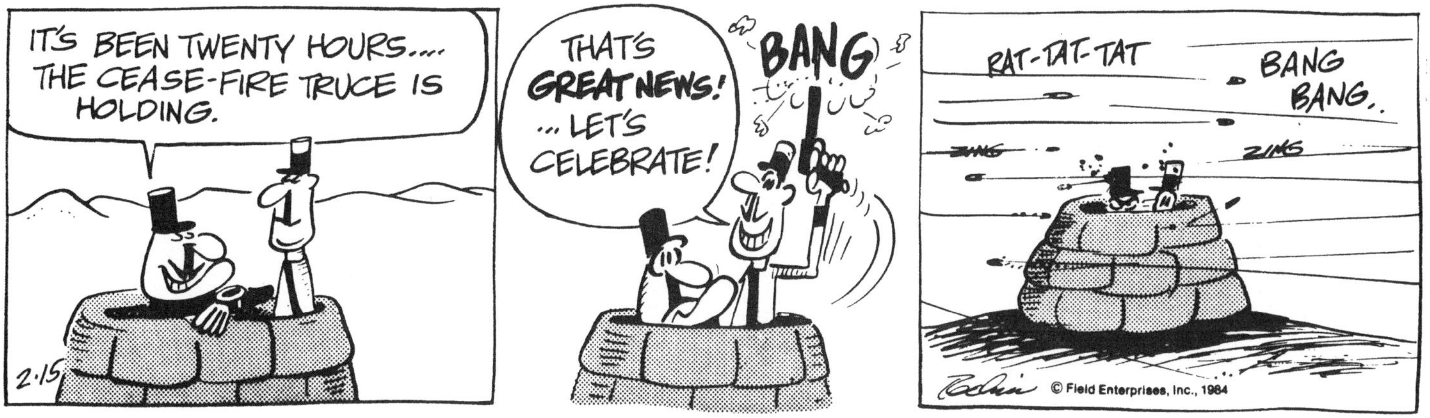
IT'S BEEN TWENTY HOURS.... THE CEASE-FIRE TRUCE IS HOLDING.
2·15
THAT'S GREAT NEWS! ...LET'S CELEBRATE!
BANG
RAT-TAT-TAT
BANG BANG.
ZING
ZING
© Field Enterprises, Inc., 1984

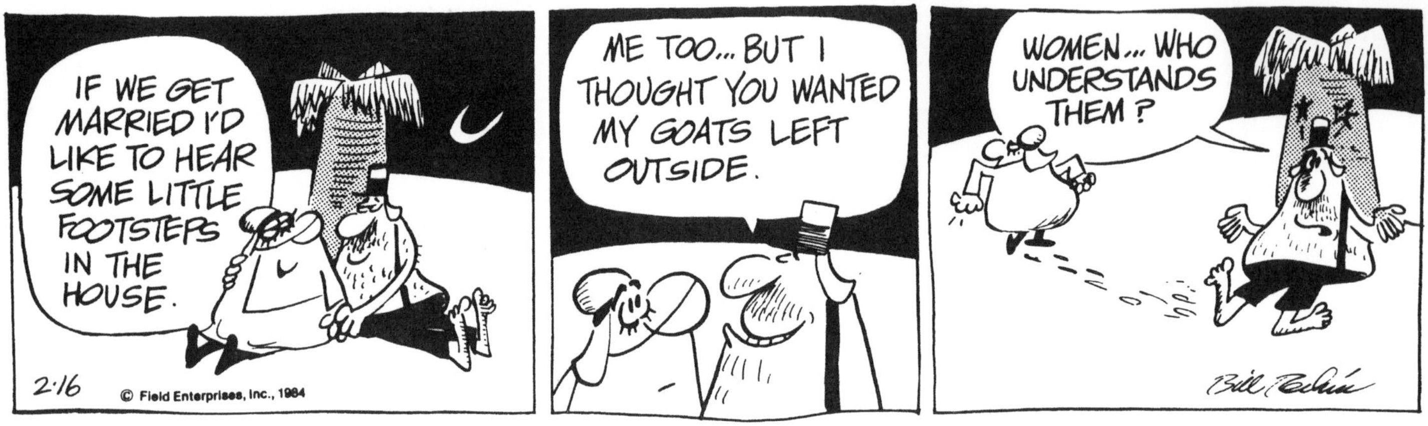
IF WE GET MARRIED I'D LIKE TO HEAR SOME LITTLE FOOTSTEPS IN THE HOUSE.
ME TOO... BUT I THOUGHT YOU WANTED MY GOATS LEFT OUTSIDE.
WOMEN... WHO UNDERSTANDS THEM?
2·16
© Field Enterprises, Inc., 1984
Bill Rechin

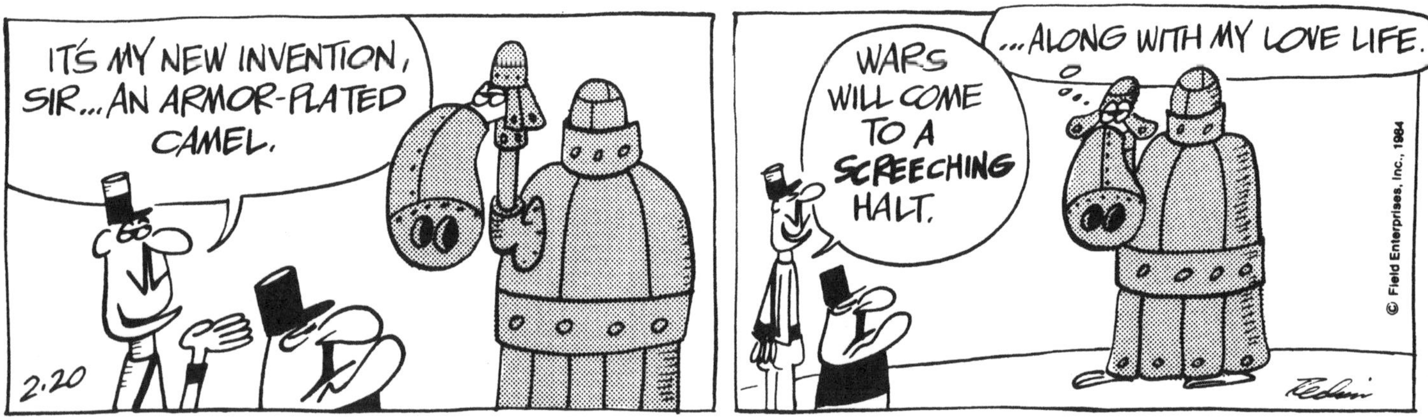
IT'S MY NEW INVENTION, SIR... AN ARMOR-PLATED CAMEL.
2·20
WARS WILL COME TO A SCREECHING HALT.
...ALONG WITH MY LOVE LIFE.
© Field Enterprises, Inc., 1984
Rechin

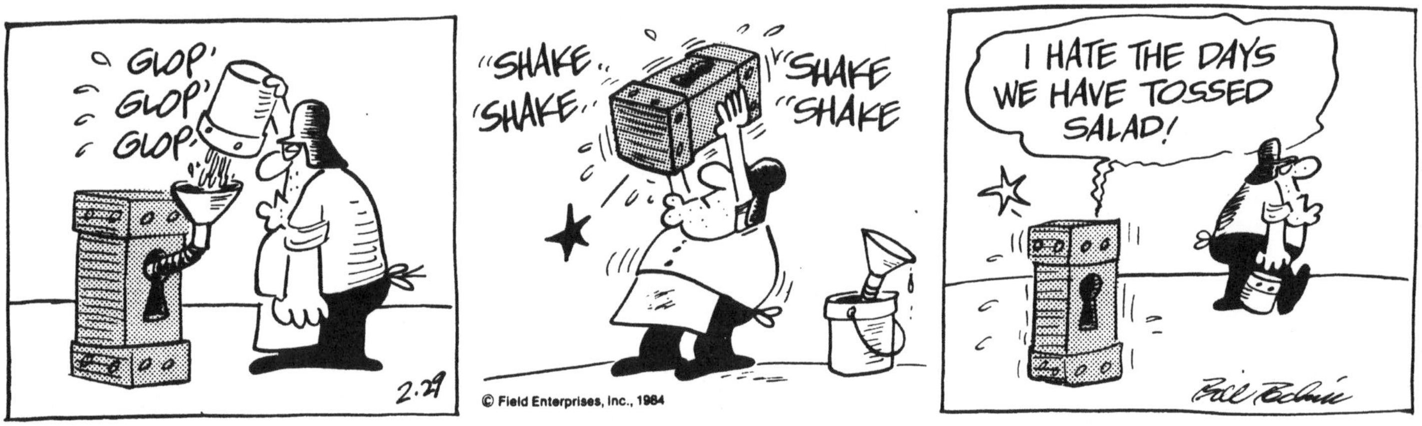
GLOP GLOP GLOP
2·29
SHAKE SHAKE SHAKE SHAKE
© Field Enterprises, Inc., 1984
I HATE THE DAYS WE HAVE TOSSED SALAD!
Bill Rechin

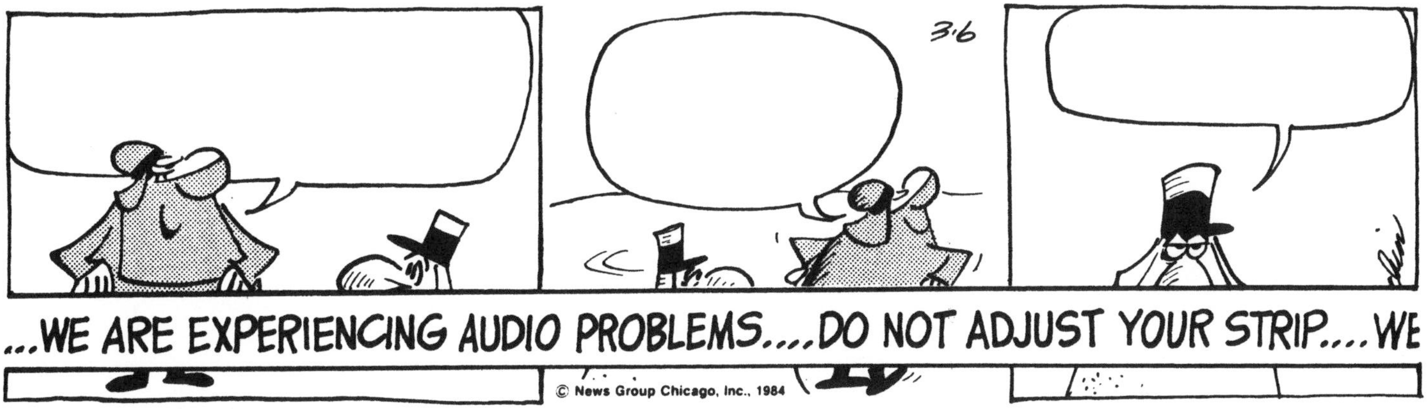
3·6
...WE ARE EXPERIENCING AUDIO PROBLEMS....DO NOT ADJUST YOUR STRIP....WE
© News Group Chicago, Inc., 1984

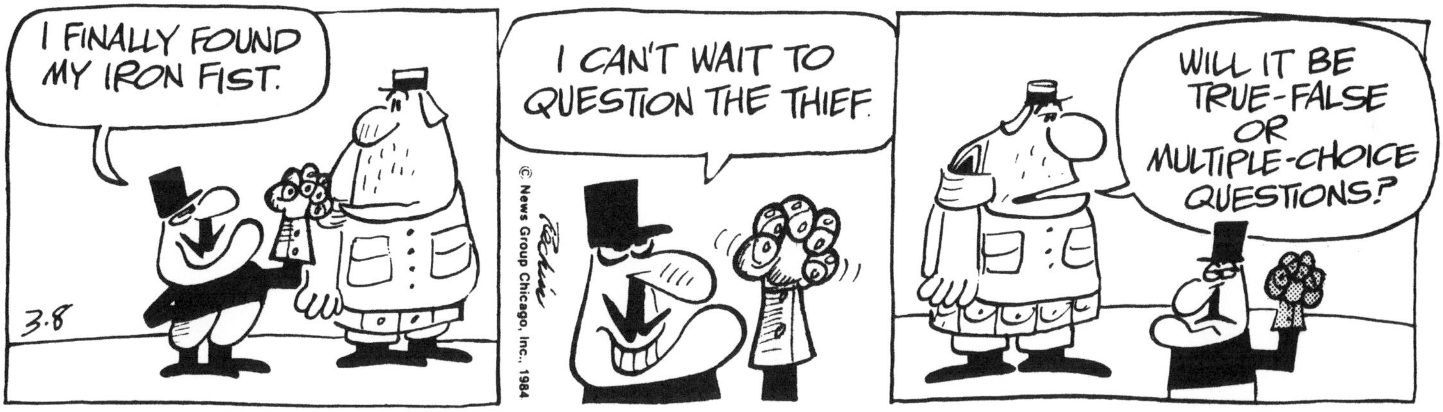
I FINALLY FOUND MY IRON FIST.
3·8
I CAN'T WAIT TO QUESTION THE THIEF.
© News Group Chicago, Inc., 1984
WILL IT BE TRUE-FALSE OR MULTIPLE-CHOICE QUESTIONS?

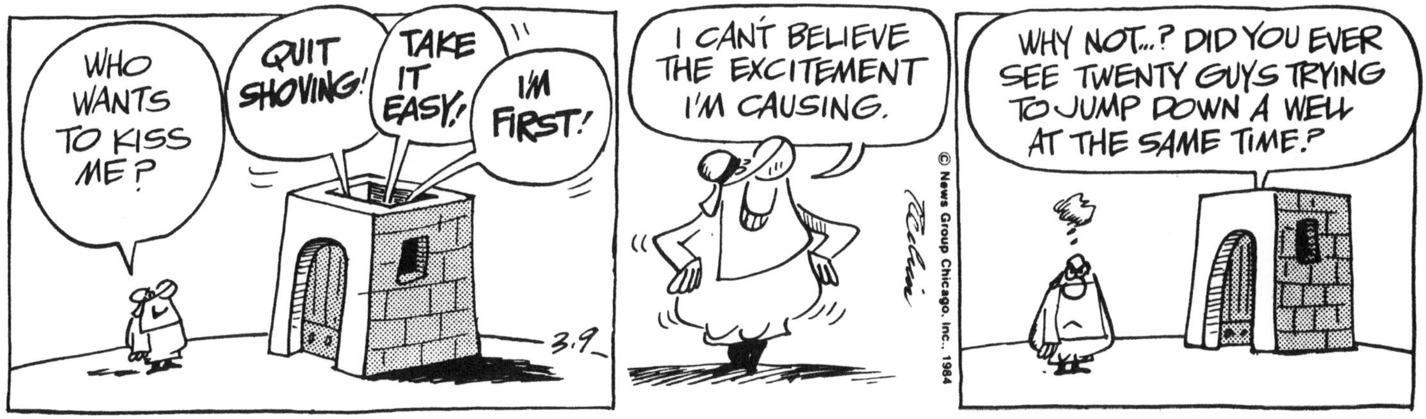
WHO WANTS TO KISS ME?
QUIT SHOVING!
TAKE IT EASY!
I'M FIRST!
3·9
I CAN'T BELIEVE THE EXCITEMENT I'M CAUSING.
© News Group Chicago, Inc., 1984
WHY NOT...? DID YOU EVER SEE TWENTY GUYS TRYING TO JUMP DOWN A WELL AT THE SAME TIME?

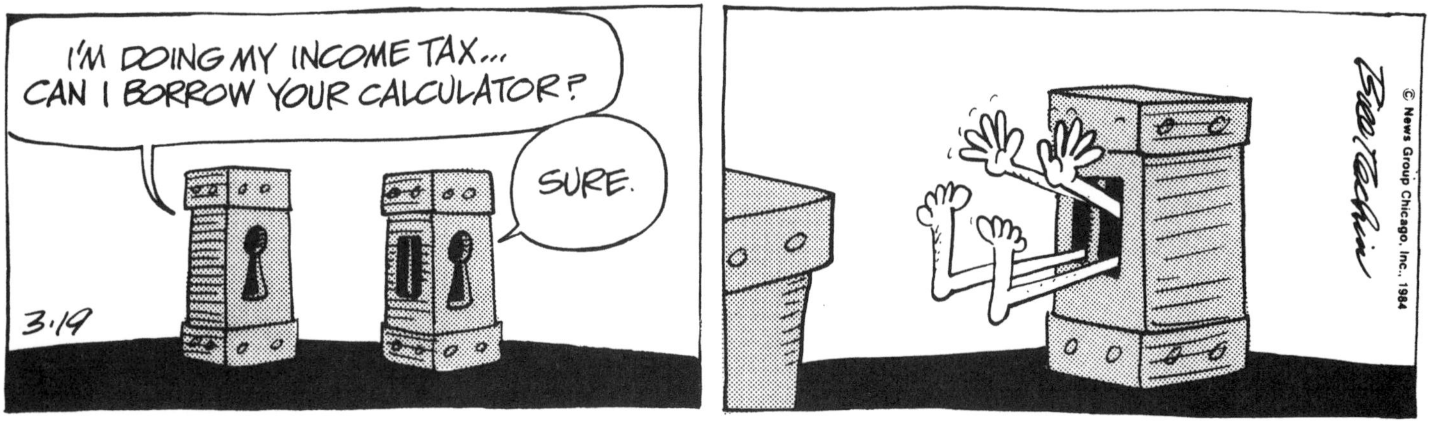
I'M DOING MY INCOME TAX...
CAN I BORROW YOUR CALCULATOR?
SURE.
3.19
© News Group Chicago, Inc., 1984

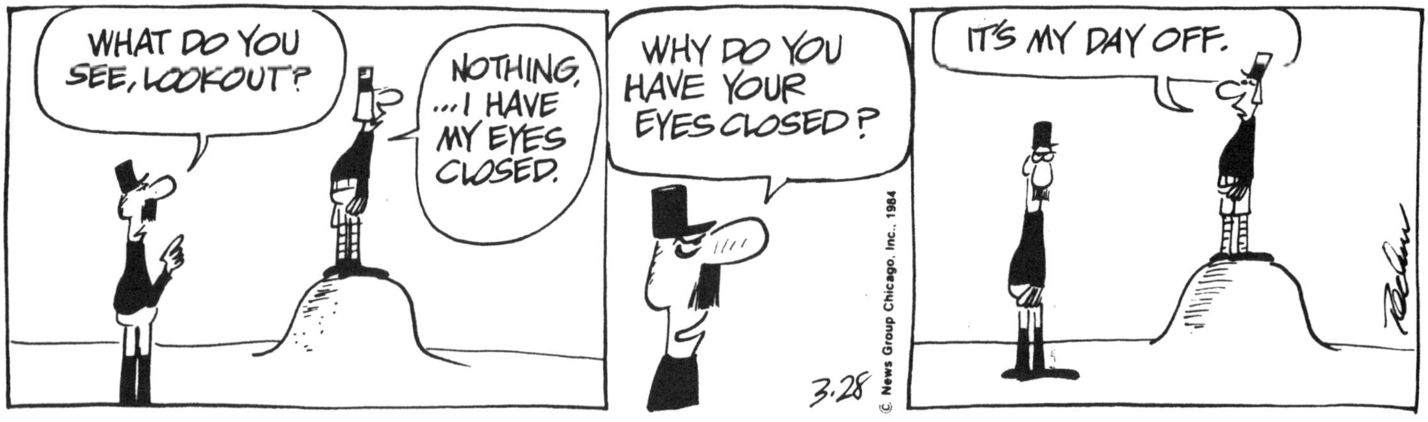
WHAT DO YOU SEE, LOOKOUT?
NOTHING, ...I HAVE MY EYES CLOSED.
WHY DO YOU HAVE YOUR EYES CLOSED?
3.28
© News Group Chicago, Inc., 1984
IT'S MY DAY OFF.

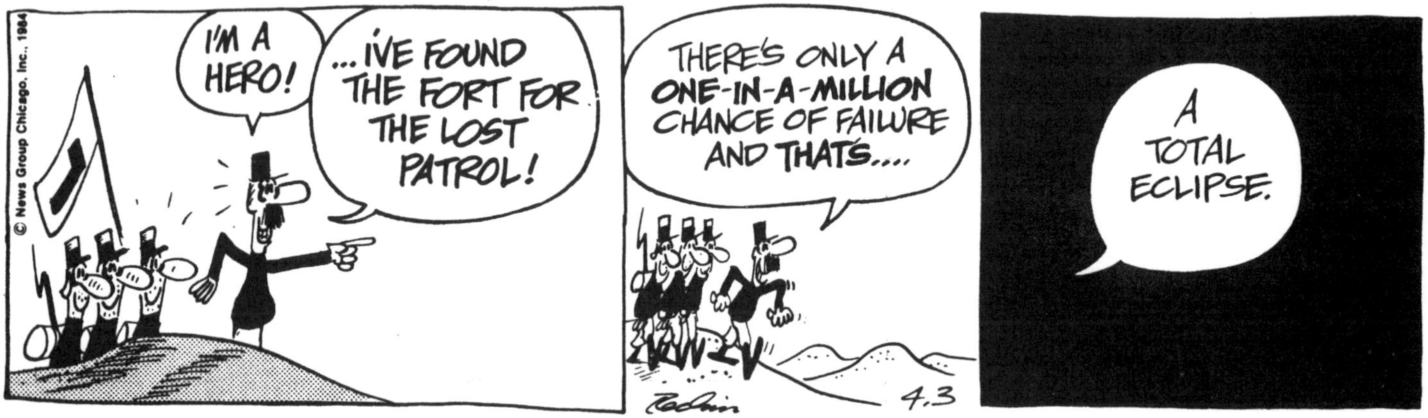
© News Group Chicago, Inc., 1984
I'M A HERO!
...I'VE FOUND THE FORT FOR THE LOST PATROL!
THERE'S ONLY A ONE-IN-A-MILLION CHANCE OF FAILURE AND THAT'S....
4.3
A TOTAL ECLIPSE.

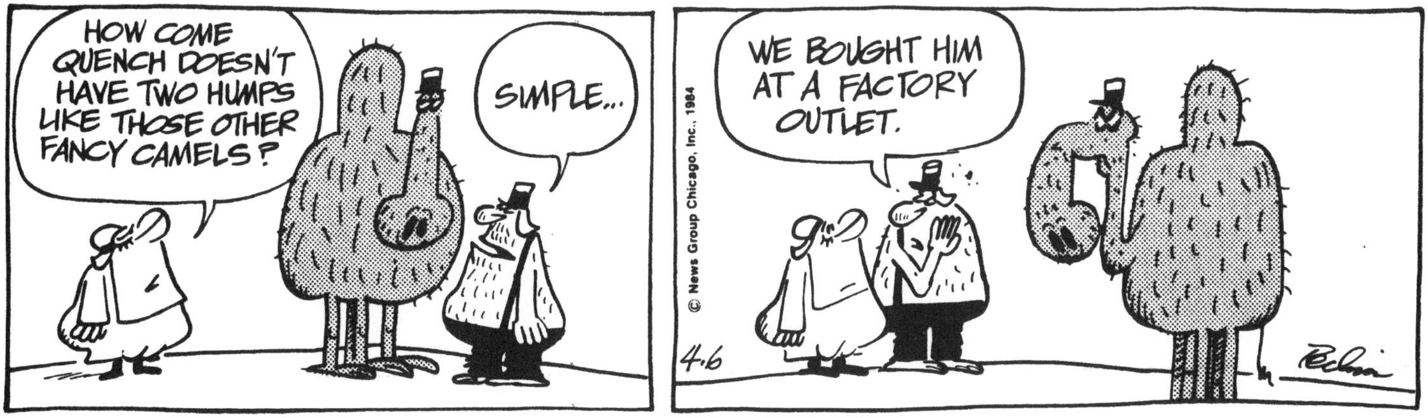
HOW COME QUENCH DOESN'T HAVE TWO HUMPS LIKE THOSE OTHER FANCY CAMELS?
SIMPLE...
WE BOUGHT HIM AT A FACTORY OUTLET.
© News Group Chicago, Inc., 1984
4.6

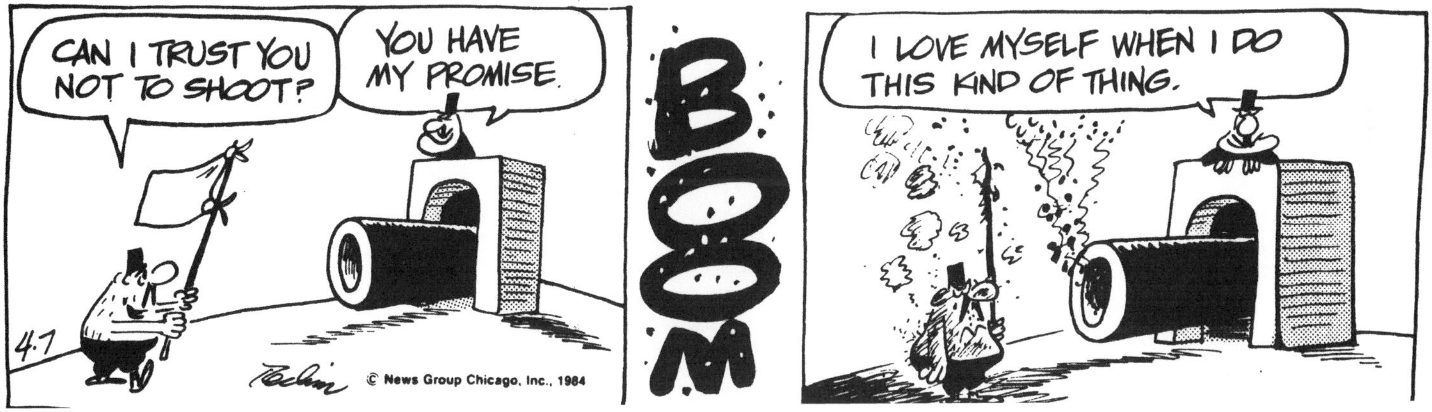
CAN I TRUST YOU NOT TO SHOOT?
YOU HAVE MY PROMISE.
4.7
© News Group Chicago, Inc., 1984
BOOM
I LOVE MYSELF WHEN I DO THIS KIND OF THING.

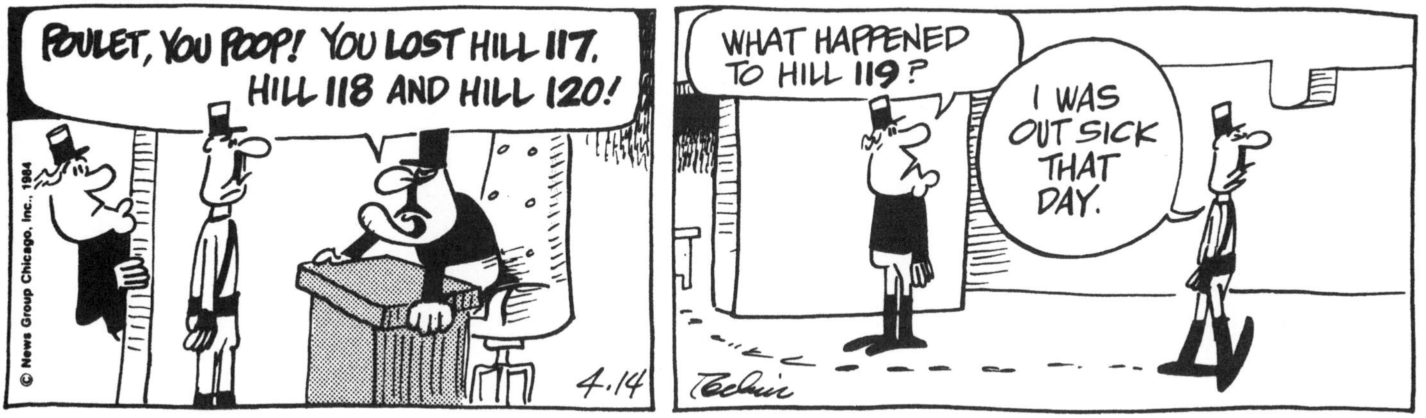
POULET, YOU POOP! YOU LOST HILL 117, HILL 118 AND HILL 120!
© News Group Chicago, Inc., 1984
4.14
WHAT HAPPENED TO HILL 119?
I WAS OUT SICK THAT DAY.

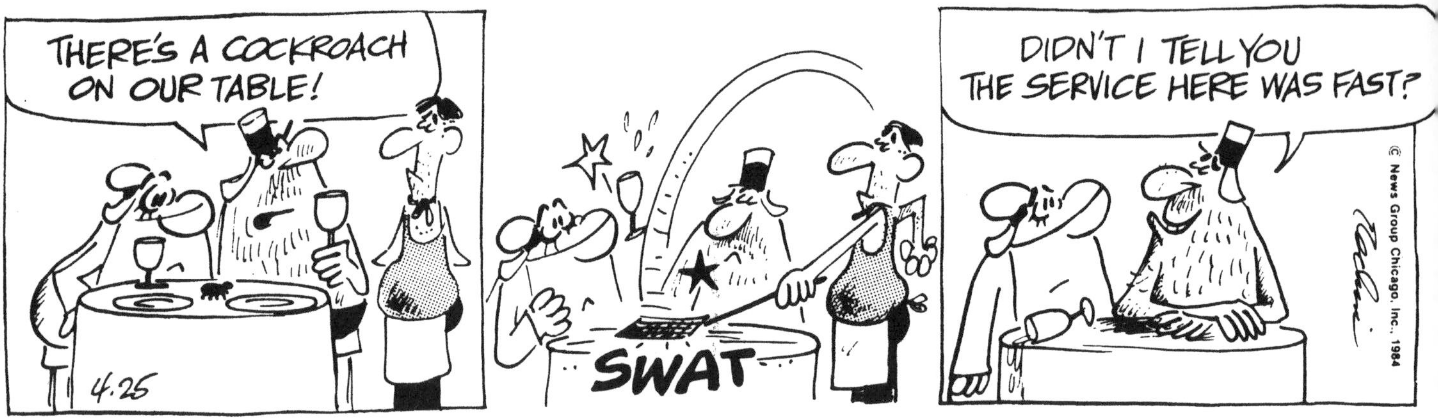
THERE'S A COCKROACH ON OUR TABLE!
4.25
SWAT
DIDN'T I TELL YOU THE SERVICE HERE WAS FAST?
© News Group Chicago, Inc., 1984

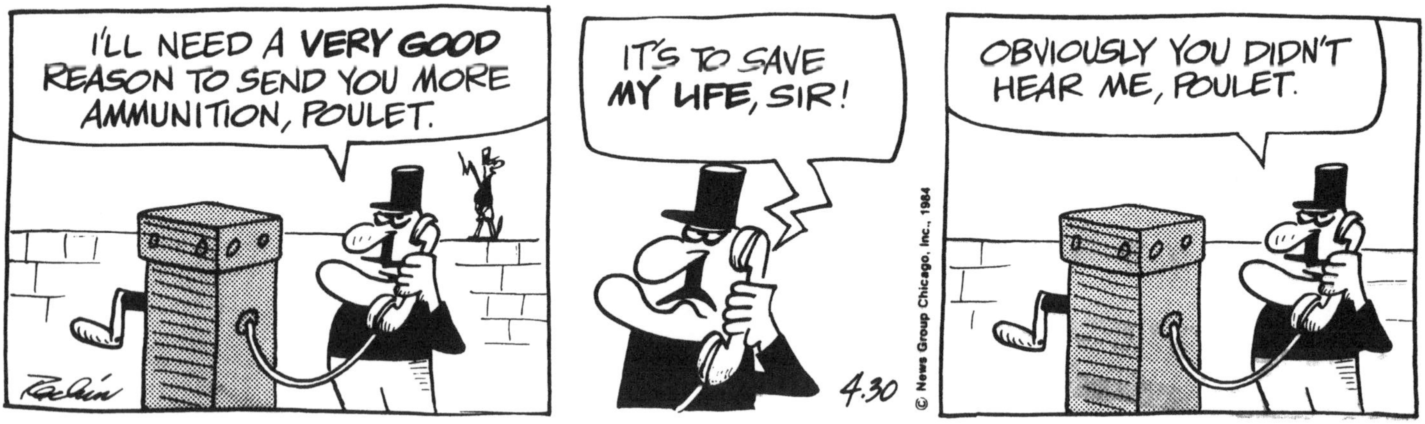
I'LL NEED A **VERY GOOD** REASON TO SEND YOU MORE AMMUNITION, POULET.
IT'S TO SAVE **MY LIFE**, SIR!
4.30
© News Group Chicago, Inc., 1984
OBVIOUSLY YOU DIDN'T HEAR ME, POULET.

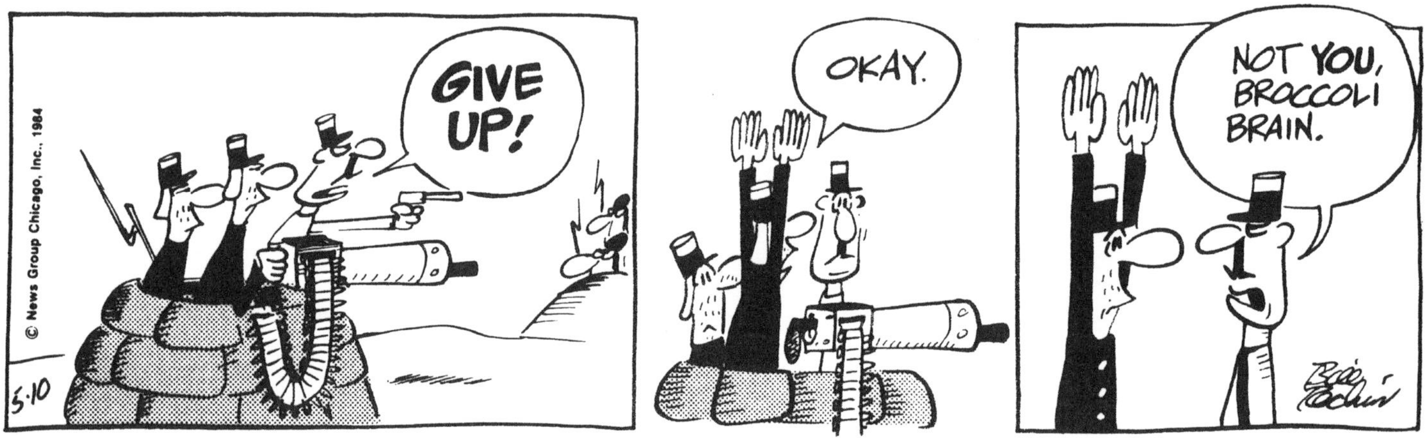
© News Group Chicago, Inc., 1984
5.10
GIVE UP!
OKAY.
NOT **YOU**, BROCCOLI BRAIN.

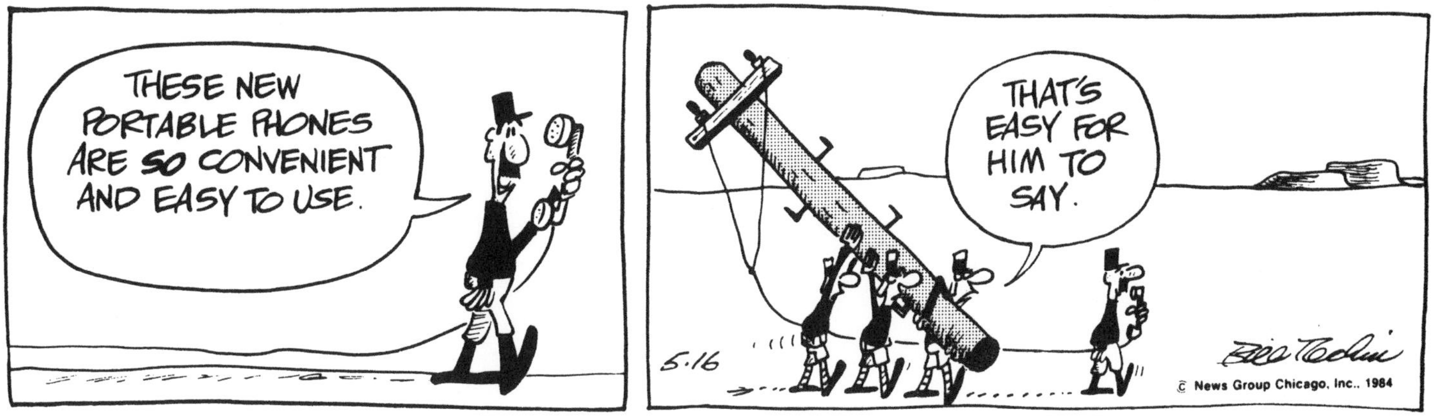
THESE NEW PORTABLE PHONES ARE SO CONVENIENT AND EASY TO USE.
THAT'S EASY FOR HIM TO SAY.
5·16
© News Group Chicago, Inc., 1984

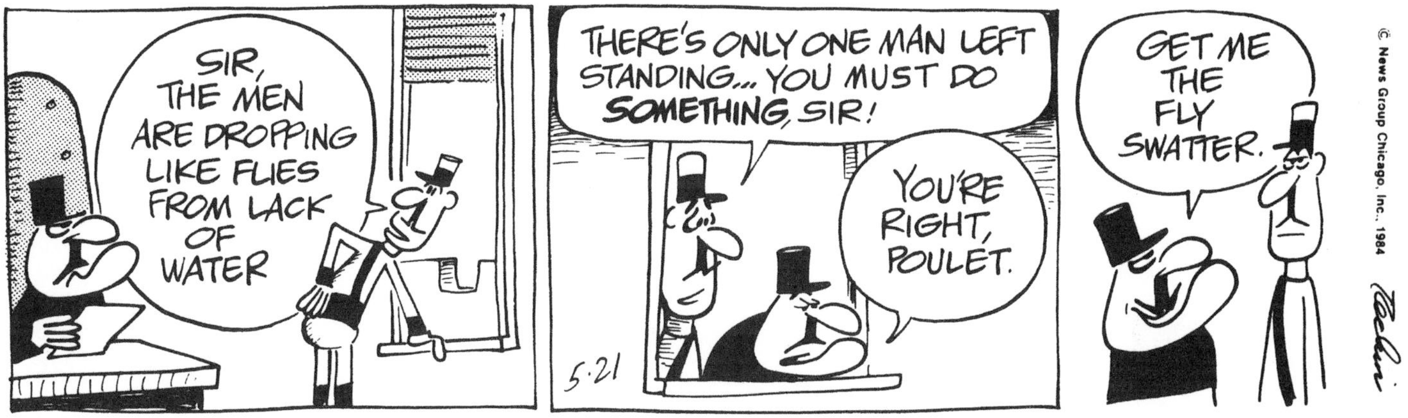
SIR, THE MEN ARE DROPPING LIKE FLIES FROM LACK OF WATER
THERE'S ONLY ONE MAN LEFT STANDING... YOU MUST DO SOMETHING, SIR!
YOU'RE RIGHT, POULET.
5·21
GET ME THE FLY SWATTER.
© News Group Chicago, Inc., 1984

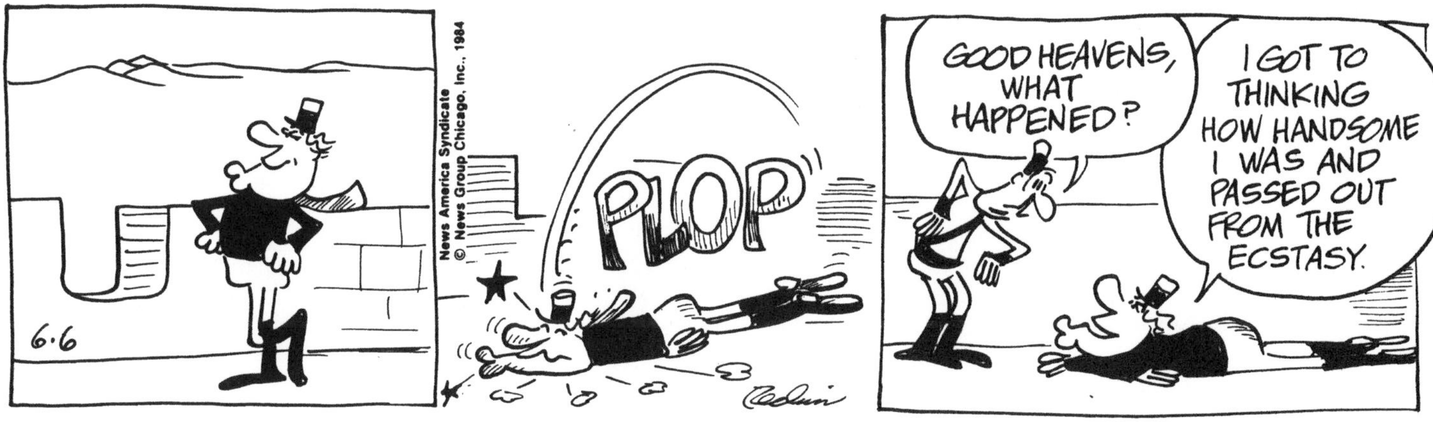
6·6
News America Syndicate
© News Group Chicago, Inc., 1984
PLOP
GOOD HEAVENS, WHAT HAPPENED?
I GOT TO THINKING HOW HANDSOME I WAS AND PASSED OUT FROM THE ECSTASY.

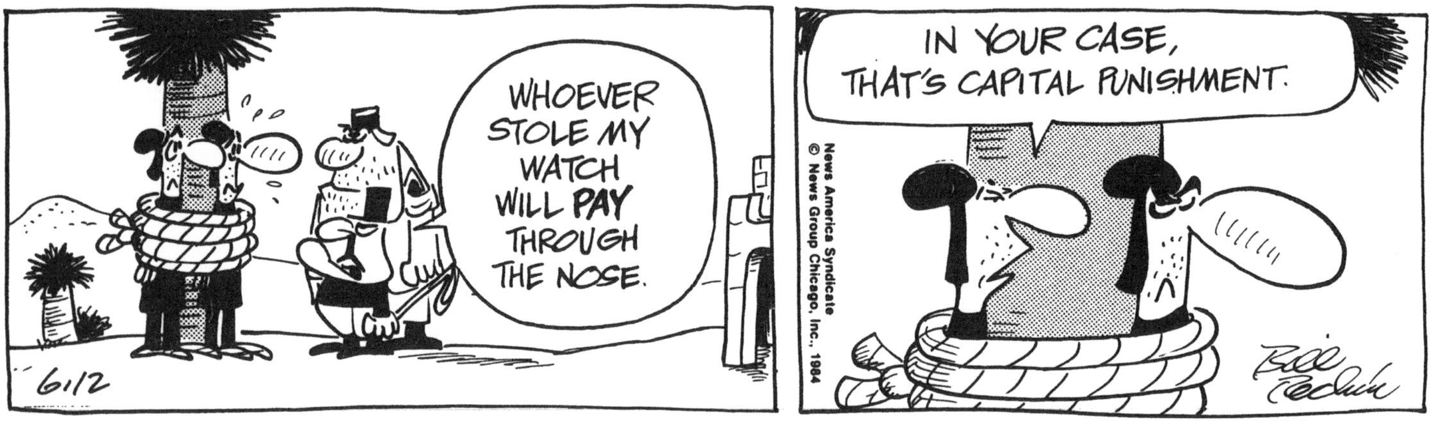
WHOEVER STOLE MY WATCH WILL PAY THROUGH THE NOSE.
6/12
IN YOUR CASE, THAT'S CAPITAL PUNISHMENT.
News America Syndicate © News Group Chicago, Inc., 1984
Bill Rechin

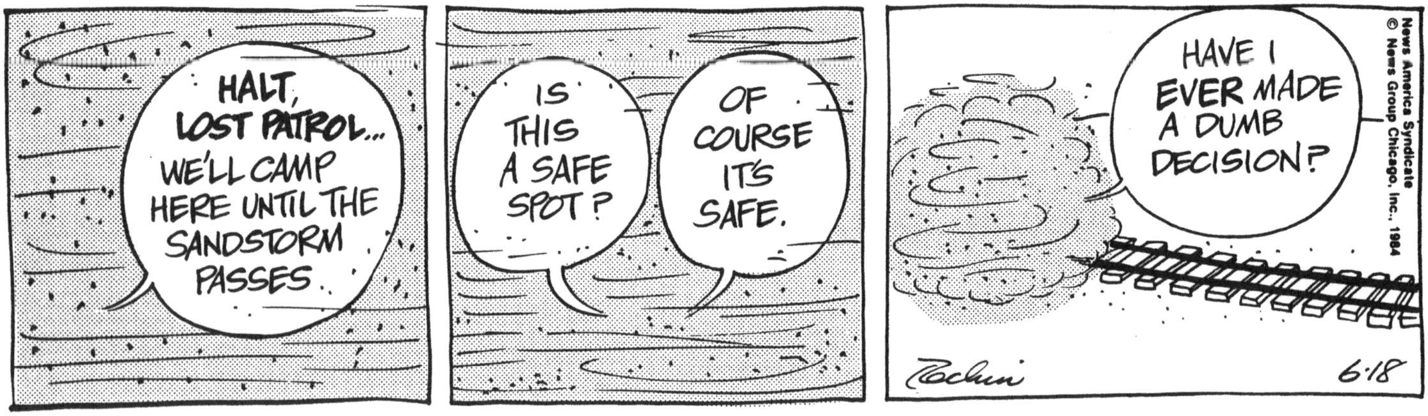
HALT, LOST PATROL... WE'LL CAMP HERE UNTIL THE SANDSTORM PASSES.
IS THIS A SAFE SPOT?
OF COURSE IT'S SAFE.
HAVE I EVER MADE A DUMB DECISION?
News America Syndicate © News Group Chicago, Inc., 1984
Rechin
6-18

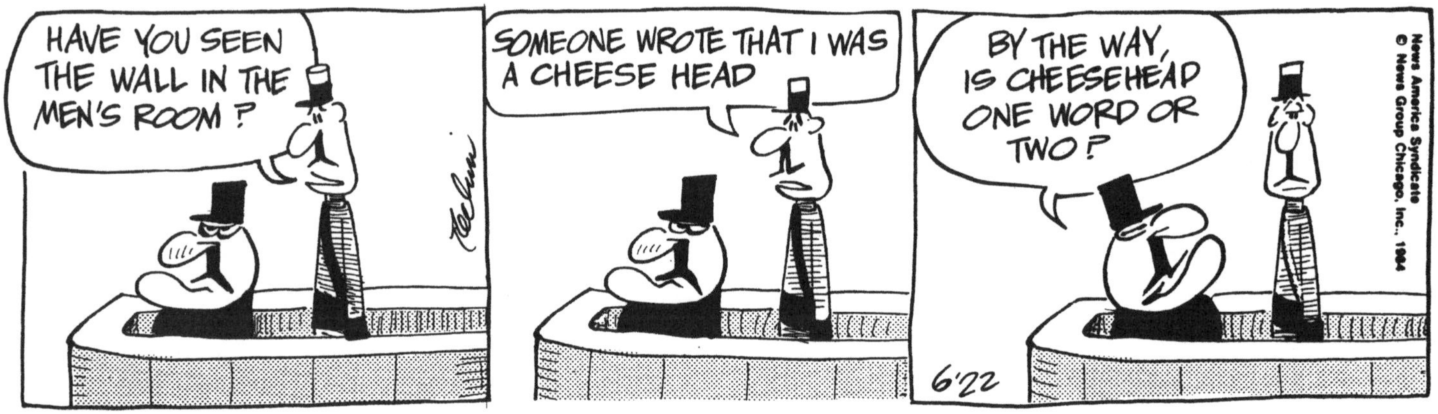
HAVE YOU SEEN THE WALL IN THE MEN'S ROOM?
Rechin
SOMEONE WROTE THAT I WAS A CHEESE HEAD
BY THE WAY, IS CHEESEHEAD ONE WORD OR TWO?
6-22
News America Syndicate © News Group Chicago, Inc., 1984

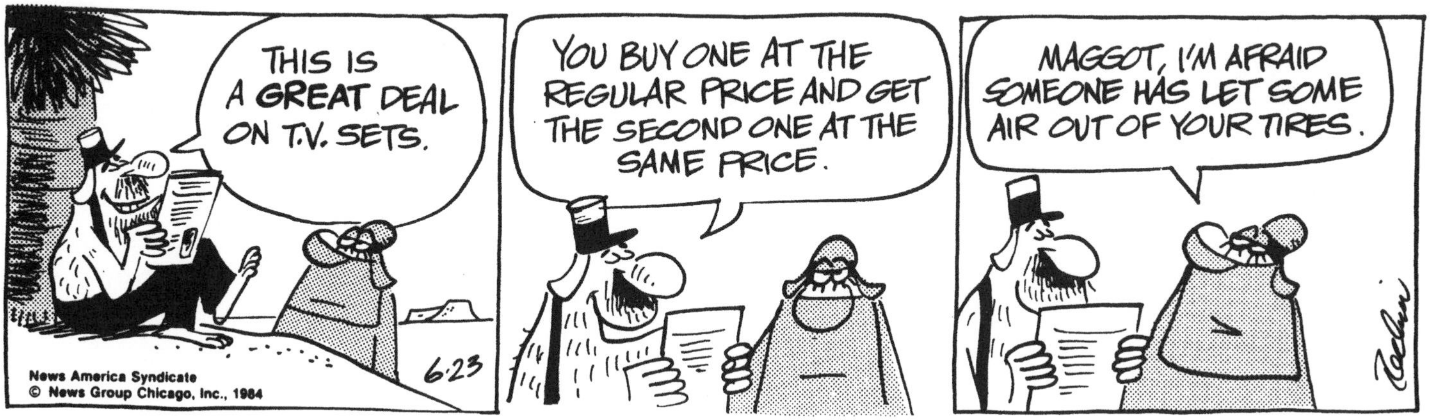
THIS IS A **GREAT** DEAL ON T.V. SETS.
News America Syndicate © News Group Chicago, Inc., 1984
6·23
YOU BUY ONE AT THE REGULAR PRICE AND GET THE SECOND ONE AT THE SAME PRICE.
MAGGOT, I'M AFRAID SOMEONE HAS LET SOME AIR OUT OF YOUR TIRES.

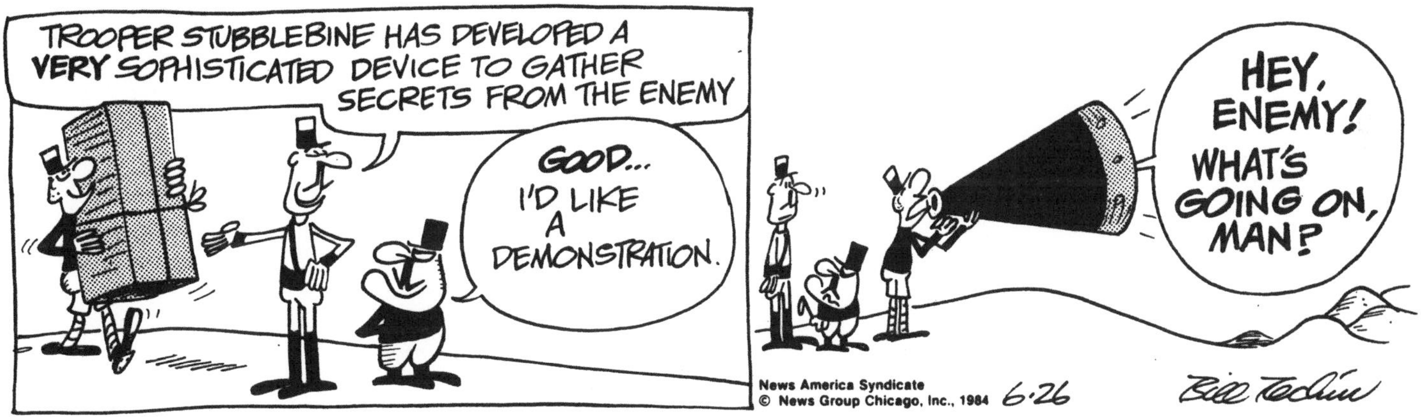
TROOPER STUBBLEBINE HAS DEVELOPED A **VERY** SOPHISTICATED DEVICE TO GATHER SECRETS FROM THE ENEMY
GOOD... I'D LIKE A DEMONSTRATION.
HEY, ENEMY! WHAT'S GOING ON, MAN?
News America Syndicate © News Group Chicago, Inc., 1984
6·26

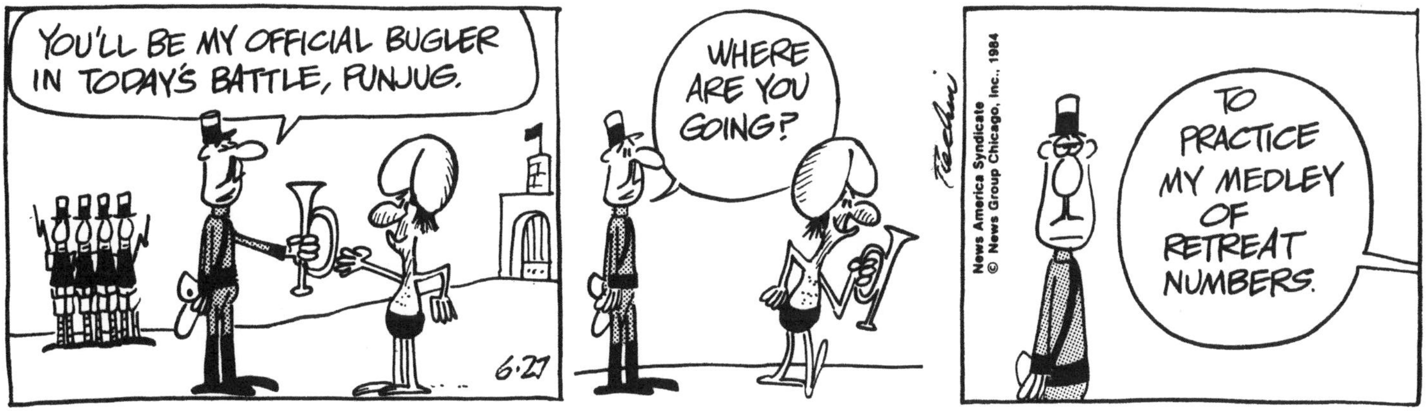
YOU'LL BE MY OFFICIAL BUGLER IN TODAY'S BATTLE, PUNJUG.
6·27
WHERE ARE YOU GOING?
News America Syndicate © News Group Chicago, Inc., 1984
TO PRACTICE MY MEDLEY OF RETREAT NUMBERS.

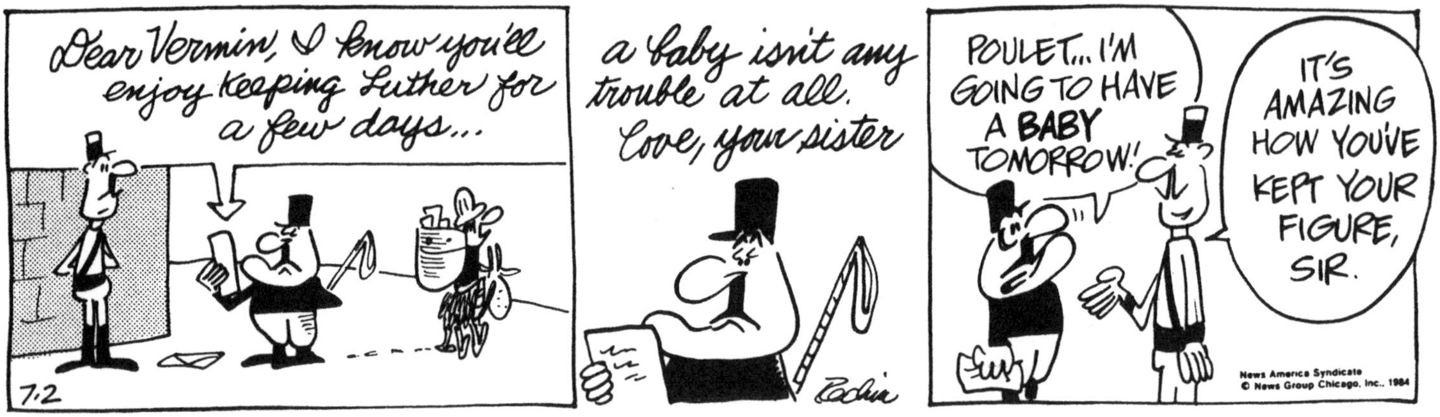
Dear Vermin, I know you'll enjoy keeping Luther for a few days...
7.2
a baby isn't any trouble at all. Love, your sister
POULET... I'M GOING TO HAVE A **BABY** TOMORROW!
IT'S AMAZING HOW YOU'VE KEPT YOUR FIGURE, SIR.
News America Syndicate © News Group Chicago, Inc., 1984

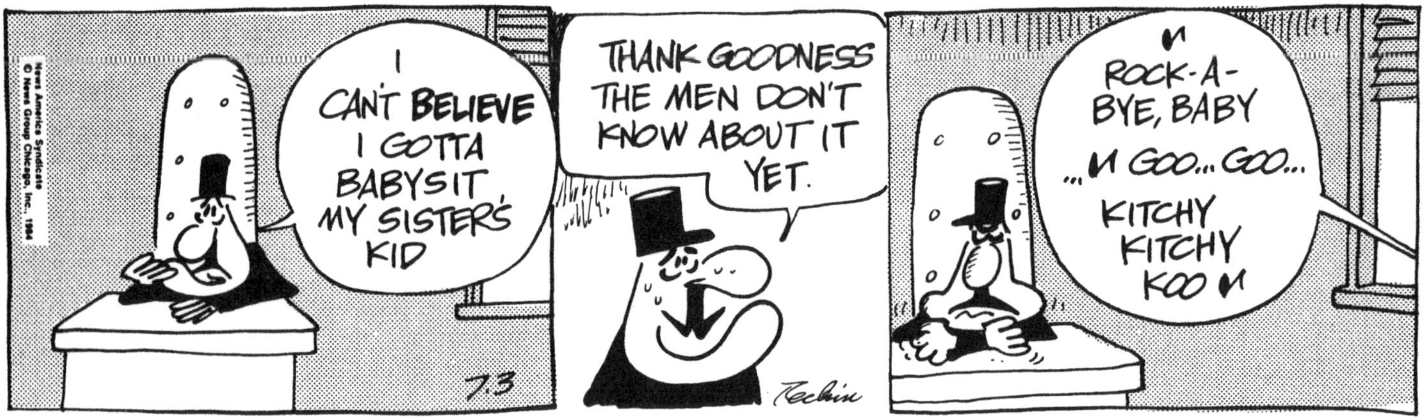
News America Syndicate © News Group Chicago, Inc., 1984
I CAN'T **BELIEVE** I GOTTA BABYSIT MY SISTER'S KID
7.3
THANK GOODNESS THE MEN DON'T KNOW ABOUT IT YET.
ROCK-A-BYE, BABY ... GOO... GOO... KITCHY KITCHY KOO

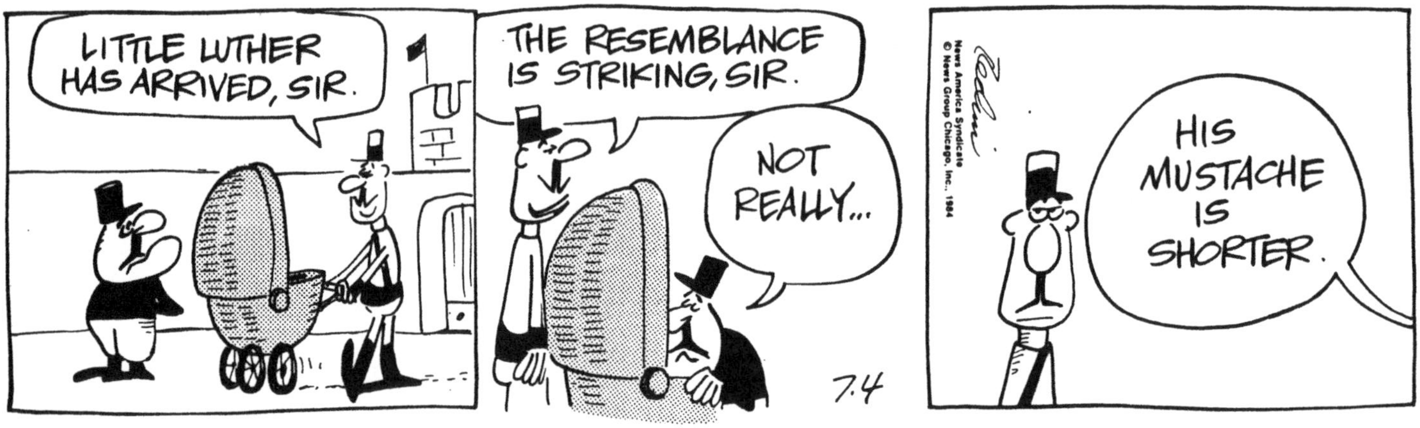
LITTLE LUTHER HAS ARRIVED, SIR.
THE RESEMBLANCE IS STRIKING, SIR.
NOT REALLY...
7.4
News America Syndicate © News Group Chicago, Inc., 1984
HIS MUSTACHE IS SHORTER.

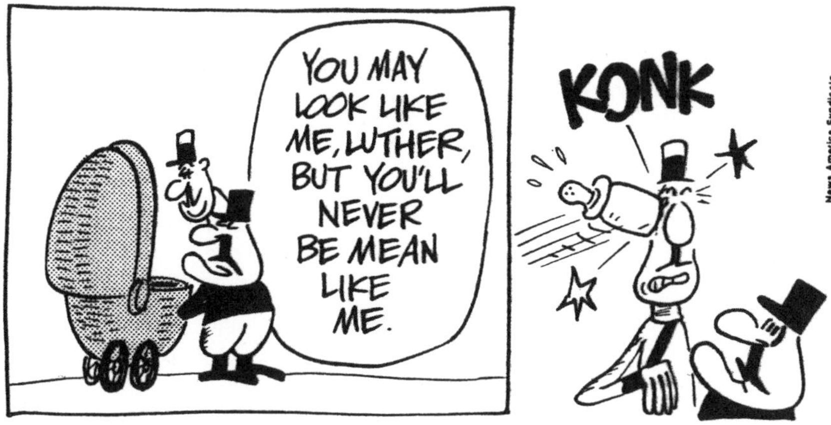
YOU MAY LOOK LIKE ME, LUTHER, BUT YOU'LL NEVER BE MEAN LIKE ME.
KONK
HOWEVER, YOU DO SHOW SOME PROMISE.
7.5

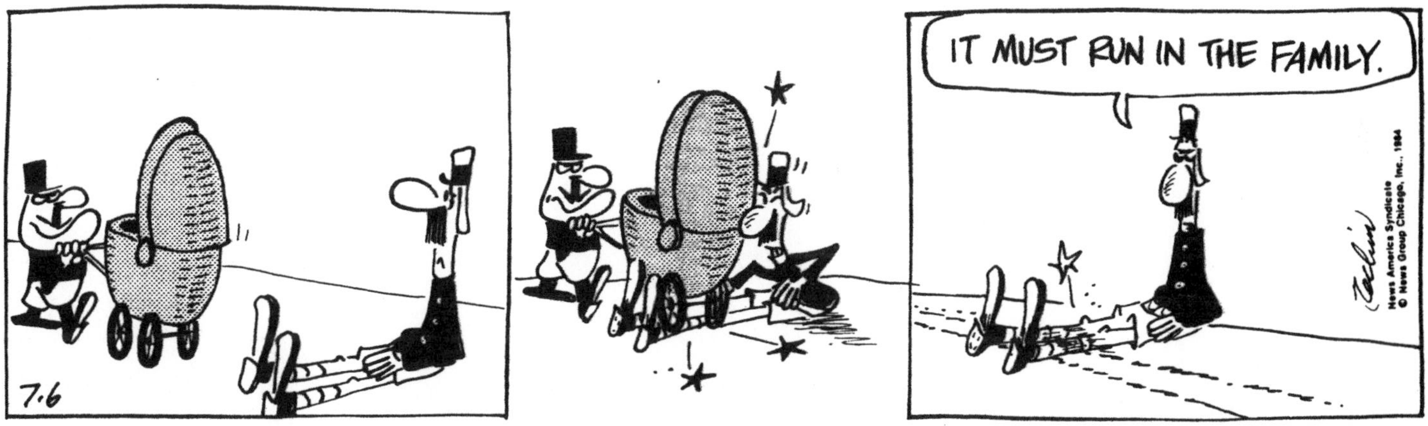
7.6
IT MUST RUN IN THE FAMILY.

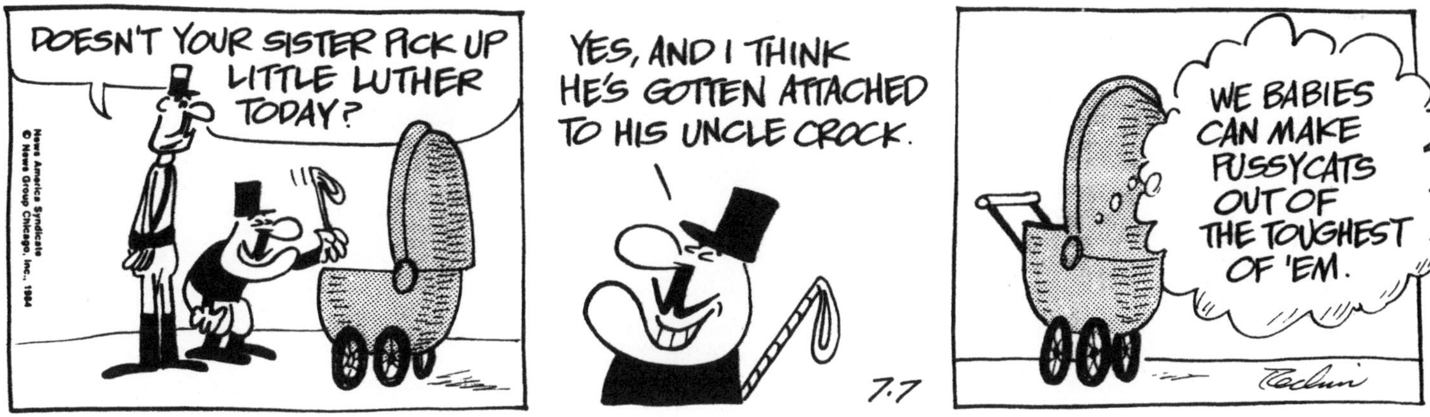
DOESN'T YOUR SISTER PICK UP LITTLE LUTHER TODAY?
YES, AND I THINK HE'S GOTTEN ATTACHED TO HIS UNCLE CROCK.
7.7
WE BABIES CAN MAKE PUSSYCATS OUT OF THE TOUGHEST OF 'EM.

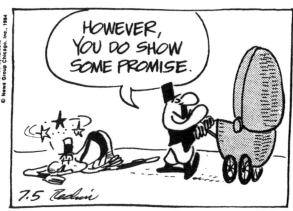

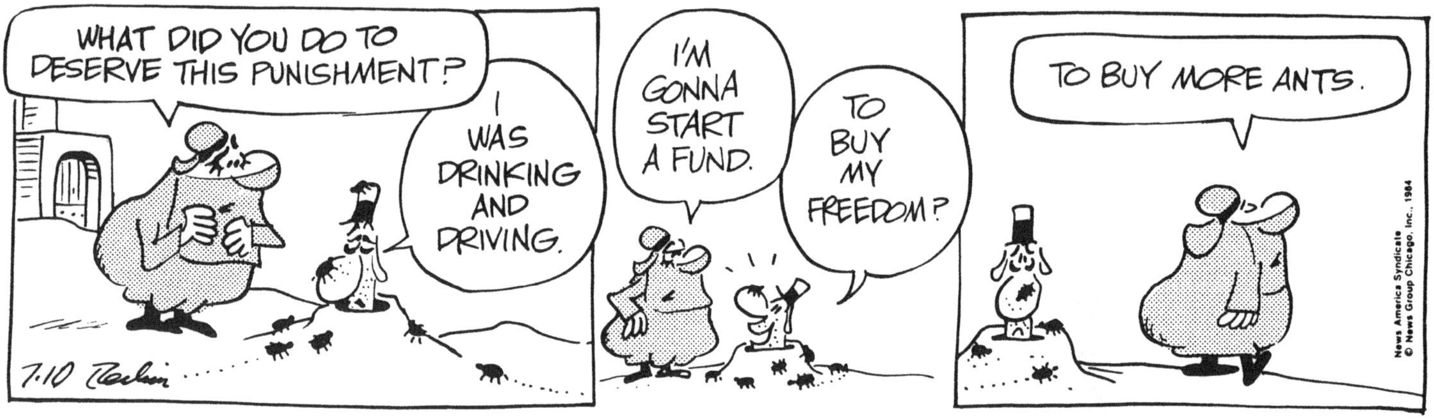
WHAT DID YOU DO TO DESERVE THIS PUNISHMENT?
I WAS DRINKING AND DRIVING.
7.10
I'M GONNA START A FUND.
TO BUY MY FREEDOM?
TO BUY MORE ANTS.
News America Syndicate © News Group Chicago, Inc., 1984

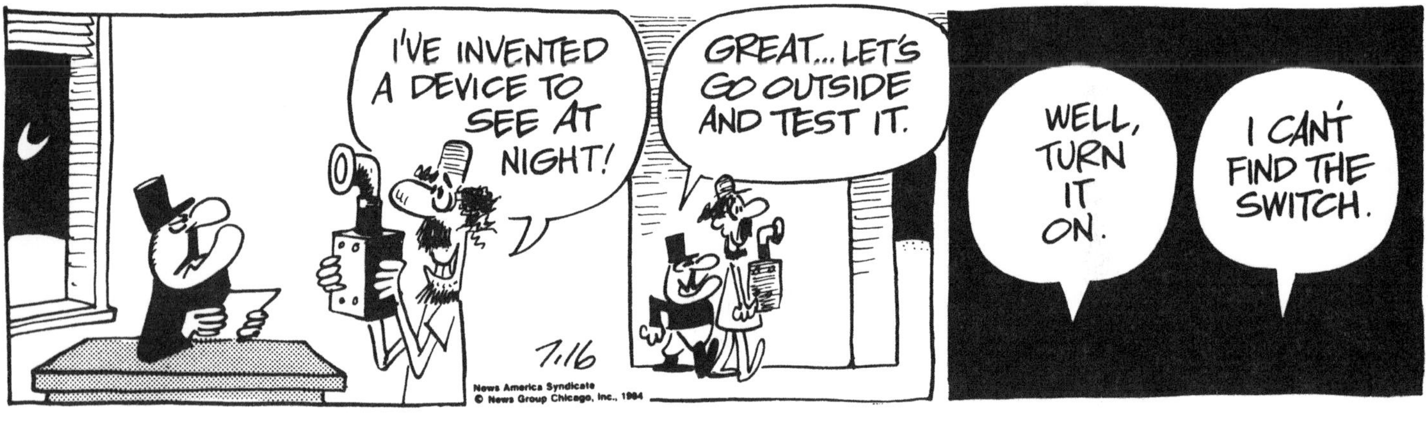
I'VE INVENTED A DEVICE TO SEE AT NIGHT!
7.16
News America Syndicate © News Group Chicago, Inc., 1984
GREAT... LET'S GO OUTSIDE AND TEST IT.
WELL, TURN IT ON.
I CAN'T FIND THE SWITCH.

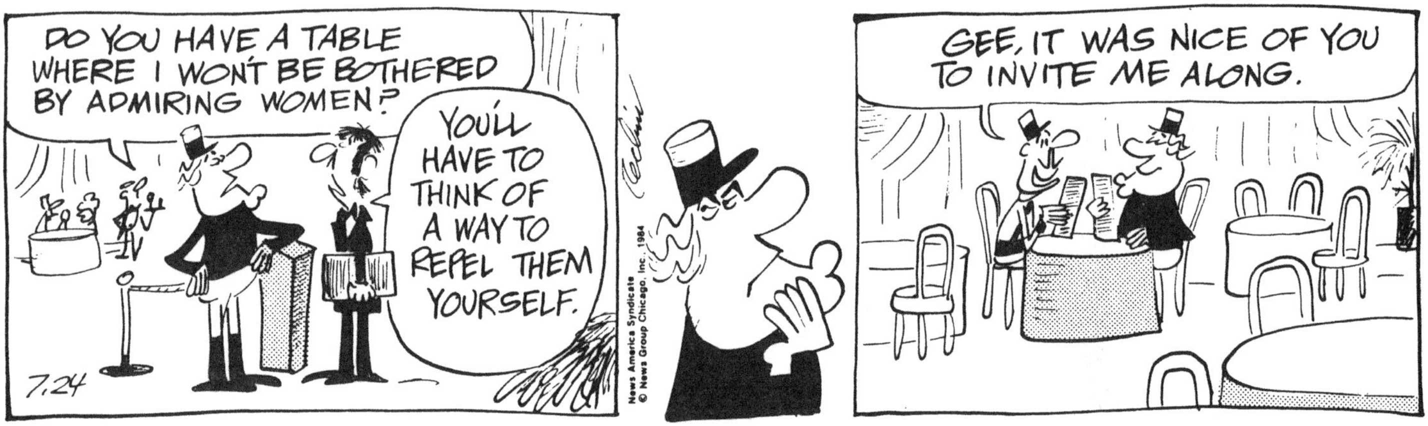
DO YOU HAVE A TABLE WHERE I WON'T BE BOTHERED BY ADMIRING WOMEN?
YOU'LL HAVE TO THINK OF A WAY TO REPEL THEM YOURSELF.
7.24
News America Syndicate © News Group Chicago, Inc., 1984
GEE, IT WAS NICE OF YOU TO INVITE ME ALONG.

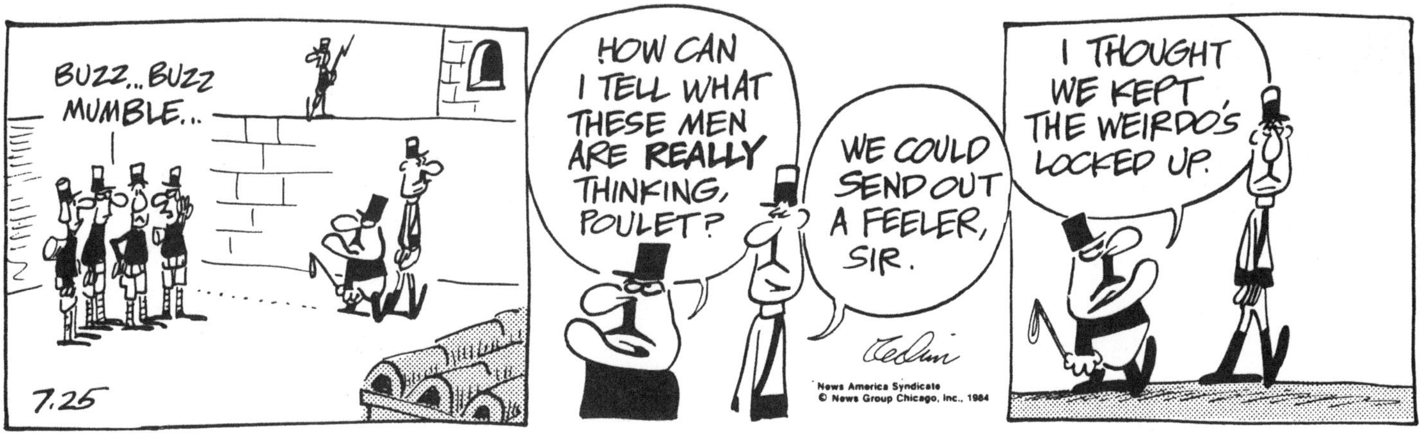
BUZZ...BUZZ MUMBLE...
7.25
HOW CAN I TELL WHAT THESE MEN ARE **REALLY** THINKING, POULET?
WE COULD SEND OUT A FEELER, SIR.
News America Syndicate © News Group Chicago, Inc., 1984
I THOUGHT WE KEPT THE WEIRDO'S LOCKED UP.

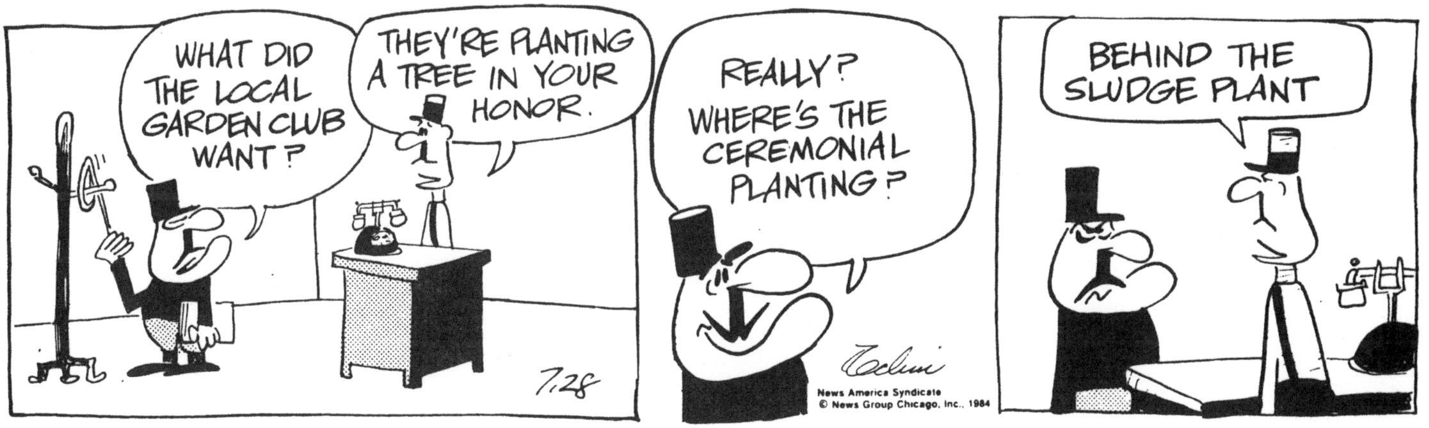
WHAT DID THE LOCAL GARDEN CLUB WANT?
THEY'RE PLANTING A TREE IN YOUR HONOR.
7.28
REALLY? WHERE'S THE CEREMONIAL PLANTING?
News America Syndicate © News Group Chicago, Inc., 1984
BEHIND THE SLUDGE PLANT

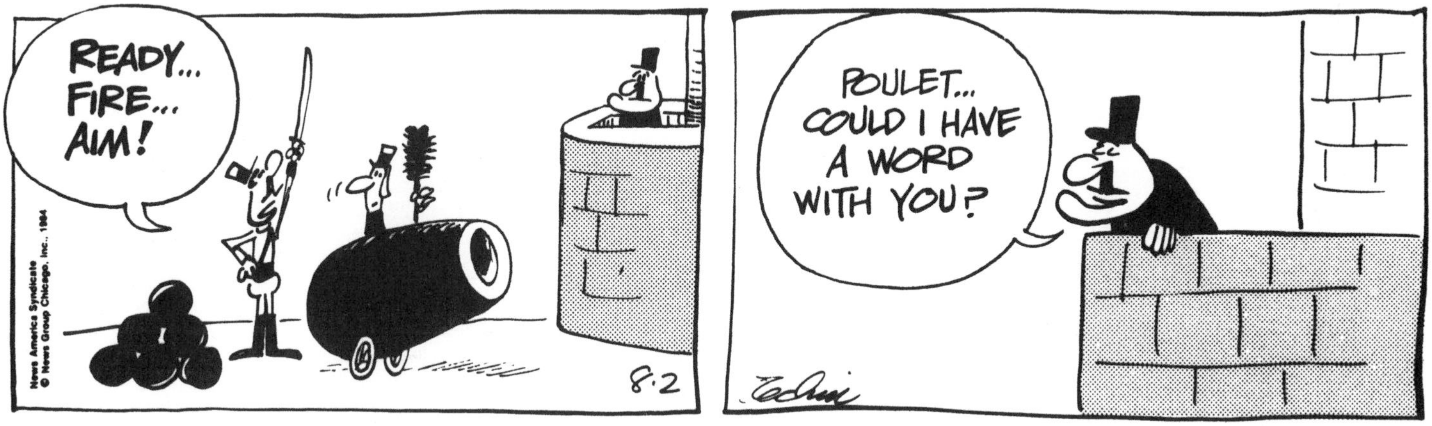
READY... FIRE... AIM!
News America Syndicate © News Group Chicago, Inc., 1984
8.2
POULET... COULD I HAVE A WORD WITH YOU?

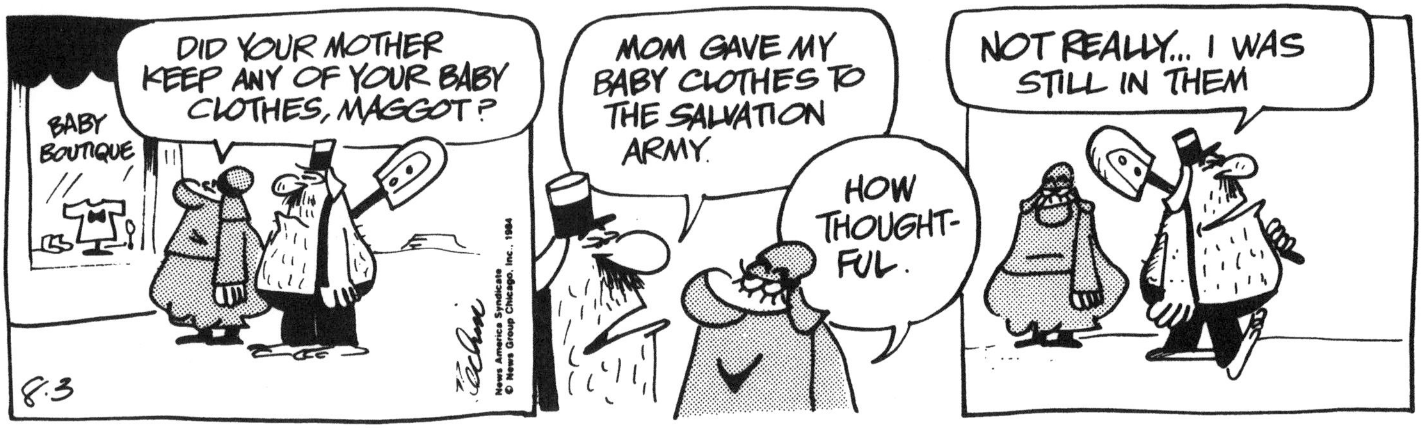
DID YOUR MOTHER KEEP ANY OF YOUR BABY CLOTHES, MAGGOT?
BABY BOUTIQUE
8.3
News America Syndicate © News Group Chicago, Inc., 1984
MOM GAVE MY BABY CLOTHES TO THE SALVATION ARMY.
HOW THOUGHT-FUL.
NOT REALLY... I WAS STILL IN THEM

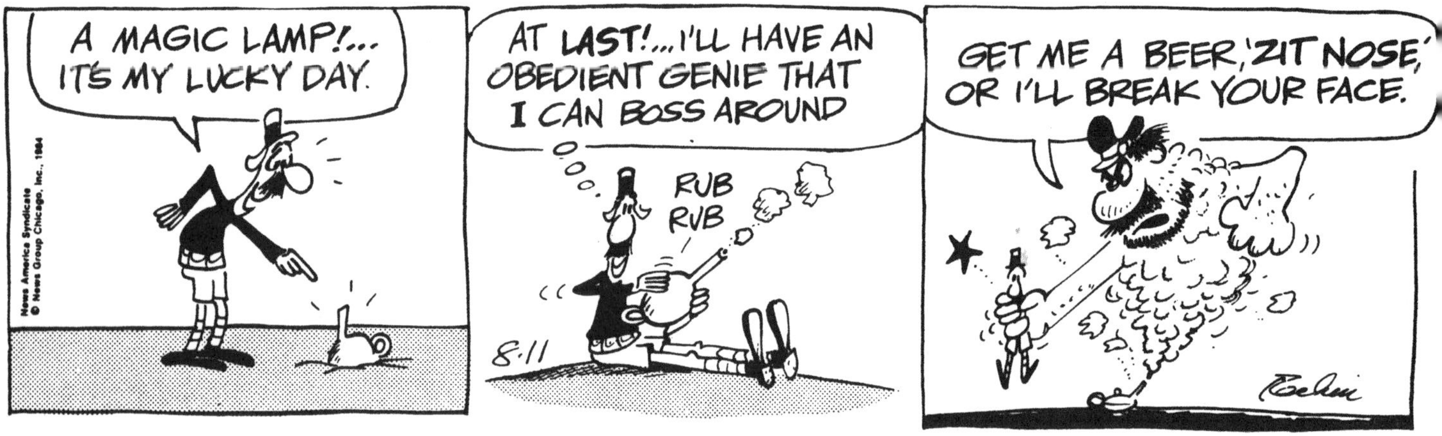
A MAGIC LAMP!... IT'S MY LUCKY DAY.
News America Syndicate © News Group Chicago, Inc., 1984
AT LAST!... I'LL HAVE AN OBEDIENT GENIE THAT I CAN BOSS AROUND
RUB RUB
8.11
GET ME A BEER, 'ZIT NOSE,' OR I'LL BREAK YOUR FACE.

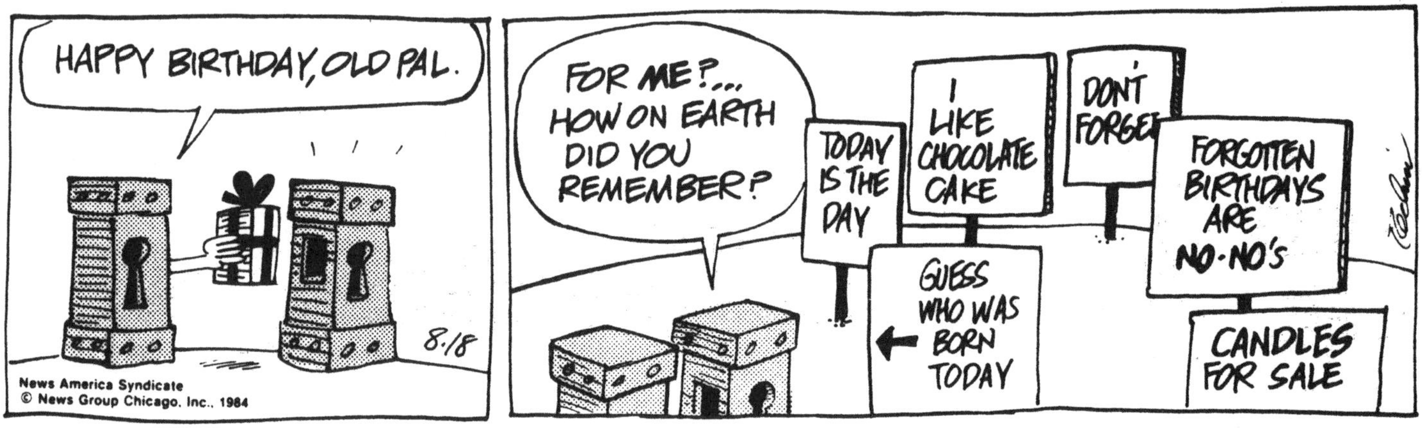
HAPPY BIRTHDAY, OLD PAL.
8.18
News America Syndicate © News Group Chicago, Inc., 1984
FOR ME?... HOW ON EARTH DID YOU REMEMBER?
TODAY IS THE DAY
I LIKE CHOCOLATE CAKE
DON'T FORGE
FORGOTTEN BIRTHDAYS ARE NO-NO'S
GUESS WHO WAS BORN TODAY
CANDLES FOR SALE

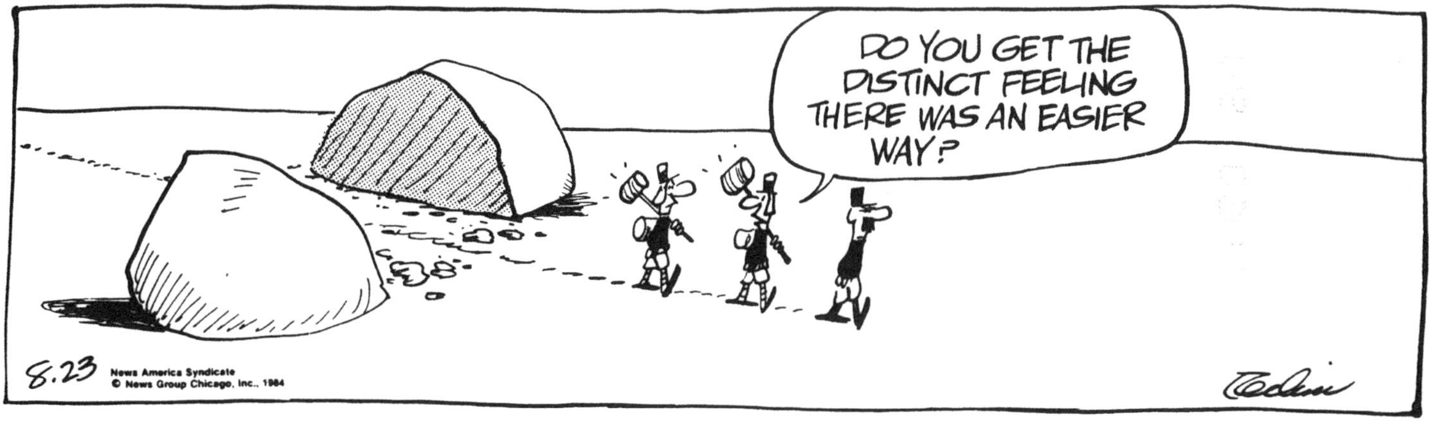
DO YOU GET THE DISTINCT FEELING THERE WAS AN EASIER WAY?
8.23
News America Syndicate
© News Group Chicago, Inc., 1984

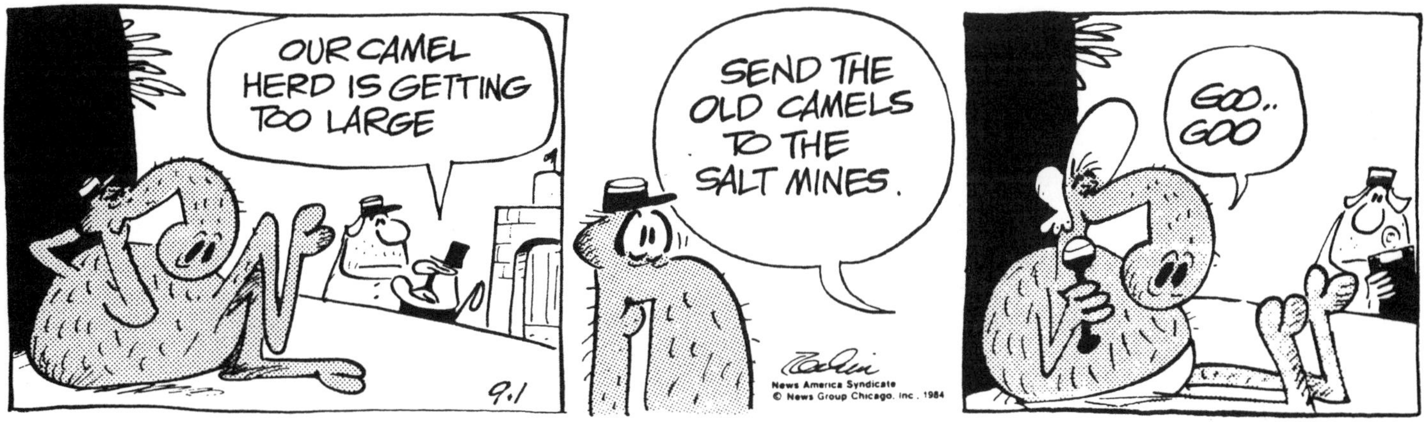
OUR CAMEL HERD IS GETTING TOO LARGE
9.1
SEND THE OLD CAMELS TO THE SALT MINES.
News America Syndicate
© News Group Chicago, Inc., 1984
GOO.. GOO

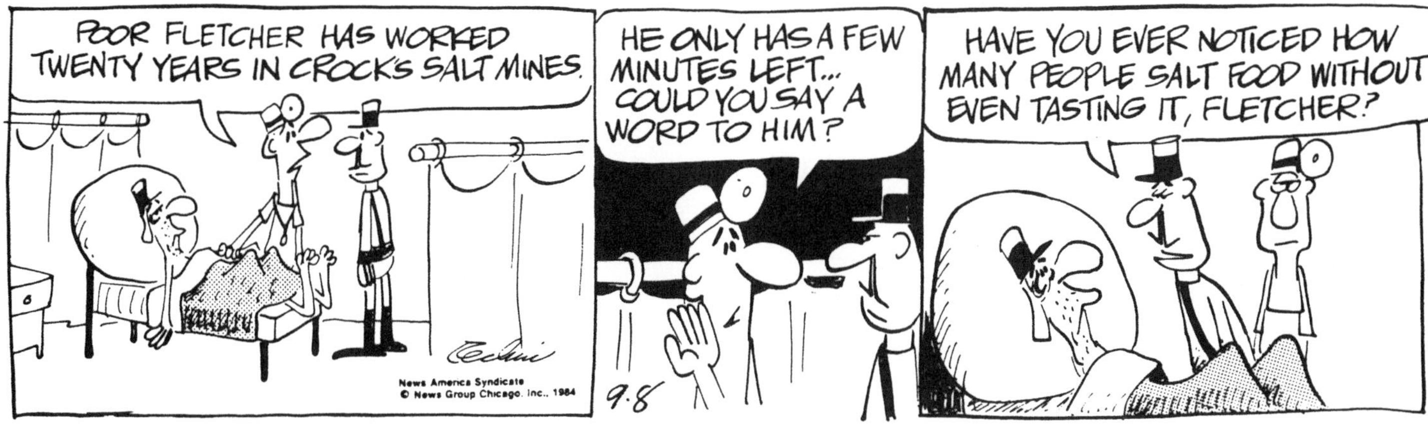
POOR FLETCHER HAS WORKED TWENTY YEARS IN CROCK'S SALT MINES.
News America Syndicate
© News Group Chicago, Inc., 1984
HE ONLY HAS A FEW MINUTES LEFT... COULD YOU SAY A WORD TO HIM?
9.8
HAVE YOU EVER NOTICED HOW MANY PEOPLE SALT FOOD WITHOUT EVEN TASTING IT, FLETCHER?

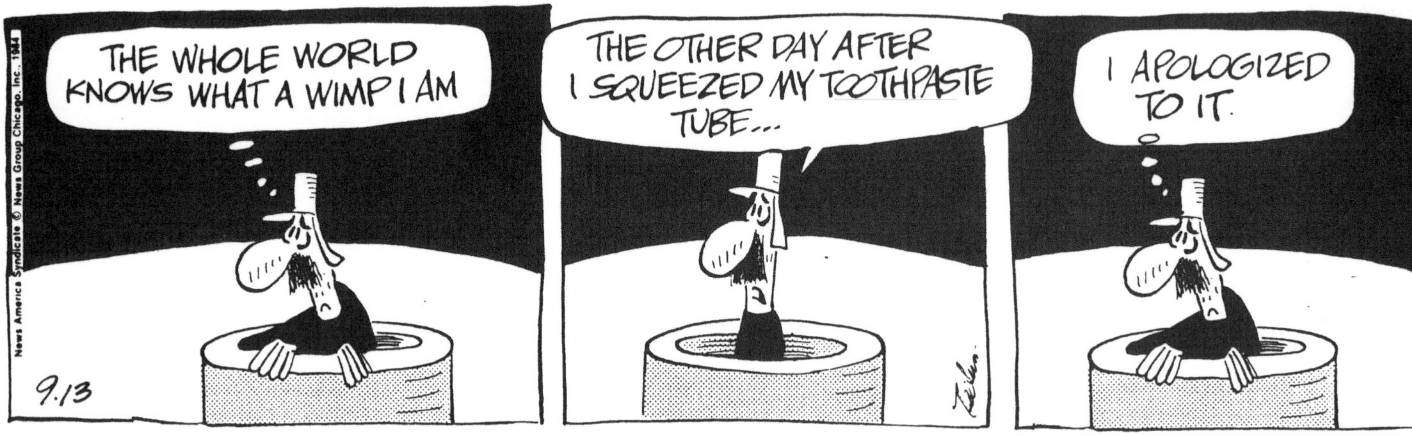
News America Syndicate © News Group Chicago, Inc., 1984
9.13
THE WHOLE WORLD KNOWS WHAT A WIMP I AM
THE OTHER DAY AFTER I SQUEEZED MY TOOTHPASTE TUBE...
I APOLOGIZED TO IT.

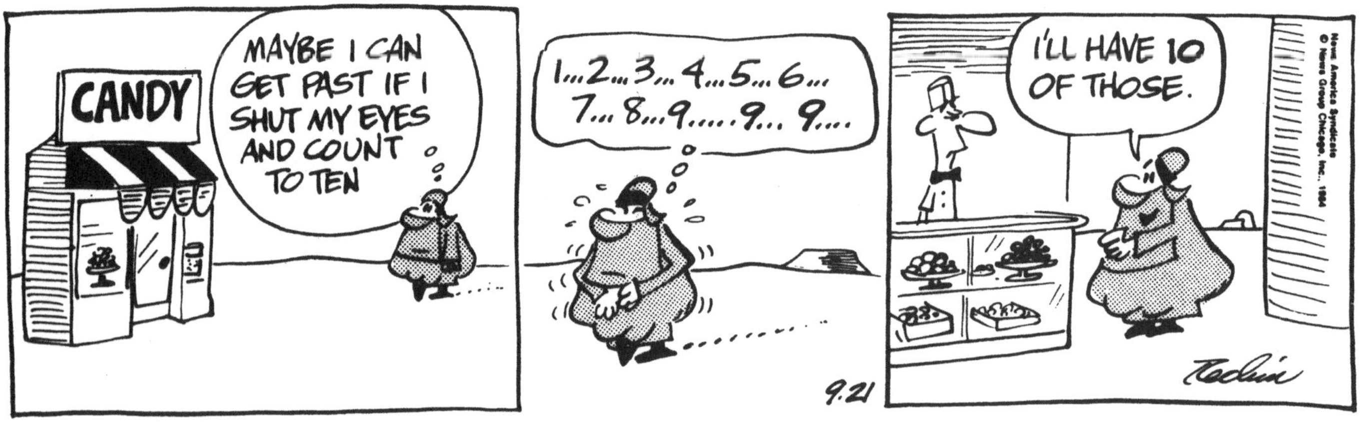
CANDY
MAYBE I CAN GET PAST IF I SHUT MY EYES AND COUNT TO TEN
1...2...3...4...5...6... 7...8...9.....9... 9....
9.21
I'LL HAVE 10 OF THOSE.
News America Syndicate © News Group Chicago, Inc., 1984

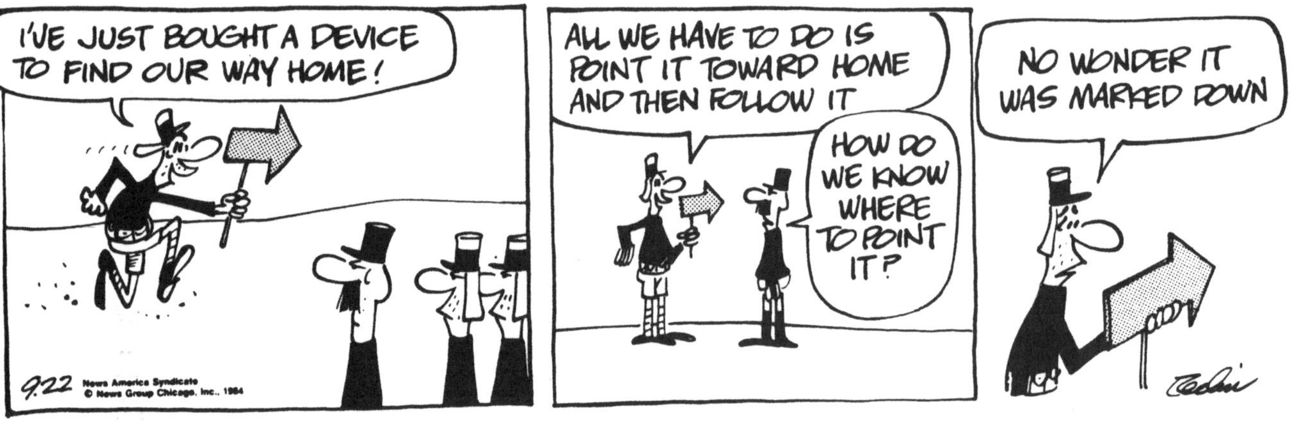
I'VE JUST BOUGHT A DEVICE TO FIND OUR WAY HOME!
9.22 News America Syndicate © News Group Chicago, Inc., 1984
ALL WE HAVE TO DO IS POINT IT TOWARD HOME AND THEN FOLLOW IT
HOW DO WE KNOW WHERE TO POINT IT?
NO WONDER IT WAS MARKED DOWN

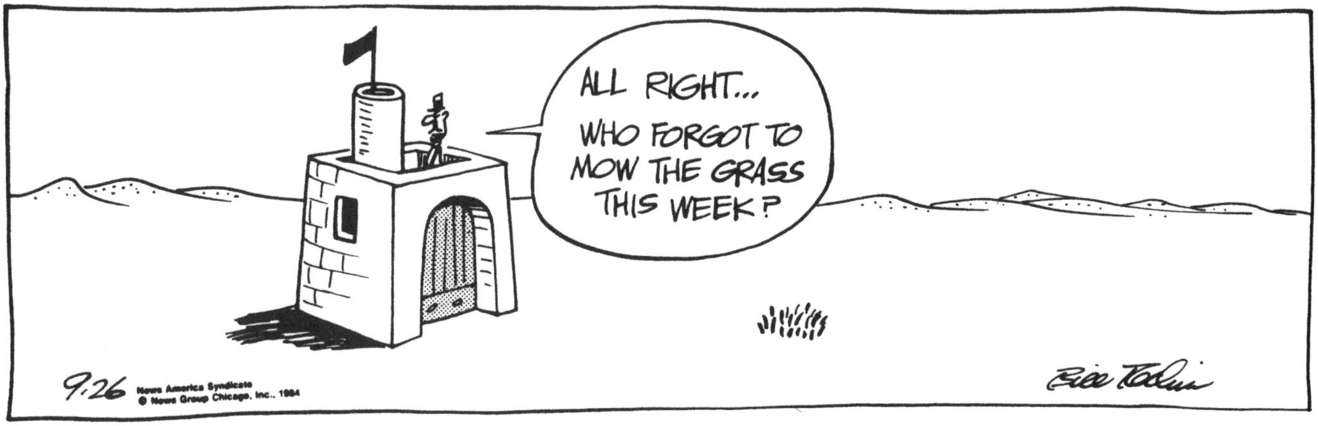
ALL RIGHT... WHO FORGOT TO MOW THE GRASS THIS WEEK?
9·26
News America Syndicate © News Group Chicago, Inc., 1984

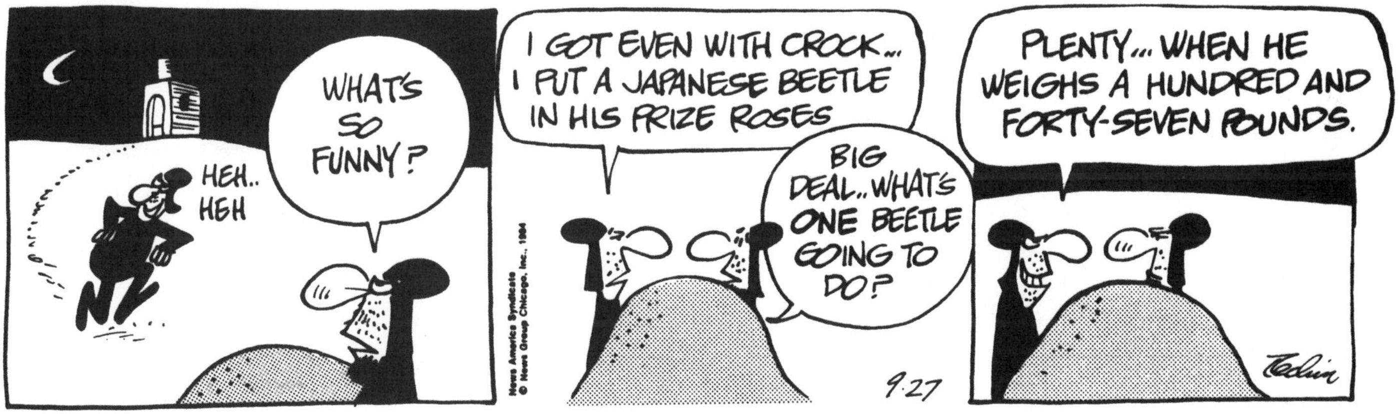
HEH.. HEH
WHAT'S SO FUNNY?
I GOT EVEN WITH CROCK... I PUT A JAPANESE BEETLE IN HIS PRIZE ROSES
BIG DEAL.. WHAT'S ONE BEETLE GOING TO DO?
PLENTY... WHEN HE WEIGHS A HUNDRED AND FORTY-SEVEN POUNDS.
News America Syndicate © News Group Chicago, Inc., 1984
9·27

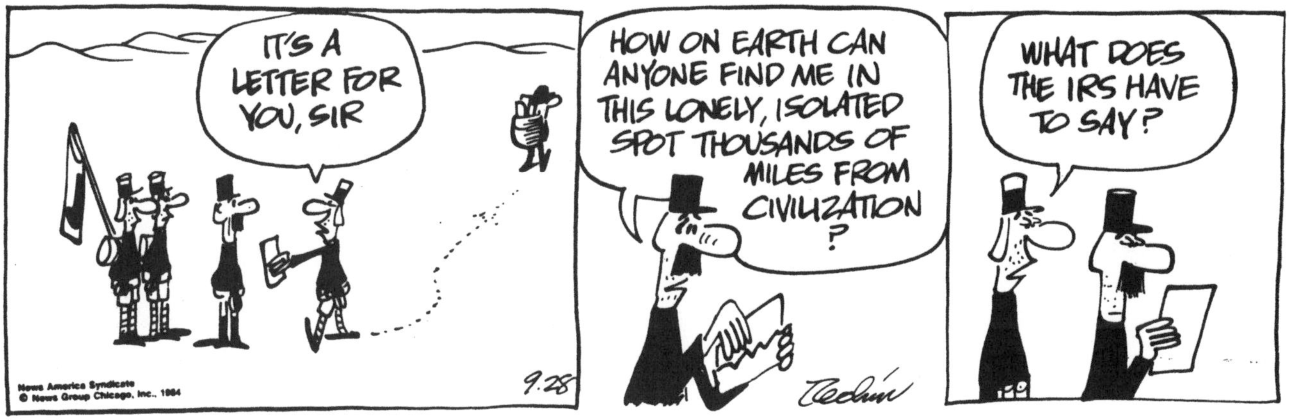
IT'S A LETTER FOR YOU, SIR
HOW ON EARTH CAN ANYONE FIND ME IN THIS LONELY, ISOLATED SPOT THOUSANDS OF MILES FROM CIVILIZATION?
WHAT DOES THE IRS HAVE TO SAY?
News America Syndicate © News Group Chicago, Inc., 1984
9·28

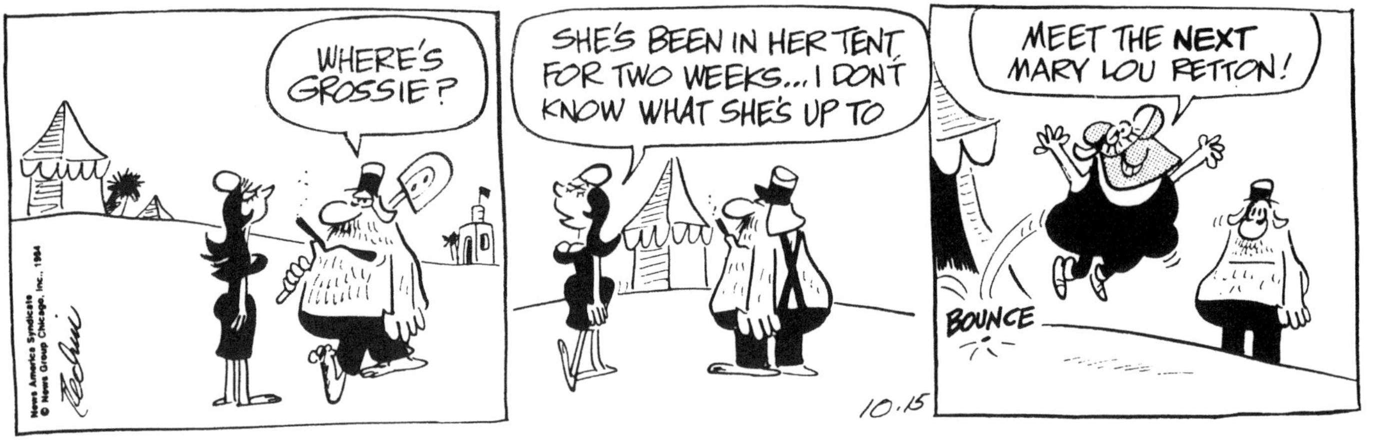
WHERE'S GROSSIE?
SHE'S BEEN IN HER TENT FOR TWO WEEKS... I DON'T KNOW WHAT SHE'S UP TO
MEET THE NEXT MARY LOU RETTON!
BOUNCE
News America Syndicate © News Group Chicago, Inc., 1984
10.15

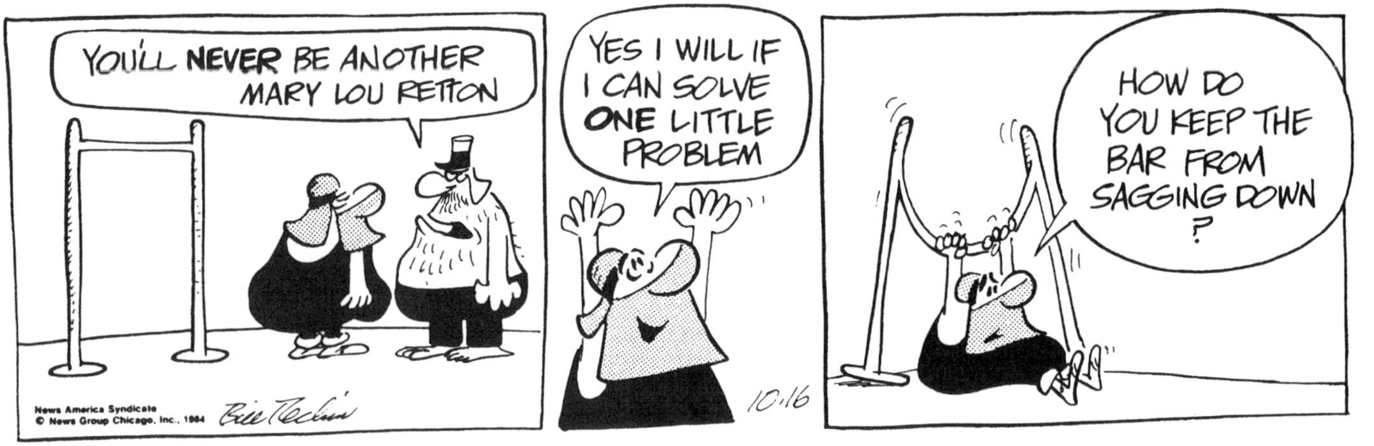
YOU'LL NEVER BE ANOTHER MARY LOU RETTON
YES I WILL IF I CAN SOLVE ONE LITTLE PROBLEM
HOW DO YOU KEEP THE BAR FROM SAGGING DOWN?
News America Syndicate © News Group Chicago, Inc., 1984
Bill Rechin
10.16

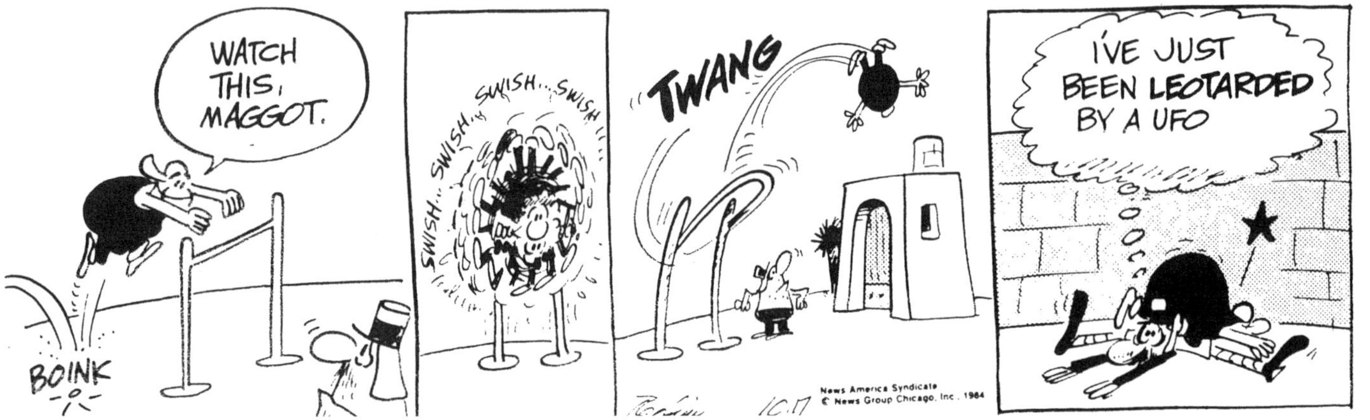
WATCH THIS, MAGGOT.
BOINK
SWISH... SWISH... SWISH... SWISH
TWANG
I'VE JUST BEEN LEOTARDED BY A UFO
10.17
News America Syndicate © News Group Chicago, Inc., 1984

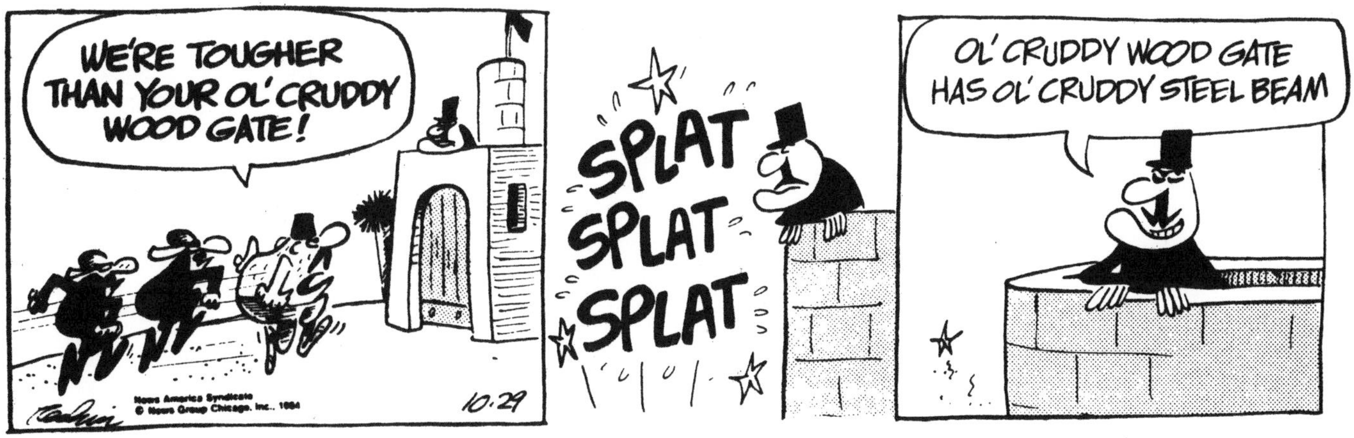
WE'RE TOUGHER THAN YOUR OL' CRUDDY WOOD GATE!
News America Syndicate © News Group Chicago, Inc., 1984
10·29
SPLAT SPLAT SPLAT
OL' CRUDDY WOOD GATE HAS OL' CRUDDY STEEL BEAM

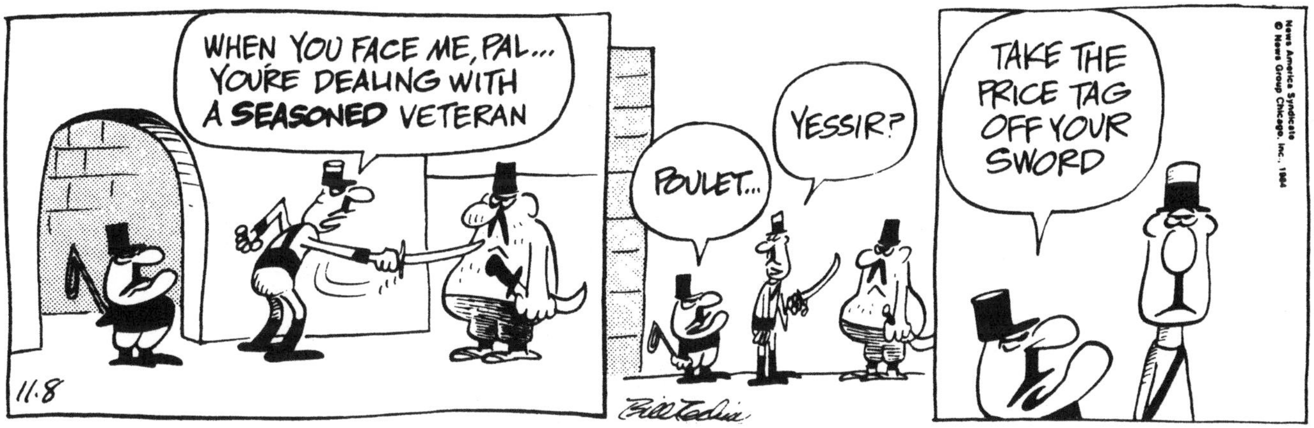
WHEN YOU FACE ME, PAL... YOU'RE DEALING WITH A SEASONED VETERAN
11·8
POULET...
YESSIR?
TAKE THE PRICE TAG OFF YOUR SWORD
News America Syndicate © News Group Chicago, Inc., 1984

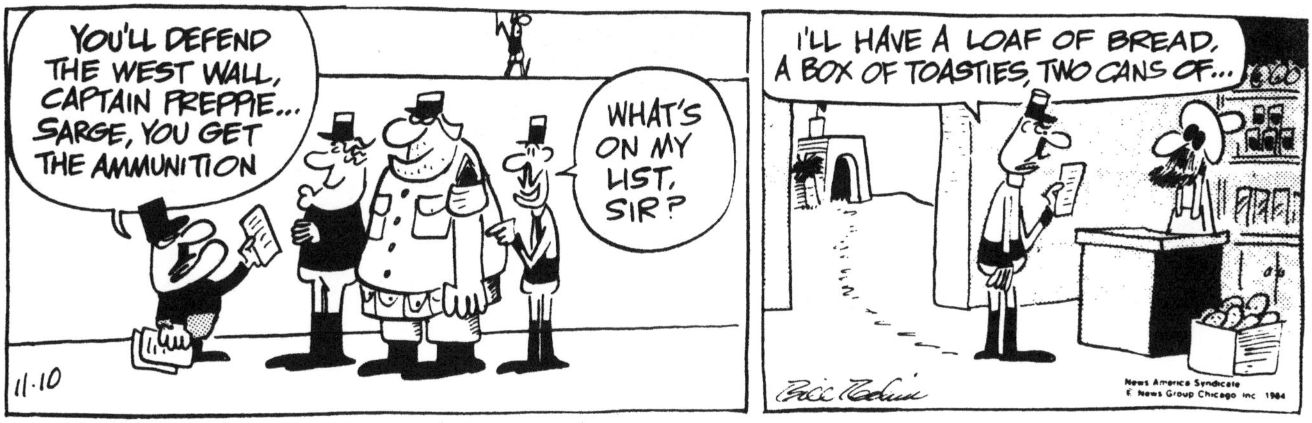
YOU'LL DEFEND THE WEST WALL, CAPTAIN PREPPIE... SARGE, YOU GET THE AMMUNITION
WHAT'S ON MY LIST, SIR?
11·10
I'LL HAVE A LOAF OF BREAD, A BOX OF TOASTIES, TWO CANS OF...
News America Syndicate © News Group Chicago Inc 1984

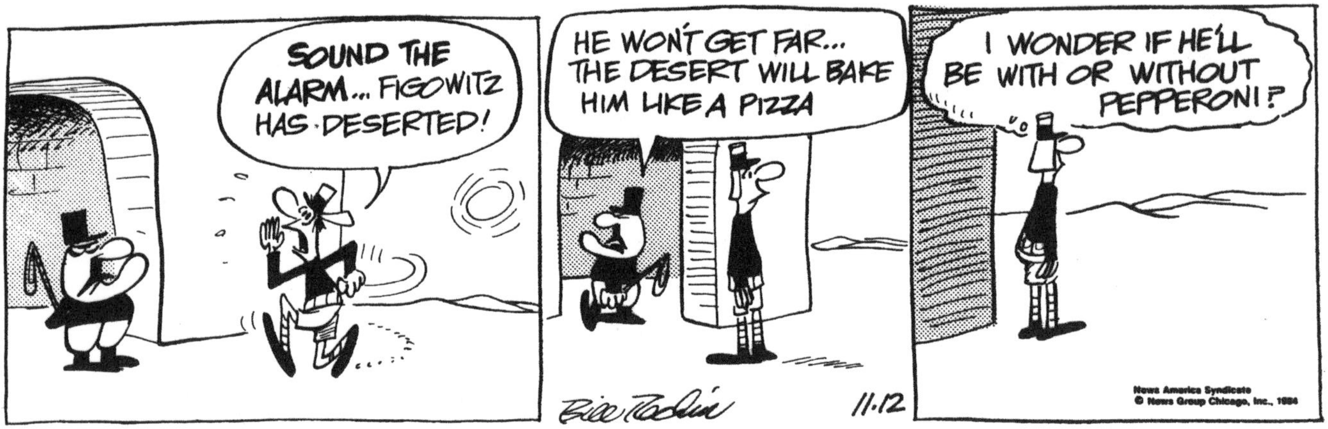
SOUND THE ALARM... FIGOWITZ HAS DESERTED!
HE WON'T GET FAR... THE DESERT WILL BAKE HIM LIKE A PIZZA
I WONDER IF HE'LL BE WITH OR WITHOUT PEPPERONI?
11.12
News America Syndicate
© News Group Chicago, Inc., 1984

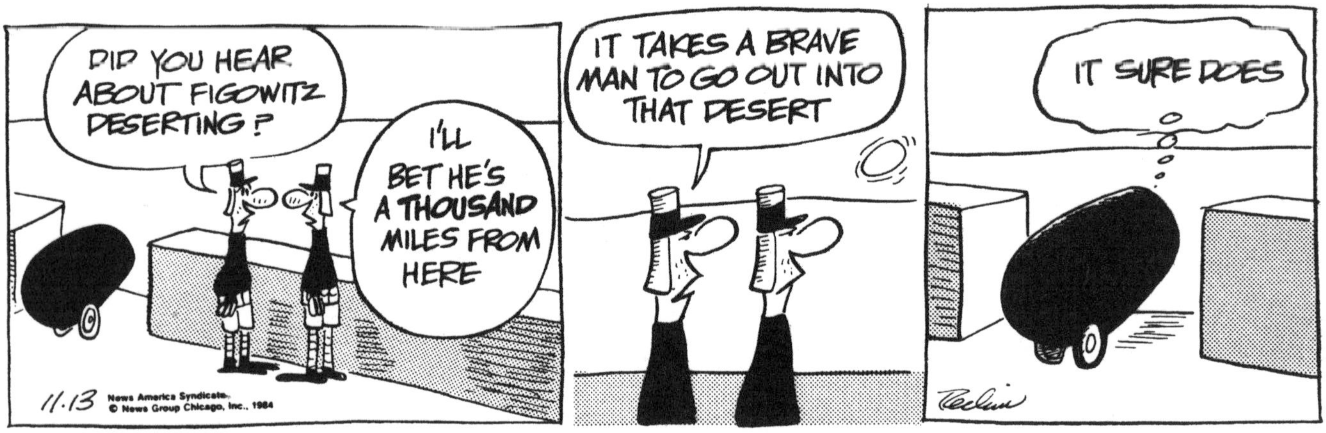
DID YOU HEAR ABOUT FIGOWITZ DESERTING?
I'LL BET HE'S A THOUSAND MILES FROM HERE
11.13
News America Syndicate
© News Group Chicago, Inc., 1984
IT TAKES A BRAVE MAN TO GO OUT INTO THAT DESERT
IT SURE DOES

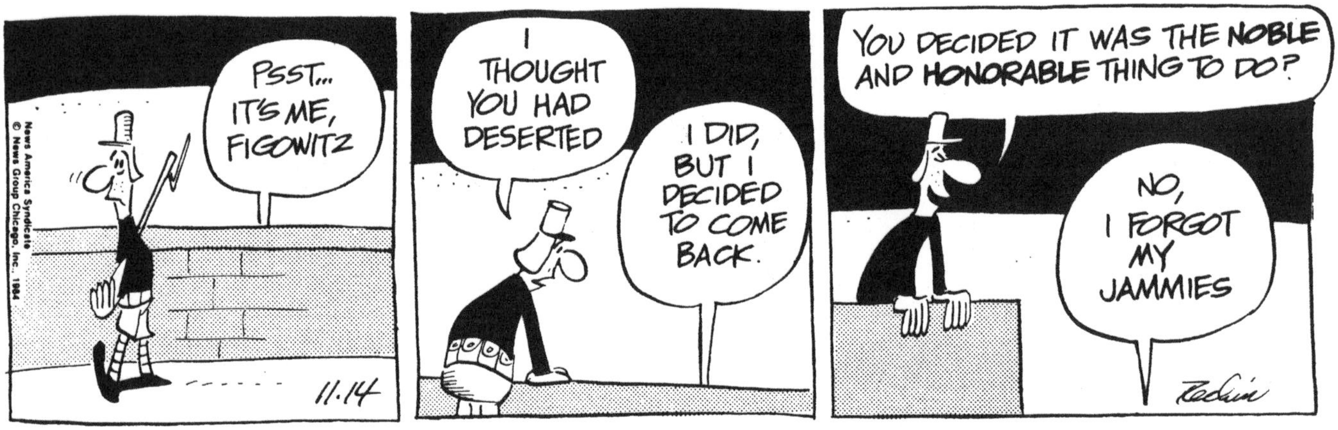
News America Syndicate
© News Group Chicago, Inc., 1984
PSST... IT'S ME, FIGOWITZ
11.14
I THOUGHT YOU HAD DESERTED
I DID, BUT I DECIDED TO COME BACK.
YOU DECIDED IT WAS THE NOBLE AND HONORABLE THING TO DO?
NO, I FORGOT MY JAMMIES

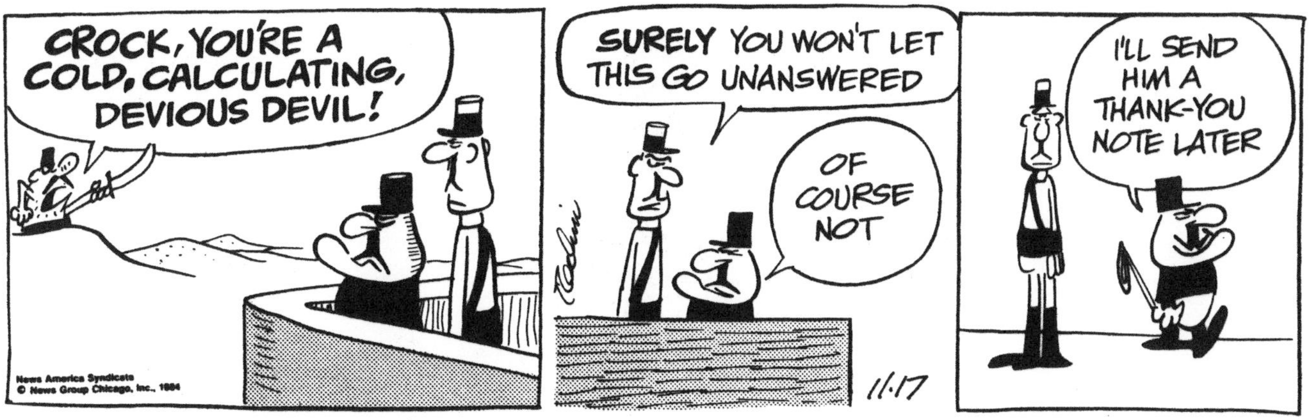
CROCK, YOU'RE A COLD, CALCULATING, DEVIOUS DEVIL!
News America Syndicate © News Group Chicago, Inc., 1984
SURELY YOU WON'T LET THIS GO UNANSWERED
OF COURSE NOT
11·17
I'LL SEND HIM A THANK-YOU NOTE LATER

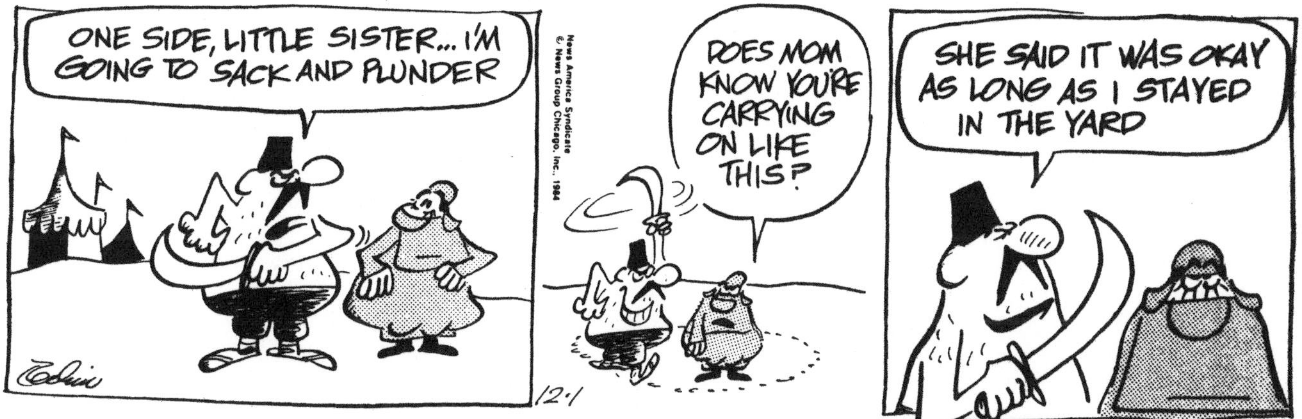
ONE SIDE, LITTLE SISTER... I'M GOING TO SACK AND PLUNDER
News America Syndicate © News Group Chicago, Inc., 1984
12·1
DOES MOM KNOW YOU'RE CARRYING ON LIKE THIS?
SHE SAID IT WAS OKAY AS LONG AS I STAYED IN THE YARD

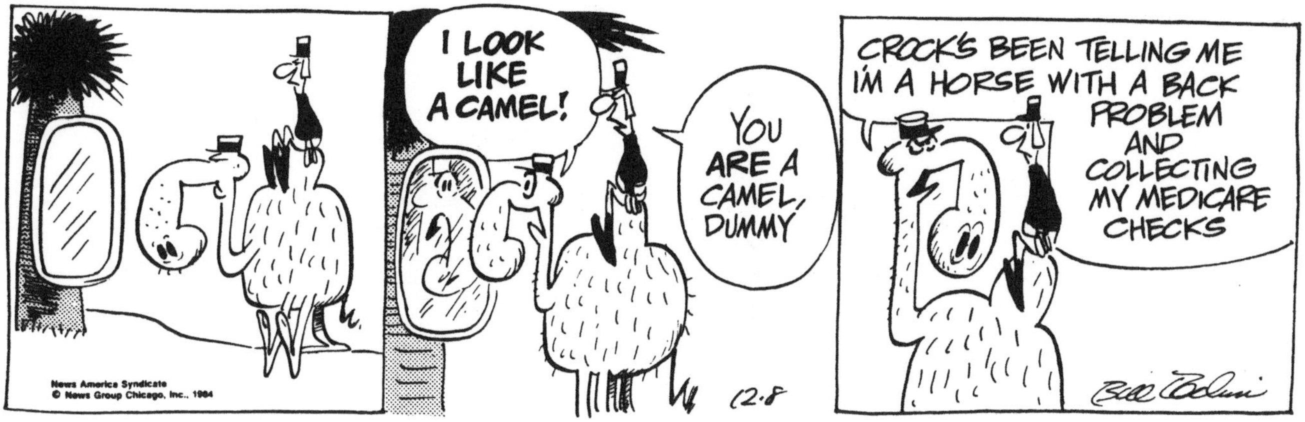
News America Syndicate © News Group Chicago, Inc., 1984
I LOOK LIKE A CAMEL!
YOU ARE A CAMEL, DUMMY
12·8
CROCK'S BEEN TELLING ME I'M A HORSE WITH A BACK PROBLEM AND COLLECTING MY MEDICARE CHECKS

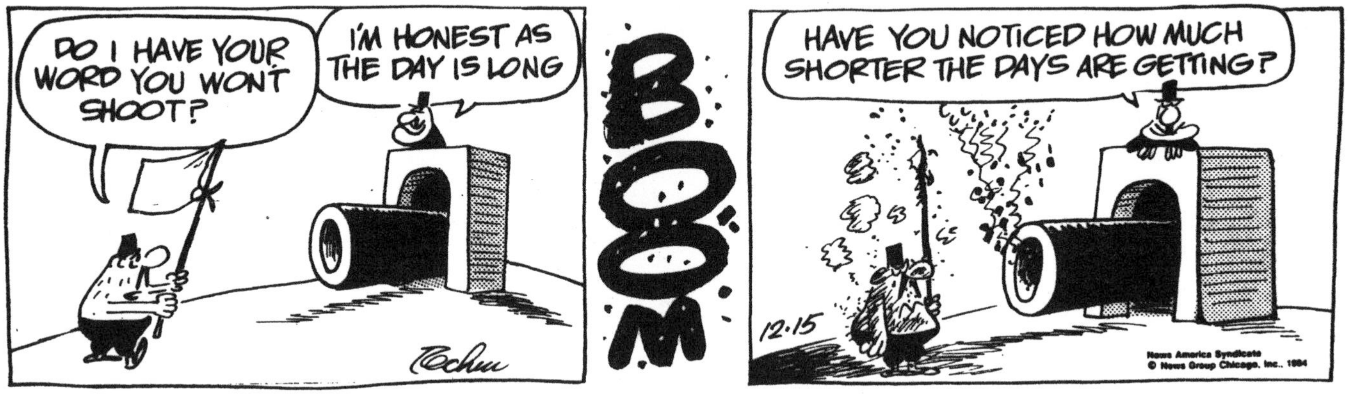
DO I HAVE YOUR WORD YOU WON'T SHOOT?
I'M HONEST AS THE DAY IS LONG
BOOM
HAVE YOU NOTICED HOW MUCH SHORTER THE DAYS ARE GETTING?
12.15
News America Syndicate
© News Group Chicago, Inc., 1984

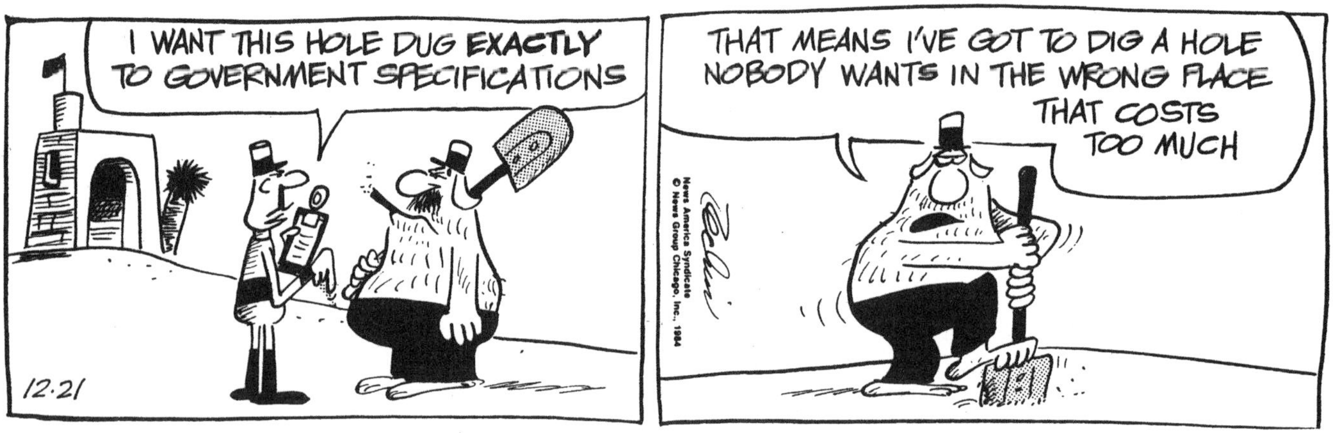
I WANT THIS HOLE DUG EXACTLY TO GOVERNMENT SPECIFICATIONS
12.21
News America Syndicate
© News Group Chicago, Inc., 1984
THAT MEANS I'VE GOT TO DIG A HOLE NOBODY WANTS IN THE WRONG PLACE THAT COSTS TOO MUCH

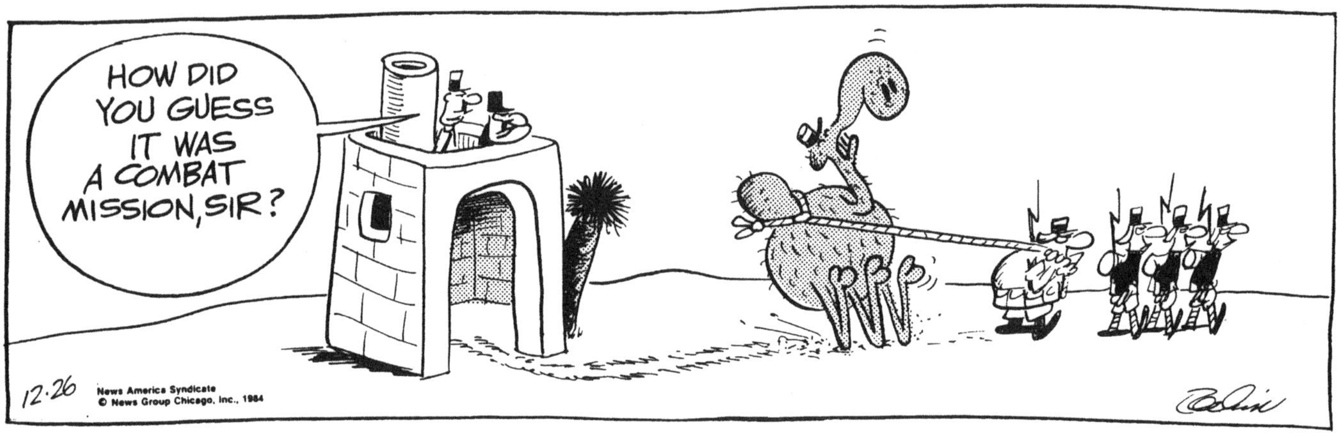
HOW DID YOU GUESS IT WAS A COMBAT MISSION, SIR?
12.26
News America Syndicate
© News Group Chicago, Inc., 1984

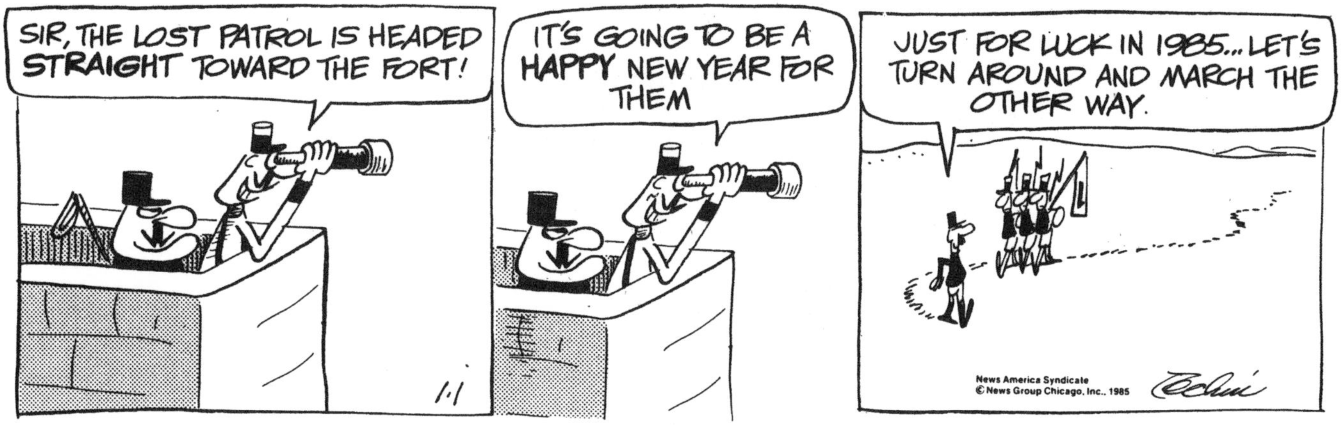
SIR, THE LOST PATROL IS HEADED STRAIGHT TOWARD THE FORT!
1.1
IT'S GOING TO BE A HAPPY NEW YEAR FOR THEM
JUST FOR LUCK IN 1985... LET'S TURN AROUND AND MARCH THE OTHER WAY.
News America Syndicate
© News Group Chicago, Inc., 1985

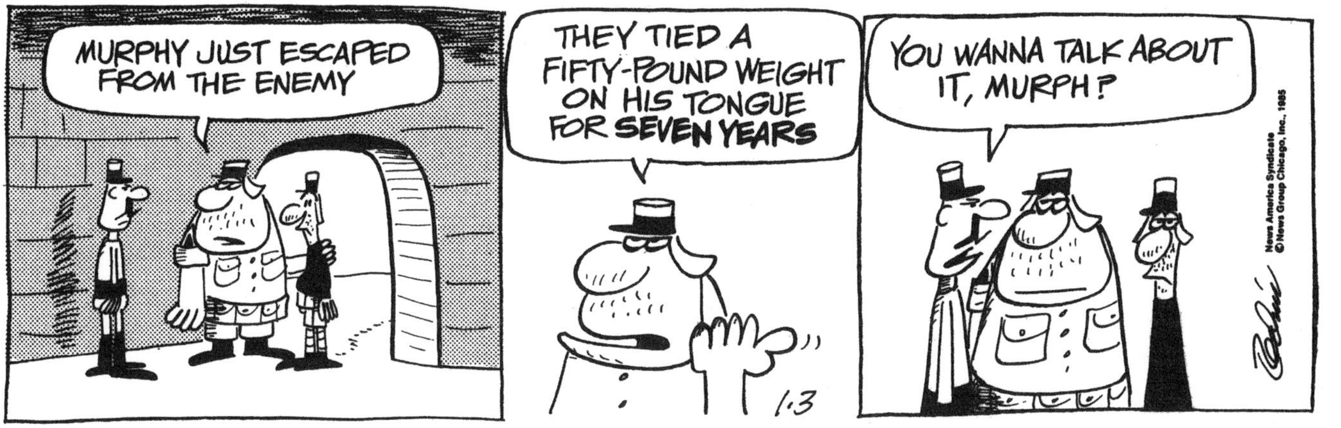
MURPHY JUST ESCAPED FROM THE ENEMY
THEY TIED A FIFTY-POUND WEIGHT ON HIS TONGUE FOR SEVEN YEARS
1.3
YOU WANNA TALK ABOUT IT, MURPH?
News America Syndicate
© News Group Chicago, Inc., 1985

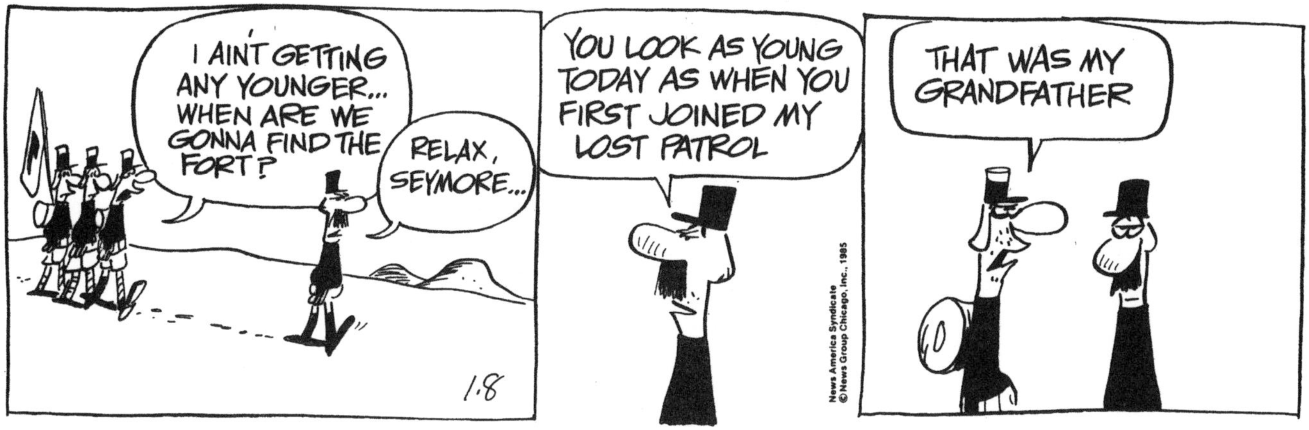
I AIN'T GETTING ANY YOUNGER... WHEN ARE WE GONNA FIND THE FORT?
RELAX, SEYMORE...
1.8
News America Syndicate
© News Group Chicago, Inc., 1985
YOU LOOK AS YOUNG TODAY AS WHEN YOU FIRST JOINED MY LOST PATROL
THAT WAS MY GRANDFATHER

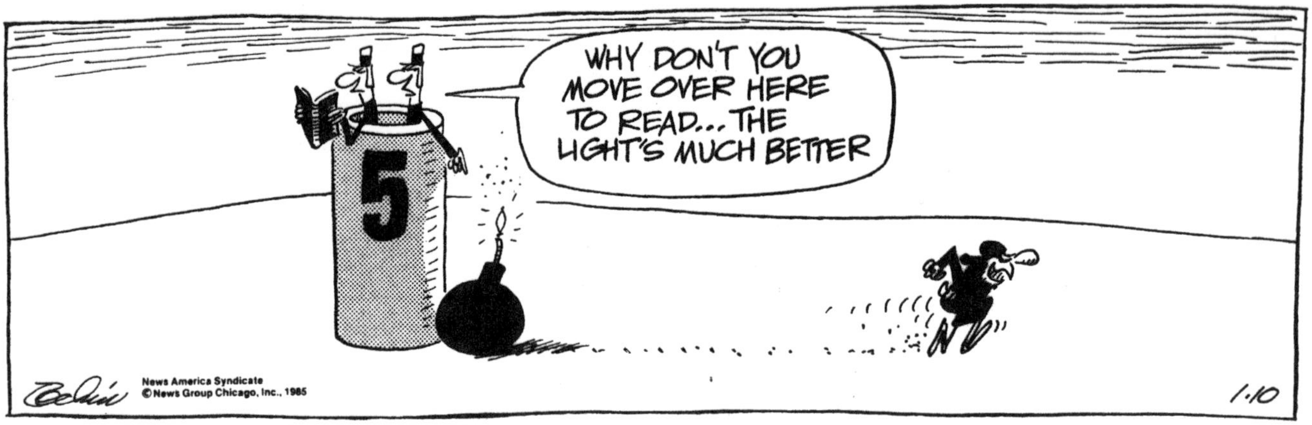
WHY DON'T YOU MOVE OVER HERE TO READ... THE LIGHT'S MUCH BETTER
5
News America Syndicate
©News Group Chicago, Inc., 1985
1.10

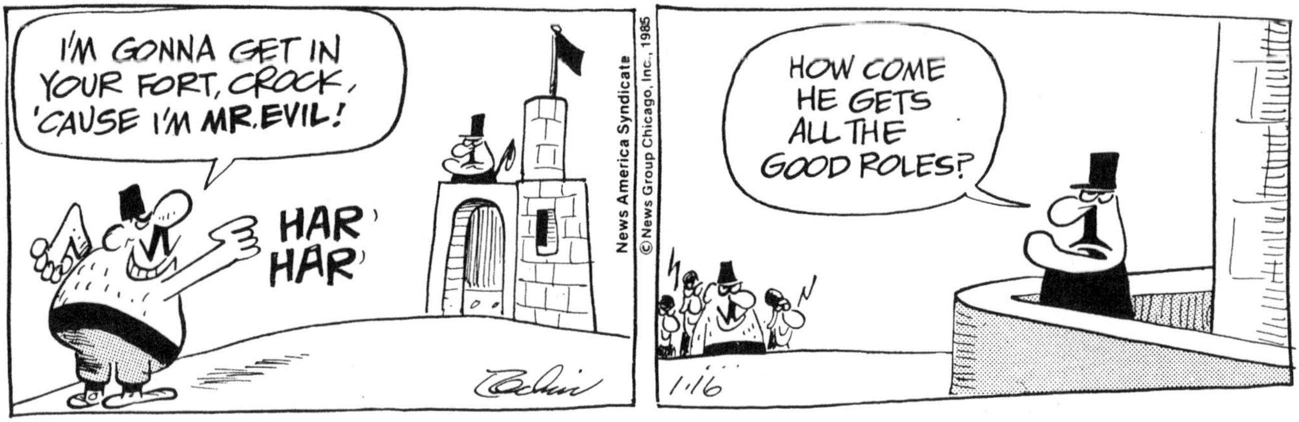
I'M GONNA GET IN YOUR FORT, CROCK, 'CAUSE I'M **MR. EVIL!**
HAR HAR
News America Syndicate
©News Group Chicago, Inc., 1985
HOW COME HE GETS ALL THE GOOD ROLES?
1.16

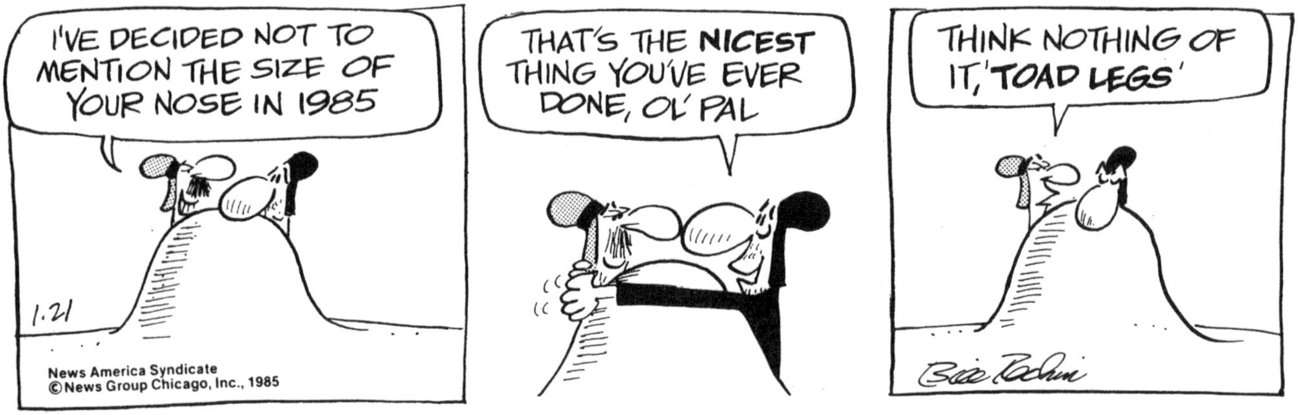
I'VE DECIDED NOT TO MENTION THE SIZE OF YOUR NOSE IN 1985
1.21
News America Syndicate
©News Group Chicago, Inc., 1985
THAT'S THE **NICEST** THING YOU'VE EVER DONE, OL' PAL
THINK NOTHING OF IT, '**TOAD LEGS**'

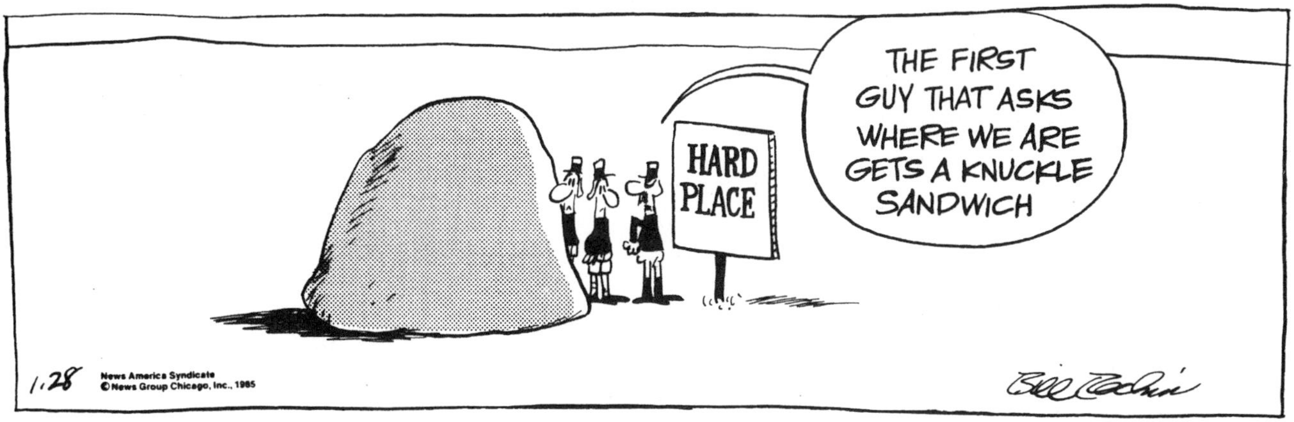
HARD PLACE
THE FIRST GUY THAT ASKS WHERE WE ARE GETS A KNUCKLE SANDWICH
1.28
News America Syndicate
© News Group Chicago, Inc., 1985

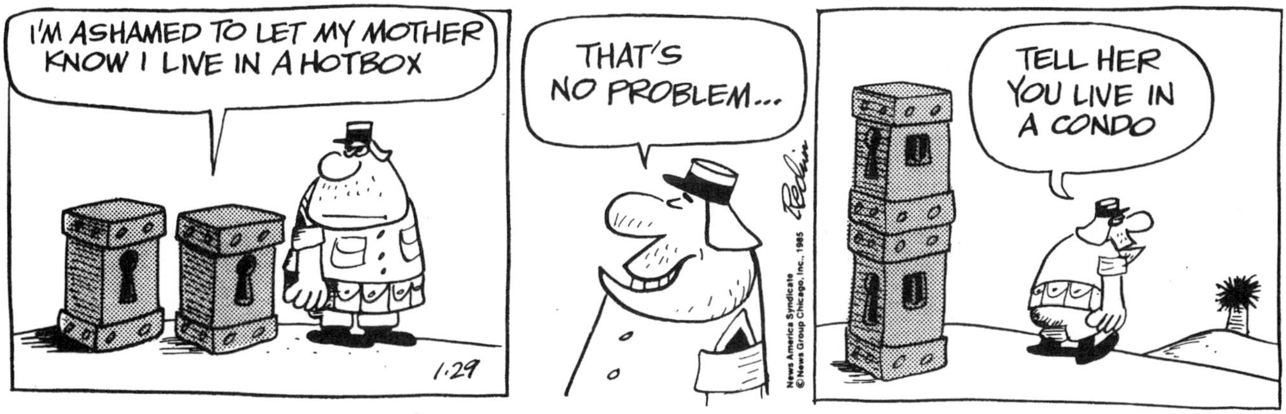
I'M ASHAMED TO LET MY MOTHER KNOW I LIVE IN A HOTBOX
THAT'S NO PROBLEM...
TELL HER YOU LIVE IN A CONDO
1.29
News America Syndicate
© News Group Chicago, Inc., 1985

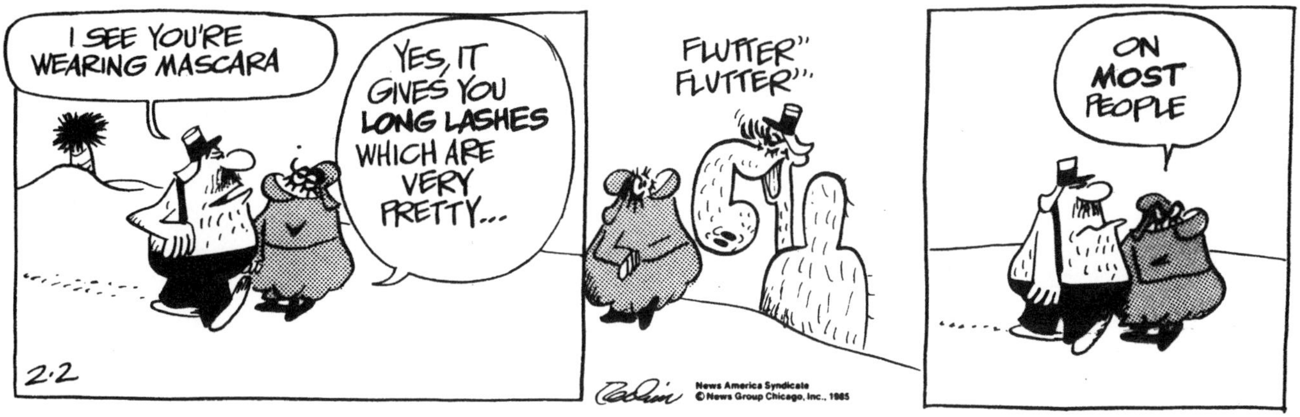
I SEE YOU'RE WEARING MASCARA
YES, IT GIVES YOU **LONG LASHES** WHICH ARE VERY PRETTY...
FLUTTER FLUTTER
ON **MOST** PEOPLE
2.2
News America Syndicate
© News Group Chicago, Inc., 1985

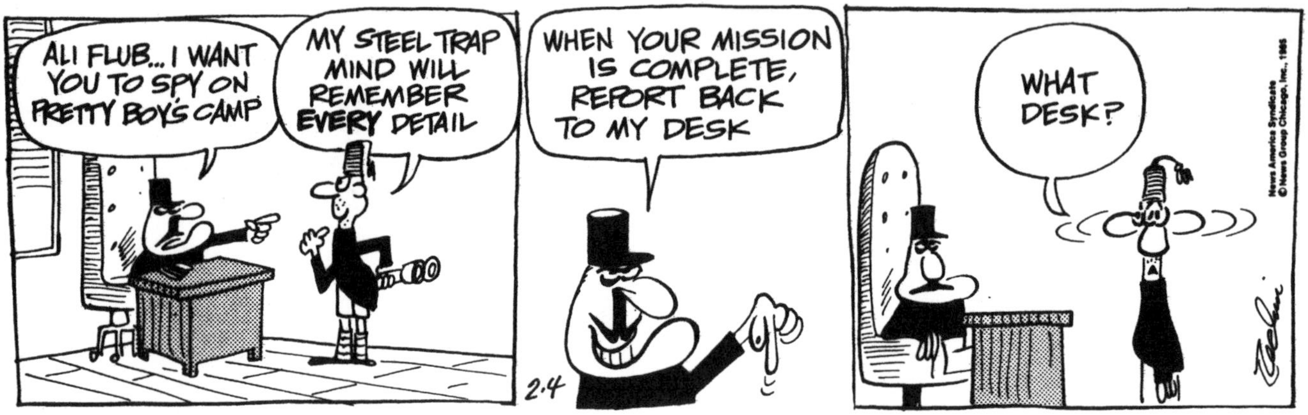
ALI FLUB... I WANT YOU TO SPY ON PRETTY BOY'S CAMP
MY STEEL TRAP MIND WILL REMEMBER EVERY DETAIL
WHEN YOUR MISSION IS COMPLETE, REPORT BACK TO MY DESK
2.4
WHAT DESK?

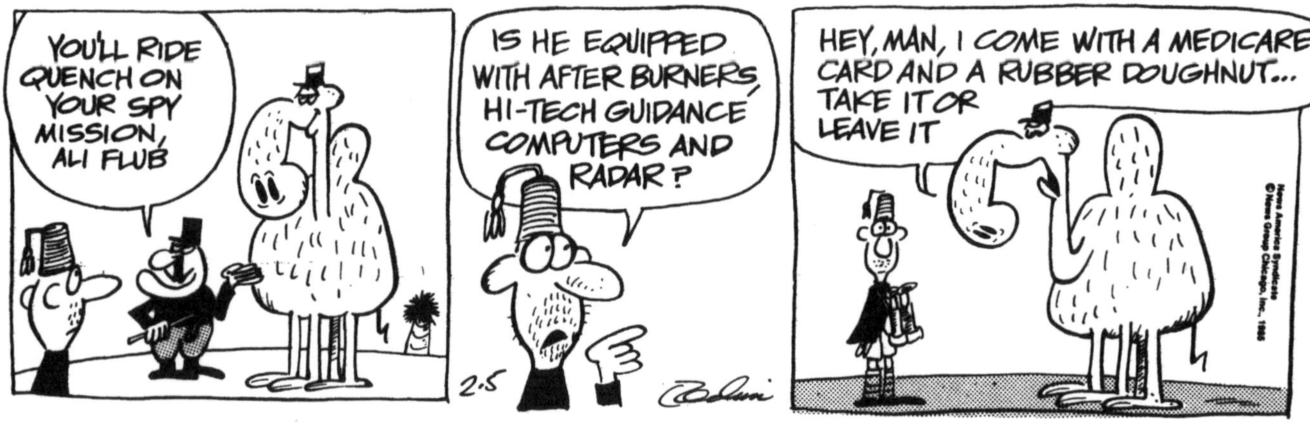
YOU'LL RIDE QUENCH ON YOUR SPY MISSION, ALI FLUB
IS HE EQUIPPED WITH AFTER BURNERS, HI-TECH GUIDANCE COMPUTERS AND RADAR?
2.5
HEY, MAN, I COME WITH A MEDICARE CARD AND A RUBBER DOUGHNUT... TAKE IT OR LEAVE IT

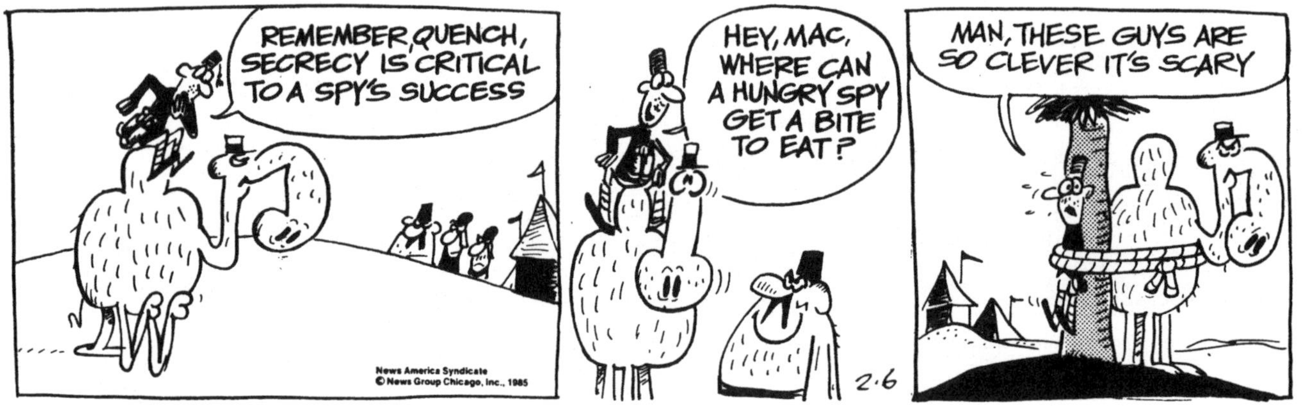
REMEMBER, QUENCH, SECRECY IS CRITICAL TO A SPY'S SUCCESS
News America Syndicate
© News Group Chicago, Inc., 1985
HEY, MAC, WHERE CAN A HUNGRY SPY GET A BITE TO EAT?
2.6
MAN, THESE GUYS ARE SO CLEVER IT'S SCARY

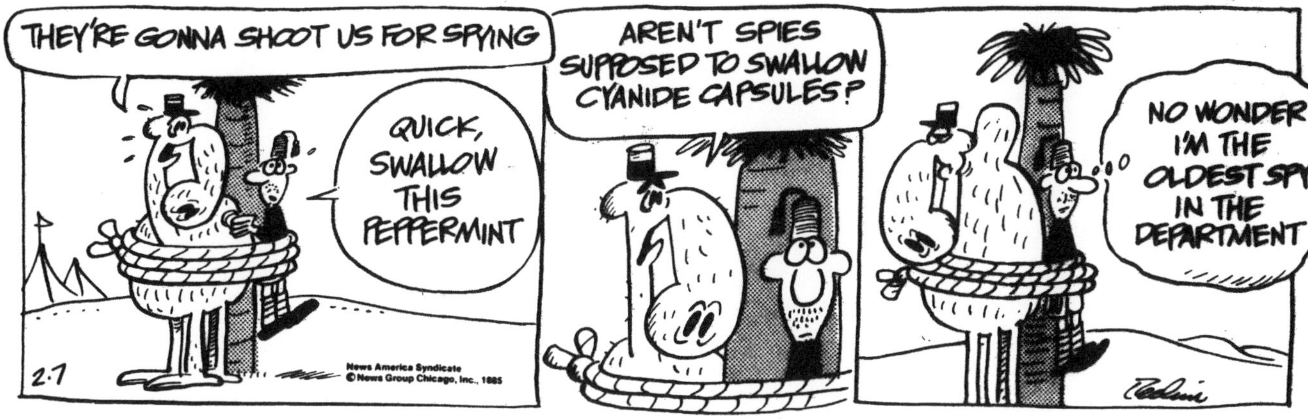
THEY'RE GONNA SHOOT US FOR SPYING
QUICK, SWALLOW THIS PEPPERMINT
2·7
News America Syndicate © News Group Chicago, Inc., 1985
AREN'T SPIES SUPPOSED TO SWALLOW CYANIDE CAPSULES?
NO WONDER I'M THE OLDEST SPY IN THE DEPARTMENT

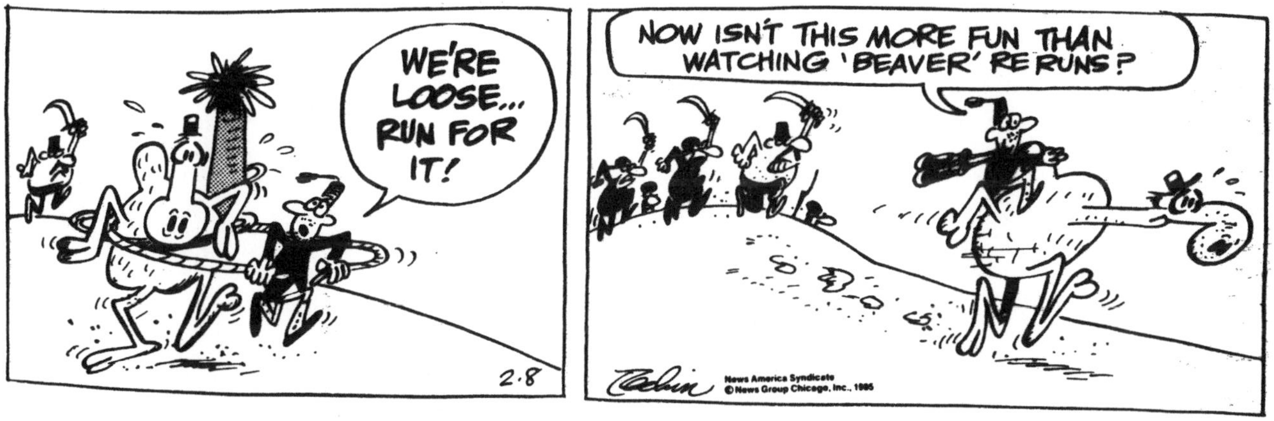
WE'RE LOOSE... RUN FOR IT!
2·8
NOW ISN'T THIS MORE FUN THAN WATCHING 'BEAVER' RE RUNS?
News America Syndicate © News Group Chicago, Inc., 1985

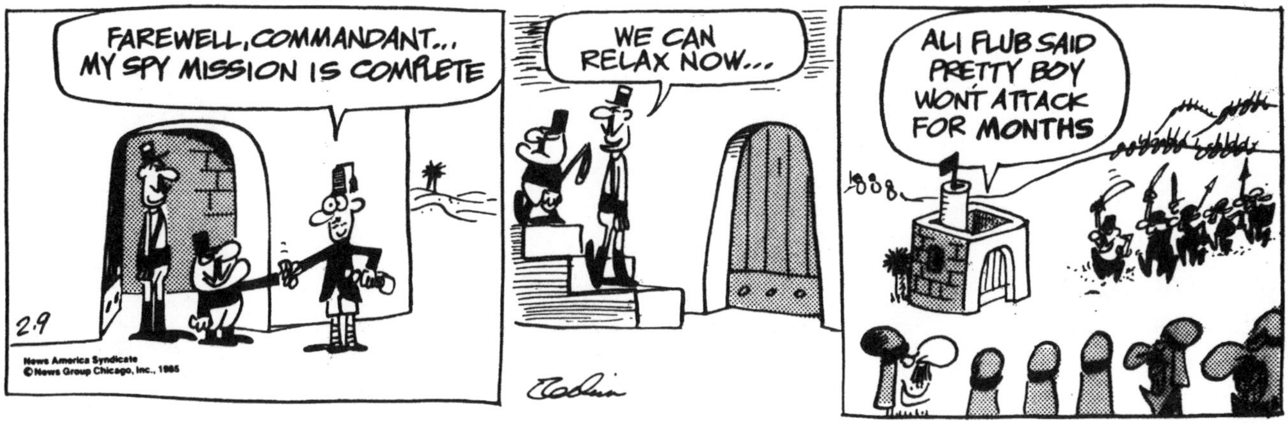
FAREWELL, COMMANDANT... MY SPY MISSION IS COMPLETE
2·9
News America Syndicate © News Group Chicago, Inc., 1985
WE CAN RELAX NOW...
ALI FLUB SAID PRETTY BOY WON'T ATTACK FOR MONTHS

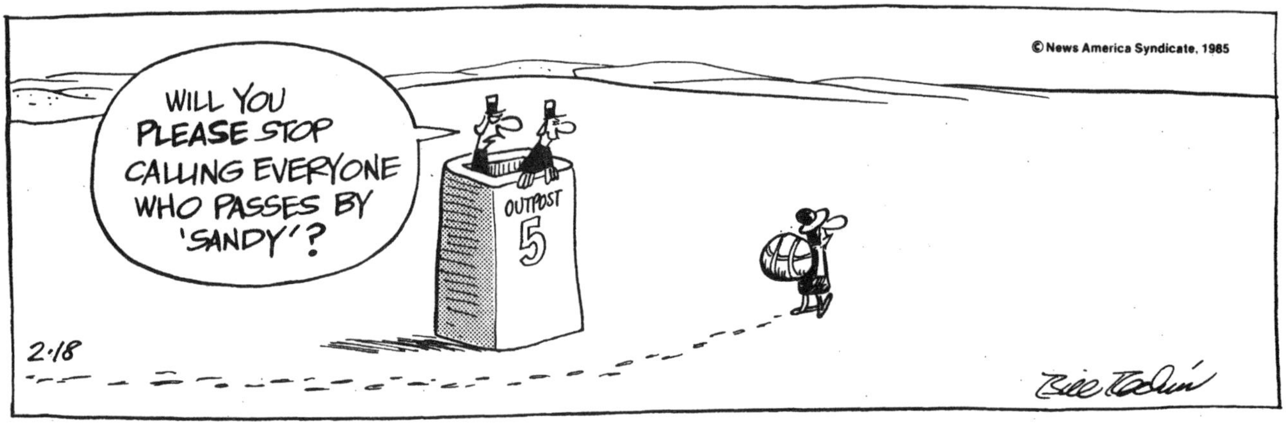
© News America Syndicate, 1985
WILL YOU PLEASE STOP CALLING EVERYONE WHO PASSES BY 'SANDY'?
OUTPOST 5
2·18

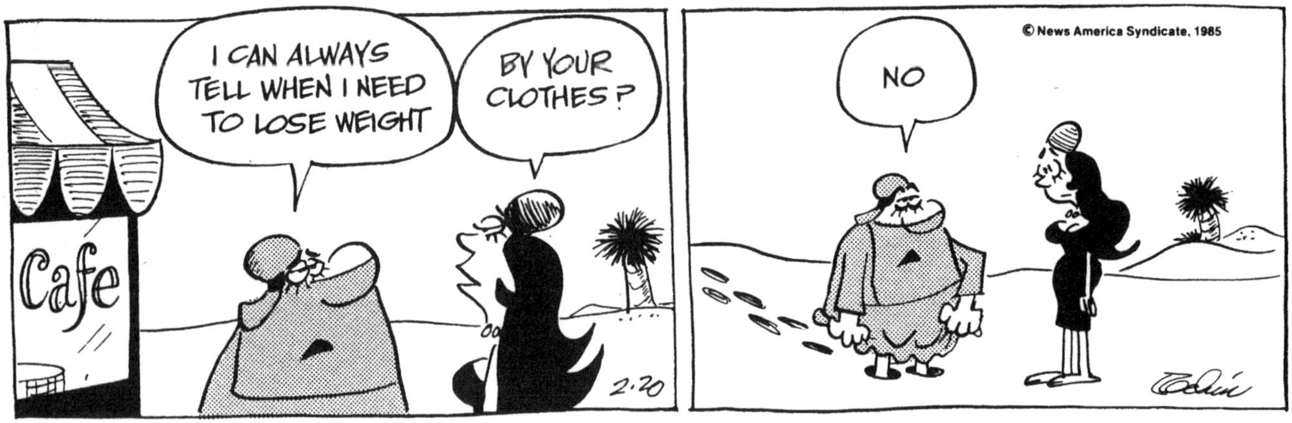
Cafe
I CAN ALWAYS TELL WHEN I NEED TO LOSE WEIGHT
BY YOUR CLOTHES?
2·20
© News America Syndicate, 1985
NO

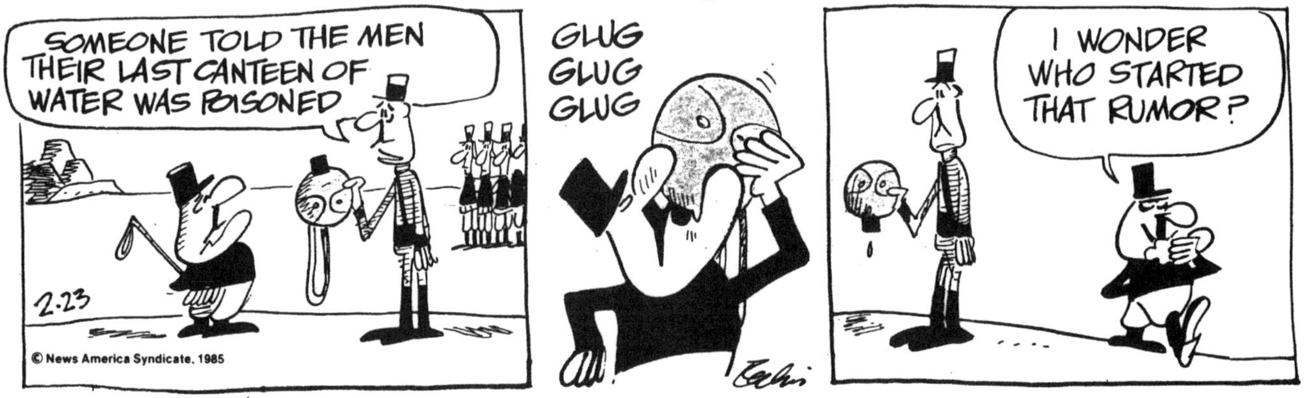
SOMEONE TOLD THE MEN THEIR LAST CANTEEN OF WATER WAS POISONED
2·23
© News America Syndicate, 1985
GLUG GLUG GLUG
I WONDER WHO STARTED THAT RUMOR?

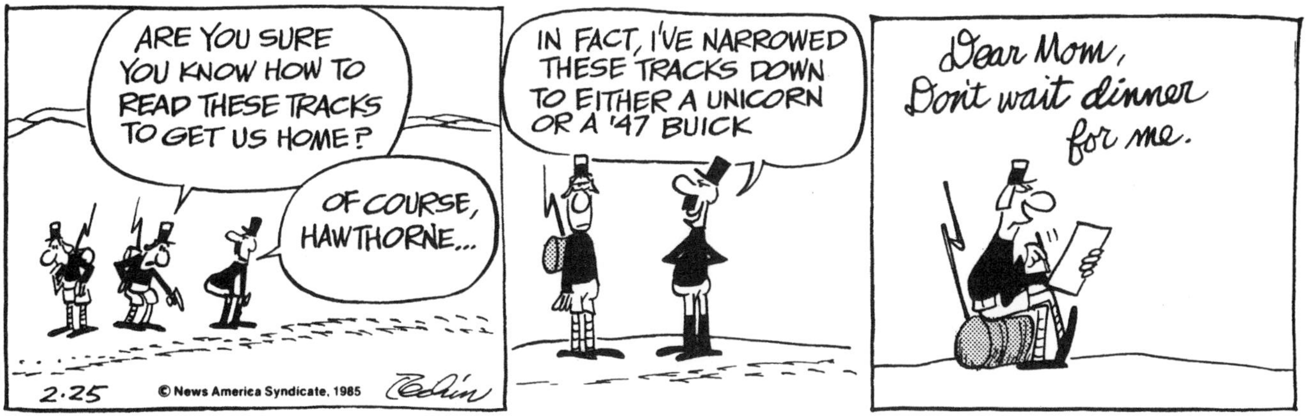
ARE YOU SURE YOU KNOW HOW TO READ THESE TRACKS TO GET US HOME?
OF COURSE, HAWTHORNE...
IN FACT, I'VE NARROWED THESE TRACKS DOWN TO EITHER A UNICORN OR A '47 BUICK
Dear Mom, Don't wait dinner for me.
2·25
© News America Syndicate, 1985

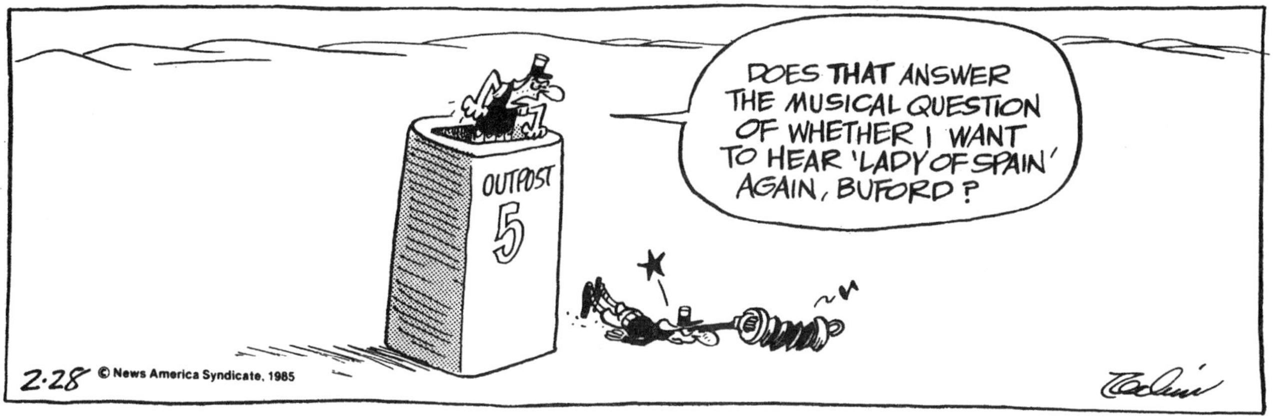
DOES THAT ANSWER THE MUSICAL QUESTION OF WHETHER I WANT TO HEAR 'LADY OF SPAIN' AGAIN, BUFORD?
OUTPOST 5
2·28
© News America Syndicate, 1985

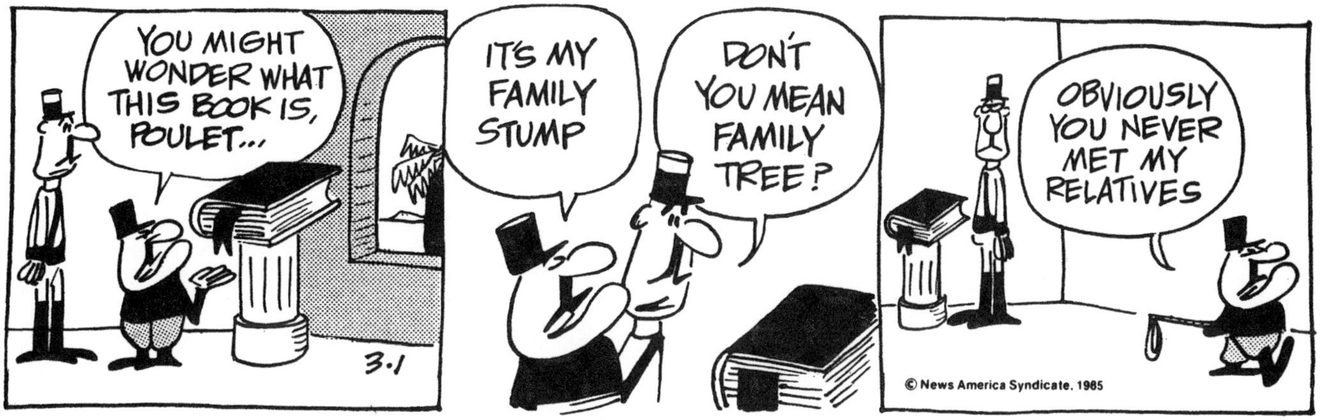
YOU MIGHT WONDER WHAT THIS BOOK IS, POULET...
IT'S MY FAMILY STUMP
DON'T YOU MEAN FAMILY TREE?
OBVIOUSLY YOU NEVER MET MY RELATIVES
3·1
© News America Syndicate, 1985

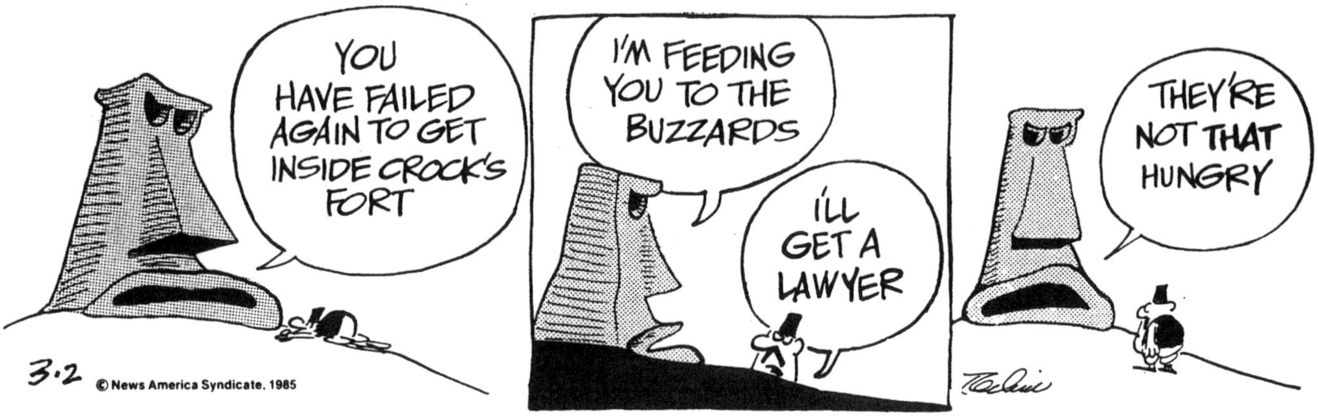
YOU HAVE FAILED AGAIN TO GET INSIDE CROCK'S FORT
3·2
© News America Syndicate, 1985
I'M FEEDING YOU TO THE BUZZARDS
I'LL GET A LAWYER
THEY'RE NOT THAT HUNGRY

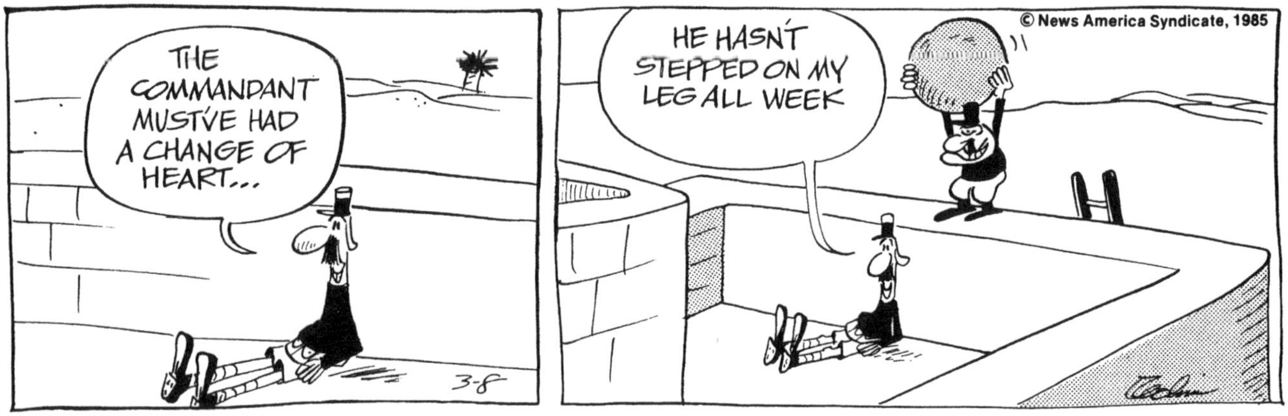
THE COMMANDANT MUST'VE HAD A CHANGE OF HEART...
3-8
© News America Syndicate, 1985
HE HASN'T STEPPED ON MY LEG ALL WEEK

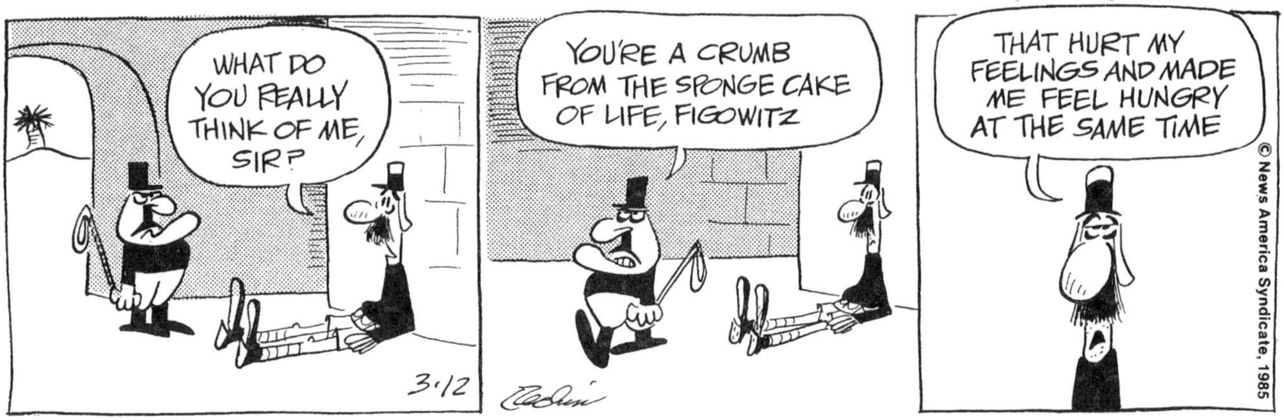
WHAT DO YOU REALLY THINK OF ME, SIR?
3·12
YOU'RE A CRUMB FROM THE SPONGE CAKE OF LIFE, FIGOWITZ
THAT HURT MY FEELINGS AND MADE ME FEEL HUNGRY AT THE SAME TIME
© News America Syndicate, 1985

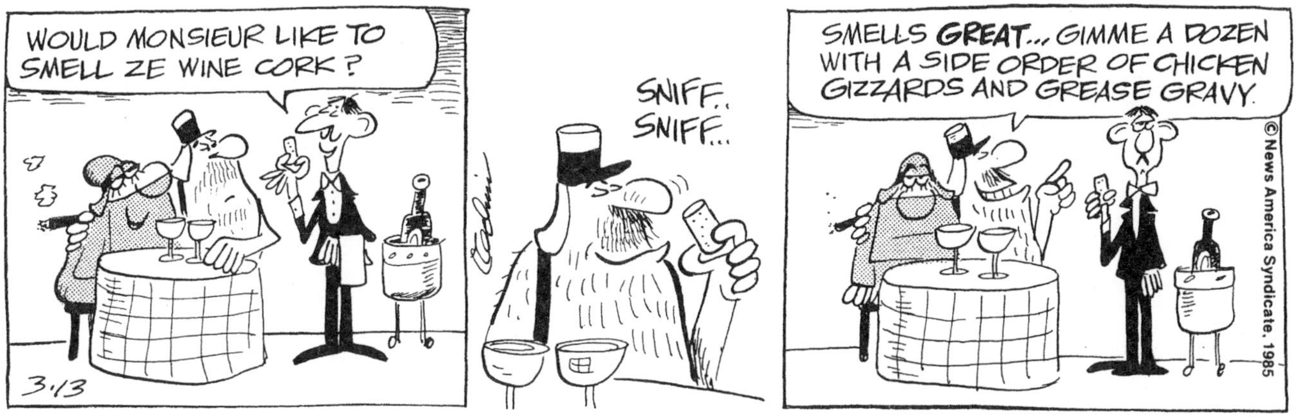
WOULD MONSIEUR LIKE TO SMELL ZE WINE CORK ?
3.13
SNIFF.. SNIFF...
SMELLS GREAT..., GIMME A DOZEN WITH A SIDE ORDER OF CHICKEN GIZZARDS AND GREASE GRAVY.
© News America Syndicate, 1985

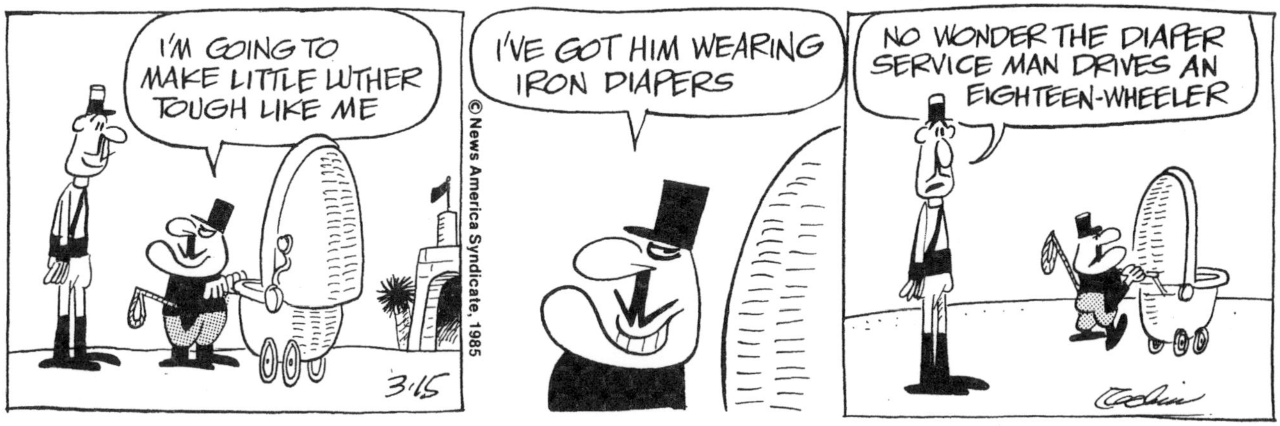
I'M GOING TO MAKE LITTLE LUTHER TOUGH LIKE ME
3.15
© News America Syndicate, 1985
I'VE GOT HIM WEARING IRON DIAPERS
NO WONDER THE DIAPER SERVICE MAN DRIVES AN EIGHTEEN-WHEELER

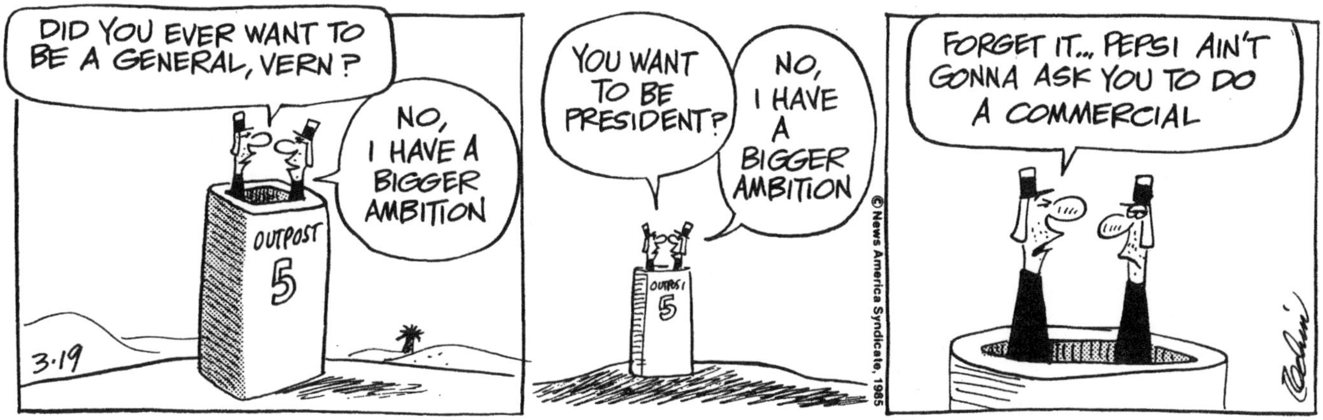
DID YOU EVER WANT TO BE A GENERAL, VERN ?
NO, I HAVE A BIGGER AMBITION
OUTPOST 5
3.19
YOU WANT TO BE PRESIDENT?
NO, I HAVE A BIGGER AMBITION
© News America Syndicate, 1985
FORGET IT..., PEPSI AIN'T GONNA ASK YOU TO DO A COMMERCIAL

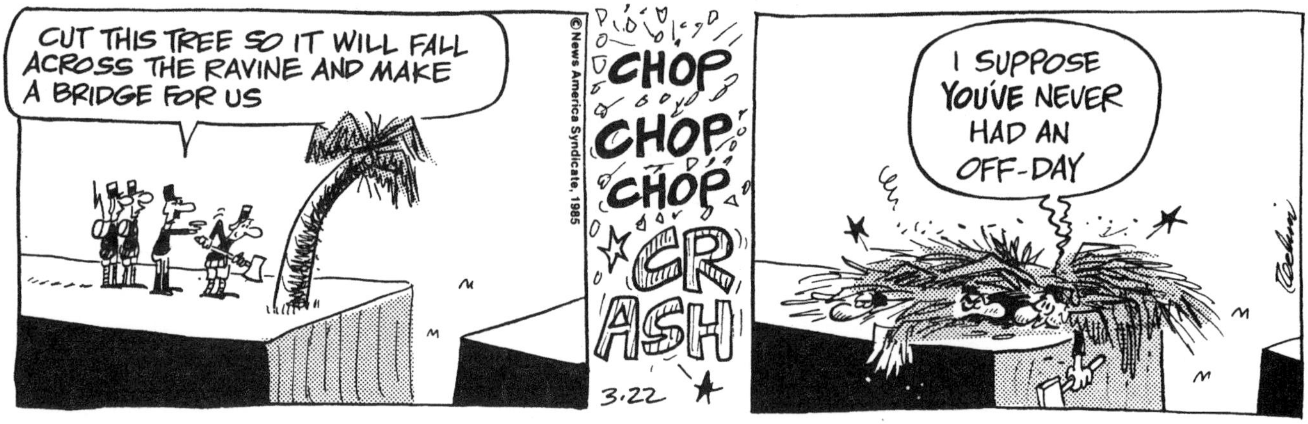
CUT THIS TREE SO IT WILL FALL ACROSS THE RAVINE AND MAKE A BRIDGE FOR US
CHOP
CHOP
CHOP
CRASH
3.22
I SUPPOSE YOU'VE NEVER HAD AN OFF-DAY
© News America Syndicate, 1985

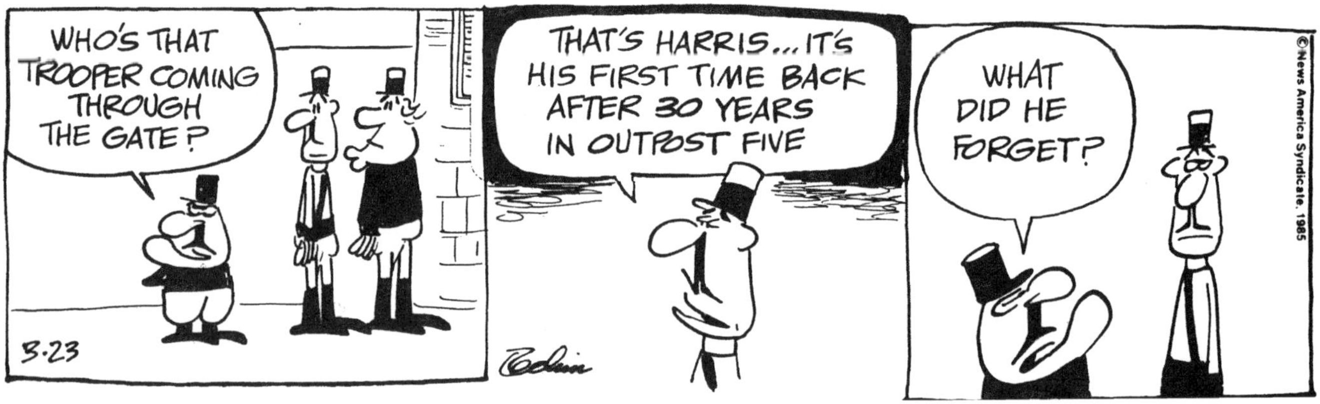
WHO'S THAT TROOPER COMING THROUGH THE GATE?
3.23
THAT'S HARRIS... IT'S HIS FIRST TIME BACK AFTER 30 YEARS IN OUTPOST FIVE
WHAT DID HE FORGET?
© News America Syndicate, 1985

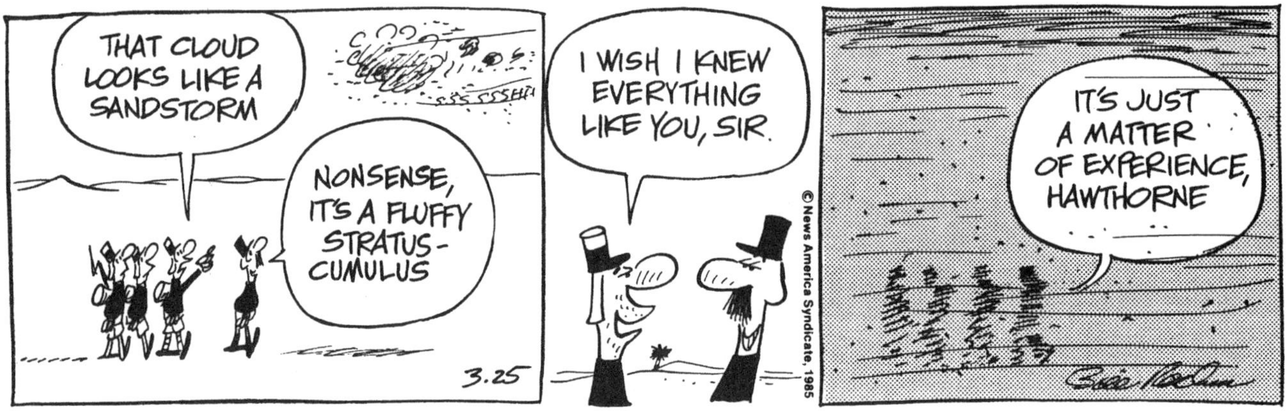
THAT CLOUD LOOKS LIKE A SANDSTORM
NONSENSE, IT'S A FLUFFY STRATUS-CUMULUS
3.25
I WISH I KNEW EVERYTHING LIKE YOU, SIR
IT'S JUST A MATTER OF EXPERIENCE, HAWTHORNE
© News America Syndicate, 1985

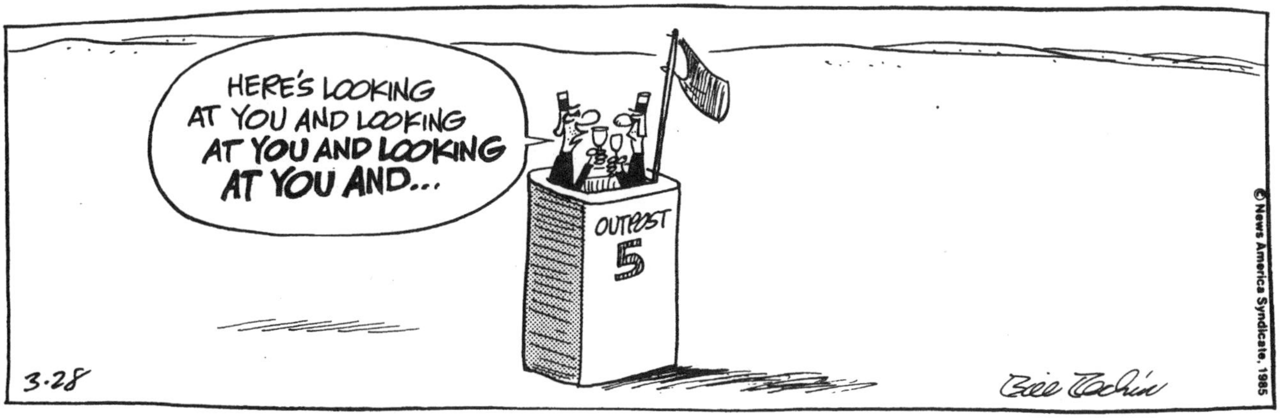
HERE'S LOOKING AT YOU AND LOOKING AT YOU AND LOOKING AT YOU AND...
OUTPOST 5
3·28
© News America Syndicate, 1985

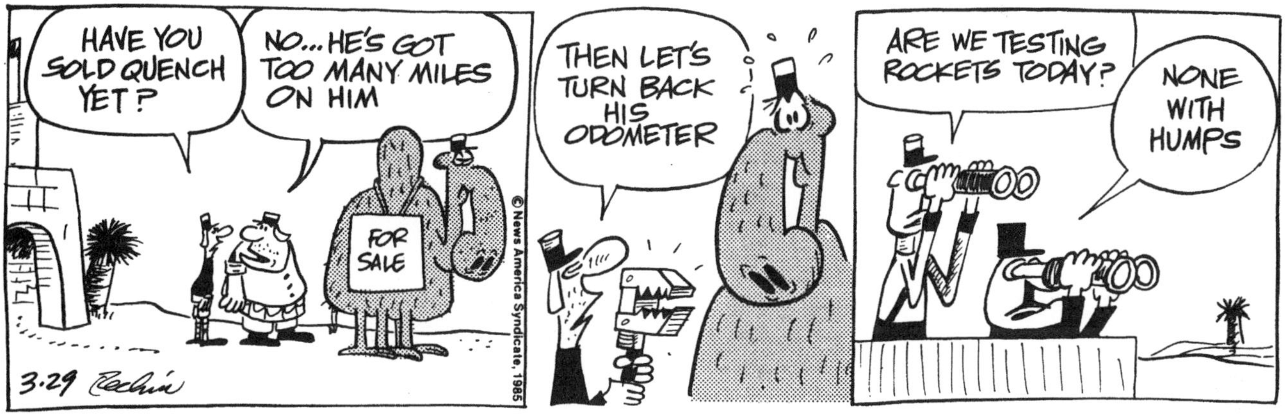
HAVE YOU SOLD QUENCH YET?
NO... HE'S GOT TOO MANY MILES ON HIM
FOR SALE
3·29
© News America Syndicate, 1985
THEN LET'S TURN BACK HIS ODOMETER
ARE WE TESTING ROCKETS TODAY?
NONE WITH HUMPS

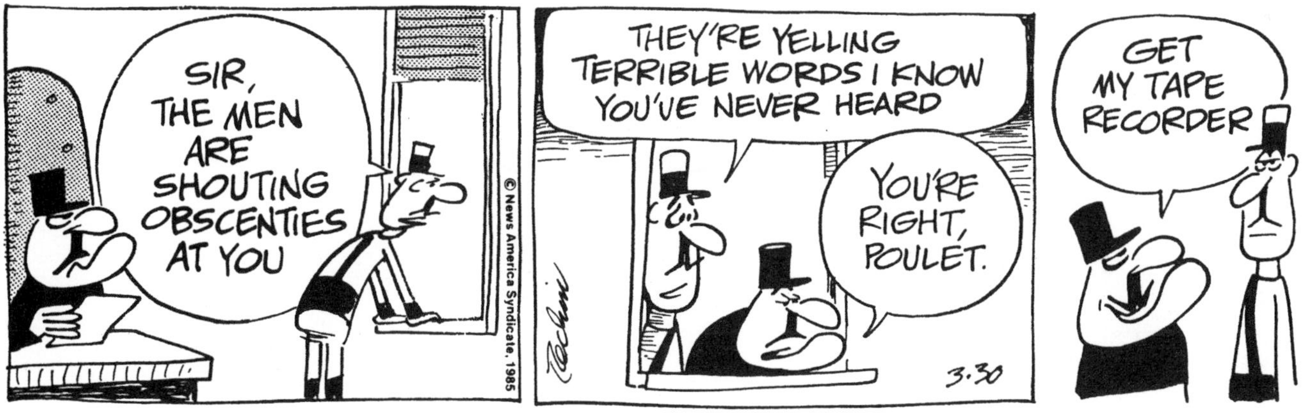
SIR, THE MEN ARE SHOUTING OBSCENTIES AT YOU
© News America Syndicate, 1985
THEY'RE YELLING TERRIBLE WORDS I KNOW YOU'VE NEVER HEARD
YOU'RE RIGHT, POULET.
3·30
GET MY TAPE RECORDER

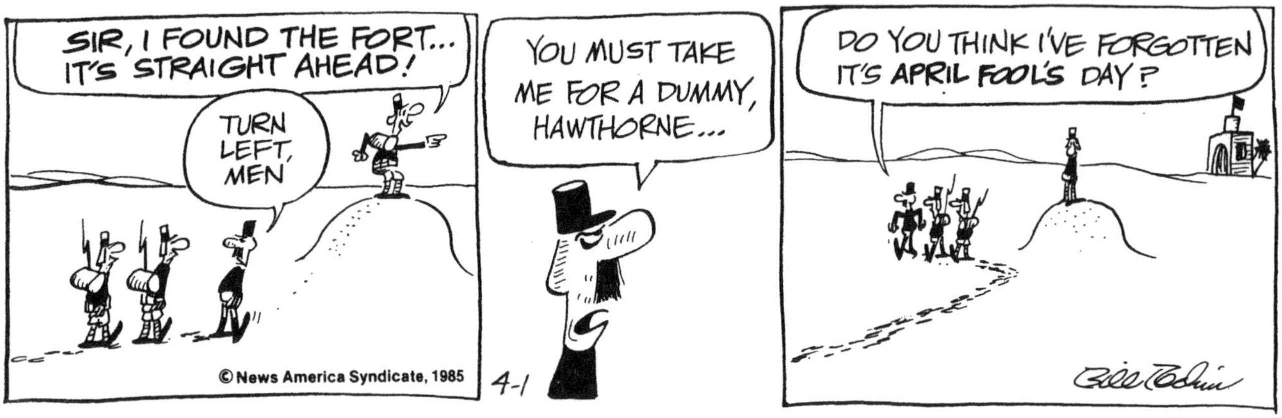
SIR, I FOUND THE FORT... IT'S STRAIGHT AHEAD!
TURN LEFT, MEN
© News America Syndicate, 1985
YOU MUST TAKE ME FOR A DUMMY, HAWTHORNE...
4-1
DO YOU THINK I'VE FORGOTTEN IT'S APRIL FOOL'S DAY?

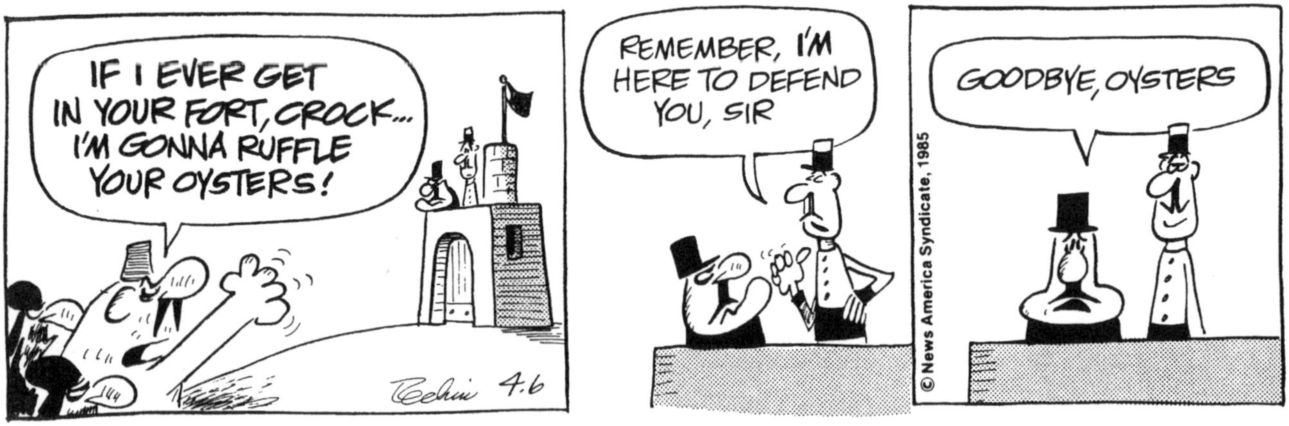
IF I EVER GET IN YOUR FORT, CROCK... I'M GONNA RUFFLE YOUR OYSTERS!
4.6
REMEMBER, I'M HERE TO DEFEND YOU, SIR
© News America Syndicate, 1985
GOODBYE, OYSTERS

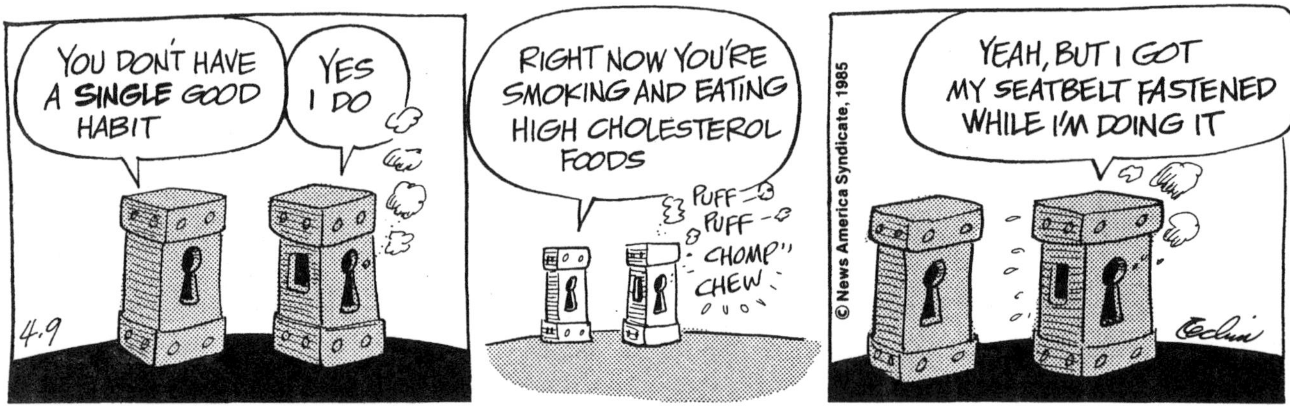
YOU DON'T HAVE A SINGLE GOOD HABIT
YES I DO
4.9
RIGHT NOW YOU'RE SMOKING AND EATING HIGH CHOLESTEROL FOODS
PUFF
PUFF
CHOMP
CHEW
© News America Syndicate, 1985
YEAH, BUT I GOT MY SEATBELT FASTENED WHILE I'M DOING IT

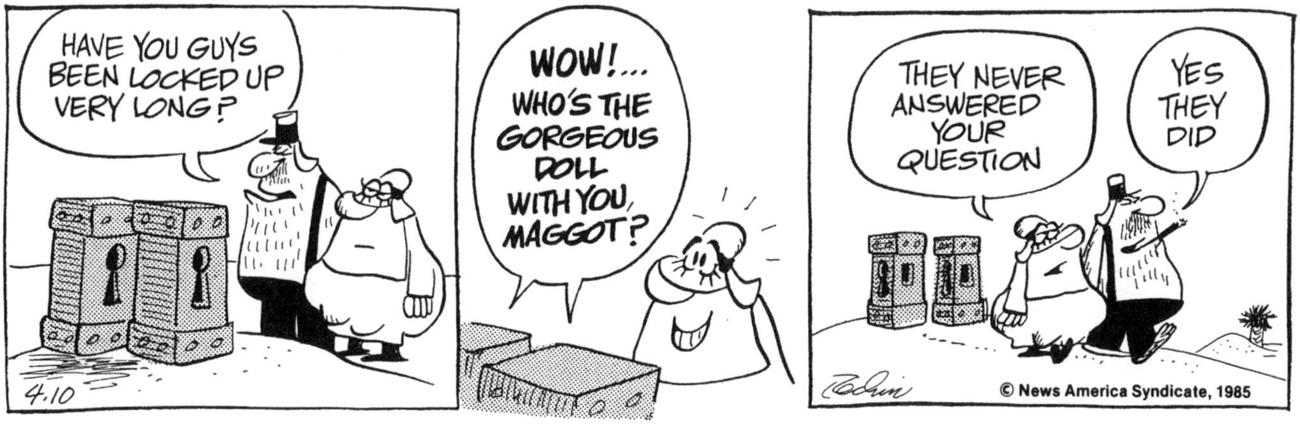
HAVE YOU GUYS BEEN LOCKED UP VERY LONG?
4.10
WOW!... WHO'S THE GORGEOUS DOLL WITH YOU, MAGGOT?
THEY NEVER ANSWERED YOUR QUESTION
YES THEY DID
© News America Syndicate, 1985

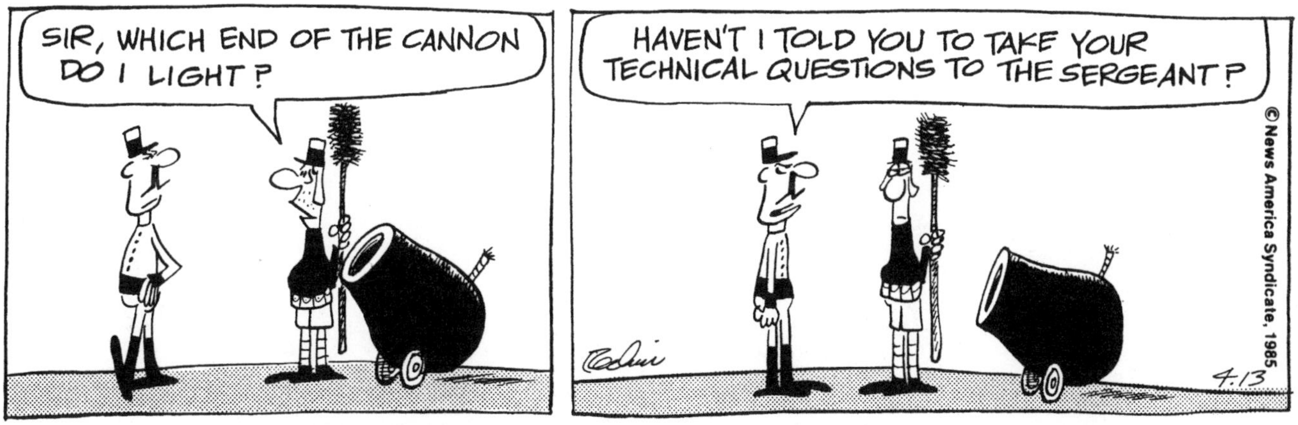
SIR, WHICH END OF THE CANNON DO I LIGHT?
HAVEN'T I TOLD YOU TO TAKE YOUR TECHNICAL QUESTIONS TO THE SERGEANT?
© News America Syndicate, 1985
4.13

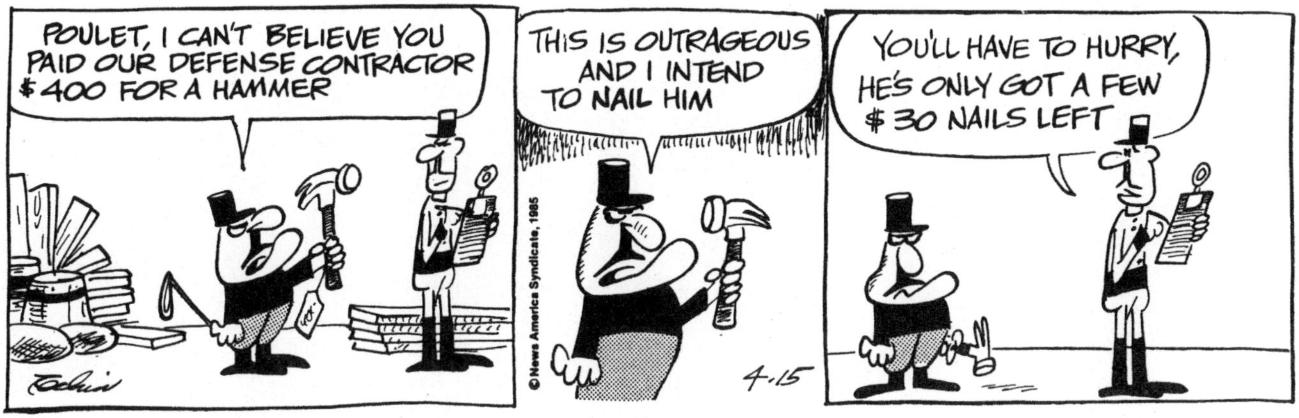
POULET, I CAN'T BELIEVE YOU PAID OUR DEFENSE CONTRACTOR $400 FOR A HAMMER
THIS IS OUTRAGEOUS AND I INTEND TO NAIL HIM
©News America Syndicate, 1985
4.15
YOU'LL HAVE TO HURRY, HE'S ONLY GOT A FEW $30 NAILS LEFT

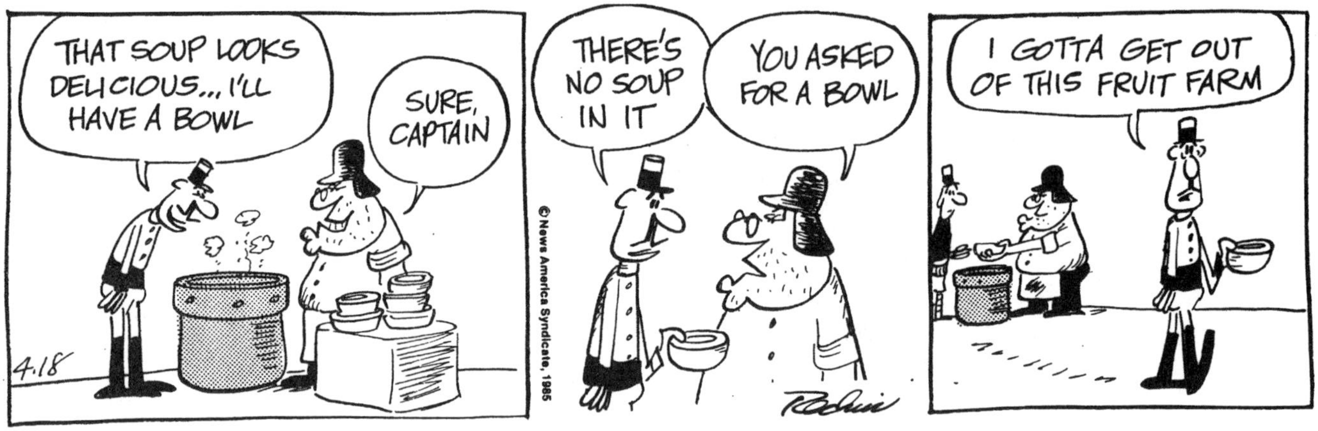
THAT SOUP LOOKS DELICIOUS... I'LL HAVE A BOWL
SURE, CAPTAIN
4.18
© News America Syndicate, 1985
THERE'S NO SOUP IN IT
YOU ASKED FOR A BOWL
I GOTTA GET OUT OF THIS FRUIT FARM

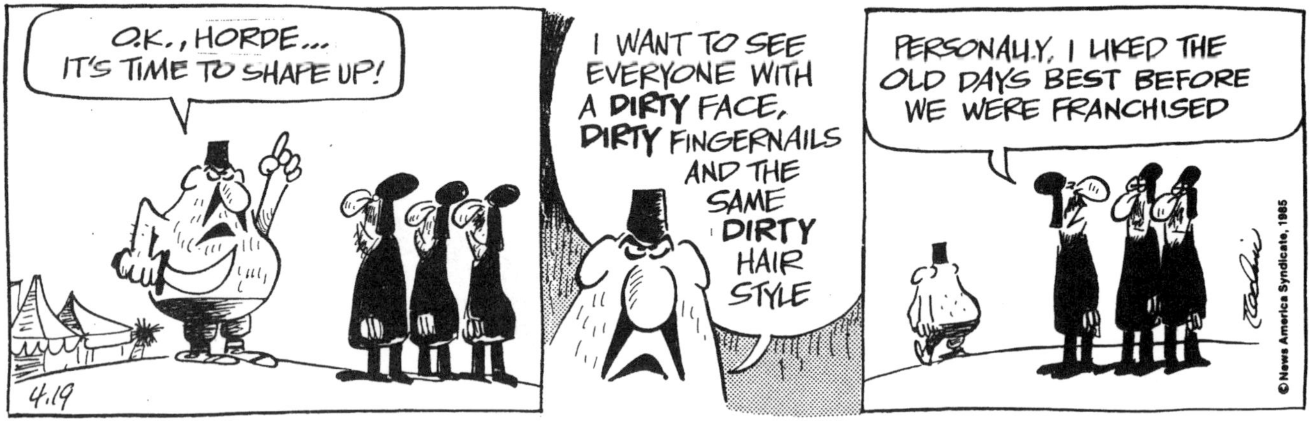
O.K., HORDE... IT'S TIME TO SHAPE UP!
4.19
I WANT TO SEE EVERYONE WITH A DIRTY FACE, DIRTY FINGERNAILS AND THE SAME DIRTY HAIR STYLE
PERSONALLY, I LIKED THE OLD DAYS BEST BEFORE WE WERE FRANCHISED
© News America Syndicate, 1985

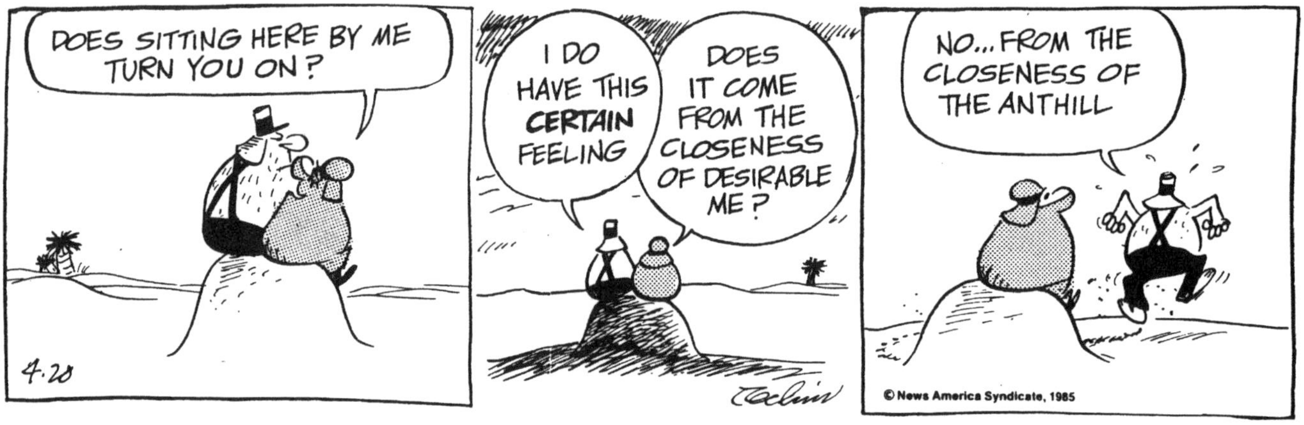
DOES SITTING HERE BY ME TURN YOU ON?
4.20
I DO HAVE THIS CERTAIN FEELING
DOES IT COME FROM THE CLOSENESS OF DESIRABLE ME?
NO... FROM THE CLOSENESS OF THE ANTHILL
© News America Syndicate, 1985

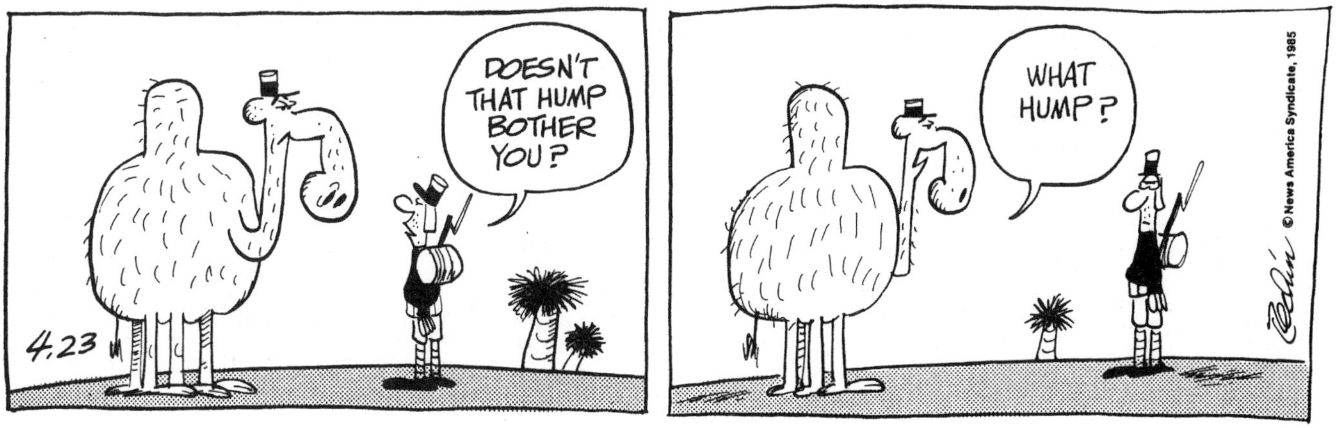
4.23
DOESN'T THAT HUMP BOTHER YOU?
WHAT HUMP?
© News America Syndicate, 1985

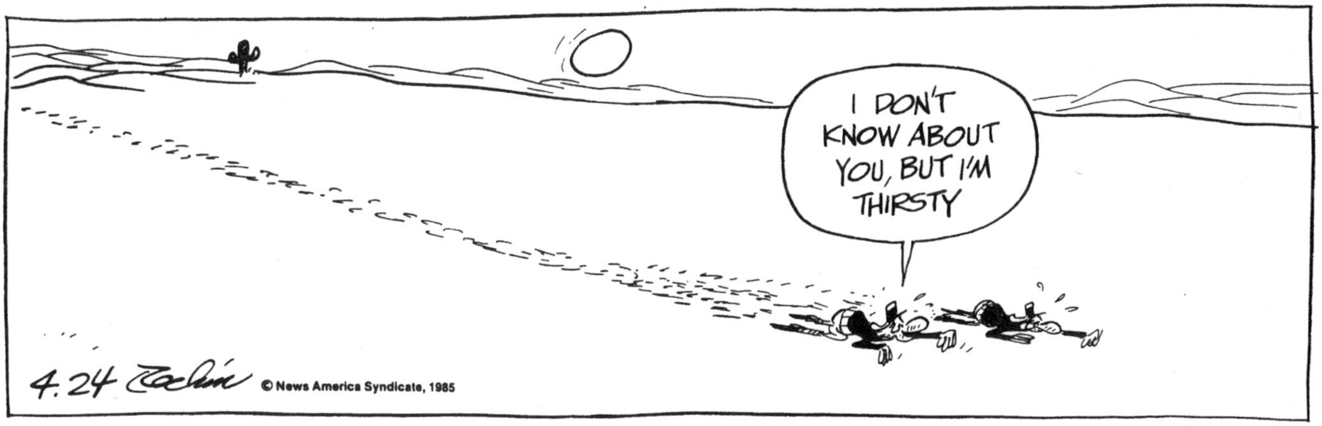
I DON'T KNOW ABOUT YOU, BUT I'M THIRSTY
4.24
© News America Syndicate, 1985

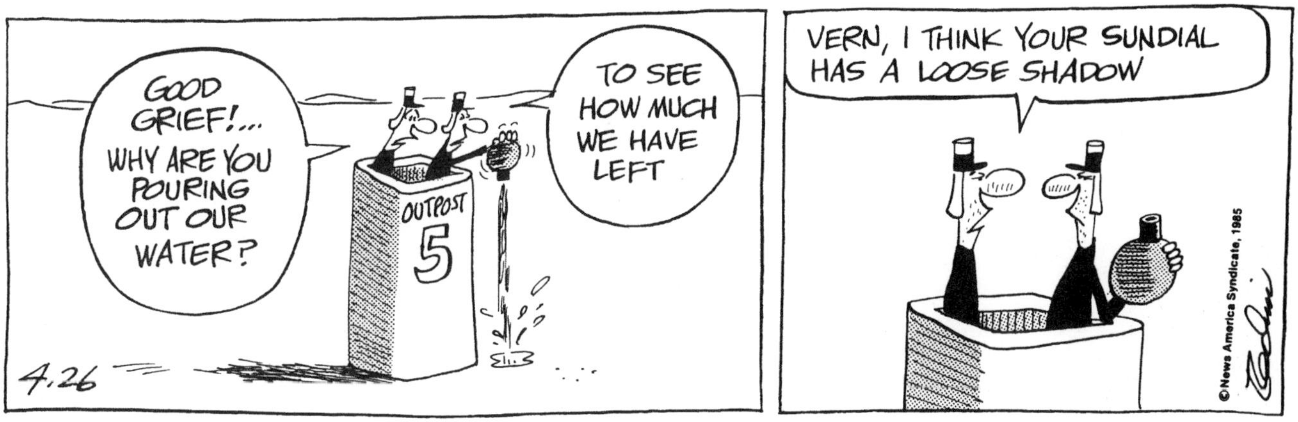
4.26
GOOD GRIEF!... WHY ARE YOU POURING OUT OUR WATER?
TO SEE HOW MUCH WE HAVE LEFT
OUTPOST 5
VERN, I THINK YOUR SUNDIAL HAS A LOOSE SHADOW
© News America Syndicate, 1985

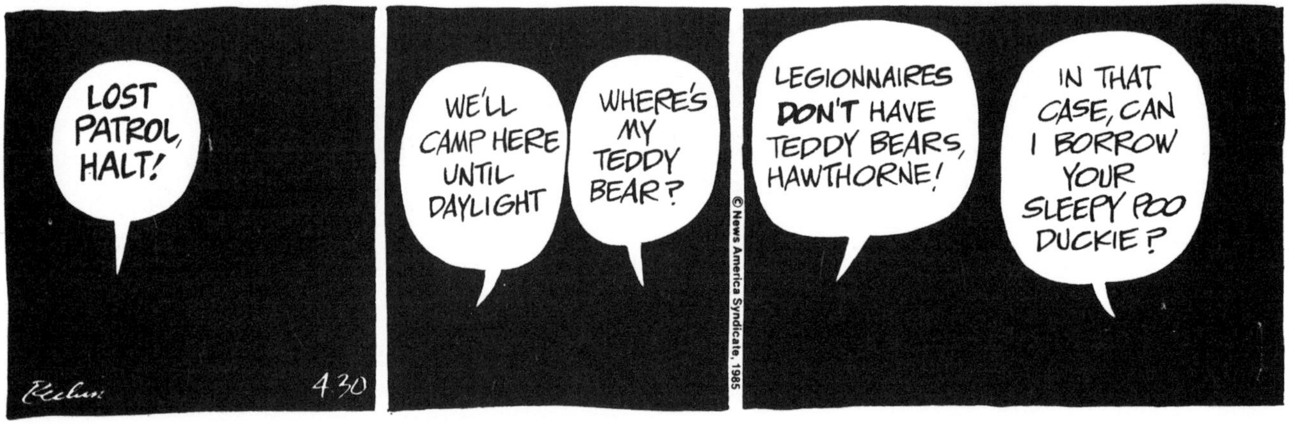
LOST PATROL, HALT!
4·30
WE'LL CAMP HERE UNTIL DAYLIGHT
WHERE'S MY TEDDY BEAR?
© News America Syndicate, 1985
LEGIONNAIRES DON'T HAVE TEDDY BEARS, HAWTHORNE!
IN THAT CASE, CAN I BORROW YOUR SLEEPY POO DUCKIE?

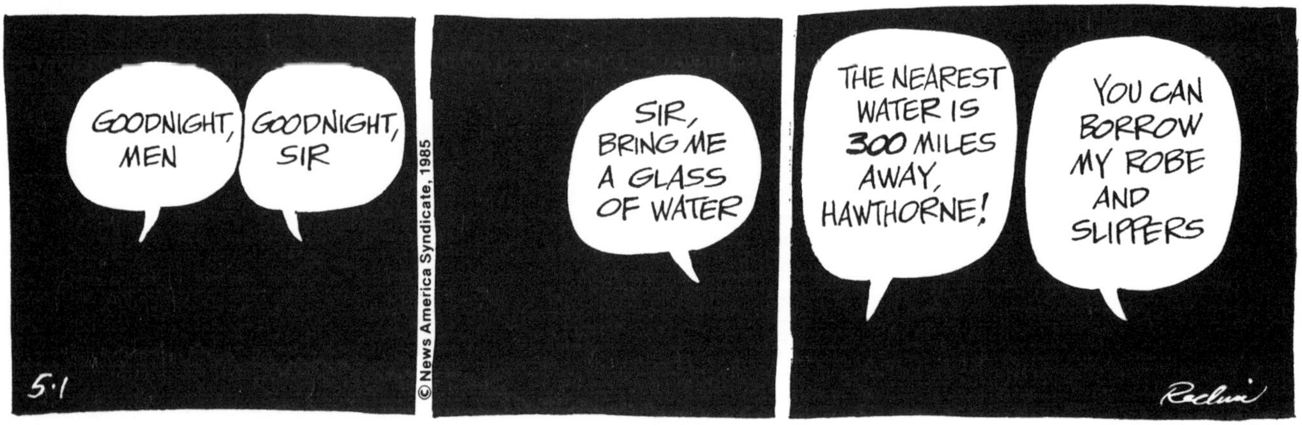
GOODNIGHT, MEN
GOODNIGHT, SIR
5·1
© News America Syndicate, 1985
SIR, BRING ME A GLASS OF WATER
THE NEAREST WATER IS 300 MILES AWAY, HAWTHORNE!
YOU CAN BORROW MY ROBE AND SLIPPERS

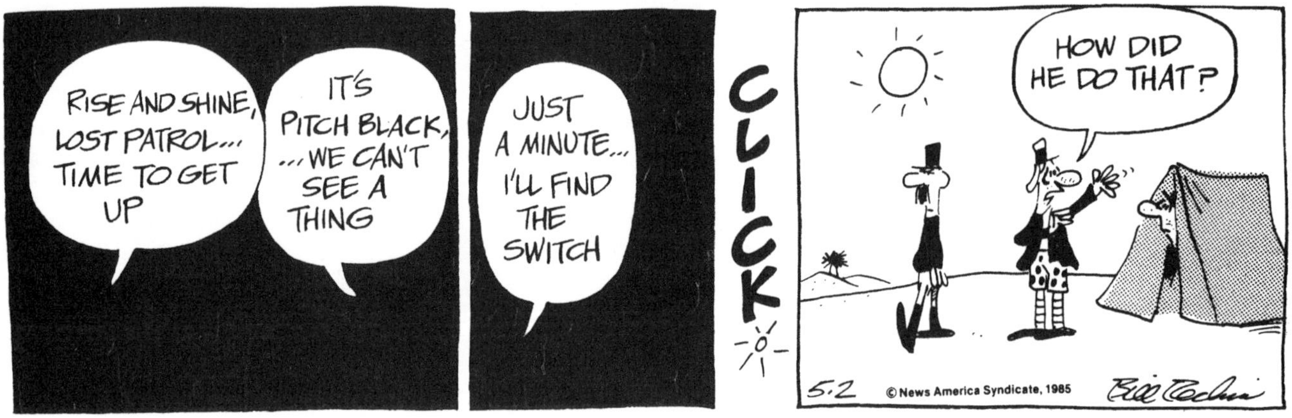
RISE AND SHINE, LOST PATROL... TIME TO GET UP
IT'S PITCH BLACK, ...WE CAN'T SEE A THING
JUST A MINUTE... I'LL FIND THE SWITCH
CLICK
HOW DID HE DO THAT?
5·2
© News America Syndicate, 1985

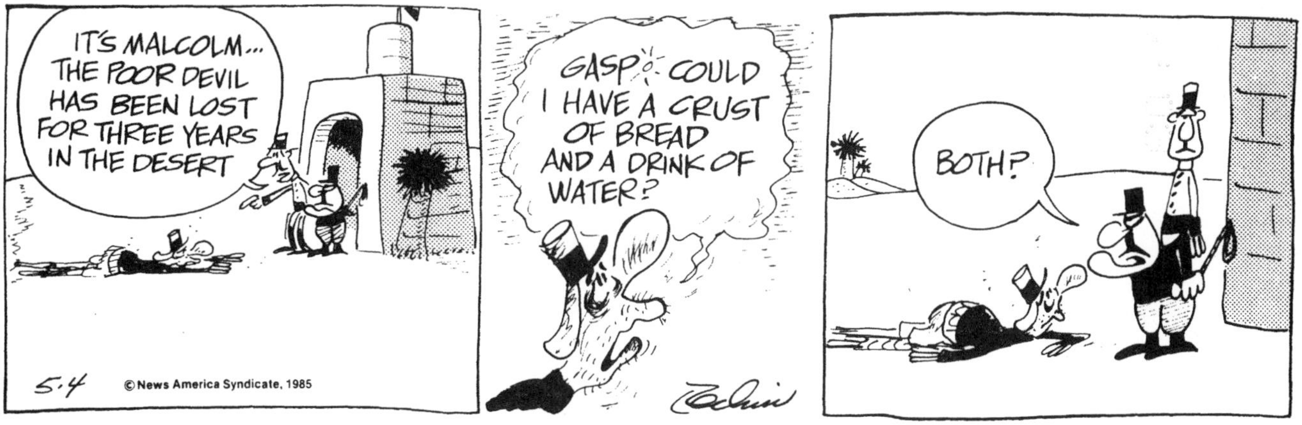
IT'S MALCOLM... THE POOR DEVIL HAS BEEN LOST FOR THREE YEARS IN THE DESERT
GASP COULD I HAVE A CRUST OF BREAD AND A DRINK OF WATER?
BOTH?
5·4
©News America Syndicate, 1985

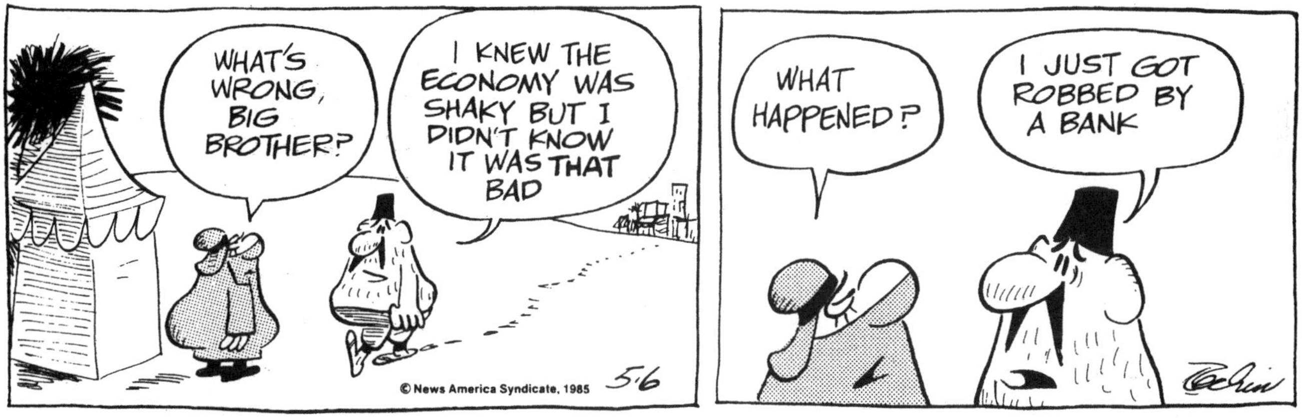
WHAT'S WRONG, BIG BROTHER?
I KNEW THE ECONOMY WAS SHAKY BUT I DIDN'T KNOW IT WAS THAT BAD
WHAT HAPPENED?
I JUST GOT ROBBED BY A BANK
5·6
©News America Syndicate, 1985

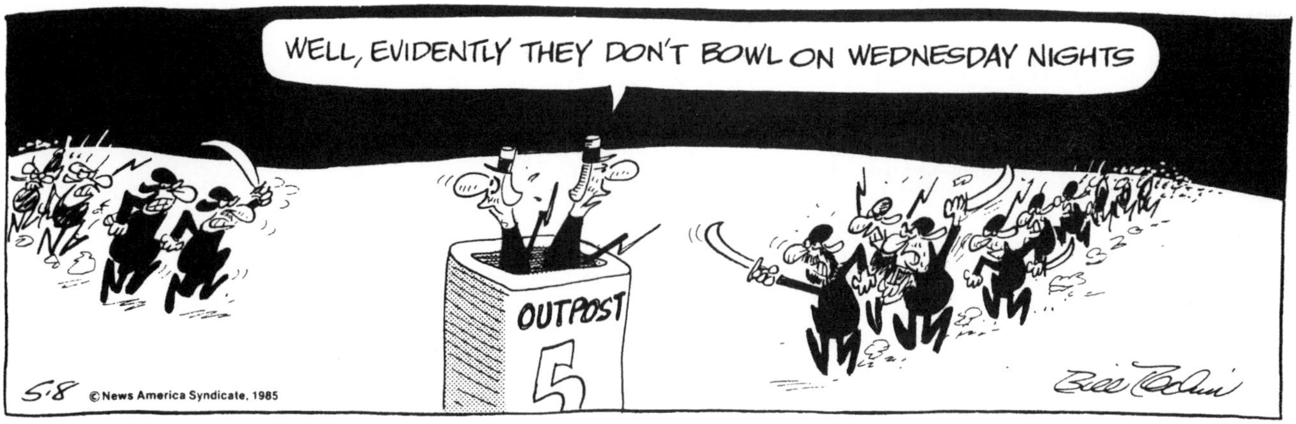
WELL, EVIDENTLY THEY DON'T BOWL ON WEDNESDAY NIGHTS
OUTPOST
5
5·8
©News America Syndicate, 1985

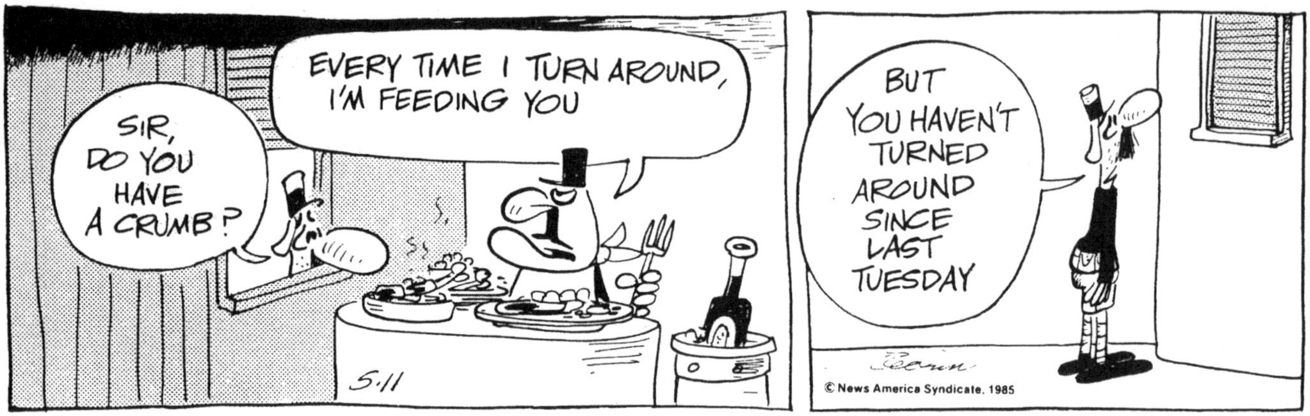
SIR, DO YOU HAVE A CRUMB?
EVERY TIME I TURN AROUND, I'M FEEDING YOU
5.11
BUT YOU HAVEN'T TURNED AROUND SINCE LAST TUESDAY
© News America Syndicate, 1985

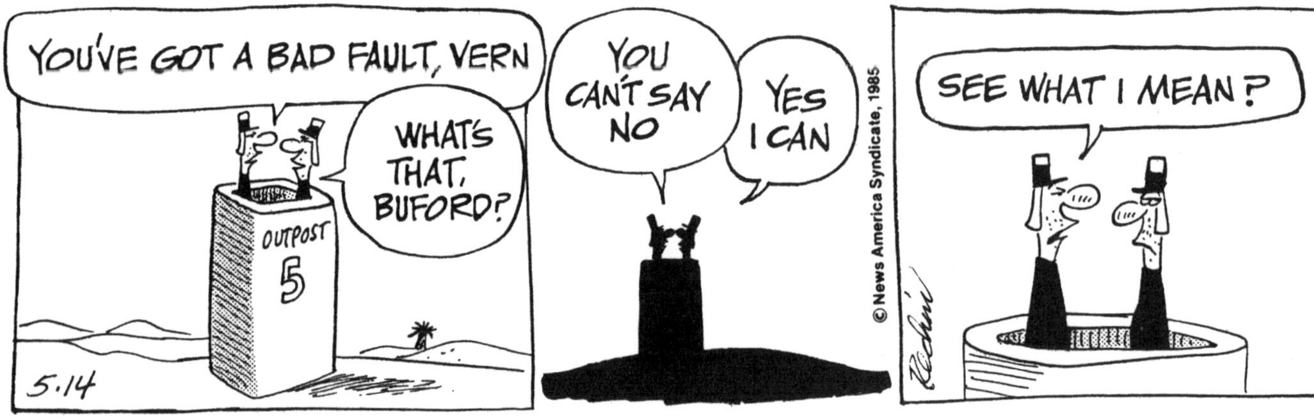
YOU'VE GOT A BAD FAULT, VERN
WHAT'S THAT, BUFORD?
OUTPOST 5
5.14
YOU CAN'T SAY NO
YES I CAN
© News America Syndicate, 1985
SEE WHAT I MEAN?

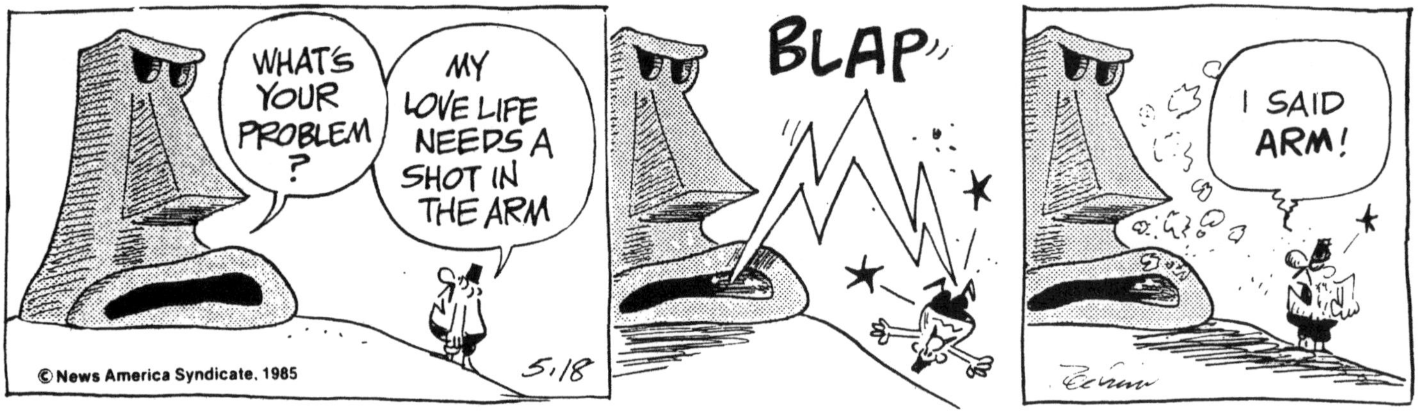
WHAT'S YOUR PROBLEM?
MY LOVE LIFE NEEDS A SHOT IN THE ARM
© News America Syndicate, 1985
5.18
BLAP
I SAID ARM!

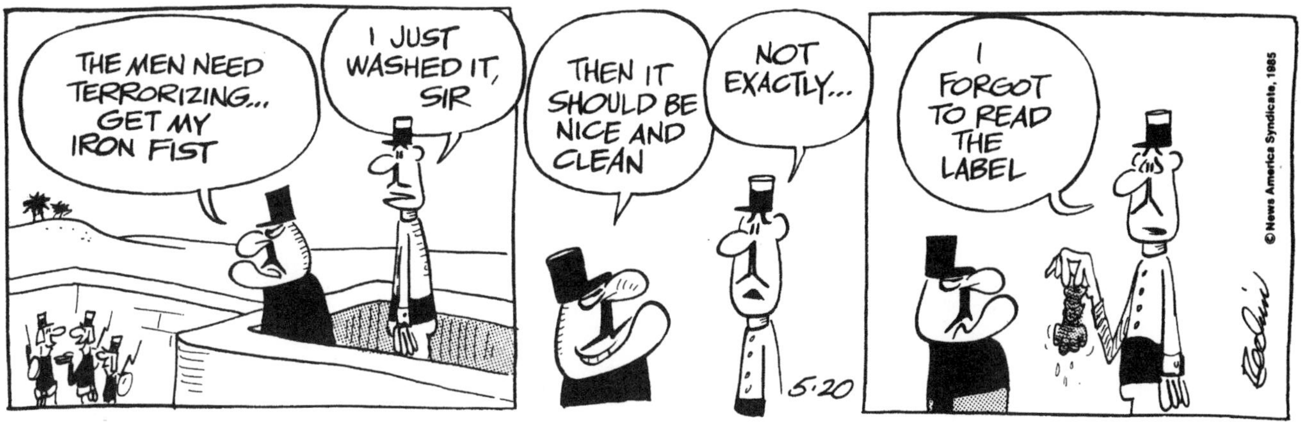
THE MEN NEED TERRORIZING... GET MY IRON FIST
I JUST WASHED IT, SIR
THEN IT SHOULD BE NICE AND CLEAN
NOT EXACTLY...
I FORGOT TO READ THE LABEL
5·20
© News America Syndicate, 1985

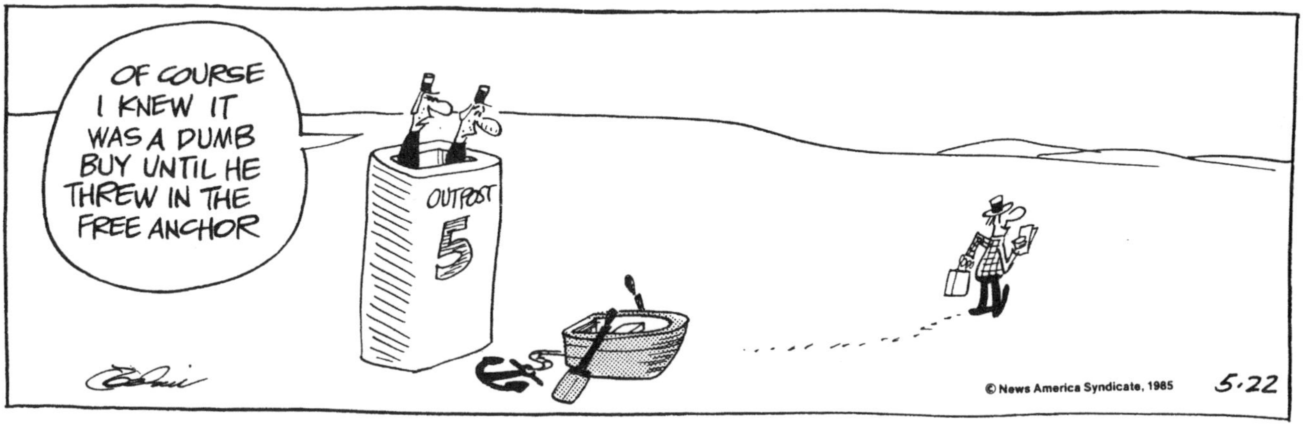
OF COURSE I KNEW IT WAS A DUMB BUY UNTIL HE THREW IN THE FREE ANCHOR
OUTPOST 5
© News America Syndicate, 1985
5·22

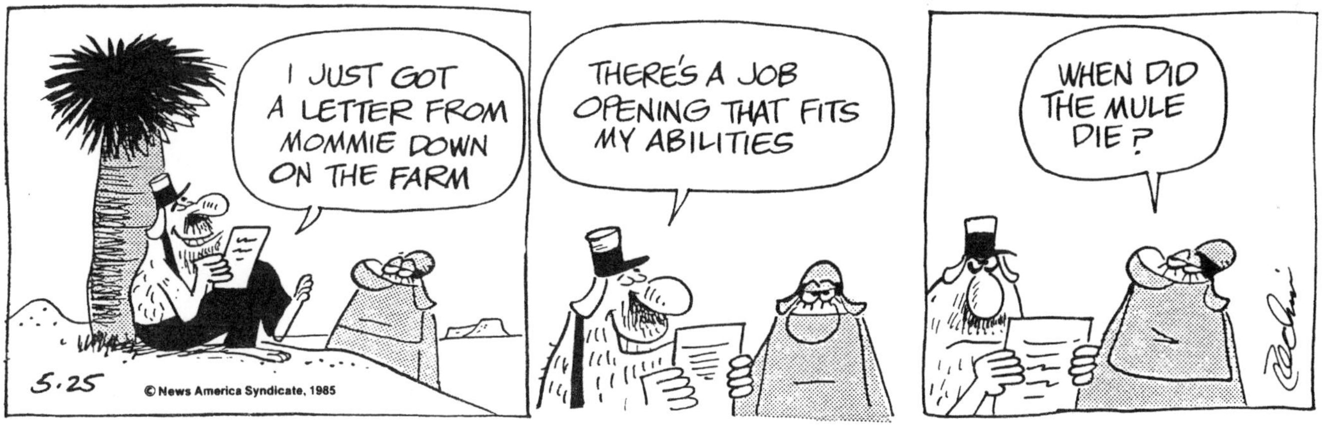
I JUST GOT A LETTER FROM MOMMIE DOWN ON THE FARM
5·25
© News America Syndicate, 1985
THERE'S A JOB OPENING THAT FITS MY ABILITIES
WHEN DID THE MULE DIE?

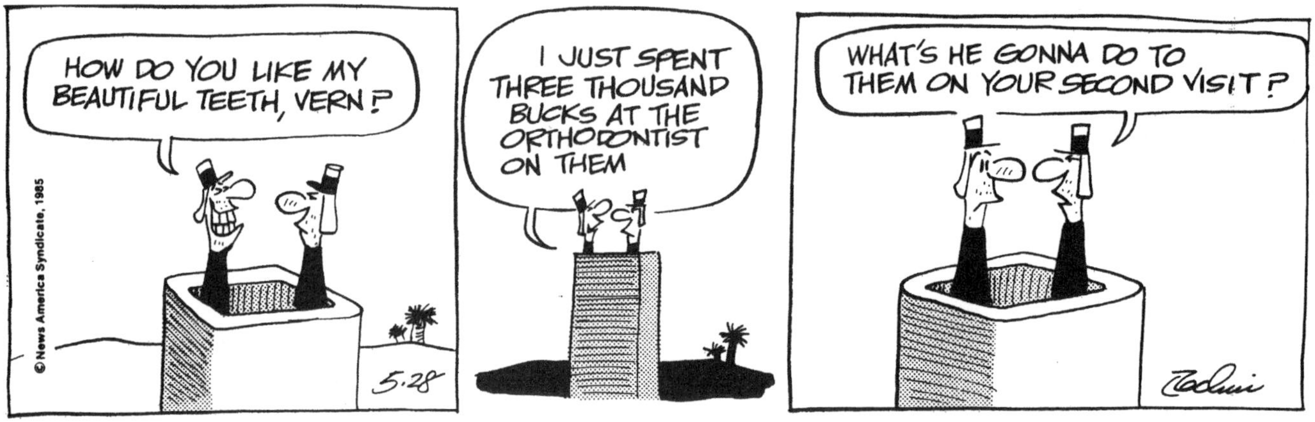
HOW DO YOU LIKE MY BEAUTIFUL TEETH, VERN?
©News America Syndicate, 1985
5-28
I JUST SPENT THREE THOUSAND BUCKS AT THE ORTHODONTIST ON THEM
WHAT'S HE GONNA DO TO THEM ON YOUR SECOND VISIT?

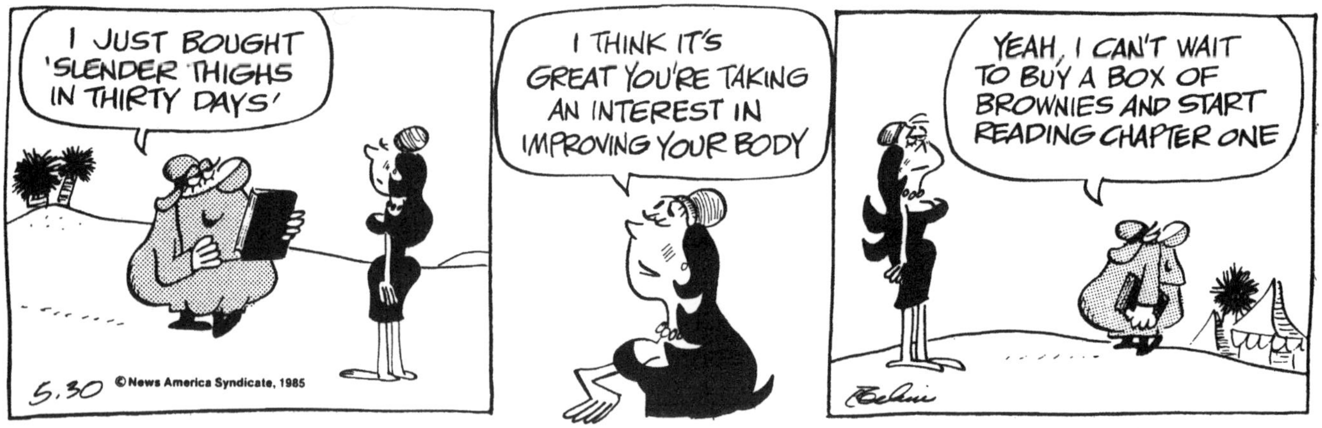
I JUST BOUGHT 'SLENDER THIGHS IN THIRTY DAYS'
5.30 ©News America Syndicate, 1985
I THINK IT'S GREAT YOU'RE TAKING AN INTEREST IN IMPROVING YOUR BODY
YEAH, I CAN'T WAIT TO BUY A BOX OF BROWNIES AND START READING CHAPTER ONE

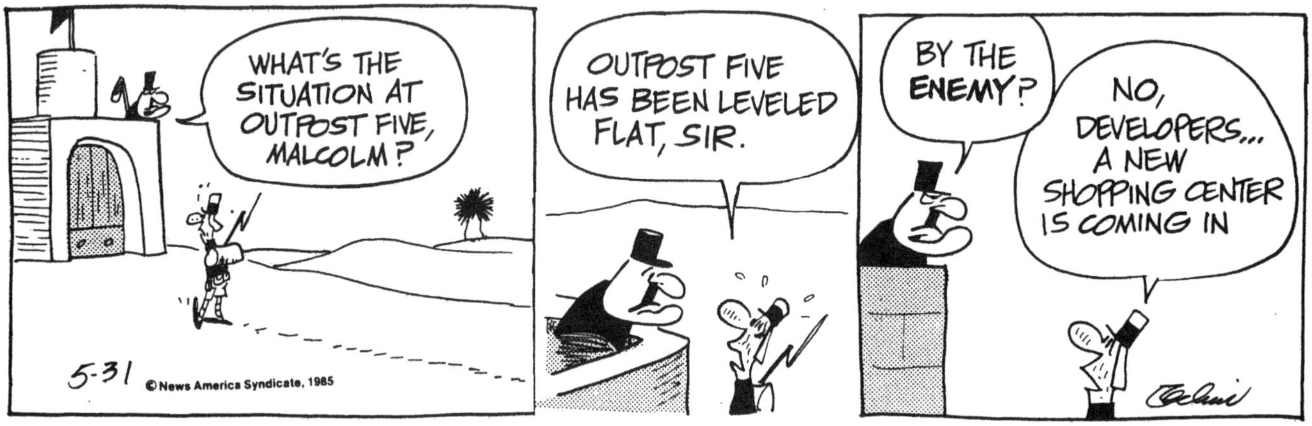
WHAT'S THE SITUATION AT OUTPOST FIVE, MALCOLM?
5-31 ©News America Syndicate, 1985
OUTPOST FIVE HAS BEEN LEVELED FLAT, SIR.
BY THE ENEMY?
NO, DEVELOPERS... A NEW SHOPPING CENTER IS COMING IN

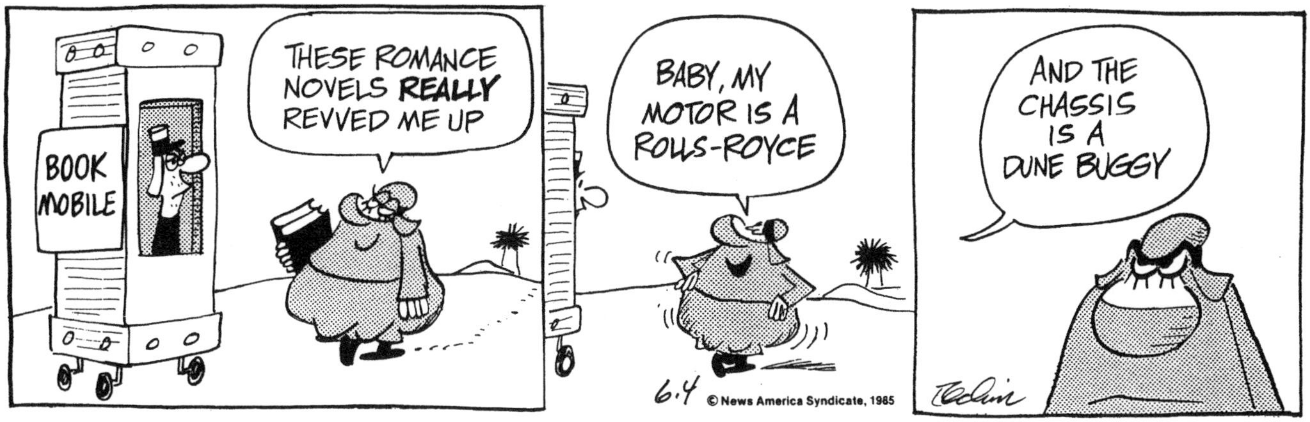
BOOK MOBILE
THESE ROMANCE NOVELS **REALLY** REVVED ME UP
BABY, MY MOTOR IS A ROLLS-ROYCE
AND THE CHASSIS IS A DUNE BUGGY
6·4
© News America Syndicate, 1985

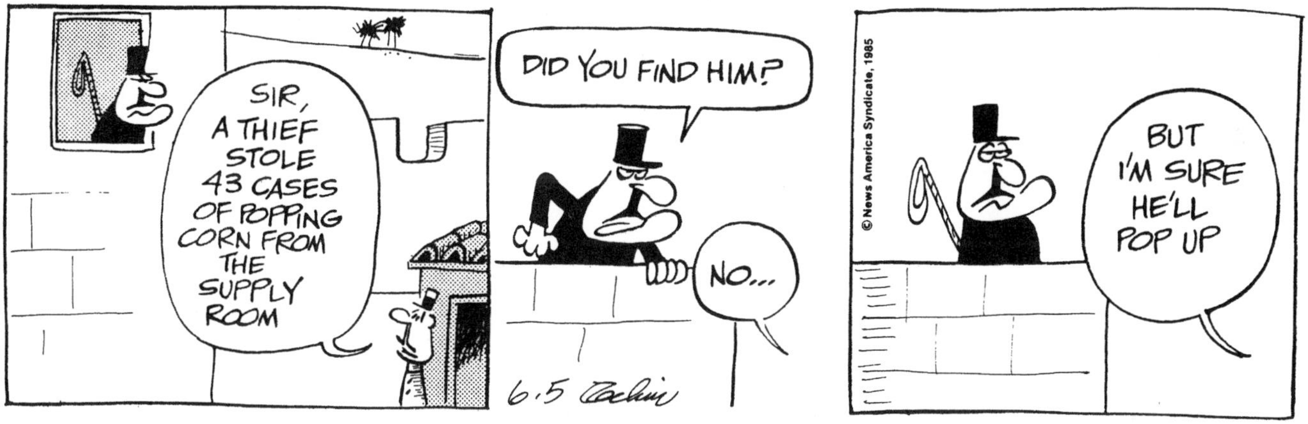
SIR, A THIEF STOLE 43 CASES OF POPPING CORN FROM THE SUPPLY ROOM
DID YOU FIND HIM?
NO...
6·5
© News America Syndicate, 1985
BUT I'M SURE HE'LL POP UP

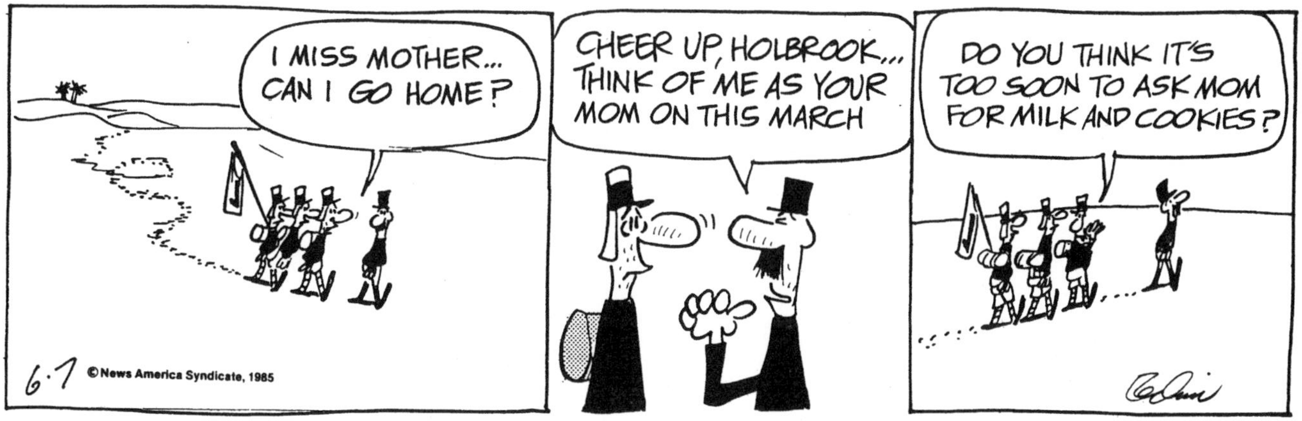
I MISS MOTHER... CAN I GO HOME?
6·7
© News America Syndicate, 1985
CHEER UP, HOLBROOK... THINK OF ME AS YOUR MOM ON THIS MARCH
DO YOU THINK IT'S TOO SOON TO ASK MOM FOR MILK AND COOKIES?

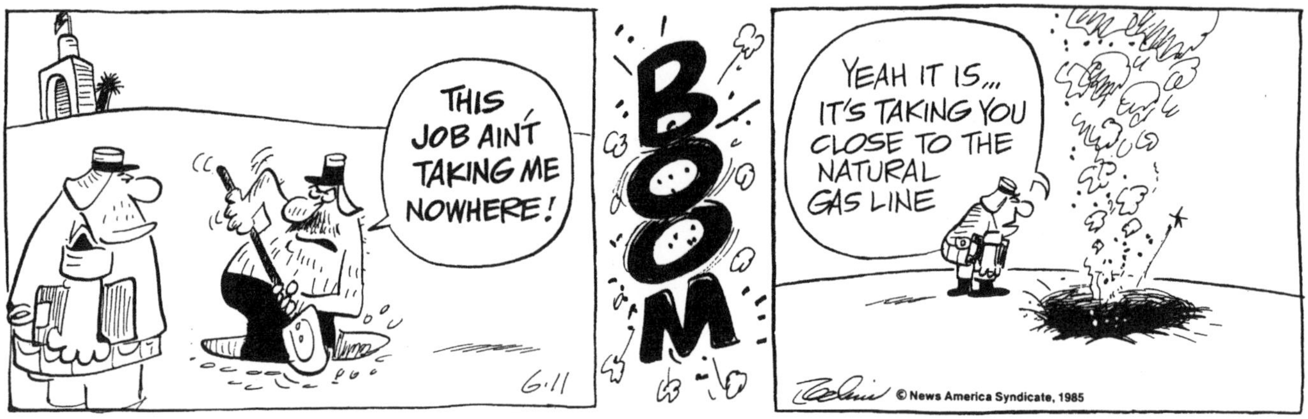
THIS JOB AIN'T TAKING ME NOWHERE!
6·11
BOOM
YEAH IT IS... IT'S TAKING YOU CLOSE TO THE NATURAL GAS LINE
© News America Syndicate, 1985

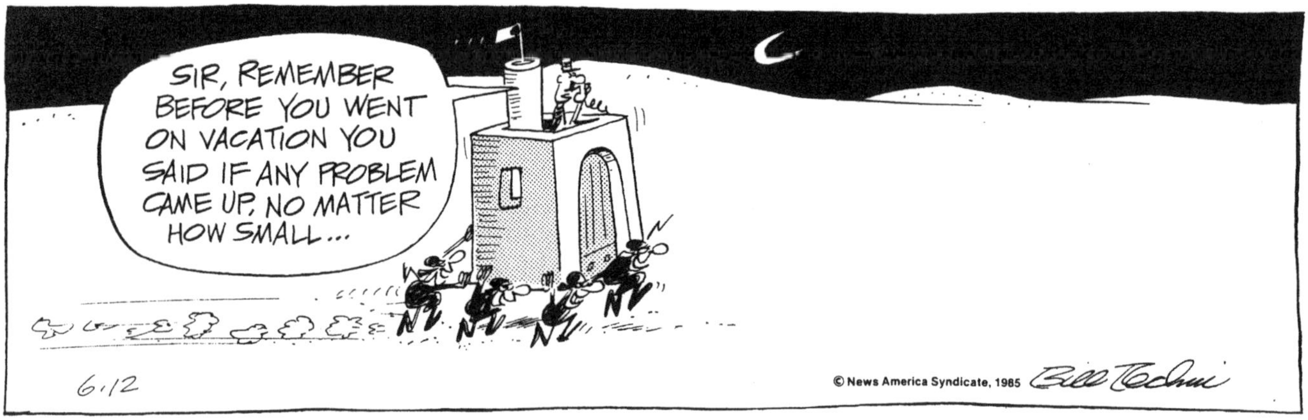
SIR, REMEMBER BEFORE YOU WENT ON VACATION YOU SAID IF ANY PROBLEM CAME UP, NO MATTER HOW SMALL...
6·12
© News America Syndicate, 1985
Bill Rechin

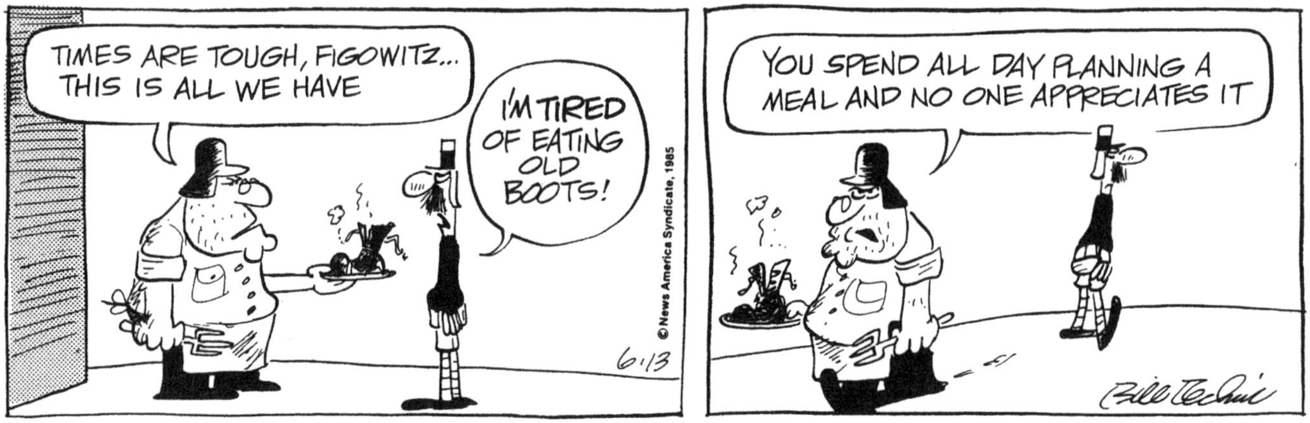
TIMES ARE TOUGH, FIGOWITZ... THIS IS ALL WE HAVE
I'M TIRED OF EATING OLD BOOTS!
© News America Syndicate, 1985
6·13
YOU SPEND ALL DAY PLANNING A MEAL AND NO ONE APPRECIATES IT
Bill Rechin

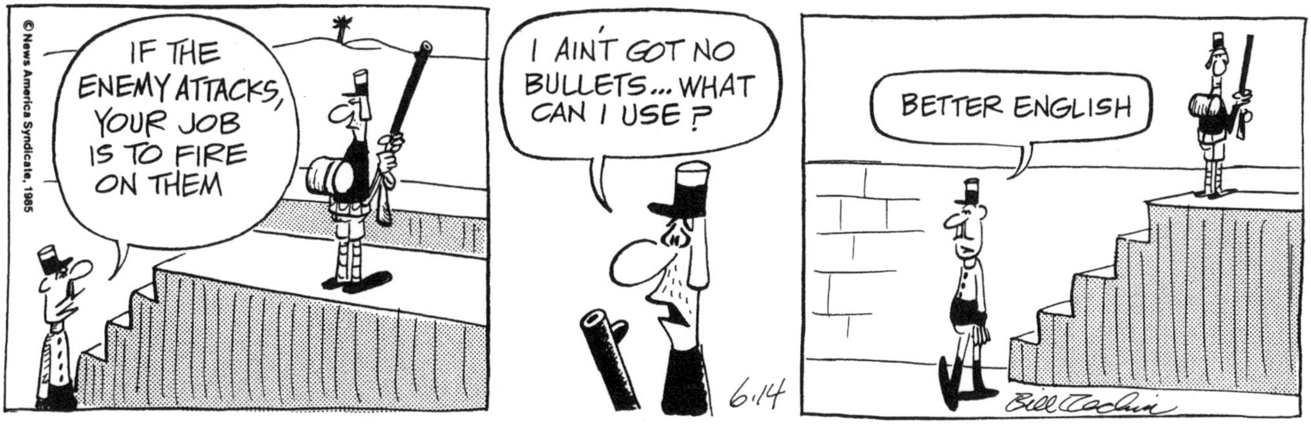
© News America Syndicate, 1985
IF THE ENEMY ATTACKS, YOUR JOB IS TO FIRE ON THEM
I AIN'T GOT NO BULLETS... WHAT CAN I USE?
6.14
BETTER ENGLISH

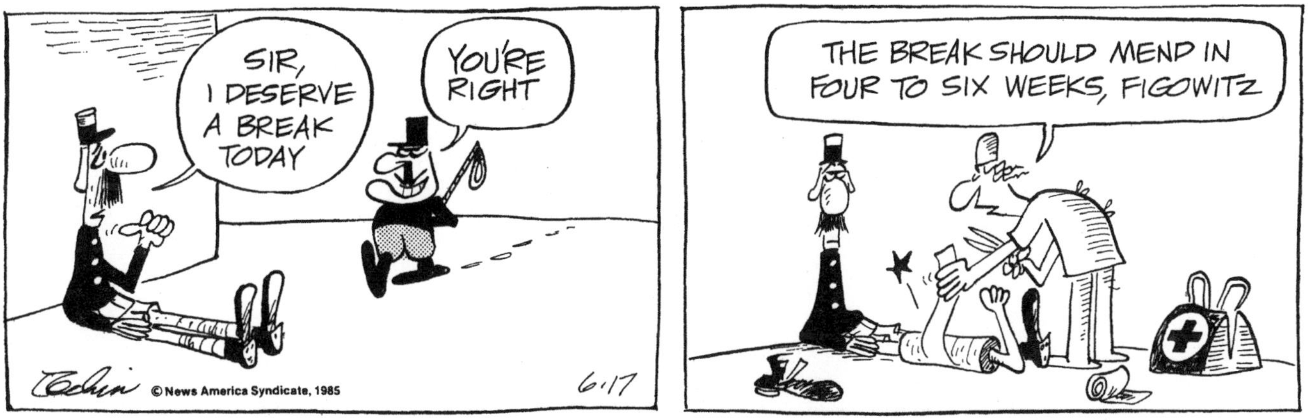
SIR, I DESERVE A BREAK TODAY
YOU'RE RIGHT
© News America Syndicate, 1985
6.17
THE BREAK SHOULD MEND IN FOUR TO SIX WEEKS, FIGOWITZ

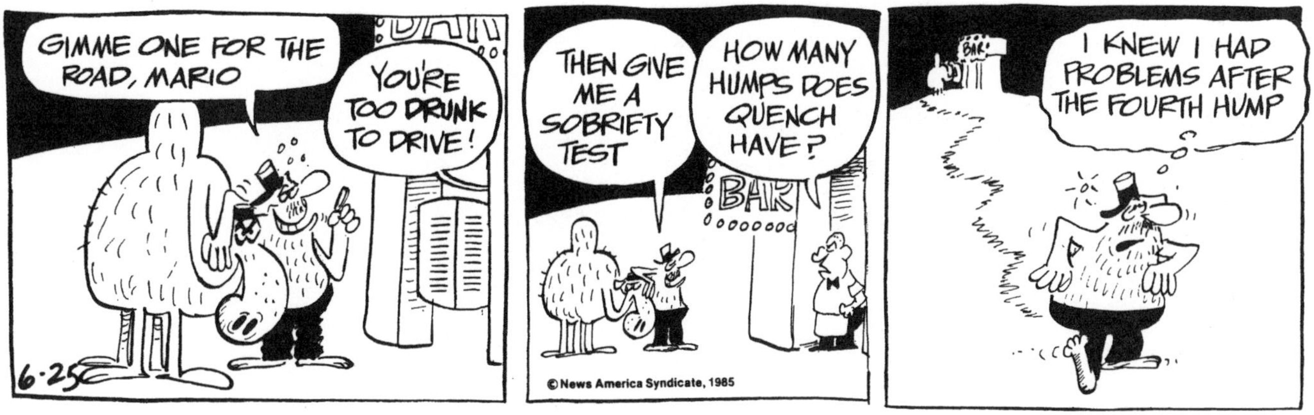
GIMME ONE FOR THE ROAD, MARIO
YOU'RE TOO DRUNK TO DRIVE!
6.25
THEN GIVE ME A SOBRIETY TEST
HOW MANY HUMPS DOES QUENCH HAVE?
BAR
© News America Syndicate, 1985
I KNEW I HAD PROBLEMS AFTER THE FOURTH HUMP

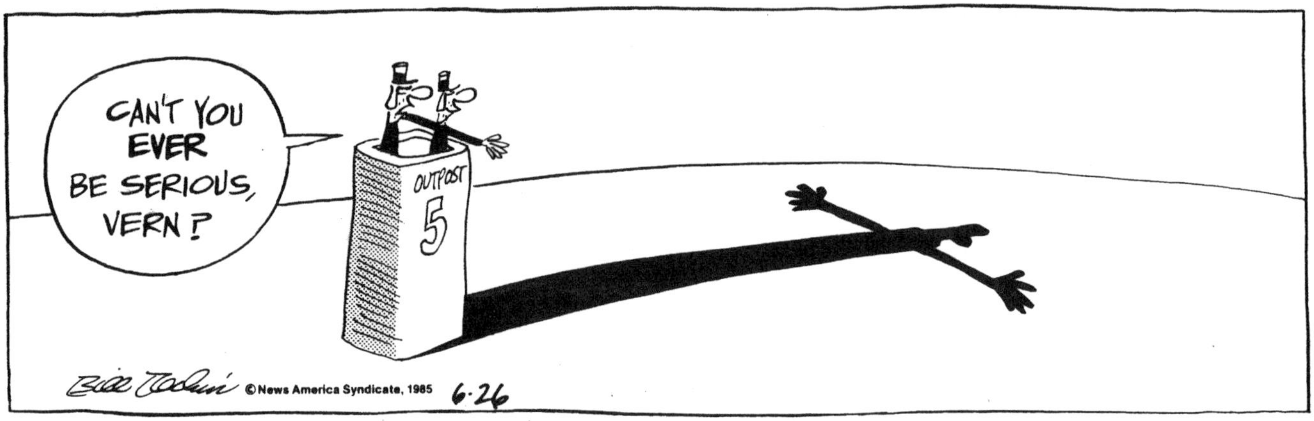
CAN'T YOU EVER BE SERIOUS, VERN?
OUTPOST 5
©News America Syndicate, 1985
6·26

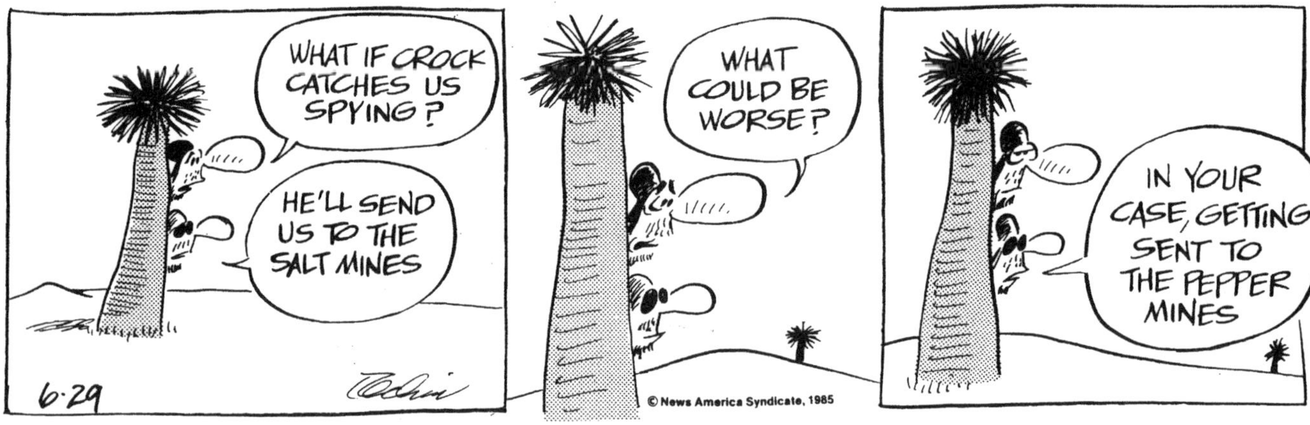
WHAT IF CROCK CATCHES US SPYING?
HE'LL SEND US TO THE SALT MINES
6·29
WHAT COULD BE WORSE?
©News America Syndicate, 1985
IN YOUR CASE, GETTING SENT TO THE PEPPER MINES

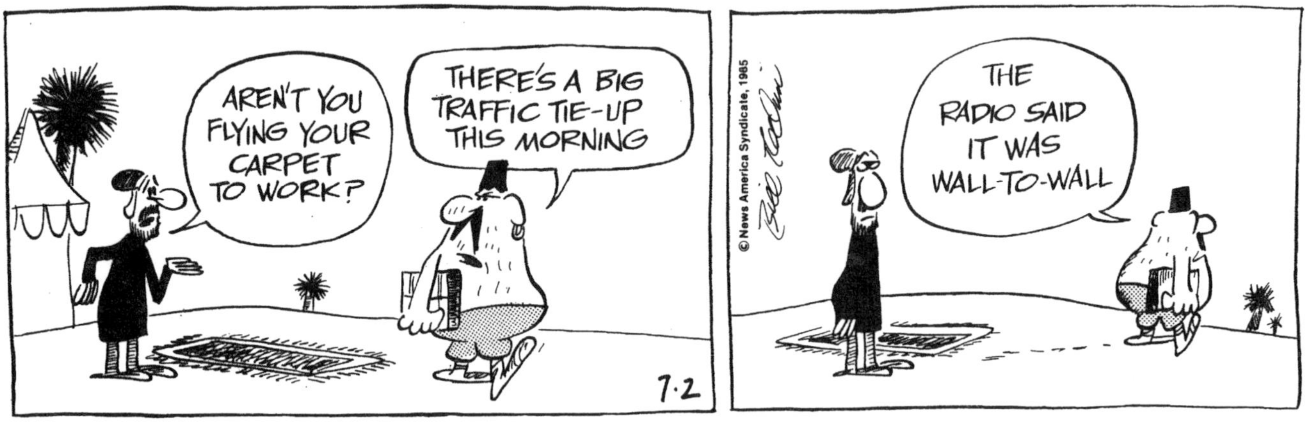
AREN'T YOU FLYING YOUR CARPET TO WORK?
THERE'S A BIG TRAFFIC TIE-UP THIS MORNING
7·2
©News America Syndicate, 1985
THE RADIO SAID IT WAS WALL-TO-WALL

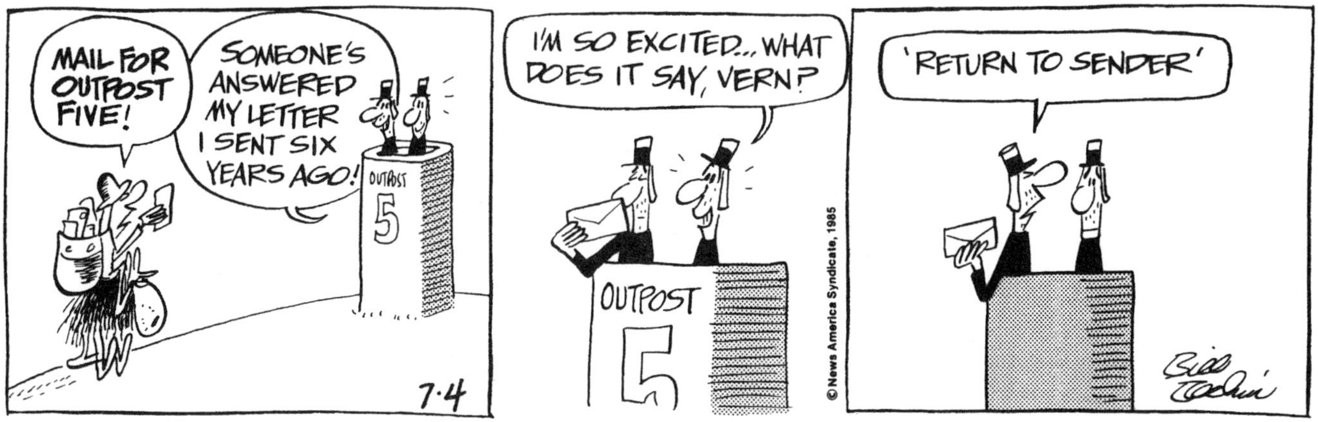
MAIL FOR OUTPOST FIVE!
SOMEONE'S ANSWERED MY LETTER I SENT SIX YEARS AGO!
OUTPOST 5
7·4
I'M SO EXCITED... WHAT DOES IT SAY, VERN?
OUTPOST 5
© News America Syndicate, 1985
'RETURN TO SENDER'

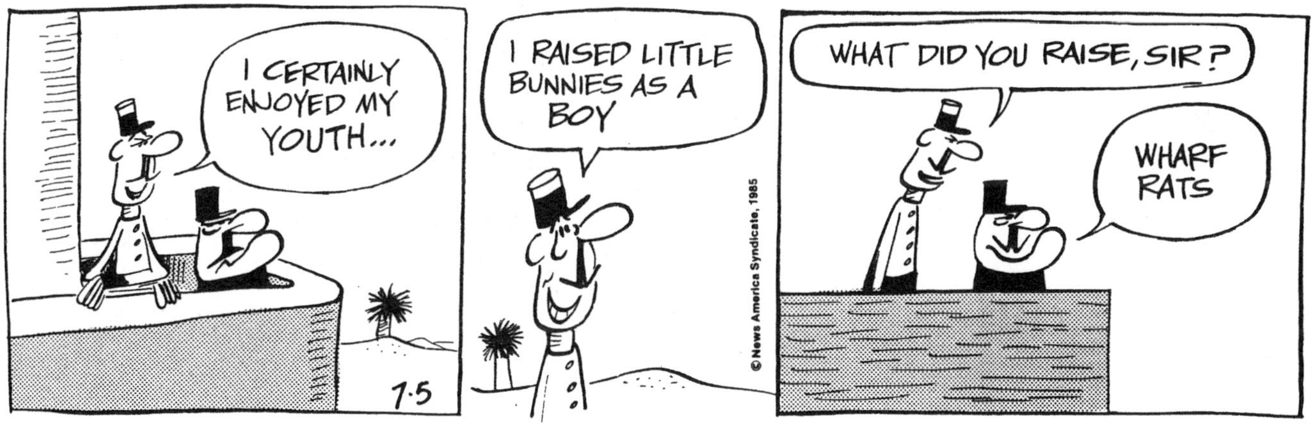
I CERTAINLY ENJOYED MY YOUTH...
7·5
I RAISED LITTLE BUNNIES AS A BOY
© News America Syndicate, 1985
WHAT DID YOU RAISE, SIR?
WHARF RATS

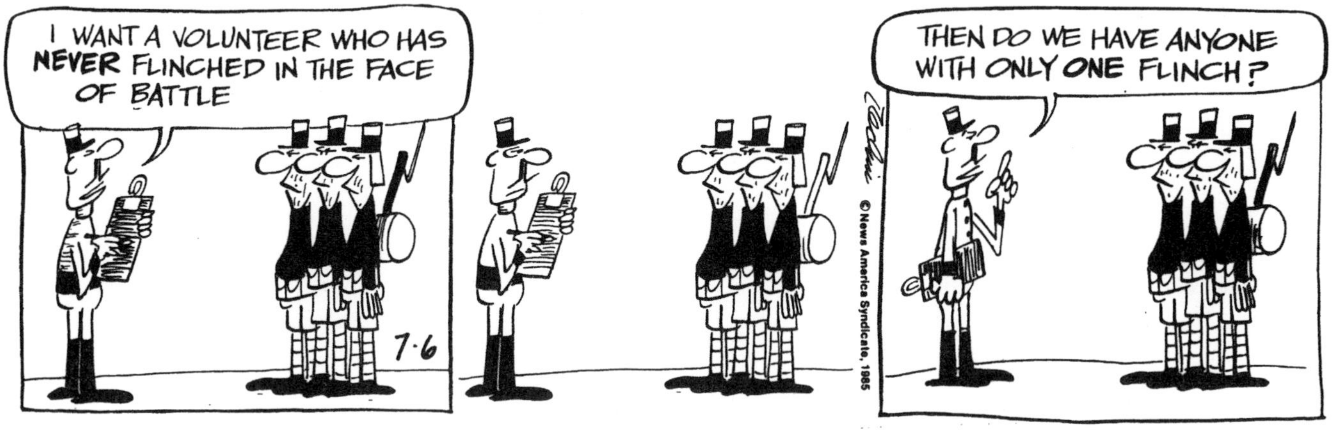
I WANT A VOLUNTEER WHO HAS NEVER FLINCHED IN THE FACE OF BATTLE
7·6
© News America Syndicate, 1985
THEN DO WE HAVE ANYONE WITH ONLY ONE FLINCH?

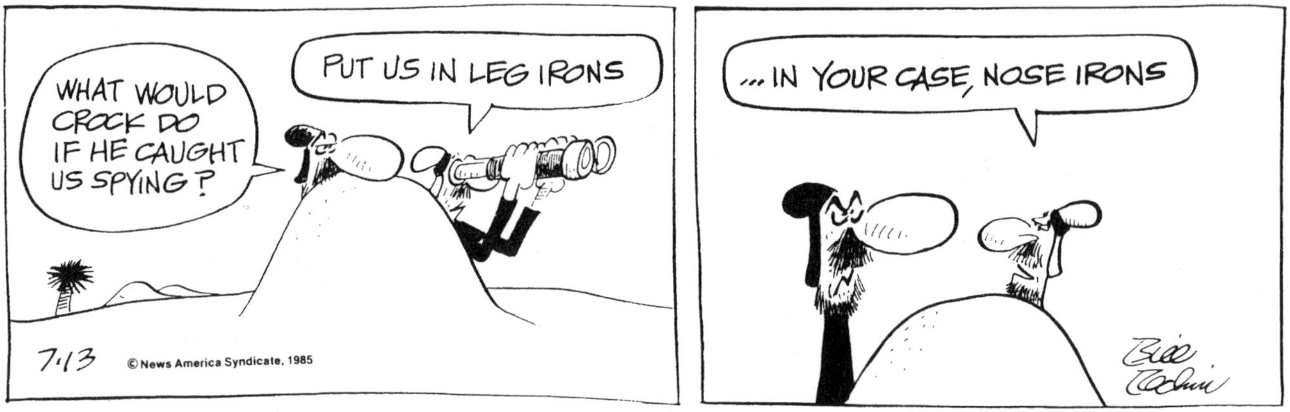
WHAT WOULD CROCK DO IF HE CAUGHT US SPYING?
PUT US IN LEG IRONS
...IN YOUR CASE, NOSE IRONS
7.13
© News America Syndicate, 1985

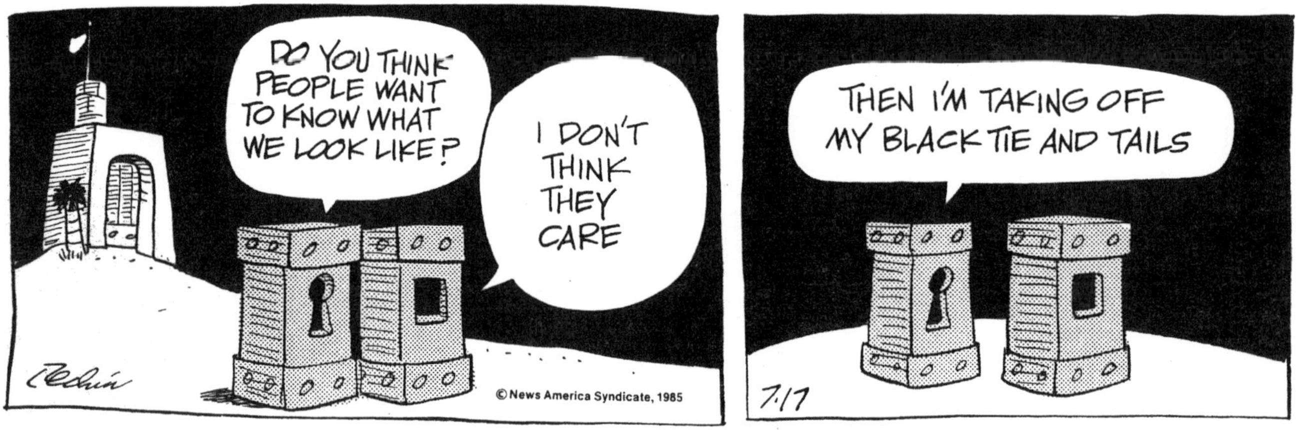
DO YOU THINK PEOPLE WANT TO KNOW WHAT WE LOOK LIKE?
I DON'T THINK THEY CARE
THEN I'M TAKING OFF MY BLACK TIE AND TAILS
© News America Syndicate, 1985
7.17

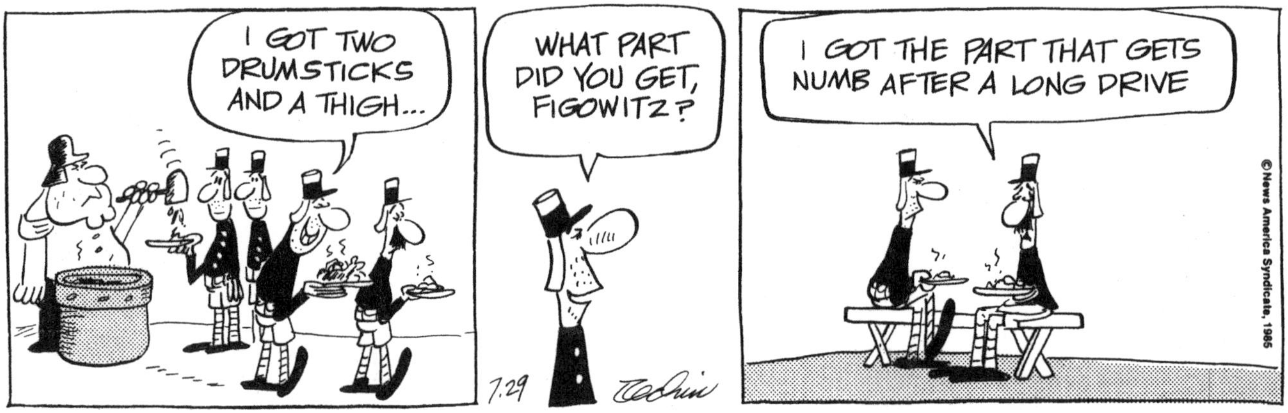
I GOT TWO DRUMSTICKS AND A THIGH...
WHAT PART DID YOU GET, FIGOWITZ?
I GOT THE PART THAT GETS NUMB AFTER A LONG DRIVE
7.29
© News America Syndicate, 1985

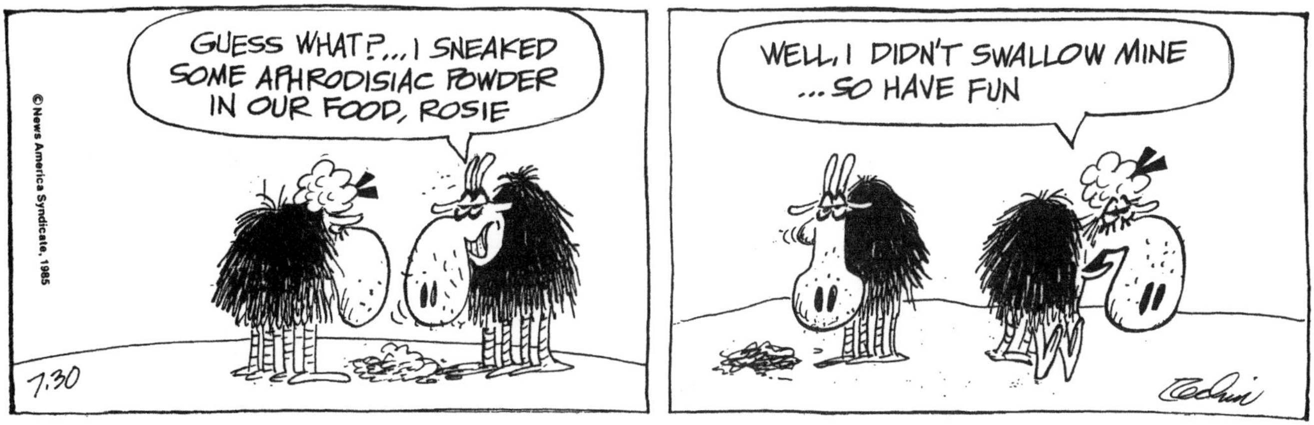
© News America Syndicate, 1985
GUESS WHAT?...I SNEAKED SOME APHRODISIAC POWDER IN OUR FOOD, ROSIE
7.30
WELL, I DIDN'T SWALLOW MINE ...SO HAVE FUN

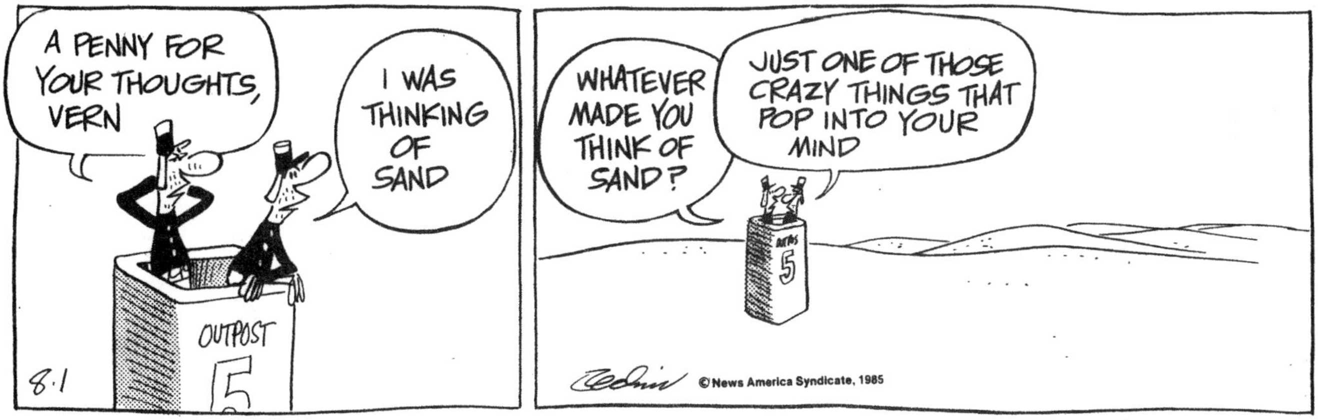
A PENNY FOR YOUR THOUGHTS, VERN
I WAS THINKING OF SAND
OUTPOST
5
8.1
WHATEVER MADE YOU THINK OF SAND?
JUST ONE OF THOSE CRAZY THINGS THAT POP INTO YOUR MIND
5
©News America Syndicate, 1985

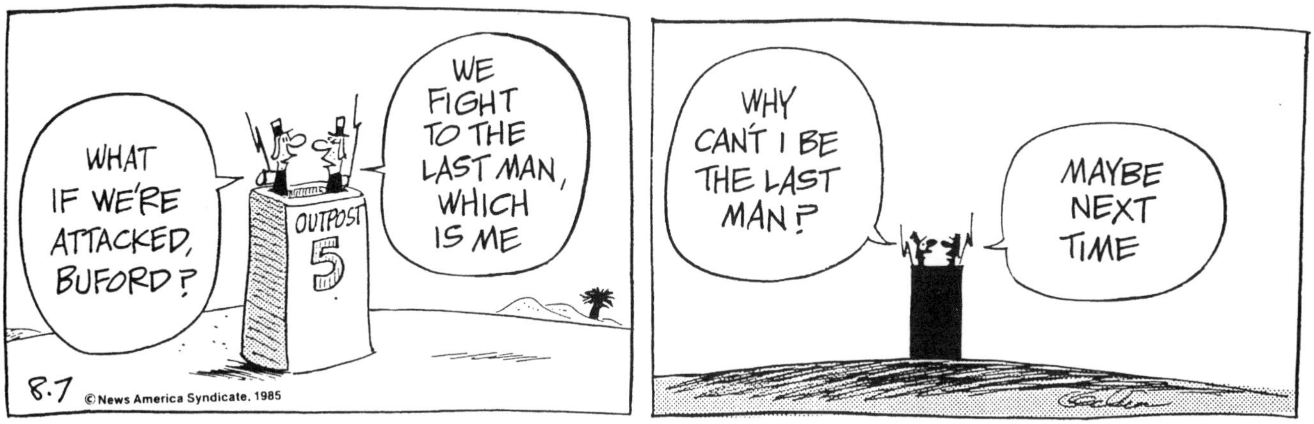
WHAT IF WE'RE ATTACKED, BUFORD?
WE FIGHT TO THE LAST MAN, WHICH IS ME
OUTPOST
5
8.7
© News America Syndicate, 1985
WHY CAN'T I BE THE LAST MAN?
MAYBE NEXT TIME

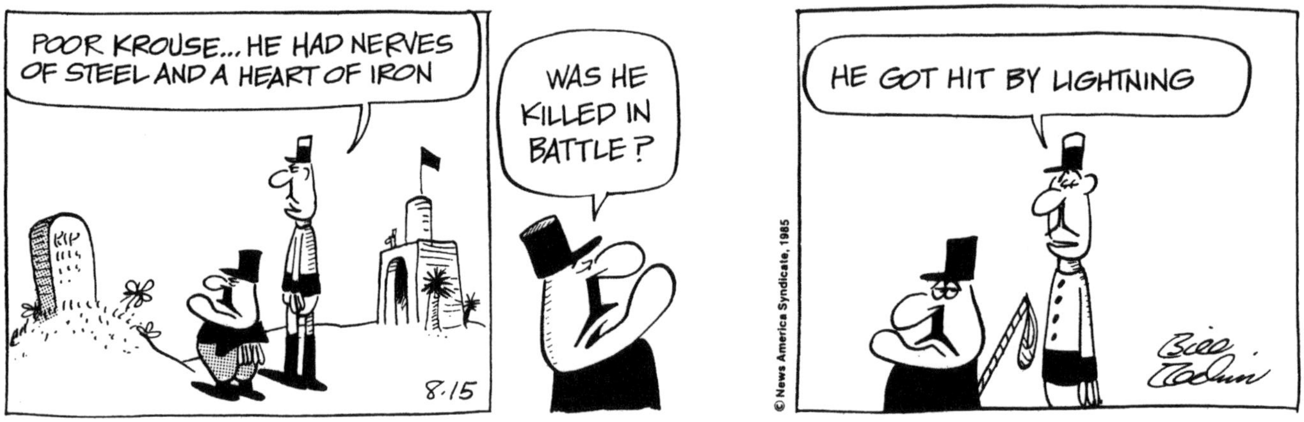
POOR KROUSE... HE HAD NERVES OF STEEL AND A HEART OF IRON
RIP
8.15
WAS HE KILLED IN BATTLE?
HE GOT HIT BY LIGHTNING
Bill Rechin
© News America Syndicate, 1985

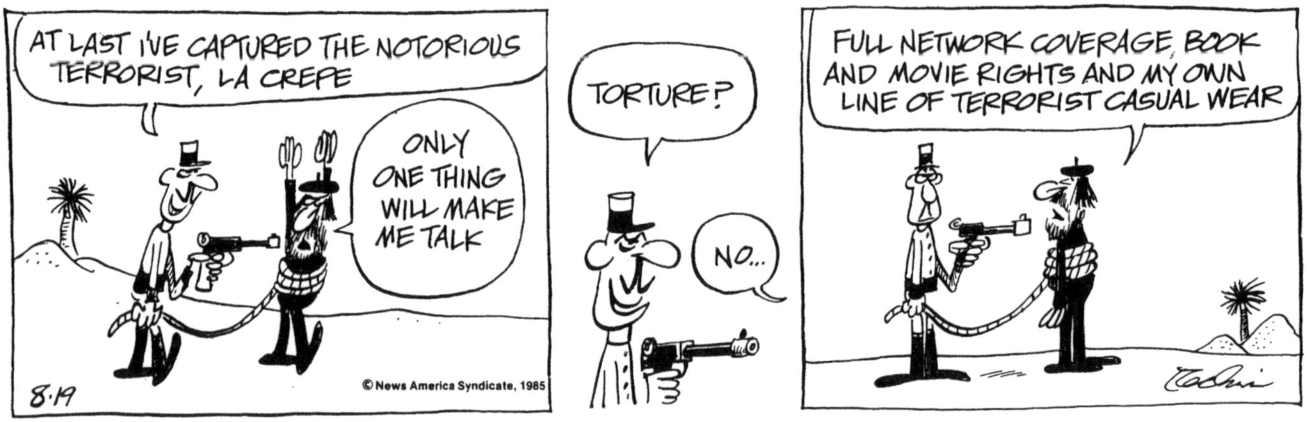
AT LAST I'VE CAPTURED THE NOTORIOUS TERRORIST, LA CREPE
ONLY ONE THING WILL MAKE ME TALK
8.19
© News America Syndicate, 1985
TORTURE?
NO...
FULL NETWORK COVERAGE, BOOK AND MOVIE RIGHTS AND MY OWN LINE OF TERRORIST CASUAL WEAR

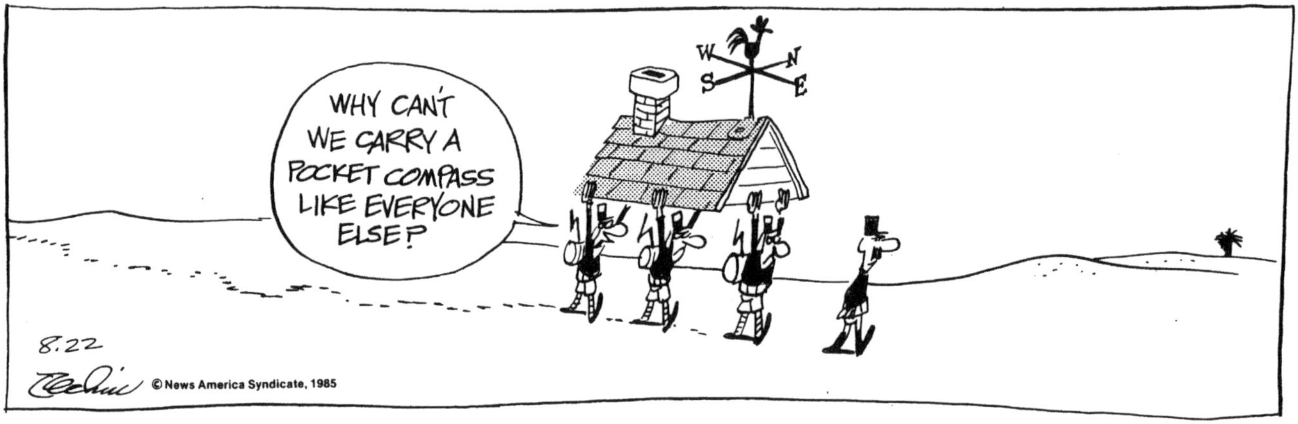
W
N
S
E
WHY CAN'T WE CARRY A POCKET COMPASS LIKE EVERYONE ELSE?
8.22
© News America Syndicate, 1985

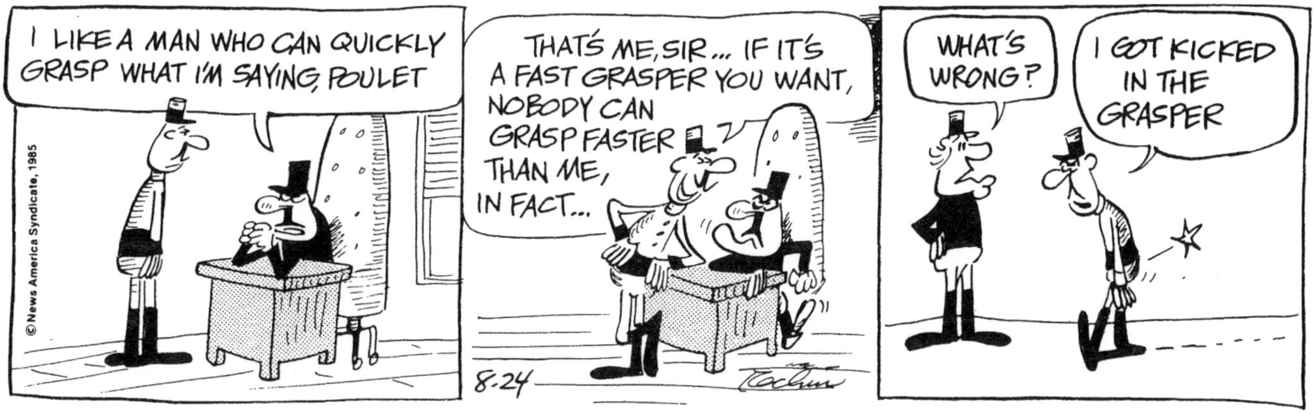
I LIKE A MAN WHO CAN QUICKLY GRASP WHAT I'M SAYING, POULET
© News America Syndicate, 1985
THAT'S ME, SIR... IF IT'S A FAST GRASPER YOU WANT, NOBODY CAN GRASP FASTER THAN ME, IN FACT...
8-24
WHAT'S WRONG?
I GOT KICKED IN THE GRASPER

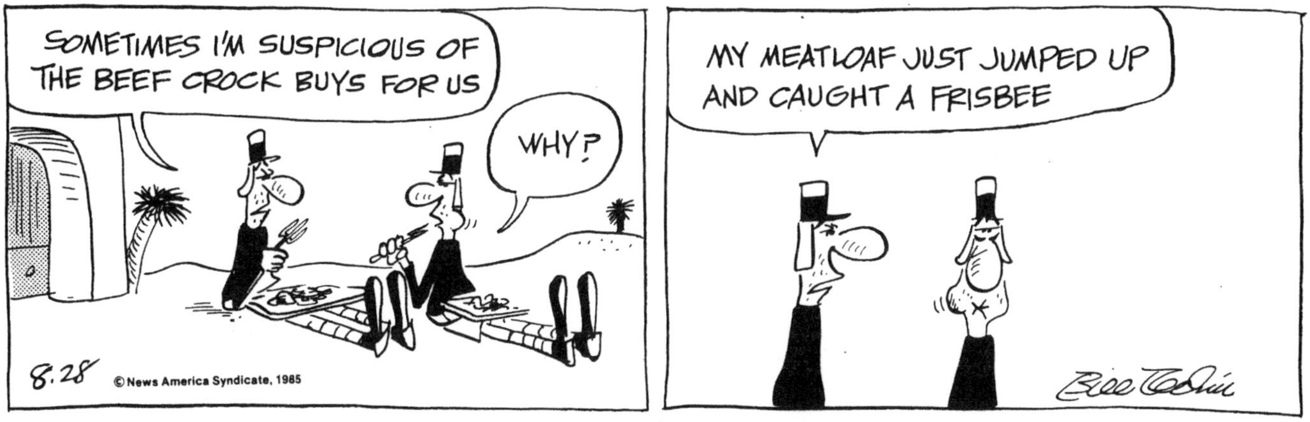
SOMETIMES I'M SUSPICIOUS OF THE BEEF CROCK BUYS FOR US
WHY?
8.28
© News America Syndicate, 1985
MY MEATLOAF JUST JUMPED UP AND CAUGHT A FRISBEE

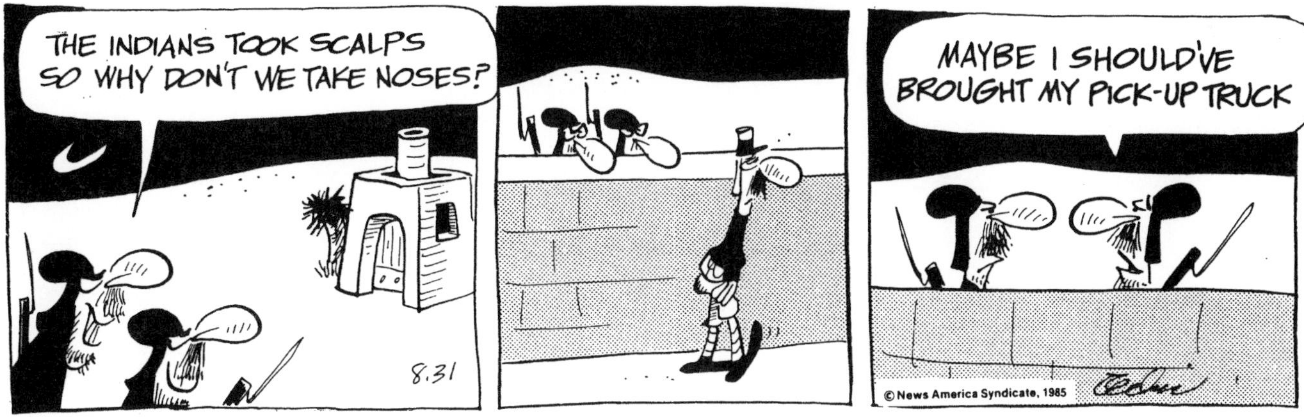
THE INDIANS TOOK SCALPS SO WHY DON'T WE TAKE NOSES?
8.31
MAYBE I SHOULD'VE BROUGHT MY PICK-UP TRUCK
© News America Syndicate, 1985

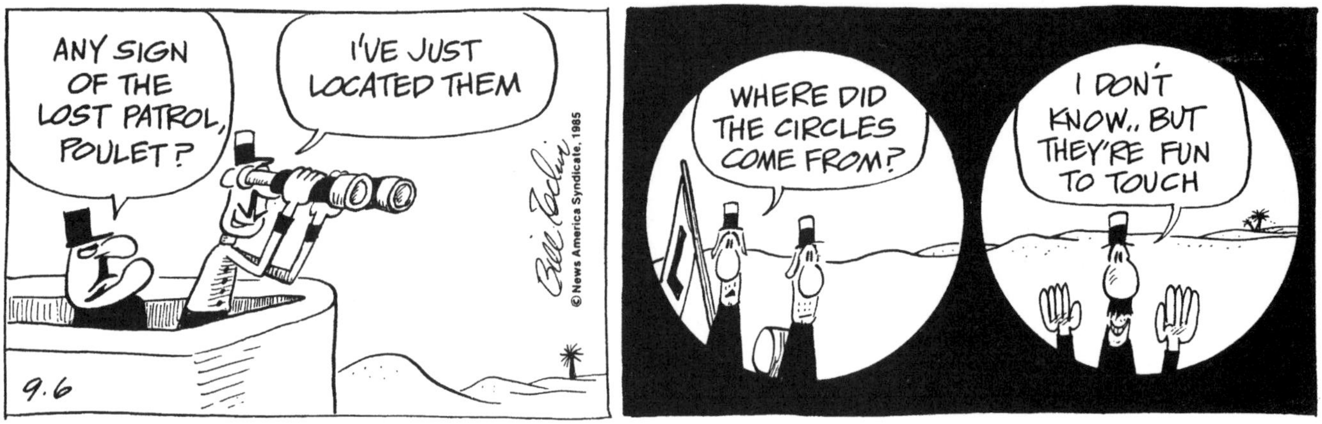
ANY SIGN OF THE LOST PATROL, POULET?
I'VE JUST LOCATED THEM
©News America Syndicate, 1985
9.6
WHERE DID THE CIRCLES COME FROM?
I DON'T KNOW.. BUT THEY'RE FUN TO TOUCH

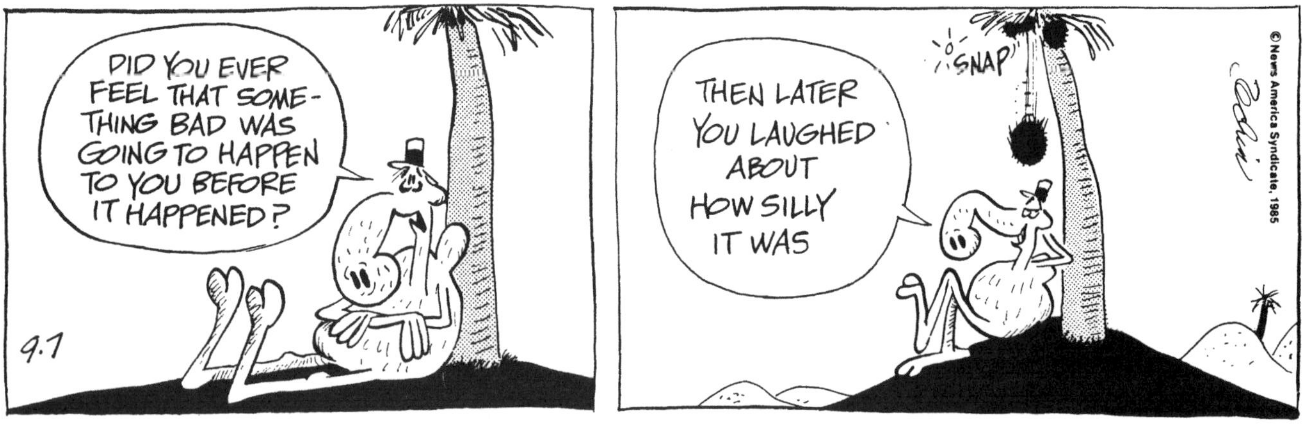
DID YOU EVER FEEL THAT SOME-THING BAD WAS GOING TO HAPPEN TO YOU BEFORE IT HAPPENED?
9.7
SNAP
THEN LATER YOU LAUGHED ABOUT HOW SILLY IT WAS
©News America Syndicate, 1985

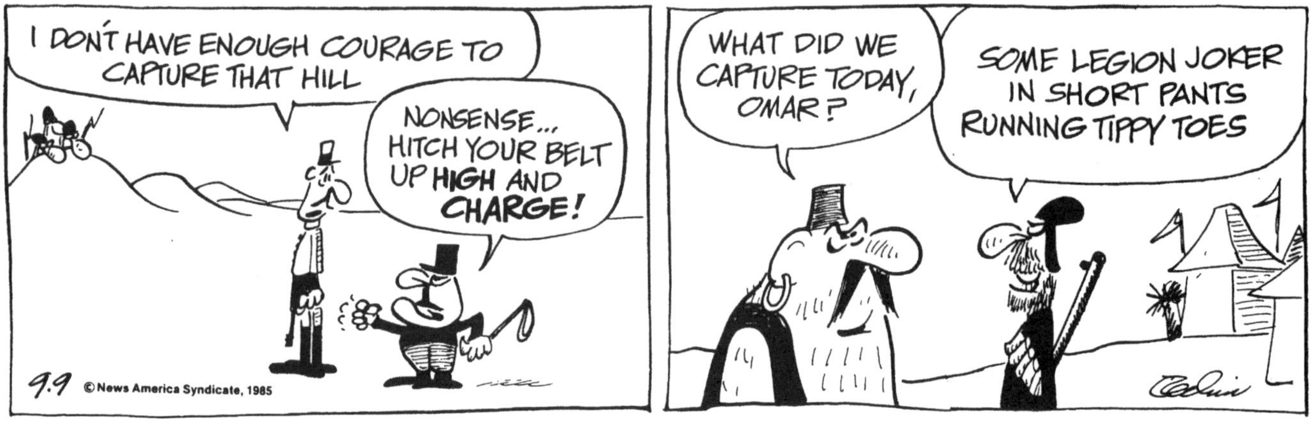
I DON'T HAVE ENOUGH COURAGE TO CAPTURE THAT HILL
NONSENSE... HITCH YOUR BELT UP **HIGH** AND **CHARGE!**
9.9
©News America Syndicate, 1985
WHAT DID WE CAPTURE TODAY, OMAR?
SOME LEGION JOKER IN SHORT PANTS RUNNING TIPPY TOES

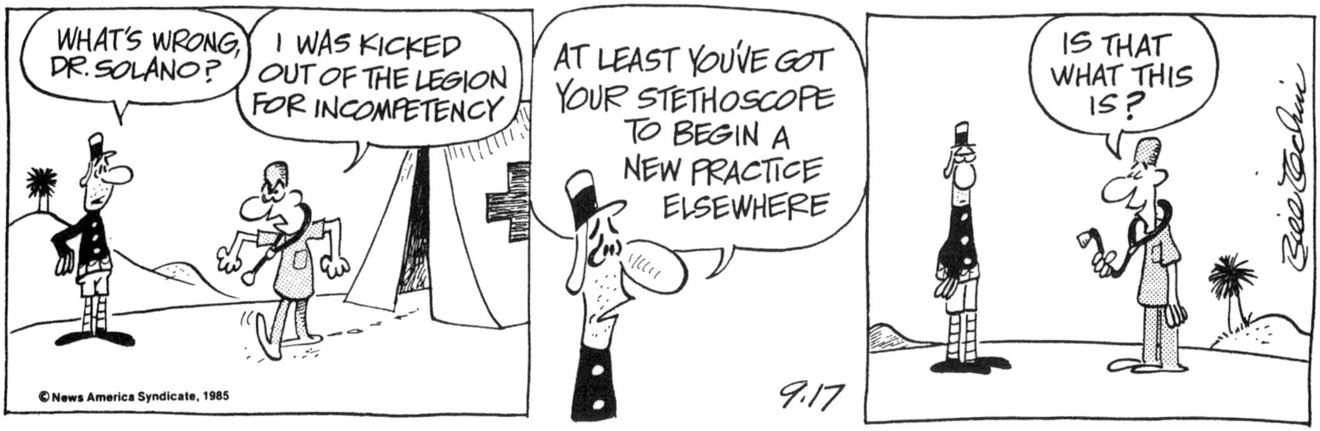
WHAT'S WRONG, DR. SOLANO?
I WAS KICKED OUT OF THE LEGION FOR INCOMPETENCY
AT LEAST YOU'VE GOT YOUR STETHOSCOPE TO BEGIN A NEW PRACTICE ELSEWHERE
IS THAT WHAT THIS IS?
©News America Syndicate, 1985
9.17

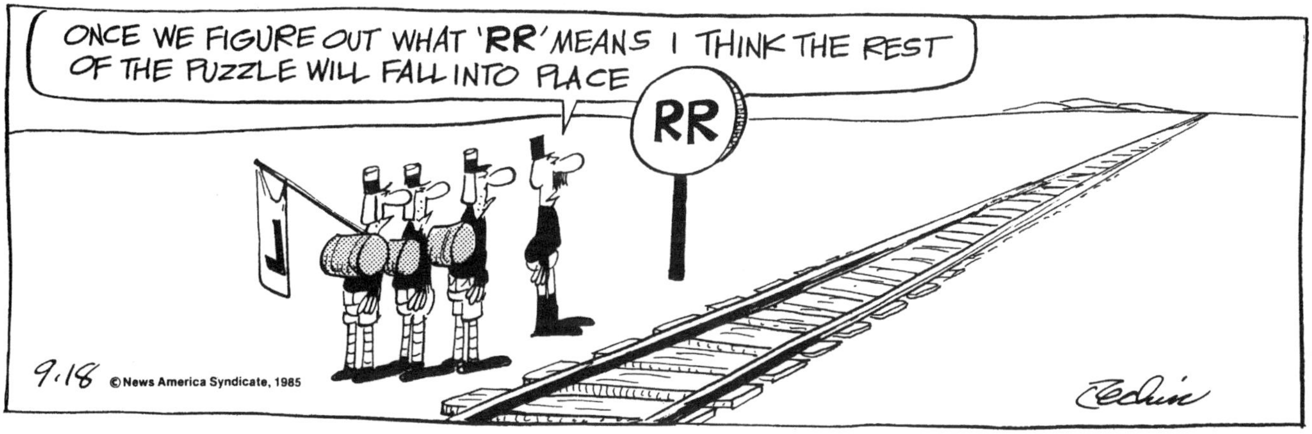
ONCE WE FIGURE OUT WHAT 'RR' MEANS I THINK THE REST OF THE PUZZLE WILL FALL INTO PLACE
RR
9.18
©News America Syndicate, 1985

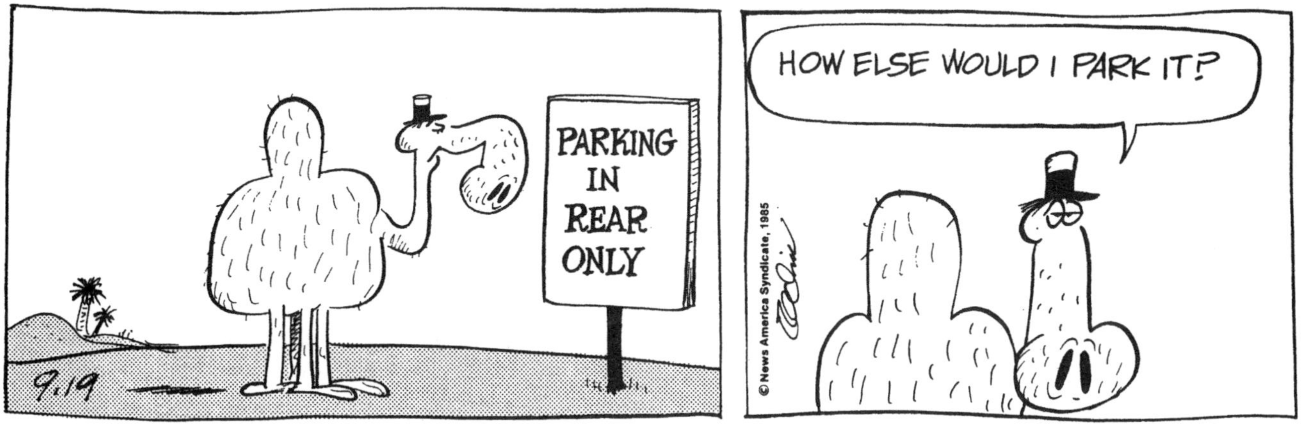
PARKING IN REAR ONLY
9.19
HOW ELSE WOULD I PARK IT?
©News America Syndicate, 1985

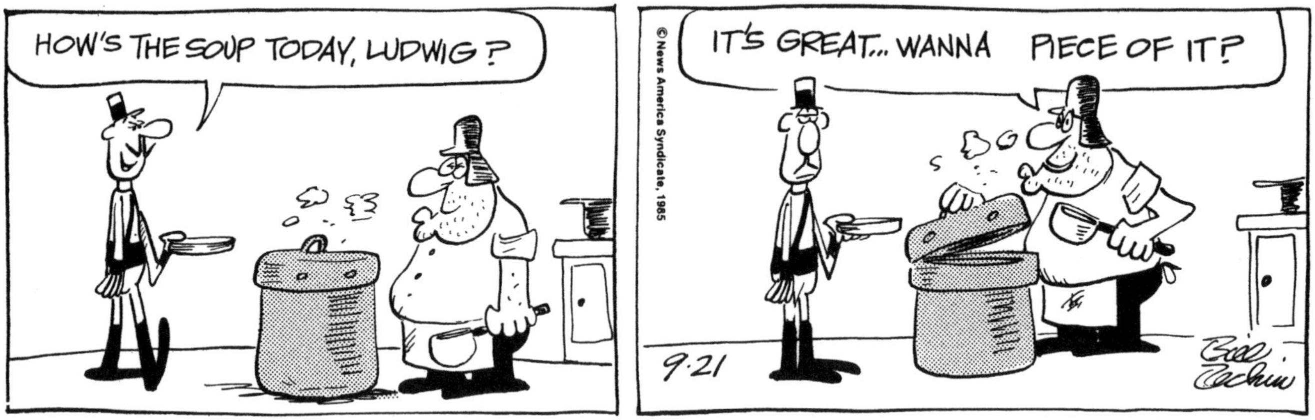
HOW'S THE SOUP TODAY, LUDWIG ?
© News America Syndicate, 1985
IT'S GREAT... WANNA PIECE OF IT?
9·21

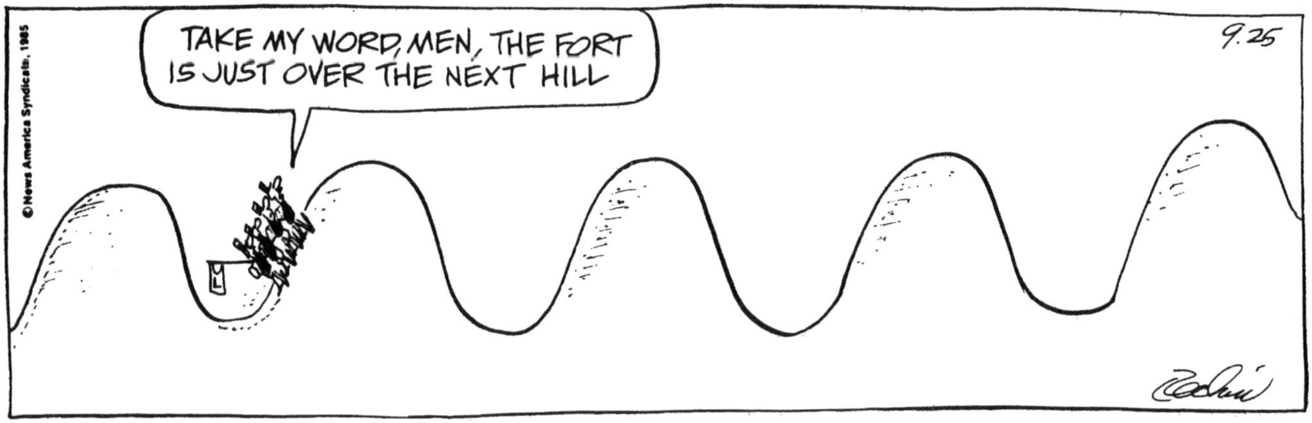
© News America Syndicate, 1985
TAKE MY WORD, MEN, THE FORT IS JUST OVER THE NEXT HILL
9·25

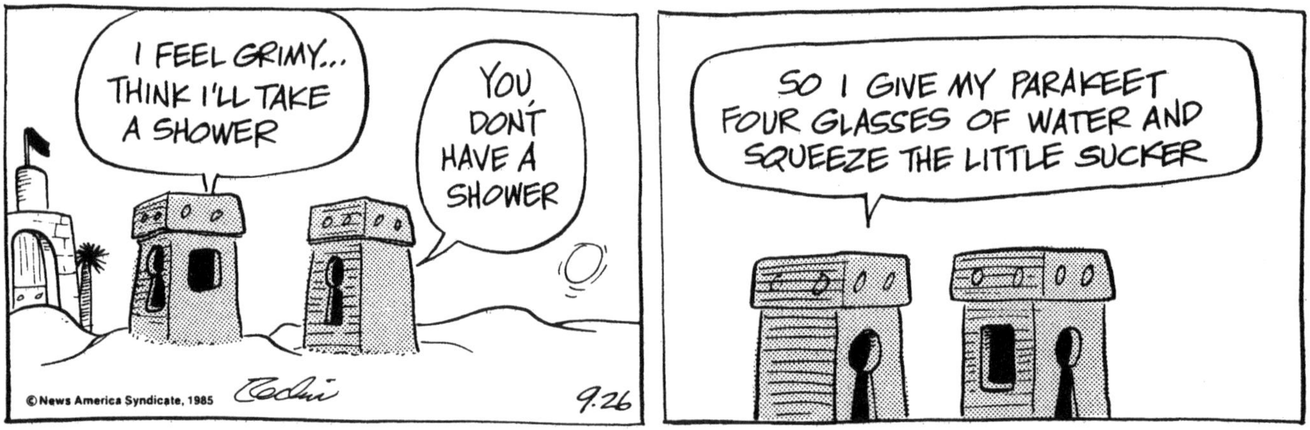
I FEEL GRIMY... THINK I'LL TAKE A SHOWER
YOU DON'T HAVE A SHOWER
© News America Syndicate, 1985
9·26
SO I GIVE MY PARAKEET FOUR GLASSES OF WATER AND SQUEEZE THE LITTLE SUCKER

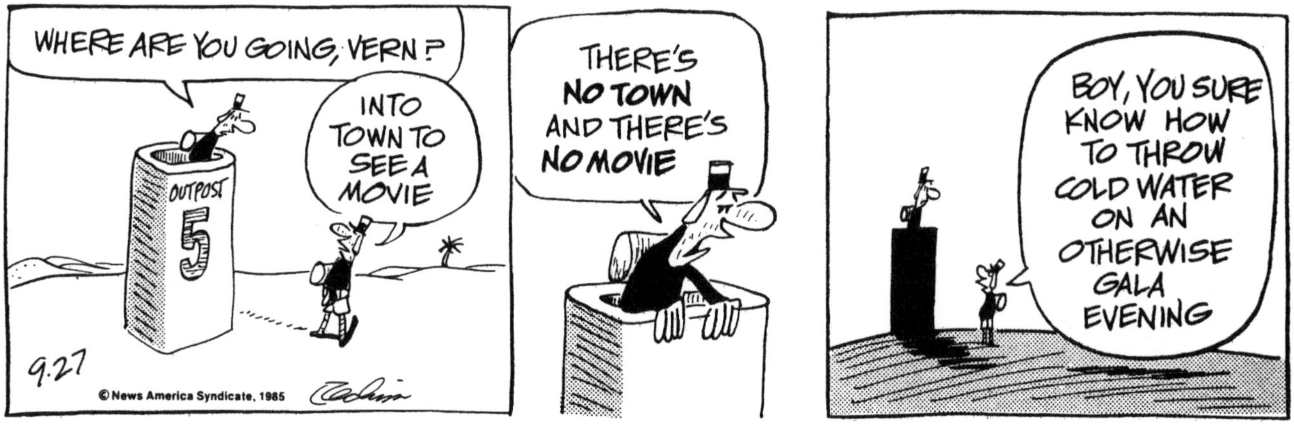
WHERE ARE YOU GOING, VERN?
INTO TOWN TO SEE A MOVIE
OUTPOST 5
9.27
© News America Syndicate, 1985
THERE'S NO TOWN AND THERE'S NO MOVIE
BOY, YOU SURE KNOW HOW TO THROW COLD WATER ON AN OTHERWISE GALA EVENING

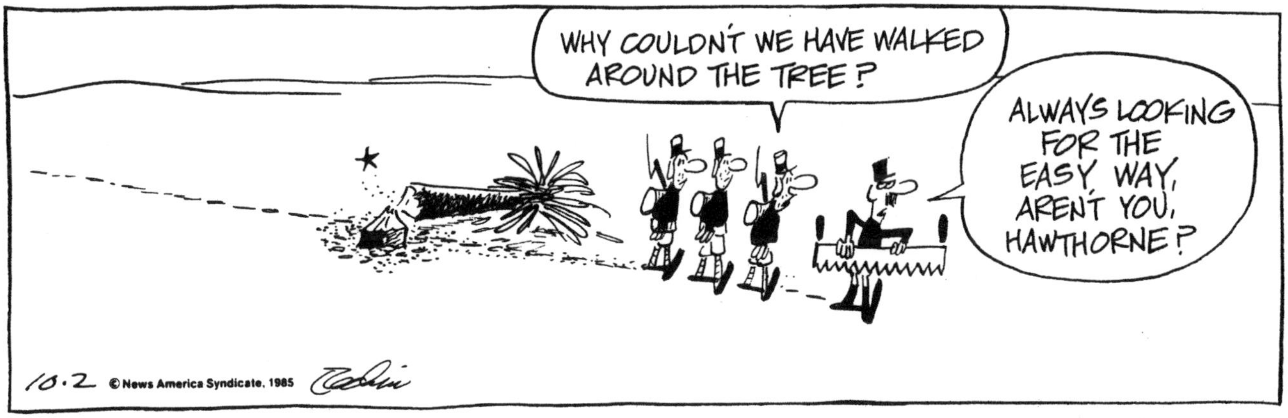
WHY COULDN'T WE HAVE WALKED AROUND THE TREE?
ALWAYS LOOKING FOR THE EASY WAY, AREN'T YOU, HAWTHORNE?
10.2
© News America Syndicate, 1985

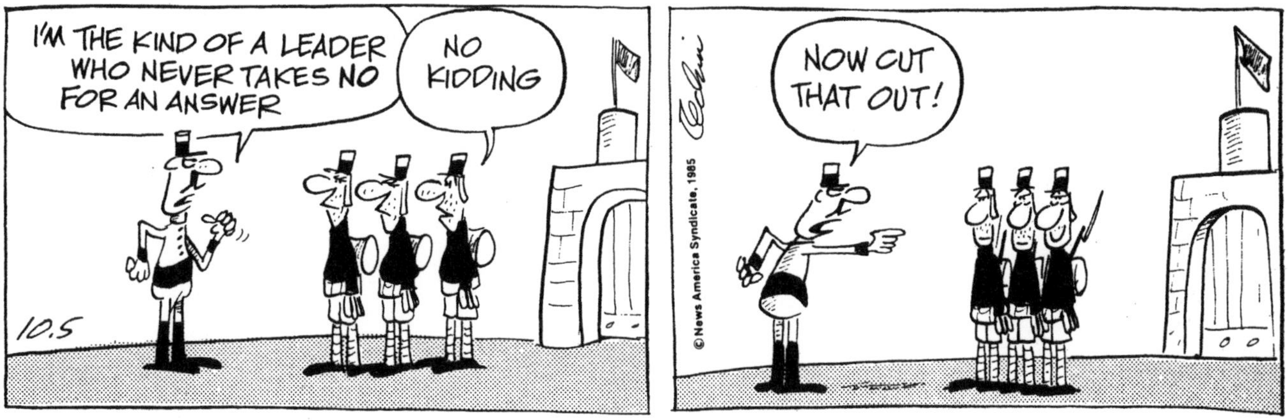
I'M THE KIND OF A LEADER WHO NEVER TAKES NO FOR AN ANSWER
NO KIDDING
10.5
© News America Syndicate, 1985
NOW CUT THAT OUT!

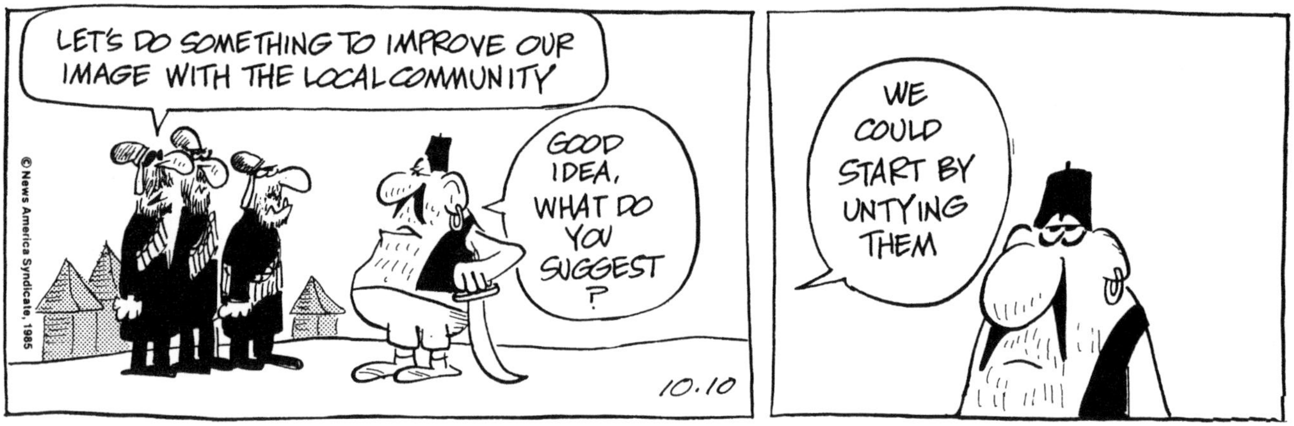
LET'S DO SOMETHING TO IMPROVE OUR IMAGE WITH THE LOCAL COMMUNITY
GOOD IDEA, WHAT DO YOU SUGGEST ?
WE COULD START BY UNTYING THEM
© News America Syndicate, 1985
10.10

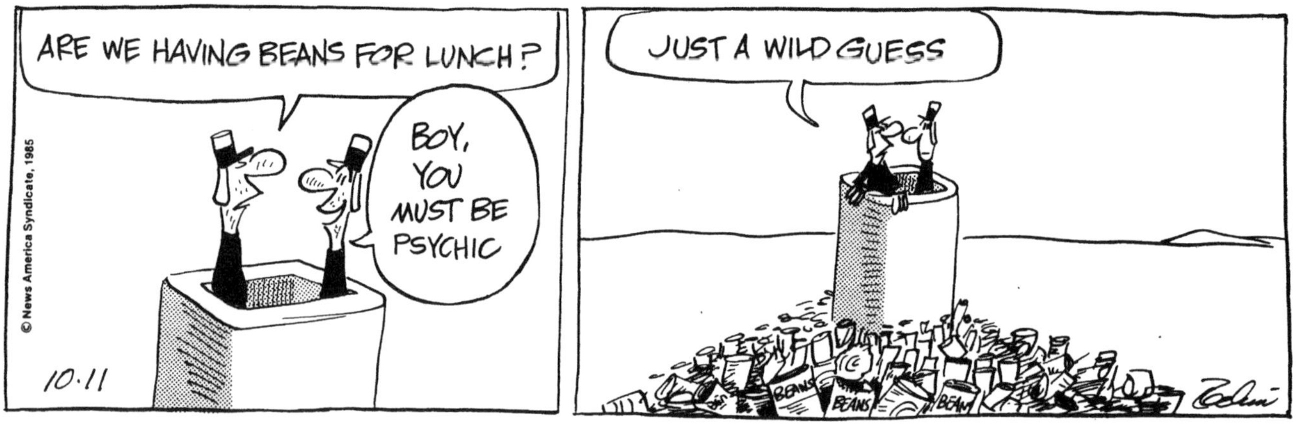
ARE WE HAVING BEANS FOR LUNCH ?
BOY, YOU MUST BE PSYCHIC
JUST A WILD GUESS
BEANS
BEANS
BEANS
© News America Syndicate, 1985
10.11

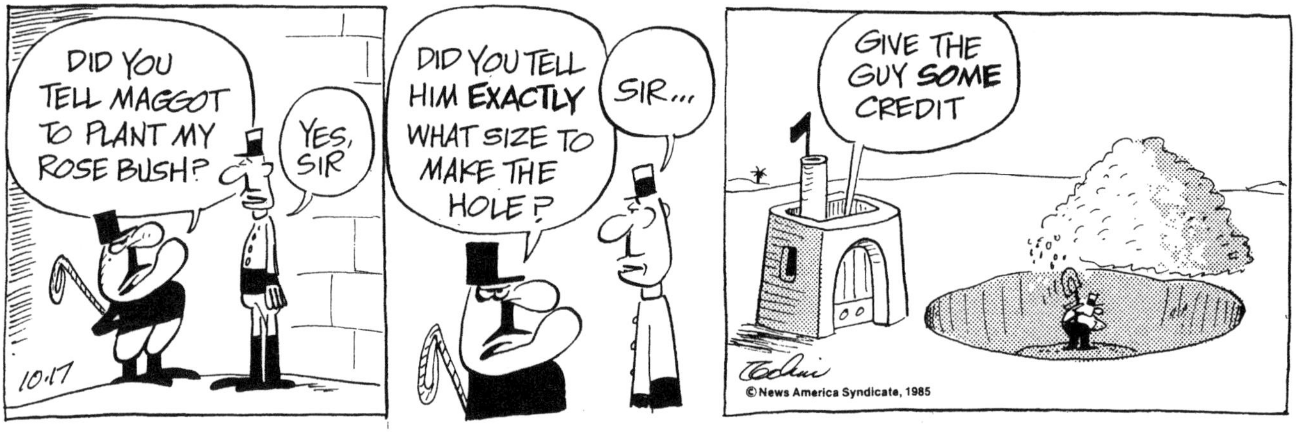
DID YOU TELL MAGGOT TO PLANT MY ROSE BUSH?
YES, SIR
DID YOU TELL HIM EXACTLY WHAT SIZE TO MAKE THE HOLE?
SIR...
GIVE THE GUY SOME CREDIT
10.17
©News America Syndicate, 1985

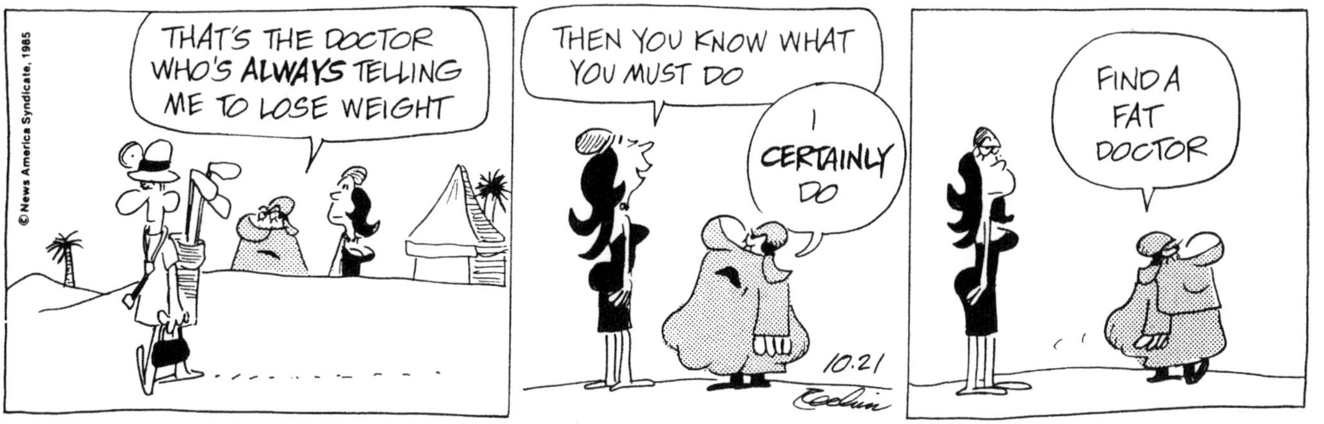
© News America Syndicate, 1985
THAT'S THE DOCTOR WHO'S ALWAYS TELLING ME TO LOSE WEIGHT
THEN YOU KNOW WHAT YOU MUST DO
I CERTAINLY DO
10.21
FIND A FAT DOCTOR

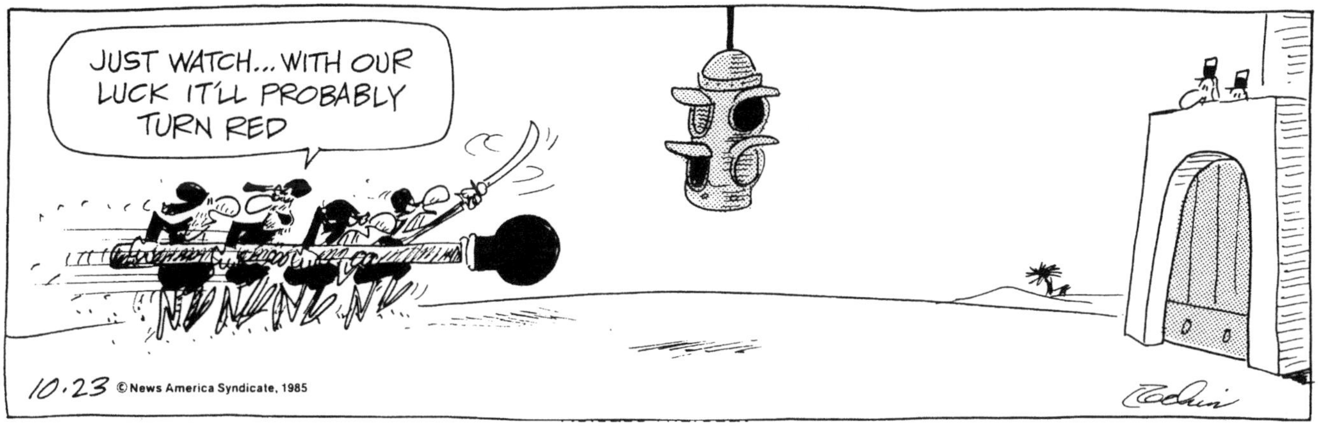
JUST WATCH... WITH OUR LUCK IT'LL PROBABLY TURN RED
10.23 © News America Syndicate, 1985

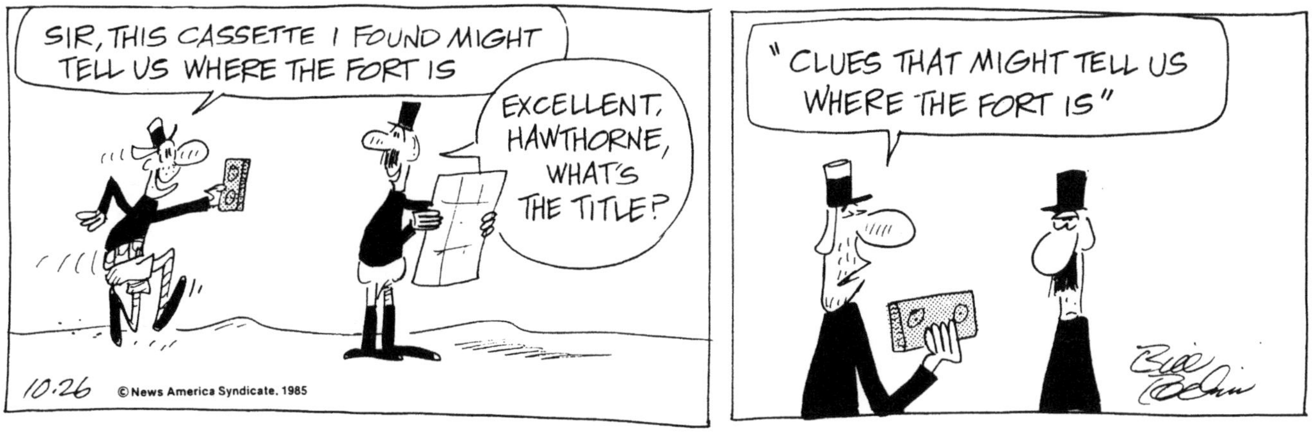
SIR, THIS CASSETTE I FOUND MIGHT TELL US WHERE THE FORT IS
EXCELLENT, HAWTHORNE, WHAT'S THE TITLE?
10.26 © News America Syndicate, 1985
"CLUES THAT MIGHT TELL US WHERE THE FORT IS"

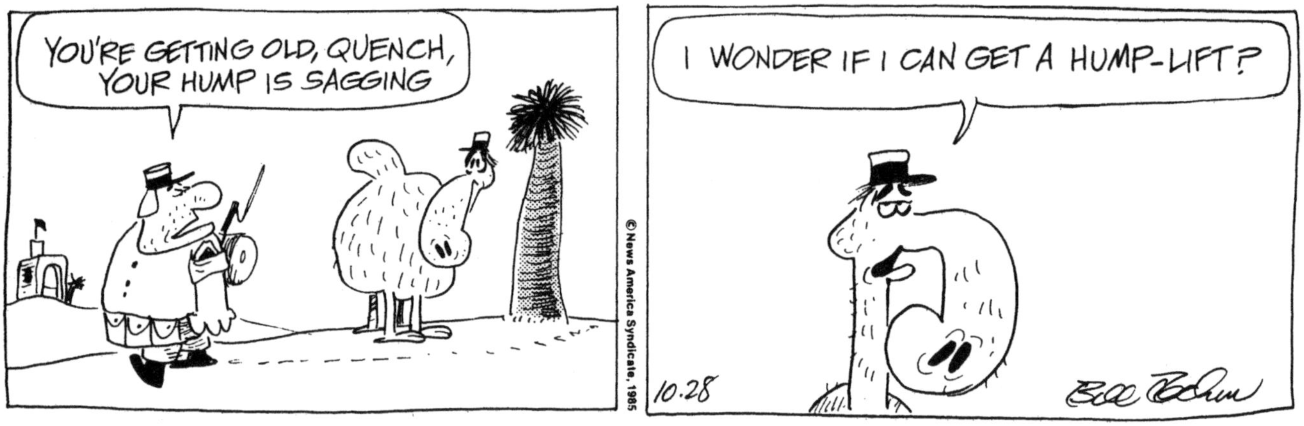
YOU'RE GETTING OLD, QUENCH, YOUR HUMP IS SAGGING
© News America Syndicate, 1985
I WONDER IF I CAN GET A HUMP-LIFT?
10.28

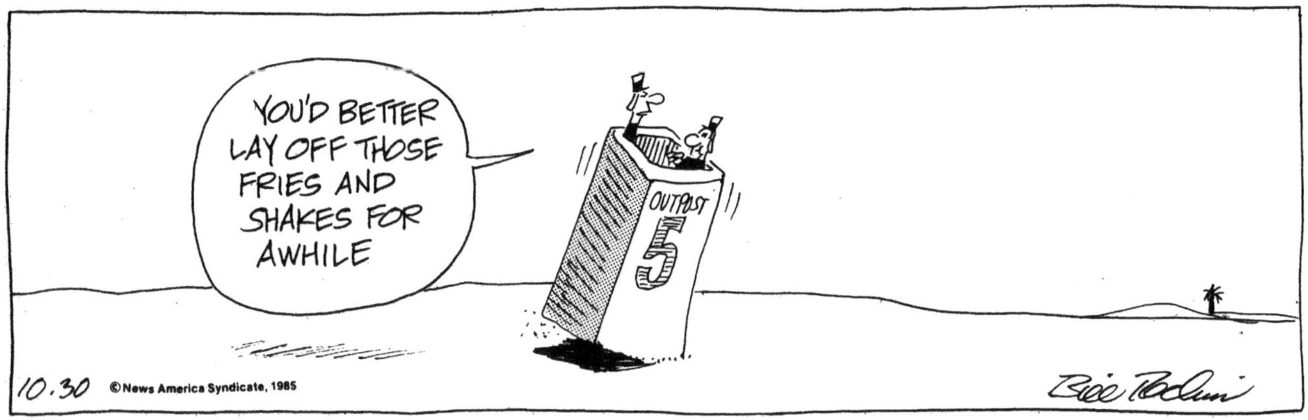
YOU'D BETTER LAY OFF THOSE FRIES AND SHAKES FOR AWHILE
OUTPOST 5
10.30
©News America Syndicate, 1985

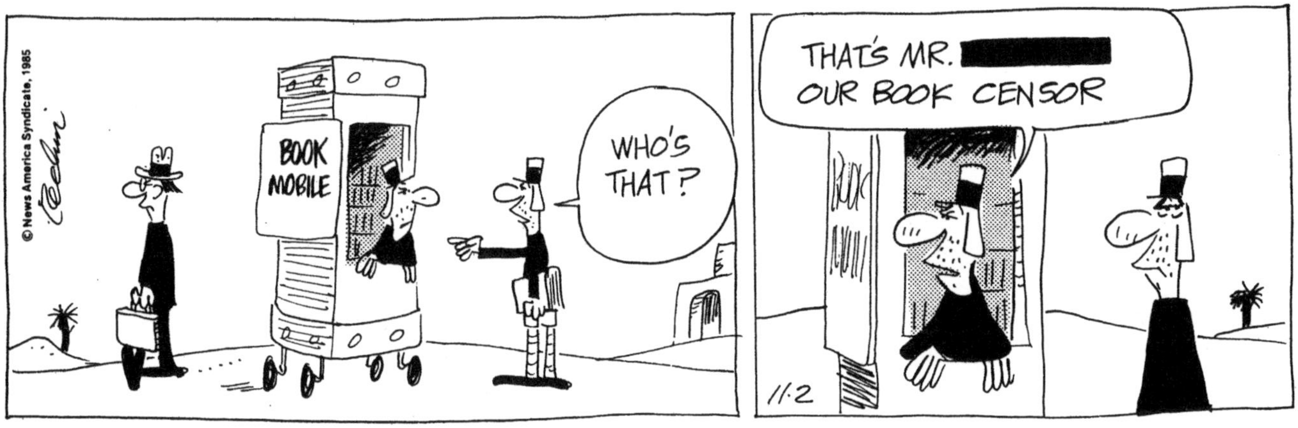
© News America Syndicate, 1985
BOOK MOBILE
WHO'S THAT?
THAT'S MR. [redacted] OUR BOOK CENSOR
11.2

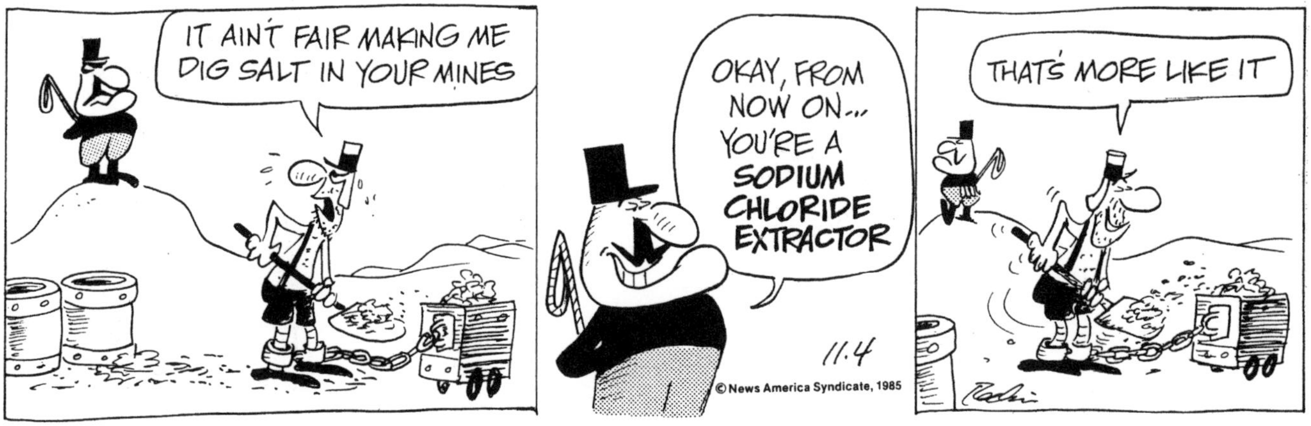
IT AIN'T FAIR MAKING ME DIG SALT IN YOUR MINES
OKAY, FROM NOW ON... YOU'RE A **SODIUM CHLORIDE EXTRACTOR**
11.4
© News America Syndicate, 1985
THAT'S MORE LIKE IT

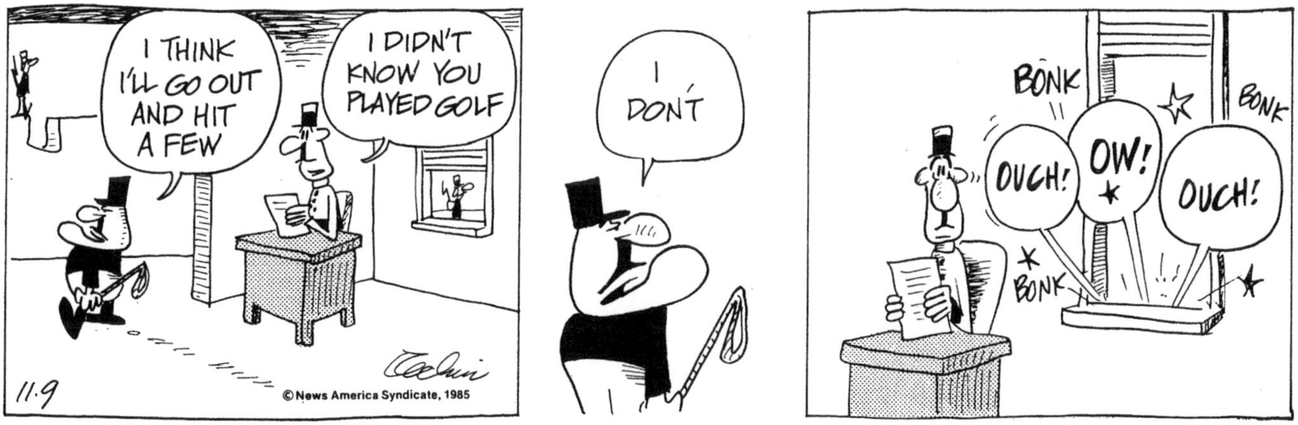
I THINK I'LL GO OUT AND HIT A FEW
I DIDN'T KNOW YOU PLAYED GOLF
11.9
© News America Syndicate, 1985
I DON'T
BONK
BONK
OUCH!
OW!
OUCH!
BONK

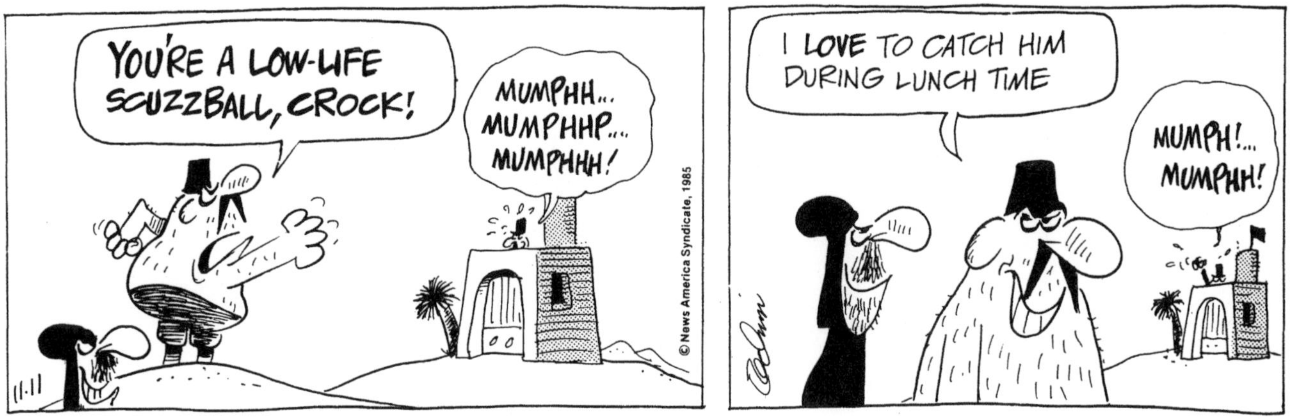
YOU'RE A LOW-LIFE SCUZZBALL, CROCK!
MUMPHH... MUMPHHP... MUMPHHH!
11.11
© News America Syndicate, 1985
I **LOVE** TO CATCH HIM DURING LUNCH TIME
MUMPH!... MUMPHH!

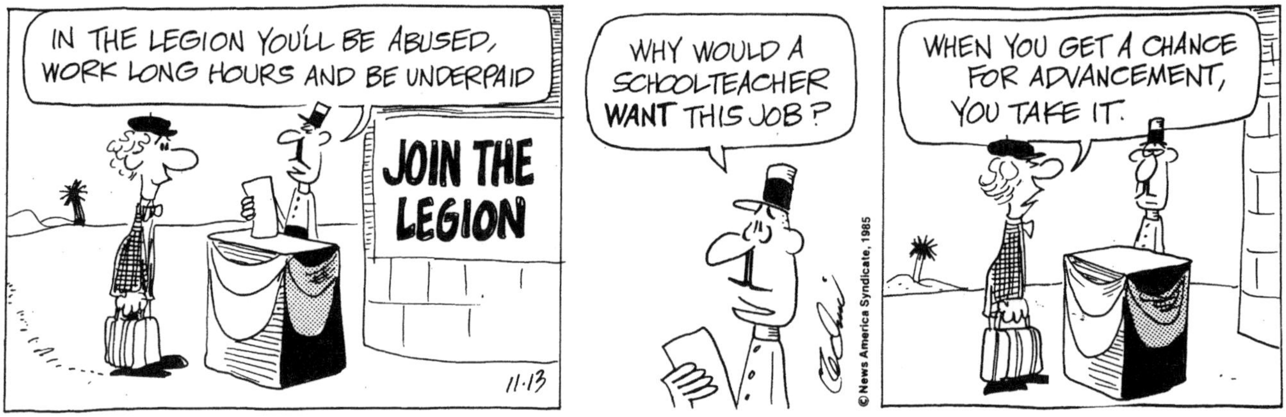
IN THE LEGION YOU'LL BE ABUSED, WORK LONG HOURS AND BE UNDERPAID
JOIN THE LEGION
11.13
WHY WOULD A SCHOOLTEACHER WANT THIS JOB?
© News America Syndicate, 1985
WHEN YOU GET A CHANCE FOR ADVANCEMENT, YOU TAKE IT.

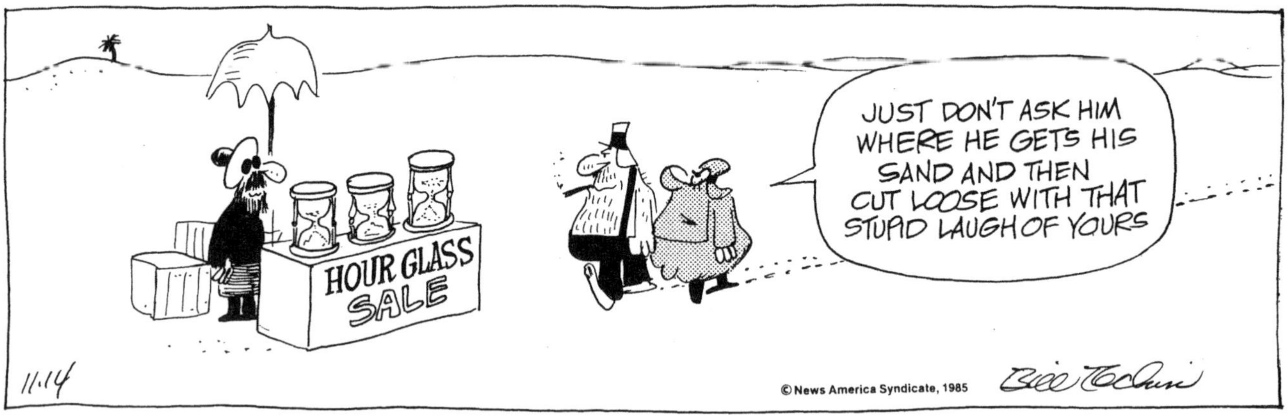
HOUR GLASS SALE
JUST DON'T ASK HIM WHERE HE GETS HIS SAND AND THEN CUT LOOSE WITH THAT STUPID LAUGH OF YOURS
11.14
© News America Syndicate, 1985
Bill Rechin

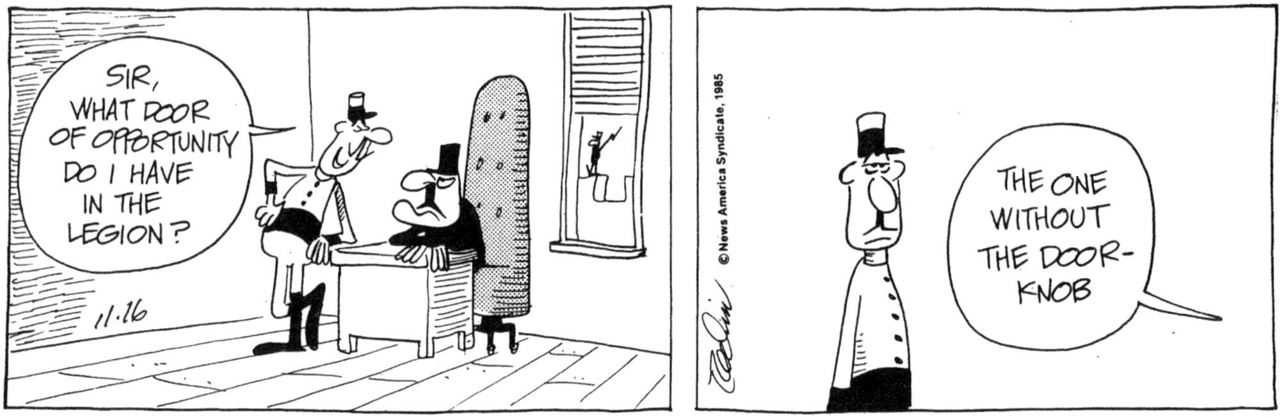
SIR, WHAT DOOR OF OPPORTUNITY DO I HAVE IN THE LEGION?
11.16
© News America Syndicate, 1985
THE ONE WITHOUT THE DOOR-KNOB

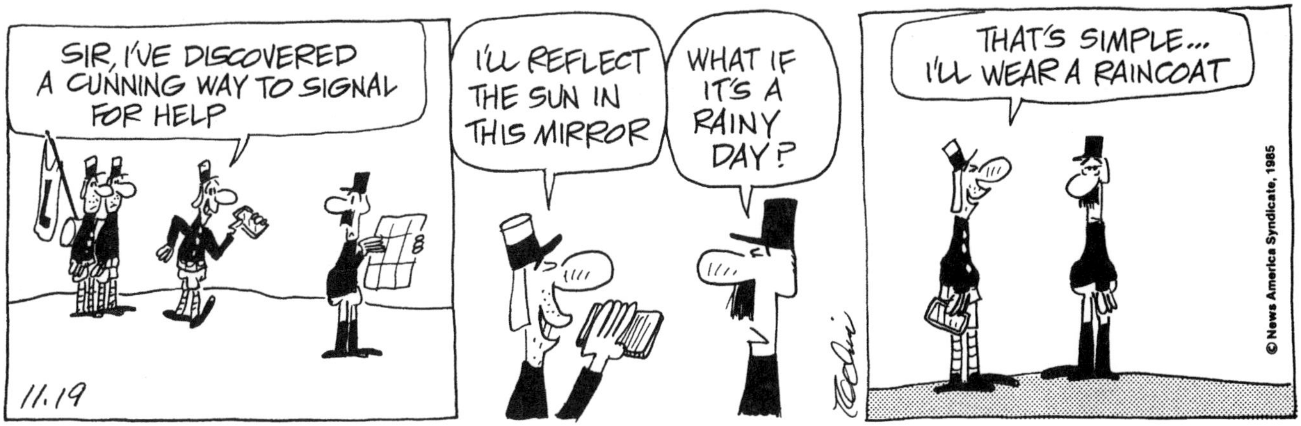
SIR, I'VE DISCOVERED A CUNNING WAY TO SIGNAL FOR HELP
I'LL REFLECT THE SUN IN THIS MIRROR
WHAT IF IT'S A RAINY DAY?
THAT'S SIMPLE... I'LL WEAR A RAINCOAT
11.19
© News America Syndicate, 1985

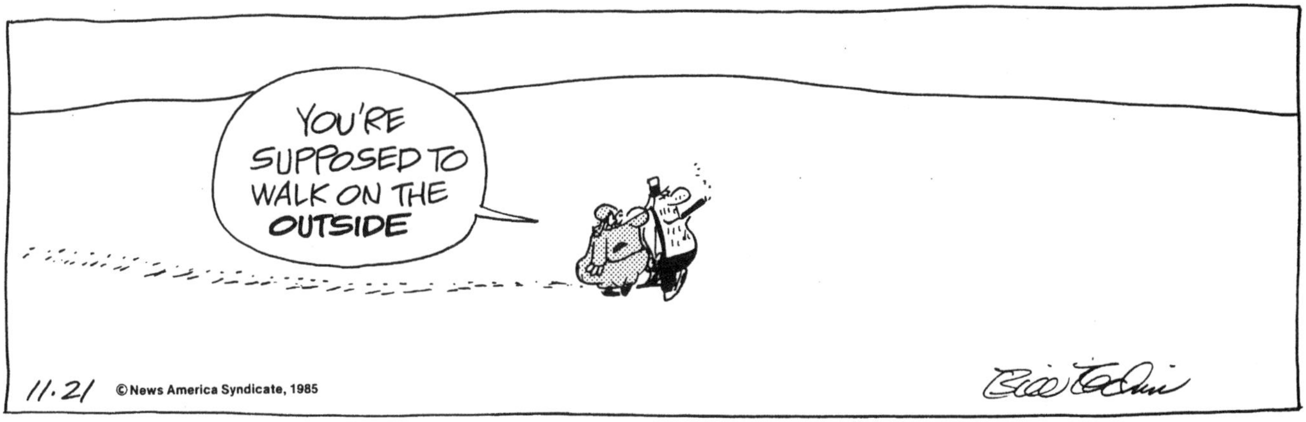
YOU'RE SUPPOSED TO WALK ON THE **OUTSIDE**
11.21
©News America Syndicate, 1985

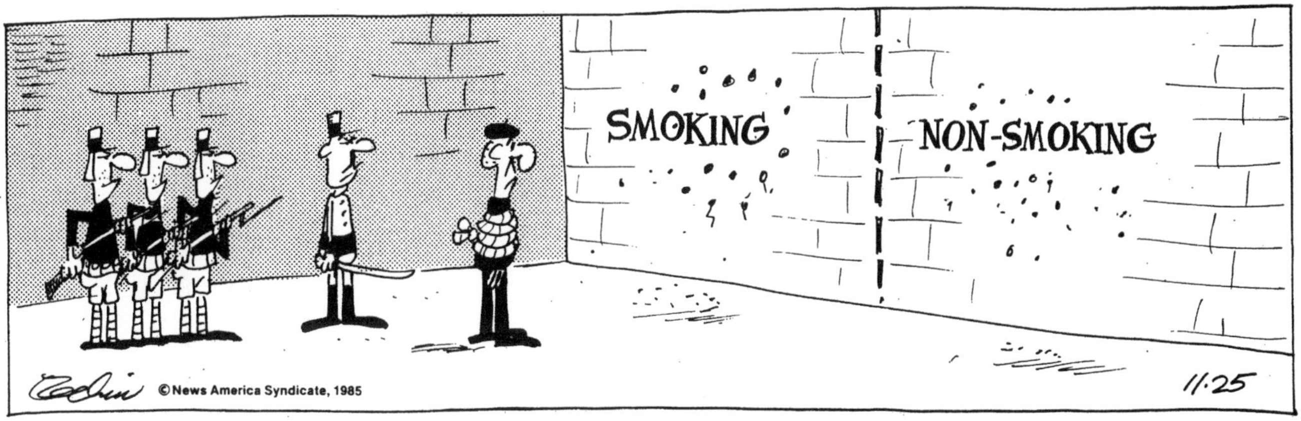
SMOKING
NON-SMOKING
©News America Syndicate, 1985
11.25

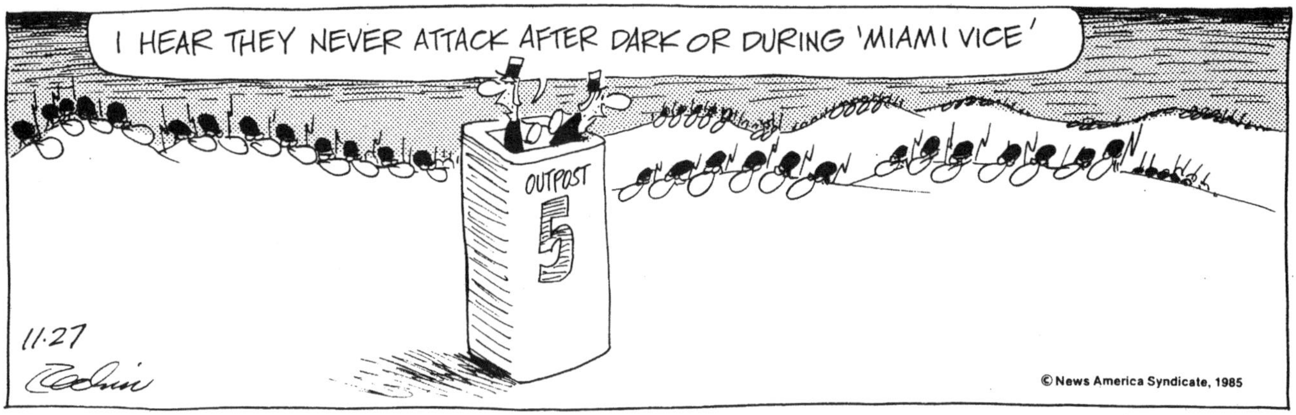
I HEAR THEY NEVER ATTACK AFTER DARK OR DURING 'MIAMI VICE'
OUTPOST 5
11·27
© News America Syndicate, 1985

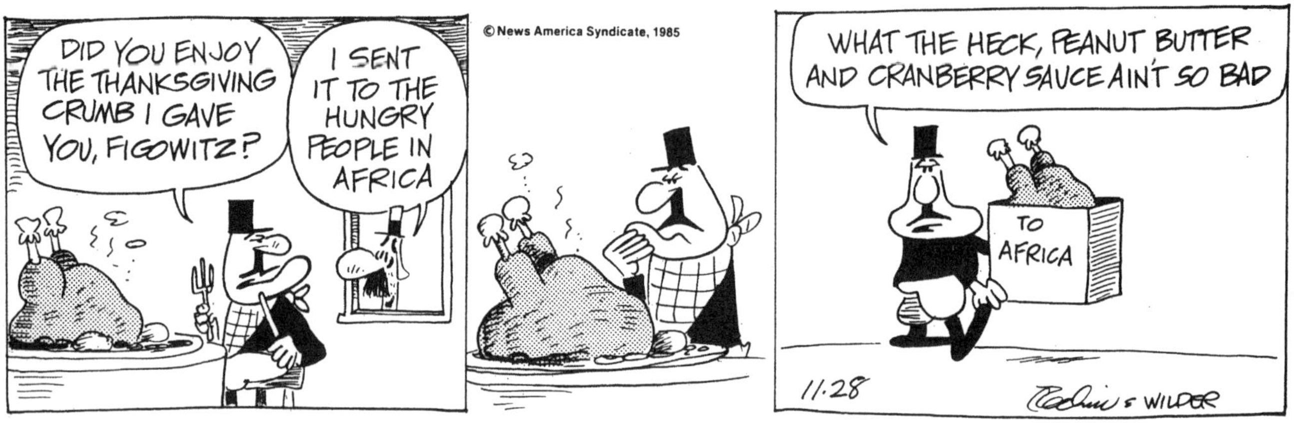
DID YOU ENJOY THE THANKSGIVING CRUMB I GAVE YOU, FIGOWITZ?
I SENT IT TO THE HUNGRY PEOPLE IN AFRICA
© News America Syndicate, 1985
WHAT THE HECK, PEANUT BUTTER AND CRANBERRY SAUCE AIN'T SO BAD
TO AFRICA
11·28
& WILDER

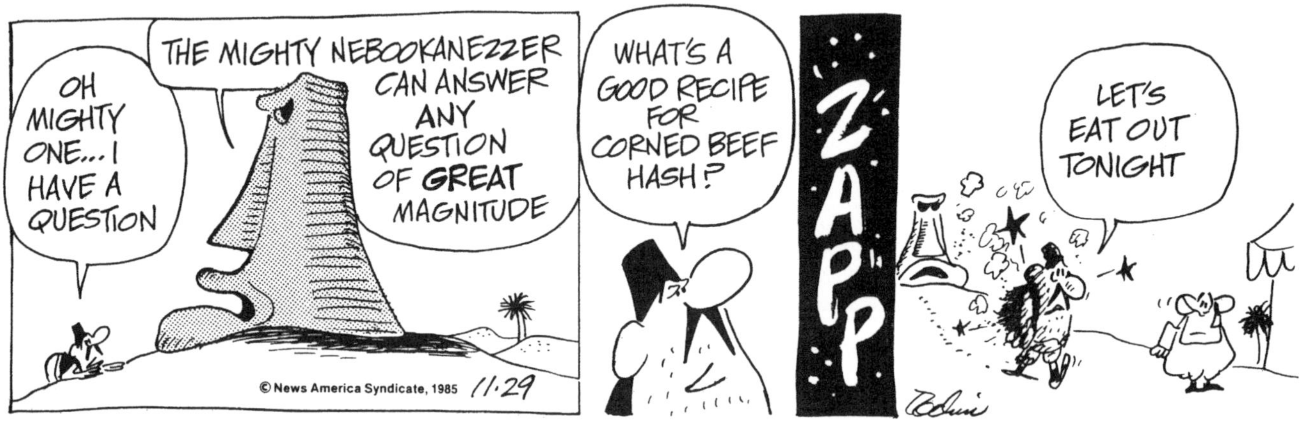
OH MIGHTY ONE... I HAVE A QUESTION
THE MIGHTY NEBOOKANEZZER CAN ANSWER ANY QUESTION OF GREAT MAGNITUDE
© News America Syndicate, 1985
11·29
WHAT'S A GOOD RECIPE FOR CORNED BEEF HASH?
ZAPP
LET'S EAT OUT TONIGHT

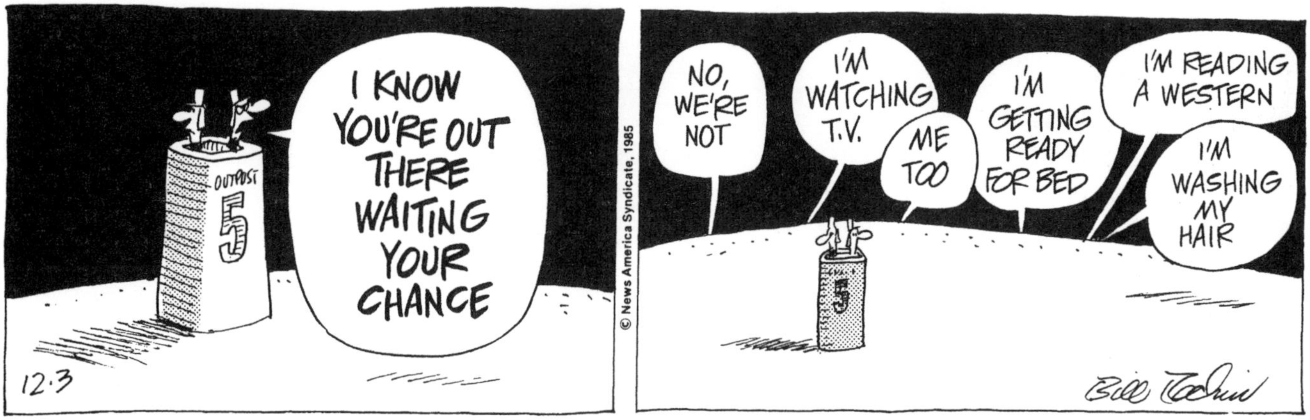
OUTPOST
5
I KNOW YOU'RE OUT THERE WAITING YOUR CHANCE
12·3
© News America Syndicate, 1985
NO, WE'RE NOT
I'M WATCHING T.V.
ME TOO
I'M GETTING READY FOR BED
I'M READING A WESTERN
I'M WASHING MY HAIR
Bill Rechin

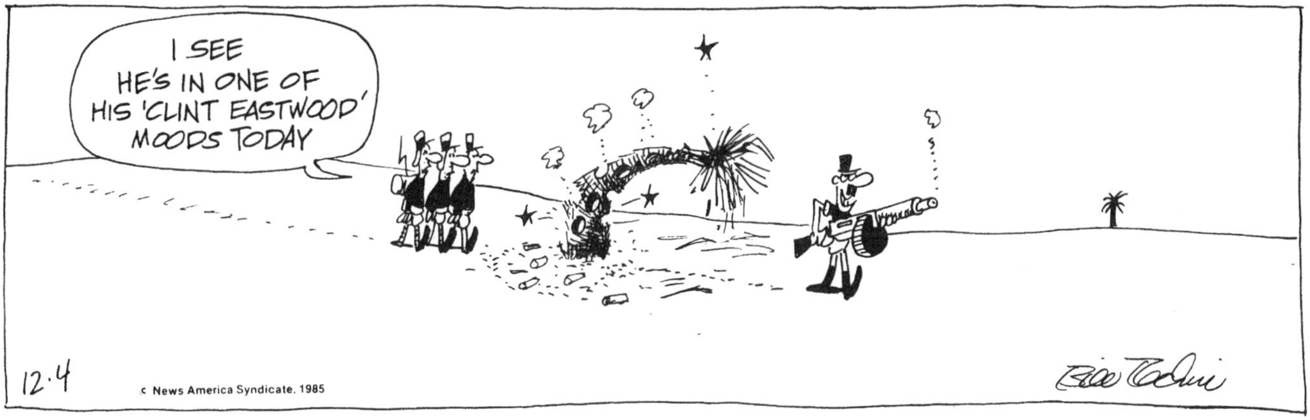
I SEE HE'S IN ONE OF HIS 'CLINT EASTWOOD' MOODS TODAY
12·4
© News America Syndicate, 1985
Bill Rechin

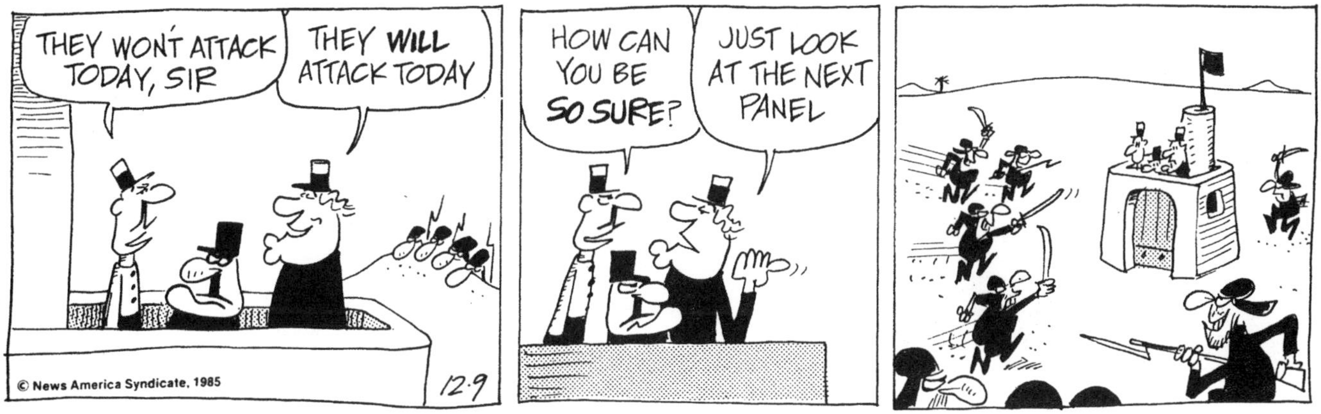
THEY WON'T ATTACK TODAY, SIR
THEY **WILL** ATTACK TODAY
© News America Syndicate, 1985
12·9
HOW CAN YOU BE **SO SURE**?
JUST LOOK AT THE NEXT PANEL

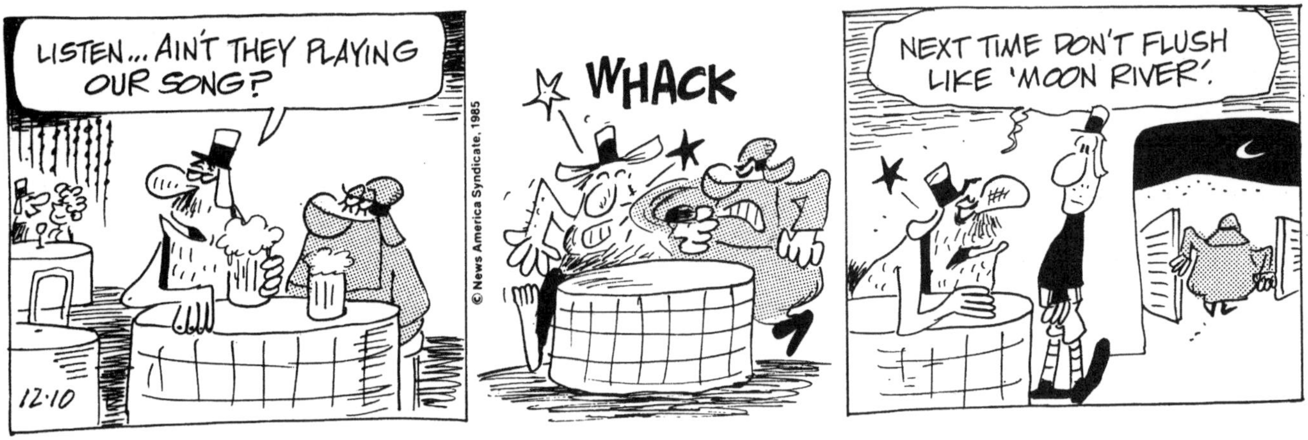
LISTEN... AIN'T THEY PLAYING OUR SONG?
12·10
© News America Syndicate, 1985
WHACK
NEXT TIME DON'T FLUSH LIKE 'MOON RIVER'.

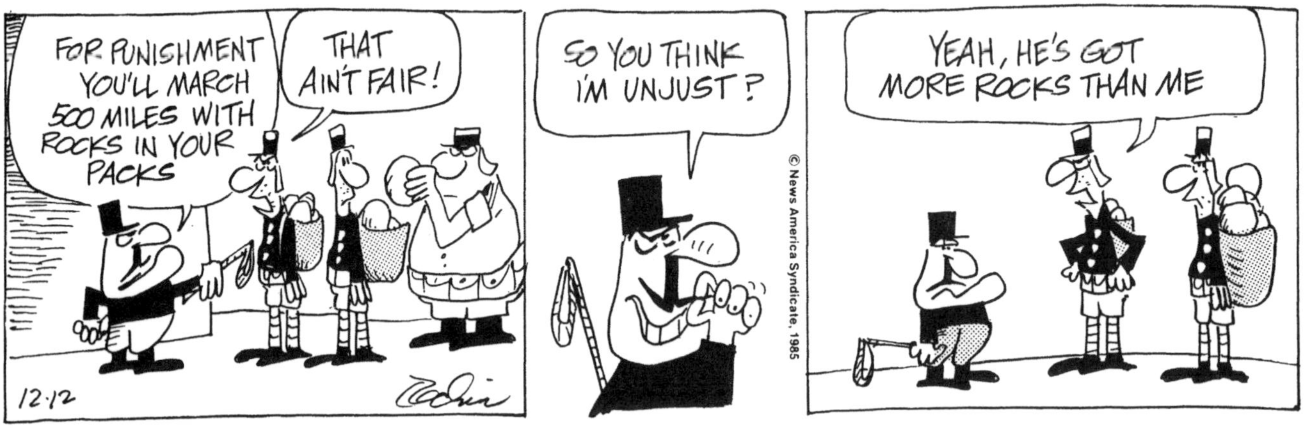
FOR PUNISHMENT YOU'LL MARCH 500 MILES WITH ROCKS IN YOUR PACKS
THAT AIN'T FAIR!
12·12
SO YOU THINK I'M UNJUST?
© News America Syndicate, 1985
YEAH, HE'S GOT MORE ROCKS THAN ME

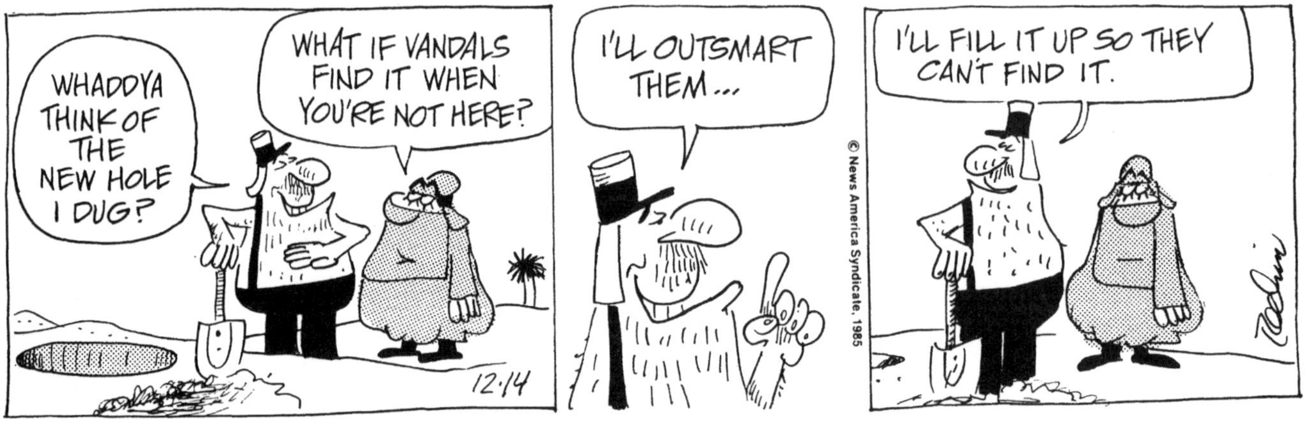
WHADDYA THINK OF THE NEW HOLE I DUG?
WHAT IF VANDALS FIND IT WHEN YOU'RE NOT HERE?
12·14
I'LL OUTSMART THEM...
© News America Syndicate, 1985
I'LL FILL IT UP SO THEY CAN'T FIND IT.

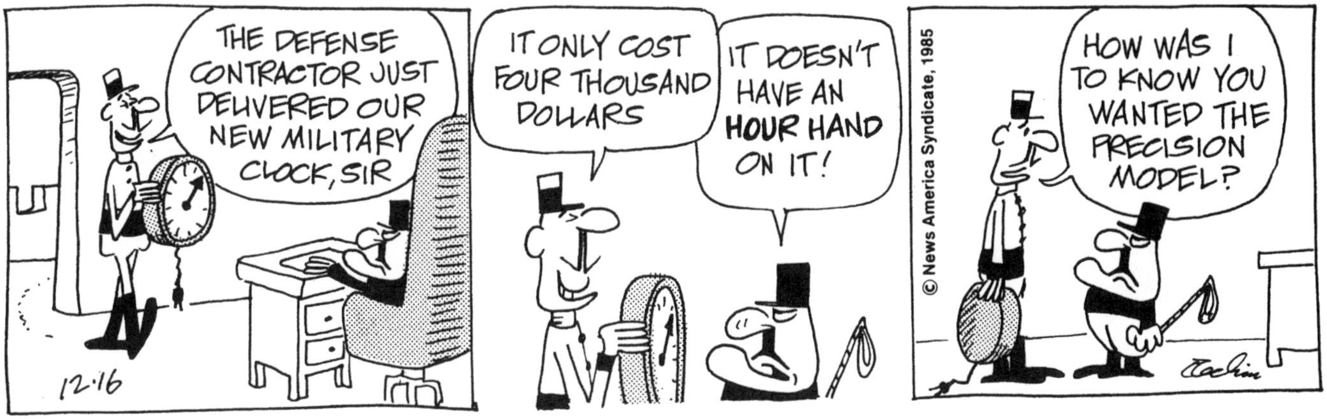
THE DEFENSE CONTRACTOR JUST DELIVERED OUR NEW MILITARY CLOCK, SIR
IT ONLY COST FOUR THOUSAND DOLLARS
IT DOESN'T HAVE AN **HOUR HAND** ON IT!
HOW WAS I TO KNOW YOU WANTED THE PRECISION MODEL?
12·16
© News America Syndicate, 1985

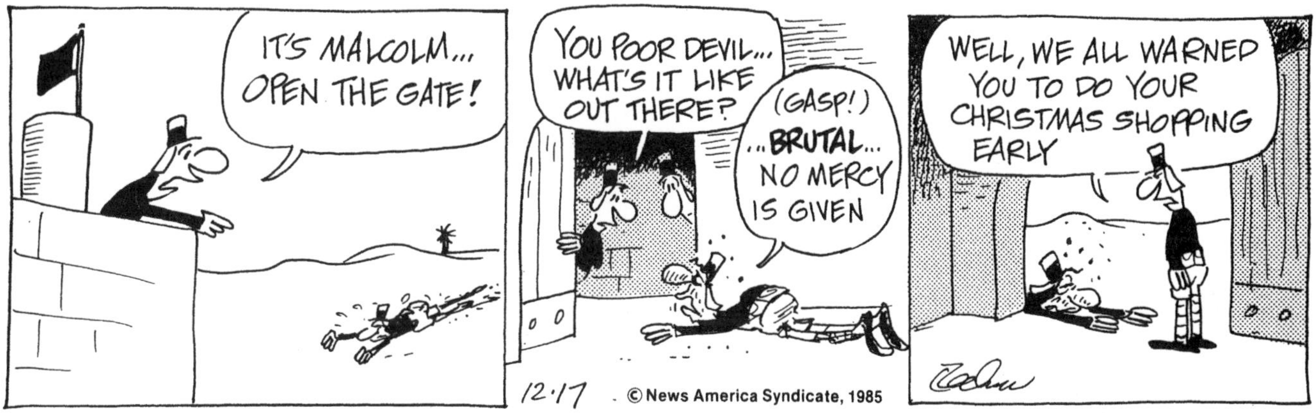
IT'S MALCOLM... OPEN THE GATE!
YOU POOR DEVIL... WHAT'S IT LIKE OUT THERE?
(GASP!) ...**BRUTAL**... NO MERCY IS GIVEN
WELL, WE ALL WARNED YOU TO DO YOUR CHRISTMAS SHOPPING EARLY
12·17
© News America Syndicate, 1985

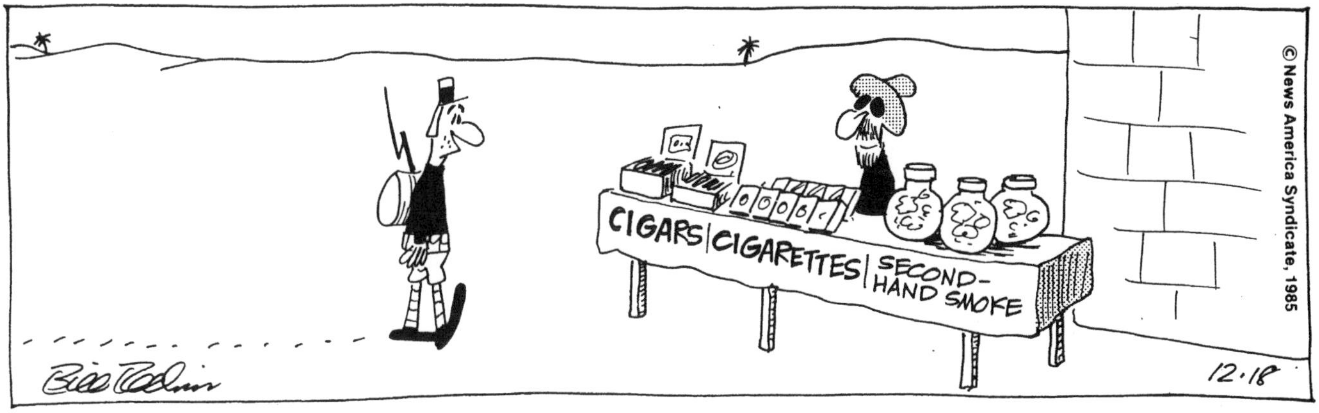
CIGARS | CIGARETTES | SECOND-HAND SMOKE
© News America Syndicate, 1985
12·18

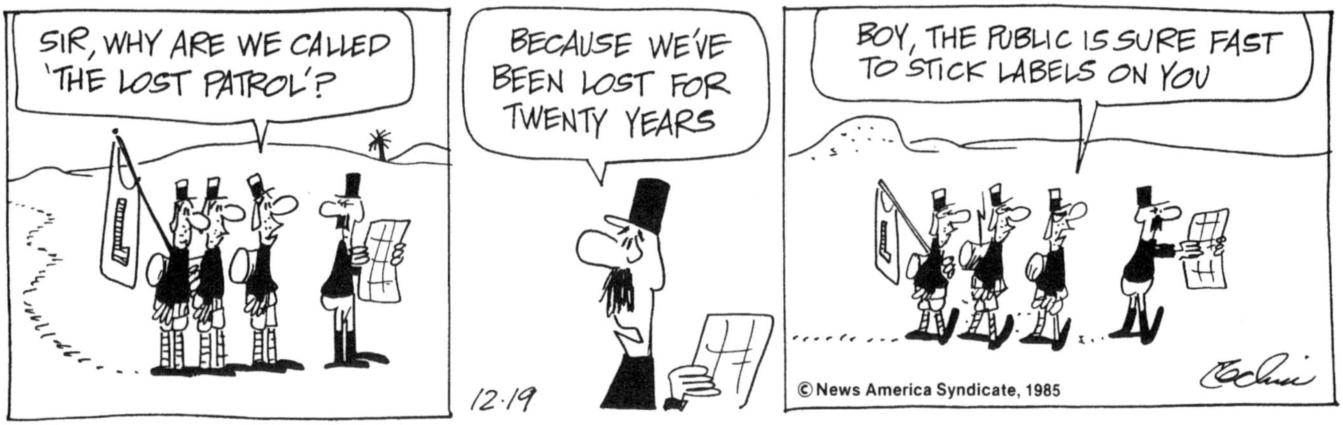
SIR, WHY ARE WE CALLED 'THE LOST PATROL'?
BECAUSE WE'VE BEEN LOST FOR TWENTY YEARS
12·19
BOY, THE PUBLIC IS SURE FAST TO STICK LABELS ON YOU
© News America Syndicate, 1985

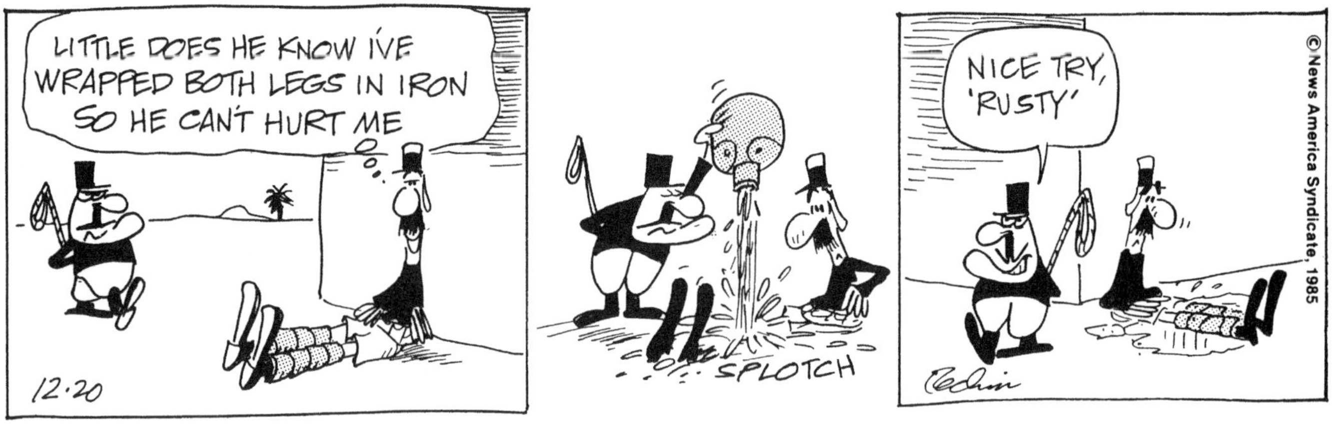
LITTLE DOES HE KNOW I'VE WRAPPED BOTH LEGS IN IRON SO HE CAN'T HURT ME
12·20
SPLOTCH
NICE TRY, 'RUSTY'
© News America Syndicate, 1985

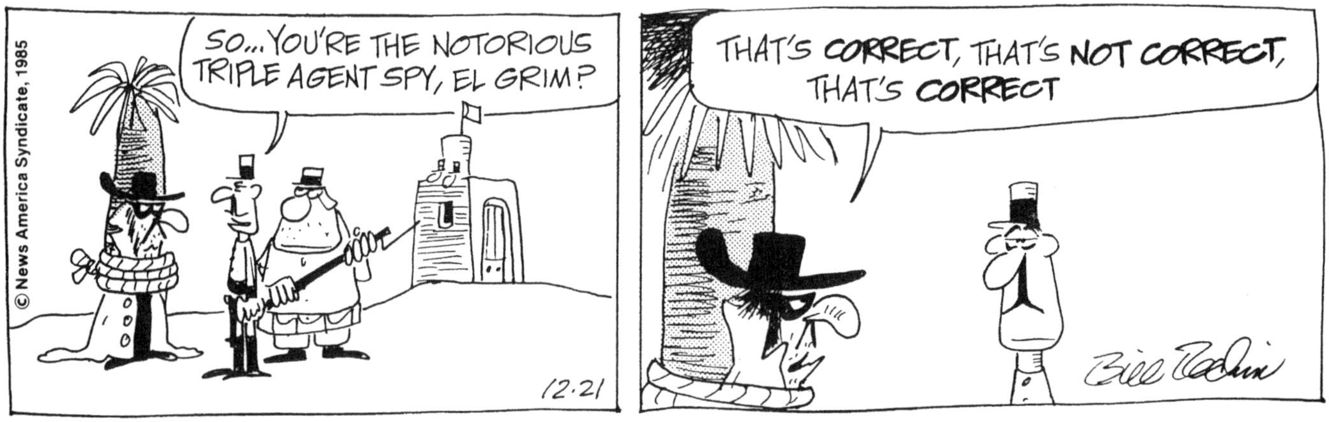
© News America Syndicate, 1985
SO... YOU'RE THE NOTORIOUS TRIPLE AGENT SPY, EL GRIM?
12·21
THAT'S CORRECT, THAT'S NOT CORRECT, THAT'S CORRECT

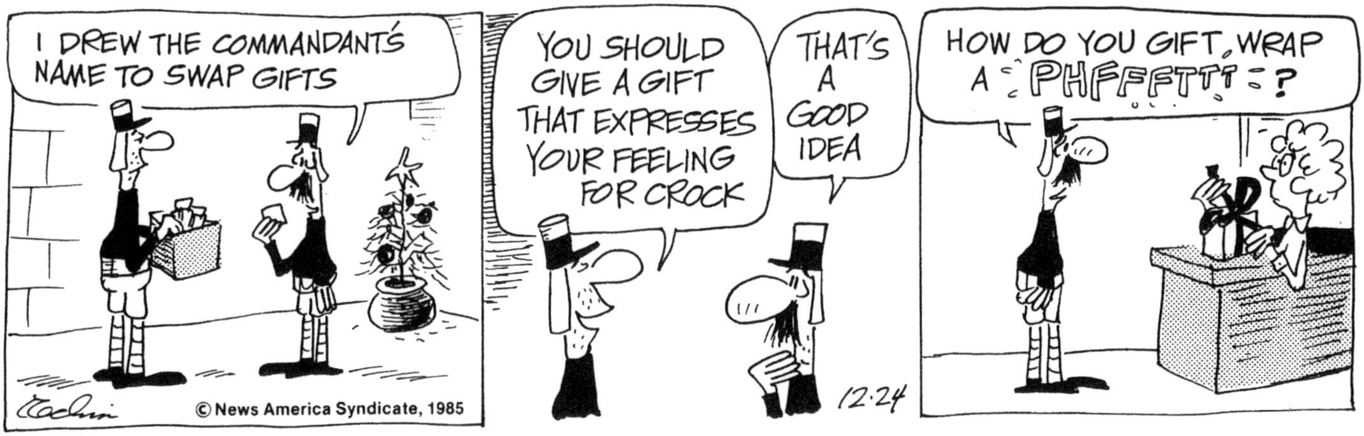
I DREW THE COMMANDANT'S NAME TO SWAP GIFTS
YOU SHOULD GIVE A GIFT THAT EXPRESSES YOUR FEELING FOR CROCK
THAT'S A GOOD IDEA
HOW DO YOU GIFT WRAP A PHFFFTTT?
© News America Syndicate, 1985
12·24

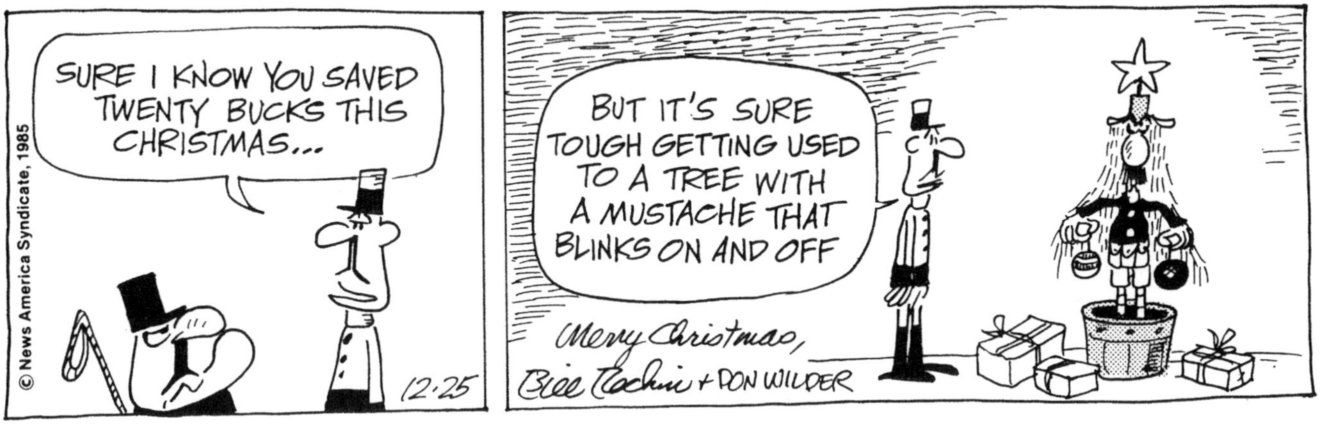
SURE I KNOW YOU SAVED TWENTY BUCKS THIS CHRISTMAS...
BUT IT'S SURE TOUGH GETTING USED TO A TREE WITH A MUSTACHE THAT BLINKS ON AND OFF
Merry Christmas,
Bill Rechin + DON WILDER
© News America Syndicate, 1985
12·25

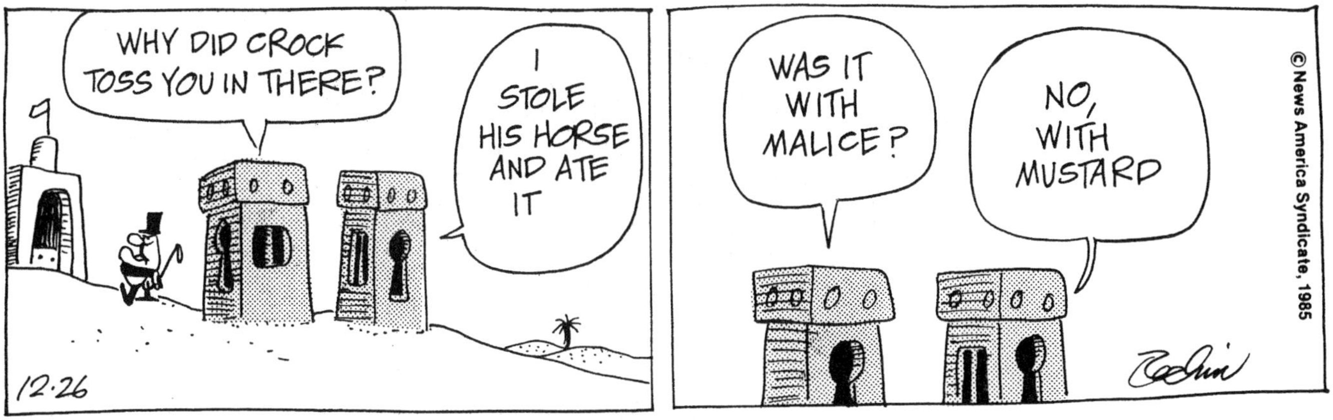
WHY DID CROCK TOSS YOU IN THERE?
I STOLE HIS HORSE AND ATE IT
WAS IT WITH MALICE?
NO, WITH MUSTARD
© News America Syndicate, 1985
12·26

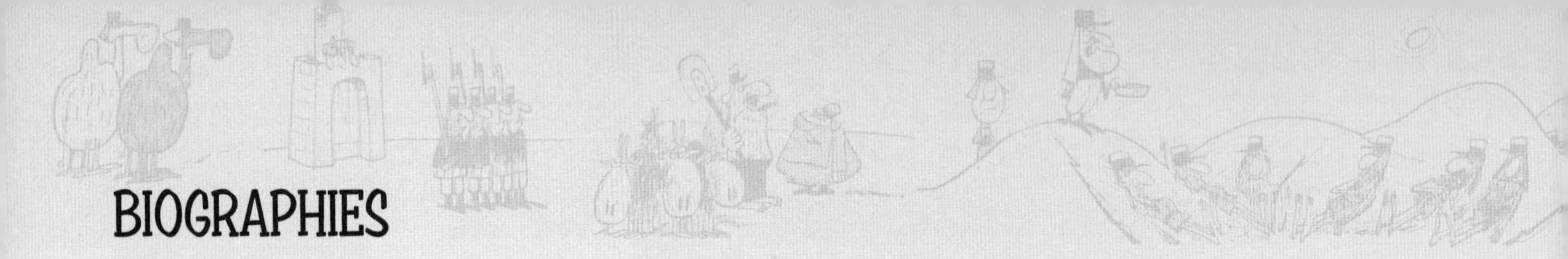

BILL RECHIN
1930-2011

Born in Buffalo, New York on August 20, 1930, Bill Rechin studied at Buffalo's Albright Academy of Art. In 1970 he drew his first strip, *Pluribus*, and five years later began collaborating with Don Wilder and Brant Parker to create *Crock*, a comic strip depicting life in the French Foreign Legion. He continued working on this through the years, and also worked with Wilder on a new strip, *Out of Bounds*, in 1986. In 1992, he received the National Cartoonists Society's Newspaper Panel Cartoon Award for his work on *Out of Bounds.*

Rechin lived in Spotsylvania County, Virginia, with his wife Trish and their family, and passed away on May 21, 2011. His son, Kevin Rechin, took over illustration duties on *Crock* that year, with his brother-in-law, Bob Morgan, writing the scripts.

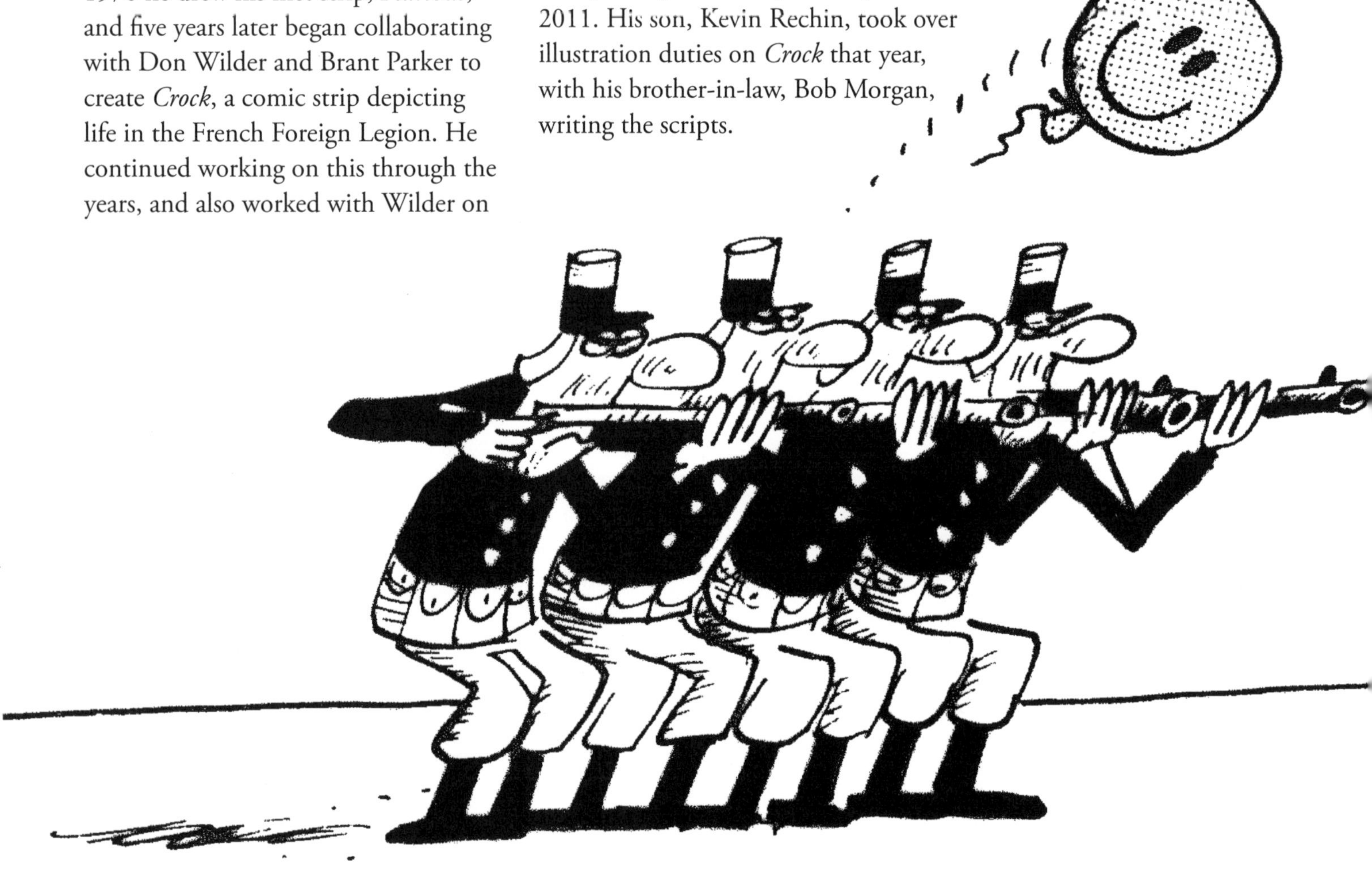

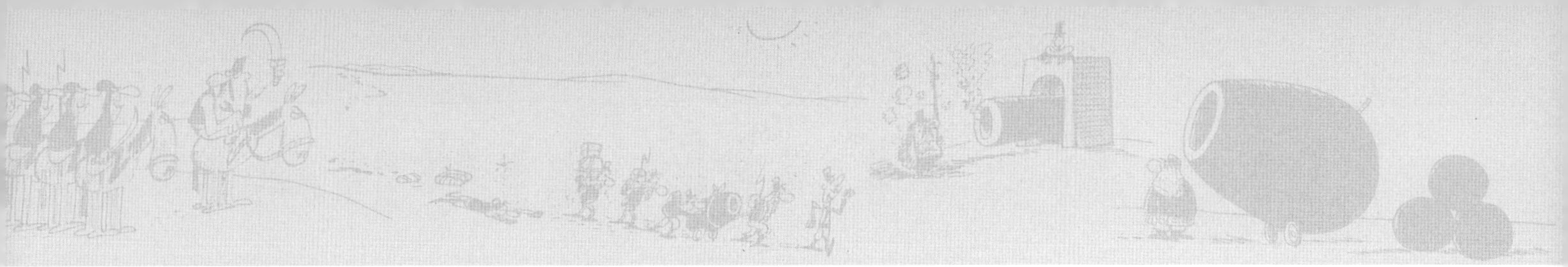

DON WILDER
1934-2008

Kentucky native Don Wilder was born in the city of Middlesboro, on June 23, 1934. He graduated from East Tennessee State University with a bachelor's degree in art, and undertook further study at the Philadelphia Museum of Art. Wilder produced cartoons for his college newspaper, and was soon selling his work to major magazines before finding employment as a technical illustrator, visual-media coordinator, and publications specialist at Lockheed Aircraft, RCA, and General Electric. Wilder also spent 17 years as a visual information specialist for the CIA.

For more than three decades, Wilder wrote the *Crock* comic strip in partnership with artist Bill Rechin, syndicated worldwide by Kings Features.

Wilder died on September 24, 2008.

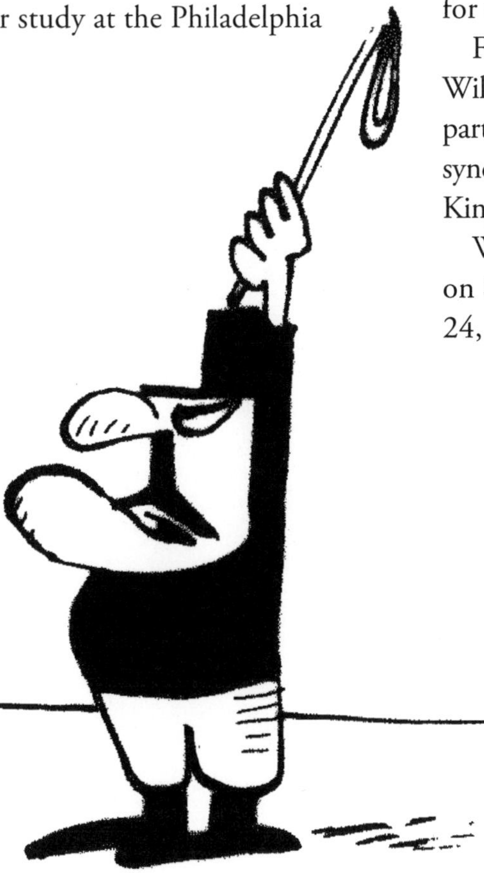

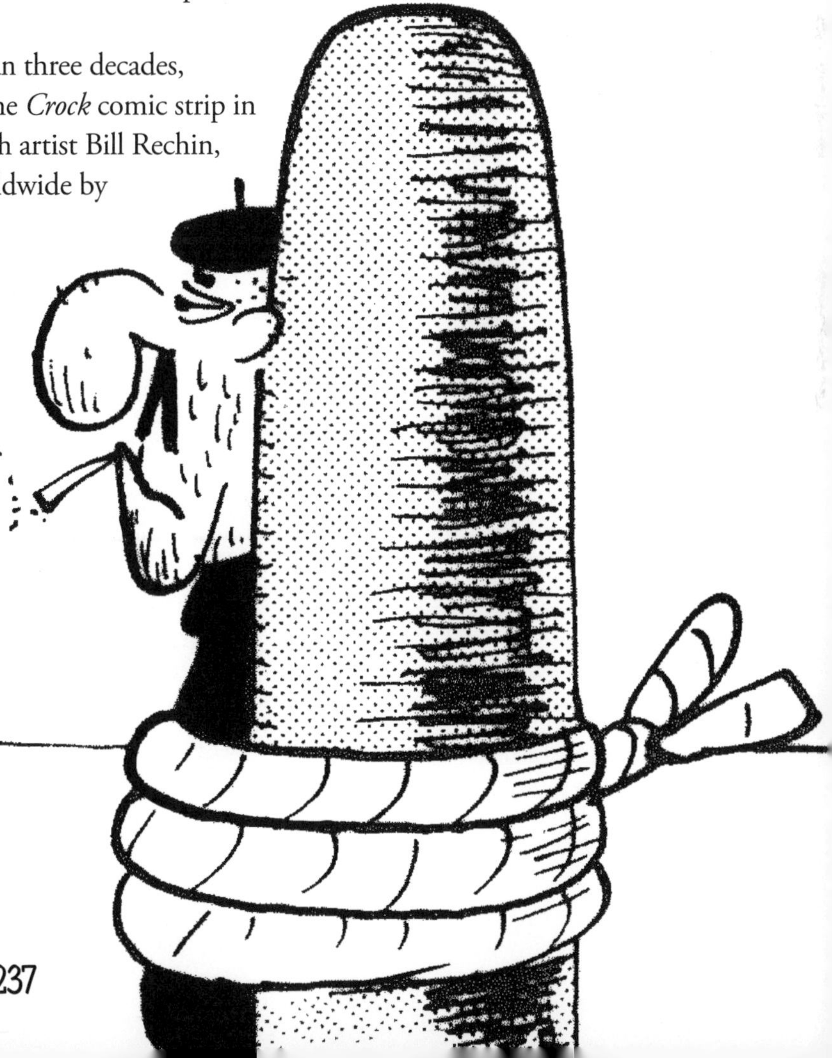

THE 'BEST OF' LIBRARY

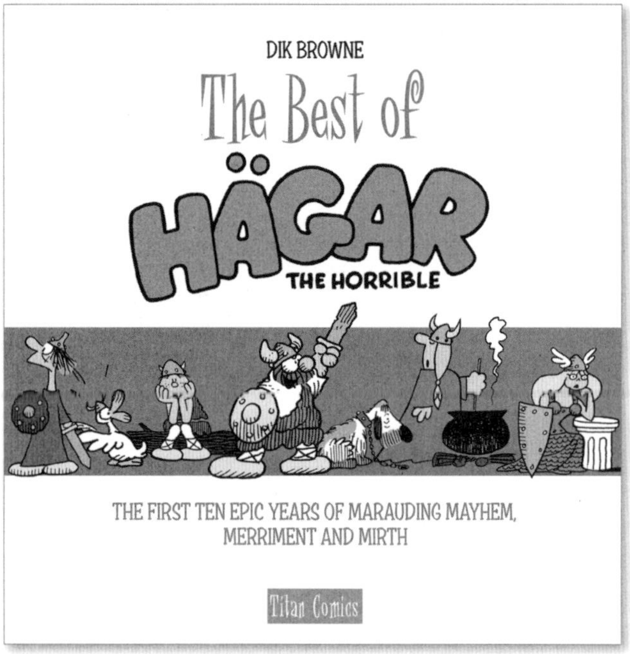
DIK BROWNE
The Best of
HÄGAR
THE HORRIBLE
THE FIRST TEN EPIC YEARS OF MARAUDING MAYHEM, MERRIMENT AND MIRTH
Titan Comics

THE BEST OF HAGAR THE HORRIBLE

By Dik Browne

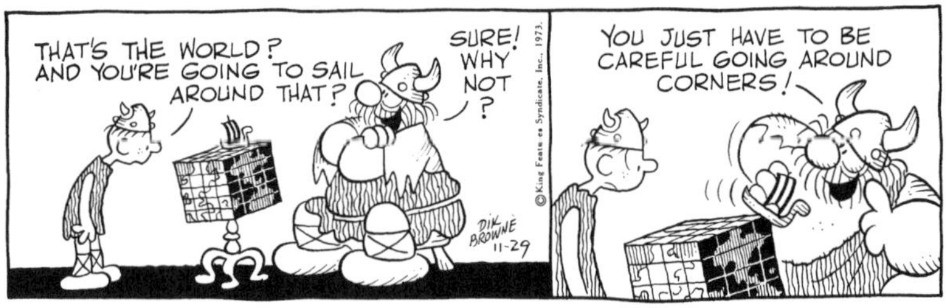
THAT'S THE WORLD? AND YOU'RE GOING TO SAIL AROUND THAT?
SURE! WHY NOT?
YOU JUST HAVE TO BE CAREFUL GOING AROUND CORNERS!

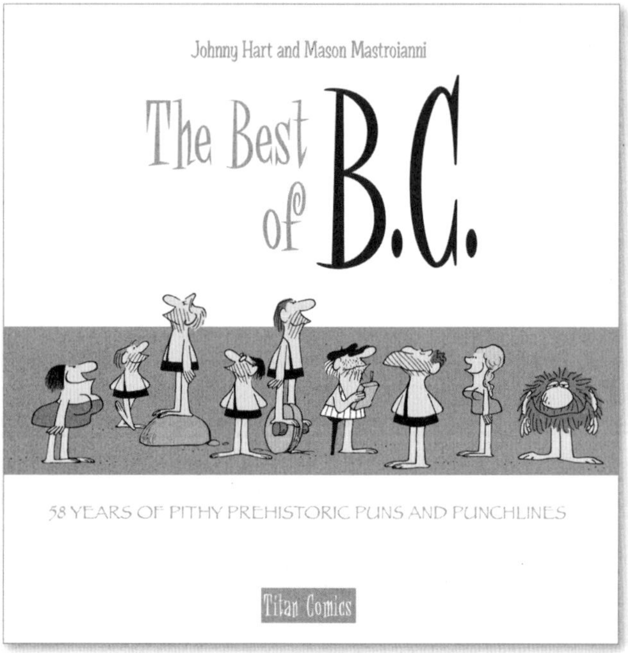
Johnny Hart and Mason Mastroianni
The Best of B.C.
58 YEARS OF PITHY PREHISTORIC PUNS AND PUNCHLINES
Titan Comics

THE BEST OF B.C.

By Johnny Hart and Mason Mastroianni

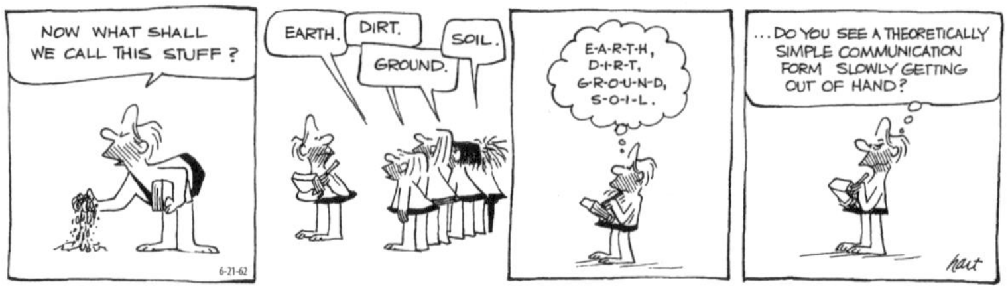
NOW WHAT SHALL WE CALL THIS STUFF?
EARTH.
DIRT.
GROUND.
SOIL.
E-A-R-T-H, D-I-R-T, G-R-O-U-N-D, S-O-I-L.
...DO YOU SEE A THEORETICALLY SIMPLE COMMUNICATION FORM SLOWLY GETTING OUT OF HAND?

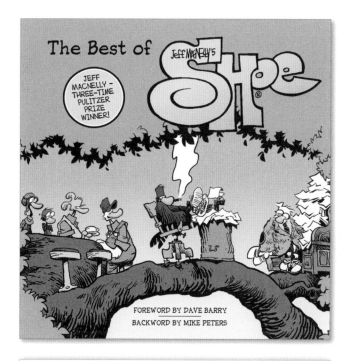

THE BEST OF SHOE

By Jeff MacNelly

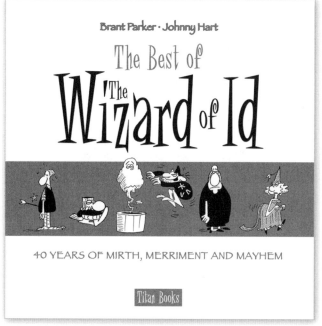

THE BEST OF
THE WIZARD OF ID

By Brant Parker, Johnny Hart

WWW.TITANBOOKS.COM - WWW.TITAN-COMICS.COM